HISTORY

OF

KERSHAW'S BRIGADE,

WITH

COMPLETE ROLL OF COMPANIES, BIOGRAPHICAL SKETCHES, INCIDENTS, ANECDOTES, ETC.

BY

D. AUGUSTUS DICKERT.

INTRODUCTION BY

ASSOCIATE JUSTICE Y. J. POPE.

NEWBERRY, S. C.
ELBERT H. AULL COMPANY.
1899.

To the soldiers of the old First Brigade (Kershaw's), of the First Division of the First Corps of the Army of Northern Virginia, this work is affectionately dedicated, not as a testimonial of their worth, nor as a memorial of their services, for this is beyond human pen; but as a slight tribute to their trials, their endurance, their loyalty, and their courage during the four years in which the author had the honor to call them,

COMRADE.

INTRODUCTION.

More than thirty-four years have passed away since the soldiers who composed the Second South Carolina Regiment of Infantry, the Third South Carolina Regiment of Infantry, the Eighth South Carolina Regiment of Infantry, the Fifteenth South Carolina Regiment of Infantry, the Twentieth South Carolina Regiment of Infantry, and the Third South Carolina Battalion of Infantry, which commands made up Kershaw's Brigade, laid down their arms; and yet, until a short time ago, no hand has been raised to perpetuate its history. This is singular, when it is remembered how largely the soldiers of this historic brigade contributed to win for the State of South Carolina the glory rightfully hers, by reason of the splendid heroism of her sons in the war between the States, from the year 1861 to that of 1865. If another generation had been allowed to pass, it is greatly feared that the power to supply the historian with the information requisite to this work would have passed away forever.

The work which assumes to perpetuate the history of Kershaw's Brigade should not be a skeleton, consisting of an enumeration of the battles, skirmishes, and marches which were participated in —with the names of the commanding officers. What is needed is not a skeleton, but a body with all its members, so to speak. It should be stated who they were, the purposes which animated these men in becoming soldiers, how they lived in camp and on the march, how they fought, how they died and where, with incidents of bravery in battle, and of fun in camp. No laurels must be taken from the brow of brave comrades in other commands; but the rights of the soldiers of Kershaw's Brigade must be jealously upheld—everyone of these rights. To do this work, will require that the writer of this history shall have been identified with this command during its existence—*he must have been a soldier*. Again, he must be a man who acts up to his convictions; no toady nor any apologist is desired. If he was a Confederate soldier from principle, say so, and apologize to no one for the fact. If he loved his State and the Southland and wished their independence, say so, and "forget not the field where they perished." Lastly, he ought to have the ability to tell the story well.

The friends of Captain D. Augustus Dickert, who commanded Company H of the Third South Carolina Regiment of Infantry, are confident that he possesses all the quality essential to this work. He was a splendid soldier—brave in battle, clear-headed always, and of that equilibrium of temperament that during camp life, amid the toil of the march, and in battle the necessity for discipline was recognized and enforced with justice and impartiality. He *was and is* a patriot. His pen is graceful, yet strong. When he yielded to the importunities of his comrades that he would write this history, there was only one condition that he insisted upon, and that was that this should be solely a work of love. Captain Dickert has devoted years to the gathering together of the materials for this history. Hence, the readers are now prepared to expect a success. Maybe it will be said this is the finest history of the war!

Y. J. POPE.

Newberry, S. C., August 7, 1899.

CAPT D. AUGUSTUS DICKERT.
Company H 3d S C. Regiment.

AUTHOR'S ANNOUNCEMENT.

COMRADES: Years ago I was asked by the members of a local camp (James D. Nance Camp, United Confederate Veterans, Newberry, S. C.,) of Veterans to write a history of Kershaw's "Old First Brigade in the Civil War," in order that the part taken by you in that memorable struggle might be transmitted to posterity through the instrumentality of a proud and loving participant in all the events that went to make up the life of an organization second to none, that has ever stood face to face with an invading foe upon the face of earth.

This request was not based upon a supposition of superior educational qualifications on my part, for the parties who made it know that my school days ended at twelve, and that the time usually devoted to instruction of youth was spent by many of us, from '61 to '65, on the northern side of Richmond. Consequently, to the love that I treasure in my heart for the "Old First" is due whatever of distinction attaches to the position of recorder of actions which prove the worth and heroism of each constituent part of the brigade. In accepting this trust I shall repress all desire for rhetorical display. I will not even attempt to do that justice, which is beyond the power of mortals; but shall simply try to be your faithful chronicler or recorder of facts as they appeared to me and others, who have so kindly assisted me in the compilation of these records, and shall confine myself to the effort to attain my highest ambition—absolute correctness. It is true that inaccuracies may have crept in; but these will be found to be mostly among proper names—due in a great measure to the illegibility of the manuscripts furnished me by correspondents. Again, apparent errors will be explained, when it is recalled to your minds that no two men see the same circumstance from the same standpoint. Honest differences will appear, no matter how trivial the facts are upon which they are based.

I have endeavored to be fair and just, and in so doing have laid aside a soldier's pardonable pride in his own regiment, and have accorded "honor to whom honor was due." Despite all that may be alleged to the contrary, ours was not a "War of the Roses," of brother against brother, struggling for supremacy; but partook more of the nature of the inhuman contest in the Netherlands, waged by the unscrupulous and crafty Duke of Alva at the instance Philip (the Good!), or rather like that in which the rich and fruitful Province of the Palatine was subjected to fire and rapine under the mailed hand of that monster of iniquity—Turenne.

How well the men of Kershaw's Brigade acted their part, how proudly they faced the foe, how grandly they fought, how nobly they died, I shall attempt not to depict; and yet—

Could heart and brain and hand and pen
But bring to earth and life again
        The scenes of old,
Then all the world might know and see;
Your deeds on scrolls of fame would be
        Inscribed in gold

———

I am indebted to many of the old comrades for their assistance, most notably Judge Y. J. Pope, of the Third South Carolina; Colonel Wm. Wallace, of the Second; Captain L. A. Waller, for the Seventh; Captains Malloy, Harllee, and McIntyre, of the Eighth; Captain D. J. Griffith and Private Charles Blair, of the Fifteenth; Colonel Rice and Captain Jennings, of the Third Battalion, and many others of the Twentieth. But should this volume prove of interest to any of the "Old Brigade," and should there be any virtue in it, remember it belongs to Y. J. Pope. Thrice have I laid down my pen, after meeting with so many rebuffs; but as often taken it up after the earnest solicitation of the former Adjutant of the Third, who it was that urged me on to its completion.

To the publisher, E H. Aull, too much praise cannot be given. He has undertaken the publication of this work on his individual convictions of its merit, and with his sole conviction that the old comrades would sustain the efforts of the author. Furthermore, he has undertaken it on his own responsibility, without one dollar in sight—a recompence for time, material, and labor being one of the remotest possibilities.

D. AUGUSTUS DICKERT.

Newberry, S. C., August 15, 1899.

CHAPTER I

SECESSION.

Its Causes and Results.

The secession bell rang out in South Carolina on the 20th of December, 1860, not to summon the men to arms, nor to prepare the State for war. There was no conquest that the State wished to make, no foe on her border, no enemy to punish. Like the liberty bell of the revolution that electrified the colonies from North to South, the bell of secession put the people of the State in a frenzy from the mountains to the sea. It announced to the world that South Carolina would be free—that her people had thrown off the yoke of the Union that bound the States together in an unholy alliance. For years the North had been making encroachments upon the South: the general government grasping, with a greedy hand, those rights and prerogatives, which belonged to the States alone, with a recklessness only equalled by Great Britain towards the colonies; began absorbing all of the rights guaranteed to the State by the constitution, and tending towards a strong and centralized government. They had made assaults upon our institutions, torn away the barriers that protected our sovereignty. So reckless and daring had become these assaults, that on more than one occasion the States of the South threatened dissolution of the Union. But with such master minds as Clay, Webster, and Calhoun in the councils of the nation, the calamity was averted for the time. The North had broken compact after compact, promises after promises, until South Carolina determined to act upon those rights she had retained for herself in the formation of the Union, and which the general government guaranteed to all, and withdrew when that Union no longer served the purposes for which it was formed.

Slavery, it has been said, was the cause of the war. Incidentally it may have been, but the real cause was far removed from the institution of slavery. That institution existed at the formation of the Union, or compact. It had existed for several hundred years, and in every State; the federation was fully cognizant of the fact when the agreement of the Union was reached. They promised not to disturb it, and allow each State to control it as it seemed best. Slavery was gradually but surely dying out. Along the border States it scarcely existed at all, and the mighty hand of an All-wise Ruler could be plainly seen in the gradual emancipation of all the slaves on the continent. It had begun in the New England States then. In the Carribbean Sea and South America emancipation had been gradually closing in upon the small compass of the Southern States, and that by peaceful measures, and of its own volition; so much so that it would have eventually died out, could not be denied by any who would look that far into the future, and judge that future by the past. The South looked with alarm and horror at a wholesale emancipation, when they viewed its havoc and destruction in Hayti and St. Domingo, where once existed beautiful homes and luxuriant fields, happy families and general progress; all this wealth, happiness, and prosperity had been swept away from those islands as by a deadly blight. Ruin, squalor, and beggary now stalks through those once fair lands.

A party sprang up at the North inimical to the South: at first only a speck upon the horizon, a single sail in a vast ocean; but it grew and spread like contagion. They were first called agitators, and consisted of a few fanatics, both women and men, whose avowed object was emancipation—to do by human hands that which an All-wise Providence was surely doing in His own wise way. At first the South did not look with any misgivings upon the fanatics. But when Governors of Northern States, leading statesmen in the councils of the nation, announced this as their creed and guide, then the South began to consider seriously the subject of secession. Seven Governors and their legislatures at the North had declared, by acts regularly passed and ratified, their determination "not to allow the laws of the land to be administered or carried out in their States." They made preparation to nullify the laws of Congress and the constitution. That party, which was first called "Agitators," but now took the name of "Republicans"

—called at the South the "black Republicans"—had grown to such proportions that they put in the field candidates for President and Vice-President of the United States. Numbers increased with each succeeding campaign. In the campaign of 1860 they put Abraham Lincoln and Hannibal Hamlin forward as their standard bearers, and whose avowed purpose was the "the liberation of the slaves, regardless of the consequences." This party had spies all over the Southern States, and these emisaries incited insurrection, taught the slaves "that by rising at night and murdering their old masters and their families, they would be doing God's will;" that "it was a duty they owed to their children;" this "butchery of the sleeping and innocent whites was the road to freedom." In Virginia they sent down armed bands of whites, roused the negroes at night, placed guns, pikes, and arms of every kind in the hands of the poor, deluded creatures, and in that one night they butchered, in cold blood, the families of some of the best men in the State. These cold blooded butcheries would have done credit to the most cruel and blood thirsty of the primeval savages of the forest. These deeds were heralded all over the North as "acts of God, done by the hands of men." The leader of this diabolical plan and his compeers were sainted by their followers and admirers, and praises sung over him all over the North, as if over the death of saints. By a stupendous blunder the people of the South, and the friends of the Union generally, allowed this party to elect Lincoln and Hamlin. The South now had no alternative. Now she must either remain in a Union, where our institutions were to be dragged down; where the laws were to be obeyed in one section, but not in another; where existed open resistance to laws in one State and quiet obedience in another; where servile insurrections were being threatened continuously; where the slaves were aided and abetted by whites at the North in the butcheries of their families; or *secede and fight.* These were the alternatives on the one part, or a severance from the Union and its consequences on the other. From the very formation of the government, two constructions were put upon this constitution—the South not · viewing this compact with that fiery zeal, or fanatical adulation, as they did at the North. The South looked upon it

more as a confederation of States for mutual protection in
times of danger, and a general advancement of those interests
where the whole were concerned. Then, again, the vast
accumulation of wealth in the Southern States, caused by the
the overshadowing of all other commodities of commerce—
cotton—created a jealousy at the North that nothing but the
prostration of the South, the shattering of her commerce,
the destruction of her homes, and the freedom of her slaves,
could answer. The wealth of the South had become a
proverb. The "Wealthy Southern Planter" had become an
eyesore to the North, and to humble her haughty pride, as the
North saw it, was to free her slaves. As one of the first
statesmen of the South has truly said, "The seeds of the Civil
War were sown fifty years before they were born who fought
her battles."

A convention was called to meet in Columbia, in December,
1860, to frame a new constitution, and to take such steps as
were best suited to meet the new order of things that would
be brought about by this fanatical party soon to be at the
head of the government. Feeling ran high—people were
excited—everywhere the voice of the people was for secession.
The women of the South, who would naturally be the first
sufferers if the programme of the "Agitators" were carried
out, were loud in their cries for separation. Some few people
were in favor of the South moving in a body, and a feeble
opposition ticket for the delegates to the convention was put in
the field. These were called "Co-operationists," i. e., in favor
of secession, but to await a union with the other Southern
States. These were dubbed by the most fiery zealots of secession, "Submissionists" in derision. The negroes, too, scented
freedom from afar. The old cooks, mammas, house servants,
and negro eavesdroppers gathered enough of "freedom of
slaves," "war," "secession," to cause the negroes to think
that a great measure was on foot somewhere, that had a direct
bearing on their long looked for Messiah—"Freedom." Vigilance committees sprung up all over the South, to watch parties of Northern sentiment, or sympathy, and exercise a more
guarded scrutiny over the acts of the negroes. Companies
were organized in towns and cities, who styled themselves
"Minute Men," and rosettes, or the letters "M. M.," adorned

the lapels of the coats worn by those in favor of secession. The convention met in Columbia, but for some local cause it was removed to Charleston. After careful deliberation, a new constitution was framed and the ordinance of secession was passed without a dissenting voice, on the 20th of December, 1860, setting forth the State's grievances and acting upon her rights, declaring South Carolina's connection with the Union at an end. It has been truly said, that this body of men who passed the ordinance of secession was one of the most deliberate, representative, and talented that had ever assembled in the State of South Carolina. When the news flashed over the wires the people were in a frenzy of delight and excitement— bells tolled, cannons boomed, great parades took place, and orators from street corners and hotel balconies harangued the people. The ladies wore palmetto upon their hats or dresses, and showed by every way possible their earnestness in the great drama that was soon to be enacted upon the stage events. Drums beat, men marched through the streets, banners waved and dipped, ladies from the windows and from the housetops waved handkerchiefs or flags to the enthusiastic throng moving below. The bells from historic old St. Michael's, in Charleston, were never so musical to the ears of the people as when they pealed out the chimes that told of secession. The war was on.

Still with all this enthusiasm, the sober-headed, patriotic element of the South regretted the necessity of this dissolution. They, too, loved the Union their ancestors had helped to make—they loved the name, the glory, and the prestige won by their forefathers upon the bloody field of the revolution. While they did not view this Union as indispensable to their existence, they loved and reverenced the flag of their country. As a people, they loved the North; as a nation, they gloried in her past and future possibilities. The dust of their ancestors mingled in imperishable fame with those of the North. In the peaceful "Godsacre" or on the fields of carnage they were ever willing to share with them their greatness, and equally enjoyed those of their own, but denied to them the rights to infringe upon the South's possessions or rights of statehood. We all loved the Union, but we loved it as it was formed and made a compact by the blood of our ancestors. Not as contorted and misconstrued by dema-gogueism aud fanaticism. We almost deified the flag of the Union, under whose folds it was made immortal by the Huguenots, the Roundheads, the Cavaliers, and men of every faith and conviction in the crowning days of the revolution. The deeds of her great men, the history of the past, were an equal heritage of all—we felt bound together by natural bonds equal to the ties of blood or kindred. We loved her towering mountains, her rolling prairies, her fertile fields, her enchant-ing scenery, her institutions, her literature and arts, all; all were equally the South's as well as the North's. Not for one moment would the South pluck a rose from the flowery wreath of our goddess of liberty and place it upon the brow of our Southland alone. The Mississippi, rising among the hills and lakes of the far North, flowing through the fertile valleys of the South, was to all our "Mother Nile." The great Rocky Mountains and Sierra Nevada chained our Western border together from Oregon to the Rio Grande. The Cumberland, the Allegheny, and the Blue Ridge, lifting their heads up from among the verdant fields of Vermont, stretching southward, until from their southern summit at "Lookout" could be viewed the borderland of the gulf. In the sceneries of these mountains, their legends and traditions, they were to all the people of the Union what Olympus was to the ancients. Where the Olympus was the haunts, the wooing places of the gods of the ancient Greeks, the Apalachian was the reveling grounds for the muses of song and story of the North and South alike. And while the glories of the virtues of Greece and Rome, the birthplace of republicanism and liberty, may have slept for centuries, or died out entirely, that spirit of national liberty and personal freedom was transplanted to the shores of the New World, and nowhere was the spirit of freedem more cherished and fostered than in the bright and sunny lands of the South. The flickering torch of freedom, borne by those sturdy sons of the old world to the new, nowhere took such strong and rapid growth as did that planted by the Huguenots on the soil of South Carolina. Is it any wonder, then, that a people with such high ideals, such lofty spirits, such love of freedom, would tamely submit to a Union where such ideals and spirits were so lightly considered as by those

who were now in charge of the government—where our women
and children were to be at the mercies of a brutal race, with all
of their passions aroused for rapine and bloodshed; where we
would be continually threatened or subjected to a racial
war, one of supremacy; where promises were made to
be broken, pledges given to be ignored; where laws made for
all were to be binding only on those who chose to obey? Such
were some of the conditions that confronted South Carolina
and her sister States at this time, and forced them into measures that brought about the most stupendous civil war in
modern or ancient times.

To sum up: It was not love for the Union, but jealousy of
the South's wealth. It was not a spirit of humanity towards
the slaves, but a hatred of the South, her chivalry, her honor,
and her integrity. A quality wanting in the one is always
hated in that of the other.

CHAPTER II

ENROLMENT OF TROOPS.

Troops Gathered at Charleston---First Service as a Volunteer.

The Legislature, immediately after the passage of the ordinance of secession, authorized the Governor to organize ten
regiments of infantry for State service. Some of these regiments were enlisted for twelve months, while Gregg's, the First,
was for six, or, as it was understood at the time, its main duties
were the taking of Sumter. The first regiments so formed
were: First, Gregg's; Second, Kershaw's; Third, Williams';
Fourth, Sloan's; Fifth, Jenkins'; Sixth, Rion's; Seventh,
Bacon's: Eighth, Cash's; Ninth, Blanding's; besides a regiment of regulars and some artillery and cavalry companies.
There existed a nominal militia in the State, and numbered by
battalions and regiments. These met every three months by
companies and made some feeble attempts at drilling, or "mus-
tering," as it was called. To the militia was intrusted the

care of internal police of the State. Each company was divided into squads, with a captain, whose duties were to do the policing of the neighborhood, called "patrolling." They would patrol the country during Sundays, and occasionally at nights, to prevent illegal assemblies of negroes, and also to prevent them from being at large without permission of their masters. But this system had dwindled down to a farce, and was only engaged in by some of the youngsters, more in a spirit of fun and frolic than to keep order in the neighborhood. The real duties of the militia of the State consisted of an annual battalion and regimental parade, called "battalion muster" and "general muster." This occasioned a lively turnout of the people, both ladies and gentlemen, not connected with the troops, to witness the display of officers' uniforms, and bright caparisoned steeds, the stately tread of the "muster men," listen to the rattle of the drums and inspiring strains of the fifes, and horns of the rural bands.

From each battalion a company was formed for State service. These companies elected their captains and field officers, the general officers being appointed by the Governor. Immediately after the call of the Governor for troops, a great military spirit swept the country, volunteer companies sprang up like magic all over the land, each anxious to enter the service of the State and share the honor of going to war. Up to this time, few thought there would be a conflict. Major Anderson, U. S. A., then on garrison duty at Fort Moultrie, heard of the secession of the State, and (whether by orders or his own volition, is not known and immaterial,) left Fort Moultrie, after spiking the guns and destroying the carriages; took possession of Fort Sumter. The State government looked with some apprehension upon this questionable act of Maj. Anderson's. Fort Sumter stood upon grounds of the State, ceded to the United States for purposes of defence. South Carolina now claimed the property, and made demands upon Maj. Anderson and the government at Washington for its restoration. This was refused.

Ten companies, under Col. Maxcy Gregg, were called to Charleston for the purpose of retaking this fort by force of arms, if peaceful methods failed. These companies were raised mostly in towns and cities by officers who had been commissioned by the Governor. College professors formed companies of their classes, and hurried off to Charleston. Companies of town and city volunteers offered their services to the Governor—all for six months, or until the fall of Sumter.

On the 9th of January, 1861, the State was thrown into a greater paroxysm of excitement by the "Star of the West," a Northern vessel, being fired on in the bay of Charleston by State troops. This steamer, laden with supplies for Sumter, had entered the channel with the evident intention of reinforcing Anderson, when the Citadel guards, under Captain Stevens, fired several shots across her bow, then she turned about and sped away to the sea. In the meantime the old battalions of militia had been called out at their respective "muster grounds," patriotic speeches made, and a call or volunteers made. Companies were easily formed and officers elected. Usually in selecting the material for officers, preference was given to soldiers of the Mexican war, graduates of the military schools and the old militia of officers. These companies met weekly, and were put through a course of instructions in the old Macomb's tactics. In this way the ten regiments were formed, but not called together until the commencement of the bombardment of Sumter, with the exception of those troops enlisted for six months, now under Gregg at Charleston, and a few volunteer companies of cavalry and artillery.

The writer was preparing to enter school in a neighboring county when the first wave of patriotism struck him. Captain Walker's Company, from Newberry, of which I was a member, had been ordered to Charleston with Gregg, and was stationed at Morris' Island before I could get off. Two of my brothers and myself had joined the company made up from the Thirty-ninth Battalion of State militia, and which afterwards formed a part of the Third S. C. Volunteers (Colonel Williams). But at that time, to a young mind like mine, the war looked too remote for me to wait for this company to go, so when on my way to school I boarded a train filled with enthusiasts, some tardy soldiers on their way to join their companies, and others to see, and if need be, "take old Anderson out of his den." Nothing on the train could be heard but war, war—"taking of Sumter," "Old Anderson," and

2

"Star of the West." Everyone was in a high glee—palmetto cockades, brass buttons, uniforms, and gaudy epaulettes were seen in every direction. This was more than a youthful vision could withstand, so I directed my steps towards the seat of war instead of school. By this time the city of Charleston may be said to have been in a state of siege—none could leave the islands or lands without a permit from the Governor or the Adjutant and Inspector General. The headquarters of Governor Pickens and staff were in the rooms of the Charleston Hotel, and to that place I immediately hied and presented myself before those "August dignitaries," and asked permission to join my company on Morris' Island, but was refused. First, on account of not having a permit of leave of absence from my captain; secondly, on account of my youth (I then being on the rise of 15); and thirdly, having no permission from my parents. What a contrast with later years, when boys of that age were pressed into service. The city of Charleston was ablaze with excitement, flags waved from the house tops, the heavy tread of the embryo soldiers could be heard in the streets, the corridors of hotels, and in all the public places. The beautiful park on the water front, called the "Battery," was thronged with people of every age and sex, straining their eyes or looking through glasses out at Sumter, whose bristling front was surmounted with cannon, her flags waving defiance. Small boats and steamers dotted the waters of the bay. Ordnance and ammunition were being hurried to the islands. The one continual talk was "Anderson," "Fort Sumter," and "war." While there was no spirit of bravado, or of courting of war, there was no disposition to shirk it. A strict guard was kept at all the wharves, or boat landings, to prevent any espionage on our movements or works. It will be well to say here, that no moment from the day of secession to the day the first gun was fired at Sumter, had been allowed to pass without overtures being made to the government at Washington for a peaceful solution of the momentous question. Every effort that tact or diplomacy could invent was resorted to, to have an amicable adjustment. Commissioners had been sent to Washington, asking, urging, and almost begging to be allowed to leave the Union, now odious to the people of the State, without bloodshed. Commissioners of the North came to Charleston to treat for peace, but they demanded peace without any concessions, peace with submission, peace with all the chances of a servile war. Some few leaders at the North were willing to allow us the right, while none denied it. The leading journal at the North said: "Let the erring sisters depart in peace." But all of our overtures were rejected by the administration at Washington, and a policy of evasion, or dilly-dallying, was kept up by those in authority at the North. All the while active preparations were going on to coerce the State by force of arms. During this time other States seceded and joined South Carolina, and formed the "Confederate States of America," with Jefferson Davis as President, with the capital at Montgomery, Ala.

Being determined to reach my company, I boarded a steamer, bound for Morris' Island, intending, if possible, to avoid the guard. In this I was foiled. But after making several futile attempts, I fell in with an officer of the First South Carolina Regiment. who promised to pilot me over. On reaching the landing, at Cummings Point, I was to follow his lead, as he had a passport, but in going down the gang plank we were met by soldiers with crossed bayonets, demanding "passports." The officer, true to his word, passed me over, but then my trouble began. When I reached the shore I lost my sponsor, and began to make inquiries for my company. When it was discovered that there was a stranger in the camp without a passport, a corporal of the guards was called. I was placed under arrest, sent to the guardhouse, and remained in durance vile until Captain Walker came to release me. When I joined my company I found a few of my old school-mates, the others were strangers. Everything that met my eyes reminded me of war. Sentinels patrolled the beach; drums beat; soldiers marching and countermarching; great cannons being drawn along the beach, hundreds of men pulling them by long ropes, or drawn by mule teams. Across the bay we could see on Sullivan's Island men and soldiers building and digging out foundations for forts. Morris' Island was lined from the lower point to the light house, with batteries of heavy guns. To the youthful eye of a Southerner, whose mind had been fierd by Southern sentiment and literature of the day, by reading the stories of heroes and soldiers in our old "Southern Reader," of the thrilling romances of Marion and his men, by William Gilmore Simms, this sight of war was enough to dazzle and startle to an enthusiasm that scarcely knew any bounds.   The South were "hero worshipers."   The stories of Washington and Putnam, of Valley Forge, of Trenton, of Bunker Hill, and Lexington never grew old, while men, women, and children never tired of reading of the storming of Mexico, the siege of Vera Cruz, the daring of the Southern troops at Moli.io del Rey.

My first duty as a soldier, I will never forget.   I went with a detail to Steven's Iron Battery to build embrasures for the forts there.   This was done by filling cotton bags the size of 50-pound flour sacks with sand, placing them one upon the top of the other at the opening where the mouths of cannons projected, to prevent the loose earth from falling down and filling in the openings.   The sand was first put upon common wheel-barrows and rolled up single planks in a zig-zag way to the top of the fort, then placed in the sacks and laid in position.   My turn came to use a barrow, while a comrade used the shovel for filling up.   I had never worked a wheel-barrow in my life, and like most of my companions, had done but little work of any kind.   But up I went the narrow zig-zag gangway, with a heavy loaded barrow of loose sand.   I made the first plank all right, and the second, but when I undertook to reach the third plank on the angles, and about fifteen feet from the ground, my barrow rolled off, and down came sand, barrow, and myself to the ground below.   I could have cried with shame and mortification, for my misfortune created much merriment for the good natured workers.   But it mortified me to death to think I was not man enough to fill a soldier's place.   My good coworker and brother soldier exchanged the shovel for the barrow with me, and then began the first day's work I had ever done of that kind.   Hour after hour passed, and I used the shovel with a will.   It looked as if night would never come.   At times I thought I would have to sink to the earth from pure exhaustion, but my pride and youthful patriotism, animated by the acts of others, urged me on.   Great blisters formed and bursted in my hand, beads of perspiration dripped from my brow, and towards night the blood began to show at the root of my fingers.   But I was not by myself; there were many others as tender as myself. Young men with wealthy parents, school and college boys, clerks and men of leisure, some who had never done a lick of manual labor in their lives, and would not have used a spade or shovel for any consideration, would have scoffed at the idea of doing the laborious work of men, were now toiling away with the farmer boys, the overseers' sons, the mechanics—all with a will—and filled with enthusiasm that nothing short of the most disinterested patriotism could have endured. There were men in companies raised in Columbia, Charleston, and other towns, who were as ignorant and as much strangers to manual labor as though they had been infants, toiling away with pick and shovel with as much glee as if they had been reared upon the farm or had been laborers in a mine.

Over about midway in the harbor stood grim old Sumter, from whose parapets giant guns frowned down upon us; while around the battlements the sentinels walked to and fro upon their beats. All this preparation and labor were to reduce the fort or prevent a reinforcement. Supplies had been cut off, only so much allowed as was needed for the garrison's daily consumption. With drill every two hours, guard duty, and working details, the soldiers had little time for rest or reflection. Bands of music enlivened the men while on drill, and cheered them while at work by martial and inspiring strains of "Lorena," "The Prairie Flower," "Dixie," and other Southern airs. Pickets walked the beach, every thirty paces, night and day; none were allowed to pass without a countersign or a permit. During the day small fishing smacks, their white sails bobbing up and down over the waves, dotted the bay; some going out over the bar at night with rockets and signals to watch for strangers coming from the seaward. Days and nights passed without cessation of active operations—all waiting anxiously the orders from Montgomery to reduce the fort.

General G. T. Beauregard, a citizen of Louisiana, resident of New Orleans, a veteran of the Mexican War, and a recent officer in the United States Engineering Corps, was appointed Brigadier General and placed in command of all the forces around Charleston. A great many troops from other States, which had also seceded and joined the Confederacy, had come to South Carolina to aid in the capture of Sumter. General Beauregard was a great favorite with all the people, and the greatest confidence felt in his skill and ability by the soldiers. The State officers and troops obeyed him cheerfully, and had implicit faith in his military skill. As he was destined to play an important part in the great role of war that was soon to follow. I will give here a short sketch of his life.

General G. T. Beauregard was born near the city of New Orleans, May 18th, 1818. His first ancestors were from Wales, but engaging in an insurrection, they were forced to flee from their country, and sought an asylum in France. In the last of the thirteenth century one of them became attached to the Court of Phillip the IV, surnamed the "Fair." He then married Mademorselle de Lafayette, maid of honor to the sister of Philip. When Edward, King of England, married the sister of Philip, he followed with his wife the fortunes of the English King, and became a member at the Court of St. James. He was afterwards assigned to a British post on the continent. And again this family of the early Beauregards, then called Toutant-Beauregard, became citizens of France. Jacques Beauregard came to Louisiana from France with a colony sent out by Louis XIV. The grandson of this Jacques is the present Gustav Toutant Beauregard. At the early age of eleven years he was taken to New York and placed under a private tutor, an exile from France, and who had fled the Empire on the downfall of Napoleon. At sixteen he entered West Point as a cadet, and graduated July 1st, 1838, being second in a class of forty-five. He entered the service of the United States as Second Lieutenant of Engineers. He served with distinction through the Mexican War, under Major General Scott, in the engineer corps. For gallant and meritorious conduct he was twice promoted—first to the Captaincy and then to the position of Major. For a short time he was Superintendent of the West Point Military Academy, but owing to the stirring events just preceding the late war, he resigned on the first of March, 1861. He entered the service of the Confederate States; was appointed Brigadier General and assigned to the post of Charleston. Soon after the fall of Sumter he was made full General, and assigned to a command on the Potomac, and with J. E. Johnston fought the memorable battle

of Bull Run. He was second in command at Shiloh with
A. S. Johnston, then the "Department of South Carolina,
Georgia, and Florida." With J. E. Johnston he commanded
the last remnant of a once grand army that surrendered at
Greensboro, N. C. He returned to his old home in New
Orleans at the close of the war, to find it ruined, his fortune
wrecked, his wife dead, and his country at the feet of a merciless foe. He took no further part in military or political
affairs, and passed away gently and peacefully at a ripe old
age, loved and admired by his many friends, and respected by
his enemies. Such, in brief, was the life of the man who came
to control the destinies of South Carolina at this most critical
moment of her history.

On March 6th he placed Morris' Island under the immediate
command of Brigadier General James Simonds, while the
batteries were under the command of Lieutenant Colonel
W. G. DeSaussure. Sullivan's Island was under the command
of General R. G. M. Dunovant, and the batteries of this island
were under Lieutenant Colonel Ripley. Captain Calhoun
commanded at Fort Moultrie, and Captain Thomas at Fort
Johnston. A floating battery had been constructed by Captain
Hamilton, and moved out to the western extremity of Sullivan's Island. This was under command of its inventor and
builder. It consisted of very heavy timbers; its .oof overlaid
with railroad iron in a slanting position, through which trap
doors had been cut for the cannon to project. The Stevens'
Battery, as it was called, was constructed on the same principle; was built at Cummings' Point, on Morris' Island, and
commanded by Captain Stevens, of the Citadel Academy. It
was feared at this time that the concussion caused by the
heavy shells and solid shots striking the iron would cause
death to those underneath, or so stun them as to render them
unfit for further service; but both these batteries did excellent
service in the coming bombardment. Batteries along the
water fronts of the islands were manned by the volunteer companies of Colonel Gregg's Regiment, and other regiments that
had artillery companies attached.

On the 8th of April a message was received at Montgomery
to the effect that a fleet was then en route to reinforce Sumter,
"peaceably if they could, but forcibly if necessary."

General Beauregard was instructed to demand the immediate evacuation of the fort; Anderson failing to comply with this demand, he was to proceed to reduce it. The demand was made upon Major Anderson, and was refused. General Beauregard had everything in readiness, only waiting the result of the negotiations for the surrender or evacuation, to give the command to fire. The night of the 11th was one of great excitement. It was known for a certainty that on to-morrow the long looked for battle was to take place. Diplomacy had done its work, now powder and ball must do what diplomacy had failed to accomplish. All working details had been called in, tools put aside, the heating furnaces fired, shells and red-hot solid shot piled in close proximity to the cannon and mortars. All the troops were under arms during the night, and a double picket line stretched along the beach, and while all seemed to be life and animation, a death-like stillness pervaded the air. There was some apprehension lest the fleet might come in during the night, land an army on Morris' Island in small boats, and take the forts by surprise. Men watched with breathless interest the hands on the dials as they slowly moved around to the hour of four, the time set to open the fire. At that hour gunners stood with lanyards in their hands. Men peered through the darkness in the direction of Sumter, as looking for some invisible object. At half past four Captain James, from Fort Johnston, pulled his lanyard; the great mortar belched forth, a bright flash, and the shell went curving over in a kind of semi-circle, the lit fuse trailing behind, showing a glimmering light, like the wings of a fire fly, bursting over the silent old Sumter. This was the signal gun that unchained the great bull-dogs of war around the whole circle of forts. Scarcely had the sound of the first gun died away, ere the dull report from Fort Moultrie came rumbling over the waters, like an echo, and another shell exploded over the deserted parade ground of the doomed fort. Scarcely had the fragments of this shell been scattered before General Stevens jerked the lanyard at the railroad battery, and over the water gracefully sped the lighted shell, its glimmering fuse lighting its course as it, too, sped on in its mission of destruction. Along the water fronts, and from all the forts, now a perfect sheet of flame flashed out, a deafening roar, a rumbling deadening sound, and the war was on. The men as a whole were alive to their work; shot after shot was fired. Now a red-hot solid shot, now a shell, goes capering through the air like a shower of meteors on a frolic. The city was aroused. Men, women, and children rush to the housetops, or crowd each other along the water front of the battery.

But Sumter remained silent, grim, defiant. All there seemed to be in peaceful, quiet slumber, while the solid shot battered against her walls, or the shells burst over their heads and in the court yard below. Round after round is fired. The gunners began to weary of their attempt to arouse the sleeping foe. Is the lion so far back in his lair as not to feel the prods of his tormentors? or is his apathy or contempt too great to be aroused from his slumber by such feeble blows? The grey streaks of morning came coursing from the east, and still the lion is not angry, or is loath to take up the struggle before he has had his morning meal. At seven o'clock, however, if there had been any real anxiety to rouse his temper, it was appeased. The stars and stripes ran up the flag staff, and from out the walls of the grim old stronghold burst a wreath of smoke—then a report, and a shot comes whizzing through the air, strikes the iron battery, and ricochets over in the sand banks. He then pays his respects to Moultrie. From the casements and barbette guns issue a flame and smoke, while the air is filled with flying shot. The battle is general and grand. Men spring upon ramparts and shout defiance at Sumter, to be answered by the crashing of shot against the walls of their bomb-proof forts. All day long the battle rages without intermission or material advantages to either side. As night approached, the fire slackened in all direction, and at dark Sumter ceased to return our fire at all. By a preconcerted arrangement, the fire from our batteries and forts kept up at fifteen-minute intervals only. The next morning the firing began with the same vigor and determination as the day before. Sumter, too, was not slow in showing her metal and paid particular attention to Moultrie. Early in the forenoon the smoke began to rise from within the walls of Sumter; "the fort was on fire." Shots now rain upon the walls of the burning fort with greater fury than ever. The flag was seen to waver, then slowly bend over the staff and fall. A shout of triumph rent the air from the thousands of spectators on the islands and the mainland. Flags and handkerchiefs waved from the hands of excited throngs in the city, as tokens of approval of eager watchers. Soldiers mount the ramparts and shout in exultation, throwing their caps in the air. Away to the seaward the whitened sails of the Federal fleet were seen moving up towards the bar. Anxiety and expectation are now on tip-toe. Will the fleet attempt the succor of their struggling comrades? Will they dare to run the gauntlet of the heavy dahlgreen guns that line the channel sides? From the burning fort the garrison was fighting for their existence. Through the fiery element and hail of shot and shell they see the near approach of the long expected relief. Will the fleet accept the guage of battle? No. The ships falter and stop. They cast anchor and remain a passive spectator to the exciting scenes going on, without offering aid to their friends or battle to their enemies.

General Beauregard, with that chivalrous spirit that characterized all true Southerners, when he saw the dense curling smoke and the flames that now began to leap and lick the topmost walls of the fort, sent three of his aids to Major Anderson, offering aid and assistance in case of distress. But the brave commander, too proud to receive aid from a generous foe when his friends are at hand yet too cowardly to come to the rescue, politely refused the offer. But soon thereafter the white flag was waving from the parapets of Fort Sumter. Anderson had surrendered; the battle was over; a victory won by the gallant troops of the South, and one of the most miraculous instances of a bloodless victory, was the first battle fought and won. Thousands of shots given and taken, and no one hurt on either side.

A remarkable instance of Southern magnanimity was that of W. T. Wigfall, a volunteer aide to General Beauregard. As he stood watching the progress of the battle from Cummings' Point and saw the great volume of black smoke curling and twisting in the air—the storm of shot and shell plunging into the doomed walls of the fort, and the white flag flying from its burning parapets—his generous, noble, and sympathetic heart was fired to a pitch that brooked no consideration, "a brave foe in distress" is to him a friend in need. Before orders could be given to cease firing, or permission granted by the commanding general, he leaped into a small boat, and with a single companion rowed away to the burning fortress, shells shrieking over his head, the waves rocking his frail little craft like a shell in a vast ocean, but the undaunted spirit of the great man overcame all obstacles and danger, and reached the fort in safety. Here a hasty consultation was had. Anderson agreed to capitulate and Wigfall hastened to so inform General Beauregard.

It was agreed that Major Anderson should leave the fort—not as a prisoner of war, but as a brave foe, who had done all in human power to sustain the dignity of his country and the honor of his flag. He was allowed to salute his flag, by firing a number of guns, and with his officers and troops and all personal belongings placed upon a transport, was carried out to the fleet.

The only melancholy event of the memorable bombardment was the sudden death of one of the soldiers of the garrison, caused by the premature explosion of a shell while firing the salute to the flag.

The prominence given to Wigfall's exertion, and erratic conduct at the time, and his meritorious career during the existence of the Confederacy, prompt me to give a short sketch of this meteoric character. He was born in Edgefield County along in the first quarter of the century of good old South Carolina stock, and educated in the common schools and in South Carolina College. His large means, inherited from a long line of wealthy ancestors, afforded him opportunities to enjoy life at his pleasure. He was full of that fiery zeal for honor, hot headed and impulsive. His hasty and stubborn nature caused him many enemies; yet his charitable disposition and generous impulses gave him many friends. He could brook no differences; he was intolerant, proud of his many qualities, gifted, and brave to rashness. In early life he had differences with Whitfield Brooks, the father of Preston S. Brooks, Congressman from South Carolina, but at that time a student of South Carolina College. While the son was in college, Wigfall challenged the elder Brooks to a duel. Brooks, from his age and infirmities, refused. According to the rules

of the code duello, Wigfall posted Brooks at Edgefield Court
House, and guarded the fatal notice during the day with a
loaded pistol.   A relative of Brooks, a feeble, retiring, and unassuming young man, braved the vengeance of Wigfall, and
tore the degrading challenge from the court house door in spite
of the warning and threats of the Knight of the Code.   A pistol shot rang out, and the young champion of Brooks fell dead
at his feet.   Preston Brooks, hearing of the indignity placed
upon his father, the death of his kinsman and defender of his
family honor, now entered the list, and challenged the slayer
of his father's protector.   Wigfall accepted the challenge with
eagerness, for now the hot Southern blood was thoroughly
aroused, and party feelings had sprung up and ran high.   The
gauge of battle was to be settled at Sand Bar Ferry, on the
Savannah River near Augusta, Ga., the noted duelling ground
of the high tempered sons of Georgia and the Carolinas.   It
was fought with dueling pistols of the old school, and at the
first fire Brooks was severely wounded.   Wigfall had kindled
a feeling against himself in the State that his sensitive nature
could not endure.   He left for the rising and new born State
of Texas.   Years rolled by, and the next meeting of those
fiery antagonists was at the Capital of the United States—
Brooks in Congress, and Wigfall in the Senate.

CHAPTER III.

Reorganization of the Troops--Volunteers for Confederate Service--Call from Virginia. Troops Leave the State.

INCIDENTS ON THE WAY.

There was much discussion at the time as to who really fired
the first gun at Sumter.   Great importance was attached to
the episode, and as there were different opinions, and it was
never satisfactorily settled, it is not expected that any new
light can be thrown on it at this late day.   It was first said to
have been General Edmond Ruffin, a venerable octogenarian

from Virginia, who at the secession of South Carolina came to this State and offered his services as a volunteer. He had at one time been a citizen of South Carolina, connected with a geological survey, and had written several works on the resources and possibilities of the State, which created quite an interest at that day and time. He was one of the noblest types of elderly men it has ever been my fortune to look upon. He could not be called venerable, but picturesque. His hair hung in long silvery locks, tied in a queue in the fashions of the past centuries. His height was very near six feet, slender and straight as an Indian brave, and his piercing black eyes seemed to flash fire and impressed one as being able to look into your very soul. He joined the "Palmetto Guards," donned the uniform of that company, and his pictures were sold all over the entire South, taken, as they were, in the habiliments of a soldier. These showed him in an easy pose, his rifle between his knees, coat adorned with palmetto buttons closely buttoned up to his chin, his hair combed straight from his brow and tied up with a bow of ribbon that streamed down his back, his cap placed upon his knee bearing the monogram "P. G.," the emblem of his company, worked in with palmetto.

The other aspirant for the honor of firing the first gun was Captain George S. James, afterwards the Colonel of James' Battalion, or "Third Battalion," as it was known in Kershaw's Brigade. It has been said that this honor was granted him, at his special request, by Captain Stephen D. Lee, on General Beauregard's staff (afterwards a Lieutenant General of the Confederate Army). Captain James' claim appears to be more valid than that of General Ruffin from the fact that it is positively known that James' company was on duty at Fort Johnston, on James' Island, while the Palmetto Guards, of which General Ruffin was a member, was at the railroad battery on Morris Island. However, this should not be taken as conclusive, as at that time discipline was, to a certain extent, not strictly enforced, and many independent volunteers belonged to the army over whom there was very little, if any control. So General Ruffin may have been at Fort Johnston while his company was at Cummings Point. However, little interest is attached to this incident after the lapse of so many years.

Perhaps never in the history of a State was there such a

frenzy of excitement—not even in the days of Indian insurrections or the raids of the bloody Tarleton—as when the news
flashed over the country that Sumter was being bombarded,
and a call was made for all the volunteers to assemble in
Charleston.   There were not the facilities in those days as now
for the spreading of news, there being but few telegraph lines
in the State.   Notwithstanding this, every method possible
was put into practice for gathering in the troops.   There were
no assemblages of troops outside of Charleston.   Men were following their daily vocations.   Extra trains were put in motion; couriers dashed with rapid speed across the country.
Private means, as well as public, were resorted to to arouse the
men and bring them to the front.   Officers warned the private, and he in turn rode with all the speed his horse, loosed
from the plow, could command, to arouse his comrades.   It
was on Saturday when word was first sent out, but it was late
the next day (Sunday) before men in the remote rural districts received the stirring notice.   Men left their plows standing in the field, not to return under four years, and many of
them never.   Carpenters came down from the unfinished roof,
or left their bench with work half finished.   The student who
had left his school on the Friday before never recited his Mon-
day's lesson.   The country doctor left his patients to the care
of the good housewife.   Many people had gone to church and
in places the bells were still tolling, calling the worshippers
together to listen to the good and faithful teachings of the
Bible, but the sermon was never delivered or listened to.
Hasty preparations were made everywhere.   The loyal wives
soon had the husband's clothes in the homemade knapsack;
the mother buckled on the girdle of her son, while the gray
haired father was burning with impatience, only sorrowing
that he, too, could not go.   Never before in the history of the
world, not even in Carthage or Sparta, was there ever such a
spontaneous outburst of patriotic feeling; never such a cheerful
and willing answer to the call of a mother country.   Not a regret, not a tear; no murmuring or reproaches—not one single
complaint.   Never did the faithful Scott give with better grace
his sons for the defense of his beloved chief, "Eric," than did
the fathers and mothers of South Carolina give their sons for
the defense of the beloved Southland.

The soldiers gathered at the railroad stations, and as the trains that had been sent to the farthest limits of the State came along, the troops boarded them and hurried along to Charleston, then the seat of war. General M. L. Bonham had been appointed Major General of State troops and called his brigades together. Colonel Gregg was already in Charleston with the First Regiment. Col. Joseph B. Kershaw with the Second, Colonel James H. Williams with the Third, Colonel Thomas Bacon with the Seventh, and Colonel E. B. C. Cash with the Eighth, formed their regiments by gathering the different companies along at the various railroad stations. The Second, Seventh, and Eighth came on to Charleston, reaching there while the bombardment was still in progress, but not early enough to take active part in the battle. Colonel Williams with the Third, for want of transportation, was stopped in Columbia, and took up quarters in the Fair Grounds. The other regiments went into camp in the suburbs of Charleston and on the islands. After the surrender of Sumter the troops on the islands and mainland returned to their old quarters to talk upon the incidents of the battle, write home of the memorable events and to rejoice generally. Almost as many rumors were now afloat as there were men in the army. It was the generally conceded opinion of all that the war was at an end. A great many of the Southern leaders boasted of "drinking all the blood that would be shed in the war." The whole truth of the entire matter was, both sections underrated each other. The South, proud and haughty, looked with disdain upon the courage of the North; considered the people cowardly, and not being familiar with firearms would be poor soldiers; that the rank and file of the North, being of a foreign, or a mixture of foreign blood, would not remain loyal to the Union, as the leaders thought, and would not fight. While the North looked upon the South as a set of aristocratic blusterers, their affluence and wealth having made them effeminate; a nation of weaklings, who could not stand the fatigues and hardships of a campaign. Neither understood the other, overrating themselves and underrating the strength of their antagonists. When Lincoln first called for 50,000 troops and several millions of dollars for equipment and conduct of the war, the South would ask in derision, "Where would he get them?"

When the South would talk of resistance, the North would ask,
"Where are her soldiers?"   "The rich planters' sons cannot
fight."   "The poor man will not do battle for the negroes of
the rich."   "The South has no arms, no money, no credit."
So each mistook the strength, motives, spirits, and sentiments
that actuated the other.   A great change came over the feelings of the North after the fall of Sumter.   They considered
that their flag had been insulted, their country dishonored.
Where there had been differences before at the North, there
was harmony now. · The conservative press of that section
was now defiant and called for war; party differences were
healed and the Democratic party of the North that had always
affiliated in national affairs with the South, was now bitter
against their erring sisters, and cried loudly for "Union or
coercion."   The common people of the North were taught to
believe that the Nation had been irretrievably dishonored and
disgraced, that the disruption of the Union was a death knell
to Republican institutions and personal liberty.   That the liberty and independence that their ancestors had won by their
blood in the Revolution was now to be scattered to the four
winds of heaven by a few fanatical slave holders at the South.
But up to this time the question of slavery had not been
brought into controversy on either side.   It was not discussed
and was only an after thought, a military necessity.

Virginia, three days after the fall of Sumter, joined her sister State.   This act of the old commonwealth was hailed in the
Gulf States with great rejoicing.   Bells tolled and cannon
boomed and men hurrahed.   Until now it was not certain
what stand would be taken by the Border States.   They did
not wish to leave the Union; neither would they be a party to
a war upon their seceding sisters.   They promised to be neu-
tral.   But President Lincoln soon dispelled all doubt and uncertainty by his proclamation, calling upon all States then remaining in the Union to furnish their quota of troops.   They
were then forced to take sides for or against and were not
long in reaching a conclusion.   As soon as conventions could
be assembled, the States joined the Confederacy and began
levying troops to resist invasion.   Teunessee followed Virginia, then Arkansas, the Old North State being the last of
the Atlantic and Gulf States to cross the Rubicon into the

"plains of Southern independence." The troops that had been called for six months were now disbanded, and those who had enlisted for twelve months for State service were called upon to volunteer in the Confederate Army for the unexpired time. They volunteered almost without a dissenting voice. Having left their homes so hurriedly, they were granted a furlough of a week or ten days to return to their families and put their houses in order. They then returned and went into a camp of instruction.

General Bonham had not gotten all of his regiments together up to this time. The Second, Seventh, and Eighth were around Charleston, while the Third was at Lightwood Knot Spring, four miles from Columbia. This camp was called "Camp Williams," in honor of their Colonel. That in Columbia was called "Camp Ruffin," in honor of General Ruffin. It was customary to give all the different camps a name during the first year's service, generally in honor of some favorite officer or statesman. Colonel Gregg's regiment remained on Morris Island until early in May, when it was sent to Norfolk, Va., to take charge of the large amount of government property there, now very valuable to the South.

At the reorganization of the First Regiment I came to Columbia and joined the company I had before enlisted in. I had two older brothers there, and I was given a place as Second Sergeant in the company.

At the secession of South Carolina, Colonel Williams was in Arkansas, where he had large estates, but on being notified of his election, he joined his regiment while at Lightwood Knot Springs. He was met at the railroad by his troops with great demonstrations of joy and pride. Stalwart men hoisted him upon their shoulders and carried him through the camp, followed by a throng of shouting and delighted soldiers. The regiment had been commanded up to that time by Lieutenant Colonel Foster, of Spartanburg, with James M. Baxter as Major, D. R. Rutherford as Adjutant, Dr. D. E. Ewart Surgeon, John McGowan Quartermaster.

Cadets were sent from the Citadel as drill masters to all the regiments, and for six hours daily the ears were greeted with "hep-hep" to designate the "left" foot "down" while on the drill. It took great patience, determination, and toil to bring

3

the men under military discipline. Fresh from the fields, shops, and schools they had been accustomed to the freedom of home life, and with all their patriotism, it took time to break into the harness of military restraint and discipline these lovers of personal freedom. Many amusing incidents occurred while breaking these "wild colts," but all took it good humoredly, and the best of feelings existed between officers and men. Some few, however, were nettled by the restraint and forced obedience to those whom they had heretofore been accustomed to look upon as equals, but now suddenly made superiors. The great majority entered upon the duties of camp life with rare good will. All were waiting patiently the call to Virginia. Here I will give a short description of the regiments and their officers up to the time that all were brought together as a brigade. After that time we will treat them as a whole.

The regiments were uniformed by private donations. each neighborhood uniforming the company raised in its bounds. The tents were large and old fashioned—about 8 x 10 feet square, with a separate fly on top—one of these b.ing allowed to every six or seven men. They were pitched in rows, about fifty feet apart, the front of one company facing the rear of the other. About the first of June all the regiments, except the Second, were ordered to Manassas, Va. The regiments were formed by companies from battalions of the militia from various counties, one company usually being formed from a battalion. These companies were organized into regiments, very much as at present, and like the old anti-bellum militia. At times some ambitious citizen would undertake to raise a volunteer company outside of those raised from battalions, and generally these were called "crack companies." Afterwards a few undertook to raise companies in this manner, *i. e.*, selecting the officers first, and then proceeding to select the men, refusing such as would not make acceptable soldiers. thus forming exclusive organizations. These were mostly formed in towns and cities. At other times old volunteer companies, as they were called, of the militia would enlist in a body, with such recruits as were wanted to fill up the number. In the old militia service almost all the towns and cities had these companies as a kind of city organization, and they would be handsomely uniformed, well equipped, and in many cases were almost equal to regular soldiers. Columbia had at least three of these companies in our brigade—the Governor's Guards, Richland Rifles, and one more, I think, but on this point am not positive. Charleston had two or more, the Palmetto Guards and others; Greenville, the Butler Guards; Newberry, the Quitman Rifles; while the other counties, Abbeville, Anderson, Edgefield, Williamsburg, Darlington, Sumter, and almost all the counties represented in our brigade had one of these city volunteer companies. When all the companies called for had been organized, they were notified to what regiment they had been assigned, or what companies were to constitute a regiment, and were ordered to hold an election for field officers. Each company would hold its election. candidates in the meantime having offered their services to fill the respective places of Colonel, Lieutenant Colonel, and Major. After the elections thus held, the returns would be sent up to the Adjutant and Inspector General's office and there tabulated, and the result declared. The candidates for field officers were generally Mexican War Veterans, or some popular citizen, whom the old men thought "would take care of the boys." At first the qualification of a commander, be it Colonel or Captain, mostly required was clemency. His rules of discipline, bravery, or military ability were not so much taken into consideration.

SECOND SOUTH CAROLINA REGIMENT.

Early in May or the last of April four companies of the Second Regiment, under Colonel Kershaw, volunteered for Confederate service, and were sent at once to Virginia. These companies were commandded by—

Captain John D. Kennedy, Kershaw County.

Captain W. H. Casson, Richland County.

Captain William Wallace, Richland County.

Captain John Richardson, Sumter County.

They were afterwards joined by companies under—

Captain Perryman, of Abbeville County, (formerly of the Seventh Regiment).

Captain Cuthbert. Charleston.

Captain Rhett, Charleston.

Captain Haile, Kershaw.

Captain McManus, Lancaster.

Captain Hoke, Greenville.

These were among the first soldiers from the "Palmetto State" to go to Virginia, and the regiment when fully organized stood as follows:

J. B. Kershaw, Colonel, of Camden.

E. P. Jones, Lieutenant Colonel.

Fred Gaillard, Major.

A. D. Goodwin, Adjutant.

Company A—W. H. Casson, Richland.

Company B—A. D. Hoke, Greenville.

Company C—William Wallace, Richland.

Company D—T. S. Richardson.

Company E—John L. Kennedy, Kershaw.

Company F—W. W. Perryman, Anderson.

Company G—I. Haile, Kershaw.

Company H—H. McManus, Lancaster.

Company I—G. B. Cuthbert, Charleston.

Company K—R. Rhett, Charleston.

Surgeon—Dr. F. Salmond, Kershaw.

Quartermaster—W. S. Wood, Columbia.

Commissary—J. J. Villepigue.

Chaplain—A. J. McGruder.

THIRD SOUTH CAROLINA REGIMENT.

The Third Regiment had originally twelve companies enlisted for State service, but in transferring to Confederate Army only ten were allowed by the army regulations. Two companies were left out, viz.: Captain J. C. S. Brown's, from Newberry, and Captain Mat. Jones', from Laurens. The privates, however, enlisted in the other companies as a general rule, for the companies were allowed a maximum number of 100. The Eighth and Third made no changes in their companies or officers from their first enlistment in the State service until their second enlistment in 1862, only as occasioned by resignations or the casualties of war. The two regiments remained as first organized, with few exceptions.

The Third stood, when ready for transportation to Virginia, the 7th of June, as follows:

James H. Williams, Colonel, Newberry.

B. B. Foster, Lieutenant Colonel, Spartanburg.

James M. Baxter, Major, Newberry.

W. D. Rutherford, Adjutant, Newberry.

Company A—B. Conway Garlington, Laurens.

Company B—S. Newton Davidson, Newberry.

Company C—R. C. Maffett, Newberry.

Company D—T. B. Furgerson, Spartanburg and Union.

Company E—James D. Nance, Newberry.

Company F—T. Walker, Newberry and Laurens.

Company G—R. P. Todd, Laurens.

Company H—D. Nunamaker, Lexington.

Company I—Smith L. Jones, Laurens.

Company K—Benj. Kennedy, Spartanburg.

Surgeon—Dr. D. E. Ewart, Newberry.

Quartermaster—John McGowan, Laurens.

Commissary—Sergeant J. N. Martin, Newberry.

Chaplain—Rev. Mayfield.

SEVENTH SOUTH CAROLINA REGIMENT.

Colonel, Thomas G. Bacon.

The following companies were from Abbeville:

Company A, Captain W. W. Perryman.

Company B, Captain G. M. Mattison.

Company C, Captain P. H. Bradley.

Company D, Captain S. J. Hester.

The following companies were from Edgefield:

Company E, Captain D. Dendy.

Company F, Captain John S. Hard.

Company G, Captain J. Hampden Brooks.

Company H, Captain Elbert Bland.

Company I, Captain W. E. Prescott.

Company K, Captain Bart Talbert.

Captain Perryman with his company, the "Secession Guards," volunteered for the Confederate service before the other companies, and left for Virginia on April 28th and joined the Second South Carolina Regiment. Captain Bland took his place with his company in the regiment as Company A.

The companies of the Seventh came together as a regiment at the Schutzenplatz, near Charleston, on the 16th of April. In about two weeks it was ordered to Edgefield District at a place called Montmorenci, in Aiken County. While here a company came from Edgefield County near Trenton, under Captain Coleman, and joined the regiment. But this company failed to enlist.

The Seventh Regiment elected as officers: Colonel, Thomas G. Bacon, of Edgefield District; Lieutenant Colonel, Robert A. Fair, of Abbeville; Major, Emmet Seibels, of Edgefield; Adjutant, D. Wyatt Aiken, of Abbeville. All the staff officers were appointed by the Colonels until the transfer to the Confederate service; then the medical department was made a separate branch, and the Surgeons and Assistant Surgeons were appointed by the Department. Colonel Bacon appointed on his staff: B. F. Lovelass, Quartermaster; Fred Smith, Commissary; afterwards A. F. Townsend.

Surgeon Joseph W. Hearst resigned, and A. R. Drogie was made Surgeon in his stead, with Dr. G. H. Waddell as Assistant Surgeon. A. C. Stallworth, Sergeant Major, left for Virginia about the first of June and joined the Second a few days afterwards.

EIGHTH SOUTH CAROLINA REGIMENT.

The Eighth Regiment was organized early in the year 1861, but the companies were not called together until the 14th day of April, arriving in Charleston in the afternoon of that day, just after the fall of Fort Sumter. It was composed of ten companies, as follows: Three from Chesterfield, two from Marion, two from Marlborough, and three from Darlington, with Colonel, E. B. C. Cash; Lieutenant Colonel, John W. Henegan; Major, Thomas E. Lucas; Adjutant, C. B. Weatherly.

Companies first taken to Virginia:

Company A—A. I. Hoole, Darlington.
Company B—M. I. Hough, Chesterfield.
Company C—Wm. H. Coit, Chrsterfield.
Company D—John S. Miller, Chesterfield.
Company E—W. E. Jay. Darlington.
Company F—W. H. Evans, Darlington.
Company G—John W. Harrington, Marlboro.
Company H—R. L. Singletary, Marion.
Company I—T. E. Stackhouse, Marion.
Company K—D. McD. McLeod, Marlboro.

After remaining in Charleston until the 4th of May it was moved to Florence. On the 1st of June the regiment re-enlisted for Confederate service. They were ordered to Richmond and arrived there on June 4th, and left on the 15th to join the Second then at Bull Run. On the 22nd of June they went into camp at Germantown, near Fairfax Court House, where all the regiments were soon joined together as Bonhams' Brigade.

The first real exciting incident connected with the Third South Carolina Regiment—the first panic and stampede—happened as the troops were returning from their ten days' furlough to their camp of instruction, near Columbia, just after their enlistment in the Confederate service. I record this occurrence to show what little incidents, and those of such little moment, are calculated to stampede an army, and to what foolish lengths men will go when excited. The train was rattling along at a good speed, something like ten or fifteen miles an hour, just above Columbia; a long string of box cars loaded with soldiers; the baggage of the troops scattered promiscuously around in the cars; trunks, valises, carpet bags, and boxes of all conceivable dimensions, holding the belongings of several neighborhoods of boys; spirits flowed without and within; congenial friends in a congenial cause; congenial topics made a congenial whole. When just below Littleton, with long stretches of lowlands on one side and the river on the other, the curling streaks of a little grey smoke made its appearance from under one of the forward cars. At first the merry good humor and enlivening effects of some amusing jest, the occasional round of a friendly bottle, prevented the men from noticing this danger signal of fire. However, a little later on this continuing and increasing volume of smoke caused an alarm to be given. Men ran to the doors on either side, shouted and called, waved hats, hands, and handkerchiefs, at the same time pointing at the smoke below. There being no communication between the cars, those in front and rear had to be guided by the wild gesticulations of those in the smoking car. The engineer did not notice anything amiss, and sat placidly upon his high seat, watching the fast receding rails as they flashed under and out of sight beneath the ponderous driving-wheels of the

engine.   At last someone in the forward car, not accustomed
to, but familiar with the dangers of a railroad car by the wild
rumors given currency in his rural district of railroad wrecks,
made a desperate leap from the car.   This was followed by
another, now equally excited.   Those in the front cars,
clutching to the sides of the doors, craned their necks as far as
possible outward, but could see nothing but leaping men.
They fearing a catastrophe of some kind, leaped also, while
those in the rear cars, as they saw along the sides of the railroad track men leaping, rolling, and tumbling on the ground,
took it for granted that a desperate calamity had happened to
a forward car.   No time for questions, no time for meditation.
The soldier's only care was to watch for a soft place to make
his desperate leap, and in many cases there was little choice.
Men leaped wildly in the air, some with their heels up, others
falling on their heads and backs, some rolling over in a mad
scramble to clear themselves from the threatening danger.
The engineer not being aware of anything wrong with the
train, glided serenely along, unconscious of the pandemonium
in the rear.   But when all had about left the train, and the
great driving-wheels began to spin around like mad, from the
lightening of the load, the master of the throttle looked to the
rear.   There lay stretched prone upon the ground, or limping
on one foot, or rolling over in the dirt, some bareheaded and
coatless, boxes and trunks scattered as in an awful collision,
upwards of one thousand men along the railroad track.   Many
of the men thinking, no doubt, the train hopelessly lost, or
serious danger imminent, threw their baggage out before making the dangerous leap.   At last the train was stopped and
brought back to the scene of desolation.   It terminated like
the bombardment of Fort Sumter—"no one hurt," and all
occasioned by a hot-box that could have been cooled in a very
few minutes.   Much swearing and good-humored jesting were
now engaged in.   Such is the result of the want of presence of
mind.   A wave of the hat at the proper moment as a signal to
the engineer to stop, and all would have been well.   It was
told once of a young lady crossing a railroad track in front of
a fast approaching train, that her shoe got fastened in the frog
where the two rails join.   She began to struggle, then to
scream, and then fainted.   A crowd rushed up, some grasping

the lady's body attempted to pull her loose by force; others shouted to the train to stop; some called for crow-bars to take up the iron. At last one man pushed through the crowd, untied the lady's shoe, and she was loose. Presence of mind, and not force, did it.

Remaining in camp a few days, orders came to move, and cars were gotten in readiness and baggage packed preparatory to the trip to Virginia. To many, especially those reared in the back districts, and who, before their brief army life, had never been farther from their homes than their county seat, the trip to the old "Mother of Presidents," the grand old commonwealth, was quite a journey indeed. The old negroes, who had been brought South during the early days of the century, called the old State "Virginy" and mixing it with local dialect, in some parts had got the name so changed that it was called "Ferginey." The circus troops and negro comedians, in their annual trips through the Southern States, had songs already so catchy to our people, on account of their pathos and melody, of Old Virginia, that now it almost appeared as though we were going to our old home. Virginia had been endeared to us and closely connected with the people of South Carolina by many links, not the least being its many sentimental songs of that romantic land, and the stories of her great men.

The baggage of the common soldier at this stage of the war would have thrown an ordinary quartermaster of latter day service into an epileptic fit, it was so ponderous in size and enormous in quantities—a perfect household outfit. A few days before this the soldier had received his first two months' pay, all in new crisp bank notes, fresh from the State banks or banks of deposit. It can be easily imagined that there were lively times for the butcher, the baker and candlestick maker, with all this money afloat. The Third South South Carolina was transported by way of Wilmington and Weldon, N. C. Had there ever existed any doubts in the country as to the feelings of the people of the South before this in regard to Secession, it was entirely dispelled by the enthusiastic cheers and good will of the people along the road. The conduct of the men and women through South Carolina, North Carolina, and Virginia, showed one long and continued ovation along the line of travel, looking like a general holiday. As the cars sped along through the fields, the little hamlets and towns, people of every kind, size, and complexion rushed to the railroad and gave us welcome and Godspeed. Hats went into the air as we passed, handkerchiefs fluttered, flags waved in the gentle summer breeze from almost every housetop. The ladies and old men pressed to the side of the cars when we halted, to shake the hands of the brave soldier boys, and gave them blessings, hope and encouragement. The ladies vied with the men in doing homage to the soldiers of the Palmetto State. Telegrams had been sent on asking of our coming, the hour of our passage through the little towns, and inviting us to stop and enjoy their hospitality and partake of refreshments. In those places where a stop was permitted, long tables were spread in some neighboring grove or park, bending under the weight of their bounties, laden down with everything tempting to the soldier's appetite. The purest and best of the women mingled freely with the troops, and by every device known to the fair sex showed their sympathy and encouragement in the cause we had espoused. At Wilmington, N. C., we crossed the Cape Fear River on a little river steamer, the roads not being connected with a bridge. At Petersburg and Richmond we had to march through portions of those cities in going from one depot to another, union sheds, not being in vogue at that time, and on our entry into these cities the population turned out en masse to welcome and extend to us their greeting. Every private house stood open to the soldiers and the greatest good will was everywhere manifested.

Much has been said in after years, since misfortune and ruin overtook the South, since the sad reverses of the army and the overthrow of our principles, about leaders plunging the nation into a bloody and uncalled for war. This is all the height of folly. No man or combination of men could have stayed or avoided war. No human persuasion or earthly power could have stayed the great wave of revolution that had struck the land; and while, like a storm widening and gathering strength and fury as it goes, to have attempted it would have been but to court ruin and destruction. Few men living in that period of our country's history would have had the boldness or hardihood to counsel submission or inactivity. Differences there may have been and were as to methods, but to Secession, none.

The voices of the women of the land were alone enough to have forced the measures upon the men in some shape or other. Then, as to the leaders being "shirkers" when the actual contest came, the history of the times gives contradictions sufficient without examples. Where the duties of the service called, they willingly obeyed. All could not fill departments or sit in the councils of the nation, but none shirked the responsibility the conditions called them to. Where fathers filled easy places their sons were in the ranks, and many of our leaders of Secession headed troops in the field. General Bonham, our Brigadier, had just resigned his seat in the United States Congress; so had L. M. Keitt, who fell at Cold Harbor at the head of our brigade, while Colonel of the Twentieth Regiment. James L. Orr, one of the original Secessionists snd a member of Congress, raised the first regiment of rifles. The son of Governor Gist, the last Executive of South Carolnia just previous to Secession, fell while leading his regiment, the Fifteenth, of our brigade, in the assault at Fort Loudon, at Knoxville. Scarcely was there a member of the convention that passed the Ordinance of Secession who had not a son or near kinsman in the ranks of the army. They showed by their deeds the truth and honesty of their convictions. They had trusted the North until trusting had ceased to be a virtue. They wished peace, but feared not war. All this idle talk, so common since the war, of a "rich man's war and a poor man's fight" is the merest twaddle and vilely untrue.

The men of the South had risked their all upon the cast, and were willing to abide by the hazard of the die. All the great men of South Carolina were for Secession, and they nobly entered the field. The Hamptons, Butlers, Haskells, Draytons, Bonhams, all readily grasped the sword or musket. The fire-eaters, like Bob Toombs, of Georgia, and Wigfall, of Texas, led brigades, and were as fiery upon the battlefield as they had been upon the floor of the United States Senate. So with all the leaders of Secession, without exception; they contributed their lives, their services, and their wealth to the cause they had advocated and loved so well. I make this departure here to correct an opinion or belief, originated and propagated by the envious few who did not rise to distinction in the war, or who were too young to participate in its glories—those glories that were mutual and will ever surround the Confederate soldier, regardless of rank.

After stopping a few days in Richmond, we were carried on to Manassas and Bull Run, then to Fairfax, where we joined the other regiments. The Third Regiment camped first at Mitchell's Ford, remained at that point for a week or ten days, and from thence moved to the outpost just beyond Fairfax Court House. The Eighth and Second camped for a while at Germantown, and soon the whole brigade was between Fairfax and Bull Run.

CHAPTER IV

Camp at Fairfax—Bonham's Staff—Biography of General Bonham—Retreat to Bull Run. Battle of the 18th

General Bonham had gathered around him, as staff officers, a galaxy of gentlemen as cultured, talented, and patriotic as South Carolina could produce, and as gallant as ever followed a general upon the battlefield; all of whom won promotion and distinction as the war progressed in the different branches of service.

Colonel Samuel Melton, one of the staff, writing in a pleasant mood, thirty-five years afterwards, says: "That with universal acclamation it may be said, that the retinue gathered around the General of the old First Brigade was a gorgeous one. I am proud of it 'until yet.' "

This staff of General Bonham's was the one allowed by the State service, and the appointments were made under State laws. However, all followed him into the Confederate service, and, with a few exceptions, remained until after the battle of Manassas, serving without pay. The Confederate Government was much more modest in its appointment of staff officers, and only allowed a Brigadier General three or four members as his personal staff.

The following is a list of officers who followed General Bonham to Virginia, or joined him soon after his arrival:

W. C. Morayne, Assistant Adjutant General, with rank of Colonel.

The following with rank of Lieutenant Colonel:

W. D. Simpson, Inspector General.

A. P. Aldrich, Quartermaster General.

R. B. Boylston, Commissary General.

J. N. Lipscomb, Paymaster General.

Aides, with rank of Major: S. W. Melton, B. F. Withers, T. J. Davis, E. S. Hammond, S. Warren Nelson, Samuel Tompkins, W. P. Butler, M. B. Lipscomb.

Colonel S. McGowan, Volunteer Aide.

Dr. Reeves, of Virginia, was Brigade Surgeon.

Colonels Morayne and Boylston remained only a few weeks. Captain George W. Say, an officer of the Confederate staff, succeeded Colonel Morayne, and remained a short while, when he was promoted and sent elsewhere. Colonel Lipscomb became the regular aide, with rank of First Lieutenant.

When Captain Say left, S. W. Melton was put in his place as Assistant Adjutant General, without appointment or without pay, and discharged the duties of that office until August, when he left on sick leave. When he returned he was appointed Major and Assistant Adjutant General, and assigned to duty upon the staff of Major General G. W. Smith, commanding Second Corps of the Army of the Potomac. In 1863 he was promoted to Lieutenant Colonel and assigned to duty in the war department.

William F. Nance, of Newberry, was appointed Captain and Assistant Adjutant General, and in September, 1861, was assigned to duty upon General Bonham's staff, where he remained until the General's resignation. In 1864 Nance was on duty in Charleston, where he remained on staff duty until the end.

S. McGowan and W. D. Simpson returned to South Carolina after the battle of Manassas, and assisted in raising the Fourteenth South Carolina Regiment of Volunteers, of which the former was elected Lieutenant Colonel and the latter Major. Colonel McGowan became Colonel of the regiment, and afterwards Brigadier of one of the most famous brigades

(McGowan's) in the Confederate Army. Colonel Simpson served in the Confederate Congress after his retirement from the army.

All the others of the staff filled prominent positions, either as commanding or staff officers, or serving in the departments in Richmond. I have no data at hand to give sketches of their individual services.

Fairfax Court House was the extreme limit at which the infantry was posted on that side of the Blue Ridge. Cavalry was still in advance, and under the leadership of the indefatigable Stuart scouting the whole front between the Confederate and Federal armies. The Third South Carolina was encamped about a mile north of the little old fashioned hamlet, the county seat of the county of that name. In this section of the State lived the ancestors of most of the illustrious families of Virginia, Washington, Jefferson, Madison, Monroe, and Lee. It is a rather picturesque country; not so beautiful and productive, however, as the Shenandoah and Luray Valleys. The Seventh, Eighth, and Second Regiments were encamped several miles distant, but all in the hearing of one another's drums. Our main duties outside of our regular drills consisted in picketing the highways and blockading all roads by felling the timber across for more than a hundred yards on either side of the roads. Large details armed with axes were sent out to blockade the thoroughfares leading to Washington and points across the Potomac. For miles out, in all directions, wherever the road led through wooded lands, large trees, chestnut, hickory, oak, and pine, were cut pell mell, creating a perfect abattis across the road—so much so as to cause our troops in their verdant ignorance to think it almost an impossibility for such obstructions to be cleared away in many days; whereas, as a fact, the pioneer corps of the Federal Army cleared it away as fast as the army marched, not causing as much as one hour's halt. Every morning at nine o'clock one company from a regiment would go out about two miles in the direction of Washington Falls church or Annandale to do picket duty, and remain until nine o'clock next day, when it would be relieved by another company. The "Black Horse Cavalry," an old organization of Virginia, said to have remained intact since the Revolution, did vidette duty still beyond the infantry. Their duties were to ride through the country in every direction, and on every road and by-way to give warning of approaching danger to the infantry. These were bold riders in those days, some daring to ride even within view of the spires and domes of Washington itself. On our outposts we could plainly hear the sound of the drums of the Federalists in their preparation for the "on to Richmond" move. General Bonham had also some fearless scouts at this time. Even some of the boldest of the women dared to cross the Potomac in search of information for the Confederate Generals. It was here that the noted Miss Bell Boyd made herself famous by her daring rides, her many escapades and hairbreadth escapes, her bold acts of crossing the Potomac. sometimes disguised and at other times not, even entering the City of Washington itself. In this way she gathered much valuable information for the Confederate Generals, and kept them posted on the movements of the enemy. She was one of the best horsewomen of that day; a fine specimen of womanhood, and as fearless and brave as a stout hearted cavalier. She generally carried a brace of Colt's revolvers around her waist, and was daring enough to meet any foe who was so bold as to cross her path. Bell Boyd was one of the many noble Virginia women who staked and dared all for the cause of the South. William Farley, of South Carolina, another bold scout, was invaluable to General Stuart and General Bonham. It was he that John Esten Cooke immortalized in "Surry of Eagle's Nest" and was killed at the battle of Chancellorsville. He was a native of Laurens County.

The duties of picketing were the first features of our army life that looked really like war. The soldiers had become accustomed to guard duty, but to be placed out on picket or vidette posts alone, or in company with a comrade, to stand all day and during the dead hours of the night, expecting some lurking foe every moment to shoot you in the back, or from behind some bush to shoot your head off, was quite another matter. As a guard, we watched over our friends; as a picket, we watched for our foe. For a long time, being no nearer the enemy than the hearing of their drums, the soldiers had grown somewhat careless. But there was an uncanny feeling in standing alone in the still hours of the night, in a strange country, watching, waiting for an enemy to crawl up and shoot

you unawares. This feeling was heightened, especially in my
company, by an amusing incident that happened while on
picket duty on the Annandale road. Up to this time there
had been no prisoners captured on either side, and it was
uncertain as to what would be the fate of any who would fall
in the enemy's hands. As we were considered traitors and
rebels, the penalty for that crime was, as we all knew, death.
The Northern press had kept up quite a howl, picturing the
long rows of traitors that would be hung side by side as soon
as they had captured the Confederate Army. That there was
a good deal of "squeamishness" felt at the idea of being captured, cannot be doubted. So videttes were stationed several
hundred yards down the road with a picket post of four men,
between the outside sentinels and the company, as reserve.
A large pine thicket was to our right, while on the left was an
old field with here and there a few wild cherry trees. The
cherries being ripe, some of the men had gone up in the trees
to treat themselves to this luscious little fruit. The other part
of the company lay indolently about, sheltering themselves as
best they could from the rays of the hot July sun, under the
trees. Some lay on the tops of fences, and in corners, while
not a few, with coats and vests off, enjoyed a heated game of
"old sledge." All felt a perfect security, for with the pickets
in front, the cavalry scouring the country, and the almost impassable barricades of the roads, seemed to render it impossible for an enemy to approach unobserved. The guns leaned
carelessly against the fence or lay on the ground, trappings,
etc., scattered promiscuously around. Not a dream of danger;
no thought of a foe. While the men were thus pleasantly
engaged, and the officers taking an afternoon nap, from out in
the thicket on the right came "bang-bang," and a hail of bullets came whizzing over our heads. What a scramble! What
an excitement! What terror depicted on the men's faces!
Had a shower of meteors fallen in our midst, had a volcano burst
from the top of the Blue Ridge, or had a thunder bolt fell at
our feet out of the clear blue sky, the consternation could not
have been greater. Excitement, demoralization, and panic
ensued. Men tumbled off the fences, guns were reached for,
haversacks and canteens hastily grabbed, and, as usual in
such panics, no one could get hold of his own. Some started

up the road, some down. Officers thus summarily aroused
were equally demoralized. Some gave one order, some
another. "Pandemonium reigned supreme." Those in the
cherry trees came down. nor did the "cherry pickers" stand
on the order of their coming. The whole Yankee army was
thought to be over the hills. At last the officer commanding
got the men halted some little distance up the road; a semblance of a line formed, men cocked their guns and peered
anxiously through the cracks of the rail fence, expecting to
see an enemy behind every tree. A great giant, a sergeant
from the mountain section, who stood six feet, three inches in
his stockings, and as brave as he was big, his face flushed
with excitement, his whole frame trembling with emotion, in
his shirt sleeves and bareheaded, rushed to the middle of the
road, braced himself, as waiting for some desperate shock, and
stood like Horatio Cockles at the Bridge, waving his gun in
the air, calling out in defiant and stentorian voice, "Come on,
I'll fight all of you; I'll fight old Lincoln from here to the
sea." Such a laugh as was set up afterwards, at his expense!
The amusing part of it was the parties who fired the shots at
the time the stampeding was going on with us, were running
for dear life's sake across the fields, worse scared, if possible,
than we ourselves. They were three of a scouting party, who
had eluded our pickets, and seeing our good. easy, and indifferent
condition, took it into their heads to have a little amusement
at our expense. But the sound of their guns in the quiet surrounding, no doubt excited the Yankees as much as it did the
Confederates. This was an adventure not long in reaching
home, for to be shot at by a real live Yankee was an event in
every one's life at the time not soon to be forgotten. But it
was so magnified, that by the time it reached home, had not
the battle of Bull Run come in its heels so soon, this incident
would no doubt have ever remained to those who were engaged in it as one of the battles of the war. The only casualty
was a hole shot through a hat. I write this little incident to
show the difference in raw and seasoned troops. One year
later such an incident would not have disturbed those men
any more than the buzzing of a bee. Picket duty after this
incident was much more stringent. Two men were made to
stand on post all night, without relief, only such as they gave

4

each other.   Half of the company's reserve were kept awake
all night.   Orders were given that the utmost silence should
prevail, the men were not even to speak above a whisper, and
on the approach of anyone they were to be hailed with the
command, "Halt, who comes there?"   If a satisfactory answer was given, they were allowed to pass.   If not, to remain
standing, and an officer of the guard called.   At night they
were to call "halt" three times, and if no answer, they were to
fire and retreat to the reserve.

One night, shortly after this, one of the companies from
Spartanburg had been sent out about three miles to the intersection of a country road leading off to the left.   Down this
country road, or lane, were two pickets.   They concealed
themselves during the day in the fence corners, but at night
they crawled over into a piece of timber land, and crouched
down behind a large oak.   The shooting incident of a few
days before made the two pickets feel somewhat tender at thus
being alone in the forest, when at any moment an enemy
might creep upon them sufficiently near as to shoot them in
the dark.   Everything was as quiet as the grave.   The stars,
peeping faintly out from behind the clouds, midnight came,
and each began to nod, when a twig breaks some distance in
front, then another, then the rustling of dry leaves.   Their
hearts leap to their throats and beat like sledge hammers.
One whispers to the other, "Whist, some one is coming."
They strain their ears to better catch the sound.   Surely
enough they hear the leaves rustling as if some one is approaching.   "Click," "click," the two hammers of their
trusty rifles spring back, fingers upon the triggers, while
nearer the invisible comes.   "Halt," rang out in the midnight
air; "'halt," once more, but still the steady tread keeps approaching.   When the third "halt" was given it was accompanied by the crack of their rifles.   A deafening report and
frightful squeal, as an old female porker went charging through
the underbrush like mad.   The crack of the rifles alarmed the
sleeping companions in reserve, who rushed to arms and
awaited the attack.   But after much good humored badgering
of the two frightened sentinels, "peace reigned once more at
Warsaw" till the break of day.   The company returned next
morning to camp, but the two sentinels who had fired on the

old innocent porker were glad enough to seek the quietude of their quarters to escape the jests of their comrades.

A simple system of breastworks was thrown up just beyond our camp at Fairfax on a little eminence to the right of the road. This we thought sufficient to defeat quite an army, or at least keep them at bay. General Bonham had his headquarters at Fairfax Court House, but rode out daily to examine the work done on the entrenchments, or inspect the pickets and outposts. General Bonham was one of the finest looking officers in the entire army. His tall, graceful figure, his commanding appearance, his noble bearing, and soldierly mein were all qualities to excite the confidence and admiration of his troops. He wore a broad-brimmed hat, with a waving plume floating out behind, and sat his horse as knightly as Charles the Bold, or Henry of Navarre. His soldiers were proud of him, and loved to do him homage. He endeared himself to his officers, and while he was a good disciplinarian as far as the volunteer service required, he did not treat his officers with that air of superiority, nor exact that rigid military courtesy that is required in the regular army. I will here give a short sketch of his life for the benefit of his old comrades in arms.

MILLEDGE LUKE BONHAM

Was born near Red Bank in that part of Edgefield District now included in Saluda County, South Carolina, on the 25th day of December, 1813. His father, Captain James Bonham, who had come from Virginia to South Carolina about the close of the last century, was the son of Major Absalom Bonham, who was a native of Maryland, but who enlisted for the war of the Revolution in a New Jersey regiment, and became a Major of the line on the establishment of that State. After the Revolution he moved to Virginia. Captain James Bonham was himself at the siege of Yorktown as a lad of fifteen, in a company whose captain was only twenty years old. He first settled in this State in the District of Colleton, and there married. After the death of his wife, he moved to Edgefield District, and there married Sophie Smith, who was the mother of the subject of this sketch. She was the daughter of Jacob Smith and his wife, Sallie Butler, who was a sister of that

Captain James Butler who was the forefather of the illustrious
family of that name in this State, and who with his young
son, also named James, was cruelly massacred along with
others at Cloud's Creek, in Edgefield District, by "Bloody
Bill" Cunningham.

Milledge L. Bonham received his early education in the
"old field" schools of the neighborhood, and his academic
training under instructors at Abbeville and Edgefield. He
entered the South Carolina College and graduated with second
honor in 1834. Soon thereafter the Seminole or Florida war
broke out, and he volunteered in the company from Edgefield,
commanded by Captain James Jones, and was Orderly Sergeant of the company. During the progress of the war in
Florida, he was appointed by General Bull, who commanded
the South Carolina Brigade, to be Brigade Major, a position
which corresponds with what is now known in military circles
as Adjutant General of Brigade.

Returning from the war, he resumed the study of law and
was admitted to the Bar and settled at Edgefield for the practice of his profession. In 1844 he was elected to the Legislature. He always took an ardent interest in the militia, and
was first Brigadier General and afterwards Major General of
militia. When the war with Mexico was declared, he was
appointed Lieutenant Colonel of the Twelfth United States
Infantry, one of the new regiments added to the army for that
war. With his regiment he went to Mexico and served with
distinction throughout the war, being promoted to Colonel of
the regiment, and having, by the way, for his Adjutant, Lieutenant Winfield Scott Hancock, afterwards a distinguished
Major General of the Federal Army in the late war. After
the cessation of hostilities, Colonel Bonham was retained in
Mexico as Military Governor of one of the provinces for about
a year. Being then honorably discharged, he returned to
Edgefield and resumed the practice of law. In 1848 he was
elected Solicitor of the Southern Circuit, composed of Edgefield, Barnwell, Orangeburg, Colleton, and Beaufort Districts.
The Bars of the various Districts composing this Circuit
counted among their members many of the ablest and most
distinguished lawyers of the State, and hence it required the
possession and industrious use of talents of no mean order to

sustain one's self as prosecuting officer against such an array
of ability.   But General Bonham continued to hold the office
until 1856, when, upon the death of Hon. Preston S. Brooks,
he was elected to succeed that eminent gentleman in Congress,
and again in 1858 was elected for the full term.   Those were
the stirring times preceding the bursting of the cloud of civil
war, and the debates in Congress were hot and spicy.   In all
these he took his full part.   When South Carolina seceded
from the Union, he promptly resigned his seat in Congress,
and was appointed by Governor Pickens Commander-in-Chief
of all the forces of South Carolina with the rank of Major General.   In this capacity, and waiving all question of rank and
precedence, at the request of Governor Pickens, he served on
the coast on Morris' Island with General Beauregard, who had
been sent there by the Provisional Government of the Confederacy to take command of the operations around Charleston.
On the permanent organization of the Confederate Government, General Bonham was appointed by President Davis a
Brigadier General in the Army of the Confederate States.
His brigade consisted of four South Carolina regiments, commanded respectively by Colonels Kershaw, Williams, Cash,
and Bacon, and General Bonham used to love to say that no
finer body of men were ever assembled together in one command.   With this brigade he went to Virginia, and they were
the first troops other than Virginia troops that landed in Richmond for its defense.   With them he took part in the operations around Fairfax, Vienna, Centerville, and the first battle
of Manassas.

Afterwards, in consequence of a disagreement with the
Department of War, he resigned from the army.   Soon thereafter he was elected to the Confederate Congress, in which
body he served until he was elected Governor of this State in
December, 1862.   It was a trying time to fill that office, and
President Davis, in letters, bears witness to the fact that no
one of the Governors of the South gave him more efficient aid
and support than did Governor Bonham.   At the expiration
of his term of office, in January, 1865, he was appointed to the
command of a brigade of cavalry, and at once set to work to
organize it, but the surrender of Johnston's army put an end
to the war.

Returning from the war broken in fortune, as were all of
his people, he remained for a year or more on his plantation
on Saluda River, in Edgefield County.   He then moved to
Edgefield Court House, again to take up his practice, so often
interrupted by calls to arms.   He was elected to the Legislature in 1866, just preceding Reconstruction, but with the coming of that political era he, in common with all the white men
of the State, was debarred from further participation in public
affairs.   In the movement known as the Tax-payers Convention, which had for its object the relief of the people from
Republican oppression and corruption, he took part as one of
the delegates sent by this convention to Washington to lay before President Grant the condition of the people of the "Pros-
trate State."   He took an active interest and part in the political revolution of 1876 and warmly advocated what was known
as "the straightout policy" and the nomination of Wade
Hampton as Governor.

In 1878 Governor Simpson appointed him the first Railroad
Commissioner under the Act just passed, and subsequently
when the number of the Commissioners was increased to three,
he was elected Chairman of the Commission, in which position
he continued until his death, on the 27th day of August, 1890.
He died suddenly from the rupture of a blood vessel while on
a visit to Haywood White Sulphur Springs, N. C.

General Bonham married on November 13th, 1845, Ann
Patience, a daughter of Nathan L. Griffin, Esq., a prominent
lawyer of Edgefield.   She survived him four years, and of
their union there are living eight children.

Attached to Bonham's Brigade was Kemper's Battery of
light artillery, commanded by Captain Dell Kemper.   This
company was from Alexandria, Va., just over the Potomac
from Washington.   This organization was part of the old
State militia, known as volunteer companies, and had been in
existence as such for many years.   It being in such close
proximity to Washington, the sentiment of the company was
divided, like all companies on the border.   Some of the company were in favor of joining the Union Army, while others
wished to go with the State.   Much discussion took place at
this time among the members as to which side they would
join, but Captain Kemper, with a great display of coolness and

courage, cut the Gordian knot by taking those with him of Southern sentiment, like himself, and on one dark night he pulled out from Alexandria with his cannon and horses and made his way South to join the Southern Army. That was the last time any of that gallant band ever saw their native city for more than four years, and many of the poor fellows looked upon it that night for the last time. Between them and the South Carolinians sprang up a warm attachment that continued during the war. They remained with us as a part of the brigade for nearly two years, or until the artillery was made a separate branch of the service. While in winter quarters, when many troops were granted furloughs, those men having no home to which they could visit like the others, were invited by members of the brigade to visit their own homes in South Carolina and remain with their families the length of their leave of absence. Many availed themselves of these kind invitations, and spent a pleasant month in the hospitable homes of this State. The ladies of South Carolina, appreciating their isolated condition and forced separation from their homes, with no kind mother or sister with opportunities to cheer them with their delicate favors, made them all a handsome uniform and outfit of underwear, and sent to them as a Christmas gift. Never during the long years of the struggle did the hearts of South Carolinians fail to respond to those of the brave Virginians, when they heard the sound of Kemper's guns belching forth death and destruction to the enemy, or when the battle was raging loud and furious.

On the morning of the 16th of July, when all was still and quiet in camp, a puff of blue smoke from a hill about three miles off, followed by the roar of a cannon, the hissing noise of a shell overhead, its loud report, was the first intimation the troops had that the enemy had commenced the advance. It is needless to say excitement and consternation overwhelmed the camp. While all were expecting and anxiously awaiting it, still the idea of being now in the face of a real live enemy, on the eve of a great battle, where death and horrors of war, such as all had heard of but never realized, came upon them with no little feelings of dread and emotion. No man living, nor any who ever lived, retaining his natural faculties, ever faced death in battle without some feeling of dread

or superstitious awe. The soldiers knew, too, the eyes of the
world were upon them, that they were to make the history for
their generation. ' Tents were hurriedly struck, baggage rolled
and thrown into wagons, with which the excited teamsters
were not long in getting into the pike road. Drums beat the
assembly, troops formed in line and took position behind the
breastwork; while the artillery galloped up to the front and
unlimbered, ready for action. The enemy threw twenty-
pound shells repeatedly over the camp, that did no further
damage than add to the consternation of the already excited
teamsters, who seemed to think the safety of the army depended on their getting out of the way. It was an exciting
scene to see four-horse teams galloping down the pike at
break-neck speed, urged forward by the frantic drivers.

It was the intention of McDowell, the Federal Chief, to surprise the advance at Fairfax Court House and cut off their retreat. Already a column was being hurried along the Germantown road, that intersected the main road four miles in
our rear at the little hamlet of Germantown. But soon General Bonham had his forces, according to preconcerted arrangements, following the retreating trains along the pike
towards Bull Run. Men overloaded with baggage, weighted
down with excitement, went at a double quick down the road,
panting and sweating in the noonday sun, while one of the
field officers in the rear accelerated the pace by a continual
shouting, "Hurry up, men, they are firing on our rear." This
command was repeated so often and persistently that it became a by-word in our brigade, so much so, that when anything was wanted to be done with speed the order was always
accompanied with, "Hurry up, men, they are firing on our
rear." The negro servants, evincing no disposition to be left
behind, rushed along with the wagon train like men beset.
While we were on the double-quick, some one noticed a small
Confederate flag floating lazily in the breeze from a tall pine
pole that some soldier had put up at his tent, but by the hurried departure neglected to take down. Its owner could not
entertain the idea of leaving this piece of bunting as a trophy
for the enemy, so risking the chance of capture, he ran back,
cut the staff, and returned almost out of breath to his company
with the coveted flag. We were none too precipitate in our

movement, for as we were passing through Germantown we could see the long rows of glistening bayonets of the enemy crowning the hills to our right. We stopped in Centerville until midnight, then resumed the march, reaching Bull Run at Mitchell's Ford as the sun was just rising above the hill tops.

Colonel Kershaw and Colonel Cash were filing down the east bank to the left, while Colonels Williams and Bacon occupied some earthworks on the right. These had been erected by former troops, who had encamped there before us. General Beauregard had divided his troops into six brigades, putting regiments of the same State together, as far as possible, Bonham's being First Brigade. Beauregard was determined to make Bull Run his line of defense. This is a slow, sluggish stream, only fordable at certain points, its banks steep and rather rocky with a rough plateau reaching back from either side. The western being the more elevated, gave the enemy the advantage in artillery practice. In fact, the banks on the western side at some points came up to the stream in a bluff—especially so at Blackburn's Ford. In the rear and in the direction of the railroad was the now famous Manassas Plains. The Confederate line extended five miles, from Union Mills Ford to Stone Bridge. At the latter place was General Evans, of South Carolina, with two regiments and four pieces of artillery. On the extreme right, Buell with his brigade and a battery of twelve-pounders was posted at Union Mills. McLean's Ford was guarded by D. R. Jones' brigade, with two brass six-pounders. Longstreet with two six-pounders, and Bonham with two batteries of artillery and a squadron of cavalry, guarded the fords at Blackburn's and Mitchell's respectively. Early's Brigade acted as reserve on the right. In rear of the other fords was Cooke's Brigade and one battery. The entire force on the roll on July 11th consisted of 27 pieces of light artillery and 534 men; cavalry, 1425; foot artillery, 265; infantry, 16,150—18,401, comprising the grand total of all arms of General Beauregard one week before the first battle. Now it must be understood that this includes the sick, guards, and those on outpost duty. McDowell had 37,300 of mostly seasoned troops.

The morning of the 18th opened bright and sunny. To our

rear was all bustle and commotion, and it looked like a vast
camp of wagon trains. From the surrounding country all
wagons had been called in from the foraging expeditions laden
with provisions. Herds of cattle were corralled to secure the
troops fresh beef, while the little fires scattered over the vast
plains showed that the cooking details were not idle. General
Beauregard had his headquarters on the hill in our rear.

At eight o'clock on the 18th, McDowell pushed his leading
division forward at Blackburn's Ford, where two old comrades,
but now facing each other as foes, General Tyler and General
Longstreet, were to measure strength and generalship. The
Washington Artillery, under Captain Richardson, of New
Orleans, a famous battery throughout the war, which claims
the distinction of firing the first gun at Bull Run and the last
at Appomattox, was with Longstreet to aid him with their
brass six-pounders.

The enemy advanced over the plain and up to the very bluff
overlooking the stream, and a very short distance from where
Longsteet's force lay, but the Washington Artillery had been
raking the field all the while, from an eminence in the rear,
while the infantry now began to fire in earnest. The elevated position gave the enemy great advantage, and at one
time General Longstreet had to call up his reserves, but the
advantageous assault was speedily repulsed as soon as the
Southern troops became more calm and better accustomed to
the fire and tension of the battlefield. Several assaults were
made, one immediately after the other, but each time Southern
valor overcame Northern discipline. From our position at
Mitchell's Ford, we could hear the fierce, continual roll of the
infantry fire, mingled with the deafening thunder of the
cannon. Bonham was under a continual shelling from long
range, by twenty pounders, some reaching as far in the rear
as the wagon yard. After the fourth repulse, and Longstreet
had his reserves well in hand, he felt himself strong enough
to take the initiative. Plunging through the marshes and
lagoons that bordered the stream, the troops crossed over and
up the bluff, but when on the heights they met another
advance of the enemy, who were soon sent scampering
from the field. Then was first heard the famous "Rebel
yell." The Confederates finding themselves victorious in this

their first engagement, gave vent to their feelings by uttering such a yell as suited each individual best, forming for all time the famous "Rebel Yell." Longstreet withdrew his forces to the east side, but a continual fusilade of artillery was kept up until night. Some of our soldiers visited the battlefield that night and next day, and brought in many trophies and mementoes of the day's fight, such as blankets, oilcloths, canteens, guns, etc.

CHAPTER V

The Battle of Manassas---Rout of the Enemy. Visit to the Battlefield.

Of the battle of the 18th, the enemy seemed to make little, and called it a "demoustration" at which General Tyler exceeded his orders, and pushed his troops too far. However, the Coufederates were very well satisfied with the contest where the first blood was drawn. General Johnston, who at this time was up in the Shenandoah Valley, near Winchester, was asked by General Beauregard to come to his relief. He was confronted himself by General Patterson, an able Federal General, with a largely superior army. This General Johnston had assurance to believe was preparing to advance, and his own danger great. Still by a strategem, he succeeded in quietly withdrawing his troops, and began the hazardous undertaking of re-enforcing Beauregard. Some of his troops he placed upon the cars at Piedmont, and sped along o'er mountains and glens with lightning speed, while the others on foot came over and through the torturous mountain passes without halt or rest, bending all their energies to meet Beauregard upon the plains of Manassas. Couriers came on foaming steeds, their bloody sides showing the impress of the riders' spurs, bringing the glad tidings to the Army of the Potomac that succor was near. Beauregard was busy with the disposition of his troops, preparing to give battle, while the soldiers worked with a will erecting some hasty breastworks.

At this point I will digress for the moment to relate an incident of the Federal march, to show the brutal cowardice and baseness of the Federals in making war upon the non-combatants—women and children—and also the unyielding spirit and inflexible courage of our Southern people. Those dispositions were manifested on both sides throughout the whole war. It is unnecessary to say that feeling ran high on the border, as elsewhere, and everyone was anxious to display his colors in order to show to the world how his feelings ran. Confederate flags waved from many housetops along the border, and on the morning the Federals crossed the Potomac from Washington to Alexandria, many little pieces of bunting, displaying stars and bars, floated from the houses in that old sleeping city of Alexandria. Among that number was a violent Secessionist named Jackson. Colonel Ellsworth, commanding the New York Zouaves, the advance guard, ordered all flags with Confederate devices to be torn down by force. The soldiers thus engaged in the debasing acts of entering private dwellings, insulting the inmates with the vilest epithets, ruthlessly tore down the hated emblems of the South everywhere. When they came to Jackson's house they met the fiery defender of his home on the landing of the stairs, rifle in hand, who with determined air informed the Federal soldiers that whoever lowered his flag would meet instant death. Staggered and dazed by such a determined spirit, they lost no time in reporting the fact to Colonel Ellsworth. Enraged beyond all control by this cool impudence, Ellsworth rushed to Jackson's house, followed by a squad of soldiers. On reaching the landing he, too, met Jackson with his eyes flashing fire and determination, his whole frame trembling with the emotion he felt, his rifle cocked and to his shoulder, boldly declaring, "Whoever tears down that flag, dies in his tracks." Ellsworth and party thought this threat could not be real, and only Southern braggadocio. Brushing past the determined hero, Ellsworth snatched the hated flag from its fastening, but at that instant he fell dead at the feet of his adversary. The report of Jackson's rifle told too plainly that he had kept his word. The soldiers who had followed and witnessed the death of their commander, riddled the body of the Southern martyr with bullets, and not satisfied with his death, mutilated his body beyond recognition. Thus fell the first martyr to Southern principles. The South never showed this disposition of hatred on any occasion, for in after years while marching through Pennsylvania Union flags floated unmolested from housetops, over towns, and cities. The soldiers only laughed and ridiculed the stars and stripes. The South feared no display of sentiment, neither did they insult women and non-combatants.

A like occurrence happened in New Orleans a few years later, where General Butler commanded, and gained the unenviable sobriquet of "Beast" by his war upon the women and those not engaged in the struggle, and by trampling upon every right and liberty sacred to the people. He had issued some degrading order, which the citizens were bound in pain of death to obey. One brave man, Mumford, refused, preferring death to obeying this humiliating order. For this he was torn from the embrace of his devoted family, and, in sight of his wife and children, placed in a wagon, forced to ride upon his own coffin, and in the public square was hanged like a felon.

General Johnston, with a portion of his troops, reached the field on the 20th, and his forces were placed in rear of those of Beauregard as reserves. On the night of the 20th, both opposing generals, by a strange coincidence, had formed plans of the battle for the next day, and both plans were identical. Beauregard determined to advance his right by echelon of brigades, commencing with Ewell at Union Mills, then Jones and Longstreet were to cross Bull Run, with Bonham as a pivot, and attack McDowell in flank and rear. This was the identical plan conceived and carried out by the enemy, but with little success, as events afterwards showed. The only difference was McDowell got his blow in first by pushing his advance columns forward up the Warrenton Road on our left, in the direction of the Stone Bridge. He attacked General Evans, who had the Fourth South Carolina and Wheat's Battalion of Louisiana Tigers, on guard at this point, with great energy and zeal. But under cover of a dense forest, he moved his main body of troops still higher up the Run, crossed at Sudley's Ford, and came down on Evans' rear. Fighting "Shanks Evans," as he was afterwards called, met this overwhelming force with stubborn resistance and a reckless cour-

age. The enemy from the opposite side of the Run was sending in a continued shower of shot and shell, which threatened
the annihilation of the two little six-pounders and the handful
of infantry that Evans had. But support soon reached him,
the Brigade of Bee's coming up; still he was pressed back
beyond a small stream in his rear. Bee, with his own and
Bartow's Brigade, with a battery of artillery, were all soon
engaged, but the whole column was forced back in the valley
below. Jackson came upon the crest of the hill in their rear
at this juncture, and on this column the demoralized troops
were ordered to rally. It was here Jackson gained the name
of "Stonewall," for Bee, to animate and reassure his own men,
pointed to Jackson and said: "Look at Jackson, he stands like
a stonewall." But the gallant South Carolinian who gave the
illustrious chieftain the famous name of "Stonewall" did not
live long enough to see the name applied, for in a short time he
fell, pierced through with a shot, which proved fatal. Hampton, with his Legion, came like a whirlwind upon the field,
and formed on the right, other batteries were brought into
play, still the enemy pressed forward. Stone Bridge being
uncovered, Tyler crossed his troops over, and joined those of
Hunter and Heintzelman coming from Sudley's Ford. This
united the three divisions of the enemy, and they made a
vigorous and pressing assault upon the demoralized Confederates. The roar of the cannon became continuous, the earth
trembled from this storm of battle, sulphurous smoke obscures
the sky, the air vibrates with shrieking shot and shell, men rush
madly to the charge. Our small six-pounders against their
twelve and twenty-pounders, manned by the best artillerists
at the North, was quite an uneven combat. Johnston and
Beauregard had now come upon the field and aided in giving
order and confidence to the troops now badly disorganized by
the fury of the charge. The battle raged in all its fierceness;
the infantry and artillery, by their roaring and thunder-like
tone, gave one the impression of a continued, protracted
electrical storm, and to those at a distance it sounded like
"worlds at war." On the plateau between the Lewis House
and the Henry House the battle raged fast and furious with
all the varying fortunes of battle. Now victorious—now
defeated—the enemy advances over hill, across plateaus, to be

met with stubborn resistance first, then driven flying from the
field.   Around the Henry House the battle was desperate and
hand to hand.   Here the Louisiana Battalion, under Major
Wheat, immortalized itself by the fury of its assault.   Again
and again was the house taken and lost, retaken and lost again;
the men, seeking cover, rushed up around and into it, only to
be driven away by the storm of shot and shell sent hurling
through it.   Now our troops would be dislodged, but rallying
they rushed again to the assault and retook it.   Twelve
o'clock came, and the battle was far from being decided.
Bartow fell, then Bee.   The wounded and dead lay strewn
over the entire field from the Henry House to the bridge.
Away to the left is seen the glitter of advancing bayonets,
with flags waving, and the steady tread of long lines of soldiers marching through the open field.   They are first thought
to be the enemy, seeking to turn our left.   Officers and men
turned pale at the sight of the unexpected foe.   Couriers were
sent to Longstreet and Bonham to prepare to cover the retreat,
for the day was now thought to be lost, and a retreat inevitable.   The troops proved to be friends.   Elzeys and Kirby
Smith on the way from the Valley to Manassas, hearing the
firing of the guns, left the cars and hurried to the scene of
action.   Cheer after cheer now rent the air, for relief was now
at hand.   They were put in on the left, but soon General
Kirby Smith fell wounded, and had to be borne from the
field.   Other reinforcements were on the way to relieve the
pressure that was convincing to the generals commanding, even,
that the troops could not long endure.   The Second and
Eighth South Carolina Regiments, under the command of
Colonels Kershaw and Cash, were taken from the line at
Mitchell's Ford and hurried forward.   When all the forces
were gotten well in hand, a general forward movement was
made.   But the enemy met it with a determined front.   The
shrieking and bursting of shells shook the very earth, while
the constant roll of the infantry sounded like continual peals
of heavy thunder.   Here and there an explosion, like a
volcanic eruption, told of a caisson being blown up by the
bursting of a shell.   The enemy graped the field right and
left, and had a decided advantage in the forenoon when their
long range twenty-pounders played havoc with our advancing

and retreating columns, while our small four and six-pounders could not reach their batteries. But in the after part of the day, when the contending forces were nearer together, Ricket's and Griffin's Batteries, the most celebrated at that time in the Northern Army, could not stand the precision and impetuosity of Kemper's, the Washington, Stannard's, Pendleton's, and Pelham's Batteries as they graped the field. The Second and Eighth South Carolina coming up at a double quick, joined Hampton's Legion, with Early, Cox, and the troops from the Valley just in time to be of eminent service at a critical moment. The clear clarion voice of Kershaw gave the command, "Forward!" and when repeated in the stentorian voice of Cash, the men knew what was expected of them, answered the call, and leaped to the front with a will. The enemy could no longer withstand the desperate onslaught of the Confederate Volunteers, and McDowell now began to interest himself with the doubtful problem of withdrawing his troops at this critical juncture. With the rugged banks of the deep, sluggish stream in his rear, and only a few places it could be crossed, with a long sheet of flame blazing out from the compact lines of the Confederates into the faces of his men, his position was perilous in the extreme. His troops must have been of like opinion, for the ranks began to waver, then break away, and soon they found themselves in full retreat. Kershaw, Cash, and Hampton pressed them hard towards Stone Bridge. A retreat at first now became a panic, then a rout. Men threw away their baggage, then their guns, all in a mad rush to put the stream between themselves and the dreaded "gray-backs." Cannon were abandoned, men mounted the horses and fled in wild disorder, trampling underfoot those who came between them and safety, while others limbered up their pieces and went at headlong speed, only to be upset or tangled in an unrecognizable mass on Stone Bridge. The South Carolinians pressed them to the very crossing, capturing prisoners and guns; among the latter was the enemy's celebrated "Long Tom." All semblance of order was now cast aside, each trying to leave his less fortunate neighbor in the rear. Plunging headlong down the precipitous banks of the Run, the terror-stricken soldiers pushed over and out in the woods and the fields on the other side.

The shells of our rifle and parrot guns accelerated their speed, and added to their demoralization by hissing and shrieking above their heads and bursting in the tree tops. Orders were sent to Generals Bonham, Longstreet, and Jones, who were holding the lower fords, to cross over and strike the flying fugitives in the rear near Centerville. Colonels Williams and Bacon, with their regiments, led by General Bonham, in person, crossed the stream at a double quick, and began the pursuit of the stampeded troops. When we reached the camps of the enemy, where they had bivouaced the night before, the scene beggared description. On either side of the road were piled as high as one could reach baggages of every description, which the men had discarded before going into action. Blankets rolled up, oilcloths, overcoats, tents, all of the very best material, piled up by the hundreds and thousands. Pots and camp kettles hung over fires, and from within came the savory smell of "rich viands, with rare condiments," being prepared to appease the keen appetite of the battle-worn veterans after the day's victory. Great quarters of fresh beef hung temptingly from the limbs of the trees, wagons filled with arms and accoutrements, provisions, and army supplies, with not a few well-laden with all the delicacies, tid-bits, and rarest old wines that Washington could afford, to assuage the thirst of officers and the men of note. Many of the high dignitaries and officials from the Capitol had come out to witness the fight from afar, and enjoy the exciting scene of battle. They were now fleeing through the woods like men demented, or crouched behind trees, perfectly paralyzed with uncertainty and fright. One old citizen of the North, captured by the boys, gave much merriment by the antics he cut, being frightened out of his wits with the thought of being summarily dealt with by the soldiers. Some would punch him in the back with their bayonets, then another would give him a thrust as he turned to ask quarters of the first tormentor. The crisis was reached, however, when one of the soldiers, in a spirit of mischief, called for a rope to hang him; he thought himself lost, and through his tears he begged for mercy, pleaded for compassion, and promised atonement. General Bonham riding up at this juncture of the soldiers' sport, and seeing the abject fear of the old Northern Aboli-

5

tionist, took pity and showed his sympathy by telling the
men to turn him loose, and not to interfere with non-combatants. He was told to run now, and if he kept the gait he
started with through the woods, not many hours elapsed
before he placed the placid waters of the Potomac between him
and the blood-thirsty Rebels. Strict orders were given to
"stay in ranks," but the sight of so much valuable plunder,
and actual necessaries to the soldiers, was too much for the
poorly provided Confederates; and not a few plucked from the
pile a blanket, overcoat, canteen, or other article that his
wants dictated. A joke the boys had on a major was that
while riding along the line, waving his sword, giving orders
not to molest the baggage, and crying out, "Stay in ranks,
men, stay in ranks," then in an undertone he would call to
his servant, "Get me another blanket, Harvy." The artillery that had been ordered to take part in the infantry's
pursuit were just preparing to open fire upon the fleeing
enemy, when by some unaccountable order, the pursuit was
ordered to be abandoned. Had not this uncalled for order
come at this juncture, it is not hard to conceive the results.
The greater portion of the Federal Army would have been
captured, for with the exception of General Sykes' Brigade of
regulars and a battery of regular atillery, there was not an
organization between our army and Washington City. All
night long the roads through Centerville, and the next day all
leading through Fairfax, Falls Church, and Anandale were
one continual throng of fleeing fugitives. Guns and accoutrements, camp equipage, and ordnance strewed the sides of the
road for miles; wagons, ambulances, cannon, and caissons had
been abandoned, and terror-stricken animals galloped unbri-
dled through the woods and fields. The great herds of cattle,
now free from their keepers, went bellowing through the
forest, seeking shelter in some secluded swamp.

At night, we were all very reluctantly ordered back to our
old camp to talk, rejoice, and dream of the wonderful victory.
Beauregard and Johnston had in this engagement of all arms
30,888, but 3,000 of Ewell's and part of Bonham's Brigade
were not on the field on that day. The enemy had 50,000
and 117 cannon. Confederate loss in killed and wounded,
1,485. Federal loss in killed, wounded, and captured, 4,500.

There being no enemy in our front and little danger of surprise, the soldiers were allowed to roam at will over the battlefield the next few days. Almost the entire army availed themselves of this their first opportunity of visiting a real battlefield and witnessing the real horrors and carnage of which they had often read and seen pictures but had never seen in reality.

Who is it that has ever looked upon a battlefield and could forget the sickening scene, or obliterate from his mind the memory of its dreaded sight? It was recorded of the great Napoleon, by one of his most intimate friends and historians, that after every great battle the first thing he did the next day was to ride over the field, where lay the dead and wounded, and when he would come to those points where the battle had been desperate and the dead lay thickest, he would sit as in a trance, and with silence and meditation never witnessed on other occasions, view the ghastly corpses as they lay strewn over the field. The field of carnage had a fascinating power over him he could not resist, and on which his eyes delighted to feast. With a comrade I went to visit the field of Manassas. Passing over the uneven and partly wooded country, we witnessed all the effect of the enemy's rifled guns. Trees were cut down, great holes dug in the ground where shells had exploded, broken wagons, upset ambulances, wounded and dead horses lining the whole way. The first real scene of carnage was on the plateau of the Lewis house. Here the Virginians lying behind the crest of the hill as the enemy emerged from the woods on the other side, gave them such a volley as to cause a momentary repulse, but only to renew their attack with renewed vigor. The battle here was desperate. Major Wheat with his Louisianians fought around the Henry house with a ferocity hardly equalled by any troops during the war. Their peculiar uniform, large flowing trousers with blue and white stripes coming only to the knees, colored stockings, and a loose bodice, made quite a picturesque appearance and a good target for the enemy. These lay around the house and in front in almost arm's length of each other. This position had been taken and lost twice during the day. Beyond the house and down the declivity on the other side, the enemy's dead told how destructive and deadly had been the Confederate fire. On the other plateau where Jackson had formed and where Bee and Bartow fell, the scene was sickening. There lay friend and foe face to face in the cold embrace of death. Only by the caps could one be distinguished from the other, for the ghouls of the battlefield had already been there to strip, rob, and plunder. Beyond the ravine to the left is where Hampton and his Legion fought, as well as the troops of Kirby Smith and Elzey, of Johnston's army, who had come upon the scene just in time to turn the tide of battle from defeat to victory. On the right of Hampton was the Eighth and Second South Carolina under Kershaw. From the Lewis house to the Stone Bridge the dead lay in every direction. The enemy in their precipitate flight gave the Confederates ample opportunity to slay at will. The effects of artillery here were dreadful. Rickett's Battery, the best in the North, had pushed their guns far in advance of the infantry, and swept the field with grape and canister. Here was a caisson blown up by a shell from Kemper's Battery, and the havoc was frightful. Six beautiful horses, all well caparisoned and still attached to the caisson, all stretched as they had fallen, without so much as a struggle. The drivers lay by the side of the horses, one poor fellow underneath and badly mutilated. To one side and near by lay the officer in command and his horse, the noble animal lying as he had died in the beautiful poise he must have been in when the fatal shot struck him. His hind legs straightened as if in the act of rearing, his forefeet in the air, one before the other, the whole looking more like a dismantled statue than the result of a battlefield. Fragments of shells, broken guns, knapsacks, and baggage were scattered over the plains. Details were busy gathering up the wounded and burying the dead. But from the looks of the field the task seemed difficult. In the little clusters of bushes, behind trees, in gullies, and in every conceivable place that seemed to offer shelter, lay the dead. What a shudder thrills the whole frame when you stand and contemplate the gruesome faces of the battle's dead. In every posture and all positions, with every conceivable shade of countenance, the glaring, glassy eyes meet you. Some lay as they fell, stretched full length on the ground; others show a desperate struggle for the last few remaining breaths. There lay the beardless youth with a pleasant smile yet lingering on his face as though waiting for the maternal kiss; the cold stern features of the middle aged as he lay grasping his trusty rifle, some drawn up in a perfect knot of agony, others their faces prone upon the earth, all dead, dead.   Great pools of blood here and there had saturated the earth, the victim perhaps crawling to a nearby shelter or some little glen, hoping to gain a mouthful of water to cool his parched lips, or perhaps some friendly hand had carried him away to a hospital.   Few of our troops had been molested by the body snatchers of the battle-field, but the enemy had almost invariably been stripped of his outer clothing.   On the incline of the far side of a little hill spots were pointed out where the gallant South Caroli-ian, Bee, had fallen, while rallying his men for the final as-sault, and also the brave Georgian, Colonel Bartow, in a like endeavor.

We came to the Henry house, on the opposite plateau from the Lewis house, the former at this time almost as noted as the little log hut at Waterloo that stood half a century before as a landmark to the fall of Napoleon.   They were common, old fashioned frame houses, occupied by some poor people on this frightful day.   The battle came with such suddenness and unexpectancy, the unfortunate inmates could not get away, and there throughout the bloody day these three Henry women had endured all the dread, excitement, and dangers of a great battle, and forced to remain between the opposing armies. The house was perfectly riddled with minnie balls, while great openings were torn in the side and roofs by the shells shatter-ing through.   There was no escape or place of safety.   They stretched themselves at full length upon the floor, calmly awaiting death, while a perfect storm of shot and shell raged without and within.   As we went in the house two women sat around the few mouldering embers that had answered the purpose of cooking a hasty meal.   It was a single room house, with two beds, some cheap furniture, and a few cooking uten-sils.   These were torn into fragments.   In one corner lay the dead sister, who had been shot the day before, with a sheet thrown over to shield her from the gaze of the curious.   The two sisters were eating a morsel unconcernedly, unconscious of the surroundings, while the house was crowded during the

day with sight seers and curious questioners. On the othe
side of the room were some wounded soldiers, carried in to b
shielded from the rays of the July sun, while all without la
in heaps the mangled dead. The exceeding tension of excite
ment, fright, untold fear, that had been drawn around then
during the continuous struggle of the day before, had ren
dered those women callous and indifferent to all surroundin
appearance; but their haggard faces told but too plainly thei
mental anguish and bodily suffering of yesterday. The eye
tire of the sickening scene, and the mind turns from this re
volting field of blood, and we return heartstricken to ou
camp. The poor crippled and deserted horses limp over th
field nibbling a little bunch of grass left green in places afte
the day of mad galloping of horses. Everywhere we sav
friends hunting friends. Relief corps had come up from Rich
mond and were working night and day relieving the sufferin
and moving the wounded away. Cars were run at short inter
vals from Manassas, carrying the disabled to Warrentown
Orange Court House, Culpepper, and Richmond. Presiden
Davis had come up just after the battle had gone in our favor
and the soldiers were delighted to get a glimpse at our illus
trious chieftain. It was needless to say Beauregard's sta
was still in the ascendant.

CHAPTER VI

Vienna---Flint Hill---Duel Sports---July to October.

Much discussion has taken place since the rout at Manassa
as to reasons for not following up the victory so gloriousl
won, and for not pushing on to Washington at once. It i
enough to say the two commanders at the time and on th
field saw difficulties and dangers sufficient in the way to re
on their spoils. The President, who was in council wit
them, after due consideration was convinced of the impract
cability of a forward movement. In the first place, no prepa
ration had been made for such an event; that the spoils wer
so out of proportion to their most sanguine expectations; tha

the transportation for the troops had to be employed in its removal; that no thought of a forward movement or invasion had ever been contemplated; so there were no plans or specifications at hand. Then again, the dead and wounded of both armies had to be attended to, which crippled our medical department so as to render it powerless should another engagement take place. And again, a large portion of our people thought this total defeat of the enemy at the very outset of the war would render the design of coercion by force of arms impracticable. The South was conservative, and did not wish to inflame the minds of the people of the Union by entering their territory or destroying their capital. Knowing there was a large party at the North opposed to the war, some of our leaders had reason to think this shattering of their first grand army would so strengthen their feelings and party that the whole North would call for peace. They further hugged that fatal delusion to their breast, a delusion that eventually shattered the foundation of our government and betrayed the confidence of the troops, "foreign intervention." They reasoned that a great victory by the South would cause our government to be recognized by the foreign powers and the South given a footing as a distinct, separate, and independent nation among all other great nations of the earth. That the South would no longer be looked upon as an "Insurrectionary Faction," "Erring Sisters," or "Rebellious Children." Our ports had been ordered closed by the North, and an imaginary blockade, a nominal fleet, stood out in front of our harbors. Our people thought the world's desire for the South's cotton would so influence the commercial and laboring people of Europe that the powers would force the North to declare her blockade off. Such were some of the feelings and hopes of a large body of our troops, as well as the citizens of the country at large. But it all was a fallacy, a delusion, an ignis fatuus. The North was aroused to double her former fury, her energies renewed and strengthened, tensions drawn, her ardor largely increased, her feelings doubly embittered, and the whole spirit of the North on fire. Now the cry was in earnest, "On to Richmond," "Down with the rebellion," "Peace and unity." The Northern press was in a perfect blaze, the men wild with excitement, and every art and device was re-

sorted to to arouse the people to arms.   The stain of defeat
must now be wiped out; a stigma had been put upon the
nation, her flag disgraced, her people dishonored.   Large
bounties were offered for volunteers, and the recruiting was
earnest and energetic.   Lincoln called for 300,000 more troops,
and the same question was asked at the South, "Where will
he get them and how pay them?"

We were moved out near Centerville, and a few days afterwards took up camp at Vienna, a small station on the Baltimore and Ohio railroad.   The day after our arrival all of the
troops, with the exception of the ordinary detail, were put to
work tearing up the railroad track.   It being Sunday, loud
complaints were made against this desecration of the Lord's
Day, but we were told there was no difference in days in times
of war.   The railroad was a good one and well built on a road-
bed of gravel and chips of granite, with solid heart pine or
chestnut ties, laid with "T" rails.   The cross-ties were piled
in heaps, on these were laid the rails, and all set on fire; then
for miles and miles up and down the road the crackling flames,
the black smoke twining around the trees and curling upward,
shrouded the whole earth with a canopy of black and blue,
and told of the destruction that was going on.   Here the troops
suffered as seldom during the war for provisions, especially
breadstuff.   Loud murmurings were heard on all sides against
the commissary department, and the commissary complained
of the Quartermaster for not furnishing transportation.   The
troops on one occasion here had to go three days and at hard
work without one mouthful of bread, except what little they
could buy or beg of the citizens o' the thinly settled country.
Meat was plentiful, but no bread, and any one who has ever
felt the tortures of bread hunger may imagine the sufferings
of the men.   For want of bread the meats became nauseating
and repulsive.   The whole fault lay in having too many
bosses and red tape in the Department at Richmond.   By
order of these officials, all commissary supplies, even gathered
in sight of the camps, had to be first sent to Richmond and
issued out only on requisitions to the head of the departments.
The railroad facilities were bad, irregular, and blocked, while
our wagons and teams were limited to one for each one hundred men for all purposes.   General Beauregard, now second

Brig. Gen. James Connor,
    (Page 440.)

Brig. Gen. John D. Kennedy,
    (Page 476.)

Adjt. Y. J. Pope.
    Acting Asst. Adjt. Genl. of
    Kershaw's Brigade.
        (Page 456.)
Dr. Thos. W. Salmond,
    Surgeon of Kershaw's Brigade.
        (Page 253.)

in command, and directly in command of the First Army Corps of the Army of the Potomac, of which our brigade formed a part, wishing to concentrate his troops, ordered all to Flint Hill, three miles west of Fairfax Court House. General Johnston, Commander-in-Chief, directed the movements of the whole army, but more directly the Second Army Corps, or the Army of the Shenandoah. The army up to this time had not been put into divisions, commanded by Major Generals, nor corps, by Lieutenant Generals, but the two commanders divided nominally the army into two corps, each commanded by a full General—Brigadier General Beauregard having been raised to the rank of full General the day after his signal victory at Manassas by President Davis.

In the Confederate Army the grades of the Generals were different to those in the United States Army. A brigade consisted of a number of regiments joined together as one body and commanded by a Brigadier General, the lowest in rank. Four, more or less, brigades constituted a division, commanded by a Major General. Three or four divisions constituted a corps, commanded by a Lieutenant General, and a separate army, as two or more corps, was commanded by a General, the highest in rank. Their rank is the same, but the Seniors are those whose commissions had been granted first, and take precedence where two are together. So it is with all officers in the army—age is not taken into consideration, but the date of commission. Where a brigade, from any cause, temporarily loses its commander, the Colonel with the oldest commission takes the command; where a division loses its Major General, the Senior Brigadier in that division immediately assumes command; and the same way in the corps and the army. The Major General takes command of the corps where its commander is absent, and in case of absence, either temporary or permanent, of the Commander-in-Chief of an army, the ranking Lieutenant General takes command until a full General relieves him. In no case can an officer of inferior rank command one of superior rank. Rank gives command whether ordered or not. In any case of absence, whether in battle, march, or camp, whenever an officer finds himself Senior in his organization, he is commander and so held without further orders.

The soldiers had rather a good time at Flint Hill, doing a little drilling and occasional picket duty out in the direction of Munson and Mason Hill. The Commanding General wished to advance his pickets to Munson Hill, a few miles from Washington, and to do this it was necessary to dislodge the enemy, who had possession there. The Second Regiment, under Colonel Kershaw, was sent out, and after a considerable brush he succeeded in driving the enemy away. After this one regiment at a time was sent out to do picket duty. When our South Carolina regiments would go out orders were given to be quiet, and during our stay at Mason and Munson Hill the utmost secrecy prevailed, but when Wheat's Louisiana Battalion had to relieve a regiment we could hear the beating of their drums, the loud shouts of the men on their way out, and all would rush to the side of the road to see the "tigers" pass. Down the road they would come, banners waving, the swinging step of the men keeping time to the shrill notes of the fife and the rattle of the drums. Their large flowing pants, their gaudy striped long hose, made quite an imposing spectacle. This was a noted band of men for a time, but their brave commander, Wheat, and almost all of his men, were killed in the battles that followed around Richmond. Major Wheat had been in the Turkish Army when that nation was at war with Russia, and in several other foreign wars, as well as the Mexican War. When his State seceded he returned to Louisiana and raised a battalion of the hardest set of men in New Orleans. The soldiers called them "wharf rats," "sailors," "longshoremen," "cut throats," and "gutter snipes." They knew no subordination and defied law and military discipline. While in camp here several of them were shot at the stake. Major Wheat had asked to be allowed to manage his men as he saw best, and had a law unto himself. For some mutiny and insubordination he had several of them shot. Afterwards, when the soldiers heard a volley fired, the word would go out, "Wheat is having another tiger shot."

The fields were green with the great waving corn, just in roasting ears, and it was a sight to see hundreds of men in these fields early in the morning plucking the fine ears for breakfast. In most cases the owners had abandoned their fields and homes, taking what was movable to other places in

Virginia. What was left the soldiers were at liberty to "slay and eat." At first it was determined to protect the stock, but the soldiers agreed that what the Southern soldiers left the enemy would be sure to take. I remember the first theft I was engaged in during the war. I say "first" advisedly. Now soldiers have different views as to rights of property to that of the average citizen. What he finds that will add to his comfort or welfare, or his wants dictate, or a liability of the property falling into the hands of the enemy, he takes without compunction or disposition to rob—and more often he robs in a spirit of mischief. A few fine hogs had been left to roam at will through the fields by the refugee farmers, and orders were given not to kill or molest them, to eat as much corn as we wished, but to spare the hogs. When the regiments were sent on pickets, a detail was left in camp as guard, also to watch around the fields to prevent trespass. While our regiment was on its three days' picket, I was left as one of the detail to guard the camp. Some one reported a fine hog in the yard of a house some distance away. It was agreed to kill it, divide it up, and have a rare treat for the weary pickets when they returned. How to kill it without attracting the attention of the other guards was a question of importance, because the report of a rifle and the proverbial squeal of a hog would be sure to bring down upon us the guard. One of the men had a pistol, still we were afraid to trust this. A cellar door stood temptingly open. We tried to drive the hog into it, but with a hog's perverseness it refused to be driven, and after rushing around the yard several times with no results, it was decided to shoot it. The man claimed to be a good shot, and declared that no hog would squeal after being shot by him, but, as Burns says, "The best laid plans of mice and men aft' gang a glee." So with us. After shooting, the porker cut desperate antics, and set up a frightful noise, but the unexpected always happens, and the hog took refuge in the cellar, or rather the basement of the dwelling, to our great relief. We were proceeding finely, skinning away, the only method the soldiers had of cleaning a hog, when to our astonishment and dismay, in walked the much dreaded guard. Now there is something peculiar about the soldier's idea of duty, the effects of military training, and the stern obedience to orders.

The first lesson he learns is obedience, and the longer in service the more convinced he is of its necessity.   While he may break ranks, pass guards, rob roosts, or pilfer fruits and vegetables himself, yet put a gun in his hand, place him on duty, order him to guard or protect men or property, and his integrity in that respect is as unyielding, inflexible, and stern as if his life depended upon his faithful performance.   The Roman soldiers' obedience to orders made them immortal, and their nation the greatest on earth.   But to resume the thread of my story.   When the guard came in we thought ourselves lost. To be punished for hog stealing, and it published at home, was more than our patriotism could stand.   The guard questioned us about the killing, said it was against orders to fire a gun within range of camp, and furthermore against orders to molest private property.   We tried to convince the guard that it was contraband, that the owners had left it, and to crown the argument, insisted that if we did not take the hog the Yankees would.   This was the argument always last resorted to to ease conscience and evade the law.   In this case, strange to say, it had its effect.   After some parleying, it was agreed to share the booty equally between the guard and ourselves. They helped us cut brush and cover it nicely, and after tattoo all were to return and divide up.   We did not know the guards personally, but knew their command.   And so we returned to the camp to await the return of our pickets and night.   It was soon noised in camp that there was a fine fat porker to be distributed after tattoo, and no little eagerness and inquisitiveness were manifested, as all wished a piece. Armed with a crocus-sack, we returned to the house; all was dark and still.   We whistled the signal, but no answer.   It was repeated, but still no reply.   The guard had not come. Sitting down on the door step, we began our long wait. Moments passed into minutes, minutes into hours, until at last we began to have some forebodings and misgivings.   Had we been betrayed?   Would we be reported and our tents searched next day?   Hardly; a soldier could not be so treacherous. We entered the cellar and began to fumble around without results, a match was struck, and to our unspeakable dismay not a vestige of hog remained.   Stuck against the side of the wall was a piece of paper, on which was written: "No mercy

for the hog rogue.'' Such swearing, such stamping and beating the air with our fists, in imitation of the punishment that
would be given the treacherous rascals if present; the atmosphere was perfectly sulphurous with the venom spit out
against the foul party. Here was a true verification of the old
adage, "Set a rogue to catch a rogue." Dejected and crest-
fallen, we returned to camp, but dared not tell of our misfortune, for fear of the jeers of our comrades.

Measles and jaundice began to scourge the camp; the green
corn, it was said, did the army more damage than the enemy
did in battle. Wagons and ambulances went out daily loaded
with the sick; the hospitals were being crowded in Richmond
and other cities: hotels, colleges, and churches were appropriated for hospital service, and the good people of Virginia can
never be forgotten, nor amply rewarded for the self-sacrifices
and aid rendered to the sick soldiers. Private houses were
thrown open to the sick when their homes were far distant, or
where they could not reach it. The soldier was never too
dirty or ragged to be received into palatial homes; all found a
ready welcome and the best attention.

Generals Johnston and Beauregard had now concentrated all
their forces in supporting distance around Fairfax Court
House, and were preparing for a movement across the Potomac.
Bonham's Brigade was at Flint Hill, Cox's at Centerville,
Jones's at Germantown, Hampton and Early on the Occoquon,
the Louisiana Brigade at Bull Run, and Longstreet at Fairfax
Court House. The troops were all in easy distance, and a
gigantic plan of General Beauregard, with the doubtful approval
of General Johnston and others, was for a formidable invasion
of the North. General Johnston evinced that same disposition
in military tactics that he followed during the war, "a purely
defensive war." In none of his campaigns did he exhibit any
desire to take advantage of the enemy by bold moves; his one
idea seemed to be "defensive," and in that he was a genius—
in retreat, his was a mastermind; in defense, masterly. In the
end it may have proven the better policy to have remained on
the defensive. But the quick, impulsive temperament of Beauregard was ever on the alert for some bold stroke or sudden
attack upon the enemy's weaker points. His idea coincided
with Longstreet's in this particular, that the North, Ken-

tucky, Tennessee, or Maryland should be the theatre of war
and the battleground of the Confederacy. General Lee,
according to the ideas of one of his most trusted lieutenants,
was more in accordance with the views of General Johnston,
that is, "the South should fight a defensive war"—and it was
only when in the immediate presence of the enemy, or when
he observed a weak point in his opponent, or a strategic move,
that he could not resist the temptation to strike a blow. In
several of his great battles it is reported of Lee that he intended
to await the attack of the enemy, but could not control his
impatience when the enemy began to press him; then all the
fire of his warlike nature came to the surface, and he sprang
upon his adversary with the ferocity of a wild beast. But Lee
in battle was not the Lee in camp.

The middle of summer the two commanding Generals
called President Davis to Fairfax Court House to enter a conference in regard to the projected invasion. The plans were
all carefully laid before him. First a demonstration was to
be made above Washington; then with the whole army cross
below, strike Washington on the east, crush the enemy in
their camps, march through Maryland, hoist the standard of
revolt in that State, make a call for all Southern sympathizers
to flock to their banners, and to overawe the North by this
sudden onslaught. But President Davis turned a deaf ear to
all such overtures; pleaded the want of transportation and the
necessary equipment for invasion. It was the feeling of the
South even at this late day that much could yet be done by
diplomacy and mild measures; that a great body of the North
could be won over by fears of a prolonged war; and the South
did not wish to exasperate the more conservative element by
any overt act. We all naturally looked for peace; we fully
expected the war would end during the fall and winter, and it
was not too much to say that many of our leaders hugged this
delusion to their breast.

While in camp here an incident occurred which showed that
the men had not yet fully recognized the importance of military restraint and discipline. It is well known that private
broils or feuds of any kind are strictly forbidden by army regulations. The French manner of settling disputes or vindicating
personal honor according to code duello was not countenanced

by our military laws; still the hot blood and fiery temper of the proud South Carolinians could brook no restraint at this time when an affront was given or his honor assailed.   Captain Elbert Bland, of Edgefield, and Major Emett Seibles, both of the Seventh Regiment, were engaged in a friendly game of chess, a difference arose, then a dispute, hot words, and at last insult given that could not be recalled nor allowed to pass unnoticed.   Challenge is offered and accepted, seconds appointed, pistols chosen; distance, twenty paces; time' sunrise next morning on a hillside near the outskirts of the camp. Early next morning a lone ambulance is seen moving out of camp, followed by two surgeons, then the principals with their seconds at a respectful distance.   On reaching the spot chosen lots were cast for choice of stations.   This fell to Captain Bland.   The distance was measured with mechanical exactness, dueling pistols produced, each second loading that of his principal.   The regular dueling pistol is a costly affair and of the very finest material.   Long slim rifle barrel with hammer underneath, the stock finely chiseled and elaborately ornamented with silver or gold; the whole about ten inches in length and carrying a bullet of 22 calibre.   The seconds took their places at an equal distance from each other and midway between the principals.   Captain Bland takes his position at the west end of the field, and Major Seibles the east.   Both stood confronting each other, not fierce nor glaring like two men roused in passion, or that either wished the blood of the other, but bold, calm, and defiant; an insult to be wiped out and honor to be sustained.   They turned, facing the rear, hands down, with pistols in the right.   The seconds call out in calm, deliberate tones: "Gentlemen, are you ready?" Then, "Ready, aim, fire!"   "One, two, three, stop."   The shooting must take place between the words "fire" and "stop," or during the count of one, two, three.   If the principal fires before or after this command it is murder, and he is at once shot down by the second of his opponent.   Or if in any case the principals fail to respond at the hour set, the second promptly takes his place.   But no danger of such possibilities where two such men as Major Seibles and Captain Bland are interested.   There was a matter at issue dearer than country, wife, or child.   It was honor, and a true South Carolinian of

the old stock would make any sacrifice, give or take life, to
uphold his name unsullied or the honor of his family untarnished. As the word fire was given the opponents wheeled
and two pistol shots rang out on the stillness of the morning.
Captain Bland stands still erect, commanding and motionless
as a statue. Major Seibles remains steady for a moment, then
sways a little to the left, staggers and falls into the arms of
his second and surgeon. A hasty examination is made.
"Blood," calls out the second of Major Seibles. A nod of satisfaction is given and acknowledged by both seconds. Captain
Bland retires on the arm of his friend, while the Major, now
bleeding profusely from a wound in the chest, is lifted in the
ambulance and carried to his tent. It was many months before Major Seibles was sufficiently recovered from his wound
to return to duty. The matter was kept quiet and no action
taken. Major Seibles died the following year, while the gallant Bland was killed at Chickamauga while leading as Colonel
the Seventh Regiment in battle.

While at Flint Hill, another stirring scene took place of
quite a different nature. In front of the Third Regiment was
a beautiful stretch of road, and this was selected as a course
for a race to be run between the horse of Captain Mitchell of
the Louisiana Tigers and that of the Colonel of a Virginia
regiment of cavalry. The troops now so long inactive, nothing to break the monotony between drills, guard duty, and
picketing, waited with no little anxiety the coming of the day
that was to test the metal of the little grey from the Pelican
State and the sorrel from the Old Dominion. Word had gone
out among all the troopers that a race was up, and all lovers of
the sport came in groups, companies, and regiments to the
place of rendezvous. Men seemed to come from everywhere,
captains, colonels, and even generals graced the occasion with
their presence. Never before in our army had so many distinguished individuals congregated for so trivial an occasion.
There was Wheat, fat, clean shaven, and jolly, his every
feature indicating the man he was—bold as a lion, fearless, full
of life and frolic as a school boy, but who had seen war in
almost every clime under the sun. There was Turner Ashby,
his eyes flashing fire from under his shaggy eyebrows, his
long black beard and flowing locks, looking more like

brigand than one of the most daring cavaliers of the Confederate
Army.   Fitzhugh Lee, too, was there, with colonels, majors,
and captains without number.   Nothing seemed farther from
the horizon of these jolly men than thoughts of the triumphs
of war.   Captain Mitchell's horse was more on the pony order
than a racer, but it was said by those who knew that on more
occasions than one the pony had thrown dirt into the eyes of
the fastest horse in the Crescent City, and the Louisianans
were betting on him to a man.   The wiry sorrel was equally
a favorite with the Virginians, while the South Carolinians
were divided between the two.   After a great amount of
jockeying, usual on such occasions, judges were appointed,
distance measured, horses and riders in their places, and
hundreds of men stretched along the side of the road to witness
the heated race.   No little amount of Confederate money had
been put upon the race, although it was understood to be
merely a friendly one, and for amusement only.   When the
drum sounded, the two horses almost leaped into the air,
and sped away like the wind, "little grey" shooting away
from her larger adversary like a bullet, and came flying down
the track like a streak, about a length ahead of the Virginia
horse.   The favorites on the Louisianan rent the air with their
yells, hats went into the air, while the friends of the Virginian
shouted like mad to the rider: "Let him out, let him out."
When the distance was about half run he was "let out;" the
rowels went into the side and the whip came down upon the
flanks of the thoroughly aroused racer, and the Virginian
began forging to the front, gaining at every leap.   Now he is
neck and neck, spur and whip are used without stint, he goes
ahead and is leaving the "grey" far in the rear; Captain
Mitchell is leaning far over on the withers of the faithful little
pony, never sparing the whip for a moment, but all could see
that he was running a losing race.   When about the commencement of the last quarter the "grey" leaves the track,
and off to the right he plunges through the trees, dashing
headlong by the groups of men, till at last the Captain brings
him up with one rein broken.   A g.eat crowd surround him,
questioning, swearing, and jeering, but the Captain sat as
silent, unmovable, and inattentive as a statue, pointing to the
broken rein.   It had been cut with a knife.   The Captain and

his friends claimed that the friends of the Virginian had, unnoticed by him, cut the leather to a bare thread, while the friends of the other party, with equal persistency, charged the Captain with cutting it himself.   That when he saw the race lost, he reached over and cut the rein about six inches from the bit, thus throwing the horse out of the track and saving its credit, if not the money.   No one ever knew how it happened, but that there had been a trick played and foul means employed were evident.   A great many had lost their money, and their curses were loud and deep, while the winners went away as merry as "marriage bells."

CHAPTER VII

Winter Quarters at Bull Run.

Sometime in October the brigade was withdrawn to the vicinity of Centerville for better facilities in the way of provisions, water, etc., and to be nearer the wooded section of the country.   The water had been scarce at Flint Hill, a long distance from camp, and of inferior quality.   The health of the troops was considerably impaired, a great many having been sent to the hospitals, or to their homes.   The sickness was attributed, in a large measure, to the quality of green corn and fresh meat, salt being an object now with the Confederacy, and was issued in limited quantities.   We fared sumptuously while at our camp near Centerville.   Our wagon train going weekly up towards Warrenton and the mountains, returning laden with flour, meat, and the finest beef we had ever received.   The teamsters acting as hucksters, brought in a lot of delicacies to sell on their own account—chickens, turkeys, and vegetables, and not unfrequently a keg of "Mountain Dew" would be packed in the wagon with the army supplies, and sold by the wagoners at an enormous profit.   There being no revenue officers or "dispensary constables" in those days, whiskey could be handled with impunity, and not a little found its way into camp.   The citizens, too, had an eye single to their own welfare, and would bring in loads of all kinds of country produce. Sometimes a wagon would drive into camp loaded with dressed chickens and turkeys to the number of one hundred or more. A large old-fashioned wagon-sheet would be spread over the bottom and side of the wagon body, and filled with as much as two horses could pull. I never knew until then how far a man's prejudice could overcome him. Our mess had concluded to treat itself to a turkey dinner on Christmas. Our boss of the mess was instructed to purchase a turkey of the next wagon that came in. Sure enough, the day came and a fine fat turkey bought, already dressed, and boiling away in the camp kettle, while all hands stood around and drank in the delightful aroma from turkey and condiments that so temptingly escaped from under the kettle lid. When all was ready, the feast spread, and the cook was in the act of sinking his fork into the breast of the rich brown turkey, some one said in the greatest astonishment: "Well, George Stuck, I'll be d—d if you haven't bought a goose instead of a turkey, look at its short legs." There was a go, our money gone, appetites whetted, and for a goose! Well up to that time and even now I cannot eat goose. A dispute arose, some said it was a goose, others held out with equal persistency that it was a turkey, and I not having discretion enough to judge by the color of the flesh, and so overcome by my prejudice, did not taste it, and a madder man was not often found. To this day I have never been convinced whether it was a turkey or a goose, but am rather inclined to give the benefit of the doubt to the goose.

We did not get into our regular winter quarters until after the first of January, 1862. These were established on the south Banks of Bull Run, near Blackburn's Ford, the place of the first battle of the name, where Longstreet fought on the 18th of July. Large details were sent out from camp every day to build foundations for these quarters. This was done by cutting pine poles or logs the right length of our tents, build up three or four feet, and over this pen the tent to be stretched. They were generally about ten feet square, but a man could only stand erect in the middle. The cracks between the logs were clinked with mud, a chimney built out of poles split in half and notched up in the ends of the log parts of the tent. An inside wall was made of plank or small round poles, with space between the two walls of five or six inches. This was filled with soft earth or mud, packed tightly, then a blazing fire started, the inner wall burned out, and the dirt baked hard and solid as a brick. In this way we had very good chimneys and comfortable quarters. From six to eight occupied one tent, and generally all the inmates messed together. Forks were driven into the ground, on which were placed strong and substantial cross-pieces, then round pipe poles, about the size of a man's arm, laid over all and thickly strewn with pine needles, on which the blankets are laid. There you have the winter quarters for the Southern soldiers the first year of the war.

But some of the men did not like so primitive an order of architecture and built huts entirely out of logs, and displayed as much originality as you would find in more pretentious cities. These were covered over with poles, on which straw and sand were tightly packed, enough so as to make them water-tight. Some would give names to their quarters, marked in large letters above their doors in charcoal, taxing their minds to give ingenious and unique names, such as "Uncle Tom's Cabin," "The House that Jack Built," "Park Row," "Devil's Inn," etc. To while away the long nights and cold days, the men had recourse to the soldier's game, "cards." Few ever played for the money that was in it, but more for an amusement and pastime. While almost all played cards, there were very few who could be considered gamblers, or who would take their comrades' money, if they even won it. There would be stakes played for, it is true, on the "credit system" generally, to be evened-up on pay-day. But when that time came around such good feeling existed that "poker debts," as they were called, were seldom ever thought of, and the game would continue with its varying successes without ever a thought of liquidation. You might often see a good old Methodist or a strict Presbyterian earnestly engaged in a "five cent antie" game, but never take his friend's money, even if honestly won. Something had to be done to pass away the time, and card-playing was considered an innocent amusement.

The long inactivity made men naturally think and dream of home. The soldiers had left home quite suddenly, and in many cases with little preparation, but the continual talk of "peace in the spring," and the daily vaporing of the press about England or France recognizing the South's belligerency —and the opening of her ports—buoyed up the spirits of the soldiers, and fanned the flame of hope. A great many of the old army officers of the United States, hailing from the South, had resigned their commissions on the Secession of the States, and tendered their services to the Confederacy. Of course it mattered not what was their former rank, or what service, if any they had seen, all expected places as generals. President Davis being a West Pointer himself, had great partiality for graduates of that institution. It was his weakness, this favoritism for West Pointers; and the persistency with which he appointed them above and over the generals of the volunteers, gave dissatisfaction. These appointments caused such resentment and dissatisfaction that some of our very best generals resigned their commissions, refusing to serve under men of no experience and doubtful qualifications. Longstreet, Van Dorn, McLaws, G. W. Smith, and a host of others, who had been captains and majors in the United States Army, were here or in Richmond waiting for some high grade, without first winning their spurs upon the field. McLaws, a Major in the regular army, was made a Major General, and Longstreet had been appointed over General Bonham, the latter having seen varied service in Mexico, commanding a regiment of regulars, doing staff duty, and Military Governor of one of the provinces after the war. At such injustice as this, gave General Bonham reason to resign his command and return to South Carolina, where he soon afterwards was elected to Congress, and later elected Governor of the State. This left the command to Colonel Kershaw as senior Colonel, but he was soon thereafter made Brigadier General. While the troops felt safe and confident under Kershaw, they parted with General Bonham with unfeigned reluctance and regret. Although none blamed him for the steps taken, for all felt keenly the injustice done, still they wished him to remain and lead them to victory, and share the glory they felt sure was in store for all connected with the old First Brigade.

In future we will call the brigade by the name of Kershaw, the name by which it was mostly known, and under whose

leadership the troops did such deeds of prowess, endured so
many hardships, fought so many battles, and gained so many
victories, as to shed a halo around the heads of all who
marched with him and fought under the banner of Joseph B.
Kershaw.   Here I will give a brief biography of General
Kershaw.

JOSEPH BREVARD KERSHAW

Was born January 5th, 1822, at Camden, S. C.   He was a
son of John Kershaw and Harriet DuBose, his wife.   Both of
the families of Kershaws and DuBoses were represented by
more than one member, either in the Continentals or the State
troops, during the War of the Revolution, Joseph Kershaw,
the most prominent of them, and the grandfather of the subject of this sketch, having lost his fortune in his efforts to
maintain the patriot cause.   John Kershaw died when his
son, Joseph Brevard, was a child of seven years of age.   He
attended first a "dame school" in his native town.   Afterwards he attended a school taught by a rigid disciplinarian, a
Mr. Hatfield, who is still remembered by some of the pupils
for his vigorous application of the rod on frequent occasions,
with apparent enjoyment on his part, but with quite other sentiments on the part of the boys.   He was sent at the age of
fifteen to the Cokesbury Conference school, in Abbeville District, as it was then known, where he remained for only a
brief time.   Leaving this school, after a short sojourn at home,
he went to Charleston, S. C., where he became a clerk in a
dry goods house.   This life not being congenial to him, he returned to Camden and entered as a student in the law office of
the late John M. DeSaussure, Esq., from which, at the age of
twenty-one, he was admitted to the Bar.   He soon afterwards
formed a copartnership with James Pope Dickinson, who
was subsequently killed at the battle of Cherubusco, in the
war with Mexico, gallantly leading the charge of the Palmetto
Regiment.   Both partners went to the Mexican War, young
Kershaw as First Lieutenant of the Camden company, known
as the DeKalb Rifle Guards.   Struck down by fever contracted
while in the service, he returned home a physical wreck, to be
tenderly nursed back to health by his wife, Lucretia Douglass,
whom he had married in 1844.   Upon the recovery of his

health, the war being over, he resumed the practice of law in Camden. But it was not long before his services were demanded in the State Legislature, which he entered as a member of the lower house in 1852. From this time on until the opening of hostilities in the war between the States, he practiced his profession with eminent success, and served also in the Legislature several terms, being handsomely re-elected when he stood for the place. He took a deep interest in the struggle then impending, and was a member of the Secession Convention from his native district. As it became more and more evident that there would be war, he ran for and was elected to the office of Colonel of the militia, regiment composed of companies from Kershaw and adjacent districts, which, early in 1861, by command of Governor Pickens, he mobilized and led to Charleston and thence to Morris' Island, where the regiment remained until it volunteered and was called to go to Virginia to enter the service of the Confederacy. Several of the companies then in his regiment consented to go. These were supplemented by other companies which offered their services, and the new regiment, now known as the Second South Carolina Volunteers, proceeded to Richmond, thence to Manassas.

From this time until 1864 it is unnecessary to trace his personal history in this place, because the history of the brigade, to the command of which he was elected at the reorganization in 1862, and of its commander cannot be separated. In May, 1864, he was promoted to the rank of Major General and assigned to the command of a division, of which his brigade formed a part. His was the First Brigade of the First Division of the First Corps of the Army of Northern Virginia. On the retreat from Richmond his division, with other troops, numbering in all about 6,000 men, was surrounded and captured at the battle of Sailor's Creek, April 6th, 1865. In this disastrous battle Lieutenant Ewell, Major Generals Kershaw and Custis Lee, Brigadier Generals D. M. DuBose, Semmes, Hunter, and Corse, and Commodores Hunter and Tucker, of the Confederate States' Navy, ranking on shore duty as Brigadiers, were captured, together with their respective commands, almost to a man, after a desperate and sanguinary struggle against immense odds. Those officers were all sent to Fort Warren, Boston Harbor, where they remained in prison until some time in August, 1865, when they were allowed to return to their respective homes.

General Kershaw resumed the profession of law in Camden immediately upon his return, and enjoyed a laige and lucrative practice for many years, until called to serve his State as Circuit Judge in 1877, when the government was wrested from the hands of the Republicans.   He took an active part in politics, having been elected to the State Senate in the fall of 1865. He ran for Congress from his district in 1874, but was counted out, as it was believed, at the election.   He was also summoned to Columbia by Governor Hampton after his election in 1876, and rendered important service in securing the peaceable outcome of that most trying struggle.   Upon the convening of the Legislature, he was at once elected Judge of the Fifth Circuit, a position which he held with distinguished honor for sixteen years, rendering it to Judge Ernest Gary in June, 1893, on which occasion there was tendered him a farewell probably unique in the judicial history of the State, by eminent representatives of the Bar of his Circuit.   With impaired health, but with unwavering faith and carefulness that no adversity diminished, he once more returned to the practice of his profession.   It was a gallant effort in the face of tremendous odds, but the splendid health that he had enjoyed for many years had been undermined slowly and insidiously by disease incident to a life that had ever borne the burdens of others, and that had spent itself freely and unselfishly for his country and his fellowman, and it was evident to all that his days were numbered.   Devoted friends, the names of many of whom are unknown to me, offered him pecuniary help at this trying juncture, and these the writer would wish to hold, as he would have wished, "in everlasting remembrance."   In his message to the General Assembly that year, 1893, Governor B. R. Tillman proposed him as the proper person to collect the records of the services of South Carolina soldiers in the Civil War, and to prepare suitable historical introduction to the volume. The Legislature promptly, and I believe unanimously, endorsed the nomination and made an appropriation for the work. To this he gave himself during the two succeeding months, collecting data, and even preparing in part the proposed introduction. But growing infirmities compelled him to lay it down, and in the latter part of March, 1894, he became alarmingly ill. All was done for his relief that the most competent skill and gentle care could do, but to no avail, and in the night of April 12th, just before midnight, he breathed his last. Among his last words to his son were these, spoken when he was perfectly conscious of what was before him: "My son, I have no doubts and no fears." On the occasion of his funeral there was a general outpouring of people from the town and vicinity for many miles, who sincerely mourned the departure of their friend. The State was represented by the Governor and seven members of his official family. On the modest monument that marks his last resting place is inscribed his name and the date of his birth and death. On the base the legend runs: "I have fought a good fight; I have kept the faith."

It may prove of interest to the surviving members of the old brigade to know that after the fight of Sailor's Creek, when General Kershaw and his companions were being taken back to Petersburg and thence to City Point to be shipped North, he spent a night at a farm house, then occupied as a field hospital and as quarters by the surgeons and attendants. They were South Carolinians, and were anxious to hear all about the fight. In telling of it the pride and love which he reposed in the old brigade received a wistful testimonial. It was then confronting Sherman somewhere in North Carolina. Its old commander said in a voice vibrant with feeling: "If I had only had my old brigade with me I believe we could have held these fellows in check until night gave us the opportunity to withdraw."

The roads in every direction near the army had become almost impassable—mud knee deep in the middle and ruts cut to the hubs on either side. The roads leading to Manassas were literally strewn with the carcasses of horses, some even sunk out of sight in the slough and mud. It would remind one of the passage of Napoleon across the Arabian desert, so graphically described by historians. The firewood had become scarce, and had to be carried on the men's shoulders the distance of a mile, the wagons being engaged in hauling supplies and the enormous private baggage sent to the soldiers from home. I remember once on my return from home on a short furlough, I had under my charge one whole carload of boxes for my company alone. Towards night every soldier would go out to the nearest woodland, which was usually a mile distant, cut a stick of wood the size he could easily carry, and bring into camp, this to do the night and next day. The weather being so severe, fires had to be kept up all during the night. Some constructed little boats and boated the wood across the stream, Bull Run, and a time they generally had of it, with the boat upsetting the men and the wood floundering and rolling about in the water, and it freezing cold.

The Department granted a thirty days' leave of absence to all individuals and companies that would re-enlist for the re-remaining two years or the war. Many officers were granted commissions to raise companies of cavalry and artillery out of the infantry commands, whose time was soon to expire. Lieutenant T. J. Lipscomb, of Company B, Third South Carolina Regiment, was given a commission as Captain, and he, with others, raised a company of cavalry and was given a thirty days' furlough. A great many companies volunteered in a body, not knowing at the time that the Conscript Act soon to be enacted would retain in service all between certain ages in the army, even after their time had expired.

About the middle of February President Davis called General Johnston to Richmond to confer with him upon the practicability of withdrawing the army to the south banks of the Rappahannock. It was generally understood at the time, and largely the impression since, that the army was withdrawn in consequence of McClellan's movements on the Peninsula. But such was not the case. This withdrawal was determined on long before it was known for certain that McClellan would adopt the Peninsula as his base of operations. The middle of February began the removal of the ordnance and commissary stores by railroad to the south of the rivers in our rear. These had been accumulated at Manassas out of all proportion to the needs of the army, and against the wishes of the commanding General. There seemed to be a want of harmony between the army officers and the officers of the Department in Richmond. This difference of feelings was kept up throughout the war, greatly to the embarassment at times of the Generals in the field, and often a great sacrifice to the service. The officials in Richmond, away from the seat of war, had a continual pre-dilection to meddle with the internal affairs of the army. This meddling caused Jackson, who became immortal in after years, to tender his resignation, and but for the interference of General Johnston, the world would perhaps never have heard of the daring feats of "Stonewall Jackson." He asked to be returned to the professorship at the Military Institute, but General Johnston held his letter up and appealed to Jackson's patriotism and the cause for which all were fighting, to reconsider his action and to overlook this officious intermeddling and remain at his post. This he did under protest.

Our brigade, and, in fact, all regiments and brigades, had been put in different commands at different times to suit the caprice of the President or whims of the Department, and now we were Early's Division.

On the night of the 9th of March we broke up quarters at Bull Run and commenced our long and tiresome march for the Rappahannock. We were ordered by different routes to facilitate the movement, our wagon trains moving out in the morning along the dirt road and near the railroad. All baggage that the soldiers could not carry had been sent to the rear days before, and the greater part destroyed in the great wreck and conflagration that followed at Manassas on its evacuation. In passing through Manassas the stores, filled to the very tops with commissary stores, sutler's goods, clothing, shoes, private boxes, and whiskey, were thrown open for the soldiers to help themselves. What a feast for the troops! There seemed everything at hand to tempt him to eat, drink, or wear, but it was a verification of the adage, "When it rains much you have no spoon." We had no way of transporting these goods, now piled high on every hand, but to carry them on our backs, and we were already overloaded for a march of any distance. Whiskey flowed like water. Barrels were knocked open and canteens filled. Kegs, jugs, and bottles seemed to be everywhere. One stalwart man of my company shouldered a ten gallon keg and proposed to hold on to it as long as possible, and it is a fact that a few men carried this keg by reliefs all night and next day. This was the case in other companies. When we got out of the town and on the railroad, the men were completely overloaded. All night we marched along the railroad at a slow, steady gait, but all order and discipline were abandoned. About midnight we saw in our rear great sheets of flame shooting up from the burning buildings, that illuminated the country for miles around. Manassas was on fire! Some of the buildings had caught fire by accident or carelessness of the soldeirs, for the firing was not to begin until next day, after the withdrawal of the cavalry. The people in the surrounding country had been invited to come in and get whatever they wished, but I doubt if any came in time to save much from the burning mass. A great meat curing establishment at Thoroughfare Gap, that contained millions of pounds of beef and pork, was also destroyed. We could hear the bursting of bombs as the flames reached the magazines, as well as the explosion of thousands of small arm cartridges. The whole sounded like the raging of a great battle. Manassas had become endeared to the soldiers by its many memories, and when the word went along the line, "Manassas is burning," it put a melancholy feeling upon all. Some of the happiest recollections of the soldiers that composed Kershaw's Brigade. as well as all of Johnston's Army, were centred around Manassas. It was here they had experienced their first sensations of the soldier, Manassas was the field of their first victory, and there they had spent their first winter. It seemed to connect the soldiers of the Confederacy with those of Washington at Valley Forge and Trenton, the winter quarters of the army of the patriots. It gave the recollection of rest, a contrast with the many marches, the hard fought battles, trials, and hardships.

The next day it began to rain, and a continual down-pour continued for days and nights. Blankets were taken from knapsacks to cover over the men as they marched, but they soon filled with water, and had to be thrown aside. Both sides of the railroad were strewn with blankets, shawls, overcoats, and clothing of every description, the men finding it impossible to bear up under such loads. The slippery ground and the unevenness of the railroad track made marching very disagreeable to soldiers unaccustomed to it. Some took the dirt road, while others kept the railroad track, and in this way all organizations were lost sight of, but at night they collected together in regiments, joined the wagon trains, and bivouaced for the night. Sometimes it would be midnight before the last of the stragglers came up. We crossed the Rappahannock on the railroad bridge, which had been laid with plank to accommodate the passage of wagon trains, on the 11th and remained until the 19th. Up to this time it was not fully understood by the authorities in Richmond which route McClellan would take to reach Richmond, whether by way of Fredericksburg or Yorktown, but now scouts reported large transports, laden with soldiers, being shipped down the Potomac to the mouth of the James and York Rivers. This left no doubt in the minds of the authorities that the Peninsula was to be the base of operations. We continued our march on the 19th, crossed the Rapidan, and encamped around Orange Court House.

Beauregard, whom the soldiers loved dearly, and in whom they had every confidence as a leader, was transferred to the West, to join General A. S. Johnston, who had come from California and was organizing an army in Southern Tennessee.

Magruder, commanding at Yorktown, reporting large bodies disembarking in his front, Kershaw's Brigade, with several others, were placed upon cars and hurried on through Richmond to his support, leaving the other portion of the army to continue the march on foot, or on cars, wherever met. At Richmond we were put on board small sail boats and passed down the James River for the seat of war. This was a novel mode of transportation for most of the soldiers on board. It was a most bitter day and night. A cold east wind blowing from the sea, with a mist of sleet, the cold on the deck of the little vessel became almost unbearable. About two hundred were placed on board of each, and it being so cold we were forced to go below in the "hold," leaving only a little trap door of four feet square as our only means of ventilation. Down in the hold, where these two hundred men were packed like sardines in a box, caused us to almost suffocate, while to remain on deck five minutes would be to court death by freezing. Thus one would go up the little ladder, stick his head through the door a moment for a breath of fresh air, then drop back and allow another the pleasure of a fresh breathing spell. So we alternated between freezing and smothering all the way, a distance of one hundred and fifty miles or more. I had read of the tortures of the "middle passage" and the packing of the slave ships, but I do not think it could have exceeded our condition.

Now it must be remembered that for the most of the time on our march we were separated from our wagon trains that had our tents, cooking utensils, and other baggage. Many novel arrangements were resorted to for cooking. The flour was kneaded into dough on an oil cloth spread upon the ground, the dough pulled into thin cakes, pinned to boards or barrel heads by little twigs or wooden pegs, placed before the fire, and baked into very fair bread. Who would think of baking bread on a ram-rod? But it was often done. Long slices of dough would be rolled around the iron ram-rods, then held over the fire, turning it over continually to prevent burning, and in this way we made excellent bread, but by a tedious process. It is needless to say the meats were cooked by broiling. We parched corn when flour was scarce, and often guards had to be placed over the stock at feed time to prevent soldiers from robbing the horses of their corn.

At midnight the captain of the sloop notified us that we were now at our place of disembarkation, and we began to scramble up the ladder, a small lamp hanging near by and out on deck. The wooden wharfs were even with the deck, so we had no difficulty in stepping from one to the other. But the night was pitch dark, and our only mode of keeping direction was taken from the footsteps of the soldiers on the wharf and in front. Here we came very near losing one of our best soldiers. Jim George was an erratic, or some said "half witted" fellow, but was nevertheless a good soldier, and more will be said of him in future. In going out of the hold on deck he became what is called in common parlance "wrong shipped," and instead of passing to the right, as the others did, he took the left, and in a moment he was floundering about in the cold black waves of the river below. The wind was shrieking, howling, and blowing—a perfect storm—so no one could hear his call for help. He struck out manfully and paddled wildly about in the chilly water, until fortunately a passing sailor, with the natural instinct of his calling, scented a "man overboard." A line was thrown Jim, and after a pull he was landed on shore, more dead than alive.

"How long were you in the water, Jim?" someone asked.

"Hell! more dan t'ree hours," was the laconic and good-natured reply.

Had we lost Jim here, the regiment would have lost a treat in after years, as time will show.

We went into camp a mile or so from the historic old Yorktown, if a few old tumbled down houses and a row of wooden wharfs could be called a town. The country around Yorktown was low and swampy, and the continual rains made the woods and fields a perfect marsh, not a dry foot of land to pitch a tent on, if we had had tents, and scarcely a comfortable place to stand upon. Fires were built, and around these men would stand during the day, and a pretense of sleep during the night. But the soldiers were far from being despondent; although some cursed our luck, others laughed and joked the growlers. The next day great numbers visited Yorktown through curiosity, and watched the Federal Fleet anchored off Old Point Comfort. Here happened a "wind fall" I could never account for. While walking along the beach with some comrades, we came upon a group of soldiers, who, like ourselves, were out sight-seeing. They appeared to be somewhat excited by the way they were gesticulating. When we came up, we found a barrel, supposed to be filled with whiskey, had been washed ashore. Some were swearing by all that was good and bad, that "it was a trick of the d—n Yankees on the fleet," who had poisoned the whiskey and thrown it overboard to catch the "Johnny Rebs." The crowd gathered, and with it the discussion and differences grew. Some swore they would not drink a drop of it for all the world, while others were shouting, "Open her up," "get into it," "not so much talking, but more drinking." But who was "to bell the cat?" Who would drink first? No one seemed to care for the first drink, but all were willing enough, if somebody else would just "try it." It was the first and only time I ever saw whiskey go begging among a lot of soldiers. At last a long, lank, lantern-jawed son of the "pitch and turpentine State" walked up and said:

"Burst her open and give me a drink, a man might as well die from a good fill of whiskey as to camp in this God-forsaken swamp and die of fever; I've got a chill now."

The barrel was opened. The "tar heel" took a long, a steady, and strong pull from a tin cup; then holding it to a comrade, he said: "Go for it. boys, she's all right; no poison thar, and she didn't come from them thar gun boats either. Yankees ain't such fools as to throw away truck like that. No, boys, that 'ar liquor just dropped from Heaven." The battle around the whiskey barrel now raged fast and furious; spirits flowed without and within; cups, canteens, hats, and caps were soused in the tempting fluid, and all drank with a relish. Unfortunately, many had left their canteens in camp, but after getting a drink they scurried away for that jewel of the soldier, the canteen. The news of the find spread like contagion, and in a few minutes hundreds of men were struggling around the barrel of "poison." Where it came from was never known, but it is supposed to have been dropped by accident from a Federal man-of-war. As the soldiers said, "All gifts thankfully received and no questions asked."

General J. Bankhead Magruder was in command of the Peninsula at the time of our arrival, and had established his lines behind the Warwick River, a sluggish stream rising near Yorktown and flowing southward to the James. Along this river light entrenchments had been thrown up. The river had been dammed in places to overflow the lowlands, and at these dams redoubts had been built and defended by our heaviest artillery.

In a few days all our division was in line, and soon thereafter was joined by Longstreet's, D. H. Hill's, and G. W. Smith's, with the cavalry under Stuart. General Johnston was Commander-in-Chief. We remained in camp around Yorktown about two weeks, when General Johnston decided to abandon this line of defense for one nearer Richmond. One of the worst marches our brigade ever had was the night before we evacuated our lines along the Warwick. Remember the troops had no intention of a retreat, for they were going down the river towards the enemy. It was to make a feint, however, to appear as if Johnston was making a general advance, thus to enable the wagon trains and artillery to get out of the way of the retreating army, and Kershaw was to cover this retreat.

At dark we began our march through long ponds and pools

of water, and mud up to the knees, in the direction opposite Gloucester Point, and near a point opposite to the enemy's fleet of gunboats. Through mud and water we floundered and fell, the night being dark. Mile after mile we marched at a snail's gait until we came to a large opening, surrounded by a rail fence. This was about midnight. Here we were ordered to build great fires of the rails near by. This was done, and soon the heavens were lit up by this great stretch of roaring fires. Some had spread their blankets and lay down for a good sleep, while others sat around the good, warm, crackling blaze, wondering what next. Scarcely had we all become quiet than orders came to "fall in." Back over the same sloppy, muddy, and deep-rutted road we marched, retracing the steps made only an hour before, reaching our old camp at daylight, but we were not allowed to stop or rest. The retreat had begun. Magruder, with the other of his forces, was far on the road towards Williamsburg, and we had to fall in his rear and follow his footsteps over roads now simply impassable to any but foot soldiers. We kept up the march until we had left Yorktown ten miles in our rear, after marching a distance of nearly thirty miles, and all night and day. A council of war had been held at Richmond, at which were present President Davis, Generals Lee, Smith, Longstreet, Johnston, and the Secretary of War, to determine upon the point at which our forces were to concentrate and give McClellan battle. Johnston favored Richmond as the most easy of concentration; there to gather all the forces available in Virginia, North Carolina, and South Carolina around Richmond, and as the enemy approached fall upon and crush him. G. W. Smith coincided with Johnston. Longstreet favored reinforcing Jackson in the Valley, drive the enemy out, cross the Potomac, and threaten Washington, and force McClellan to look after his Capitol. The others favored Yorktown and the Peninsula as the point of concentration. But General Johnston found his position untenable, as the enemy could easily flank his right and left with his fleet.

On May 3rd began the long, toilsome march up the York River and the James. The enemy hovered on our rear and picked up our stragglers, and forced the rear guard at every step. At Williamsburg, the evening of the 4th of May, John-

7

ston was forced to turn and fight.   Breastworks and redoubts
had been built some miles in front of the town, and it was here
intended to give battle.   The heavy down-pour of rain prevented Anderson, who was holding the rear and protecting
the wagon trains, from moving, and the enemy began pressing him hard.

Kershaw and the other brigades had passed through Williamsburg when the fight began, but the continual roar of the
cannon told of a battle in earnest going on in the rear and our
troops hotly engaged.   Kershaw and Simms, of our Division,
were ordered back at double quick.   As we passed through
the town the citizens were greatly excited, the piazzas and
balconies being filled with ladies and old men, who urged the
men on with all the power and eloquence at their command.
The woods had been felled for some distance in front of the
earthworks and forts, and as we neared the former we could see
the enemy's skirmishers pushing out of the woods in the clearing.   The Second and Eighth South Carolina Regiments were
ordered to occupy the forts and breastworks beyond Fort
Magruder, and they had a perfect race to reach them before
the enemy did.   The battle was raging in all fierceness on the
left, as well as in our front.   More troops were put in action
on both sides, and it seemed as if we were going to have the
great battle there.   D. R. Jones, Longstreet, and McLaws
were more or less engaged along their whole lines.   The
Third Regiment did not have an opportunity to fire a gun that
day, nor either the Seventh, but the other two had a considerable fight, but being mostly behind breastworks their casualties
were light.   The enemy withdrew at nightfall, and after
remaining on the field for some hours, our army took up the
line of march towards Richmond.   It has been computed that
McClellan had with him on the Peninsula, outside of his
marines, 111,000 men of all arms.

As the term of first enlistment has expired, I will give a
brief sketch of some of the field officers who led the regiments
during the first twelve months of the war.

COLONEL JAMES H. WILLIAMS, OF THE THIRD SOUTH CAROLINA VOLUNTEERS.

Colonel James H. Williams, the commander of the Third
South Carolina Regiment, was born in Newberry County,

October 4th, 1813. He was of Welsh descent, his ancestors immigrating to this country with Lord Baltimore. He was English by his maternal grandmother. The grandfather of Colonel Williams was a Revolutionary soldier, and was killed at the battle of Ninety-Six. The father of the subject of this sketch was also a soldier, and held the office of Captain in the war of 1812.

Colonel Williams, it would seem, inherited his love for the military service from his ancestors, and in early life joined a company of Nullifiers, in 1831. He also served in the Florida War. His ardor in military matters was such he gave little time for other attainments; he had no high school or college education. When only twenty-four years old he was elected Major of the Thirty-eighth Regiment of State Militia, and in 1843 took the Captaincy of the McDuffie Artillery, a crack volunteer company of Newberry. In 1846 he organized a company for the Mexican War, and was mustered into service in 1847 as Company L, Palmetto Regiment. He was in all the battles of that war, and, with the Palmetto Regiment, won distinction on every field. After his return from Mexico he was elected Brigadier General and then Major General of State Militia. He served as Mayor of his town, Commissioner in Equity, and in the State Legislature.

Before the breaking out of the Civil War, he had acquired some large estates in the West, and was there attending to some business connected therewith when South Carolina seceded. The companies that were to compose the Third Regiment elected him their Colonel, but in his absence, when the troops were called into service, they were commanded for the time by Lieutenant Colonel Foster, of Spartanburg. He joined the Regiment at "Lightwood Knot Springs," the 1st of May. He commanded the Third during the term of its first enlistment, and carried it through the first twelve months' campaign in Virginia.

At the reorganization of the regiment, the men composing it being almost wholly young men, desired new blood at the head of the volunteer service, and elected Captain James D. Nance in his stead. After his return to the State, he was placed at the head of the Fourth and Ninth Regiments of State Troops, and served as such until the close.

After the war, he returned to Arkansas and continued his planting operations until the time of his death, August 21st, 1892. He was a member of the Constitutional Convention of that State in 1874.

Colonel Williams was a born soldier, considerate of and kind to his men. He was cool and fearless to a fault. He understood tactics thoroughly, but was wanting in those elements of discipline— its sternness and rigidity that was required to govern troops in actual war. His age counted against him as a strict disciplinarian, but not as a soldier. He was elected to the Legislature of this State before Reconstruction, as well as a member of the Constitutional Convention of Arkansas in 1874.

LIEUTENANT COLONEL FOSTER, OF THE THIRD SOUTH CAROLINA VOLUNTEERS.

Lieutenant Colonel C. B. Foster, of the Third South Carolina Regiment, was born in Spartanburg County, South Carolina, at the old Foster homestead, near Cedar Springs, in 1817. His father was Anthony Foster, a native of Virginia. Colonel Foster was a member of the Legislature before the war, and represented Spartanburg County in the Secession Convention, along with Simpson Bobo, Dr. J. H. Carlisle, and others. After the Convention adjourned he returned to his home in Spartanburg and immediately began drilling a company for the war. He was elected Captain of the Blackstock Company, which was Company K, in the Third Regiment of South Carolina Volunteers. The Blackstock Company reported for duty as soon as volunteers were called for, and went immediately to the camp of instruction at Lightwood Knot Springs. Colonel Foster was elected Lieutenant Colonel of the regiment. After spending about three months at the camp of instruction, the Third Regiment was ordered to Virginia. Colonel Foster served until some time after the battle of First Manassas, having participated in that campaign. He remained in Virginia until the fall of 1861, when he was ordered to go home by the surgeon, his health having completely given way. It took long nursing to get him on his feet again. He was devoted to the Confederate cause, and was always willing and ready to help in any way its advancement. He gave two sons to his country. One, Captain Perrin Foster, also of the Third Regiment, was killed at Fredericksburg leading his command. His other son, James Anthony Foster, gave up his life in the front of his command during the frightful charge on Maryland Heights. He was a member of Company K, of the Third Regiment.

Colonel Foster was considered a wealthy man before the war, but when it ended he was left penniless. At that time be lived near Glenn Springs, Spartanburg County. In 1867 he moved to Union County and merchandised until 1884. He was also County Treasurer for a long time. He died on June 9th, 1897, at the residence of his daughter, Mrs. Benjamin Kennedy, at Jonesville, Union County. In early life Colonel Foster married Miss Mary Ann Perrin, a sister of Colonel Thomas C. Perrin, of Abbeville. She died in 1886. Three daughters survive Colonel Foster, Mrs. I. G. McKissick, Mrs. Benjamin Kennedy, and Mrs. J. A. Thompson. Colonel Foster was one of God's noblemen. He was true to his friends, his family, and his country. He never flinched from danger nor from his duty. He was faithful at all times and under all circumstances to the best principles of the Anglo-Saxon race.

COLONEL THOMAS G. BACON, OF THE SEVENTH SOUTH CAROLINA VOLUNTEERS.

Thomas Glascock Bacon was born in Edgefield Village of English ancestry on the 24th of June, 1812. He was the youngest son of Major Edmund Bacon, the eloquent and distinguished member of the Edgefield Bar, and author of the humorous "Georgia Scenes," written under the nom de plume of Ned Brace. Colonel Bacon's mother was a sister of Brigadier General Thomas F. Glascock, of Georgia, a gallant and distinguished officer of the Revolutionary War, and after whom Colonel Bacon was named. He received the early rudiments of education at the Edgefield Academy, and when at the proper age he was sent for his classical education to the Pendleton English and Classical Institute, under the tutilage of that profound scholar and educator, Prof. S. M. Shuford. Colonel Bacon was fond of the classics, and had acquired rare literary attainments, and had he cultivated his tastes in that line assiduously, he no doubt would have become the foremost scholar of the State, if not the South.   He was passionately fond of manly sports and out-door exercise.   He was a devotee of the turf, and this disposition led him early in life to the development of fast horses and a breeder of blooded stock.   He was a turfman of the old school, and there were but few courses in the South that had not tested the mettle of his stock.   But like his brother in arms, Colonel Cash, of the Eighth, and brother turfman, he became disgusted with the thievery and trickery of later day sports and quit the turf, still owning at his death some of the most noted racers of the times, Granger Lynchburg, John Payne, Glengary, Father Ryan, Ned Brace, and others of lesser note.

He paid much attention to military matters, and held several offices in the State militia before the war.   He, with his friend and superior, General M. L. Bonham, enlisted in the "Blues" and served in the Palmetto Regiment in the war with the Seminoles.   At the breaking out of the Civil War he, with Elbert Bland, afterwards Colonel of the Seventh, organized the first company from Edgefield, and was elected Captain. The companies assigned to the Seventh Regiment unanimously elected him the Colonel, and in that capacity he led his regiment to Virginia, being among the first regiments from the State to reach the seat of war.   He was at the battle of Manassas, and participated in the Peninsular campaign.   At the reorganization of the regiment at the expiration of the term of enlistment, his failing health forced him to decline a re-election as Colonel.   Returning home, and the State needing the services of trained soldiers to command the State troops, notwithstanding his failing health, he cheerfully accepted the command of the Seventh Regiment State troops. In 1863 he was elected to the State Senate.   He died at his home, Pine Pond, in Edgefield County, September 25th, 1876, leaving a widow, but no children.

Strong in his friendship and earnest in his affection, but with a peaceable and forgiving temperament, pure in his motives, charitable in all things, generous to the needy, affectionate to his friends and relatives, chivalric and honorable in every relation of life, brave in action, and with that fortitude under adverse circumstances that makes heroes of men, just and impartial to the officers and men under his command, pleasant and sociable towards his equals in rank, obedient and courteous to his superiors, few men lived or died with so much respect and admiration, genuine friendship, and love from all as Colonel Thomas G. Bacon, of the Seventh South Carolina Volunteers.

COLONEL E. B. C. CASH, OF THE EIGHTH SOUTH CAROLINA VOLUNTEERS.

Ellerbe Boggan Crawford Cash was born near Wadesboro, Anson County, North Carolina, on July 1st, 1823. His father was Boggan Cash, a Colonel in militia of that State, merchant, and member of Legislature, His mother was Miss Elizabeth Ellerbe, of Chesterfield County, S. C. He was the only child. His father died when he was near two years old, and his mother returned to her father's, in South Carolina. He was educated at Mt. Zion Institute, Winnsboro, S. C., and South Carolina College. He read law under General Blakeney, at Cheraw, S. C., and practiced in partnership a short while with Alexander McIver, Esq., the Solicitor of the Eastern Circuit, and father of Chief Justice Henry McIver, of South Carolina. But his mother owning a large landed estate, and several hundred negroes, he soon retired from the Bar to look after her affairs, and devoted himself to planting and raising fine horses and cattle. He married in 1847 his cousin, Miss Allan Ellerbe, of Kershaw, S. C. He was elected to the Legislature from his County, Chesterfield. He was elected Colonel, Brigadier General, and Major General of State militia.

When the war commenced he was one of the Major Generals of the State. He volunteered and was elected Colonel of the Eighth South Carolina Regiment. At the reorganization he did not offer for re-election, but came home and was made Colonel in State troops. He was kind to the poor the whole war, and gave away during the war over 50,000 bushels of corn and large quantities of other provisions to soldiers' families, or sold it in Confederate money at ante bellum prices. After the war all notes, claims, and mortgages he held on estates of old soldiers he cancelled and made a present of them to their families. In one case the amount he gave a widow, who had a family and small children, was over $5,000, her husband having been killed in his regiment.

After the war he continued to farm. In 1876 he took an active part in redeeming the State, and contributed his time, advice, and services, and a great deal of money. In 1881 he fought a duel with Colonel Wm. M. Shannon, in which he killed Colonel Shannon. Colonel Cash was the challeged party. His wife died in May, 1880. Colonel Cash died March 10, 1888, and was buried in the family burying ground at his residence, Cash's Depot, S. C.

Colonel Cash was a man of strong character, fearless, brave, generous and true, a good friend and patriot. He made no religious profession. He was charitable to the extreme, and was the soul of honor, and while he had many enemies, being a fearless man and a good hater, he had such qualities as inspired the respect and admiration of his fellowmen.

CHAPTER VIII

Reorganized—"New Officers"—Battle.

On the 13th of April the term for which the twelve months' troops had enlisted was now soon to expire, the great number which had not re-enlisted were looking forward with longing anticipation for orders to disband and return to their homes. On the 14th, their obligations being at an end, officers and men were making rapid preparation to depart for home—not to quit the service, however, but more to enjoy a short leave of absence with their families, and to join other branches of the services, more especially cavalry. Some of the companies had actually left, and were a mile or two from camp when orders came to return. The Conscript Act had been passed, making it obligatory on all, between the ages of eighteen and thirty-five, to enter or remain in the army The men took their sudden return in good humor, for really it was only the married men, who had left their families so unprepared twelve months before, who cared to return home; for some of the young men, who were under the conscript age, refused to leave. Those who had to return received a lot of good-natured badgering at their sudden return to the army. "Hello,

boys, when did you get back? What's the news at home?"
"How did you find all?" were some of the soothing jeers the
"returned sinners" had to endure; and as so great a number
had expressed a desire to join the cavalry, not a few were
asked: "Did you bring your horses with you?" But all was
soon forgotten, for in a few days a reorganization was ordered
to take place, and new officers elected.

The Conscript Act was condemned in unmeasured terms in
many places at the South, but its necessity and expediency
was never doubted. To have allowed so great a number to
absent themselves from the army at this time, in the face of
an overwhelming enemy, and that enemy advancing upon our
Capitol, was more than the morale of the army would admit.
Not altogether would the absence of the soldiers themselves
effect the army, but in the breaking up of organizations, for in
some companies all had re-enlisted, while in others one-half,
and in many cases none. New regiments would have had to
be formed out of the re-enlisted companies, and new companies
out of the large number of recruits, now in camps of instruction. So by keeping up the old organizations, and filling up
the ranks by the conscripts at home, the army would be
greatly benefited.

In some countries, to be called a conscript or drafted man
was considered a stigma, but not so in the South. There is
little doubt, had a call been made for volunteers, any number
could have been had at a moment's notice, for there were
hundreds and thousands at the South only awaiting an opportunity to enter the army. In fact, there were companies and
regiments already organized and officered, only awaiting arms
by the government, but these organizations were all raw men,
and at this time it was believed to fill up the old companies
with recruits, thus putting seasoned troops side by side with
raw ones, would enhance the efficiency of the army, retain its
discipline, and *esprit de corps*.

Then, again, the farms had to be managed, the slaves kept
in subjection, and the army fed, and the older men were better
qualified for this service than the young. In reality, all
were in the service of the country, for while the younger
men were fighting in the ranks, the older ones were working in the fields and factories to furnish them clothes, provis-

ions, and munitions of war.   Our government had no means
at home, no ships on the ocean, little credit abroad, and our
ports all blockaded.   So all had to enter the service either as
a fighter or a worker, and our wisest men thought it the better
policy to allow the young men the glory upon the field, while
the old men served at home.   On the 13th of May all companies were allowed to elect their officers, both company and
regimental, and enter the service for two more years.   As I
said in the commencement of this work, at the breaking out of
the war men generally selected as officers the old militia officers for company officers and veterans of the Mexican War for
field officers.   General Bonham had been a Colonel in Mexico.
Williams, of the Third, had led a company from Newberry
to that far-off land.   Kershaw went as First Lieutenant.
Cash, of the Eighth, was a Major General of the militia at
the breaking out of the war.   The greatest number of the first
Colonels of regiments under the first call were Mexican veterans.   Another qualification that was considered at the first
organization was popularity—gentle, clever, and kind-hearted.
The qualification of courage or as a disciplinarian was seldom
thought of; for a man to be wanting in the first could not be
thought possible.   Our men, who had known the proud feelings of personal freedom, dreaded discipline and restraint, naturally turned to those men for officers most conducive to their
will and wishes.   But twelve months' service in trying campaigns made quite a change.   What they had once looked upon
with dread and misgiving they now saw as a necessity.   Strict
discipline was the better for both men and the service.   A
greater number of the older officers, feeling their services
could be better utilized at home than in the army, and also
having done their duty and share by setting the example by
enlistment and serving twelve months, relinquished these offices
to the younger men and returned home.   The younger, too,
saw the advisability of infusing in the organizations young
blood—men more of their own age and temperament—the
stern necessity of military discipline, a closer attendance to
tactics and drills, better regulations, and above all, courage.
The organizations selected such men as in their opinions would
better subserve the interests of the service, and who had the
requisites for leadership.   This is said with no disparagement

to the old officers, for truer, more patriotic, nor a braver set of men ever drew a blade than those who constituted the old brigade during its first organization. In fact, some who had served during the first twelve months as officers, when they discovered their deficiency, or that the men had more confidence in others, after a short respite at home, returned and joined their old companies as privates. Was there ever greater patriotism and unselfishness and less ostentation shown as in the example of these men! It was but natural that men selected almost at random, and in many instances unacquainted with a majority of the men at enlistment unusual to military life, or the requirements of an officer in actual service, could possibly be as acceptable as those chosen after a year of service, and in close compact with the men.

SECOND REGIMENT.

The Second Regiment chose as officers—

Colonel—Jno. D. Kennedy.

Lieutenant Colonel—A. S. Goodwin.

Major—Frank Gaillard.

Adjutant—E. E. Sill.

Quartermaster—W. D. Peck.

Commissary—J. J. Villipigue.

Chief Surgeon—Dr. F. Salmond.

Chaplains—Revs. McGruder and Smith.

I give below a list of the Captains, as well as the field officers, of the Second Regiment during the war. There were many changes from Lieutenants to Captains, and subsequent elections from the ranks to Lieutenants, caused by the casualties of war, but space forbids, and want of the facts prevents me from giving more than the company commanders and the field officers.

Colonels—J. B. Kershaw, E. P. Jones, Jno. D. Kennedy, and Wm. Wallace.

Lieutenant Colonels—E. P. Jones, A. D. Goodwin, F. Gaillard, Wm. Wallace, and J. D. Graham.

Majors—A. D. Goodwin, W. H. Casson, F. Gaillard, Wm. Wallace, I. D. Graham, B. F. Clyburn, G. L. Leaphart.

Adjutants—A. D. Goodwin, E. E. Sill, and A. McNeil.

Surgeons and Assistant Surgeons—J. A. Maxwell and J. H. Nott.

Some of them went from Captains and Majors through all the grades to Colonel. The following are the Captains, some elected at the first organization, some at the reorganization, and others rose by promotion from Lieutenant:

Company A—W. H. Casson, M. A. Shelton, G. L. Leaphart, M. M. Maddrey.

Company B—A. D. Hoke, Wm. Pulliam, W. Powell, J. Caigle.

Company C—Wm. Wallace, S. Lorick, J. T. Scott, A. P. Winson.

Company D—J. S. Richardson, J. D. Graham, W. Wilder.

Company E—John D. Kennedy, elected Colonel, Z. Leitner, J. Crackeford.

Company F—W. W. Perryman, W. C. China, G. McDowell.

Company G—J. Hail, J. Friesdale, J. P. Cunningham.

Company H—H. McManus, D. Clyburn.

Company I—G. B. Cuthbreath, Ralph Elliott, R. Fishburn, B. F. Barlow.

Company K—R. Rhett, J. Moorer, K. D. Webb, J. D. Dutart, —— Burton, G. T. Haltiwanger.

Many changes took place by death and resignation. Scarcely any of the field officers remained in the end. Many Captains of a low rank went all the way to Colonels of regiments, and Third Lieutenants rose by promotion to Captains. This shows the terrible mortality among the officers. None of the first field officers but what had been killed or incapacitated for service by wounds at the close of the war.

THIRD SOUTH CAROLINA REGIMENT.

James D. Nance, of Newberry, Captain of Company E, elected Colonel.

Conway Garlington, of Laurens, Captain of Company A, elected Lieutenant Colonel.

W. D. Rutherford, of Newberry, formerly Adjutant, made Major.

Y. J. Pope, Newberry, formerly Orderly Sergeant of Company E, made Adjutant.

G. W. Shell, Laurens, Quartermaster.

J. N. Martin and R. N. Lowrance, Commissary.

Ed. Hicks, of Laurens, Sergeant Major.

All staff officers are appointed or recommended for appoint-ment by the Colonel of the regiment. The offices of Regi-mental Quartermaster and Commissary, the encumbents heretofore ranking as Captains, were abolished during the year, having one Quartermaster and one Commissary for the bri-gade, the regiments having only Sergeants to act as such. I will state here that some of the companies from each regiment had reorganized and elected officers before the time of re-enlist-ment. This is one reason why rank was not accorded in the regular order. In the Third Regiment, Company E, Captain J. D. Nance, and perhaps several others, had reorganized, taken their thirty days' furlough, and had returned before the general order to reorganize and remain for two more years or the war. The new organizations stood in the Third as fol-lows, by Captains:

Company A—Willie Hance, Laurens.

Company B—N. Davidson, Newberry.

Company C—R. C. Maffett, Newberry.

Company D—N. F. Walker, Spartanburg.

Company E—J. K. G. Nance—Newberry.

Company F—P. Williams, Laurens.

Company G—R. P. Todd—Laurens.

Company H—John C. Summer, Lexington.

Company I—D. M. H. Langston, Laurens.

Company K—S. M. Langford, Spartanburg.

Many changes took place in this regiment, some almost im-mediately after the election and others in the battle that fol-lowed in a few weeks.

Captain Davidson died in two weeks after his election from disease, and was succeeded by Lieutenant Thomas W. Gary, who had during the first twelve months been Captain David-son's Orderly Sergeant. It seems the position of Orderly Ser-geant was quite favorable to promotion, for nearly all the Orderlies during the first twelve months were made either Cap-tains or Lieutenants.

Lieutenant Colonel Garlington being killed at Savage Sta-tion, Major Rutherford was promoted to that position, while Captain Maffett was made Major and Lieutenant Herbert Cap-tain in his stead of Company C.

Captain Hance, of Company A, being killed at Fredericksburg, First Lieutenant Robert Richardson became Captain.

Lieutenant R. H. Wright became Captain of Company E after the promotion of Nance to Major in the latter part of the service.

Captain Williams, of Company F, was killed, and Lieutenant Wm. Deal made Captain and commanded at the surrender. There may have been other Captains of this company, but no data at hand.

John W. Watts became Captain of Company G after the promotion of Captain Todd to Major and Lieutenant Colonel.

Captain Summer being killed at Fredericksburg, Lieutenant G. S. Swygert became Captain, was disabled and resigned, and D. A. Dickert became Captain and commanded to the end.

Captain Langston, of Company I, being killed, Lieutenant Jarred Johnston became Captain, disabled at Chickamauga.

Company K was especially unfortunate in her commanders. Captain Sanford was killed at Savage Station; then Lieutenant L. P. Foster, son of Lieutenant Colonel Foster, was promoted to Captain and killed at Fredericksburg. Then W. H. Young was made Captain and killed at Gettysburg. Then J. H. Cunningham became Captain and was killed at Chickamauga. J. P. Roebuck was promoted and soon after taken prisoner. First Lieutenant John W. Wofford commanded the company till the surrender, and after the war became State Senator from Spartanburg.

Captain N. F. Walker was permanently disabled at Savage Station, returned home, was appointed in the conscript bureau, and never returned to active duty. He still retained his rank and office as Captain of Company D, thereby preventing promotions in one of the most gallant companies in Kershaw's Brigade.

It was at the battle of Fredericksburg that the regiment lost so many officers, especially Captains, that caused the greatest changes. Captains Hance, Foster, Summer, with nearly a dozen Lieutenants, were killed there, making three new Captains, and a lot of new Lieutenants. It was by the death of Captain Summer that I received the rank of Captain, having been a Lieutenant up to that time. From December, 1862, to the end I commanded the company, with scarcely a change.

It will be seen that at the reorganization the Third Regiment made quite a new deal, and almost a clean sweep of old officers —and with few exceptions the officers from Colonel to the Lieutenants of least rank were young men. I doubt very much if there was a regiment in the service that had such a proportion of young men for officers.

I will here relate an incident connected with the name of Captain Hance's family, that was spoken of freely in the regiment at the time, but little known outside of immediate surroundings—not about Captain Hance, however, but the name and connection that the incident recalled, that was often related by the old chroniclers of Laurens. Andrew Johnson, who was at the time I speak United States Senator from Tennessee, and was on the ticket with Lincoln, for Vice-President of the United States in his second race against McClellan, was elected, and afterwards became President.. As the story goes, and it is vouched for as facts, Andrew Johnson in his younger days had a tailoring establishment at Laurens, and while there paid court to the mother of Captain Hance. So smitten was he with her charms and graces, he paid her special attention, and asked for her hand in marriage. Young Johnson was fine looking, in fact handsome, energetic, prosperous, and well-to-do young man, with no vices that were common to the young men of that day, but the great disparity in the social standing of the two caused his rejection. The family of Hance was too exclusive at the time to consent to a connection with the plebeian Johnson, yet that plebeian rose at last to the highest office in the gift of the American people, through the force of his own endowments.

SEVENTH SOUTH CAROLINA REGIMENT.

The Seventh Regiment was reorganized by electing—
Colonel—D. Wyatt Aiken, Abbeville.
Lieutenant Colonel—Elbert Bland, Edgefield.
Major—W. C. White, Edgefield.
Adjutant—Thomas M. Childs.
Sergeant Major—Amos C. Stalworth.
Quartermaster—B. F. Lovelace.
Commissary—A. F. Townsend.
Company A—Stuart Harrison.

Company B—Thomas Huggins.
Company C—W. E. Cothran.
Company D—Warren H. Allen.
Company E—James Mitchell.
Company F—John S. Hard.
Company G—W. C. Clark.
Company H—H. W. Addison.
Company I—Benj. Roper.
Company K—Jno. L. Burris.
Company L—J. L. Litchfield.
Company M—Jerry Goggans.

I am indebted to Captain A. C. Waller, of Greenwood, for the following brief summary of the Seventh after reorganization, giving the different changes of regimental and company commanders, as well as the commanders of the regiment during battle:

Colonel Aiken commanded at Savage Station, Malvern Hill, and Antietam, till wounded at Gettysburg, after which he was ordered elsewhere.

Lieutenant Colonel Bland commanded at Fredericksburg, Chancellorsville, and Chickamauga; killed in latter battle.

Major White commanded at Antietam after the wounding of Aiken, and until he was himself killed at the enemy's battery, the farthest advance of the day. Captain Hard had command at the close. Captain Hard also led for a short while at Chickamauga after the death of Bland, and fell at the head of his regiment on top of Pea Ridge.

Captain Goggans was in command at Knoxville, Bean Station, and the Wilderness, until wounded.

Captain James Mitchell led the regiment in the charge at Cold Harbor, and was in command at Spottsylvania.

Lieutenant Colonel Maffett, of the Third, was placed in command of the Seventh during the Valley campaign under Early in 1864, and led at Fisher's Hill and Cedar Creek the 13th and 19th of September. Was captured in October.

Lieutenant Colonel Huggins commanded from October till the surrender, and at the battle of Averysboro and Bentonville.

Captain Goggans was promoted to Major after the battle of the Wilderness, but resigned.

Company E was divided into two companies, E and M. Company H took the place of Cland's, which became Company A.

Captain Stuart Harrison, Company A, resigned, being elected Clerk of Court of Edgefield, and Lieutenant Gus Bart was made Captain.

John Carwile, First Lieutenant of Company A, acted as Adjutant after the death of Adjutant Childs, and also on General Kershaw's staff.

Lieutenant James Townsend became Captain of Company B after the promotion of Huggins to Lieutenant Colonel.

After Captain Hard's promotion James Rearden was made Captain of Company E and was killed at Wilderness, and Lieutenant C. K. Henderson became Captain.

Captain Wm. E. Clark, Company G, was killed at Maryand heights. Lieutenant Jno. W. Kemp was made Captain and killed at the Wilderness.

Captain J. L. Burris, of Company K, was wounded at Antieam and resigned. First Lieutenant J. L. Talbert having been killed at Maryland Heights a few days before, Second Lieutenant Giles M. Berry became Captain; he resigued, and Lieutenant West A. Cheatham was made Captain by promotion.

Captain J. L. Litchfied, of Company I, was killed at Maryand Heights, and First Lieutenant Litchfield was made Captain.

First Lieutenant P. Bouknight became Captain of Company M after the promotion of Captain Goggans.

EIGHTH SOUTH CAROLINA REGIMENT.

The Eighth South Carolina Regiment was reorganized by electing—

Colonel—Jno. W. Henagan, Marlboro.

Lieutenant Colonel—A. J. Hoole, Darlington.

Major—McD. McLeod, Marlboro.

Adjutant—C. M. Weatherly, Darlington.

Surgeon—Dr. Pearce.

Assistant Surgeon—Dr. Maxy.

Company A—John H. Muldrow, Darlington.

Company B—Richard T. Powell, Chesterfield.

Company C—Thomas E. Powe, Chesterfield.

Company D—Robt. P. Miller, Chesterfield.

Company E—M. E. Keith, Darlington.

Company F—T. E. Howle, Darlington.

Company G—C. P. Townsend, Marlboro.

Company H—Duncan McIntyre, Marion.

Company I—A. T. Harllee, Marion.

Company K—Frank Manning, Marlboro.

Company L—Thomas E. Stackhouse, Marion.

Company M—Thomas E. Howle, Darlington.

Company L was a new company, and T. E. Stackhouse was made Captain; also A. T. Harllee was made Captain of Company I. Company M was also a new company.

————

After the reorganization the Generals' staffs were reduced to more republican simplicity. General Kershaw was contented with—

Captain C. R. Holmes—Assistant Adjutant General.

Lieutenant W. M. Dwight—Adjutant and Inspector General.

Lieutenant D. A. Doby—Aide de Camp.

Lieutenant Jno. Myers—Ordnance Officer.

Major W. D. Peck—Quartermaster.

Major Kennedy—Commissary.

With a few privates for clerical service. General Kershaw had two fine-looking, noble lads as couriers, neither grown to manhood, but brave enough to follow their chief in the thickest of battle, or carry his orders through storms of battles, W. M. Crumby, of Georgia, and DeSaussure Burrows. The latter lost his life at Cedar Creek.

As I have thus shown the regiments and brigade in their second organization, under the name it is known, "Kershaw's," and as all were so closely connected and identified, I will continue to treat them as a whole. The same camps, marches, battles, scenes, and experiences were alike to all, so the history of one is the history of all. South Carolina may have had, and I have no doubt did have, as good troops in the field, as ably commanded as this brigade, but for undaunted courage, loyalty to their leaders and the cause, for self-denials and sacrifices, united spirits, and unflinching daring in the face of death, the world has never produced their superiors. There was much to animate their feelings and stimulate their courage. The older men had retired and left the field to the leadership of the young. Men were here, too, by circumstances of birth, education, and environment that could scarcely ever expect to occupy more than a secondary place in their country's history, who were destined to inferior stations in life, both social and political,—the prestige of wealth and a long family being denied them—still upon the battlefield they were any man's equal. On the march or the suffering in camp, they were the peers of the noblest, and when facing death or experiencing its pangs they knew no superiors. Such being the feelings and sentiments of those born in the humbler stations of life, what must have been the goal of those already fortune's favorites, with a high or aristocratic birth, wealth, education, and a long line of illustrious ancestors, all to stimulate them to deeds of prowess and unparalleled heroism? Such were the men to make the name of South Carolina glorious, and that of "Kershaw" immortal. How many of these noble souls died that their country might be free? the name of her people great? In the former they lost, as the ends for which they fought and died were never consummated. To-day, after nearly a half century has passed, when we look around among the young and see the decadence of chivalry and noble aspirations, the decline of homage to women, want of integrity to men, want of truth and honor, individually and politically, are we not inclined, at times, to think those men died in vain? We gained the shadow; have we the substance? We gained an unparalleled prestige for courage, but are the people to-day better morally, socially, and politically? Let the world answer. The days of knight-errantry had their decadence; may not the days of the South's chivalry have theirs?

CHAPTER IX

Battle of Seven Pines---Seven Days' Fight Around Richmond.

It was the intention of General Johnston to fall back slowly before McClellan, drawing him away from his base, then when

the Federal Corps become separated in their marches, to concentrate his forces, turn and crush him at one blow. The
low, swampy, and wooded condition of the country from Yorktown up the Peninsula would not admit of the handling of the
troops, nor was there any place for artillery practice to be
effective. Now that he had his forces all on the South side of
the Chickahominy, and the lands more rolling and firm, he
began to contemplate a change in his tactics. Ewell, with
several detached regiments under Whiting, had been sent in
the Valley to re-enforce that fiery meteor, Stonewall Jackson,
who was flying through the Shenandoah Valley and the gorges
of the Blue Ridge like a cyclone, and General Johnston wished
Jackson to so crush his enemy that his troops could be concentrated with his own before Richmond. But the authorities at
Richmond thought otherwise. It is true Jackson had been
worsted at Kernstown by Shields, but his masterly movements
against Banks, Fremont, Siegle, and others, gave him such
prestige as to make his name almost indispensible to our army.
McDowell, with forty thousand men, lay at Fredericksburg,
with nothing in his front but a few squadrons of cavalry and
some infantry regiments. Johnston was thus apprehensive
that he might undertake to come down upon his flanks and
re-enforce "Little Mc." or the "Young Napoleon," as the
commander of the Federal Army was now called. On the
20th of May, Johnston heard of two of the Federal Corps,
Keyes' and Heintzleman's, being on the south side of the
Chickahominy, while the others were scattered along the
north banks at the different crossings. McClellan had his
headquarters six miles away, towards the Pamunkey River.
This was considered a good opportunity to strike, and had
there been no miscarriages of plan, nor refusals to obey orders,
and, instead, harmony and mutual understanding prevailed,
the South might have gained one of its greatest victories, and
had a different ending to the campaign entirely. G. W.
Smith lay to the north of Richmond; Longstreet on the Williamsburg Road, immediately in front of the enemy; Huger on
the James; Magruder, of which was Kershaw's Brigade (in a
division under McLaws), stretched along the Chickahominy
above New Bridge.

All these troops were to concentrate near Seven Pines and

there fall upon the enemy's two corps, and beat them before succor could be rendered. No Lieutenant Generals had as yet been appointed, senior Major Generals generally commanding two divisions. The night before the attack, General Johnston called his generals together and gave them such instructions and orders as were necessary, and divided his army for the day's battle into two wings, G. W. Smith to command the left and Longstreet the right; the right wing to make the first assault (it being on the south side of the York River Railroad). G. W. Smith was to occupy the Nine Mile Road, running parallel with Longstreet's front and extending to the river, near New Bridge, on the Chickahominy. He was to watch the movements of the enemy on the other side, and prevent Sumner, whose corps were near the New Bridge, from crossing, and to follow up the fight as Longstreet and D. H. Hill progressed. Magruder, with his own and McLaws' Division, supported Smith, and was to act as emergencies required. Kershaw was now under McLaws. Huger was to march up on the Charles City Road and put in on Longstreet's left as it uncovered at White Oak Swamp, or to join his forces with Longstreet's and the two drive the enemy back from the railroad. Keyes' Federal Corps lay along the railroad to Fair Oaks; then Heintzleman's turned abruptly at a right angle in front of G. W. Smith. The whole was admirably planned, and what seemed to make success doubly sure, a very heavy rain had fallen that night, May 30th, accompanied by excessive peals of thunder and livid flashes of lightning, and the whole face of the country was flooded with water. The river was overflowing its banks, bridges washed away or inundated by the rapidly swelling stream, all going to make re-enforcement by McClellan from the north side out of the question. But the entire movement seemed to be one continual routine of blunders, misunderstandings, and perverseness; a continual wrangling among the senior Major Generals. The enemy had thrown up two lines of heavy earthworks for infantry and redoubts for the artillery, one near Fair Oaks, the other one-half mile in the rear. Longstreet and D. H. Hill assaulted the works with great vigor on the morning of the 31st of May, and drove the enemy from his first entrenched camp. But it seems G. W. Smith did not press to the front, as was

expected, but understood his orders to remain and guard t
crossing of the river.   Huger lost his way and did not co:
up until the opportunity to grasp the key to the situation v
lost, and then it was discovered there was a mistake or m
understanding in regard to his and Longstreet's seniorit
Still Huger waived his rank reluctantly and allowed Lor
street and Hill to still press the enemy back to his second li
of entrenchments.   From where we lay, inactive and idle, t
steady roll of the musketry was grand and exciting.   The
was little opportunity for ability and little used, only by t
enemy in their forts.

Several ineffectual attempts were made to storm these for
and to dislodge the enemy at the point of the bayonet.   Fina
R. H. Anderson's Brigade of South Carolinians came up, a
three regiments, led by Colonel Jenkins, made a flank mor
ment, and by a desperate assault, took the redoubt on the le
with six pieces of artillery.   When Rhodes' North Caroli
Brigade got sufficiently through the tangle and undergrow
and near the opening as to see their way clear, they raised
yell, and with a mad rush, they took the fort with a bour
They were now within the strong fortress on the left and ma
ters of the situation.   Colonel Jenkins was highly compliment
by the commanding General for his skill, and the energy a
courage of his men.   The enemy worked their guns faithfu:
and swept the ranks of Rhodes and Anderson with grape a
canister, but Southern valor here, as elsewhere, overcai
Northern discipline.   Many of the enemy fell dead within t
fort, while endeavoring to spike their guns.

Sumner, from the north side of the Chickahominy, was ma
ing frantic efforts to cross the stream and come to the relief
sorely pressed comrades.   The bridges were two feet or mc
under water, swaying and creaking as if anxious to follow t
rushing waters below.   It is said the Federal General, Butl
called afterwards "Beast," covered himself with glory, by ru:
ing at the head of his troops, in and through the water, a
succeeded in getting enough men on the bridge to hold it dow
while the others crossed over.   But the reinforcements cai
too late to aid their hard pressed friends.   After the entrenc
ments were all taken, the enemy had no other alternative t
to fall back in the dense forest and undergrowth, giving the

shelter until night, with her sable curtains, hid friend and foe alike.   Just as the last charge had been made, General Johnston, riding out in an opening, was first struck by a fragment of shell, thereby disabling him for further duty upon the field for a long time.   The command of the army now fell upon General G. W. Smith, who ordered the troops to remain stationary for the night, and next morning, they were returned to their original quarters.   Kershaw and the other Brigadiers of the division did not become engaged, as they were awaiting upon a contingency that did not arise.   It is true, the enemy were driven from thier strongly fortified position, and for more than a mile to the rear, still the fruits of the victory were swallowed up in the loss of so many good men, with no tangible or lasting results.   From all the facts known at the time, and those developed since, it is the opinion that upon G. W. Smith rested the blame for the loss of the day.   Had he been as active or energetic as the other Major Generals, or had he assumed responsibility, and taken advantage of events presenting themselves during the battle, that could not be known beforehand, nor counted in the plan of the battle, the day at Seven Pines might have loomed up on the side of the Confederate forces with those at Gaines' Mills or Second Manassas. But, as it was, it must be counted as one of the fruitless victories of the war.

General Smith left the army next day, never to return to active service.   Here was a commentary on the question of the made soldier or the soldier born.   At West Point General Smith stood almost at the very head of his class; at the commencement of the war, he was considered as one of our most brilliant officers, and stood head and shoulders above some of his cotemporaries in the estimation of our leaders and the Department at Richmond.   But his actions and conduct on several momentous occasions will leave to posterity the necessity of voting him a failure: while others of his day, with no training nor experience in the science of war, have astonished the world with their achievements and soldierly conduct.   The soldiers were sorrowful and sad when they learned of the fate of their beloved Commander-in-Chief.   They had learned to love him as a father; he had their entire confidence.   They were fearful at the time lest his place could never be filled; and,

but for the splendid achievement of their new commander, R.
E. Lee, with the troops drilled and disciplined by his pre-
decessor, and who fought the battles on the plans laid down
by him, it is doubtful whether their confidence could have ever
been transferred to another.

General Lee took command the next day, June the 1st, 1862.
He did not come with any prestige of great victory to recommend him to the troops, but his bold face, manly features, distinguished bearing, soon inspired a considerable degree of
confidence and esteem, to be soon permanently welded by the
glorious victories won from the Chickahominy to the James.
He called all his Lieutenants around him in a few days and
had a friendly talk. He told none his plans—he left that to
be surmised—but he gained the confidence of his Generals at
once.

The troops were set to work fortifying their lines from the
James to the Chickahominy, and up the latter stream to near
Meadow Bridge. Engineer corps were established, and large
details from each regiment, almost one-third of the number,
were put to work under the engineers strengthening their
camps on scientific principles. The troops thought they were
to do their fighting behind these works, but strange to say,
out of the hundred of fortifications built by Kershaw's
men during the war, not one ever fired a gun from behind
them.

On the 12th of June General Stuart started on his remarkable ride around the army of McClellan, and gained for himself the name of "Prince of Raiders." Starting out in the
morning as if going away to our left at a leisurely gait, he
rode as far as Hanover Court House. Before daylight next
morning his troopers sprang into their saddles and swept down
the country between the Chickahominy and the Pamunkey
Rivers like a thunderbolt, capturing pickets. driving in outposts, overturning wagon trains, and destroying everything
with fire and sword. He rides boldly across the enemy's line
of communicators, coming up at nighfall at the Chickahominy.
with the whole of McClellan's army between him and Richmond. In this ride he came in contact with his old regiment
in the United States Army, capturing its wagon trains, one
laden with the finest delicacies and choicest of wines. After

Col. William Wallace,
2d S. C. Regiment.
(Page 479)

Col. Jno. W. Hennagan,
8th S. C. Regiment,
(Page 423)

Lieut. Col. A. J. Hoole,
8th S. C. Regiment.
(Page 284.)

John M. Kinard,
Acting Lieut. Col. 20 S. C. Reg.
(Page 441.)

putting the enemy to rout Stuart and his men regaled themselves on these tempting viands, Stuart himself drinking a
"bumper of choice old Burgundy," sending word to his
former comrades that he "was sorry they did not stay and
join him, but as it was, he would drink their health in their
absence." Finding the bridges destroyed, he built a temporary one, over which the men walked and swam their horses,
holding on to the bridles. When all were safely over Stuart
sped like a whirlwind towards the James, leaving the enemy
staring wildly in mute astonishment at the very audacity of
his daring. That night he returned to his camps, having
made in thirty-six hours the entire circuit of the Federal
Army. Stuart was a rare character. Light hearted, merry,
and good natured, he was the very idol of his cavaliers. His
boldness, dash, and erratic mode of warfare made him a
dreaded foe and dangerous enemy. One moment he was in
their camps, on the plains, shouting and slashing, and before
the frightened sleepers could be brought to the realization of
their situation, he was far over the foothills of the Blue Ridge
or across the swift waters of the Rappahannock.

During the first week after taking our position on the line,
Magruder, with his divisions of eight brigades, was posted
high up on the Chickahominy, nearly north of Richmond.
McLaws, commanding Kershaw's, Cobb's, Semmes', and
Barksdale's Brigades, was on the left, the first being South
Carolinians, the next two Georgians, and the last Mississippians. General D. R. Jones, with his own, Toombs', G. T.
Anderson's, and perhaps one other Brigade, constituted the
right of the corps. The army was divided in wings. Huger,
the senior Major General, commanded on the right, next the
James River, with Longstreet next; but before the great battle
Magruder was given the centre and Longstreet the left with
his divisions, and the two Hills', A. P. and D. H. But after
the coming of Jackson A. P. Hill's, called the "Light Brigade," was placed under the command of the Valley chieftain.

While up on the Chickahominy, the enemy were continually
watching our movements from lines of balloons floating high
up in the air, anchored in place by stout ropes. They created
quite a mystic and superstitious feeling among some of the
most credulous. One night while a member of Company C,

Third South Carolina, was on picket among some tangled brushwood on the crest of the hill overlooking the river, he created quite a stir by seeing a strange light in his front, just beyond the stream. He called for the officer of the guard with all his might and main. When the officer made his appearance with a strong reinforcement, he demanded the reason of the untimely call. With fear and trembling he pointed to the brilliant light and said:

"Don't you see 'em yonder? They are putting up a balloon."

"No," said the officer, "that's nothing but a star," which it really was.

"Star, hell! I tell you it's a balloon. Are the Yankees smart enough to catch the stars?" It is enough to say the man carried the name of "balloon" during the rest of his service.

A Federal battery was stationed immediately in our front, beyond the river, supported by infantry. Some one in authority suggested the idea of crossing over at night, break through the tangled morass on the other side, and capture the outfit by a sudden dash. The day before the Third South Carolina Regiment was formed in line and a call made for volunteers to undertake this hazardous enterprise. Only one hundred soldiers were required, and that number was easily obtained, a great number being officers. At least twenty-five Lieutenants and Captains had volunteered. The detachment was put under Captain Foster as chief of the storming party, and the next day was occupied in drilling the men and putting them in shape for the undertaking. We were formed in line about dark near the time and place allotted, and all were in high glee in anticipation of the novel assault. But just as all were ready, orders came countermanding the first order. So the officers and men returned to their quarters. Some appeared well satisfied at the turn of events, especially those who had volunteered more for the honor attached than the good to be performed. Others, however, were disappointed. An old man from Laurens was indignant. He said "the Third Regiment would never get anything. That he had been naked and barefooted for two months, and when a chance was offered to clothe and shoe himself some d—n fool had to countermand the order." Ere many days his ambition and lust for a fight were filled to overflowing.

The various grades and ranks of the Generals kept us continually moving from left to right, Generals being sometimes like a balky horse—will not pull out of his right place. We were stationed, as it appea.ed from the preparations made, permanently just in front of Richmond, or a little to the left of that place and the Williamsburg road, and began to fortify in earnest. About the middle of June Lee and his Lieutenants were planning that great campaign whereby McClellan was to be overthrown and his army sent flying back to Washington. Generals plan the moves of men like players their pieces upon the chess board—a demonstration here, a feint there, now a great battle, then a reconnoissance—without ever thinking of or considering the lives lost, the orphans made, the disconsolate widows, and broken homes that these moves make. They talk of attacks, of pressing or crushing, of long marches, the streams or obstacles encountered, as if it were only the movement of some vast machinery, where the slipping of a cog or the breaking of a wheel will cause the machine to stop. The General views in his mind his successes, his marches, his strategy, without ever thinking of the dead men that will mark his pathway, the victorious fields made glorious by the groans of the dying, or the blackened corpses of the dead. The most Christian and humane soldier, however, plans his battles without ever a thought of the conseqnences to his faithful followers.

On the 25th of June, orders came to be prepared to move at a moment's notice. This left no doubt in the minds of the men that stirring times were ahead. It had been whispered in camp that Jackson, the "ubiquitous," was on his way from the Valley to help Lee in his work of defeating McClellan.

About 4 o'clock, on the 26th of June, as the men lay lolling around in camp, the ominous sound of a cannon was heard away to our left and rear. Soon another and another, their dull rumbling roar telling too plainly the battle was about to begin. Men hasten hither and thither, gathering their effects, expecting every moment to be ordered away. Soon the roar of musketry filled the air; the regular and continual baying of the cannon beat time to the steady roll of small arms. Jackson had come down from the Valley, and was sweeping over the country away to our left like an avalanche. Fitz John Porter, one of the most accomplished soldiers in the Northern Army, was entrusted with the defense of the north side of the Chickahominy, and had erected formidable lines of breast-works along Beaver Dam Creek, already strong and unap-proachable from its natural formations. Jackson was to have encountered Porter on the extreme right flank of the Union Army at an early hour in the day, and as soon as A. P. Hill heard the sound of his guns, he was to cross over on our left at Meadow Bridge and sweep down the river on Jackson's right. But after waiting for the opening of Jackson's guns until after 3 o'clock, without any information that he was on the field, Hill crossed over the river and attacked Porter in his strong position at Mechanicsville. His task was to beat back the enemy until the bridges below were uncovered, allowing re-enforcement to reach him. Jackson being unavoidably delayed, A. P. Hill assailed the whole right wing of the Federal Army, single-handed and alone, he only having five brigades, one being left some miles above on the river, but the brigade that was left was making rapid strides to join the fighting column. The strong earthworks, filled with fighting infantry and heavy field artillery in the forts, were too much for this light column, but undaunted by the weight of num-bers and strength of arms, Hill threw himself headlong upon the entrenched positions with rare courage and determination. There were South Carolinians with him who were now engag-ing in their maiden effort, and were winning imperishable fame by their deeds of valor. Gregg, with the old First South Carolina Regiment of Veterans, with four new organizations, the Twelfth, Thirteenth, Fourteenth, and Orr's Rifles, went recklessly into the fray, and struck right and left with the courage and confidence of veteran troops. D. H. Hill, late in the evening, crossed over and placed himself on the right of those already engaged. The battle of Gaines' Mill was one continual slaughter on the side of the Confederates. The enemy being behind their protections, their loss was comparatively slight. The fight was kept up till 9 o'clock at night, with little material advantage to either, with his own and only a portion of Jackson's troops up. But the desperate onslaught

of the day convinced Porter that he could not hold his ground
against another such assault, so he fell back to a much stronger
position around Gaines' Mill.

The next day, the 27th, will be remembered as long as history records the events of our Civil War as one of the most
bloody and determined of any of the great battles of the war
for the men engaged. For desperate and reckless charges, for
brave and steady resistance, it stands second to none. Jackson, Ewell, Whiting, and D. H. Hill moved their divisions by
daylight, aroused the enemy's right, intending to reach his
rear, but at Cold Harbor they met the enemy in strong force.
D. H. Hill attacked immediately, while A. P. Hill, who had
been left in Porter's front, marched through the deserted camp,
over his fortifications, and at Gaines' Mill, he met Porter
posted on an eminence beyond the stream. This was only
passable at few places, but Hill pushed his men over under a
galling fire of musketry, while the enemy swept the plain and
valley below with shell and grape from their batteries crowning the height beyond. A. P. Hill formed his lines beyond
the stream, and advanced with a steady step and a bold front
to the assault. Charge after charge was made, only to be met
and repulsed with a courage equal to that of the Confederates.
Hill did not know then that he was fighting the bulk of the
Fifth Corps, for he heard the constant roll of Jackson and D.
H. Hill's guns away to his left; Jackson thinking the Light Division under A. P. Hill would drive the enemy from his position, withdrew from Cold Harbor and sought to intercept the
retreating foe in concealing his men for some hours on the line
of retreat. But as the day wore on, and no diminution of the
firing, at the point where A. P. Hill and his adversary had so
long kept up, Jackson and D. H. Hill undertook to relieve
him. Longstreet, too, near nightfall, who had been held in
reserve all day, now broke from his place of inaction and
rushed into the fray like an uncaged lion, and placed himself
between A. P. Hill and the river. For a few moments the earth
trembled with the tread of struggling thousands, and the
dreadful recoil of the heavy batteries that lined the crest of the
hill from right to left. The air was filled with the shrieking
shells as they sizzed through the air or plowed their way
through the ranks of the battling masses. Charges were met

by charges, and the terrible "Rebel Yell" could be heard above
the din and roar of battle, as the Confederates swept over
field or through the forest, either to capture a battery or to
force a line of infantry back by the point of the bayonet.
While the battle was yet trembling in the balance, the Confederates making frantic efforts to pierce the enemy's lines
and they, with equal courage and persistency, determined or
holding, Pickett and Anderson, of Longstreet's Division, and
Hood and Whiting, of Jackson's, threw their strength and
weight to the aid of Hill's depleted ranks. The enemy could
stand no longer. The line is broken at one point, then another,
and as the Confederates closed in on them from all sides, they
break in disorder and leave the field. It looked at one time as
if there would be a rout, but Porter in this emergency, put in
practice one of Napolean's favorite tactics. He called up his
cavalry, and threatened the weakened ranks of the Confederates with a formidable front of his best troopers. These could
not be of service in the weight of battle, but protected the
broken columns and fleeing fugitives of Porter's Army.

South Carolina will be ever proud of the men whom she had
on that memorable field who consecrated the earth at Gaines'
Mill with their blood, as well as of such leaders as Gregg,
McGowan, McCrady, Marshall, Simpson, Haskell, and Hamilton, and hosts of others, who have ever shed lustre and glory
equal to those of any of the thousands who have made the
Palmetto State renowned the world over.

McClellan was now in sore straits. He could not weaken
his lines on the south side of the Chickahominy to re-enforce
Fitz John Porter, for fear Magruder, Holmes, and Huger,
who were watching his every movements in their front, should
fall upon the line thus weakened and cut his army in twain.
The next day McClellan commenced his retreat towards the
James, having put his army over the Chickahominy the night
after his defeat. His step was, no doubt, occasioned by the
fact that Lee had sent Stuart with his cavalry and Ewell's
Division of Infantry down the north side of the Chickahominy
and destroyed McClellan's line of communication between his
army and the York River. However, the Confederate commander was equally as anxious to cut him off from the James
as the York. He aimed to force him to battle between the

two rivers, and there, cut off from his fleet, he would be utterly destroyed. Lee only wished McClellan to remain in his present position until he could reach the James with a part of his own troops, now on the north side of the Chickahominy.

On the evening of the 27th, Magruder made a feint with Kershaw's and some other brigades of this division, near Alens, as the troops in his front showed a disposition to retire. A line of battle was formed, skirmishers thrown out, and an advance ordered. Our skirmishers had not penetrated far into the thicket before they were met by a volley from the enemy's line of battle The balls whistled over our heads and through the tops of the scrubby oaks, like a fall of hail. It put chills to creeping up our backs, the first time we had ever been under a musketry fire. For a moment we were thrown into a perfect fever of excitement and confusion. The opening in the rear looked temptingly inviting in comparison to the wooded grounds in front, from whence came the volley of bullets. Here the Third South Carolina lost her first soldier in battle, Dr. William Thompson, of the medical staff, who had followed too close on the heels of the fighting column in his anxiety to be near the battle.

Early in the morning of the 28th, Lee put the columns of Longstreet and A. P. Hill in motion in the direction of Richmond around our rear. After their meeting with Holmes and Huger on our extreme right, they were to press down the James River and prevent McClellan from reaching it. Jackson, D. H. Hill, and Magruder were to follow the retreating army. We left our quarters early in the day, and soon found ourselves in the enemy's deserted camp.

The country between the James and the Chickahominy is a very flat, swampy country, grown up in great forests, with now and then a cultivated field. The forests were overrun with a tangled mass of undergrowth. It was impossible for the army to keep up with the enemy while in line of battle. So sending our skirmishers ahead the army followed the roads in columns of fours. In each regiment the right or left company in the beginning of battle is always deployed at such distance between each soldier as to cover the front of the regiment, while in line of battle the regiments being from ten to fifty yards apart. In this way we marched all day, sometimes in line of battle, at others by the roads in columns. A great siege cannon had been erected on a platform car and pushed abreast of us along the railroad by an engine, and gave out thundering evidences of its presence by shelling the woods in our front. This was one of the most novel batteries of the war, a siege gun going in battle on board of cars. Near night at Savage Station Sumner and Franklin, of the Federal Army who had been retreating all day, turned to give battle. Jackson was pressing on our left, and it became necessary that Sumner should hold Magruder in check until the army and trains of the Federals that were passing in his rear should cross White Oak Swamp to a place of safety. Our brigade was lying in a little declivity between two rises in the ground; that in our front, and more than one hundred yards distance, was thickly studded with briars, creepers, and underbrush with a sparse growth of heavy timber. We had passed numerous redoubts, where the field batteries of the enemy would occupy and shell our ranks while the infantry continued the retreat. Our brigade skirmishers, under command of Major Rutherford had been halted in this thicket while the line of battle was resting. But hardly had the skirmishers been ordered forward than the enemy's line of battle, upon which they had come, poured a galling fire into them, the bullets whistling over our heads causing a momentary panic among the skirmishers, a part retreating to the main line. A battery of six guns stationed in a fort in our front, opened upon us with shell and grape. Being in the valley, between the two hills, the bullets rattled over our heads doing no damage, but threw us into some excitement. The Third being near the center of the brigade, General Kershaw, in person, was immediately in our rear on foot. As soon as the bullets had passed over he called out in a loud clear tone the single word "charge." The troops bounded to the front with a yell, and made for the forest in front, while the batteries graped us as we rushed through the tangled morass. The topography of the country was such that our artillery could get no position to reply, but the heavy railroad siege gun made the welkin ring with its deafening reports. Semmes and Barksdale put in on our right; Cobb remaining a reserve, while the Division of D. R. Jones, which had been moving down on the left side of the railroad, soon became engaged. The enemy fought with great energy and vigor, while the Confederates pressed them hard. Much was at stake, and night was near. Sumner was fighting for the safety of the long trains of artillery and wagons seeking cover in his rear, as well as for the very life of the army itself. Soon after the first fire the settling smoke and dense shrubbery made the woods almost as dark as night in our front, but the long line of fire flashing from the enemy's guns revealed their position. The men became woefully tangled and disorganized, and in some places losing the organizations entirely, but under all these difficulties they steadily pressed to the front. When near the outer edge of the thicket, we could see the enemy lying down in some young growth of pines, with their batteries in the fort. The graping was simply dreadful, cutting and breaking through the bushes and striking against trees. I had not gone far into the thicket before I was struck by a minnie ball in the chest, which sent me reeling to the ground momentarily unconscious. Our men lost all semblance of a line, being scattered over a space of perhaps 50 yards, and those in front were in as much danger from friend as from foe. While I lay in a semi-unconscious state, I received another bullet in my thigh which I had every reason to believe came from some one in the rear. But I roused myself, and staggering to my feet made my way as well as I could out of the thicket. When I reached the place from whence we had first made the charge, our drummer was beating the assembly or long roll with all his might, and men collecting around General Kershaw and Colonel Nance. Here I first learned of the repulse. The balls were still flying overhead, but some of our batteries had got in position and were giving the enemy a raking fire. Nor was the railroad battery idle, for I could see the great black, grim monster puffing out heaps of gray smoke, then the red flash, then the report, sending the engine and car back along the track with a fearful recoil. The lines were speedily reformed and again put in motion. Jones, too, was forced by overwhelming numbers to give back, but Jackson coming up gave him renewed confidence, and a final advance was made along the whole line. The battle was kept up with varying success until after night, when Sumner withdrew over White Oak Swamp.

On the morning of the 30th, McClellan, like a quarry drive to bay, drew up his forces on the south side of White Oa Swamp and awaited the next shock of battle. Behind hi were his trains of heavy siege guns, his army wagons, poi toons, and ordnance trains, all in bog and slush, seeking safet under the sheltering wings of his gunboats and ironclads o the James. Lee met him at every point with bristling bay nets of his victorious troops. At three o'clock A. M. Lon; street and A. P. Hill moved down the Darbytown road, leavin Jackson, D. H. Hill, and Magruder to press McClellan retreating forces in the rear. Huger, with the two forme was to come down the James River and attack in the flanl Magruder, with his corps, was sent early in the day on a wil goose chase to support Longstreet's right, but by being led h guides who did not understand the roads or plan of battle Magruder took the wrong road and did not get up in time t join in the battle of Frazier's Farm. Jackson for some caus did not press the rear, as anticipated, neither did Huger com in time, leaving the brunt of the battle on the shoulders A. P. Hill and Longstreet. The battle was but a repetitio of that of Gaines' Mill, the troops of Hill and Longstre gaining imperishable glory by their stubborn and resistle attacks, lasting till nine o'clock at night, when the enem finally withdrew.

Two incidents of these battles are worthy of record, showin the different dispositions of the people of the North and Soutl At night the division commanded by General McCall, wh had been fighting Longstreet so desperately all day, was ca; tured and brought to Longstreet's headquarters. Gener McCall had been Captain of a company in the United Stat Army, in which Longstreet had been a Lieutenant. Whe General Longstreet saw his old comrade brought to him as prisoner of war, he sought to lighten the weight of his feelin; as much as circumstances would admit. He dismounte pulled his gloves, and offered his hand in true knightly fashic to his fallen foe. But his Federal antagonist, becoming i censed, drew himself up haughtily and waved Longstre away, saying, "Excuse me, sir, I can stand defeat but n insult." Insult indeed! to shake the hand of one of the mo illustrious chieftains of the century, one who had tendered th hand in friendly recognition of past associations, thus to smooth and soften the humiliation of his foe's present condition! Insult—was it?

When Bob Toombs, at the head of his brigade, was sweeping through the tangled underbrush at Savage Station, under a terrific hail of bullets from the retreating enemy, he was hailed by a fallen enemy, who had braced himself against a tree:

"Hello, Bob Toombs! Hello, Bob Toombs! Don't you know your old friend Webster?"

Dismounting, Toombs went to the son of his old friend but political adversary, Daniel Webster, one of the great trio at Washington of twenty years before, and found his life slowly ebbing away. Toombs rendered him all the assistance in his power—placed him in comfortable position that he might die at ease—and hastened on to rejoin his command, after promising to perform some last sad rites after his death. When the battle was ended for the day, the great fiery Secessionist hastened to return to the wounded enemy. But too late; his spirit had flown, and nothing was now left to Toombs but to fulfill the promises he made to his dying foe. He had his body carried through the lines that night under a flag of truce and delivered with the messages left to his friends. He had known young Webster at Washington when his illustrious father was at the zenith of his power and fame. The son and the great Southern States' Rights champion had become fast friends as the latter was just entering on his glorious career.

Our brigade lost heavily in the battle of Savage Station both in officers and men. Lieutenant Colonel Garlington, of the Third, was killed, and so was Captain Langford and several Lieutenants. Colonel Bland, of the Seventh, was wounded and disabled for a long time. The casualties in the battle of Savage Station caused changes in officers in almost every company in the brigade.

When I came to consciousness after being wounded the first thing that met my ears was the roar of musketry and the boom of cannon, with the continual swish, swash of the grape and canister striking the trees and ground. I placed my hand in my bosom, where I felt a dull, deadening sensation. There I found the warm blood, that filled my inner garments and

now trickled down my side as I endeavored to stand upright.
I had been shot through the left lung, and as I felt the great
gaping wound in my chest, the blood gushing and spluttering
out at every breath, I began to realize my situation.   I tried
to get off the field the best I could, the bullet in my leg not
troubling me much, and as yet, I felt strong enough to walk.
My brother, who was a surgeon, and served three years in the
hospitals in Richmond, but now in the ranks, came to my aid
and led me to the rear.   We stopped near the railroad battery,
which was belching away, the report of the great gun bringing upon us the concentrated fire of the enemy.   As I sat upon
the fallen trunk of a tree my brother made a hasty examination of my wound.   All this while I was fully convinced I was
near death's door.   He pronounced my wound at first as fatal,
a bit of very unpleasant information, but after probing my
wound with his finger he gave me the flattering assurance that
unless I bled to death quite soon my chances might be good!
Gentle reader, were you ever, as you thought, at death's door,
when the grim monster was facing you, when life looked
indeed a very brief span? If so, you can understand my feelings—I was scared! As Goldsmith once said, "When you
think you are about to die, this world looks mighty tempting
and pretty." Everything in my front took on the hue of
da.k green, a pleasant sensation came over me, and I had the
strangest feeling ever experienced in my life. I thought sure
I was dying then and there and fell from the log in a death-
like swoon.   But I soon revived, having only fainted from loss
of blood, and my brother insisted on my going back up the
railroad to a farmhouse we had passed, and where our surgeons had established a hospital.   The long stretch of wood
we had to travel was lined with the wounded, each wounded
soldier with two or three friends helping him off the field.
We had no "litter bearers" or regular detail to care for the
wounded at this time, and the friends who untertook this service voluntarily oftentimes depleted the ranks more than the
loss in battle.   Hundreds in this way absented themselves for
a few days taking care of the wounded.   But all this was
changed soon afterwards.   Regular details were made from
each regiment, consisting of a non-commissioned officer and
five privates, whose duty it was to follow close in rear of the

line of battle with their "stretchers" and take off the disabled.

I will never forget the scene that met my eyes as I neared the house where the wounded had been gathered. There the torn and mangled lay, shot in every conceivable part of the body or limbs—some with wounds in the head, arms torn off at the shoulder or elbow, legs broken, fingers, toes, or foot shot away; some hobbling along on inverted muskets or crutches, but the great mass were stretched at full length upon the ground, uttering low, deep, and piteous moans, that told of the great sufferings, or a life passing away. The main hall of the deserted farm house, as well as the rooms, were filled to overflowing with those most seriously wounded. The stifling stench of blood was sickening in the extreme. The front and back yards, the fence corners, and even the outbuildings were filled with the dead and dying. Surgeons and their assistants were hurrying to and fro, relieving the distress as far as their limited means would allow, making such hasty examinations as time permitted. Here they would stop to probe a wound, there to set a broken limb, bind a wound, stop the flow of blood, or tie an artery.

But among all this deluge of blood, mangled bodies, and the groans of the wounded and dying, our ears were continually greeted by the awful, everlasting rattle of the musketry, the roar of the field batteries, and the booming, shaking, and trembling of the siege guns from friend and foe.

The peculiar odor of human blood, mingling with the settling smoke of the near by battlefield, became so oppressive I could not remain in the house. My brother helped me into the yard, but in passing out I fell, fainting for the third time; my loss of blood had been so great I could stand only with difficulty. I thought the end was near now for a certainty, and was frightened accordingly. But still I nerved myself with all the will power I possessed, and was placed on an oil cloth under the spreading branches of an elm. From the front a continual stream of wounded kept coming in till late at night. Some were carried on shoulders of friends, others leaning their weight upon them and dragging their bodies along, while the slightly wounded were left to care for themselves. Oh, the horrors of the battlefield! So cruel, so sickening, so heart-rending to those even of the stoutest nerves!—once seen, is indelibly impressed upon your mind forever.

The firing ceased about 9 o'clock, and all became still as death, save the groaning of the wounded soldiers in the hospital, or the calls and cries of those left upon the battlefield. Oh, such a night, the night after the battle! The very remembrance of it is a vivid picture of Dante's "Inferno." To lie during the long and anxious watches of the night, surrounded by such scenes of suffering and woe, to continually hear the groans of the wounded, the whispered consultations of the surgeons over the case of some poor boy who was soon to be robbed of a leg or arm, the air filled with stifled groans, or the wild shout of some poor soldier, who, now delirious with pain, his voice sounding like the wail of a lost soul—all this, and more—and thinking your soul, too, is about to shake off its mortal coil and take its flight with the thousands that have just gone, are going, and the many more to follow before the rising of the next sun—all this is too much for a feeble pen like mine to portray.

The troops lay on the battlefield all night under arms. Here and there a soldier, singly or perhaps in twos, were scouring through the dense thicket or isolated places, seeking lost friends and comrades, whose names were unanswered to at the roll call, and who were not among the wounded and dead at the hospital. The pale moon looked down in sombre silence upon the ghastly upturned faces of the dead that lay strewn along the battle line. The next day was a true version of the lines—

> "Under the sod, under the clay,
> Here lies the blue, there the grey."

for the blue and grey fell in great wind rows that day, and were buried side by side.

The Confederates being repulsed in the first charge, returned to the attack, broke the Federal lines in pieces, and by 9 o'clock they had fled the field, leaving all the fruits of victory in the hands of the Confederates.

No rest for the beaten enemy, no sleep for the hunted prey. McClellan was moving heaven and earth during the whole night to place "White Oak Swamp" (a tangled, swampy wilderness, of a half mile in width and six or eight miles in

length,) between his army and Lee's. By morning he had
the greater portion of his army and supply trains over, but
had left several divisions on the north side of the swamp to
guard the crossings. Jackson and Magruder began pressing
him early on the 30th in his rear, while Longstreet, A. P.
Hill, and others were marching with might and main to intercept him on the other side. After some desultory firing,
Jackson found McClellan's rear guard too strong to assail, by
direct assault, so his divisions, with Magruder's, were ordered
around to join forces with Hill and Longstreet. The swamp
was impassable, except at the few crossings, and they were
strongly guarded, so they were considered not practicable of
direct assault. But in the long winding roads that intervened
between the two wings, Magruder and Jackson on the north
and Longstreet and A. P. Hill on the south, Magruder was
misled by taking the wrong road (the whole Peninsula being
a veritable wilderness), and marched away from the field
instead of towards it, and did not reach Longstreet during the
day. But at 3 o'clock Longstreet, not hearing either Jackson's
or Magruder's guns, as per agreement, and restless of the
delays of the other portions of the army, feeling the danger of
longer inactivity, boldly marched in and attacked the enemy
in his front.

Here was Frazier's Farm, and here was fought as stubbornly
contested battle, considering the numbers engaged, as any
during the campaign. Near nightfall, after Longstreet had
nearly exhausted the strength of his troops by hard fighting,
A. P. Hill, ever watchful and on the alert, threw the weight
of his columns on the depleted ranks of the enemy, and forced
them from the field. The soldiers who had done such deeds
of daring as to win everlasting renown at Gaines' Mill and
Cold Harbor, did not fail their fearless commander at Frazier's
Farm. When the signal for battle was given, they leaped to
the front, like dogs unleashed, and sprang upon their old
enemies, Porter, McCall, Heintzelman, Hooker, and Kearny.
Here again the steady fire and discipline of the Federals had to
yield to the impetuosity and valor of Southern troops. Hill
and Longstreet swept the field, capturing several hundred
prisoners, a whole battery of artillery, horses, and men.

McClellan brought up his beaten army on Malvern Hill, to

make one last desperate effort to save his army from destruction or annihilation.   This is a place of great natural defenses. Situated one mile from the James River, it rises suddenly on all sides from the surrounding marshy lowlands to several hundred feet in height, and environed on three sides by branches and and by Turkey Creek.   On the northern eminence McClellan planted eighty pieces of heavy ordnance, and on the eastern, field batteries in great numbers.   Lee placed his troops in mass on the extreme east of the position occupied by the enemy, intending to park the greater number of his heaviest batteries against the northern front of the eminence, where McClellan had his artiilery pointing to the east, and where the Confederates massed to sweep the field as Lee advanced his infantry.   The object of Lee was to concentrate all his artillery on the flank of McClellan's artillery, then by an enfilade fire from his own, he could destroy that of his enemy, and advance his infantry through the broad sweep of lowlands, separating the forces, without subjecting them to the severe cannonading.   He gave orders that as soon as the enemy's batteries were demolished or silenced, Armistead's Virginia Brigade, occupying the most advanced aud favorable position for observation, was to advance to the assault, with a yell and a hurrah, as a signal for the advance of all the attacking columns.   But the condition of the ground was such that the officers who were to put the cannon in position got only a few heavy pieces in play, and these were soon knocked in pieces by the numbers of the enemy's siege guns and rifled field pieces.   Some of the brigade commanders, thinking the signal for combat had been given, rushed at the hill in front with ear piercing yells without further orders.   They were mown down like grain before the sickle by the fierce artillery fire and the enemy's infantry on the crest of the hill.   Kershaw following the lead of the brigade on his left, gave orders, "Forward, charge!"   Down the incline, across the wide expanse, they rushed with a yell, their bayonets bristling and glittering in the sunlight, while the shells rained like hail stones through their ranks from the cannon crested hill in front.   The gunboats and ironclad monitors in the James opened a fearful fusilade from their monster guns and huge mortars, the great three-hundred-pound shells from the latter rising high in the air, then curling in a beautiful bow to fall among the troops, with a crash and explosion that shook the ground like the trembling of the earth around a volcano. The whole face of the bluff front was veiled by the white smoke of the one hundred belching cannon, the flashing of the guns forming a perfect rain of fire around the sides of the hill. It was too far to fire and too dense and tangled to charge with any degree of progress or order, so, in broken and disconnected ranks, Kershaw had to advance and endure this storm of shot and shell, that by the time he reached the line of the enemy's infantry, his ranks were too much broken to offer a very formidable front. From the enemy's fortified position their deadly fire caused our already thinned ranks to melt like snow before the sun's warm rays. The result was a complete repulse along the whole line. But McClellan was only too glad to be allowed a breathing spell from his seven days of continual defeat, and availed himself of the opportunity of this respite to pull off his army under the protecting wings of his ironclad fleet.

The Confederates had won a glorious victory during the first six days. The enemy had been driven from the Chickahominy to the James, his army defeated and demoralized beyond months of recuperation. Lee and his followers should be satisfied. But had none of his orders miscarried, and all of his Lieutenants fulfilled what he had expected of them, yet greater results might have been accomplished—not too much to say McClellan's Army would have been entirely destroyed or captured, for had he been kept away from the natural defenses of Malvern Hill and forced to fight in the open field, his destruction would have followed beyond the cavil of a doubt. The Southern soldiers were as eager and as fresh on the last day as on the first, but a land army has a superstitious dread of one sheltered by gunboats and ironclads.

All the troops engaged in the Seven Days' Battle did extremely well, and won imperishable fame by their deeds of valor and prowess. Their commanders in the field were matchless, and showed military talents of high order, the courage of their troops invincible, and to particularize would be unjust. But truth will say, in after years, when impartial hands will record the events, and give blame where blame belongs, and justice where justice is due, that in this great Seven Days' Conflict, where so much heroism was displayed on both sides, individually and collectively, that to A. P. Hill and the brave men under him belongs the honor of first scotching at Gaines' Mill the great serpent that was surrounding the Capital with bristling bayonets, and were in at the breaking of its back at Frazier's Farm.

It was due to the daring and intrepidity of Hill's Light Division at Gaines' Mill, more than to any other, that made it possible for the stirring events and unprecedented results that followed.

Among the greater Generals, Lee was simply matchless and superb; Jackson, a mystic meteor or firey comet; Longstreet and the two Hills, the "Wild Huns" of the South, masterful in tactics, cyclones in battle. Huger, Magruder, and Holmes were rather slow, but the courage and endurance of their troops made up for the shortcomings of their commanders.

Among the lesser lights will stand Gregg, Jenkins, and Kershaw, of South Carolina, as foremost among the galaxy of immortal heroes who gave the battles around Richmond their place as "unparalleled in history."

CHAPTER X

The March to Maryland—Second Manassas. Capture of Harper's Ferry—Sharpsburg.

The enemy lay quietly in his camps at Harrison's Landing for a few days, but to cover his meditated removal down the James, he advanced a large part of his army as far as Malvern Hill on the day of the 5th of August as if to press Lee back. Kershaw, with the rest of McLaw's Division, together with Jones and Longstreet, were sent to meet them. The troops were all placed in position by nightfall, bivouaced for the night on the field, and slept on their arms to guard against any night attack. The soldiers thought of tomorrow—that it perhaps might be yet more sanguinary than any of the others. Our ranks, already badly worn by the desperate conflicts at

Savage Station, Frazier's Farm, Cold Harbor, etc., still showed
a bold front for the coming day. Early in the morning the
troops were put in motion, skirmishers thrown out, and all
preparations for battle made, but to the surprise and relief of
all, the "bird had flown," and instead of battle lines and bristling steel fronts we found nothing but deserted camps and evidences of a hasty flight. In a few days we were removed further back towards Richmond and sought camp on higher
ground, to better guard against the ravages of disease and to
be further removed from the enemy. The troops now had
the pleasure of a month's rest, our only duties being guard and
advance picket every ten or twelve days.

While McClellan had been pushing his army up on the
Peninsula the Federals were actively engaged in organizing a
second army in the vicinity of Manassas and Fredericksburg
under General John Pope, to operate against Richmond by the
flank. General Pope from his infamous orders greatly incensed
the people of the South, and from his vain boasting gained for
himself the sobriquet of "Pope the Braggart." He ordered
every citizen within his lines or living near them to either take
the oath of allegiance to the United States or to be driven out
of the country as an enemy of the Union. No one was to
have any communication with his friends within the Confederate lines, either by letter or otherwise, on the penalty of
being shot as a spy and his property confiscated. Hundreds of
homes were broken up by the order. Men and women were
driven South, or placed in Federal prisons, there to linger for
years, perhaps, with their homes abandoned to the malicious
desecration of a merciless enemy, all for no other charges than
their refusal to be a traitor to their principles and an enemy to
their country. Pope boasted of "seeing nothing of the enemy
but his back," and that "he had no headquarters but in the
saddle." He was continually sending dispatches to his chief,
General Halleck, who had been appointed Commander-in-
Chief of all the Federal forces in the field, of the "victories
gained over Lee," his "bloody repulses of Jackson," and "successful advances," and "the Confederates on the run," etc.,
etc., while the very opposites were the facts. On one occasion
he telegraphed to Washington that he had defeated Lee, that
the Confederate leader was in full retreat to Richmond, when,

as a fact, before the dispatch had reached its destination his own army was overwhelmed, and with Pope at its head, flying the field in every direction, seeking safety under the guns at Washington. It is little wonder he bore the name he had so deservedly won by his manifestoes, "Pope the Braggart."

About the middle of July Jackson, with Ewell and A. P. Hill, was sent up to the Rapidan to look after Pope and his wonderful army, which had begun to be re-enforced by troops from the James. On the 9th of August Jackson came up with a part of Pope's army at Cedar Mountain, and a fierce battle was fought, very favorable to the Confederate side. A month after Jackson had left Richmond, Longstreet, with three divisions, headed by Lee in person, was ordered to re-enforce Jackson, and began the offensive. While the Federal commander was lying securely in his camp, between the Rappahannock and the Rapidan, unconscious of the near approach of the Confederate Army, his scouts intercepted an order written by General Lee to his cavalry leader, giving details of his intended advance and attack. Pope, being thus apprised, hurriedly re-crossed the Rappahannock and concentrated his forces behind that stream. Lee followed his movements closely, and while watching in front, with a portion of his army, he started Jackson on his famous march around the enemy's rear. Pulling up at night, Jackson marched to the left, crossed the Rappahannock on the 25th, and by the night of the 26th he had reached the railroad immediately in Pope's rear, capturing trains of cars, prisoners, etc. On learning that large quantities of provisions and munitions of war were stored at Manassas Junction, feebly guarded, General Trimble, with a small number of brave Alabamians, Georgians, and North Carolinians, not five hundred all told, volunteered to march still further to that point, a distance of some miles, notwithstanding they had marched with Jackson thirty miles during the day, and capture the place. This was done in good time, defeating a brigade doing guard duty, and capturing a large number of prisoners, one entire battery of artillery, and untold quantities of provisions. Jackson now appeared to retreat, but only withdrew in order to give Longstreet time to come up, which he was doing hard upon Jackson's track, but more than twenty-four hours behind. This was one of the most hazardous feats accomplished by Lee during the war, with the possible exception of Chancellorsville, "dividing his army in the face of superior numbers," a movement denounced by all successful Generals and scientists of war. But Lee attempted this on more occasions than one, and always successfully.

Jackson concealed his forces among the hills of Bull Run, giving time for Longstreet, who was fighting his way through Thoroughfare Gap at the very point of the bayonet, to come up, while Pope was racing around the plains of Manassas, trying to intercept Jackson's imaginary retreat. It seems as if the one single idea impressed itself upon the Federal commander, and that was that Jackson was trying to get away from him. But before many days Pope found the wily "Stonewall," and when in his embrace endeavoring to hold him, Pope found himself in the predicament of the man who had essayed to wrestle with a bear. When the man had downed his antagonist he had to call lustily for friends. So Pope had to call for help to turn Jackson loose—to pull him loose. On the 29th the forces of Pope, the "Braggart," came upon those of Jackson hidden behind a railroad enbankment on the plains of Manassas, and a stubborn battle ensued, which lasted until late at night. Longstreet came upon the field, but took no further part in the battle than a heavy demonstration on the right to relieve the pressure from Jackson. Longstreet's left, however, turned the tide of battle. Lee turned some prisoners loose at night that had been captured during the day, leaving the impression on their minds that he was beating a hasty retreat. Reporting to their chief that night, the prisoners confirmed the opinion that Pope was fooled in believing all day, that "Lee was in full retreat," trying to avoid a battle. Pope sent flaming messages to that effect to the authorities at Washington, and so anxious was he lest his prey should escape, he gave orders for his troops to be in motion early in the morning. On the 30th was fought the decisive battle of Second Manassas, and the plains above Bull Run were again the scence of a glorious Confederate victory, by Lee almost annihilating the army of John Pope, "the Braggart." Had it not been for the steady discipline, extraordinary coolness, and soldierly behavior of Sykes and his regulars at Stone Bridge, the rout of the Federal Army at Second Manassas would have been but little less complete than on the fatal day just a little more than one year before.

At Ox Hill, 1st September, Pope had to adopt the tactics of McClellan at Malvern Hill, face about and fight for the safety of his great ordnance and supply trains, and to allow his army a safe passage over the Potomac. At Ox Hill, the enemy under Stephens and Kearny, displayed extraordinary tenacity and courage, these two division commanders throwing their columns headlong upon those of Jackson without a thought of the danger and risks such rash acts incurred. Both were killed in the battle. Phil. Kearney had gained a national reputation for his enterprising warfare in Calafornia and Mexico during the troublesome times of the Mexican War, and it was with unfeigned sorrow and regret the two armies heard of the sad death of this veteran hero.

During the time that all these stirring events were taking place and just before Magruder, with McLaw's and Walker's divisions, was either quietly lying in front of Richmond watching the army of McClellan dwindle away, leaving by transports down the James and up the Potomac, or was marching at a killing gait to overtake their comrades under Lee to share with them their trials, their battles and their victories in Maryland. Lee could not leave the Capital with all his force so long as there was a semblance of an army threatening it.

As soon as it was discovered that Manassas was to be the real battle ground of the campaign, and Washington instead of Richmond the objective point, Lee lost no time in concentrating his army north of the Rappahannock. About the middle of August McLaws, with Kershaw's, Sumner's, Cobb's, and Barksdale's Brigades, with two brigades under Walker and the Hampton Legion Cavalry, turned their footsteps Northward, and bent all their energies to reach the scene of action before the culminating events above mentioned.

At Orange C. H., on the 26th, we hastened our march, as news began to reach us of Jackson's extraordinary movements and the excitement in the Federal Army, occasioned by their ludicrous hunt for the "lost Confederate." Jackson's name had reached its meridian in the minds of the troops, and they were ever expecting to hear of some new achievement or brilliant victory by this strange, silent, and mysterious man. The very mystery of his movements, his unexplainable absence and sudden reappearance at unexpected points, his audacity in the face of the enemy, his seeming recklessness, gave unbounded confidence to the army. The men began to feel safe at the very idea of his disappearance and absence. While the thunder of his guns and those of Longstreet's were sounding along the valleys of Bull Run, and reverberating down to the Potomac or up to Washington, McLaws with his South Carolinians, Georgians, and Mississippians was swinging along with an elastic step between Orange C. H. and Manassas.

McClellan himself had already reached Alexandria with the last of his troops, but by the acts of the ubiquitous Jackson his lines of communication were cut and the Federal commander had to grope his way in the dark for fear of running foul of his erratic enemy.

When we began nearing Manassas, we learned of the awful effect of the two preceding days' battle by meeting the wounded. They came singly and in groups, men marching with arms in slings, heads bandaged, or hopping along on improvised crutches, while the wagons and ambulances were laden with the severely wounded. In that barren country no hospital could be established, for it was as destitute of sustenance as the arid plains of the Arabian Desert when the great Napoleon undertook to cross it with his beaten army. All, with the exception of water; we had plenty of that. Passing over a part of the battlefield about the 5th of September, the harrowing sights that were met with were in places too sickening to admit of description. The enemy's dead, in many places, had been left unburied, it being a veritable instance of "leaving the dead to bury the dead." Horses in a rapid state of decomposition literally covered the field. The air was so impregnated with the foul stench arising from the plains where the battle had raged fiercest, that the troops were forced to close their notrils while passing. Here and there lay a dead enemy overlooked in the night of the general burial, stripped of his outer clothing, his blackened features and glassy eyes staring upturned to the hot September sun, while our soldiers hurried past, leaving them unburied and unnoticed. Some lay in the beaten track of our wagon trains, and had been run over ruthlessly by the teamsters, they not

having the time, if the inclination, to remove them. The hot
sun made decomposition rapid, and the dead that had fallen on
the steep incline their heads had left the body and rolled
several paces away. All the dead had become as black as
Africans, the hot rays of the sun changing the features quite
prematurely. In the opening where the Washington Battalion
of Artillery from New Orleans had played such havoc on the
30th with the enemy's retreating columns, it resembled some
great railroad wreck—cannon and broken caissons piled in
great heaps; horses lying swollen and stiff, some harnessed,
others not; broken rammers, smashed wheels, dismounted
pieces told of the desperate struggle that had taken place.
One of the strange features of a battlefied is the absence of the
carrion crow or buzzard—it matters little as to the number of
dead soldiers or horses, no vultures ever venture near—it
being a fact that a buzzard was never seen in that part of
Virginia during the war.

All was still, save the rumble of the wagon trains and the
steady tread of the soldiers. Across Bull Run and out towards
Washington McLaws followed with hasty step the track of
Longstreet and Jackson.

On the 5th or 6th we rejoined at last, after a two months'
separation from the other portion of the army. Lee was now
preparing to invade Maryland and other States North, as the
course of events dictated. Pope's Army had joined that of
McClellan, and the authorities at Washington had to call on the
latter to "save their Capital." When the troops began the
crossing of the now classic Potomac, a name on every tongue
since the commencement of hostilities, their enthusiasm knew
no bounds. Bands played "Maryland, My Mrryland," men
sang and cheered, hats filled the air, flags waved, and shouts
from fifty thousand throats reverberated up and down the
banks of the river, to be echoed back from the mountains and
die away among the hills and highlands of Maryland. McLaws
stopped midway in the stream and sang loudly the cheering
strains of Randall's, "Maryland, My Maryland." We were
overjoyed at rejoining the army, and the troops of Jackson,
Longstreet, and the two Hills were proud to feel the elbow
touch of such chivalrous spirits as McLaws, Kershaw, Hampton, and others in the conflicts that were soon to take place.

Never before had an occurrence so excited and enlivened the spirits of the troops as the crossing of the Potomac into the land of our sister, Maryland. It is said the Crusaders, after months of toil, marching, and fighting, on their way through the plains of Asia Minor, wept when they saw the towering spires of Jerusalem, the Holy City, in the distance; and if ever Lee's troops could have wept for joy, it was at the crossing of the Potomac. But we paid dearly for this pleasure in the death of so many thousands of brave men and the loss of so many valuable officers. General Winder fell at Cedar Mountain, and Jackson's right hand, the brave Ewell, lost his leg at Manassas.

The army went into camp around Frederick City, Md. From here, on the 8th, Lee issued his celebrated address to the people of Maryland, and to those of the North generally, telling them of his entry into their country, its cause and purpose; that it was not as a conqueror, or an enemy, but to demand and enforce a peace between the two countries. He clothed his language in the most conservative and entreating terms, professing friendship for those who would assist him, and protection to life and the property of all. He enjoined the people, without regard to past differences, to flock to his standard and aid in the defeat of the party and people who were now drenching the country in blood and putting in mourning the people of two nations. The young men he asked to join his ranks as soldiers of a just and honorable cause. Of the old he asked their sympathies and prayers. To the President of the Confederate States he also wrote a letter, proposing to him that he should head his armies, and, as the chieftain of the nation, propose a peace to the authorities at Washington from the very threshold of their Capital. But both failed of the desired effect. The people of the South had been led to believe that Maryland was anxious to cast her destinies with those of her sister States, that all her sympathies were with the people of the South, and that her young men were anxious and only awaiting the opportunity to join the ranks as soldiers under Lee. But these ideas and promises were all delusions, for the people we saw along the route remained passive spectators and disinterested witnesses to the great evolutions now taking place. What the people felt on the ''eastern

10

shore" is not known; but the acts of those between the
Potomac and Pennsylvania above Washington indicated but
little sympathy with the Southern cause; and what enlistments
were made lacked the proportions needed to swell Lee's army
to its desired limits.   Lee promised protection and he gáve it.
The soldiers to a man seemed to feel the importance of obeying
the orders to respect and protect the person and property of
those with whom we came in contact.   It was said of this,
as well as other campaigns in the North, that "it was conducted with kid gloves on."

While lying at Frederick City, Lee conceived the bold and
perilous project of again dividing his army in the face of his
enemy, and that enemy McClellan.   Swinging back with a
part of his army, he captured the stronghold of Harper's
Ferry, with its 11,000 defenders, while with the other he held
McClellan at bay in front.   The undertaking was dangerous
in the extreme, and with a leader less bold and Lieutenants
less prompt and skillful, its final consummation would have
been more than problematical.   But Lee was the one to propose his subalterns to act.   Harper's Ferry, on the Virginia
side of the Potomac, where that river is intersected by the
Shenandoah, both cutting their way through the cliffs and
crags of the Blue Ridge, was the seat of the United States
Arsenal, and had immense stores of arms and ammunition, as
well as army supplies of every description.   The Baltimore
and Ohio Railroad and the canal cross the mountains here on
the Maryland side, both hugging the precipitous side of the
mountain and at the very edge of the water.   The approaches
to the place were few, and they so defended that capture seemed
impossible, unless the heights surrounding could be obtained,
and this appeared impossible from a military point of view.
On the south side are the Loudon and Bolivar Heights.   On
the other side the mountains divide into two distinct ranges,
and gradually bear away from each other until they reach a
distance of three miles from crest to crest.   Between the two
mountains is the beautiful and picturesque Pleasant Valley.
The eastern ridge, called South Mountain, commencing from
the rugged cliff at Rivertoria, a little hamlet nestled down
between the mountains and the Potomac, runs northwards,
while the western ridge, called Elk Mountain, starts from the

bluff called Maryland Heights, overlooking the town of Harper's Ferry, and runs nearly parallel to the other.   Jackson passed on up the river with his division, Ewell's, and A. P. Hill's, recrossed the Potomac into Virginia, captured Martinsburg, where a number of prisoners and great supplies were taken, and came up and took possession of Bolivar Heights, above Harper's Ferry.   Walker's Division marched back across the Potomac and took possession of Loudon Heights, a neck of high land between the Shenandoah and Potomac overlooking Harper's Ferry from below, the Shenandoah being between his army and the latter place.   On the 11th McLaws moved out of Frederick City, strengthened by the brigades of Wilcox, Featherstone, and Pryor, making seven brigades that were to undertake the capture of the stronghold by the mountain passes and ridges on the north.   Kershaw, it will be seen, was given the most difficult position of passage and more formidable to attack than any of the other routes of approach. Some time after Jackson and Walker had left on their long march, McLaws followed.   Longstreet and other portions of the army and wagon trains kept the straight road towards Hagerstown, while Kershaw and the rest of the troops under McLaws took the road leading southwest, on through the town of Burkettville, and camped at the foothills of the mountain, on the east side.   Next morning Kershaw, commanding his own brigade and that of Barksdale, took the lead, passed over South Mountain, through Pleasant Valley, and to Elk Ridge, three miles distance, thence along the top of Elk Ridge by a dull cattle path.   The width of the crest was not more than fifty yards in places, and along this Kershaw had to move in line of battle, Barksdale's Brigade in reserve.   Wright's Brigade moved along a similar path on the crest of South Mountain, he taking with him two mountain howitzers, drawn by one horse each.   Mc-Laws, as Commander-in-Chief, with some of the other brigades, marched by the road at the base of the mountain below Wright, while Cobb was to keep abreast of Kershaw and Barksdale at the base of Elk Ridge.   Over such obstacles as were encountered and the difficulties and dangers separating the different troops, a line of battle never before made headway as did those of Kershaw and the troops under McLaws.

We met the enemy's skirmishers soon after turning to the left on Elk Ridge, and all along the whole distance of five miles we were more or less harassed by them. During the march of the 12th the men had to pull themselves up precipitous inclines by the twigs and undergrowth that lined the mountain side, or hold themselves in position by the trees in front. At night we bivouaced on the mountain. We could see the fires all along the mountain side and gorges through Pleasant Valley and up on South Mountain, where the troops of Wright had camped opposite. Early next morning as we advanced we again met the enemy's skirmishers, and had to be continually driving them back. Away to the south and beyond the Potomac we could hear the sound of Jackson's guns as he was beating his way up to meet us. By noon we encountered the enemy's breastworks, built of great stones and logs, in front of which was an abattis of felled timber and brushwood. The Third, under Nance, and the Seventh, under Aiken, were ordered to the charge on the right. Having no artillery up, it was with great difficulty we approached the fortifications. Men had to cling to bushes while they loaded and fired. But with their usual gallantry they came down to their work. Through the tangled undergrowth, through the abattis, and over the breastworks they leaped with a yell. The fighting was short but very severe. The Third did not lose any field officers, but the line suffered considerably. The Third lost some of her most promising officers. Of the Seventh, Captain Litchfield, of Company L, Captain Wm. Clark, of Company G, and Lieutenant J. L. Talbert fell dead, and many others wounded.

The Second and Eighth had climbed the mountains, and advanced on Harper's Ferry from the east. The Second was commanded by Colonel Kennedy and the Eighth by Colonel Henegan. The enemy was posted behind works, constructed the same as those assaulted by the Third and Seventh, of cliffs of rocks, trunks of trees, covered by an abattis. The regiments advanced in splendid style, and through the tangled underbrush and over boulders they rushed for the enemy's works. Colonel Kennedy was wounded in the early part of the engagement, but did not leave the field. The Second lost some gallant line officers. When the order was given to charge the color bearer of the Eighth, Sergeant Strother, of Chesterfield, a tall, handsome man of six feet three in height, carrying the beautiful banner presented to the regiment by the ladies of Pee Dee, fell dead within thirty yards of the enemy's works. All the color guard were either killed or wounded. Captain A. T. Harllee, commanding one of the color companies, seeing the flag fall, seized it and waving it aloft, called to the men to forward and take the breastworks. He, too, fell desperately wounded, shot through both thighs with a minnie ball. He then called to Colonel Henegan, he being near at hand, to take the colors. Snatching them from under Captain Harllee, Colonel Henegan shouted to the men to follow him, but had not gone far before he fell dangerously wounded. Some of the men lifted up their fallen Colonel and started to the rear; but just at this moment his regiment began to waver and break to the rear. The gallant Colonel seeing this ordered his men to put him down, and commanded in a loud, clear voice, "About face! Charge and take the works," which order was obeyed with promptness, and soon the flags of Kershaw's Regiments waved in triumph over the enemy's deserted works.

Walker had occupied Loudon Heights, on the Virginia side, and all were waiting now for Jackson to finish the work assigned to him and to occupy Bolivar Heights, thus finishing the cordon around the luckless garrison. The enemy's cavalry under the cover of the darkness crossed the river, hugged its banks close, and escaped. During the night a road was cut to the top of Maryland Heights by our engineer corps and several pieces of small cannon drawn up, mostly by hand, and placed in such position as to sweep the garrison below. Some of Jackson's troops early in the night began climbing around the steep cliffs that overlook the Shenandoah, and by daylight took possession of the heights opposite to those occupied by Walker's Division. But all during the day, while we were awaiting the signal of Jackson's approach, we heard continually the deep, dull sound of cannonading in our rear. Peal after peal from heavy guns that fairly shook the mountain side told too plainly a desperate struggle was going on in the passes that protected our rear. General McLaws, taking Cobb's Georgia Brigade and some cavalry, hurried back over the rugged by-paths that

had been just traversed, to find D. H. Hill and Longstreet in a
hand-to-hand combat, defending the routes on South Moun
tain that led down on us by the mountain crests. The nex
day orders for storming the works by the troops beyond the
river were given. McLaws and Walker had secured thei
position, and now were in readiness to assist Jackson. All the
batteries were opened on Bolivar Heights, and from the thre
sides the artillery duel raged furiously for a time, while Jack
son's infantry was pushed to the front and captured the work
there. Soon thereafter the white flag was waving over Har
per's Ferry, "the citadel had fallen." In the capitulatio
eleven thousand prisoners, seventy-two pieces of artillery
twelve thousand stands of small arms, horses, wagons
munitions, and supplies in abundance passed into the hands o
the Confederates. Jackson's troops fairly swam in the deli
cacies, provisions, and "drinkables" constituting a part of the
spoils taken, while Kershrw's and all of McLaw's and Walker'
troops, who had done the hardest of the fighting, got none
Our men complained bitterly of this seeming injustice. I
took all day to finish the capitulation, paroling prisoners, and
dividing out the supplies; but we had but little time to rest
for Lee's Army was now in a critical condition. McClellan
having by accident captured Lee's orders specifying the route
to be taken by all the troops after the fall of Harper's Ferry
knew exactly where and when to strike. The Southern Arm
was at this time woefully divided, a part being between th
Potomac and the Shenandoah, Jackson with three division
across the Potomac in Virginia, McLaws with his own and
part of Anderson's Division on the heights of Maryland, wit
the enemy five miles in his rear at Crompton Pass cutting hir
off from retreat in that direction. Lee, with the rest of hi
army and reserve trains, was near Hagerstown.

On the 16th we descended the mountain, crossed the Poto
mac, fell in the rear of Jackson's moving army, and marche
up the Potomac some distance, recrossed into Maryland, o
our hunt for Lee and his army. The sun poured down it
blistering rays with intense fierceness upon the already fatigue
and fagged soldiers, while the dust along the pikes, tha
wound over and around the numerous hills, was almost stifling
We bivouaced for the night on the roadside, ten miles from

Antietam Creek, where Lee was at the time concentrating his army, and where on the next day was to be fought the most stubbornly contested and bloody battle of modern times, if we take in consideration the number of troops engaged, its duration, and its casualties. After three days of incessant marching and fighting over mountain heights, rugged gorges, wading rivers—all on the shortest of rations, many of the men were content to fall upon the bare ground and snatch a few moments of rest without the time and trouble of a supper.

CHAPTER XI

Sharpsburg or Antietam---Return to Virginia.

When Lee crossed the Potomac the Department at Washington, as well as the whole North, was thrown into consternation, and the wildest excitement prevailed, especially in Maryland and Pennsylvania. "Where was Lee?" "Where was he going?" were some of the questions that flitted over the wires to McClellan from Washington, Philadelphia, and Baltimore. But the personage about whose movements and whereabouts seemed to excite more anxiety and superstitious dread than any or all of Lee's Lieutenants was Jackson. The North regarded him as some mythical monster, acting in reality the parts assigned to fiction. But after it was learned that Lee had turned the head of his columns to the westward, their fears were somewhat allayed. General Curtis, of Pennsylvania, almost took spasms at the thought of the dreaded rebels invading his domain, and called upon the militia "to turn out and resist the invader." In less than three weeks after the battle of Manassas, the North, or more correctly, New York, Pennsylvania, New Jersey, Delaware, and Maryland, had out 250,000 State troops behind the Susquehanna River.

The great horde of negro cooks and servants that usually followed the army were allowed to roam at will over the surrounding country, just the same as down in Virginia. The

negroes foraged for their masters wherever they went; and in
times of short rations they were quite an adjunct to the Commissary Department, gathering chickens, butter, flour, etc.
Even now, when so near the Free States, with nothing to prevent them from making their escape, the negroes showed no
disposition to take advantage of their situation and conditions,
their owners giving themselves no concern whatever for their
safety. On more occasions than one their masters told them
to go whenever they wished, that they would exercise no
authority over them whatever, but I do not believe a single
negro left of his own accord. Some few were lost, of course,
but they were lost like many of the soldiers—captured by foraging parties or left broken down along the roadside. It is a
fact, though, that during the whole war the negroes were as
much afraid of the "Yankee" as the white soldier, and dreaded
capture more.

It might be supposed that we fared sumptuously, being in
an enemy's country at fruit and harvest time, with great waving fields of corn, trees bending under loads of choice ripe
fruits, but such was far from being the case. Not an apple,
peach, or plum was allowed to be taken without payment, or
at the owner's consent. Fields, orchards, and farmhouses
were strictly guarded against depredations. The citizens as a
whole looked at us askance, rather passive than demonstrat-
ive. The young did not flock to our standards as was
expected, and the old men looked on more in wonder than in
pleasure, and opened their granaries with willingness, but not
with cheerfulness. They accepted the Confederate money
offered as pay for meals or provisions more as a respect to an
overpowering foe than as a compensation for their wares. A
good joke in this campaign was had at the expense of Captain
Nance, of the Third. It must be remembered that the privates played many practical jokes upon their officers in camps,
when at other times and on other occasions such would be no
joke at all, but a bit of downright rascality and meanness—
but in the army such was called fun. A nice chicken, but too
old to fry, so it must be stewed. As the wagons were not up,
cooking utensils were scarce—about one oven to twenty-five
men. Captain Nance ordered Jess to bake the biscuit at night
and put away till morning, when the chicken would be cooked

and a fine breakfast spread. Now the Captain was overflowing in good humor and spirits, and being naturally generoushearted, invited the Colonel and Lieutenant Colonel Rutherford, the latter his prospective brother-in-law, down to take breakfast with him. The biscuits were all baked nicely and piled high up on an old tin plate and put in the Captain's tent at his head for safe keeping during the night. Early next morning the fowl was "jumping in the pan," as the boys would say, while the Captain made merry with the others over their discomfiture at seeing him and his guests eating "chicken and flour bread," while they would be "chewing crackers." All things must come to an end, of course; so the chicken was at last "cooked to a turn," the Colonel and the future brother-in-law are seated expectantly upon the ground waiting the breakfast call. The Captain was assisting Jess in putting on the finishing touches to the tempting meal, as well as doing the honors to his distinguished guests. When all was ready he ordered Jess to bring out the biscuits. After an unusual long wait, as it may have appeared to Captain Nance under the condition of his appetite and the presence of his superiors, he called out, "Why in the thunder don't you bring out the biscuits, Jess?" Still blankets were overturned and turned again, knapsacks moved for the fourth or fifth time, yet Jess hunted faithfully in that little four by six tent for the plate of biscuits. "Why in the h—l don't you come on with the biscuits, Jess?" with a pronounced accent on the word "Jess." Meanwhile Jess poked his black, shaggy head through the tent door, the white of his eyes depicting the anguish of his mind, his voice the despair he felt, answered: "Well, Marse John, before God Almighty, ef somebody ain't tooken stole dem bisket." Tableaux!! Twenty-five years afterwards at a big revival meeting at Bethel Church, in Newberry County, a great many "hard cases," as they were called, were greatly impressed with the sermons, and one especially seemed on the point of "getting religion," as it is called. But he seemed to be burdened with a great weight. At the end of the service he took out Captain Nance and expressed a desire to make a confession. "Did you ever know who stole your biscuits that night at Frederick City?" "No." "Well, I and Bud Wilson—" But Captain Nance never allowed John Mathis to

finish, for as the light of that far-off truth dawned upon him
and seemed to bring back the recollection of that nice brown
chicken and the missing biscuits he said: "No, I'll never forgive you; go home and don't try for religion any longer, for a
crime as heinous as yours is beyond forgiveness.   Oh, such
depravity!"   It appears since that two of his most intimate
friends had robbed him just for the fun they would have over
his disappointment in the morning and the chagrin the Captain
would experience, but the biscuits were too tempting to keep.

On the morning of the 17th we were yet ten miles from
Sharpsburg, where Lee had drawn up his army around that
little hamlet and along Antietam Creek, to meet the shock of
battle that McClellan was preparing to give.   The battleground chosen was in a bend of the Potomac, Lee's left resting
on the river above and around to the front to near the point
where the Antietam enters the Potomac on the right.   The
little sluggish stream between the two armies, running at the
base of the heights around and beyond Sharpsburg, was not
fordable for some distance above the Potomac, and only crossed
by stone bridges at the public roads.   Up near Lee's left it
could be crossed without bridges.   The Confederate Army now
lay in a small compass in this bend of the river, the Federal
Army extending in his front from the river above to the
Antietam below, just above its junction with the Potomac.
That stream rolled in a deep, strong current in the rear of
Lee.

Even before the sun had spread its rays over the heights of
this quaint old Quaker town sufficient to distinguish objects a
few feet away, the guns were booming along the crossings of
Antietam.   With a hurried breakfast Kershaw took up the
line of march along the dusty roads in the direction of the
firing, which had begun by daylight and continued to rage
incessantly during the day and till after dark, making this the
most bloody battle for the men engaged fought during the
century.   In its casualties—the actual dead upon the field and
the wounded—for the time of action, it exceeded all others
before or since.   When we neared General Lee's headquarters,
some distance in rear of the town, D. H. Hill and part of
Jackson's forces were already in the doubtful toils of a raging
conflict away to our left and front, where Hooker was endeav-

oring to break Lee's left or press it back upon the river.
Barksdale's Brigade, of our division, was in front, and when
near the battlefield formed in line of battle.   Kershaw formed
his lines with the Third, Colonel Nance, in front, nearly parallel with a body of woods, near the Dunker Church, and left
of the road leading to it, the enemy being about five hundred
yards in our front.   The other regiments were formed in line
on our left as they came up, Colonel Aiken, of the Seventh,
Lieutenant Colonel Hoole, of the Eighth, and Colonel Kennedy, of the Second, in the order named, Barksdale moving in
action before our last regiment came fairly in line.   Sumner,
of the Federal Army, was pushing his forces of the Second
Army Corps forward at this point of the line in columns of
brigades, having crossed the Antietam at the fords above.
Sedgwick, of his leading division, had already formed in line
of battle awaiting our assault.   One of the Georgia Brigades of
the division formed on Kershaw's left, while the other acted as
reserve, and a general advance was ordered against the troops
in the woods.   The battle was in full blast now along the
greater part of the line.   General Longstreet, speaking of the
time Kershaw came in action, says: "The fire spread along
both lines from left to right, across the Antietam, and back
again, and the thunder of the big guns became continuous and
increased to a mighty volume.   To this was presently added
the sharper rattle of musketry, and the surge of mingling
sound sweeping up and down the field was multiplied and confused by the reverberations from the rocks and hills.   And in
the great tumult of sound, which shook the air and seemed to
shatter the cliffs and ledges above the Antietam, bodies of the
facing foes were pushed forward to closer work, and soon
added the clash of steel to the thunderous crash of cannon
shot.   Under this storm, now Kershaw advanced his men.
Through the open, on through the woods, with a solid step
these brave men went, while the battery on their left swept
their ranks with grape and canister."   In the woods the brigade was moved to the left to evade this storm of shot and
shell.   The Mississippians on the left were now reforming
their broken ranks.   Colonel Aiken, of the Seventh, had fallen
badly wounded in the first charge, and the command was
given to Captain White.   This was the first battle in a fair

field in which the new commanders of the regiments had had
an opportunity to show their mettle and ability, and well did
they sustain themselves.   Savage Station and Maryland
Heights were so crowded with underbrush and vision so
obscured that they were almost battles in the dark.   Colonel
Kennedy, of the Second, and Lieutenant Colonel Hoole, of the
Eighth, were handling their men in splendid style, the Seventh
changing its commander three times while in battle.   Colonel
Nance changed his front in the lull of battle, and moved under
the friendly cover of a hill, on which was posted the battery
that had been graping the field so desperately during the first
advance.   The brigade had now passed through the field of
waving corn, over the rail fence, and driven Sedgwick from
his position.   Barksdale, who had been staggered by the first
impact, was now moving up in beautiful harmony; the steady, .
elastic step of his men, the waving banners, the officers marching in the rear, their bright blades glittering in the sunlight,
made a most imposing spectacle.   Up the slope, among the
straggling oaks, they bent their steps, while the grape, shell,
and canister thinned their ranks to such an extent that when
the enemy's infantry was met, their galling fire forced Barksdale to retire in great disorder.   The enemy's troops were
being hurried over the creek and forming in our front.   Kershaw moved forward in line with those on the right to meet
them, and swept everything from his front.   The enemy had
been massing along the whole line, and when Kershaw reached
the farthest limit of the open field he was met by overwhelming numbers.   Now the fight waged hot and fierce, but the line
on the right having retired left the right flank of the Third
Regiment entirely exposed both to the fire of the artillery and
infantry, forcing the brigade to retire to its former ground,
leaving, however, the second commander of the Seventh dead
upon the field.   It was here the famous scout and aide to
General Stuart, Captain W. D. Farley, killed at the Rappahannock, came to visit his brother, Lieutenant Farley, of the
Third.   He was made doubly famous by the fiction of Captain
Estine Cooke.

McClellan was now growing desperate, his lines making no
headway either on the left or centre.   His forces were held at
bay on our right across the Antietam, having failed to force a

crossing at the bridges. Jackson and Hill, on the left, were being sorely pressed by the corps of Mansfield and Hooker, but still doggedly held their ground. Jackson had left the division of A. P. Hill at Harper's Ferry to settle the negotiations of surrender, and had but a comparative weak force to meet this overwhelming number of two army corps. Again and again the Confederate ranks were broken, but as often reformed. Stuart stood on the extreme left, with his body of cavalry, but the condition of the field was such as to prevent him from doing little more service than holding the flanks. General Toombs, with his Georgia Brigade, and some detached troops, with two batteries, held the lower fords all day against the whole of Burnside's corps, notwithstanding the imperative orders of his chief "to cross and strike the Confederates in the rear." Assaults by whole divisions were repeatedly made against the small force west of the stream, but were easily repulsed by Toombs and his Georgians. In all probability these unsuccessful attacks would have continued during the day, had not the Federals found a crossing, unknown to the Confederate Generals, between the bridges. When the crossing was found the whole slope on the western side of the stream was soon a perfect sheet of blue. So sure were they of victory that they called upon the Confederates to "throw down their arms and surrender." This was only answered by a volley and a charge with the bayonet point. But there was a factor in the day's battle not yet taken account of, and which was soon to come upon the field like a whirlwind and change the course of events. A. P. Hill, who had been left at Harper's Ferry, was speeding towards the bloody field with all the speed his tired troops could make. Gregg, Branch, and Archer, of Hill's Division, were thrown into the combat at this most critical moment, after the enemy had forced a crossing at all points and were pushing Lee backwards towards the Potomac. Short and decisive was the work. An advance of the whole right was made. The enemy first staggered, then reeled, and at last pressed off the field. The batteries lost in the early part of the day were retaken, and the enemy was glad to find shelter under his heavy guns on the other side of the Antietam. But the battle on the left was not so favorable. Jackson's, D. H. Hill's, and McLaw's troops, jaded and fagged by the forced marches in the morning, their ranks woefully thinned by the day's continuous fighting, their ammunition sadly exhausted, could do no more than hold their ground for the remainder of the day. The enemy now being re-enforced by Porter's Corps, his batteries enfilading our ranks. McLaws was forced to move Kershaw and the troops on his right to the left and rear, nearly parallel to the line first formed during the day. There had been no material advantage on either side. On the right the enemy had crossed the Antietam, it is true, but to a position no better than the night before. Our left and centre were bent back in somewhat more acute angle than on the morning, but to an equally good position. Not many prisoners were taken on either side in proportion to the magnitude of the battle. The enemy's loss in killed and wounded was a little more than ours, but so far as the day's battle goes, the loss and gain were about equal. It is true Lee lost thousands of good and brave troops whose places could scarcely be filled; yet he inflicted such punishment upon the enemy that it took him months to recuperate. The moral effect was against us and in favor of the enemy It had a decided bearing upon the coming elections at the North, and a corresponding depression upon the people at the South. The Southern Army, from its many successive victories in the past, had taught themselves to believe that they were simply invincible upon the field of battle, and the people of the South looked upon the strategy and military skill of Lee and Jackson as being far beyond the cope of any Generals the North could produce. But this battle taught the South a great lesson in many ways. It demonstrated the fact that it was possible to be matched in generalship, it was possible to meet men upon the field equal in courage and endurance to themselves. But it also proved to what point of forbearance and self-sacrifice the Southern soldier could go when the necessity arose, and how faithful and obedient they would remain to their leaders under the severest of tests. The Confederate soldier had been proven beyond cavil the equal in every respect to that of any on the globe. After fighting all day, without food and with little water, they had to remain on the field of battle, tired and hungry, until details returned to the wagons and cooked their rations. It may be easily imagined that both armies were glad enough to fall upon the ground and rest after such a day of blood and carnage, with the smoke, dust, and weltering heat of the day. Before the sound of the last gun had died away in the distance one hundred thousand men were stretched upon the ground fast asleep, while near a third of that number were sleeping their last sleep or suffering from the effects of fearful wounds. The ghouls of the battlefield are now at their wanton work. Stealthily and cautiously they creep and grope about in the dark to hunt the body of an enemy, or even a comrade, and strip or rob him of his little all. Prayers, groans, and curses mingle, but the robber of the battlefield continues his work. Friends seek lost comrades here and there, a brother looks, perhaps, in vain for a brother.

The loss in some of our regiments was appalling, especially the Seventh. Two regimental commanders of that command had fallen, Colonel Aiken and Captain White, leaving Captain Hard, one of the junior Captains, in command. The regiment lost in the two battles of Maryland Heights and Sharpsburg, two hundred and fifty-three out of four hundred and forty-six.

General McClellan, in his testimony before the War Investigating Committee, says: "We fought pretty close upon one hundred thousand men. Our forces were, total in action, eighty-seven thousand one hundred and sixty-four." Deducting the cavalry division not in action of four thousand three hundred and twenty, gives McClellan eighty-two thousand eight hundred and forty-four, infantry and artillery.

General Lee says in his report: "The battle was fought by less than forty thousand men of all arms on our side." The actual numbers were:

Jackson, including A. P. Hill . . .	10,000
Longstreet	12,000
D. H. Hill and Walker	7,000
Cavalry	8,000
	37,000

Deduct four thousand cavalry on detached service and not on the field from Lee's force, and we have of infantry, artillery, and cavalry, thirty-three thousand. Jackson only had four

thousand on the left until the arrival of A. P. Hill, and withstood the assaults of forty thousand till noon; when re-enforced
by Hill he pressed the enemy from the field.

The next day was employed in burying the dead and
gathering up the wounded. Those who could travel were
started off across the Potomac on foot, in wagons and ambulances, on the long one hundred miles march to the nearest
railroad station, while those whose wounds would not admit of
their removal were gathered in houses in the town and surgeons
detailed to remain and treat them. On the morning of the
19th some hours before day the rumbling of the wagon trains
told of our march backward. We crossed the Potomac, Longstreet leading, and Jackson bringing up the rear. A great
many that had been broken down by the rapid marches and
the sun's burning rays from the time of our crossing into
Maryland till now, were not up at the battle of the 17th, thus
weakening the ranks of Lee to nearly one-half their real
strength, taking those on detached service into consideration
also. But these had all come up and joined their ranks as we
began crossing the Potomac. None wished to be left behind;
even men so badly wounded that at home they would be confined to their beds marched one hundred miles in the killing
heat. Hundreds of men with their arms amputated left the
operating table to take up their long march. Some shot
through the head, body, or limbs preferred to place the Potomac
between themselves and the enemy.

Lee entered Maryland with sixty-one thousand men all told,
counting Quartermaster and Commissary Departments, the
teamsters, and those in the Medical and Engineer Department.
Lee lost thirteen thousand six hundred and eighty-seven men
killed and wounded on the field of battle, and several thousand
in capture and broken down by the wayside, most of the latter,
however, reporting for duty in a few days.

McClellan had of actual soldiers in the lines of battle and
reserve eighty-seven thousand one hunhred and sixty-four, his
losses in battle being twelve thousand four hundred and ten,
making his casualties one thousand two hundred and seventy-
seven less than Lee's. The prisoners and cannon captured in
action were about equal during the twelve days north of the
Potomac, while at Harper's Ferry Lee captured sufficient

ammunition to replenish that spent in battle, and horses and
wagons enough to fully equip the whole army, thousands of
improved small arms, seventy-two cannon and caissons, and
eleven thousand prisoners. While the loss of prisoners,
ammunition, horses, ordnance, etc., did not materially cripple
the North, our losses in prisoners and killed and wounded
could hardly be replaced at that time. So in summing up the
results it is doubtful whether or not the South gained any
lasting benefit from the campaign beyond the Potomac. But
Lee was forced by circumstances after the enemy's disaster at
Manassas to follow up his victories and be guided by the
course of events, and in that direction they lead. McClellan
offered the gauge of battle; Lee was bound to accept. The
North claimed Sharpsburg or Antietam as a victory, and the
world accepted it as such. This gave Lincoln the opportunity
he had long waited for to write his famous Emancipation
Proclamation. It was not promulgated, however, till the first
of January following. Among military critics this battle
would be given to Lee, even while the campaign is voted a
failure. It is an axiom in war that when one army stands
upon the defensive and is attacked by the other, if the latter
fails to force the former from his position, then it is considered
a victory for the army standing on the defensive. (See Lee
at Gettysburg and Burnsides at Fredericksburg.) While Lee
was the invader, he stood on the defensive at Sharpsburg or
Antietam, and McClellan did no more than press his left and
centre back. Lee held his battle line firmly, slept on the
field, buried his dead the next aay, then deliberately withdrew. What better evidence is wanting to prove Lee not
defeated. McClellan claimed no more than a drawn fight.

On the 19th the enemy began pressing our rear near Shep-
ardstown, and A. P. Hill was ordered to return and drive
them off. A fierce and sanguinary battle took place at
Bateler's Ford, between two portions of the armies, A. P. Hill
gaining a complete victory, driving the enemy beyond the
river. The army fell back to Martinsburg and rested a few
days. Afterwards they were encamped at Winchester, where
they remained until the opening of the next campaign.

Before closing the account of the First Maryland campaign,
I wish to say a word in regard to the Commissary and Quar-

11

termaster's Departments.   Much ridicule, and sometimes
abuse, has been heaped upon the heads of those who composed
the two Departments.   I must say, in all justice, that much of
this was ill timed and ill advised.   It must be remembered
that to the men who constituted these Departments belonged
the duty of feeding, clothing, and furnishing the transportation for the whole army.   Often without means or ways,
they had to invent them.   In an enemy's country, surrounded
by many dangers, in a hostile and treacherous community,
and mostly unprotected except by those of their own force,
they had to toil night and day, through sunshine and rain,
that the men who were in the battle ranks could be fed and
clothed.   They had no rest.   When the men were hungry
they must be fed; when others slept they had to be on the
alert.   When sick or unable to travel a means of transportation
must be furnished.   The Commissary and the Quartermaster
must provide for the sustenance of the army.   Kershaw's Brigade was doubly blessed in the persons of Captain, afterwards
Major W. D. Peck and Captain Shell, of the Quartermaster
Department, and Captain R. N. Lowrance, and Lieutenant
J. X. Martin, of the Commissary.   The troops never wanted
or suffered while it was in the power of those officers to supply
them.

Major Peck was a remarkable man in many respects.   He
certainly could be called one of nature's noblemen.   Besides
being a perfect high-toned gentleman of the old school, he
was one of the most efficient officers in the army, and his popularity was universal   His greatest service was in the Quartermaster's Department, but he served for awhile in the ranks
in Captain Wm. Wallace's Company, Second Regiment, as
Orderly Sergeant --served in that capacity at the bombardment
of Fort Sumter and the first battle of Manassas.   On the death
of Quartermaster W. S. Wood, Colonel Kershaw appointed
him his Regimental Quartermaster to fill the place made
vacant by Captain Wood, in July, 1861, with the rank of
Captain.   When Kershaw was made Brigadier General, on
the resignation of General Bonham, he had him promoted to
Brigade Quartermaster with the rank of Major.   On the resignation of Major McLaws, Division Quartermaster, he was
made Division Quartermaster in his stead, and held this position

during the war. He received his last appointment only one
month before his illustrious chief, J. B. Kershaw, was made
Major General. It seems a strange coincidence in the rise of
these two men, who entered the service together—each took
different arms, but rose in parallel grades to the highest
position in the division. Major Peck was seldom absent from
duty, and a complaint against him was never heard. He was
a bold, gallant officer, and when in the discharge of his duties
he laid aside every other consideration. Major Peck had a
very striking appearance, tall, erect, and dignified, and upon
horseback he was a perfect cavalier. It might be truly said
he was one of the handsomest men in the army. His commanding appearance attracted attention wherever he went,
and he was often taken for a general officer. For cordiality,
generosity, and unselfishness he was almost without a rival.
It required no effort on his part to display the elegance of his
character—his gentlemanly qualities and deportment were as
natural to him as it is for the "sparks to fly upward." He
was born in Columbia April 4th, 1833, and died there April
25th, 1870.

The mere fact of Captain G. W. Shell being appointed to such
a responsible position as Quartermaster by so strict a disciplinarian as Colonel Nance is a sufficient guarantee of his qualifications. Captain Shell entered the army as a private in the
"State Guards," from Laurens, served one year as such, then
as Regimental Quartermaster with rank of Captain for a part
of two years. Then that office in the army was abolished
and put in charge of a non-commissioned officer. Appreciating his great services while serving his regiment, the officials
were loath to dispense with his services, and gave him a
position in the brigade department and then in the division as
assistant to Major Peck, retaining his rank. All that has
been said of Major Peck can be truly said of Captain Shell.
He was an exceptional executive officer, kind and courteous to
those under his orders, obedient and respectful to his superiors.
He was ever vigilant and watchful of the wants of the troops,
and while in the abandoned sections of Virginia, as well as in
Maryland and Pennsylvania, he displayed the greatest activity
in gathering supplies for the soldiers. He was universally
loved and admired. He was of the same age of Captain Peck,

born and reared in Laurens County, where he returned after the close of the war and still resides, enjoying all the comforts emanating from a well spent life. For several terms he filled the office of Clerk of the Court of his native county, and served two terms in the United States Congress. He was the leading spirit in the great reform movement that overspread the State several years ago. in which Ben Tillman was made Governor, and South Carolina's brightest light, both political and military, General Wade Hampton, was retired to private life.

COLONEL D. WYATT AIKEN, OF THE SEVENTH.

As Colonel Aiken saw but little more service with the First Brigade, I will here give a short sketch of his life. I have made it a rule in this work, as far as practicable, to give a sketch at the end of the officer's service in the Brigade, but in this case I make an exception.

Colonel Aiken was born in Winnsboro, Fairfield County, S. C., March 17th, 1828. He graduated at the South Carolina College in the class of 1849. Was professor at Mt. Zion College for two years, and married Miss Mattie Gaillard in 1852, settling at "Bellevue" Farm, near Winnsboro. He became county editor of Winnsboro News and Herald, and was married the second time to Miss Smith, of Abbeville, and removed to that county in 1858. Was fond of agriculture, and was editor of various periodicals devoted to that and kindred pursuits.

In 1861 he volunteered as a private in the Seventh South Carolina Volunteers, and was appointed Adjutant of that regiment. At the reorganization of the regiment in 1862 he was elected Colonel to succeed Colonel Bacon. who declined re-election. At Sharpsburg he received a wound in the body, which for a long time was feared to be fatal. He, however, returned in June, 1863. and commanded his regiment in the Gettysburg battle, after which he was deemed unable for further active service in the field, and was appointed "commandant of the post" at Macon, Ga. This position he held for one year. and then discharged from the army as being unfit for further service.

After the war he was selected for three terms to the State

Legislature. He was "Master of State Grange Patrons of Husbandry," and was twice President of the "State Agricultural and Mechanical Society of South Carolina." He was chosen Democratic standard bearer for Congress in the memorable campaign of 1876, and continually re-elected thereafter until his death, which occurred on April 6th, 1887.

Colonel Aiken was also one of nature's noblemen, bold, fearless, and incorruptible. He did as much, or perhaps more, than any of the many great and loyal men of that day to release South Carolina from the coils of the Republican ring that ruled the State during the dark days of Reconstruction.

CHAPTER XII

From Winchester to Fredericksburg.

The brigade remained in camp in a beautiful grove, about four miles beyond Winchester, until the last of October. Here the regiments were thoroughly organized and put in good shape for the next campaign. Many officers and non-commissioned officers had been killed, or totally disabled in the various battles, and their places had to be filled by election and promotion. All officers, from Colonel down, went up by regular grades, leaving nothing but the Third Lieutenants to be elected. The non-commissioned officers generally went up by promotion also, where competent, or the Captains either promoted them by regular grade or left the selection to the men of the company. We had lost no field officer killed, except Lieutenant Colonel Garlington, of the Third, and Major Rutherford was promoted to that position, and Captain R. C. Maffett made Major. Several Lieutenants in all the regiments were made Captains, and many new Lieutenants were chosen from the ranks, so much so that the rolls of the various companies were very materially changed, since the reorganization in April last. Many of the wounded had returned, and large bodies of men had come in from the conscript camps since the reorganization. The Seventh Regiment

had lost heavier, in officers and men, than any of the regi
ments.   Colonel Aiken was wounded at Sharpsburg, and neve
returned only for a short time, but the regiment was com
manded by Lieutenant Colonel Bland until the resignation c
Colonel Aiken, except when the former was himself disable
by wounds.

Camp guards were kept up around the brigade, and reg
mental pickets, some two or three miles distant, about ever
two weeks. We had company and regimental drills abou
four times per week, and, in fact, we drilled almost every day
now that we were not on the actual march.   The turn-pik
road from Winchester to Staunton, ninety miles, for week
was perfectly lined with soldiers returning at the expiration c
their furloughs, or discharged from hospital, and our conva
lescent sick and wounded from the Maryland campaign goin;
homeward.

On the 27th or 28th of October orders came to move
Longstreet took the lead, with McLaws' and Anderson'
Divisions in front.   General Lee had divided his army int
two corps; the Department of Richmond having created th
rank of Lieutenant General, raised Longstreet and Jackson t
that grade in Lee's Army.   Longstreet's Corps consisted c
McLaws' Division, composed of Kershaw's, Barksdale's
Cobb's, and Semmes' Brigades, and Anderson's, Hood's
Pickett's, and Ransom's Divisions.   Jackson's Corps consiste
of D. H. Hill's, A. P. Hill's, Ewell's, and Taliaferro'
Divisions.   We marched by way of Chester Gap over th
Blue Ridge, and came into camp near Culpepper on the 9t
of November.   The enemy had crossed the Potomac and wa
moving southward, by easy stages, on the east side of th
mountain.

On the 5th of October General McClellan was removed fror
the command of the Army of the Potomac and Major Gener
Burnsides, a corps commander, was made Commander-ir
Chief in his stead.   This change was universally regretted b
both armies, for the Northern Army had great confidence i
the little "Giant," while no officer in the Union Army wa
ever held in higher esteem by the Southern soldiers than littl
"Mack," as General McClellan was called.   They admire
him for his unsurpassed courage, generalship, and his kin

and gentlemanly deportment, quite in contrast to the majority of Union commanders.

General Burnsides, who had succeeded McClellan, now divided his army by corps in three grand divisions—General Sumner, commanding the Right Grand Division, composed of the Second and Ninth Corps; General Hooker, the center, with the Third and Fifth Corps; and General Franklin, the left, with the First and Sixth Corps. So both armies had undergone considerable changes, and were now moving along on converging lines towards a meeting point to test the mettle of the new commanders and organizations. .

We remained in camp around Culpepper until the morning of the 18th of November, when the march was resumed, by McLaws taking the road leading to Fredericksburg, headed by General Longstreet in person, and another division south along the line of the railroad in the direction of the North Anna River, the other divisions of the corps remaining stationary, awaiting developments. Jackson had not yet crossed the Blue Ridge, and General Lee was only waiting and watching the move of Burnsides before concentrating his army at any particular place. It was unknown at this time whether the Federal commander would take the route by way of Fredericksburg, or follow in a straight course and make the North Anna his base of operations. The cavalry, making a demonstration against the enemy's outposts, found the Union Army had left and gone in the direction of Fredericksburg. Then Lee began the concentration of his army by calling Jackson on the east side of the Blue Ridge and Longstreet down on the south side of the Rappahannock. We crossed the north fork of the Rappahannock at a rocky ford, two miles above the junction of the Rapidan and just below the railroad bridge, on a cold, blustery day, the water blue and cold as ice itself, coming from the mountain springs of the Blue Ridge, not many miles away. Some of the men took off their shoes and outer garments, while others plunged in just as they marched from the road. Men yelled, cursed, and laughed. Some climbed upon the rocks to allow their feet and legs to warm up in the sun's rays, others held up one foot for awhile, then the other, to allow the air to strike their naked shins and warm them. Oh! it was dreadfully cold, but such fun! The water being about three feet deep, we could easily see the rocks and sands in the bottom. The men who had pulled off their shoes and clothing suffered severely.

There was a man in my company who was as brave and as good a soldier as ever lived, but beyond question the most awkward man in the army. His comrades called him "mucus," as some one said that was the Latin for "calf." This man would fall down any time and anywhere. Standing in the road or resting on his rifle, he would fall—fall while marching, or standing in his tent. I saw him climb on top of a box car and then fall without the least provocation backwards into a ten-foot ditch. But in all his falling he was never known to hurt himself, but invariably blamed somebody for his fall. When he fell from the car, and it standing perfectly still, he only said: "I wish the d—n car would go on or stand still, one or the other." The road leading to the river makes a bend here, and between the bend and river bank an abutment of logs, filled in with stone to the height of fifteen feet, was built to prevent the water from encroaching upon the land. "Mucus," for no cause whatever that anyone could learn, quit the ranks and walked out on this abutment and along down its side, keeping near the edge of the water, but fifteen feet above, when, to the unaccountability of all, he fell headlong down into the river. The water at this point was not more than three or four feet deep, but deep enough to drench him from head to foot. He rose up, and as usual, quick to place the blame, said: "If I knew the d—n man who pushed me off in the water, I'd put a ball in him." No one had been in twenty feet of him. All the consolation he got was "how deep was the water, 'Mucus'?" "Was the water cold?" But awkward as he was, he was quick-witted and good at repartee. He answered the question "how deep was the water?" "Deep enough to drown a d—n fool, if you don't believe it, go down like I did and try it."

When we reached the other side we were told "no use to put on your shoes or clothing, another river one mile ahead," the Rapidan here joining the Rappahannock. Those who had partly disrobed put their clothing under their arms, shoes in their hands, and went hurrying along after the column in advance. These men, with their bare limbs, resembled the

Scotch Highlanders in the British Army, but their modesty was put to the test; when about half-way to the other stream they passed a large, old-fashioned Virginia residence, with balconies above and below, and these filled with ladies of the surrounding country, visitors to see the soldiers pass. It was an amusing sight no less to the ladies of the house than to the men, to witness this long line of soldiers rushing by with their coat-tails beating a tatto on their naked nether limbs. The other stream was not so wide, but equally as cold and deep.

General Kershaw, sitting on his horse at this point, amusing himself at the soldiers' plight, undertook to encourage and soothe their ruffled feelings by giving words of cheer. "Go ahead, boys," remarked the General, "and don't mind this; when I was in Mexico—" "But, General, it wasn't so cold in Mexico, nor did they fight war in winter, and a horse's legs are not so tender as a man's bare shins," were some of the answers given, and all took a merry laugh and went scudding away.

Passing over, we entered the famous Wilderness, soon to be made renowned by the clash of arms, where Lee and Hooker met and shook the surrounding country with the thunder of their guns a few months afterwards, and where Grant made the "echoes ring" and reverberate on the 5th and 6th of May, the year following. We found, too, the "Chancellor House," this lone, large, dismal-looking building standing alone in this Wilderness and surrounded on all sides by an almost impenetrable forest of scrubby oaks and tangled vines. The house was a large, old-fashioned hotel, situated on a cleared plateau, a piaza above and below, reaching around on three sides. It was called "Chancellorsville," but where the "ville" came in, or for what the structure was ever built, I am unable to tell. This place occupied a prominent place in the picture of the Battle of Chancellorsville, being for a time the headquarters of General Hooker, and around which the greater part of his cannon were placed. We took up camp in rear of Fredericksburg, about two miles south of the city.

While here we received into our brigade the Fifteenth South Carolina Regiment, commanded by Colonel DeSaussure, and the Third Battalion, composed of eight companies and commanded by Lieutenant Colonel Rice. As these are new additions, it will be necessary to give a brief sketch of their organization and movements prior to their connection with Kershaw's Brigade.

Soon after the battle of Bull Run or First Manassas, the Richmond Government made a call upon the different States for a new levy to meet the call of President Lincoln for three hundred thousand more troops to put down the Rebellion. The companies that were to compose the Fifteenth Regiment assembled at the old camping ground at Lightwood Knot Spring, three miles above Columbia. They were:

Company A—Captain Brown, Richland.

Company B—Captain Gist, Union.

Company C—Captain Lewie, Lexington.

Company D—Captain Warren, Kershaw.

Company E—Captain Davis, Fairfield.

Company F—Captain Boyd, Union.

Company G—Captain McKitchen, Williamsburg.

Company H—Captain Farr, Union.

Company I—Captain Koon, Lexington.

Company K—Captain Bird, ———

(These names are given from the best information obtainable and may not be exactly correct, but as the fortunes of war soon made radical changes it is of little moment at this late date.) These companies elected for their field officers:

Colonel—Wm. DeSaussure.

Lieutenant Colonel—Joseph Gist.

Major———

The regiment remained in camp undergoing a thorough course of instruction until Hilton Head, on the coast of South Carolina, was threatened; then the Fifteenth was ordered in the field and hurried to that place, reaching it on the afternoon of the day before the battle of that name. The Fifteenth, with the Third Battalion and other State troops, was placed under the command of Brigadier General Drayton, also of South Carolina, and put in position. The next day, by some indiscretion of General Drayton, or so supposed at that time, the Fifteenth was placed in such position as to be greatly exposed to the heavy fire from the war vessels in the harbor. This caused the loss of some thirty or forty in killed and wounded. The slaughter would have been much greater had

it not been for the courage and quick perception of Colonel
DeSaussure in manœuvering them into a place of safety.
After the battle the regiment lay for some time about Hardees-
ville and Bluffton doing guard and picket duty, still keeping
up their course of daily drills. They were then sent to James
Island, and were held in reserve at the battle of Secessionville.
After the great Seven Days' Battles around Richmond it and
the Third Battalion were ordered to Virginia and placed with
a regiment from Alabama and one from Georgia in a brigade
under General Drayton. They went into camp below Richmond as a part of a division commanded by Brigadier General
D. R. Jones, in the corps commanded by Longstreet. When
Lee began his march northward they broke camp on the 13th
of August, and followed the lead of Longstreet to Gordonsville, and from thence on to Maryland. They were on the
field during the bloody battle of Second Manassas, but not
actually engaged, being held in the reserve line on the extreme
right. At South Mountain they received their first baptism of
fire in a battle with infantry. On the memorable 17th of
September at Sharpsburg they were confirmed as veteran soldiers in an additional baptism of blood. However, as yet
considered raw and undisciplined troops, they conducted
themselves on each of these trying occasions like trained soldiers. Colonel DeSaussure was one of the most gallant and
efficient officers that South Carolina ever produced. He was a
Mexican War veteran and a born soldier. His attainments
were such as fitted him for much higher position in the service than he had yet acquired. Had not the fortunes of war
laid him low not many miles distant one year later, he would
have shown, no doubt, as one of the brightest stars in the constellation of great Generals that South Carolina ever produced.
After the return to Virginia Drayton's Brigade was broken
up, and the Fifteenth and Third Battalion were assigned to
the brigade of General J. B. Kershaw, and began its service
in that organization on the heights of Fredericksburg.

THE THIRD BATTALION.

I am indebted to Colonel W. G. Rice for a brief sketch of
the Third Battalion, or as it was more generally known in the
army, "James' Battalion," after its first commander, (who

fell at South Mountain, Md.,) up to the time of joining the brigade:

"On the fall of Hilton Head and the occupation of Port Royal by the enemy, the Governor of South Carolina issued a call for volunteers for State service. Among the companies offering their services were four from Laurens County. Lieutenant Geo. S. James having resigned from the United States Army, and being personally known to several of the officers of said four companies, they united in forming a battalion and electing him Major. The companies became known thereafter as:

"Company A—Captain W. G. Rice.

"Company B—Captain J. G. Williams.

"Company C—Captain J. M. Shumate.

"Company D—Captain G. M. Gunnels.

"All of Laurens County, the organization being effected at Camp Hampton, near Columbia, November, 1861, and where Major James assumed command. In December the battalion was ordered to Charleston, and from thence to White Point, near the coast. Here the battalion was strengthened by three more companies, making it now a compound battalion and entitled to a Lieutenant Colonel and Major. The additional companies were:

"Company E, from Laurens—Captain M. M. Hunter.

"Company F, from Richland—Captain D. B. Miller.

"Company G, from Fairfield—Captain A. P. Irby.

"Major James was promoted to Lieutenant Colonel, and Captain W. G. Rice, as senior Captain, made Major, while Lieutenant J. M. Townsend was raised to the grade of Captain in place of Major Rice.

"In April, 1862, a reorganization was ordered, and the troops enlisted in the Confederate States' service. Both Colonel James and Major Rice were elected to their former positions, with the following company commanders:

"J. M. Townsend—Captain Company A.

"O. A. Watson—Captain Company B.

"William Huggins—Captain Company C.

"G. M. Gunnels—Captain Company D.

"W. H. Fowler—Captain Company E.

"D. B. Miller—Captain Company F.

"B. M. Whitener—Captain Company G.

"Early in June the battalion was ordered to James' Island, arriving there two days before the battle of Secessionville, but not participating in it. A short while afterwards it was ordered to Richmond, and there remained until the great forward movement of General Lee's, which resulted in the Second Manassas Battle and the invasion of Maryland. The battalion was now brigaded with Philip's Georgia Legion, Fiftieth and Fifty-first Georgia, and Fifteenth South Carolina Regiments, and commanded by Brigadier General Drayton. The battalion was under fire at Waterloo Bridge and at Thoroughfare Gap, and the brigade held the extreme right of Lee's Army at the Second Manassas Battle, but was not seriously engaged. The topography of the country was such that while the incessant roar of artillery could be distinctly heard during the day, no infantry could be heard, and the extreme right did not hear of the result of the great battle until General Robert Toombs marched by and shouted to his fellow Georgians: 'Another great and glorious Bull Run.' After repeated marches and counter-marches during the day, night put an end to the bloody struggle, and the troops lay down to rest. A perfect tornado of shot and shell tore through the woods all around us until deep darkness fell and the enemy withdrew, leaving the entire field to the Confederates."

After resting for nearly a week at Frederick City, Md., the battalion, with the Fifteenth South Carolina and the Georgians of Drayton's Brigade, was ordered to re-enforce General D. H. Hill, who was guarding Lee's rear at Crompton's Gap, in South Mountain. Here the South Carolinians were for the first time thoroughly baptized with fire and blood, and in which the gallant Colonel Jones lost his life. Of this battle Colonel Rice says:

"Late in the evening of September 14th the brigade reached the battlefield and deployed in an old disused road that crossed the mountain some four hundred yards to the right of the turnpike. No enemy in sight. Failing to drive D. H. Hill from their front, the Federals made a detour and approached him by the flank. Two hundred yards from the road mentioned above was a belt of woods saddling the mountain, and at this point running parallel with the road. General Drayton,

not seeing the enemy, ordered forward Captain Miller's
Company as skirmishers to ascertain their whereabouts.
Captain Miller had advanced but a short distance when he
met the enemy in force. General Drayton ordered the command to forward and drive them from the woods. In the
execution of this order some confusion arose, and a part of the
brigade gave way, leaving the battalion in a very peculiar and
isolated condition. There was a low rock fence running at
right angles to the battle line, and behind this the battalion
sought to protect itself, but it seemed and was in reality a
death trap, for it presented its right flank to the enemy. It
thus became only a question of a very short time when it must
either leave the field or surrender. Right nobly did this little
band of heroes hold their ground against overwhelming
numbers, and their front was never successfully approached;
but as both flanks were so mercilessly assailed, a short time
was sufficient to almost annihilate them. Colonel James
was twice admonished by his second in command of his untenable position, and that death or surrender was inevitable if he
persisted in holding his ground, but without avail. The true
soldier that he was preferred death to yielding. Just as night
approached and firing began to cease, Colonel James was
pierced through the breast with a minnie ball, from the effects
of which he soon died."

Colonel Rice was dangerously wounded and left on the field
for dead. But recovering consciousness, he found himself
within the enemy's lines, that portion of his command nearest
him having been withdrawn some distance in the rectifying of
the lines. Colonel Rice escaped capture by crawling in a deep
wash in the road, and was rescued by some skirmishers who
were advancing to establish a new line. Colonel Rice gives
this information in a foot-note: "The road in which the brigade
was stationed was as all roads crossing hills, much washed and
worn down, thus giving the troops therein stationed the
advantage of first-class breastworks. I do not know that the
Fifteenth South Carolina and the other portion of the brigade
were thus sheltered—have heard indeed that all were not—but
within my vision the position was most admirable, now almost
impregnable with good troops to defend it. To leave such a
position was suicidal, especially when we were ordered to

march through open ground and attack the enemy, sheltered
behind trees and rocks. This is my estimate at least, and the
result proved most disastrous to the brigade and General Drayton himself, as he was soon afterwards relieved of his command.''

It has been the aim of the writer of this History not to criti-
cize, condemn, nor make any comments upon the motives or
acts of any of the officers whom he should have cause to mention, and he somewhat reluctantly gives space to Colonel Rice's
stricture of General Drayton.   It is difficult for officers in subaltern position to understand all that their superiors do and do
not.   The Generals, from their positions, can see differently
from those in the line amid the smoke of battle, and they often
give commands hard to comprehend from minor officers' point
of view.   General Drayton was an accomplished and gallant
officer, and while he might have been rash and reckless at
South Mountain, still it is hard to conceive his being relieved
of his command through the charge of ''rashness,'' especially
when his brigade held up successfully for so long a time one
of the most stubborn battles of the war.

At the Battle of Sharpsburg or Antietam, the little remnant
of the battalion was again engaged.   On Lee's return to Virginia, and during the last days of November or early in December, the Third Battalion and the Fifteenth Regiment were
transferred to Kershaw's Brigade, and from thence on it will
be treated as a part of the old First Brigade.   At Fredericksburg, on the day of the great battle, the battalion held the
railroad cut running from near the city to the right of
Mayree's Hill, and was well protected by a bluff and the railroad, consequently did not suffer as great a loss as the other
regiments of the brigade.

COLONEL GEORGE S. JAMES,

The first commander of the Third Battalion, and who fell at
South Mountain, was born in Laurens County, in 1829.   He
was the second son of John S. James, a prominent lawyer of
Laurens, who, meeting with misfortune and losing a handsome
fortune, attempted to retain it by moving to Columbia and
engaging in mercantile pursuits.   This he followed with success.   Colonel George S. James received his early education

in the academies of the up-country.   While yet a youth so
seventeen years of age, war with Mexico was declared, a
his patriotic and chivalric spirit sent him at once to the ra
of the Palmetto Regiment, and he shared the triumphs and
tunes of that command to the close of the war.

After his return to his native State, he entered the So
Carolina College, along with many others, who in after ye
made their State and themselves immortal by their fiery a
in the War of Secession.   At the college young James wa
great favorite of all who knew him best, and while not a cl
student of text-books, he was an extensive reader, alwa
delighting his friends with wit and humor.   The student l
however, failed to satisfy his adventurous spirit, and wand
ing away to the far distant West, seeking adventure or con
nial pursuits, he received a commission of Lieutenant in
United States Army.

The storm cloud of war, so long hovering over the la
was now about to burst, and Lieutenant James seeing sepa
tion and perhaps war inevitable, resigned his commission, a
hastened to offer his sword to his native State.   He co
manded a battery at Fort Johnson, on James' Island, a
shared with General Ruffin the honor of firing the first gur
Fort Sumter, a shot that was to electrify the world and
in motion two of the grandest and mightiest armies of
times.

CHAPTER XII

Battle of Fredericksburg—The Fifteenth Re
ment and Third Battalion Join Brigade.

A portion of the Federal Army had preceded Lee, reach
the heights opposite Fredericksburg two days before
arrival of Kershaw's Brigade and the other parts of
division.   The Federals had been met by a small body
Confederates doing outpost duty there and held at bay till
coming of Longstreet with his five divisions.   General

was not long in determining the route Burnsides had selected
and hurried Jackson on, and placed him some miles to our
right, near Hamilton's Crossing, on the Richmond and Fredericksburg Railroad. When Burnsides became aware of the
mighty obstacle of Lee's battalions between him and his goal,
the deep, sluggish river separating the two armies, he realized
the trouble that lay in his path. He began fortifying the
ridges running parallel to and near the river, and built a great
chain of forts along "Stafford Heights," opposite Fredericksburg. In these forts he mounted one hundred and thirty-
seven guns, forty being siege pieces brought down from Washington by way of the Potomac and Acquia Creek, and lined the
entire range of hills with his heaviest and long-distanced field
batteries. These forts and batteries commanded the river and
plain beyond, as well as every height and elevation on the
Southern side. The range of hills on the opposite side were
much higher and more commanding than those on the Southern side, still Lee began fortifying Taylor's, Mayree's, and
Lee's Heights, and all the intervening hills also, by building
forts and heavy redoubts, with protected embrasures on the
flanks. Between these hills and along their crests the infantry
threw up light earthworks. It could not be said that ours
was a fortified position in any sense, only through natural
barriers. There is a plain of a half to a mile in width between
the river and the range to the South, commencing at Taylor's
Hill, half a mile above the city, and widening as it diverges
from the river below, terminating in a broken plateau down
near Hamilton's Crossing. The highlands on the opposite
side come rather precipitous to the water's edge. Along the
banks, on either side, were rifle pits, in which were kept from
three to five pickets, and on our side a brigade was stationed
night and day in the city as a support to the videttes guarding
the river front. These pickets were directed to prevent a
crossing at all hazards until the troops at camp in the rear
were all in position in front of Fredericksburg. Stuart, with
the body of his cavalry, guarded the river and country on our
right below Jackson, while Hampton kept a lookout at the
crossings above on the left of Longstreet.

On the morning of the 11th, at 3 o'clock, when all was still
and the soldiers fast asleep, they were rudely aroused from

12

their slumbers by the deep boom of a cannon away to the front
and across the river. Scarcely had the sound of the first gun
died away than another report thundered out on the stillness
of that December night, its echo reverberating from hill to hill
and down along the river side. These sounds were too ominous to be mistaken; they were the signal guns that were to
put in motion these two mighty armies. "Fall in" was the
word given, and repeated from hill to hill and camp to camp.
Drums beat the long roll at every camp, while far below and
above the blast of the bugle called the troopers to "boots and
saddle." Couriers dashed headlong in the sombre darkness
from one General's headquarters to another's. Adjutants' and
Colonels' orderlies were rushing from tent to tent, arousing
the officers and men to arms, and giving instructions for the
move.

I can remember well the sharp, distinct voice of Adjutant
Y. J. Pope on that morning, coming down the line of the
officers' tents and calling out to each as he came opposite:
"Captain ———, get your company ready to move at once."

Under such orders, companies have that same rivalry to be
first on the parade ground as exists among fire companies in
towns and cities when the fire bell rings. We were all soon
in line and marching with a hasty step in the direction of the
breastworks above the city, Kershaw taking position immediately to the right of the Telegraph Road. This is a public
highway leading into the city, curving in a semi-circle around
Mayree Hill on the left. From this road the hill rises on the
west and north in a regular bluff—a stone wall of five feet in
height bordering either side of the road. "Deep Run", a
small ravine, runs between the hill on which Kershaw was
stationed and that of Mayree's. Daylight was yet some hours
off when we took position, but we could hear the rattle of the
guns of Barksdale's Mississippians, whose turn it was to be on
picket in the city, driving off the enemy's pontoon corps and
bridge builders.

The city was almost deserted, General Lee advising the citizens to leave their homes as soon as it became apparent that a
battle would be fought here. Still a few, loath to leave their
all to the ravages of an army, decided to remain and trust to
fate. But soon after the firing along the river began, we saw

groups of women and children and a few old men in the glim twilight of the morning rushing along the roads out from the city as fast as their feeble limbs and tender feet could carry them, hunting a safe retreat in the backwoods until the cloud of war broke or passed over. Some were carrying babes in their arms, others dragging little children along by the hands, with a few articles of bedding or wearing apparel under their arms or thrown over their shoulders. The old men tottered along in the rear, giving words of comfort and cheer to the excited and frightened women and little ones. It was a sickening sight to see these helpless and inoffensive people hurrying away from the dangers of battle in the chilly morning of December, seeking some safe haunt in the backwoods, yet they bore it all without murmur or complaint.

Anderson's Division of Longstreet's Corps rested on the river on the extreme left, at Taylor's Hill; then Ransom's along the crest of the ridge between Taylor's and Mayree's, and McLaws' from his left across Deep Run Valley and along the ridge to Lee's Hill, where Pickett was posted; Hood extending from Pickett's right, touching the left of the troops of Jackson's Corps. Three of Cobb's regiments and one from North Carolina were posted behind the stone wall lining the sunken road, while two of Cooke's North Carolina regiments were on the crest of Mayree's Hill overlooking Cobb. Kershaw's Brigade, with the Third South Carolina on the left, was resting on the ridge running at right angles to the Telegraph Road, the left resting on the road, the Second South Carolina next, and so on to the left of Semmes' Brigade. Barksdale being in the city on picket, was relieved and placed in reserve.

As soon as the signal guns gave evidence of an impending battle, D. H. Hill, who had been sent on detached service down the river, was recalled and placed in line with the other portion of Jackson's Corps. Jackson had his entire force closely massed in the woodland around Hamilton's Crossing and along the Richmond and Fredericksburg Railroad, one mile from the river. The Light Division of A. P. Hill occupied the front line, with a heavy battery of fourteen guns on his right, supported by Archer's Brigade; then Lane's and Pender's in front, with Gregg's and Thomas' in reserve.

Behind the Light Division lay Early on the right, Taliafer
on the left, with D. H. Hill in rear of all along the Mi
Road, the right of these divisions resting on Hamilton's Cro
ing.   Hood occupied the valley between Lee's Hill and tl
highland around Hamilton's Crossing; Pickett on the rid;
between Hood and McLaws; Stuart's Cavalry ran at rig
angles to the infantry line from Hamilton's Crossing to tl
river, hemming the Federal Army in the plain between Har
ilton's Crossing and Taylor's Hill above the city, a space thr
miles long by one wide.

Before day the enemy's pontoon corps came cautiously
the river and began operations at laying down the bridge, b
the pickets in the rifle pits kept them off for a time by the
steady fire.   The manner of putting down army bridges
much more simple and rapid than the old country mode
building.   Large boats are loaded on long-coupled wagor
the boats filled with plank for flooring and cross beams, wi
a large iron ring in the rear end of each boat, through whi
a stout rope is to run, holding them at equal distance when
the water.   When all is ready the boats are launched at eqt
distance so that the beams can reach, then pushed out in t
stream, and floated around in a semi-circle, until the oppos:
bank is reached, the rope fastened to trees on either ban
cross pieces are laid, the flooring put down, and the bridge
ready for crossing.

After making several ineffectual attempts in placing t
bridge, the destructive fire of Barksdale's Riflemen forci;
them back, the enemy attempted the bold project of filling t
boats with armed soldiers, pushing out in the stream, a
fighting their way across, under cover of their artillery fir
While the dense fog was yet hanging heavily over the wate
one hundred and forty guns, many siege pieces, were open
upon the deserted city and the men along the water front.   T
roar from the cannon-crowned battlements shook the very eart
Above and below us seemed to vibrate as from the effects of
mighty upheaval, while the shot and shell came whizzing a
shrieking overhead, looking like a shower of falling meteo
For more than an hour did this seething volcano vomit ir
like hail upon the city and the men in the rifle pits, t
shells and shot from the siege guns tearing through t

houses and plunging along the streets, and ricocheting to the hills above. Not a house nor room nor chimney escaped destruction. Walls were perforated, plastering and ceiling fell, chimneys tottering or spreading over yards and out into the streets. Not a place of safety, save the cellars and wells, and in the former some were forced to take refuge. Yet through all this, the brave Mississippians stood and bravely fought the bridge builders, beating them back till orders were given to retire. They had accomplished the purpose of delaying the enemy's crossing until our troops were in position. The Federals now hurried over in swarms, by thousands and tens of thousands, and made their way down the river, stationing a strong cordon of guards around the point of landing. The space between was soon a seething mass of humanity, the houses and streets crowded to overflowing. A second bridge was laid a mile below at the mouth of Deep Run, and here a continuous stream of all arms were soon pouring over. General Kershaw rode along our lines, encouraging the men, urging them to stand steadfast, assuring them that there was to be neither an advance nor retreat, that we were but to hold our ground, and one of the greatest victories of the war would be gained. How prophetic his words! All during the day and night the deep rumbling sound of the long wagon trains, artillery, and cavalry could be heard crossing the pontoon bridges above and below.

The next morning, the 12th, as the fog lifted, Stafford Heights and the inclines above the river were one field of blue. Great lines of infantry, with waving banners, their bright guns and bayonets glittering in the sunlight, all slowly marching down the steep inclines between the heights and the river on over the bridges, then down the river side at a double-quick to join their comrades of the night before. These long, swaying lines, surging in and out among the jutting of the hillsides beyond, down to the river, over and down among the trees and bushes near the water, resembled some monster serpent dragging its "weary length along." Light batteries of artillery came dashing at break-neck speed down the hillsides, their horses rearing and plunging as if wishing to take the river at a leap. Cavalry, too, with their heavy-bodied Norman horses, their spurs digging the flanks, sabres bright and glistening

and dangling at their sides, came at a canter, all seeming anx—
ious to get over and meet the death and desolation awaiting
them. Long trains of ordnance wagons, with their black oil—
cloth covering, the supply trains and quartermaster depart—
ments all following in the wake of their division or corps head—
quarters, escorts, and trains. All spread out over the hills
and in the gorges lay men by the thousands, awaiting their
turn to move. Not a shot nor shell to mar or disturb "the
even tenor of their way."   Bands of music enlivened the scene
by their inspiring strains, and when some national air, or
specially martial piece, would be struck up, shouts and yells
rended the air for miles, to be answered by counter yells from
the throats of fifty thousand "Johnny Rebs," as the Southern
soldiers were called. The Confederate bands were not idle,
for as soon as a Federal band would cease playing, some of the
Southern bands would take up the refrain, and as the notes,
especially Dixie, would be wafted over the water and hills, the
"blue coats" would shout, sing, and dance—hats and caps
went up, flags waved in the breeze—so delighted were they at
the sight and sound of Dixie. The whole presented more the
spectacle of a holiday procession, or a gala day, rather than
the prelude to the most sanguinary battle of modern times.

The night following was cold, and a biting wind was blowing. Only a few days before a heavy snow had fallen. and in
some places it still remained banked up in shaded corners.
To those who had to stand picket out in the plain between
the armies the cold was fearful. The enemy had no fires
outside of the city, and their sufferings from cold must have
been severe. My company, from the Third, as well as one
from each of the other regiments, were on picket duty, posted
in an open cornfield in the plain close to the enemy, near
enough, in fact, to hear voices in either camp—with no fire,
and not allowed to speak above a whisper. The night became
so intensely cold just before day that the men gathered corn-
stalks and kindled little fires along the beat, and at early dawn
we were withdrawn.

All knew full well, as the day preceding had passed without
any demonstrations, only manouvering. this day, the 13th,
would be a day of battle. A heavy fog, as usual, rose from
the river and settled along the plains and hillsides, so much so

that objects could not be distinguished twenty paces. However, the least noise could be heard at a great distance. Activity in the Federal camp was noticed early in the morning. Officers could be heard giving commands, wagons and artillery moving to positions. At half past ten the fog suddenly lifted, and away to our right and near the river great columns of men were moving, marching and counter-marching. These were in front of A. P. Hill, of Jackson's Corps. In front of us and in the town all was still and quiet as a city of the dead. The great siege guns from beyond the river on Stafford Heights opened the battle by a dozen or more shells screaming through the tree tops and falling in Jackson's camp. From every fort soon afterwards a white puff of smoke could be seen, then a vivid flash and a deafening report, telling us that the enemy was ready and waiting. From the many field batteries between Jackson and the river the smoke curled up around the tree tops, and shell went crashing through the timbers. Our batteries along the front of Longstreet's Corps opened their long-ranged guns on the redoubts beyond the river, and our two siege guns on Lee's Hill, just brought up from Richmond, paid special attention to the columns moving to the assault of A. P. Hill. For one hour the earth and air seemed to tremble and shake beneath the shock of three hundred guns, and the bursting of thousands of shells overhead, before and behind us, looked like bursting stars on a frolic. The activity suddenly ceases in front of Hill, and the enemy's infantry lines move to the front. First the skirmishers meet, and their regular firing tells the two armies that they are near together. Then the skirmish fire gives way to the deep, sullen roar of the line of battle. From our position, some three hundred yards in rear and to the right of Mayree's Hill, we could see the Union columns moving down the river, our batteries raking them with shot and shell. In crossing an old unfinished railroad cut the two siege guns played upon the flank with fearful effect. Huddling down behind the walls of the cut to avoid the fire in front, the batteries from Mayree's and in the fields to the right enfiladed the position, the men rushing hither and thither and falling in heaps from the deadly fire in front and flank. Jackson has been engaged in a heavy battle for nearly an hour, when suddenly in our front tens of

thousands of "blue coats" seemed to spring up out of the
earth and make for our lines. Near one-half of the army had
concealed themselves in the city and along the river banks,
close to the water's edge. The foliage of the trees and the
declivity of the ground having hidden them thus far from
view. From out of the streets and from behind walls and
houses men poured, as if by some magical process or super-
human agency, and formed lines of battle behind a little rise in
the ground, near the canal. But in a few moments they
emerged from their second place of protection and bore down
upon the stone wall, behind which stood Cobb's Georgians and
a Regiment of North Carolinians. When midway between
the canal and stone fence, they met an obstruction—a plank
fence—but this did not delay them long. It was soon dashed
to the ground and out of their way, but their men were falling
at every step from Cobb's infantry fire and grape and canister
from the Washington Artillery of New Orleans on the hill.
They never neared the wall nor did they take more time than to
fire a volley or two before they fled the field. This retreating
column of Franklin's met that of Hancock's, formed, and on
its way to try issues with the troops behind the stone wall.
Longstreet now saw what had never been considered before—
that Burnsides was determined to possess himself of the key to
Lee's position, "Mayree's Hill," in front of which was the
stone wall. He ordered the two regiments of North Carolinians that were posted on the crest of the hill down behind the
stone wall, to the left of Cobb and Kershaw, to reinforce the
position with his brigade.

The Third Regiment being ordered to the top of Mayree's
Hill, Colonel Nance, at the head of his regiment, entered the
Telegraph Road, and down this the men rushed, followed by
the Second, led by Colonel Kennedy, under one of the heaviest
shellings the troops ever experienced. This two hundred yards'
stretch of road was in full view and range of the heavy gun
batteries on Stafford Heights, and as the men scattered out
along and down the road, the shells passed, plowing in the
road, bursting overhead, or striking the earth and ricocheting
to the hills far in the rear. On reaching the ravine, at the
lower end of the incline, the Third Regiment was turned to
the left and up a by-road to the plateau in rear of the "Mayree

Col. William Drayton Rutherford,
3d S. C. Regiment.
(Page 485.)

Col. D. Wyatt Aiken,
7th S. C. Regiment.
(Page 100.)

Col. E. T Stackhouse,
8th S. C. Regiment.
(Page 285.)

Lieut. Col. B. B. Foster,
3d S. C. Regiment.
(Page 164.)

Mansion." The house tops in the city were lined with sharp-shooters, and from windows and doors and from behind houses the deadly missiles from the globe-sighted rifles made sad havoc in our ranks.

When the Third reached the top of the plateau it was in column of fours, and Colonel Nance formed line of battle by changing "front forward on first company." This pretty piece of tactics was executed while under the galling fire from the artillery and sharp-shooters, but was as perfect as on dress parade. The regiment lined up, the right resting on the house and extending along a dull road to the next street leading into the city. We had scarcely gotten in position before Nance, Rutherford, and Maffett, the three field officers, had fallen. Colonel Kennedy, with the Second, passed over the left of the plateau and down the street on our left, and at right angles with our line, being in a position to give a sweeping fire to the flank of the columns of assault against the stone fence. From the preparation and determination made to break through the line here, Kershaw ordered Lieutenant Colonel Bland, with the Seventh, Colonel Henegan, with the Eighth, and Colonel DeSaussure, with the Fifteenth, to double-up with Cobb's men, and to hold their position "at the sacrifice of every man of their commands."

All of the different regiments, with the exception of the Third South Carolina, had good protection in the way of stone walls, this being the sole occasion that any of Kershaw's troops had been protected by breastworks of any kind during the whole war. The Second was in a sunken road leading to the city, walled on either side with granite, the earth on the outside being leveled up with the top. The manouvering into position had taken place while Hancock was making the first assault upon the wall defended by Cobb. Howard was now preparing to make the doubtful attempt at taking the strong-hold with the point of the bayonet, and without firing a gun. But with such men as the Georgians, South Carolinians, and North Carolinians in their front, the task proved too Hercu-lean. Howard moved to the battle in beautiful style, their line almost solid and straight, their step in perfect unison with the long, moving columns, their guns carried at a trail, and the stars and stripes floating proudly above their heads. The

shot and shell plunging through their ranks from the hill
above, the two siege guns on Lee's Hill now in beautiful play
the brass pieces of the Washington Artillery firing with grap
and shrapnell—but all this made no break nor halt in tha
long line of blue.   The double column behind the stone wal
and the Third South Carolina on the crest of the Hill me
them in front with a cool and steady fire, while the Secon
South Carolina directed its attention to the flank.   But th
boldest and stoutest hearts could not withstand this withering
blast of bullets and shells without returning the fire.   Th
enemy opened upon us a terrific fire, both from the column
in front and from the sharp-shooters in the housetops in th
city.   After giving us battle as long as human enduranc
could bear the ordeal, they, like their companions before them
fled in confusion.

Before making the direct attack, Howard attempted a diver
sion by endeavoring to turn Cobb's left.   Passing out into th
plain above the city, he was met by some of Cooke's Nortl
Carolinians, and there around the sacred tomb of Mary Wash
ington was a hand to hand encounter between some New Yorl
and Massachusetts troops and those from the Pine Tree State
Sons of the same ancestry, sons of sires who fought with th
"Father of his Country" in the struggle for the nation's inde
pendence, now fighting above the grave of the mother for it
dissolution!   Thrice were the Confederates driven from th
position, but as often retaken, and at last held at the point o
the bayonet by the hardy sons of North Carolina.

The battle, grand and awful in its sublimity, raged from th
morning's opening till two o'clock, without the least abate
ment along the whole line.   From the extreme right to ou
left at Taylor's Hill was a sea of fire.   But Mayree's Hill wa
the center, around which all the other battles revolved.   I
was the key to Lee's position, and this had become the boo
of contention.   It was in the taking of Mayree's Hill and th
defeat of the troops defending it that the North was pourin
out its river of blood.   Both commanders were still preparin
to stake their all upon this hazard of the die—the discipline o
the North against the valor of the South.

Our loss was heavy, both in officers and men.   The brave
chivalric Cobb, of Georgia, had fallen.   Of the Third Soutl

Carolina, Colonel Nance, Lieutenant Colonel Rutherford, and Major Maffett had all been severely wounded in the early part of the engagement. Captain Hance, while commanding, fell pierced through the heart. Then the next in command, Captain Summer, met a similar fate; then Captain Foster. Captain Nance, the junior Captain in the regiment, retained the command during the continuance of the fight, although painfully wounded. The dead of the Third Regiment lay in heaps, like hogs in a slaughter pen. The position of the Second Regiment gave it great advantage over the advancing column. From a piaza in rear of the sunken road, Colonel Kennedy posted himself, getting a better view, and to better direct the firing Lieutenant Colonel William Wallace remained with the men in the road, and as the column of assault reached the proper range, he ordered a telling fire on the enemy's flank. Men in the road would load the guns for those near the wall, thus keeping up a continual fire, and as the enemy scattered over the plain in their retreat, then was the opportunity for the Second and Third, from their elevated positions and better view, to give them such deadly parting salutes. The smoke in front of the stone wall became so dense that the troops behind it could only fire at the flashing of the enemy's guns. From the Third's position, it was more dangerous for its wounded to leave the field than remain on the battle line, the broad, level plateau in rear almost making it suicidal to raise even as high as a stooping posture.

From the constant, steady, and uninterrupted roll of musketry far to the right, we knew Jackson was engaged in a mighty struggle. From the early morning's opening the noise of his battle had been gradually bearing to the rear. He was being driven from position to position, and was meeting with defeat and possibly disaster. From the direction of his fire our situation was anything but assuring.

General Meade, of the Federal Army, had made the first morning attack upon the Light Brigade, under A. P. Hill, throwing that column in confusion and driving it back upon the second line. These troops were not expecting the advance, and some had their guns stacked. The heavy fog obscured the Federal lines until they were almost within pistol shot. When it·was discovered that an enemy was in their front (in fact some thought them their friends), in this confusion of troops a retreat was ordered to the second line. In this surprise and disorder South Carolina lost one of her most gifted sons, and the South a brave and accomplished officer, Brigadier General Maxcy Gregg.

General Hood, on Hill's left, failing to move in time to give him the support expected, the whole of Jackson's Corps was forced to retire. But the tide at length begins to turn. Meade is driven from the field. Division after division was rushed to the front to meet and check Jackson's steady advance. Cannon now boom as never before heard, even the clear ringing of Pelham's little howitzers, of Stuart's Cavalry, could be heard above the thunder of the big guns, telling us that Stuart was putting his horse artillery in the balance. His brave artillery leader was raking the enemy's flank as they fell back on the river. In our front new troops were being marshalled and put in readiness to swell the human holocaust before the fatal wall.

Franklin, Hancock, and Howard had made unsuccessful attempts upon this position, leaving their wounded and dead lying in heaps and wind rows from the old railroad cut to the suburbs. Now Sturgis, of the Ninth Corps, was steadily advancing. The Washington Artillery, from New Orleans, occupying the most conspicuous and favorable position on the right of the "Mayree House," had exhausted their shot and shell. The infantry in the road and behind the wall, Cobb's and part of Kershaw's, were nearly out of ammunition, and during the last charge had been using that of their dead and wounded. Calls were made on all sides for "more ammunition," both from the artillery and infantry. Orders and details had been sent to the ordnance trains to bring supplies to the front. But the orders had miscarried, or the trains were too far distant, for up to three o'clock no sign of replenishment was in sight. The hearts of the exhausted men began to fail them—the batteries silent, the infantry short of ammunition, while a long line of blue was making rapid strides towards us in front.

But now all hearts were made glad by the sudden rush of Alexander's Battery coming to the relief of the Washington Artillery. Down the Telegraph Road the battery came, their horses rearing and plunging, drivers burying the points of their spurs deep into the flanks of the foaming steeds; riders in front bending low upon the saddle bows to escape the shells that now filled the air, or plowing up the earth beneath the horses hoofs; the men on the caissons clinging with a death-like grip to retain their seats, the great heavy wheels spinning around like mad and bounding high in the air; while the officers riding at the side of this charging column of artillerists, shouted at the top of thier voices, giving directions to the leaders. Down this open and exposed stretch of road, up over the plateau, then wheel to the right, they make a rush through the gauntlet that separates them from the fort in which stood the Washington Artillery. Over the dead and dying the horses leap and plunge, dragging the cannon and ammunition chests—they enter the fort at a gallop. Swinging into line, their brass pieces are now belching forth grape and canister into the ranks of the advancing columns. All this takes place in less time than it takes to record it. The bold dash and beautiful piece of evolution so excite the admiration of all who witnessed it, that a yell went up that drowns for a time the heavy baying of the siege guns on Stafford Heights.

About this time Jackson seems to have reached his limit of retreat, and was now forging steadily to the front, regaining every inch of the lost ground of the morning. The Federal Commander-in-Chief, seeing the stubborn resistance he is met with in front of the city, and Jackson's gray lines pressing his left back upon the river, began to feel the hopelessness of his battle, and sent orders to Franklin to attack Jackson with his entire force. Hooker was to reinforce Sumner on the right, the latter to take the stone wall and the heights beyond before night. Sturgis had met the fate of those who had assaulted before him. Now Getty and Griffin were making frantic efforts to reach the wall. Griffin had his men concealed and protected in the wet, marshy bed of the old canal. He now undertook to accomplish that which Howard had attempted in the morning, and failed—the feat of taking the stone walls with empty guns.

In this column of assault was the famous Meager's Irish Brigade, of New York,—all Irishmen, but undoubtedly the finest body of troops in the Federal Army. When the signal for advance was given, from out of their hiding places they sprang—from the canal, the bushes on the river bank, the side streets in the city, one compact row of glittering bayonets came —in long battle lines. General Kershaw, seeing the preparation made for this final and overwhelming assault upon our jaded troops, sent Captain Doby, of his staff, along our lines with orders to hold our position at all hazards, even at the point of the bayonet.

As the rifle balls from the housetops and shells from the batteries along the river banks sang their peculiar death notes overhead and around us, this brave and fearless officer made the entire length of the line, exhorting, entreating, and urging the men to redoubled efforts. How Captain Doby escaped death is little less than miraculous.

The casualties of battle among the officers and the doubling up process of the men behind the wall caused all order of organization to be lost sight of, and each man loaded and fired as he saw best. The men in the road, even the wounded, crowded out from the wall by force of number, loaded the guns for the more fortunate who had places, and in many instances three and four men loaded the guns for one, passing them to those who were firing from the top of the stone fence. Each seemed to fight on his own responsibility, and with the same determined spirit to hold the wall and the heights above. Each felt as if the safety of the army depended upon his exertions alone.

With a firm and elastic step this long, swaying line of Irishmen moved to the assault with as much indifference apparently to their fate as "sheep going to the shambles." Not a shot was fired from this advancing column, while the shells from our batteries cut swath after swath through their ranks, only to be closed again as if by some mechanical means; colors fall, but rise and float again, men bounding forward and eagerly grasping the fallen staff, indifferent of the fate that awaited them. Officers are in front, with drawn swords flashing in the gleam of the fading sunlight, urging on their men to still greater deeds of prowess, and by their individual courage set examples in heroism never before witnessed on this continent. The assault upon Mayree's Hill by the Irish Brigade and their compatriots will go down in history as only equalled by the famous ride of the "Six Hundred at Hohenlinden," and the "Charge of the Light Brigade at Balaclava." They forge their way forward over the heap of dead and dying that now strew the plain, nearer to the deadly wall than any of the troops before them. It began to look for the moment as if their undaunted courage would succeed, but the courage of the defenders of Mayree's Hill seemed to increase in ardour and determination in proportion to that of the enemy. The smoke and flame of their battle is now less than one hundred paces from the wall, but the odds are against them, and they, too, had to finally yield to the inevitable and leave the field in great disorder.

From both sides hopes and prayers had gone up that this charge would prove the last attempt to break our lines. But Humphries met the shattered columns with a fresh advance. Those who were marching to enter this maelstrom of carnage were entreated and prayed to by all of those who had just returned from the sickening scene not to enter this death trap, and begged them not to throw away their lives in the vain attempt to accomplish the impossible. But Humphries, anxious of glory for himself and men, urged on by the imperative orders from his Commander-in-Chief, soon had his men on the march to the "bloody wall." But as the sun dropped behind the hills in our rear, the scene that presented itself in the fading gloom of that December day was a plain filled with the dead and dying—a living stream of flying fugitives seeking shelter from the storm of shot and shell by plunging over the precipitous banks of the river, or along the streets and protecting walls of the city buildings.

Jackson had pressed all in his front back to the water's edge, while his batteries, with those of Stuart's, were still throwing shells into the huddled, panic-stricken, and now thoroughly vanquished army of the enemy.

That night the Federal Commander-in-Chief sat in his tent alone, and around him the groans of the wounded and the agonizing wails of the dying greet his ear—the gentle wind singing a requiem to his dead. He nursed alone the bitter consciousness of the total defeat of his army, now a scattered mass—a skeleton of its former greatness—while the flower of the Northern chivalry lie sleeping the sleep of death on the

hills and plains round about. His country and posterity woul
charge him with all the responsibility of defeat, and he fel
that his brief command of the once grand and mighty Arm
of the Potomac was now at an end. Sore and bitter recollec
tions!

Burnsides had on the field one hundred and thirty-two thou
sand and seventeen men; of these one hundred and sixtee
thousand six hundred and eighty-three were in line of battle
Lee had upon the field and ready for action sixty-nine thou
sand three hundred and ninety-one infantry and artillery, an
about five thousand cavalry. Burnsides had three hundre
and seventy pieces of field artillery and forty siege gun
mounted on Stafford's Heights. Lee had three hundred an
twelve pieces of field and heavy artillery, with two siege guns
both exploding, one in the early part of the day.

The enemy's loss was twelve thousand six hundred an
fifty-three, of which at least eight thousand fell in front of th
stone wall. It has been computed by returns made since tha
in the seven different charges there were engaged at leas
twenty-five thousand infantry alone in the assaults against th
stone wall, defended by not more than four thousand men
exclusive of artillery. Lee's entire loss was five thousan
three hundred and twenty-two killed, wounded, and missing
and one of the strangest features of this great battle, one i
which so many men of all arms were engaged, the enormou
loss of life on both sides, and the close proximity of such
large body of cavalry, the returns of the battle only giv
thirteen wounded and none killed of the entire cavalry force o
the Confederate side.

The men who held the stone wall and Mayree's Hill wer
three regiments of Cooke's North Carolina Brigade; the Six
teenth Georgia, Colonel Bryan; the Eighteenth Georgia, Lieu
tenant Colonel Ruff; the Twenty-fourth Georgia, Colone
McMillan; the Cobb Legion and Philip Legion, Colonel Cool
of General T. R. R. Cobb's Brigade; the Second South Care
lina, Colonel Kennedy; the Third South Carolina, Colone
Nance, Lieutenant Colonel Rutherford, Major Maffett, Cap
tains Summer, Hance, Foster, and Nance; the Seventh Sout
Carolina, Lieutenant Colonel Bland; the Eighth South Care
lina, Colonel Henegan and Major Stackhouse; the Fifteent

South Carolina, Colonel DeSaussure; the Third Battalion, Major Rice, of Kershaw's Brigade; the Washington Battery, of New Orleans, and Alexander's Battery, from Virginia. The brigades from Hood's and Pickett's Divisions, Jenkins, of South Carolina, being from the latter, were sent to the support of McLaws, at Mayree's Hill, and only acted as reserve and not engaged.

The next day, as if by mutual consent, was a day of rest. The wounded were gathered in as far as we were able to reach them. The enemy's wounded lay within one hundred yards of the stone wall for two days and nights, and their piteous calls for help and water were simply heart-rending. Whenever one of our soldiers attempted to relieve the enemy lying close under our wall, he would be fired upon by the pickets and guards in the house tops.

On the night of the 15th, the Federal Army, like strolling Arabs "folded their tents and silently stole away." The 16th was given up entirely to the burial of the dead. In the long line of pits, dug as protection for the enemy while preparing for a charge, these putrefying bodies were thrown headlong, pell mell, like the filling of blind ditches with timbers. One Confederate would get between the legs of the dead enemy, take a foot in either hand, then two others would each grasp an arm, and drag at a run the remains of the dead enemy and heave it over in the pit. In this way these pits or ditches were filled almost to a level of the surface, a little dirt thrown over them, there to remain until the great United States Government removed them to the beautiful park around Mayree's Heights. There to this day, and perhaps for all time, sleep the "blue and the gray," while the flag so disastrously beaten on that day now floats in triumph over all.

It must be said to the credit of General Burnsides, that the responsibility for this disastrous battle should not rest upon his shoulders. He felt his incapacity for handling so great a body of troops. Again and again he wrote the authorities in Washington protesting against the command being given him. "I am unable to handle so great an army," he wrote his chief, but in vain. The fiat had gone forth, "Go and crush Lee," and the result was to have been expected.

CHAPTER XIV

Incidents of the Battle—Comparisons With Other Engagements.

The Battle of Fredericksburg was not the most desperate nor bloody of the war, nor was it so fruitful of events as others in its bearing on future results. Really neither side gained nor lost any great advantage; nor was the battle any more to the Confederate side than a great victory barren of ulterior results; the loss to the Federals no more than the loss of a number of men and the lowering of the morale among the troops. Within a day or two both armies occupied the same positions as before the battle. Not wishing to attempt any invidious comparisons or reflections upon troops in wars of other periods, but for the information of those who are not conversant with the magnitude of the Civil War, as compared with the Revolution and Mexican War, I will here give a few statistics. The reader then can draw his own conclusions as to the sanguinary effects and extent of some of our battles. Of course the different kinds of weapons used in the late war— their deadly effect, long range, better mode of firing—will have to be considered in comparison to the old.

As the Revolutionary War was more of a guerilla than actual war, I will speak more directly of the Mexican War. It will be noticed the difference in the killed to the wounded was far out of proportion in favor of the latter. This I attribute to the smallness of the gun's calibre, and in many instances buck-shot were used in connection with larger balls by the soldiers of the old wars, while the Mexicans used swords and lances, as well as pistols. During the three days' battle at Molino del Rey, Chapultepec, and the storming of the City of Mexico, considered the most bloody and sanguinary of that war, the four divisions of Scott's Army, of two thousand each, lost as follows: Pillow lost one officer killed and fourteen wounded, twenty-one privates killed and ninety-seven wounded. Worth lost two officers killed and nine wounded, twenty-three privates killed and ninety-five wounded.

Quitman lost four officers killed and thirty wounded, thirty-seven privates killed and two hundred and thirty-seven wounded. Smith's Brigade, with Quitman, lost ten officers wounded and none killed, twenty-four privates killed and one hundred and twenty-six wounded. Twigg's Division lost three officers killed and twelve wounded, fifteen privates killed and seventy-seven wounded. This, with some few missing, making a grand total loss, out of Scott's Army of nine to ten thousand men, of between six hundred and fifty and seven hundred killed, wounded, and missing—a number that Kershaw's Brigade alone frequently lost in three or four hours.

The heaviest casualties in the three days' battle of Mexico in regiments were in the Palmetto Regiment and the Kentucky Rifles, where the former lost two officers killed and nine wounded, fourteen privatas killed and seventy-five wounded; the latter lost six officers wounded and none killed, nine privates killed and sixty-four wounded. When it is remembered that the Third Regiment in the battle with about three hundred and fifty and four hundred men in line lost six regimental commanders killed and wounded, not less than three times that number of other officers killed and wounded, and more than one hundred and fifty men killed and wounded, some idea can be had of its bloody crisis and deadly struggle, in which our troops were engaged, in comparison to the patriots in Mexico.

But considering the close proximity of the troops engaged at Fredericksburg, the narrow compass in which they were massed, the number of elevated positions suitable for artillery on either side, and the number of troops on the field, the wonder is why the casualties were not even greater than the reports make them. Burnsides, from the nature of the ground, could not handle more than half his army, as by official returns not more than fifty thousand were in line of battle and in actual combat. There were only two points at which he could extend his line, and if at one he found a "Scylla," he was equally sure to find a "Charybdis" at the other. On his left flank Jackson's whole corps was massed, at Hamilton's Crossing; at his right was the stone wall and Mayree's Hill. To meet Hood and Pickett he would have had to advance between a quarter and half mile through a plain, where his army could be enfiladed by the guns of Longstreet and Jackson, and in front by the batteries of Hood and Pickett. It seems from reports since come to light that the authorities at Washington apprehended more danger in Burnsides crossing the river than in the battle that was to follow. Lincoln in giving him orders as to his movements instructed his Secretary of War, Stanton, to write Burnsides to be very careful in the crossing, to guard his flanks well, and not allow Lee to fall upon one part that had crossed and crush it before the other part could come to the rescue; nor allow that wing of the army yet remaining on the Northern side to be attacked and destroyed while the other had crossed to the Southern side. It is said Stanton wrote the order couched in the best of English, and phrased in elegant terms the instructions above, telling him to guard his flanks, etc., then read the order to Lincoln for his approval. Taking up the pen, the President endorsed it, and wrote underneath, in his own hand: "In crossing the river don't allow yourself to be caught in the fix of a cow, hurried by dogs, in jumping a fence, get hung in the middle, so that she can't either use her horns in front, nor her heels behind."

Many incidents of courage and pathos could be written of this, as well as many other battles, but one that I think the crowning act of courage and sympathy for an enemy in distress is due was that of a Georgian behind the wall. In one of the first charges made during the day a Federal had fallen and to protect himself as much as possible from the bullets of his enemies, he had by sheer force of will pulled his body along until he had neared the wall. Then he failed through pure exhaustion. From loss of blood and the exposure of the sun's rays, he called loudly for water. "Oh, somebody bring me a drink of water!—water! water!!" was the piteous appeal heard by those behind the stone wall. To go to his rescue was to court certain death, as the housetops to the left were lined with sharpshooters, ready to fire upon anyone showing his head above the wall. But one brave soldier from Georgia dared all, and during the lull in the firing leaped the wall, rushed to the wounded soldier, and raising his head in his arms, gave him a drink of water, then made his way back a an

Over the wall amid a hail of bullets knocking the dirt up all around him.

The soldier, like the sailor, is proverbial for his superstition. But at times certain incidents or coincidents take place in the life of the soldier that are inexplainable, to say the least. Now it is certain that every soldier going into battle has some dread of death. It is the nature of man to dread that long lost sleep at any time and in any place. He knows that death is a master of all, and all must yield to its inexorable summons, and that summons is more likely to come in battle than on ordinary occasions. That at certain times soldiers do have a premonition of their coming death, has been proven on many occasions. Not that I say all soldiers foretell their end by some kind of secret monster, but that some do, or seem to do so. Captain Summer, of my company, was an unusually good-humored and lively man, and while he was not what could be called profane, yet he had little predilection toward piety or the Church. In other battles he advanced to the front as light-hearted and free from care as if going on drill or inspection. When we were drawn up in line of battle at Fredericksburg the first morning an order came for the Captain. He was not present, and on enquiry, I was told that he had gone to a cluster of bushes in the rear. Thinking the order might be of importance, I hastened to the place, and there I found Captain Summer on his knees in prayer. I rallied him about his "sudden piety," and in a jesting manner accused him of "weakening." After rising from his kneeling posture, I saw he was calm, pale, and serious—so different from his former moods in going into battle. I began teasing him in a bantering way about being a "coward." "No," said he, "I am no coward, and will show I have as much nerve, if not more, than most men in the army, for all have doubts of death, but I have none. I will be killed in this battle. I feel it as plainly as I feel I am living, but I am no coward, and shall go in this battle and fight with the same spirit that I have always shown." This was true. He acted bravely, and for the few moments that he commanded the regiment he exhibited all the daring a brave man could, but he fell shot through the brains with a minnie ball. He had given me messages to his young wife, to whom he had been married only about two months, before entering the services, as to the disposition of his effects, as well as his body after death.

Another instance was that of Lieutenant Hill, of Company G, Third South Carolina Regiment. The day before the battle he asked permission to return to camp that night, a distance perhaps of three miles. With a companion he returned to the camp, procured water, bathed himself, and changed his under-clothing. On being asked by his companion why he wished to walk three miles at night to simply bathe and change his clothing, with perfect unconcern he replied: "In the coming battle I feel that I will be killed, and such being the case, I could not bear the idea of dying and being buried in soiled clothes." He fell dead at the first volley. Was there ever such courage as this—to feel that death was so certain and that it could be prevented by absenting themselves from battle, but allowed their pride, patriotism, and moral courage to carry them on to sure death?

In the case of a private in Company C, Third Regiment, it was different. He did not have the moral courage to resist the "secret monitor," that silent whisperer of death. He had always asserted that he would be killed in the first battle, and so strong was this conviction upon him, that he failed to keep in line of battle on another occasion, and had been censured by his officers for cowardice. In this battle he was ordered in charge of a Sergeant, with instructions that he be carried in battle at the point of the bayonet. However, it required no force to make him keep his place in line, still he continued true to his con-victions, that his death was certain. He went willingly, if not cheerfully, in line. As the column was moving to take position on Mayree's Hill, he gave instructions to his compan-ions as he advanced what messages should be sent to his wife, and while giving those instructions and before the command reached its position he fell pierced through the heart.

Another instance that came under my own observation, that which some chose to call "presentiment," was of a member in my company in East Tennessee. He was an exceptionally good soldier and the very picture of an ideal hero, tall, erect, and physically well developed, over six feet in height, and always stood in the front rank at the head of the company. While Longstreet was moving upon Knoxville, the morning he crossed the Tennessee River before dawn and before there was any indication of a battle, this man said to me, with as much coolness and composure, as if on an ordinary subject, without a falter in his tone or any emotion whatever: "Captain, I will be killed to-day. I have some money in my pocket which I want you to take and also to draw my four months' wages now due, and send by some trusty man to my wife. Tell her also—" but here I stopped him, told him it was childish to entertain such nonsense, to be a man as his conduct had so often in the past shown him to be. I joked and laughed at him, and in a good-natured way told him the East Tennessee climate gave him that disease known among soldiers as "crawfishing." This I did to withdraw his mind from this gloomy brooding. We had no real battle, but a continual skirmish with the enemy, with stray shots throughout the day. As we were moving along in line of battle, I heard that peculiar buzzing noise of a bullet, as if in ricochet, coming in our direction, but high in the air. As it neared the column it seemed to lower and come with a more hissing sound. It struck the man square in the breast, then reeling out of ranks he made a few strides towards where I was marching, his pocket-book in hand, and fell dead at my feet without a word or groan. He was the only man killed during the day in the brigade, and not even then on the firing line. Of course all will say these are only "coincidences," but be what they may, I give them as facts coming under my own eyes, and facts of the same nature came to the knowledge of hundreds and thousands of soldiers during every campaign, which none endeavor to explain, other than the facts themselves. But as the soldier is nothing more than a small fraction of the whole of a great machine, so much happens that he cannot fathom nor explain, that it naturally makes a great number of soldiers, like the sailor, somewhat superstitious. But when we speak of moral courage, where is there a courage more sublime than the soldier marching, as he thinks, to his certain death, while all his comrades are taking their chances at the hazard of war?

There are many unaccountable incidents and coincidents in a soldier's experience. Then, again, how differently men enter battle and how differently they act when wounded.

Some men, on the eve of battle, the most trying time in a soldier's life, will stand calm and impassive, awaiting the command, "forward," while his next neighbor will tremble and shake, as with a great chill, praying, meditating, and almost in despair, awaiting the orders to advance. Then when in the heat of the conflict both men seem metamorphosed. The former, almost frightened out of his wits, loses his head and is just as apt to fire backwards as forwards; while the latter seems to have lost all fear, reckless of his life, and fights like a hero. I have known men who at home were perfect cowards, whom a schoolboy could run away with a walking cane, become fearless and brave as lions in battle; while on the other hand men who were called "game cocks" at home and great "crossroads bullies," were abject cowards in battle. As to being wounded, some men will look on a mortal wound, feel his life ebbing away, perfectly calm and without concern, and give his dying messages with the composure of an every day occurrence; while others, if the tip of the finger is touched, or his shin-bone grazed, will "yell like a hyena or holler like a loon," and raise such a rumpus as to alarm the whole army. I saw a man running out of battle once (an officer) at such a gait as only fright could give, and when I asked him if he was wounded, he replied, "Yes, my leg is broken in two places," when, as a matter of fact, he had only a slight flesh wound. These incidents the reader may think merely fiction, but they are real facts. A man in Company E, Third South Carolina Regiment, having a minnie ball lodged between the two bones of his arm, made such a racket when the surgeons undertook to push it out, that they had to turn him loose; while a private in Company G, of the same regiment, being shot in the chest, when the surgeon was probing for the ball with his finger, looked on with unconcern, only remarking, "Make the hole a little larger, doctor, and put your whole hand in it." In a few days he was dead. I could give the names of all these parties, but for obvious reasons omit them. I merely single out these cases to show how differently men's nervous systems are constructed. And I might add, too, an instance of a member of my company at the third day of the battle of Gettysburg Lying under the heavy cannonading while Pickett was making his famous charge, and most of the men asleep, this man had his foot in the fork of a little bush, to better rest himself. In this position a shot struck him above the ankle; he looked at the wound a moment, then said: "Boys, I'll be —— if that ain't a thirty days' furlough." Next day his foot had to be amputated, and to this day he wears a cork. Such is the difference in soldiers, and you cannot judge them by outward appearance.

I here insert a few paragraphs from the pen of Adjutant Y. J. Pope, of the Third, to show that there was mirth in the camps, notwithstanding the cold and hardships:

PLAYING "ANTHONY OVER" AT HEADQUARTERS ON THE SEVENTH OF DECEMBER, 1862.

There was one thing that always attracted my attention during the war, and that was the warm fellowship which existed amongst the soldiers. If a man got a trunk or box laden with good things from home, there was no selfishness about it; the comrades were expected and did share in the feast. While out on picket on the banks of the Rappahannock River, when we were told that another regiment had come to relieve ours, at the same time we were told that Colonel Rutherford had come back to us; he had been absent since September, and we were all very anxious to see him, for he was a charming fellow—whole-souled, witty, and always an addition to any party. We knew, too, that he would bring something good to eat from home. My feathers fell, though, when Colonel Nance said to me, "Go yourself and see that every company is relieved from picket duty, and bring them to the regiment." I knew what this meant. It was at night, the ground was covered with snow, and the companies would take a long time to march back to camp. A soldier is made to obey orders, whether pleasant or unpleasant, so I rode at the head of the battalion; I was chilled through; my ears felt— well I rubbed a little feeling into them. At last we reached camp. Before I did so I could hear the merry laughter of the group about our regimental headquarter fire. Rutherford greeted me with the utmost cordiality, and had my supper served, having had the servants to keep it hot. But I could not forget my having to ride three miles at the head of the four companies, and how cold I had got in doing so. Therefore, I was in a bad humor, and refusing to join the merry group around the fire, went to bed at once. About twelve o'clock that night I heard the voices in the game of "Anthony over," and was obliged to laugh. Of course the merry cup had circulated. We lived in a Sibley tent that had a cap to fit over the top. And that night, as it was very cold, it had been determined to put the cap on the tent. So the merry-makers formed themselves into two groups, and pitched the cap to the top, and when it failed to lodge the other side would try its hand. One side would call out, "Anthony," to which call the other party would reply, "over." Then the first crowd would sing out, "Here she comes," throwing the cap with the uttering of those words. The peals of laughter from both sides, when the effort to lodge the cap would fail and the teasing of each side, made me laugh whether I wished to do so or not. After awhile it lodged alright, then "goodnights" were exchanged, and then to bed.

I need not add that on the next day all was good humor at headquarters, and in six days afterwards Colonel Nance, Colonel Rutherford, and Major Maffett were all painfully wounded in battle.

IN DECEMBER, 1862.

While Longstreet's troops occupied the City of Fredericksburg in the winter of 1862, I had learned that at night one of the quartermasters of McLaws' Division was in the habit of going across to an island in the Rappahannock River, just above the city, to obtain hay and corn, and to come down to the main incentive, that there was a very charming old Virginia family who lived there, and that a bright-eyed daughter was of that family. I set about getting a sight of this "Island enchantress," and at last Captain Franks, who was Quartermaster of the Seventeenth Regiment of Barksdale's Brigade, agreed to take me with him one night. Here I was, the Adjutant of a Regiment, going over to an island without leave, with the enemy in strong force just across the river, and therefore liable to be captured. Nevertheless, the hope of a peep at bright eyes has got many a man into dangerous ventures, and my case was not different from the rest. So I went. I saw the fair maid. She was not only beautiful, but very interesting. After it was all over prudence whispered to me not to tempt my fate again—especially as a fair lady in another State would have had a right to except to such conduct on my part. I never regretted my visit to the island, though!

AN ACT OF HEROIC FIDELITY OF A NEGRO SLAVE IN THE WAR.

In looking back at the incidents of the War Between the States, it is with great pleasure that an incident highly honorable to the African slave race is recalled.

It was on the 13th of December, 1862, when the Third South Carolina Regiment of Infantry was ordered from the position at the foot of Lee's Hill, at Fredericksburg, Va., to Mayree's House, near but to the right of the sunken road protected by the rock fence, that in going down the Telegraph Road the regiment was for a time exposed to the fire of the Federal batteries on the Stafford Heights. A shell from those batteries was so accurately directed that it burst near by Company C, of that regiment, and one of the results was that Lieutenant James Spencer Piester, of that company, was instantly killed. His body lay in that road and his faithful body servant, Simpson Piester, went to the body of his master and tenderly taking it into his arms, bore it to the rear, so that it might be sent to his relatives in Newberry, South Carolina. Anyone who had occasion to go upon the Telegraph Road in that day must appreciate the courage and fidelity involved in the act performed by Simpson Piester.

CHAPTER XV

Reminiscences.

After the smoke of the great battle had cleared away and the enemy settled permanently in their old quarters north of the Rappahannock, Lee moved his army some miles south of Fredericksburg, on the wooded highlands, and prepared for winter quarters. This was not a very laborious undertaking, nor of long duration, for all that was necessary was to pitch our old wornout, slanting-roof tents, occupied by six or eight

men each.   The troops had become too well acquainted with
the uncertainty of their duration in camp to go into any very
laborious or elaborate preparations.   Kershaw had a very
desirable location among the wooded hills, but this was soon
denuded of every vestige of fuel of every kind, for it must be
understood the army had no wagons or teams to haul their
fire wood, but each had to carry his share of the wood required for the daily use, and often a mile or mile and a half
distant.   At the close of the year the Eastern Army found
itself in quite easy circumstances and well pleased with the
year's campaign, but the fruits of our victory were more in
brilliant achievements than material results.

In the Western Army it was not so successful.   On the first
of the year General Albert Sidney Johnston had his army at
Bowling Green, Ky.   But disaster after disaster befell him,
until two states were lost to the Confederacy, as well as that
great commander himself, who fell at the moment of victory
on the fatal field of Shiloh.   Commencing with the fall of
Fort Henry on the Tennessee, then Fort Donaldson on the
Cumberland, which necessitated the evacuation of the lines of
defense at Bowling Green, and the withdrawal of the army
from Kentucky.   At Pittsburg Landing Grant was over-
whelmingly defeated by the army under Beauregard, but by
the division of the army under the two Confederate leaders,
and the overpowering numbers of the enemy under some of
the greatest Generals in the Union Army, Beauregard was
forced to withdraw to Shiloh.   Here the two combined armies
of Beauregard and Johnston attacked the Union Army under
Grant, Sherman, Buell, Lew Wallace, and other military
geniuses, with over one hundred and sixteen thousand men, as
against an army of forty-eight thousand Confederates.   After
one of the most stubborn, as well as bloodiest battles of the
war, the Confederates gained a complete victory on the first
day, but through a combined train of circumstances, they
were forced to withdraw the second.   After other battles,
with varied results, the end of the year found the Western
Army in Northern Mississippi and Southern Tennessee.

The Eastern Army, on the other hand, had hurled the
enemy from the very gates of the Capital of the Confederacy,
after seven days fighting, doubling it up in an indefinable

mass, and had driven it northward in haste; on the plains of
Manassas it was overtaken, beaten, and almost annihilated,
only failing in a repetition of the same, ending as the first battle of that name and place; by the same causes, viz., Sykes'
Regulars, the enemy pushed across the Potomac, putting the
Capitol, as well as the whole North, in a perfect state of panic;
the Confederates entered the enemy's own country, capturing
one of their strongholds, with eleven thousand prisoners and
munitions of war, enough to equip an army; fought one of the
most sanguinary battles of modern times almost within sight
of the Capitol itself, if not to a successful finish to a very cred-
itable draw; returned South, unmolested, with its prisoners
and untold booty; fought the great battle of Fredericksburg,
with the results just enumerated.   Could Napoleon, Frederick
the Great, or the "Madman of the North" have done better
with the forces at hand and against an enemy with odds of
two and three to one?   So Lee's Army had nothing of which
to complain, only the loss of so many great and chivalrous
comrades.

We had little picketing to do, once perhaps a month, then
in the deserted houses of Fredericksburg.   Guard duty around
camp was abolished for the winter; so was drilling, only on
nice, warm days; the latter, however, was rarely seen during
that season.   The troops abandoned themselves to base ball,
snow fights, writing letters, and receiving as guests in their
camps friends and relatives, who never failed to bring with
them great boxes of the good things from home, as well as
clothing and shoes for the needy soldiers.   Furloughs were
granted in limited numbers.   Recruits and now the thoroughly
healed of the wounded from the many engagements flocked to
our ranks, making all put on a cheerful face.

That winter in Virginia was one of the most severe known
in many years, but the soldiers had become accustomed to the
cold of the North, and rather liked it than otherwise, especially when snow fell to the depth of twelve to sixteen inches,
and remained for two or three weeks.   So the reader can see
that the soldier's life has its sunny side, as well as its dark.
The troops delight in "snow balling," and revelled in the sport
for days at a time.   Many hard battles were fought, won, and
lost; sometimes company against company, then regiment

against regiment, and sometimes brigades would be pitted against rival brigades. When the South Carolinians were against the Georgians, or the two Georgia brigades against Kershaw's and the Mississippi brigades, then the blows would fall fast and furious. The fiercest fight and the hardest run of my life was when Kershaw's Brigade, under Colonel Rutherford, of the Third, challenged and fought Cobb's Georgians. Colonel Rutherford was a great lover of the sport, and wherever a contest was going on he would be sure to take a hand. On the day alluded to Colonel Rutherford martialed his men by the beating of drums and the bugle's blast; officers headed their companies, regiments formed, with flags flying, then when all was ready the troops were marched to the brow of a hill, or rather half way down the hill, and formed line of battle, there to await the coming of the Georgians. They were at that moment advancing across the plain that separated the two camps. The men built great pyramids of snow balls in their rear, and awaited the assault of the fast approaching enemy. Officers cheered the men and urged them to stand fast and uphold the "honor of their State," while the officers on the other side besought their men to sweep all before them off the field.

The men stood trembling with cold and emotion, and the officers with fear, for the officer who was luckless enough as to fall into the hands of a set of "snow revelers," found to his sorrow that his bed was not one of roses. When the Georgians were within one hundred feet the order was given to "fire." Then shower after shower of the the fleecy balls filled the air. Cheer after cheer went up from the assaulters and the assaultant—now pressed back by the flying balls, then to the assault again. Officers shouted to the men, and they answered with a "yell." When some, more bold than the rest, ventured too near, he was caught and dragged through the lines, while his comrades made frantic efforts to rescue him. The poor prisoner, now safely behind the lines, his fate problematical, as down in the snow he was pulled, now on his face, next on his back, then swung round and round by his heels—all the while snow being pushed down his back or in his bosom, his eyes, ears, and hair thoroughly filled with the "beautiful snow." After a fifteen minutes' struggle, our lines gave way. The fierce looks of a tall, muscular, wild-eyed Georgian, who stood directly in my front, seemed to have singled me out for sacrifice. The stampede began. I tried to lead the command in the rout by placing myself in the front of the boldest and stoutest squad in the ranks, all the while shouting to the men to "turn boys turn." But they continued to charge to the rear, and in the nearest cut to our camp, then a mile off, I saw the only chance to save myself from the clutches of that wild-eyed Georgian was in continual and rapid flight. The idea of a boy seventeen years old, and never yet tipped the beam at one hundred, in the grasp of that monster, as he now began to look to me, gave me the horrors. One by one the men began to pass me, and while the distance between us and the camp grew less at each step, yet the distance between me and my pursuer grew less as we proceeded in our mad race. The broad expanse that lay between the men and camp was one flying, surging mass, while the earth, or rather the snow, all around was filled with men who had fallen or been overtaken, and now in the last throes of a desperate snow battle. I dared not look behind, but kept bravely on. My breath grew fast and thick, and the camp seemed a perfect menage, now near at hand then far in the distance. The men who had not yet fallen in the hands of the reckless Georgians had distanced me, and the only energy that kept me to the race was the hope that some mishap might befall the wild-eyed man in my rear, otherwise I was gone. No one would have the temerity to tackle the giant in his rage. But all things must come to an end, and my race ended by falling in my tent, more dead than alive, just as I felt the warm breath of my pursurer blowing on my neck. I heard, as I lay panting, the wild-eyed man say, "I would rather have caught that d—n little Captain than to have killed the biggest man in the Yankee Army."

CHAPTER XVI

Campaign of 1863---Battle of Chancellorsville.

On the morning of April 29th the soldiers were aroused from their ·slumbers by the beating of the long roll. What an ominous sound is the long roll to the soldier wrapped in his blanket and enjoying the sweets of sleep. It is like a fire bell at night. It denotes battle. It tells the soldier the enemy is moving; it means haste and active preparation. A battle is imminent. The soldiers thus roused, as if from their long sleep since Fredericksburg, feel in a touchous mood. The frightful scenes of Fredericksburg and Mayree's Hill rise up before them as a spectre. Soldiers rush out of their tents, asking questions and making suppositions. Others are busily engaged folding blankets, tearing down tents, and making preparations to move; companies formed into regiments and regiments into brigades. The distant boom of cannon beyond the Rappahannock tells us that the enemy is to cross the river again and try conclusions with the soldiers of Lee. All expected a bloody engagement, for the Federal Army had been greatly recruited, under excellent discipline, and headed by Fighting Joe Hooker. He was one of the best officers in tha army, and he himself had boasted that his was the "fine army that had ever been organized upon the planet." numbered one hundred and thirty-one thousand men of arms, while Lee had barely sixty thousand. We moved rapid in the direction of Fredericksburg. I never saw Kershaw lo so well. Riding his iron-gray at the head of his columns, could not but be impressed with his soldierly appearance. seemed a veritable knight of old. Leading his brigade abo the city, he took position in the old entrenchments.

Before reaching the battle line, the enemy had alrea placed pontoons near the old place of landing, crossed over portion of their army, and was now picketing on the sou side of the river. One company from each regiment thrown out as sharp-shooters or skirmishers, under Capt

Goggans, of the Seventh, and deployed in the valley below, where we could watch the enemy. My company was of the number. Nothing was done during the day but a continual change of positions. We remained on the skirmish line during the night without fire or without any relief, expecting an advance next morning, or to be relieved at least. The sun was obscured by the densest fog the following morning I had almost ever witnessed. When it cleared up, about 10 o'clock, what was our astonishment?—to find no enemy in our front, nor friends in our rear. There were, however, some Federals opposite and below the city, but they belonged to another division. We could hear occasional cannonading some miles up the Rappahannock. By some staff officers passing, we ascertained that Hooker had withdrawn during the night in our front, recrossed the river at Ely's and Raccoon fords, or some of the fords opposite the Wilderness. This was on Friday, May the first. After a consultation with the officers of our detachment, it was agreed to evacuate our position and join our regiments wherever we could find them. We had no rations, and this was one of the incentives to move. But had the men been supplied with provisions, and the matter left to them alone, I doubt very much whether they would have chosen to leave the ground now occupied, as we were in comparative safety and no enemy in sight, while to join our commands would add largely to the chances of getting in battle. I am sorry to say a majority of the officers were of that opinion, too. Some brought to bear one of Napoleon's maxims I had heard when a boy, "When a soldier is in doubt where to go, always go to the place you hear the heaviest firing," and we could indistinctly hear occasional booming of cannon high up the river, indicating that a part of the army at least was in that direction.

So we moved back and over the breastworks, on to the plank road leading to Orange Court House. Making our way, keeping together as a battalion, up that road in the direction of the Wilderness, near noon we could hear the deep bay of cannon, now distant and indistinct, then again more rapidly and quite distinguishable, showing plainly that Lee was having a running fight. Later in the day we passed dead horses and a few dead and wounded soldiers. On every hand were indi-

14

cations of the effects of shot and shell. Trees were shattered
along the road side, fences torn down and rude breastworks
made here and there, the evidence of heavy skirmishing in
our front. Lee was pressing the advance guard that had
crossed at one of the lower fords back on the main army, crossing then at fords opposite and above the Chancellor's House.
Near sundown the firing was conspicuously heavy, especially
the artillery. The men of most of the companies evinced a
desire to frequently rest, and in every way delay our march as
much as possible. Some of the officers, too, joined with the
men and offered objections to rushing headlong into battle
without orders. I knew that our brigade was somewhere in
our front, and from the firing I was thoroughly convinced a
battle was imminent, and in that case our duty called us to
our command. Not through any cowardice, however, did the
men hesitate, for all this fiction written about men's eagerness
for battle, their ungovernable desire to throw themselves upon
the enemy, their great love of hearing the bursting of shells
over their heads, the whizzing of minnie balls through their
ranks is all very well for romance and on paper, but a soldier
left free to himself, unless he seeks notoriety or honors, will
not often rush voluntarily into battle, and if he can escape it
honorably, he will do it nine times out of ten. There are
times, however, when officers, whose keen sense of duty and
honorable appreciation of the position they occupy, will lead
their commands into battle unauthorized, when they see the
necessity, but a private who owes no obedience nor allegiance
only to his superiors, and has no responsibility, seldom ever
goes voluntarily into battle; if so, once is enough.

Under these circumstances, as the sun was near setting, we
learned from some wounded soldier that Kershaw was moving
in line of battle to the left of the plank road. Another Captain and myself deserted our companions and made our way to
our regiments with our companies. As we came upon it, it
was just moving out from a thicket into an open field under a
heavy skirmish fire and a fierce fire from a battery in our front.
We marched at a double-quick to rejoin the regiment, and the
proudest moments of my life, and the sweetest words to hear,
was as the other portion of the regiment saw us coming they
gave a cheer of welcome and shouted, "Hurrah! for the Dutch;

the Dutch has come; make way to the left for the Dutch," and such terms of gladness and welcome, that I thought, even while the "Dutch" and its youthful commander were but a mere speck of the great army, still some had missed us, and I was glad to feel the touch of their elbow on the right and left when a battle was in progress.

Companies in the army, like school boys, almost all have "nick-names." Mine was called the "Dutch" from the fact of its having been raised in that section of the country between Saluda River and the Broad, known as "Dutch Fork." A century or more before, this country, just above Columbia and in the fork of the two rivers, was settled by German refugees, hence the name "Dutch Fork."

After joining the regiment, we only advanced a little further and halted for the night, sleeping with guns in arms, lest a night attack might find the troops illy prepared were the guns in stack. We were so near the enemy that fires were not allowed, and none permitted to speak above a whisper. Two men from each company were detailed to go to the rear and cook rations. It is not an easy task for two men, who had been marching and fighting all day, to be up all night cooking three meals each for thirty or forty men, having to gather their own fuel, and often going half mile for water. A whole day's ration is always cooked at one time on marches, as night is the only time for cooking. The decrees of an order for a detail are inexorable. A soldier must take it as it comes, for none ever know but what the next duties may be even worse than the present. As a general rule, soldiers rarely ever grumble at any detail on the eve of an engagement, for sometimes it excuses them from a battle, and the old experienced veteran never refuses that.

At daylight a battery some two hundred yards in our front opened a furious fire upon us, the shells coming uncomfortably near our heads. If there were any infantry between the battery and our troops, they must have laid low to escape the shots over their heads. But after a few rounds they limbered up and scampered away. We moved slowly along with heavy skirmishing in our front all the morning of the second. When near the Chancellor's House, we formed line of battle in a kind of semi-circle, our right resting on the river and extending

over the plank road, Kershaw being some distance to the left
of this road, the Fifteenth Regiment occupying the right.
Here we remained for the remainder of the day. We heard
the word coming up the line, "No cheering, no cheering."
In a few moments General Lee came riding along the lines.
going to the left. He had with him quite a number of his
staff and one or two couriers. He looked straight to the front
and thoughtful, noticing none of the soldiers who rushed to
the line to see him pass. He no doubt was then forming the
masterful move, and one, too, in opposition to all rules or
order of military science or strategy, "the division of his
army in the face of the enemy," a movement that has caused
many armies, before, destruction and the downfall of its commander. But nothing succeeds like success. The great disparity in numbers was so great that Lee could only watch and
hope for some mistake or blunder of his adversary, or by some
extraordinary strategic manoeuvre on his own part. gain the
advantage by which his opponent would be ruined. Hooker
had one hundred and thirty thousand men, while Lee had
only sixty thousand. With this number it 'seemed an easy
task for Hooker to threaten Lee at Fredericksburg, then fall
upon him with his entire force at Chancellorsville and crush
him before Lee could extricate himself from the meshes that
were surrounding him, and retreat to Richmond. The dense
Wilderness seemed providential for the movement upon which
Lee had now determined to stake the fate of his army and the
fortunes of the Confederacy. Its heavy, thick undergrowth
entirely obstructed the view and hid the movements to be
made. Jackson, with Rhodes, Colston's, and A. P. Hill's
Divisions, were to make a detour around the enemy's right,
march by dull roads and bridle paths through the tangled
forest, and fall upon the enemy's rear, while McLaws, Anderson's, and Early's Divisions were to hold him in check in
front. Pickett's Division had, before this time, been sent to
Wilmington, N. C., while Ransom's Division, with Barksdale's Mississippi Brigade, of McLaws' Division, were to keep
watch of the enemy at Fredericksburg. The Federal General,
Stoneman, with his cavalry, was then on his famous but disastrous raid to Richmond. Jackson commenced his march
early in the morning, and kept it up all day, turning back

towards the rear of the enemy when sufficiently distant that
his movement could not be detected. By marching eighteen
or twenty miles he was then within three miles of his starting
point. But Hooker's Army stood between him and Lee.
Near night Jackson struck the enemy a terrific blow, near the
plank road, just opposite to where we lay, and the cannonading was simply deafening. The shots fired from some of the
rifled guns of Jackson passed far overhead of the enemy and
fell in our rear. Hooker, bewildered, and lost in the meshes
of the Wilderness, had formed his divisions in line of battle in
echelon, and moved out from the river. Great gaps would
intervene between the division in front and the one in rear.
Little did he think an enemy was marching rapidly for his
rear, another watching every movement in front, and those
enemies, Jackson and Lee, unknown to Hooker, his flank
stood exposed and the distance between the columns gave an
ordinary enemy an advantage seldom offered by an astute
General, but to such an enemy as Jackson it was more than he
had hoped or even dared to expect. As he sat watching the
broken columns of the enemy struggling through the dense
undergrowth, the favorable moment came. Seizing it with
promptness and daring, so characteristic of the man, he, like
Napoleon at Austerlitz, when he saw the Russians passing by
his front with their flanks exposed, rushed upon them like
a wild beast upon its prey, turning the exposed column back
upon its rear. Colston, commanding Jackson's old Division,
led the attack, followed by A. P. Hill. Rhodes then fell like
an avalanche upon the unexpectant and now thoroughly disorganized divisions of the retreating enemy. Volley after
volley was poured into the seething mass of advancing and
receding columns. Not much use could be made of artillery
at close range, so that arm of the service was mainly occupied
in shelling their trains and the woods in rear. Until late in
the night did the battle rage in all its fury. Darkness only
added to its intensity, and the fire was kept up until a shot
through mistake lay the great Chieftain, Stonewall Jackson,
low. General A. P. Hill now took command of the corps,
and every preparation was made for the desperate onslaught of
to-morrow. By some strange intuition peculiar to the soldier,
and his ability to gather news, the word that Jackson had

fallen burst through the camp like an explosion, and cast a gloom of sorrow over all.

As our brother South Carolinians, of McGowan's Brigade, were on the opposite side of us, and in the heat of the fray, while we remained idle, I take the liberty of quoting from "Caldwell's History" of that brigade a description of the terrible scenes being enacted on that memorable night in the Wilderness in which Jackson fell:

"Now it is night. The moon a day or two past full, rose in cloudless sky and lighted our way. We were fronted, and then advanced on the right of the road into a thick growth of pines. Soon a firing of small arms sprang up before us, and directly afterwards the enemy's artillery opened furiously, bearing upon us. The scene was terrible. Volley after volley of musketry was poured by the Confederate line in front of us upon the enemy. The enemy replied with equal rapidity; cheer, wild and fierce, rang over the whole woods; officers shouted at the top of their voices, to make themselves heard; cannon roared and shells burst continuously. We knew nothing, could see nothing, hedged in by the matted mass of trees. Night engagements are always dreadful, but this was the worst I ever knew. To see your danger is bad enough, but to hear shells whizzing and bursting over you, to hear shrapnell and iron fragments slapping the trees and cracking off limbs, and not know from whence death comes to you, is trying beyond all things. And here it looked so incongruous—below raged, thunder, shout, shriek, slaughter—above soft, silent, smiling moonlight, peace!"

The next morning A. P. Hill was moving early, but was himself wounded, and General Jeb. Stuart, of the cavalry, took command. The fighting of Jackson's Corps to-day surpassed that of the night before, and after overcoming almost insurmountable obstacles, they succeeded in dislodging Hooker from his well fortified position.

Kershaw remained in his line of battle, keeping up a constant fire with his skirmishers. An advance upon the Chancellor's House was momentarily expected. The long delay between the commencement of Jackson's movement until we heard the thunder of his guns immediately in our front and in rear of the enemy, was taken up in conjecturing, "what move was next.'' All felt that it was to be no retreat, and as we failed to advance, the mystery of our inactivity was more confounding.

Early next morning, however, the battle began in earnest. Hooker had occupied the night in straightening out his lines and establishing a basis of battle, with the hope of retrieving the blunder of the day before. Stuart (or rather A. P. Hill, until wounded,) began pressing him from the very start. We could hear the wild yells of our troops as line after line of Hooker's were reformed, to be brushed away by the heroism of the Southern troops. Our skirmishers began their desultory firing of the day before. The battle seemed to near us as it progressed, and the opening around Chancellor's House appeared to be alive with the enemy's artillery. About two o'clock our lines were ordered forward, and we made our way through the tangled morass, in direction of our skirmish line. Here one of the bravest men in our regiment was killed, private John Davis, of the ''Quitman Rifles.'' He was reckless beyond all reason. He loved danger for danger's sake. Stepping behind a tree to load (he was on skirmish line) he would pass out from this cover in plain view, take deliberate aim, and fire. Again and again he was entreated and urged by his comrades to shield himself, but in vain. A bullet from the enemy's sharp-shooters killed him instantly.

A singular and touching incident of this family is here recorded. Davis had an only brother, who was equally as brave as John and younger, James, the two being the only children of an aged but wealthy couple, of Newberry County. After the death of John, his mother exerted herself and hired a substitute for her baby boy, and came on in a week after the battle for the body of her oldest son and to take James home with her, as the only hope and solace of the declining years of this aged father and mother. Much against his will and wishes, but by mother's entreaties and friends' solicitations, the young man consented to accompany his mother home. But fate seemed to follow them here and play them false, for in less than two weeks this brave, bright, and promising boy lay dead from a malignant disease.

As our brigade was moving through the thicket in the interval between our main line and the skirmishers, and under

a heavy fire, we came upon a lone stranger sitting quietly
upon a log. At first he was thought an enemy, who in the
denseness of the undergrowth had passed our lines on a tour
of observation. He was closely questioned, and it turned out
to be Rev. Boushell, a methodist minister belonging to one of
McGowan's South Carolina regiments, who became lost from
his command in the great flank movement of Jackson (Mc-
Gowan's Brigade belonged to Jackson's Corps), and said he
came down "to see how the battle was going and to lend aid
and comfort to any wounded soldier should he chance to find
one in need of his services."

The batteries in our front were now raking the matted brush
all around and overhead, and their infantry soon became aware
of our presence, and they, too, began pouring volleys into our
advancing column. The ranks became confused, for in this
wilderness we could not see twenty paces in front. Still we
moved forward with such order as was under the conditions
permissible. When near the turn-pike road General Kershaw
gave the command to "charge." The Fifteenth raised the
yell; then the Third dashed forward; the Seventh was somewhat late on account of the almost impassable condition of the
ground, but still it and the Third Battalion, with the Second
on the left, made a mad rush for the public road, and entered
it soon after the Fifteenth and Third. A perfect sea of fire
was in our faces from the many cannon parked around the
Chancellor House and graping in all directions but the rear.
Lee on the one side and Stuart on the other had closed upon
the enemy, their wings joining just in front of the house.
Some of the pieces of the enemy's artillery were not more than
fifty yards in our front, and the discharges seemed to blaze fire
in our very ranks. Infantry, too, was there massed all over
the yard, and in rear of this one vast, mingling, moving body
of humanity, dead horses lay in all directions, while the dead
and wounded soldiers lay heaped and strewn with the living.
But a few volleys from our troops in the road soon silenced all
opposition from the infantry, while cannoneers were hitching
up their horses to fly away. Some were trying to drag away
their caissons and light pieces by hand, while thousands of
"blue coats," with and without arms, were running for cover
to the rear. In less than twenty minutes the firing ceased in

our front, and men were ordered to prepare breastworks. Our soldiers, like the beaver, by this time had become accustomed to burrow in the ground as soon as a "halt" was made. A shovel and a spade were carried at all times by each company to guard against emergencies. The bursting of a shell near my company caused a fragment to strike one of my own men on the shoulder. He claimed to be desperately wounded, and wished to go to the hospital. I examined him hastily to see if I could give him any assistance. He claimed his shoulder was broken. Just then the order was given to "commence to fortify." "G.," the wounded man, was the first to grasp the shovel, and threw dirt with an energy that caused my Orderly Sergeant, a brave and faithful soldier, but who never allowed the comic side of any transaction to pass him, to say: "Captain, look at the 'wild pigeon;' see how he scratches dirt." All soldiers carried a "nick-name," a name given by some physical disability or some error he had made, or from any circumstance in his life out of the usual order. Hardly had we taken possession of the turn-pike road and began fortifying, than the sound of shells down the river was heard, and we were hurriedly marched down the road. McLaws' and Anderson's Divisions were doubled-quicked down the turn-pike road and away from the battle to meet Sedgwick, who had crossed the Rappahannock at Fredericksburg, stormed Mayree's Heights, routed and captured the most of Barksdale's Mississippi Brigade, and was making his way rapidly upon Lee's rear.

This Battle of Chancellorsville certainly had its many sides, with its rapid marching, changing of positions, and generalship of the highest order. On the day before Jackson had gone around the right flank of Hooker and fell upon his rear, while to-day we had the novel spectacle of Sedgwick in the rear of Lee and Stuart in rear of Hooker. No one can foretell the result of the battle, had Hooker held his position until Sedgwick came up. But Lee's great mind ran quick and fast. He knew the country and was well posted by his scouts of every move and turn of the enemy on the chess-board of battle. Anderson, with his division, being on our right, led the advance down the road to meet Sedgwick. We passed great parks of wagons (ordnance and commissary) on either side of the road.   Here and there were the field infirmaries where their wounded were being attended to and where all the surplus baggage had been stacked before the battle.

On reaching Zoar Church, some five miles in rear, we encountered Sedgwick's advance line of skirmishers, and a heavy fusilade began.   Anderson formed line of battle on extreme right, and on right of plank road, with the purpose of sweeping round on the enemy's left.   McLaws formed on left of the corps, his extreme left reaching out toward the river and across the road; Kershaw being immediately on right of the road, with the Second resting on it, then the Fifteenth, the Third Battalion, the Eighth, the Third, and the Seventh on the right.   On the left of the road leading to Fredericksburg was a large open field extending to the bluff near the river; on the right was a dense thicket of pines and undergrowth.   In this we had to form.   The Seventh experienced some trouble in getting into line, and many camp rumors were afloat a few days afterwards of an uncomplimentary nature of the Seventh's action.   But this was all false; for no more gallant regiment nor better officered, both in courage and ability, was in the Confederate service than the "bloody Seventh."   But it was the unfavorable nature of the ground, the difficulties experienced in forming a line, and the crowding and lapping of the men that caused the confusion.

Soon after our line of battle was formed and Kershaw awaiting orders from McLaws to advance, a line of support came up in our rear, and mistaking us for the enemy, commenced firing upon us.   Handkerchiefs went up, calls of "friends," "friends," but still the firing continued.   One Colonel seeing the danger—the enemy just in front, and our friends firing on us in the rear—called out, "Who will volunteer to carry our colors back to our friends in rear?"   Up sprang the handsome and gallant young Sergeant, Copeland, of the "Clinton Divers," (one of the most magnificent and finest looking companies in his service, having at its enlistment forty men over six feet tall), and said, "Colonel, send me."   Grasping the colors in his hand, he carried them, waving and jesticulating in a friendly manner, until he convinced the troops that they were friends in their front.

While thus waiting for Anderson to swing around the left of

the enemy, a desperate charge was made upon us. The cannonading was exceedingly heavy and accurate. Great trees all around fell, snapped in twain by the shell and solid shot, and many men were killed and wounded by the falling timber. Trees, a foot in diameter, snapped in two like pipe stems, and fell upon the men. It was growing dark before Anderson could get in position, and during that time the troops never experienced a heavier shelling. It was enough to make the stoutest hearts quake. One of my very bravest men, one who had never failed before, called to me as I passed, "Captain, if I am not here when the roll is called, you may know where I am. I don't believe I can stand this." But he did, and like the man he was, withstood it. Another, a young recruit, and under his first fire, almost became insane, jumping upon me and begging "for God's sake" let him go to the rear. I could not stand this piteous appeal, and knowing he could not be of any service to us in that condition, told him "to go." It is needless to say he obeyed my orders. Dr. Evans, our surgeon, told me afterwards that he came to his quarters and remained three days, perfectly crazy.

At last the order came after night to advance. In a semicircle we swept through the thicket; turning, we came into the road, and over it into the opening in front. The enemy was pushed back into the breastworks on the bluff at the river. These breastworks had been built by our troops during the Fredericksburg battle, and afterwards to guard and protect Raccoon and Ely's fords, just in rear. As night was upon us, and the enemy huddled before us at the ford, we were halted and lay on the field all night. This was the ending of the battle of Chancellorsville.

Next morning the sun was perfectly hidden by a heavy fog, so much so that one could not see a man twenty yards distant. Skirmishers were thrown out and our advance made to the river, but nothing was found on this side of the river but the wounded and the discarded rifles and munitions of war. The wounded lay in all directions, calling for help and heaping curses upon their friends, who had abandoned them in their distress. Guns, tent flies, and cartridge boxes were packed up by the wagon loads. Hooker's Army was thoroughly beaten, disheartened, and disorganized. Met and defeated at every turn and move, they were only too glad to place themselves across the river and under the protection of their siege guns on Stafford's Heights. Hooker's losses were never correctly given, but roughly computed at twenty-five .thousand, while those of Lee's were ten thousand two hundred and eighty-one. But the Confederates counted it a dear victory in the loss of the intrepid but silent Stonewall Jackson. There was a magic in his name that gave enthusiasm and confidence to the whole army. To the enemy his name was a terror and himself an apparition. He had frightened and beaten Banks out of the Shennandoah Valley, had routed Fremont, and so entangled and out-generaled Seigle that he was glad to put the Potomac between himself and this silent, mysterious, and indefatigable chieftain, who oftened prayed before battle and fought with a Bible in one hand and a sword in the other. He came like a whirlwind upon the flank of McClellan at Mechanicsville, and began those series of battles and victories that terminated with the "Little Giant" being hemmed in at Drury's Bluff and Malvern Hill. While Pope, the "Braggart," was sweeping the fields before him in Northern Virginia, and whose boast was he "saw only the enemy's back," and his "headquarters were in the saddle," Jackson appeared before him like a lion in his path. He swings around Pope's right, over the mountains, back through Thoroughfare Gap; he sweeps through the country like a comet through space, and falls on Pope's rear on the plains of Manassas, and sent him flying across the Potomac like McDowell was beaten two years before. While pursuing the enemy across the river and into Maryland, he turns suddenly, recrosses the river, and stands before Harper's Ferry, and captures that stronghold with scarcely a struggle. All this was enough to give him the sobriquet of the "Silent Man," the man of "mystery," and it is not too much to say that Jackson to the South was worth ten thousand soldiers, while the terror of his name wrought consternation in the ranks of the enemy.

CHAPTER XVII

From Chancellorsville to Gettysburg---Camp, March, and Battle.

Again we are in our old quarters. Details were sent out every day to gather up the broken and captured guns, to be shipped to Richmond for repairs. The soldiers had gathered a great amount of camp supplies, such as oil cloths, tents, blankets, etc. When a soldier captured more than a sufficiency for his own wants, he would either sell to his comrades or to the brigade sutler. This was a unique personage with the soldiers. He kept for sale such articles as the soldier mostly needed, and always made great profits on his goods. Being excused from military duty, he could come and go at will. But the great danger was of his being captured or his tent raided by his own men, the risk therefore being so great that he had to ask exorbitant prices for his goods. He kept crackers, cards, oysters and sardines, paper and envelopes, etc., and often a bottle; would purchase all the plunder brought him and peddle the same to citizens in the rear. After the battle of Chancellorsville a member of Company D, from Spartanburg, took the sutler an oil cloth to buy. After the trade was effected, the sutler was seen to throw the cloth behind a box in the tent. Gathering some of his friends, to keep the man of trade engaged in front, the oil cloth man would go in the rear, raise the tent, extract the oil cloth, take it around, and sell it again. Paying over the money, the sutler would throw the cloth behind the box, and continue his trade with those in front. Another would go behind the tent, get the cloth, bring it to the front, throw it upon the counter, and demand his dollar. This was kept up till everyone had sold the oil cloth once, and sometimes twice, but at last the old sutler began to think oil cloths were coming in too regularly, so he looked behind the box, and behold he had been buying the same oil cloth all night. The office was abolished on our next campaign.

Lee began putting his army in splendid trim. All furloughs were discontinued and drills (six per week) were now begun. To an outsider this seemed nonsensical and an useless burden upon the soldiers, but to a soldier nothing is more requisite to the discipline and morale of an army than regular drills, and the army given a good share of what is called "red tape." By the last of May, or the first of June, Lee had recruited his army, by the non-extension of all furloughs and the return of the slightly wounded, to sixty-eight thousand. It is astonishing what a very slight wound will cause a soldier to seek a furlough. He naturally thinks that after the marches, danger, and dread of battle, a little blood drawn entitles him to at least a thirty days' furlough. It became a custom in the army for a man to compute the length of his furlough by the extent of his wound. The very least was thirty days, so when a soldier was asked the nature of his wound he would reply, "only a thirty days'," or "got this time a sixty days';" while with an arm or foot off he would say, "I got my discharge" at such battle.

On the 27th of June Hooker was superseded by General Geo. B. Meade, and he bent all his energies to the discipline of his great army.

General Kershaw, on his promotion to Brigadier, surrounded himself with a staff of young men of unequalled ability. tireless, watchful, and brave to a fault. Captain C. R. Holmes, as Assistant Adjutant General, was promoted to that position from one of the Charleston companies. I fear no contradiction when I say he was one of the very best staff officers in the army, and had he been in line of promotion his merits would have demanded recognition and a much higher position given him. Captain W. M. Dwight, as Adjutant and Inspector General, was also an officer of rare attainments. Cool and collected in battle, his presence always gave encouragement and confidence to the men under fire. He was captured at the Wilderness the 6th of May, 1864. Captain D. A. Doby was Kershaw's Aide-de-Camp, or personal aid, and a braver, more daring, and reckless soldier I never saw. Wherever the battle raged fiercest, Captain Doby was sure to be in the storm center. Riding along the line where shells were plowing up great furrows, or the air filled with flying fragments, and bullets following like hail from a summer cloud, Doby would give words of cheer and encouragement to the men. It seemed at times that he lived a charmed life, so perilous was his situation in times of battle. But the fatal volley that laid the lamented Jenkins low, and unhorsed Longstreet at the Wilderness, gave Doby his last long furlough, felling from his horse dead at the feet of his illustrious chieftain. Lieutenant John Myers was Brigade Ordnance officer, but his duties did not call him to the firing line, thus he was debarred from sharing with his companions their triumphs, their dangers, and their glories, the halo that will ever surround those who followed the plume of the knightly Kershaw.

The Colonels of the different regiments were also fortunate in their selection of Adjutants. This is one of the most important and responsible offices in the regimental organization. The duties are manifold, and often thankless and unappreciated. He shares more dangers (having to go from point to point during battle to give orders) than most of the officers, still he is cut off, by army regulation, from promotion, the ambition and goal of all officers. Colonel Kennedy, of the Second, appointed as his Adjutant E. E. Sill, of Camden, while Colonel Nance, of the Third, gave the position to his former Orderly Sergeant, Y. J. Pope, of Newberry. Colonel Aiken, of the Seventh, appointed as Adjutant Thomas M. Childs, who was killed at Sharpsburg. Colonel Elbert Bland then had Lieutenant John R. Carwile, of Edgefield, to fill the position during the remainder of the service, or until the latter was placed upon the brigade staff. Colonel Hennegan made Lieutenant Colin M. Weatherly, of Bennettsville, S. C., Adjutant of the Eighth. All were young men of splendid physique, energetic, courteous, and brave. They had the love and confidence of the entire command. W. C. Hariss, Adjutant of the Third Battalion, was from Laurens. Of the Fifteenth, both were good officers, but as they were not with the brigade all the while, I am not able to do them justice.

The troops of Lee were now at the zenith of their perfection and glory. They looked upon themselves as invincible, and that no General the North could put in the field could match our Lee. The cavalry of Stuart and Hampton had done some remarkably good fighting, and they were now looked upon as an indispensable arm of the service. The cavalry of the West were considered more as raiders than fighters. but our dismounted cavalry was depended upon with almost as much confidence as our infantry. This was new tactics of Lee's, never before practiced in any army of the world. In other times, where the cavalry could not charge and strike with their sabres, they remained simply spectators. But Lee, in time of battle, dismounted them, and they, with their long-ranged carbines, did good and effective service.

Grant had been foiled and defeated at Vicksburg. At Holly Springs, Chickasaw Bayou, Yazo Pass, and Millikin's Bend he had been successfully met and defeated. The people of West Virginia, that mountainous region of the old commonwealth, had ever been loyal to the Union, and now formed a new State and was admitted into the Union on the 20th of April, 1863, under the name of "West Virginia." Here it is well to notice a strange condition of facts that prevailed over the whole South, and that is the loyalty to the Union of all mountainous regions. In the mountains of North Carolina, where men are noted for their hardihood and courage, and who, once in the field, made the very best and bravest of soldiers, they held to the Union, and looked with suspicion upon the heresy of Secession. The same can be said of South Carolina, Tennessee, Georgia, and Alabama. These men would often go into hiding in the caves and gorges of the mountains, and defy all the tact and strategy of the conscript officers for months, and sometimes for years. It was not for want of courage, for they had that in abundance, but born and reared in an atmosphere of personal independence, they felt as free as the mountains they inhabited, and they scorned a law that forced them to do that which was repugnant to their ideas of personal liberty. Living in the dark recesses of the mountains, far from the changing sentiments of their more enlightened neighbors of the lowland, they drank in, as by inspiration with their mother's milk, a loyalty to the general government as it had come down to them from the days of their forefathers of the Revolution. As to the question of slavery, they had neither kith nor kin in interest or sentiment with that institution. As to State's rights, as long as they were allowed to roam at will over the mountain sides, distill the product of their valley and mountain patches, and live undisturbed in their glens and mountain homes, they looked upon any changes that would effect their surroundings as innovations to be resisted to the death.   So the part that West Virginia and the mountainous regions of the South took in the war was neither surprising to nor resented by the people of the Confederacy.

By the middle of June Lee began to turn his eyes again to the tempting fields of grain and army supplies of Pennsylvania and Maryland.   The Valley had been laid waste, West Virginia given up, the South was now put to her utmost resources to furnish supplies for her vast armies.   All heavy baggage was sent to the rear, and Lee's troops began moving by various routes up and across the river in the direction of Culpepper Court House.   But before the march began, General Lee renewed the whole of Longstreet's Corps, and the sight of this magnificent body of troops was both inspiring and encouraging. The corps was formed in two columns, in a very large and level old field.   The artillery was formed on the right, and as General Lee with his staff rode into the opening thirteen guns were fired as a salute to the Chief.   Certain officers have certain salutes.   The President has, I think, twenty-one guns, while the Commander-in-Chief has thirteen, and so on.   Wofford's Georgia regiment was on the right, then Birkdales's Mississippi, Kershaw's South Carolina and Cobb's Georgia constituted McLaws' division.   The columns wheeled by companies into line and took up the march of review.   The bands headed each brigade, and played National airs as the troops marched by.

Birksdale had a magnificent brass band, while Kershaw had only a fife corps headed by that prince of players, Sam Simmonds, who could get more real music out of a fife or flute than some musicians could out of a whole band.   The music of the fife and drum, while it may not be so accomplished, gives out more inspiring strains for the marching soldier than any brass band.   The cornet, with its accompanying pieces, makes fine music on the stillness of the night, when soldiers are preparing for their night's rest, but nothing gives the soldier on the march more spirit than the fife and drum.   When a company nears the reviewing officer they give the salute by bringing their pieces from "right shoulder" to "carry," while on the march, and from "carry" to "present arms" when stationary. The officers raise the hilt of the sword, grasped firmly in the right hand, till the hilt is opposite the chin, the point of the blade extending outward about eighteen inches from the eyes, then, with a quick movement, to the side, the point downward and forward, and kept in this position till the reviewing officer has passed about eighteen paces.

The army had been placed under three Lieutenant Generals: Longstreet, with McLaw's, Hood's and Pickett's first corps; General Ewell, with Early's, Rhodes' and Trimble's constituting the 2d; while General A. P. Hill commanded Anderson's, Heath's and Pendar's, the 3d. Colonel James D. Nance commanded the 3d South Carolina, Colonel John D. Kennedy the 2d, Lieutenant Colonel Bland the 7th, Colonel Henegan the 8th, Colonel Dessausure the 15th, and Lieutenant Colonel W. C. G. Rice the 3d battallion, which had now been recruited by one man from each company in the brigade, forming two new companies, and formed a battalliou of sharpshooters and skirmishers.

The great army was now ready for the ever memorable second invasion of Maryland and Pennsylvania, which culminated in Gettysburg. The army was never before nor afterwards under betteer discipline nor in better fighting trim.

I will say here, that Colonel Aiken soon joined the brigade and took command of his regiment until after the great battle, and then retired permanently from active service.

On the 3d of June McLaws led off, Hood following on the 4th. Pickett followed Hood. On the 4th and 5th Ewell broke camp and followed in the wake of Longstreet. A. P. Hill, with 3d corps, was left at Fredericksburg to watch the movements of the enemy. After some delay, the enemy threatening a crossing, the 3d corps followed the other troops, all congregating near Culpepper Court House. Reaching the Blue Ridge mountains at Ashby's Gap on the 12th of June, at the western base of which runs the Shenandoah, we forded the stream, it being somewhat swollen, so much so, indeed, that men had to link hands as a protection. The water came up under the armpits, and four men marched abreast, holding each other by the hands. Some caught hold of horses belonging to officers of the regimental staff. In this way we crossed

over, and took up camp in the woods beyond. The wagon
trains were in advance, and the march was slow and much impeded. Very few of the men had divested themselves of their
clothing in crossing, and consequently when we went into
quarters it was a very wet army. The soldiers had built fires
and were rinsing out their clothes, when an order came to "fall
in ranks at once." The men hastily drew on their now thoroughly wet clothes, with all haste got into line and took up the
march back towards the river. A rumor was started "the
cavalry was pressing our rear." Kershaw's Brigade was
marched back over the river, much to their disgust, and posted
on the right and left of the road on top of the mountain. Here
we were stationed all night, and being on the watch for the
enemy, no fires were allowed. Towards day a cold mountain
wind set in, and the troops suffered no little from the chilly
wind and wet clothing. At sun-up we were marched for the
third time across the river, and prepared our meals for the
morning in the quarters of the evening before. Up to this
time no intimation was given us of our destination, but while
preparing our breakfast Adjutant Pope came around with orders stating we were on our way to Hagerstown, Md. At first
some seemed to regard this as a joke, but as Adjutant Pope was
so noted for his truthfulness and lack of jesting in business
matters, we were compelled to take the matter seriously. Of
all the officers in the 3d South Carolina, Adjutant Pope, I believe, was the most beloved. His position kept him in close
contact with the officers and men, and all had the utmost confidence in his honor and integrity and none doubted his impartiality. He had to keep the list of companies, to do picket duty,
and detail, and he was never accused of showing preferment
to any company. He was kind and courteous to all, and while
he mingled and caroused with the men, he never forgot his
dignity nor the respect due to his superiors. Whenever a favor
was wanted, or a "friend at court" desired, he never failed to
relieve and assist the poorest private the same as the highest
officer. While a strict disciplinarian, he was indulgent to
almost a fault, and was often seen to dismount and walk with
the troops and allow some tired or sick soldier to ride his horse.
Adjutant Pope and old "Doc," the name of his horse, were
indispensable to the 3d South Carolina regiment. The trusty

old horse, like his master, survived the war and did good service after its close.

The next day, the 13th, we took up our march in earnest. No straggling under any circumstances was allowed. The greatest respect was to be paid to all property, no pilfering of hen roosts, no robbery of orchards nor burning of palings or fences along the march. Somes mile in front we struck the Staunton and Winchester turnpike, and at regular intervals the troops were halted for a few minutes' rest. Occasionally the bands struck up a march and the soldiers were ordered into line and to take up the step.

So away down the valley we marched with banners flying, bands playing and the soldiers with a swinging step. Our march was regulated to about eighteen miles a day. But with all the orders and strict discipline, a great many of the soldiers who were given the name of "Foragers" could leave camp at night and often cross the mountain into the Luray valley, a valley, strictly speaking, laden with "milk and honey." It had never suffered the ravages of the Shenandoah, and there everything enticing to the appetite of the soldier was found. Before day the forager would return with butter, bread, and often canteens filled with pure old "Mountain Corn" or "Apple Jack." How men, after an all-day's straggling march, which is far more tiresome than an ordinary walk, could go from ten to fifteen miles over the mountains at night in search of something to eat or drink, is more than I could understand.

In a day or two we heard the news of Ewell capturing Milroy at Winchester, with 500 prisoners, and on the way a part of their troops passed us in high glee on their way to Richmond prison. I always noticed that the Federals, on their march to Richmond, were generally in better spirits when being escorted by Confederates than when commanded by their own officers with the Confederates between them and the Southern Capital.

On the fifth day of our march we passed through Winchester, with A. P. Hill marching parallel to us, some eight or ten miles to our right. Ewell had pushed on to the Potomac, and was turning Washington wild and frantic at the sight of the "Rebels" so close to their capital. As we neared the border we could discover Union sentiment taking the place of that of the South. Those who ever sympathized with us had to be very cautious and circumspect. Now and then we would see a window slowly raise in a house by the roadside, or on a hill in the distance, and the feeble flutter of a white handkerchief told of their Confederate proclivities. Generally the doors of all dwellings in the extreme northern portion of Virginia, and in Maryland and Pennsylvania, were mostly closed.

On the morning of the 25th of June we crossed the Potomac at Williamsport. Here was shouting and yelling. Hats went into the air, flags dipped and swayed, the bands played "Maryland, My Maryland," while the men sang "All Quiet on the Potomac To-night." We were now in the enemy's country, and scarcely a shot fired. We had lost Stuart. "Where was he?" "Stewart has left us." These and like expressions were heard on all sides. That bold and audacious cavalier, in a sudden fit of adventure, or hardihood unequalled, had crossed the Potomac in sight of the spires of Washington, almost under its very guns, and had frightened the authorities out of their wits. Every citizen that could possibly get out of the place was grabbing his valuables and fleeing the city on every train. The Cabinet officers were running hither and thither, not able to form a sensible or rational idea. Had it been possible to have evacuated the city, that would have been done. A Confederate prison or a hasty gibbet stared Staunton in the face, and he was sending telegrams like lightning over the land. Lincoln was the only one who seemingly had not lost his head. But Stuart pushed on toward York and Carlisle, while Ewell had carried fear and trembling to Philadelphia and Baltimore. Mead was marching with the energy of despair to head off Lee and his victorious troops.. Longstreet halted at Chambersburg and awaited developments. The troops lived in clover. The best of everything generally was given freely and willingly to them. Great herds of the finest and fattest beeves were continually being gathered together. Our broken down artillery horses and wagon mules were replaced by Pennsylvania's best. But in all, duly paid for in Confederate notes given by our Commissaries and Quartermasters.

At Hagerstown, Hill's troops came up with those of Longstreet, both moving on to Chambersburg, and there remained until the 27th.

General Lee had issued an address to the people of Maryland setting forth the reasons and causes of his army invading their country, offering peace and protection, and calling upon them to repair to his standard and throw off the tyranny and oppression that were bearing them down. He claimed to come, not as a conqueror, nor as one in pursuit of conquest, but as a liberator. But the people seemed to be in a state of lethargy, and to take little interest in the contest one way or the other. Guards were placed at all homes where such protection was asked for, and their fields of grain and orchards, as well as their domestic possessions, were sacredly guarded.

It was the general plan of Lee not to fight an aggressive battle in the enemy's country, but to draw the army of the North away from his lines of communities, and fight him on the defensive at favorable points.

Ewell had been sent on towards Carlisle and York, both those places being probably delivered to the Confederates by the civil authorities.

In passing through Pennsylvania, many curious characters were found among the quaint old Quaker settlers, who viewed the army of Lee not with "fear" or "trembling," but more in wonder and Christian abhorrence. When the front of the column came to the line dividing Pennsylvania and Maryland, it was met by a delegation of those rigorously righteous old Quakers who, stepping in the middle of the road, commanded, as in the name of God, "So far thou canst go, but no farther." After performing this seemingly command of God, and in accordance with their faith, a perfect abhorrence to war and bloodshed, they returned to their homes perfectly satisfied. It is needless to say the commander of Lee's 2d corps paid little heed to the command of the pious Quakers.

After remaining near Chambersburg Kershaw, with the other portion of the division, marched on to a little hamlet called Greenwood, leaving a part of Pickett's division at Chambersburg to guard our trains.

On the 29th the troops in advance began gradually to concentrate in the direction of Cashtown, some eight or ten miles west of Gettysburg. Ewell was bearing down from Carlisle, A. P. Hill was moving east, while Longstreet was moved up to Greenwood.

On the first of July A. P. Hill had met the enemy near Gettysburg, and fought the first day's battle of that name, driving the enemy back and through that city, part of his lines occupying the streets of Gettysburg and extending north and around the city. The distance intervening and the mountainous condition of the country prevented us from hearing the roar of the guns, and little did any of us think, while enjoying the rest in our tents, one portion of our army was in the throes of a desperate battle. Up to this time. not a word had been heard from Stuart and his cavalry, and this seriously disturbed the mind of our great commander. The positions of the enemy, moving against our rear and flank, necessitated a battle or a withdrawal, and to fight a great battle without the aid of cavalry simply seemed preposterous. General Stuart has been greatly censured for his conduct during these stirring times, just on the eve of this, the greatest battle fought in modern times.

Near sun-down, June 1st, we got orders to move along a dull road over hills, mountains and valleys. We marched with elastic step, every one feeling the time had come for active work. Early on our march we encountered General J. E. Johnston's brigade of Early's division, that had been left at Chambersburg, together with all of Ewell's wagon trains. This delayed our march until it was thought all were well out of the way. But before midnight it was overtaken again, and then the march became slow and tedious. To walk two or three steps, and then halt for that length of time, was anything but restful and assuring to troops who had marched all night without sleep or rest. About three o'clock at night, when we had reached the summit of an eminence, we saw in the plain before us a great sea of white tents, silent and still, with here and there a groan, or a surgeon passing from one tent to another relieving the pain of some poor mortal who had fallen in battle on the morning of the day before. We had come upon the field hospital of Hill, where he had his wounded of the day before encamped. Here we first heard of the fight in which so many brave men had fallen, without any decided results. As we had friends and relatives in A. P. Hill's corps, all began to make inquiries for Gregg's old brigade. We heard with delight and animation of the grand conduct of the banner brigade of South

Carolina, "Gregg's" or McGowan's, and listened with no little pride to the report of their desperate struggle through the streets of Gettysburg, and to learn that the flag in the hands of a member of a Palmetto regiment first waved over the city.

heard here of the desperate wounding of an old friend and school-mate, Lieutenant W. L. Leitsey, and left the ranks long enough to hunt him up in one of the many tents to the left. I found him severely wounded, so much so that I never met him afterwards. While marching along at a "snail' gait" among the wagons and artillery trains, with a long row of tents to the left, tired and worn out and so dark that you could not distinguish objects a few feet distant, a lone man was standing by the road side viewing, as well as he could in the dark, the passing troops. The slowness of our march enabled me to have a few words of conversation with him At its end, and just as I was passing him, I heard, or thought I heard him say, "I have a drink in here," pointing to a tent "if you feel like it." Reader, you may have heard of angel' voices in times of great distress, but if ever an angel spoke, it was at that particular moment, and to me. I was so tired sleepy and worn out I could scarcely stand, and a drink would certainly be invigorating, but for fear I had not heard or un derstood him clearly I had him to repeat it. In fact, so timely was it that I felt as if I could have listened all night, so much like the voice of a syren was it at that moment. I said "Yes Yes!!" But just then I thought of my friend and compan ion, my next Color Captain John W. Watts, who was just ahead of me and marching under the same difficulties as my self. I told the man I had a friend in front who wanted drink worse than I did. He answered "there is enough for two," and we went in. It was Egyptian darkness, but we found a jug and tin cup on the table, and helped ourselves It may have been that in the darkness we helped ourselves to bountifully, for that morning Watts found himself in an ambu lance going to the rear. Overcome by weariness and the potion swallowed in the dark perhaps, he lay down by the roadside to snatch a few moments sleep, and was picked up by the driver of the ambulance as one desperately wounded, and the driver was playing the Good Samaritan. Just before we went into action that day, I saw coming through an old field my lost

R. C. Carlisle,
　Major and Surgeon,
　　7th S. C. Regiment.
Capt. D. J. Griffith,
　　Co. C, 15th S. C. Regiment.

Capt. J. A. Mitchell,
　Co. E, 7th S. C. Regiment.
Capt. Andrew T. Harllee,
　Co. I, 8th S. C. Regiment.
　　(Page 482.)

friend, and right royally glad was I to see him, for I was always glad when I had Watts on my right of the colors.   Our brigade lay down by the roadside to rest and recuperate for a few hours, near Willoughby's Run, four miles from Gettysburg.

CHAPTER XVIII.

Battle of Gettysburg---July 2d.

When the troops were aroused from their slumbers on that beautiful clear morning of the 2d of July, the sun had long since shot its rays over the quaint old, now historic, town of Gettysburg, sleeping down among the hills and spurs of the Blue Ridge.   After an all-night's march, and a hard day's work before them, the troops were allowed all the rest and repose possible.   I will here state that Longstreet had with him only two divisions of his corps, with four regiments to a division.   Pickett was left near Chambersburg to protect the numerous supply trains.   Jenkins' South Carolina brigade of his division had been left in Virginia to guard the mountain passes against a possible cavalry raid, and thus had not the opportunity of sharing with the other South Carolinians in the glories that will forever cluster around Gettysburg.   They would, too, had they been present, have enjoyed and deserved the halo that will for all time surround the "charge of Pickett," a charge that will go down in history with Balaclava and Hohenlinden.

A. P. Hill, aided by part of Ewell's corps, had fought a winning fight the day before, and had driven the enemy from the field through the streets of the sleepy old town of Gettysburg to the high ground on the east.   But this was only the advance guard of General Meade, thrown forward to gain time in order to bring up his main army.   He was now concentrating it with all haste, and forming in rear of the rugged ridge running south of Gettysburg and culminating in the promontories at the Round Top.   Behind this ridge was soon to assemble an army, if not the largest, yet the grandest, best disciplined, best equipped of all time, with an incentive to do successful battle as seldom falls to the lot of an army, and on its success or defeat depended the fate of two nations.

There was a kind of intuition, an apparent settled fact, among
the soldiers of Longstreet's corps, that after all the other troops
had made their long marches, tugged at the flanks of the enemy,
threatened his rear. and all the display of strategy and generalship had been exhausted in the dislodgement of the foe, and all
these failed, then when the hard, stubborn, decisive blow was
to be struck, the troops of the first corps were called upon to
strike it. Longstreet had informed Lee at the outset. "My
corps is as solid as a rock--a great rock. I will strike the
blow, and win, if the other troops gather the fruits of victory."

How confident the old "War Horse," as General Lee called
him, was in the solidity and courage of his troops. Little did
he know when he made the assertion that so soon his seventeen
thousand men were to be pitted against the whole army of the
Potomac. Still, no battle was ever considered decisive until
Longstreet, with his cool. steady head. his heart of steel and
troops who acknowledged no superior, or scarcely equal,
in ancient or modern times, in endurance and courage, had
measured strength with the enemy. This I give. not as a personal view, but as the feelings, the confidence and pardonable
pride of the troops of the 1st corps.

As A. P. Hill and Ewell had had their bout the day before,
it was a foregone conclusion that Longstreet's time to measure
strength was near at hand, and the men braced themselves accordingly for the ordeal.

A ridge running parallel with that behind which the enemy
stood, but not near so precipitous or rugged, and about a mile
distant. with a gentle decline towards the base of the opposite
ridge, was to be the base of the battle ground of the day. This
plain or gentle slope between the two armies, a mile in extent,
was mostly open fields covered with grain or other crops, with
here and there a farm house, orchard and garden. It seems
from reports since made that Lee had not matured his plan of
battle until late in the forenoon. He called a council of war
of his principal Lieutenant to discuss plans and feasibilities.
It was a long time undecided whether Ewell should lead the
battle on the right, or allow Longstreet to throw his whole
corps on the Round Top and break away these strongholds, the
very citadel to Meade's whole line. The latter was agreed upon,
much against the judgment of General Longstreet, but Lee's

orders were imperative, and obeyed with alacrity. At ten
o'clock the movement began for the formation of the columns
of assault. Along and in rear of the ridge we marched at a
slow and halting gait. The Washington artillery had preceded
us, and soon afterwards Alexander's battery passed to select
positions. We marched and countermarched, first to the right,
then to the left. As we thus marched we had little opportunity as yet to view the strongholds of the enemy on the opposite ridge, nor the incline between, which was soon to be strewn
with the dead and dying. Occasionally a General would
ride to the crest and take a survey of the surroundings. No
cannon had yet been fired on either side, and everything was
quiet and still save the tread of the thousands in motion, as if
preparing for a great review.

Longstreet passed us once or twice, but he had his eyes cast
to the ground, as if in a deep study, his mind disturbed, and
had more the look of gloom than I had ever noticed before.
Well might the great chieftain look cast down with the weight
of this great responsibility resting upon him. There seemed to
be an air of heaviness hanging around all. The soldiers trod
with a firm but seeming heavy tread. Not that there was any
want of confidence or doubt of ultimate success, but each felt
within himself that this was to be the decisive battle of the
war, and as a consequence it would be stubborn and bloody.
Soldiers looked in the faces of their fellow-soldiers with a silent
sympathy that spoke more eloquently than words an exhibition of brotherly love never before witnessed in the 1st corps.
They felt a sympathy for those whom they knew, before the
setting of the sun, would feel touch of the elbow for the last
time, and who must fall upon this distant field and in an enemy's country.

About now we were moved over the crest and halted behind
a stone wall that ran parallel to a county road, our center being
near a gateway in the wall. As soon as the halt was made
the soldiers fell down, and soon the most of them were fast
asleep. While here, it was necessary for some troops of Hill's
to pass over up and through the gate. The head of the column was lead by a doughty General clad in a brilliant new
uniform, a crimson sash encircling his waist, its deep, heavy
hanging down to his sword scabbard, while great golden curls

hung in maiden ringlets to his very shoulders. His movement
was superb and he sat his horse in true Knightly manner. On
the whole, such a turn-out was a sight seldom witnessed by the
staid soldiers of the First Corps. As he was passing a man in
Company D, 3d South Carolina, roused up from his broken
sleep, saw for the first time the soldier wonder with the long
curls. He called out to him, not knowing he was an officer of
such rank, "Say, Mister, come right down out of that hair," a
foolish and unnecessary expression that was common throughout the army when anything unusual hove in sight.

This had roused all the ire in the flashy General, he became
as "mad as a March hare," and wheeling his horse, dashed up
to where the challenge appeared to have come from and
demanded in an angry tone, "Who was that spoke? Who
commands this company?" And as no reply was given he
turned away, saying, "D—d if I only knew who it was that
insulted me, I would put a ball in him." But as he rode off
the soldier gave him a Parthian shot by calling after him, "Say,
Mister, don't get so mad about it, I thought you were some
d—n wagon master."

Slowly again our column began moving to the right. The
center of the division was halted in front of little Round Top.
Kershaw was then on the right. Barksdale with his Mississippians on his left, Wofford and Sumner with their Georgians in
rear as support. Everything was quiet in our front, as if the
enemy had put his house in order and awaited our coming.
Kershaw took position behind a tumbled down wall to await
Hood's movements on our right, and who was to open the battle by the assault on Round Top. The country on our right,
through which Hood had to manœuvre, was very much broken
and thickly studded with trees and mountain undergrowth,
which delayed that General in getting in battle line. Anderson's Georgians, with Hood's old Texas Brigade under Robertson, was on McLaws' immediate right, next to Kershaw.
Law's Alabama Brigade was on the extreme right, and made
the first advance. On McLaws' left was Wilcox, of General
"Tige" Anderson's Division of the 3d Corps, with Posey and
other troops to his left, these to act more as a brace to Long-
srreet as he advanced to the assault; however, most of them
were drawn into the vortex of battle before the close of the day.

In Kershaw's Brigade, the 2d under Colonel John D. Kennedy and Lieutenant Colonel Frank Gilliar 1, the 15th under Colonel W. D. Dessausure and Major Wm. Gist, the 3d under Colonel James D. Nance and Major R. C. Maffett, the 7th under Colonel D. Wyatt Aiken and Lieutenant Colonel Elbert Bland, the 3d Battallion under Lieutenant Colonel W. G. Rice, the 8th under Colonel John W. Henegan, Lieutenant Colonel Hood and Major McLeod, went into battle in the order named, as far as I remember Major Wm. Wallace of the 2d commanded the brigade skirmish line or sharpshooters, now some distance in our front. A battery of ten guns was immediately in our rear, in a grove of oaks, and drew on us a heavy fire when the artillery duel began. All troops in line, the batteries in position, nothing was wanting but the signal gun to put these mighty forces in motion. Ewell had been engaged during the morning in a desultory battle far to our left and beyond the town, but had now quieted down. A blue puff of smoke, a deafening report from one of the guns of the Washington Artillery of New Orleans, followed in quick succession by others, gave the signal to both armies—the battle was now on.

It was the plan of action for Hood to move forward first and engage the enemy, and when once the combat was well under way on the right, McLaws to press his columns to the front. Law, with his Alabamians, was closing around the southern base of greater Round Top, while Robertson, with his three Texas regiments and one Arkansas, and Anderson with his Georgians, were pushing their way through thickets and over boulders to the front base of the Round Tops and the gorges between the two. We could easily determine their progress by the "rebel yell" as it rang out in triumph along the mountain sides.

The battery in our rear was drawing a fearful fire upon us, as we lay behind the stone fence, and all were but too anxious to be ordered forward. Barksdale, on our left, moved out first, just in front of the famous Peach Orchard. A heavy battery was posted there, supported by McCandless' and Willard's Divisions, and began raking Barksdale from the start. The brave old Mississippian, who was so soon to lose his life, asked permission to charge and take the battery, but was refused. Kershaw next gave the command, "forward," and the men

sprang to their work with a will and determination and spread
their steps to the right and left as they advanced. Kershaw
was on foot, prepared to follow the line of battle immediately
in rear, looking cool, composed and grand, his steel-gray eyes
flashing the fire he felt in his soul.

The shelling from the enemy on the ridge in front had, up to
this time, been mostly confined to replying to our batteries,
but as soon as this long array of bristling bayonets moved over
the crest and burst out suddenly in the open, in full view of
of the cannon-crowned battlements, all guns were turned upon
us. The shelling from Round Top was terrific enough to
make the stoutest hearts quake, while the battery down at the
base of the ridge, in the orchard, was raking Barksdale and
Kershaw right and left with grape and shrapnell. Semms'
Georgians soon moved up on our right and between Kershaw
and Hood's left, but its brave commander fell mortally wounded at the very commencement of the attack. Kershaw advanced directly against little Round Top, the strongest point
in the enemy's line, and defended by Ayer's Regulars, the
best disciplined and most stubborn fighters in the Federal
army. The battery in the orchard began grapeing Kershaw's
left as soon as it came in range, the right being protected by a
depression in the ground over which they marched. Not a
gun was allowed to be fired either at sharpshooters that were
firing on our front from behind boulders and trees in a grove
we were nearing, or at the commoners who were raking our
flank on the left. Men fell here and there from the deadly
minnie-balls, while great gaps or swaths were swept away in
our ranks by shells from the batteries on the hills, or by the
destructive grape and canister from the orchard. On marched
the determined men across this open expanse, closing together
as their comrades fell out. Barksdale had fallen, but his troops
were still moving to the front and over the battery that was
making such havoc in their ranks. Semms, too, had fallen,
but his Georgians never wavered nor faltered, but moved like a
huge machine in the face of these myriads of death-dealing
missiles. Just as we entered the woods the infantry opened
upon us a withering fire, especially from up the gorge that
ran in the direction of Round Top. Firing now became general along the whole line on both sides. The Fifteenth Regi-

ment met a heavy obstruction, a mock-orange hedge, and it was just after passing this obstacle that Colonel Dessausure fell. The center of the Third Regiment and some parts of the other regiments, were practically protected by boulders and large trees, but the greater part fought in the open field or in sparsely timbered groves of small trees. The fight now waged fast and furious.

Captain Malloy writes thus of the 8th: "We occupied the extreme left of the brigade, just fronting the celebrated 'Peach Orchard.' The order was given. We began the fatal charge, and soon had driven the enemy from their guns in the orchard, when a command was given to 'move to the right,' which fatal order was obeyed under a terrible fire, this leaving the 'Peach Orchard' partly uncovered. The enemy soon rallied to their guns and turned them on the flank of our brigade. Amid a storm of shot and shell from flank and front, our gallant old brigade pushed towards the Round Top, driving all before them, till night put an end to the awful slaughter. The regiment went in action with 215 in ranks, and lost more than half its number. We lost many gallant officers, among whom were Major McLeod, Captain Thomas E. Powe, Captain John McIver, and others." The move to the right was to let Wofford in between Barksdale and Kershaw.

Barksdale was pressing up the gorge that lay between little Round Top and the ridge, was making successful battle and in all likelihood would have succeeded had it not been for General Warren. General Meade's Chief Engineer being on the ground and seeing the danger, grasped the situation at once, called up all the available force and lined the stone walls that led along the gorge with infantry. Brigade after brigade of Federal infantry was now rushed to this citadel, while the crown of little Round Top was literally covered with artillery. Ayer's Regulars were found to be a stubborn set by Kershaw's troops. The Federal volunteers on our right and left gave way to Southern valor, but the regulars stood firm, protected as they were by the great boulders along their lines. Barksdale had passed beyond us as the enemy's line bent backward at this point, and was receiving the whole shock of battle in his front, while a terrific fire was coming from down the gorge and from behind hedges on the hill-side. But the Mississippians held on like grim death till Wofford, with his Georgians, who was moving in majestic style across the open field in the rear, came to his support.

General Wofford was a splendid officer, and equally as hard a fighter. He advanced his brigade through the deadly hail of bullets and took position on Bardsdale's right and Kershaw's left, and soon the roar of his guns were mingling with those of their comrades. The whole division was now in action. The enemy began to give way and scamper up the hill-side. But Meade, by this time, had the bulk of his army around and in rear of the Round Top, and fresh troops were continually being rushed in to take the places of or reinforce those already in action. Hood's whole force was now also engaged, as well as a part of A. P. Hill's on our left. The smoke became dense, the noise of small arms and the tumult raised by the "Rebel Yell," so great that the voices of officers attempting to give commands were hushed in the pandemonium. Along to the right of the 3d, especially up the little ravine, the fire was concentrated on those who held this position and was terrific beyond description, forcing a part of the line back to the stone house. This fearful shock of battle was kept up along the whole line without intermission till night threw her sable curtains over the scene of carnage and bloodshed and put an end to the strife. Wofford and Barksdale had none to reinforce them at the gorge, and had to fight it out single-handed and alone, while the Regulars, with their backs to the base of little Round Top, protected by natural formations, were too strong to be dislodged by Kershaw. As soon as the firing ceased the troops were withdrawn to near our position of the forenoon.

The work of gathering up the wounded lasted till late at night. Our loss in regimental and line officers was very great. Scarcely a regiment but what had lost one of its staff, nor a company some of its officers. Dr. Salmond, the Brigade Surgeon, came early upon the field and directed in person the movements of his assistants in their work of gathering up the wounded. "The dead were left to take care of the dead" until next day.

When the brigade was near the woodland in its advance, a most deadly fire was directed towards the center of the 3d both by the battery to our left, and sharpshooting in the front. It was thought by some that it was our flag that was drawing the fire, four color guards having gone down, some one called out ''Lower the colors, down with the flag.'' Sergant Lamb, color bearer, waved the flag aloft, and moving to the front where all could see, called out in loud tones, "This flag never goes down until I am down.''

Then the word went up and down the line ''Shoot that officer, down him, shoot him,'' but still he continued to give those commands, ''Ready, aim, fire,'' and the grape shot would come plunging into our very faces. The sharpshooters, who had joined our ranks, as we advanced, now commenced to blaze away, and the connoneers scattered to cover in the rear. This officer finding himself deserted by his men, waved his sword defiantly over his head and walked away as deliberately as on dress parade, while the sharpshooters were plowing up the dirt all around him, but all failed to bring him down. We bivouaced during the night just in rear of the battle ground.

CHAPTER XIX.

Gettysburg Continued—Pickett's Charge.

The next morning, July the 3rd, the sun rose bright and clear. Rations were brought to the men by details, who, after marching and fighting all day, had to hunt up the supply train, draw rations and cook for their companies for the next day—certainly a heavy burden on two men, the usual detail from each company.

No one could conjecture what the next move would be, but the army felt a certainty that Lee would not yield to a drawn battle without, at least, another attempt to break Meade's front. Either the enemy would attempt to take an advantage of our yesterday's repulse and endeavor to break our lines, crush Lee by doubling him back on the Patomac, or that Lee would undertake the accomplishment of the work of the day before. After the heavy battle of yesterday and the all night's march preceding, the soldiers felt little like renewing the fight of today, still there was no despondency, no lack of ardor, or morale, each and every soldier feeling, while he had done his best the day before, still he was equal to that before him for today.

In the First Corps all was still and quiet, scarcely a shot from either side, a picket shot occasionally was the only reminder that the enemy was near.

Away to our left, aud beyond the city, the Federals had assaulted Ewell's lines, and a considerable battle was raging from daylight till 10 o'clock.

The enemy were endeavoring to regain some of the trenches they had lost two days before.

General Pickett, who had been left at Chambersburg, had now come up with his three Virginia Brigades, Garnett's, Kemper's, and Armstead's, (Pickett being left in Virginia) and was putting them in position for his famous charge.

While this has no real connection with the work in hand, still, since the "Charge of Pickett," has gone in song and story, as the most gallant, dashing, and bloody of modern times, I am tempted here to digress somewhat, and give, as far as I am able, an impartial account of this memorable combat, being an eye witness. While Pickett led the storming party, in person, still the planning and details were entrusted to another head, namely, General Longstreet. In justice to him I will say he was opposed to this useless sacrifice of life and limb. In his memoirs he tells how he pleaded with Lee, to relieve him from the responsibility of command, aud when the carnage was at its zenith, riding through the hail from three hundred cannons and shells bursting under and over him, the Old Chieftain says, "I raised my eyes heavenward and prayed that one of these shots might lay me low and relieve me from this awful responsibility." While I would, by no word, or intimation detract one iota from the justly earned fame of the great Virginian, nor the brave men under him, still it is but equal justice to remember and record that there were other Generals and troops from other States as justly meritorious and deserving of honor as participants in the great charge, as Pickett and his Virginians. On the day before, Kershaw, in the battle before little "Round Top," Semms to the right, Wofford and Barksdale in front of the peach orchard and up the deadly gorge around Little Round Top to say nothing of Hood at Round Top, charged and held in close battle, two thirds of the Army of the Potomac, without any support whatever. See now how Pickett was braced and supported. Cemetery Ridge was a long ridge of considerable elevation, on which, and behind it the enemy was marshalled in mass; opposite this ridge was another of less eminence, and one mile, or near so, distant, behind which the Confederates were concentrating for the assault. Longstreet moved McLaws up near to the right of the assaulting columns in two lines, Semms and Wofford in the front and Barksdale and Kershaw in the rear lines as support. I continue to retain the names of the Brigade Commanders to designate the troops, although Barksdale and Semms had fallen the day before.

Kemper and Garnett were on the right of the assaulting column, with Armstead as support, all Virginians and of Pickett's Division. Wilcox, with his Alabama Brigade was to move some distance in rear of Pickett's right to take any advantage of the break in the line, and to protect Pickett's flank. On the left of Pickett, and on the line of attack was Heath's Division, commanded by General Pettigrew, composed of Archer's Brigade, of Alabama and Tennesseeans, Pettigrew's, North Carolina, Brockenboro's, Virginia, and Davis' Brigade, composed of three Mississippi Regiments and one North Carolina, with Scales' and Lanes' North Carolina Brigade in support. Hood and McLaws guarding the right and A. P. Hill the left. I repeat it, was there ever an assaulting column better braced or supported?

General Alexander had charge of the artillery at this point, and the gunners along the whole line were standing to their pieces, ready to draw the lanyards that were to set the opposite hills ablaze with shot and shell, the moment the signal was given.

Every man, I dare say, in both armies held his breath in anxious and feverish suspense, awaiting the awful crash. The enemy had been apprised of the Confederate movements, and were prepared for the shock.

When all was ready the signal gun was fired, and almost simultaneously one hundred and fifty guns belched forth upon the enemy's works, which challenge was readily accepted by Meade's cannoneers, and two hundred shrieking shells made answer to the Confederate's salute. Round after round were fired in rapid succession from both sides, the air above seemed filled with shrieking, screaming, bursting shells. For a time it looked as if the Heavens above had opened her vaults of thunder bolts, and was letting them fall in showers upon the heads of mortals below. Some would burst overhead, while others would go whizzing over us and explode far in the rear. It was the intention of Lee to so silence the enemy's batteries that the assaulting column would be rid of this dangerous annoyance. Longstreet says of the opening of the battle: "The signal guns broke the silence, the blaze of the second gun, mingling in the smoke of the first, and salvos rolled to the left and repeating themselves along the ridges the enemy's fine metal spreading its fire to the converging lines of the Confederates, plowing the trembling ground, plunging through the line of batteries and clouding the heavy air. Two or three hundred guns seemed proud of their undivided honors of organized confusion. The Confederates had the benefit of converging fire into the enemy's massed position, but the superior metal of the enemy neutralized the advantages of position. The brave and steady work progressed."

After almost exhausting his amunition, General Alexander sent a message to General Pickett, "If you are coming, come at once, or I cannot give you proper support. Ammunition nearly exhausted; eighteen guns yet firing from the cemetery." This speaks volumes for our artillerist, who had silenced over one hundred and fifty guns, only eighteen yet in action, but these eighteen directly in front of Pickett. Under this deadly cannonade, Pickett sprang to the assault. Kemper and Garnett advanced over the crest, closely followed by Armstead. Wilcox, with his Alabamians, took up the step and marched a short distance in rear of the right. The Alabamians, Tennesseeans, North Carolinians, and Virginians under Pettigrew lined up on Pickett's left, followed by Trimble, with his two North Carolina Brigades and the columns were off. The batteries on the ridges in front now turned all their attention to this dreaded column of gray, as soon as they had passed over the crest that up to this time had concealed them. To the enemy even this grand moving body of the best material in the world must have looked imposing as it passed in solid phalanx over this broad expanse without scarcely a bush or tree to screen it. And what must have been the feelings of the troops that were to receive this mighty shock of battle?

The men marched with firm step, with banners flying, the thunder of our guns in rear roaring and echoing to cheer them on, while those of the enemy were sweeping wind rows through their ranks. McLaws was moved up nearer the enemy's lines to be ready to reap the benefit of the least signs of success. Brockenborro and Davis were keeping an easy step with Kemper and Garnett, but their ranks were being thinned at every advance. Great gaps were mown out by the bursting of shells while the grape and canister caused the soldiers to drop by ones, twos and sections along the whole line. Men who were spectators of this carnage, held their breath in horror, while others turned away from the sickening scene, in pitying silence. General Trimble was ordered to close up and fill the depleted ranks, which was done in splendid style, and on the assaulting columns sped.

Trimble had fallen, Garnett was killed, with Kemper and Gibbon being borne from the field more dead than alive. At last the expected crash came, when infantry met infantry. Pickett's right strikes Hancock's center, then a dull, sullen roar told too well that Greek had met Greek. Next came Davis, then Brockenborro, followed on the left by Archer's and Pettigrew's Brigade, and soon all was engulfed in the smoke of battle and lost to sight. Such a struggle could not last long for the tension was too great. The Confederates had driven in the first line, but Meade's whole army was near, and fresh battalions were being momentarily ordered to the front. The enemy now moved out against Pickett's right, but Semms and Wofford of McLaws' Division were there to repulse them.

For some cause, no one could or ever will explain, Pickett's Brigades wavered at a critical moment, halted, hesitated, then the battle was lost. Now began a scene that is as unpleasant to record as it is sickening to contemplate. When Pickett saw his ruin, he ordered a retreat and then for a mile or more these brave men, who had dared to march up to the cannon's mouth with twenty thousand infantry lying alongside, had to race across this long distance with Meade's united artillery playing upon them, while the twenty thousand rifles were firing upon their rear as they ran.

Pettigrew's Division, which was clinging close to the battle, saw the disaster that had befallen the gallant Virginians, then in turn they, too, fled the field and doubling up on Lane and

Scales, North Carolinians, made "confusion worse confounded."
This flying mass of humanity only added another target for
the enemy's guns and an additional number to the death roll,

Alexander's batteries, both of position, and the line now
turned loose with redoubled energy on those of the enemy's
to relieve, as far as possible, our defeated, flying, and demoralized troops. For a few moments (which seemed like days to
the defeated) it looked as if all nature's power and strength
were turned into one mighty upheaval; Vessuvius, Etna, and
Popocatepetl were emptying their mighty torrents upon the
heads of the unfortunate Confederates. Men fell by the hundreds, officers ceased to rally them until the cover of the ridge
was reached. The hills in front were ablaze from the flashes
of near two hundred guns, while the smoke from almost as
many on our lines slowly lifted from the ridge behind us,
showing one continued sheet of flames, the cannoneers working their guns as never before. The earth seemed to vibrate
and tremble under the recoil of these hundreds of guns, while
the air overhead was filled with flying shells. Not a twink-
ling of the eye intervened between the passing of shots or
shells. The men who were not actively engaged became
numbed and a dull heavy sleep overcame them as they lay
under this mighty unnatural storm, shells falling short came
plowing through the ground, or bursting prematurely overhead, with little or no effect upon the slumberers, only a cry
of pain as one and another received a wound or a death shot
from the flying fragments. The charge of Pickett is over, the
day is lost, and men fall prone upon the earth to catch breath
and think of the dreadful ordeal just passed and of the many
hundreds lying between them and the enemy's line bleeding,
dying without hope or succor.

Farnsworth, of Kilpatrick's Cavalry, had been watching the
fray from our extreme right, where Hood had stationed scattered troops to watch his flank, and when the Union General
saw through the mountain gorges and passes the destruction of
Pickett he thought his time for action had come. The battle-
scarred war horses snuffed the blood and smoke of battle from
afar, and champed their bits in anxious impatience. The
troopers looked down the line and met the stern faces of their
comrades adjusting themselves to their saddles and awaiting
the signal for the charge. Farnsworth awaits no orders, and

when he saw the wave of Pickett's recede he gave the command to "charge," and his five hundred troopers came thundering down upon our detachments on the extreme right. But Farnsworth had to ride over and between the Fourth, Fourteenth, and Fifteenth Alabama Regiments, the Eleventh Georgia and the First Texas, and it is needless to add, his ride was a rough and disastrous one. Farnsworth, after repeated summons to surrender, fell, pierced with five wounds, and died in a few moments. His troopers who had escaped death or capture fled to the gorges and passes of the mountains through which they had so recently ridden in high expectation.

The enemy, as well as the Confederates, had lost heavily in general officers. Hancock had fallen from his horse, shot through the side with a minnie ball, disabling him for a long time. General Dan Sickles, afterwards military Governor of South Carolina, lost a leg. General Willard was killed. Generals Newton, Gibbon, Reynolds, Barlow were either killed or wounded, with many other officers of note in the Federal Army.

The soldier is not the cold unfeeling, immovable animal that some people seem to think he is. On the contrary, and paradoxical as it may appear, he is warm-hearted, sympathetic, and generous spirited and his mind often reverts to home, kindred, and friends, when least expected. His love and sympathy for his fellow-soldier is proverbial in the army. In the lull of battle, or on its eve, men with bold hearts and strong nerves look each other in the face with grim reliance. With set teeth and nerves strung to extreme tension, the thoughts of the soldier often wander to his distant home. The panorama of his whole life passes before him in vivid colors. His fisrt thoughts are of the great beyond—all soldiers, whatever their beliefs or dogmas, think of this. It is natural, it is right, it is just to himself. He sees in his imagination the aged father or mother or the wife and little ones with outstretched arms awaiting the coming of him who perhaps will never come. These are some of the sensations and feelings of a soldier on the eve of, or in battle, or at its close. It is no use denying it, all soldiers feel as other people do, and when a soldier tells as a fact that he "went into battle without fear," he simply tells "what George Washington never told." It is human, and "self-preservation

is the first law of nature." No one wants to die. Of co
ambition, love of glory, the plaudits of your comrades
countrymen, will cause many a blade to flash where other
it would not. But every soldier who reads this will say that
is honest and the whole truth. I am writing a truthful his
of the past and honesty forces me to this confession. '
men are cowards" in the face of death. Pride, ambitio
keen sense of duty, will make differences outwardly, but
heart is a coward still when death stares the possessor in
face. Men throw away their lives for their country's sake
for honor or duty like a cast off garment and laugh at de
but this is only a sentiment, for all men want to live. I w
so much to controvert the rot written in history and fictio
soldiers anxious to rush headlong into eternity on the bayo
of the enemy.

Historians of all time will admit the fact that at Gettysb
was fought a battle, not a skirmish, but it was not w
Northern writers like to call it, "Lee's Waterloo." '
Wilderness, Spottsylvania, and Petersburg were yet to come

CHAPTER XX.

Gettysburg---Fourth Day---Incidents of th Battle---Sketch of Dessausure, McLeod, and Salmonds.

A flag of truce now waves over both armies, granting a
pite to bury the dead and care for the wounded. The bu
of the dead killed in battle is the most trying of all duties
the soldier. Not that he objects to paying these last sad r
to his fallen comrades, but it is the manner in which he n
leave them with his last farewell.

A detail from each company is formed into a squad,
armed with spades or shovels they search the field for the de
When found a shallow pit is dug, just deep enough to co
the body, the blanket is taken from around the person, his b
being wrapped therein, laid in the pit, and sufficient dirt thro
upon it to protect it from the vultures. There
is systematic work, time being too precious, and

dead are buried where they fell. Where the battle was fierce and furious, and the dead lay thick, they were buried in groups. Sometimes friendly hands cut the name and the company of the deceased upon the flap of a cartridge box, nail it to a piece of board and place at the head, but this was soon knocked down, and at the end of a short time all traces of the dead are obliterated.

The wounded were gathered in the various farm houses, and in the city of Gettysburg. Those who were too badly wounded to be moved were left in charge of Surgeons, detailed by the Medical Directors to remain with the wounded. Surgeons in the discharge of their duties are never made prisoners, and the yellow flag flies as much protection as the white. A guard is placed around the hospitals to prevent those who may convalesce while there from escaping, but notwithstanding this vigilance many made their escape and came south, as the soldiers had a horror of the Federal prison pen. Ambulances and empty wagons were loaded to their full capacity with the wounded, unable to walk, while hundreds with arms off, or otherwise wounded as not to prevent locomotion, "hit the dust," as the soldiers used to say, on their long march of one hundred and fifty miles to Staunton, Va.

The Confederate forces numbered in the battles around Gettysburg on May 31st, 75,000, including Pickett's Division. The Federals had 100,000 ready and equipped for action, divided in seven army corps, under General Doubleday commanding First Corps, General Hancock Second Corps, General Sickles Third Corps, General Sykes Fifth Corps, General Sedgwick Sixth Corps, General Howard Eleventh Corps, General Slocum Twelfth Corps, and three divisions of cavalry under Pleasanton. The Confederate losses were : Longstreet, 7,539; Ewell, 5,973; A. P. Hill, 6,735; Cavalry under Stuart, 1,426; in all 21,643. Enemy's loss, 23,049.

I herewith give sketches of Colonel Dessausure and Major McLeod, killed in action, and of Doctor Salmond, Brigade Surgeon. As the latter acted so gallantly, and showed such generous impulses during and after the engagement, I think it a fitting moment to give here a brief sketch of his life.

COLONEL WILLIAM DAVIE DESSAUSURE OF THE THIRTEENTH.

Colonel Dessausure was certainly the Bayard of South Carolina, having served during his entire manhood, with little exception, amid the exciting, bustling scenes of army life. He was a hero of both the Mexican and Civil wars, and served in the Old Army for many years on the great Western Plains. A friend of his, an officer in his command who' was very close to the Colonel, writes me a letter, of which I extract the following:

"In my judgment, he was the superior of Kershaw's fine set of Colonels, having, from nature, those rare qualities that go to make up the successful war commander, being reticent, observant, far-seeing, quick, decided, of iron will, inspiring confidence in his leadership, cheerful, self-possessed, unaffected by danger, and delighting like a game cock in battle. He was singularly truth loving and truth speaking, and you could rely with confidence on the accuracy of his every statement. He understood men, was clear sighted, quick and sound of judgment, and seemed never to be at a loss what to do in emergencies. He exposed himself with reckless courage, but protected his men with untiring concern and skill. He was rather a small man, physically, but his appearance and bearing were extremely martial, and had a stentorian voice that could be heard above the din of battle."

Colonel Dessausure was born in Columbia, S. C., December 12th, 1819, was reared and educated there, graduated at the South Carolina College, and studied law in the office of his father, Hon. Wm. F. Dessausure. He raised a company in Columbia for the Mexican war, and served through that war as Captain of Company H, Palmetto Regiment. After that he was commissioned Captain of Cavalry, and assigned to General (then Colonel) Joseph E. Johnston's Regiment in the United States Army, and served on the Plains until the Civil war commenced, when he resigned, returned to his native State and organized the Fifteenth Regiment, and was assigned to Drayton's Brigade, then on the coast.

After the Seven Days' Battle around Richmond he went with his Regiment, as a part of Drayton's Brigade, in the first Maryland campaign. On Lee's return to Virginia, just before the Fredericksburg battle, his regiment was assigned to Kershaw.

he papers promoting him to the rank of Brigadier General
: in the hands of the Secretary of War at the time he was
d.   He was buried in a private cemetery near Breane's
:rn, in Pennsylvania, and his body removed to the family
ing ground after the war.
e was married to Miss Ravenel of Charleston, who sur-
1 him some years.

DONALD MCDIARMID MCLEOD

as descended from Scotch ancestors who immigrated to
country about 1775 and settled in Marlboro District, near
t's Bluff, on Big Pee Dee River.   He was son of Daniel
eod and Catherine Evans McLeod.   He graduated from
South Carolina College about 1853, and for some time en-
d in teaching school in his native county; then married
Margaret C. Alford and engaged in planting near where he
born.   He was then quietly leading a happy and contented
vhen South Carolina seceded.   When the toscin of war
ded he raised the first company of volunteers in Marlboro
was elected Captain of it.   This company, with another
Marlboro organized about the same time under Captain
'. Hamington, formed part of the Eighth Regiment, of Ker-
-'s Brigade.   Capt. McLeod was of commanding presence,
; six feet four inches tall, erect, active, and alert, beloved
iis company, and when the test came proved himself
by of their love and confidence.   On the field of battle his
ntry was conspicuous, and he exhibited undaunted cour-
and was faithful to every trust.
the reorganization of the Regiment he was elected Major
served as such through the battles of Savage Station, Mal-
Hill, Sharpsburg, Fredericksburg, Chancellorsville, and
ysburg.   In the last named he was killed while gallantly
ng the Regiment in the desperate charge on the enemy's
ty pieces of artillery, in the celebrated peach orchard,
e in a few minutes the Eighth Regiment, being on the lef,
e Brigade, without support, assailed in front and flankt
one hundred and eleven of the one hundred and seventy
were engaged in the battle.   Of this number twenty-eight
killed and buried on the field of battle.   Notwithstanding
slaughter the Old Eighth never faltered, but with the other
nents drove the enemy from the field, pursuing them upon

the rugged slopes of Round Top Hill.   Thus ended the life
one of the noblest and most devoted of Carolina's sons.

DR. T. W. SALMOND

Was born in Camden, S. C., on 31st of August, 1825.
ceived his diploma from the Medical College, in Charlest
S. C., in 1849.   Practiced medicine in Camden till the
came on.   Married first, Miss Mary Whitaker, afterwards N
Isabel Scota Whitaker.   He had two daughters, one by e
marriage.   When the troops were ordered to Charleston, he l
with General Kershaw as Surgeon of his regiment.   Gene
Kershaw was Colonel of the Second South Carolina Regime
His regiment was at the bombardment of Sumter.   His s
consisted of Dr. T. W. Salmond, Surgeon; Fraser, Quart
Master; J. I. Villipigne, Commissary; A. D. Goodwyn, /
jutant.

At the reorganization of the Brigade, Dr. Salmond was p
moted to Brigade Surgeon and was in all of the battles in \
ginia.   He went with General Kershaw to Tennessee a
came home when General Kershaw went back to Virgia
owing to ill health in the spring of 1864.

He resumed his practice after the war and continued till
death, August 31st, 1869.

I give below a short sketch concerning the Brigade Surge
copied from a local paper, as showing the kind of meta
which Dr. Salmond was made:

To the Editor of The Kershaw Gazette:

I never look upon a maimed soldier of the "Lost Caus
who fought manfully for the cause which he deemed to
right, without being drawn towards him with I may
brotherly love, commingled with the profoundest resp
And I beg space in your valuable columns to relate an in
dent in connection with the battle of Gettysburg, which
think, will equal the one between General Hagood and i
Federal officer, Daley.

In that memorable battle, whilst we were charging a b
tery of sixteen pieces of artillery, when great gaps were bei
made in the lines by the rapid discharge of grape and caniste
when the very grass beneath our feet was being cut to piec
by these missiles of death, and it looked as if mortal men cou
not possibly live there; Capt. W. Z. Leitner of our town w

shot in the midst of this deadly shower at the head of his company. When his comrades were about to remove him from the field he said, "Men I am ruined but never give up the battle. I was shot down at the head of my company, and I would to God that I was there yet." He refused to let them carry him off the field. Dr. Salmond, then Brigade Surgeon of Kershaw's Brigade, learning that his friend Captain Leitner was seriously wounded, abandoned his post at the infirmary, mounted his horse and went to the field where Captain Leitner lay, amid the storm of lead and iron, regardless of the dangers which encompassed him on every hand. He placed Captain Leitner on his horse, and brought him off the field. The writer of this was wounded severely in this charge, and while he was making his way as best he could to the rear, he met the Brigade Surgeon on his mission of mercy to his fallen friend, ordering those to the front who were not wounded, as he went along. Brave man, he is now dead. Peace to his ashes. As long as I live, I shall cherish his memory and think of this circumstance.

A Member of the Old Brigade.

Taken from Kershaw Gazette of February 26, 1880.

Judge Pope gives me several instances of devotion and courage during the Gettysburg campaign, which I take pleasure in inserting.

"DID THE NEGROES WISH FREEDOM?"

I have listened to much which has been said and written as to the aspiration of the negroes for freedom while they were slaves, but much that I saw myself makes me doubt that this aspiration was general.

Let me relate an instance that fell under my immediate observation. An officer had lost his bodyservant in May, 1863, when he mentioned the fact to some of the gentlemen of the and regiment, the reply was made: "There is a mess in Company A or I of the Third Regiment who have an excellent free negro boy in their employment, but they must give him up and no doubt you can get him." I saw the soldiers they referred to and they assured me that they would be glad if I would take the servant off their hands. The result was the servant came to me and I hired him. Soon afterwards we began the march to the Valley of Virginia, then to Maryland and

Pennsylvania. The servant took care of my horse, amongst his other duties. Having been wounded at Gettysburg and placed in a wagon to be transported to Virginia this boy would ride the horse near by the wagon, procuring water and something to eat. As the caravan of wagons laden with wounded soldiers was drawing near to Hagerstown, Maryland, a flurry was discovered and we were told the Yankees were capturing our train. At this time the servant came up and asked me what he should do. I replied, "Put the Potomac River between you and the Yankees." He dashed off in a run. When I reached the Potomac River I found William there with my horse. The Yankees were about to attack us there. I was to be found across the river. I said to William, "What can you do?" He replied that he was going to swim the horse across the Potomac River, but said he himself could not swim. I saw him plunge into the river and swim across. The soldiers who were with me were sent from Winchester to Staunton, Virginia. While in Staunton, I was assured that I would receive a furlough at Richmond, Virginia, so William was asked if he wished to accompany me to South Carolina. This seemed to delight him. Before leaving Staunton, the boy was arrested as a runaway slave, being owned by a widow lady in Abbeville County. The servant admitted to me, when arrested, that he was a slave. A message was sent to his mistress how he had behaved while in my employment—especially how he had fled from the Yankees in Pennsylvania and Maryland. This was the last time I ever saw him. Surely a desire for freedom did not operate very seriously in this case, when the slave actually ran from it.

In parting I may add that, left to themselves negroes are very kind-hearted, and even now I recall with lively pleasure the many kindnesses while I was wounded, from this servant, who was a slave.

HE WOULD FIGHT.

Why is it that memory takes us away back into our past experiences without as much saying, "With your leave, sir"? Thirty-six years ago I knew a fine fellow just about eighteen years old and to-day he comes back to us so distinctly! He was a native of Newberry and when the war first broke out he left Newberry College to enlist as a private in Company E of the

Third South Carolina Infantry. With his fine qualities of head and heart, it was natural that he should become a general favorite—witty, very ready, and always kind. His was a brave heart, too. Still he was rather girlish in appearance, for physically he was not strong. This latter condition may explain why he was called to act as Orderly at Regimental Headquarters when J. E. Brown gave up that position for that or courier with General Longstreet early in the year 1863. Just before the Third Regiment went into action at Gettysburg, Pennsylvania, and while preparing for that event, it became necessary, under general orders, that the field and staff of the regiment should dismount. It was the habit during battles to commit the horses to the control of the Regimental Orderly. On this occasion the Adjutant said to young Sligh: "Now, Tom, get behind some hill and the moment we call you, bring up the horses; time is often of importance." To the Adjutant's surprise Sligh burst into tears and besought that officer not to require him to stay behind, but on the contrary, to allow him to join his company and go into battle. At first this was denied, but so persistent was he in his request that the Adjutant, who was very fond of him, said: "Well Tom, for this one time you may go, but don't ask it again." Away he went with a smile instead of a tear. Poor fellow! The Orderly, Thomas W. Sligh, was killed in that battle while assisting to drive back General Sickles from the "Peach Orchard" on the 2d day of July, 1863.

RETURN TO VIRGINIA.

At daylight on the morning of the 5th the remnant of that once grand army turned its face southward. I say remnant, for with the loss of near one-third its number in killed, wounded, and prisoners the pride, prestige of victory, the feelings of invincibility, were lost to the remainder, and the army was in rather ill condition when it took up the retreat. Lee has been severely criticised for fighting the battle of Gettysburg, especially the last charge of Pickett; but there are circumstances of minor import sometimes that surround a commander which force him to undertake or attempt that which his better judgment might dictate as a false step. The world judges by results the successes and achievements of a General, not by his motives or intentions. Battles, however, are in a great measure but series

of accidents at best.   Some unforeseen event or circumstance
in the battles of Napoleon might have changed some of his
most brilliant victories to utter defeats and his grandest triumphs into disastrous routs.   Had not General Warren seen
the open gap at little Round Top, and had it been possible for
Federal troops to fill it up, or that Hancock had been one
hour later, or that our troops had pushed through the gorge of
litle Round Top before seen by Warren and gained Meade's
rear—suppose these, and many other things, and then reflect what momentous results depended upon such trivial circumstances, and we will then fail to criticise Lee.   His chances
were as good as Meade's.   The combination of so many little
circumstances, and the absence of his cavalry, all conduced to
our defeat.

Hill took the lead, Longstreet followed, while Ewell brought
up the rear.   Our wagon trains had gone on, some of them
the day before, towards Williamsport.   Kilpatrick made a
dash and captured and destroyed a goodly number of them, but
the teamsters, non-combatants and the wounded succeeded in
driving them off after some little damage.

Along down the mountain sides, through gorges and over
hills, the army slowly made its way.   No haste, no confusion.
The enemy's cavalry harassed over rear, but did little more.
Meade had had too severe a lesson to hover dangerously close
on the heels of Lee, not knowing what moment the wily
Confederate Chieftain might turn and trike him a blow he would
not be able to receive.   The rain fell in torrents, night and
day.   The roads were soon greatly cut up, which in a measure was to Lee's advantage, preventing the enemy from following him too closely, it being almost impossible to follow
with his artillery and wagons after our trains had passed.
We passed through Fairfield and Hagerstown and on to Williamsport.   Near Funkstown we had some excitement by being called upon to help some of Stuart's Cavalry, who were being hard pressed at Antietam Creek.

After remaining in line of battle for several hours, on a
rocky hillside, near the crossing of a sluggish stream, and our
pickets exchanging a few shots with those of the enemy, we
continued our march.   On the night of the 6th and day of the
7th our army took up a line of battle in a kind of semi-circle,
from Williamsport to Falling Waters.   The Potomac was too

much swollen from the continuous rains to ford, and the enemy having destroyed the bridge at Falling Waters we were compelled to entrench ourselves and defend our numerous trains of wagons and artillery until a bridge could be built. In the enclosure of several miles the whole of Lee's army, with the exception of some of his cavalry, were packed. Here Lee must have been in the most critical condition of the war, outside of Appomattox. Behind him was the raging Potomac, with a continual downpour of rain, in front was the entire Federal army. There were but few heights from which to plant our batteries, and had the enemy pressed sufficiently near to have reached our vast camp with shells, our whole trains of ordnance would have been at his mercy. We had no bread stuff of consequence in the wagons, and only few beef cattle in the enclosure. For two days our bread supply had been cut off. Now had such conditions continued for several days longer, and a regular siege set in, Lee would have had to fight his way out. Lumber was difficult to obtain, so some houses were demolished, and such planks as could be used in the construction of boats were utilized, and a pontoon bridge was soon under way.

In this dilemma and strait an accident in the way of a "wind fall" (or I might more appropriately say, "bread fall") came to our regiment's relief. Jim George, a rather eccentric and "short-witted fellow," of Company C, while plundering around in some old out-buildings in our rear, conceived the idea to investigate a straw stack, or an old house filled with straw. After burrowing for some time away down in the tightly packed straw, his comrades heard his voice as he faintly called that he had struck "ile." Bounding out from beneath the straw stack, he came rushing into camp with the news of his find. He informed the Colonel that he had discovered a lot of flour in barrels hidden beneath the straw. The news was too good to be true, and knowing Jim's fund of imagination, few lent ear to the story, and most of the men shook their heads credulously. "What would a man want to put flour down in a straw stack for when no one knew of 'Lee's coming?' " and, moreover, "if they did, they did not know at which point he would cross." Many were the views expressed for and against the idea of investigating further, until "Old Uncle" Joe Culbreath, a veteran of the Mexican War, and

17

a Lieutenant in Jim George's company, said: "Boys, war is a trying thing; it puts people to thinking, and these d—n Yankees are the sharpest rascals in the world. No doubt they heard of our coming, and fearing a raid on their smoke houses, they did not do like us Southern people would have done— waited until the flour was gone before we thought of saving it —so this old fellow, no doubt, put his flour there for safety." That settled it. "Investigate" was the word, and away went a crowd. The straw was soon torn away, and there, snugly hidden, were eight or ten barrels of flour. The Colonel ordered an equal division among the regiment, giving Jim an extra portion for himself.

By the 13th the bridge was completed, and the waters had so far subsided that the river was fordable in places. An hour after dark we took up the line of march, and from our camp to the river, a distance of one mile or less, beat anything in the way of marching that human nature ever experienced. The dust that had accumulated by the armies passing over on their march to Gettysburg was now a perfect bog, while the horses and vehicles sinking in the soft earth made the road appear bottomless. We would march two or three steps, then halt for a moment or two; then a few steps more, and again the few minutes' wait. The men had to keep their hands on the backs of their file leaders to tell when to move and when to halt. The night being so dark and rainy, we could not see farther than "the noses on our faces," while at every step we went nearly up to our knees in slash and mud. Men would stand and sleep—would march (if this could be called march- ing) and sleep. The soldiers could not fall out of ranks for fear of being hopelessly lost, as troops of different corps and divisions would at times be mingled together. Thus we would be for one hour moving the distance of a hundred paces, and any soldier who has ever had to undergo such marching, can well understand its laboriousness. At daybreak we could see in the gloomy twilight our former camp, almost in hollering distance. Just as the sun began to peep up from over the eeastern hills, we came in sight of the rude pontoon bridge, lined from one end to the other with hurrying wagons and artillery—the troops at opened ranks on either side. If it had been fatiguing on the troops, what must it have been on the poor horses and mules that had fasted for days and now dra

ing great trains, with roads almost bottomless? It was with a
mingled feeling of delight and relief that the soldiers reached
the Virginia side of the river—but not a murmur or harsh
word for our beloved commander—all felt that he had done
what was best for our country, and it was more in sorrow and
sympathy that we beheld his bowed head and grief-stricken
face as he rode at times pass the moving troops.

General Pettigrew had the post of rear guard. He, with his
brave troops, beat back the charge after charge of Kirkpat-
rick's Cavalry as they attempted to destroy our rear forces. It
was a trying time to the retreating soldiers, who had passed
over the river to hear their comrades fighting, single-handed
and alone, for our safety and their very existence, without any
hope of aid or succor. They knew they were left to be lost,
and could have easily laid down their arms and surrendered,
thus saving their lives; but this would have endangered Lee's
army, so they fought and died like men. The roar of their
powitzers and the rattle of their musketry were like the blasts
of the horn of Roland when calling Charlemagne to his aid
along the mointain pass of Roncesvalles, but, unlike the latter,
we could not answer our comrades' call, and had only to leave
them alone to "die in their glory." The brave Pettigrew fell
while heading his troops in a charge to beat back some of the
furious onslaughts of the enemy. The others were taken prisoners, with the exception of a few who made their escape by
plunging in the stream and swimming across.

At first our march was by easy stages, but when Lee discovered the enemy's design of occupying the mountain passes
along the Blue Ridge to our left, no time was lost. We hastened along through Martinburg and Winchester, across the
Shennandoah to Chester Gap, on the Blue Ridge. We camped
at night on the top of the mountain.

Here an amusing, as well as ludicrous, scene was enacted, but
not so amusing to the participants however. Orders had been
given when on the eve of our entrance into Maryland, that "no
private property of whatever description should be molested."
As the fields in places were enclosed by rail fences, it was
strictly against orders to disturb any of the fences. This order
had been religiously obeyed all the while, until this night on
the top of the Blue Ridge. A shambling, tumble-down rail
fence was near the camp of the Third South Carolina, not

around any field, however, but apparently to prevent stock
from passing on the western side of the mountain. At night
while the troops lay in the open air, without any protection
whatever, only what the scrawny trees afforded, a light rain
came up. Some of the men ran to get a few rails to make a
hurried bivouac, while others who had gotten somewhat damp
by the rain took a few to build a fire. As the regiment was
formed in line next morning, ready for the march, Adjutant
Pope came around for company commanders to report to
Colonel Nance s headquarters. Thinking this was only to
receive some instructions as to the line of march, nothing was
thought of it until met by those cold, penetrating, steel-gray
eyes of Colonel Nance. Then all began to wonder "what was
up." He commenced to ask, after repeating the instructions
as to private property, whose men had taken the rails. He
commenced with Captain Richardson, of Company A.

"Did your men take any rails?"

"Yes, sir."

"Did you have them put back?"

"Yes, sir."

"Captain Gary, did your men use any rails?"

"Yes, sir."

"Did you have them replaced?"

"No, sir."

And so on down to Company K. All admitted that their
men had taken rails and had not put them back, except Captain Richardson. Then such a lecture as those nine company
commanders received was seldom heard. To have heard
Colonel Nance dilate upon the enormity of the crime of "disobedience to orders," was enough to make one think he had
"deserted his colors in the face of the enemy," or lost a battle
through his cowardice. "Now, gentlemen, let this never
occur again. For the present you will deliver]your swords to
Adjutant Pope, turn your companies over to your next officer
in command, and march in rear of the regiment until further
orders." Had a thunder bolt fallen, or a three hundred-pound
Columbiad exploded in our midst, no greater consternation
would they have caused. Captain Richardson was exhonor-
ated, but the other nine Captains had to march in rear of the
regiment during the day, subject to the jeers and ridicule of
all the troops that passed, as well as the negro cooks.' "Great

Scott, what a company of officers!'' "Where are your men?"
"Has there been a stampede?" "Got furloughs?" "Lost your
swords in a fight?'' were some of the pleasantries we were
forced to hear and endure. Captain Nance, of Company G,
had a negro cook, who undertook the command of the officers,
and as the word from the front would come down the line to
"halt" or "forward" or "rest," he would very gravely repeat
it, much to the merriment of the troops next in front and those
in our rear. Near night, however, we got into a brush with
the enemy, who were forcing their way down along the eastern
side of the mountain, and Adjutant Pope came with our swords
and orders to relieve us from arrest. Lieutenant Dan Maffett
had not taken the matter in such good humor, and on taking
command of his company, gave this laconic order, "Ya hoo!''
(That was the name given to Company C.) "If you ever
touch another rail during the whole continuance of the war,
G—d d—n you, I'll have you shot at the stake."

"How are we to get over a fence," inquired someone.

"Jump it, creep it, or go around it, but death is your portion if you ever touch a rail again.''

On the 13th of August the whole army was encamped on the
south side of the Rapidan. We were commencing to settle
down for several months of rest and enjoy a season of furloughs, as it was evident neither side would begin active operations until the armies were recruited up and the wounded
returned for duty. This would take at least several months.
But, alas! for our expectations—a blast to our fondest dreams
—heavy fighting and hard marching was in store for our corps.
Bragg was being slowly driven out of Tennessee and needed
help; the "Bull Dog of the Confederacy" was the one most
likely to stay the advancing tide of Rosecrans' Army.

CHAPTER XXI

Transferred to Georgia—Scenes Along the Route.

While in camp great stress was laid on drills. The brigade drill was the most important. Every day at 3 o'clock the whole brigade was marched to a large old field, and all the evolutions of the brigade drill were gone through with. Crowds of citizens from the surrounding country came to witness our manoeuvers, especially did the ladies grace the occasions with their presence. The troops were in the very best of spirits—no murmurs nor complaints. Clothing and provision boxes began coming in from home. A grand corps review took place soon after our encampment was established, in which Generals Lee and Longstreet reviewed the troops.

All expected a good, long rest after their many marches and bloody battles in Maryland and Pennsylvania, but we were soon to be called upon for work in other fields. General Bragg had been driven out of Tennessee to the confines of Georgia, and it seemed that, without succor from the Army of the East to aid in fighting their battles, and to add to the morale of the Western Army, Bragg would soon be forced through Georgia. It had long been the prevailing opinion of General Longstreet that the most strategic movement for the South was to reinforce General Bragg with all the available troops of the East (Lee standing on the defensive), crush Rosecrans, and, if possible, drive him back and across the Ohio. With this end in view, General Longstreet wrote, in August, to General Lee, as well as to the Secretary of War, giving these opinions as being the only solution to the question of checking the continued advance of Rosecrans—renewing the morale of the Western Army and reviving the waning spirits of the Confederacy, thus putting the enemy on the defensive and regaining lost territory.

It should be remembered that our last stronghold on the

Mississippi, Vicksburg, had capitulated about the time of the disastrous battle of Gettysburg, with thirty thousand prisoners. That great waterway was opened to the enemy's gun boats and transports, thus cutting the South, with a part of her army, in twain.

This suggestion of General Longstreet was accepted, so far as sending him, with a part of his corps, to Georgia, by his receiving orders early in September to prepare his troops for transportation.

The most direct route by railroad to Chattanooga, through Southwest Virginia and East Tennessee, had for some time been in the hands of the enemy at Knoxville. We were, therefore, forced to take the circuitous route by way of the two Carolinas and Georgia. There were two roads open to transportation, one by Wilmington and one by Charlotte, N. C., as far as Augusta, Ga., but from thence on there was but a single line, and as such our transit was greatly impeded.

On the morning of the 15th or 16th of September Kershaw's Brigade was put aboard the trains at White Oak Station, and commenced the long ride to North Georgia. Hood's Division was already on the way. Jenkins' (S. C.) Brigade had been assigned to that division, but it and one of the other of Hood's brigades failed to reach the battleground in time to participate in the glories of that event. General McLaws, also, with two of his brigades, Bryan's and Wofford' (Georgians), missed the fight, the former awaiting the movements of his last troops, as well as that of the artillery.

Long trains of box cars had been ordered up from Richmond and the troops were loaded by one company being put inside and the next on top, so one-half of the corps made the long four days' journey on the top of box cars. The cars on all railroads in which troops were transported were little more than skeleton cars; the weather being warm, the troops cut all but the frame work loose with knives and axes. They furthermore wished to see outside and witness the fine country and delightful scenery that lay along the route; nor could those inside bear the idea of being shut up in a box car while their comrades on top were cheering and yelling themselves hoarse at the waving of handkerchiefs and flags in the hands of the pretty women and the hats thrown in the air by the old men and boys along the roadside as the trains sped through the

towns, villages, and hamlets of the Carolinas and Georgia.
No, no; the exuberant spirits of the Southern soldier were
too great to allow him to hear yelling going on and not yell
himself. He yelled at everything he saw, from an ox-cart to a
pretty woman, a downfall of a luckless cavalryman to a charge
in battle.

The news of our coming had preceded us, and at every station and road-crossing the people of the surrounding country,
without regard to sex or age, crowded to see us pass, and gave
us their blessings and God speed as we swept by with lightning
speed. Our whole trip was one grand ovation. Old men
slapped their hands in praise, boys threw up their hats in joy,
while the ladies fanned the breeze with their flags and handkerchiefs; yet many a mother dropped a silent tear or felt a
heart-ache as she saw her long absent soldier boy flying pass
without a word or a kiss.

At the towns which we were forced to stop for a short time
great tables were stretched, filled with the bounties of the
land, while the fairest and the best women on earth stood by
and ministered to every wish or want. Was there ever a
purer devotion, a more passionate patriotism, a more sincere
loyalty, than that displayed by the women of the South towards
the soldier boys and the cause for which they fought? Was
there ever elsewhere on earth such women? Will there ever
again exist circumstances and conditions that will require such
heroism, fortitude, and suffering? Perhaps so, perhaps not.

In passing through Richmond we left behind us two very
efficient officers on a very pleasant mission, Dr. James Evans,
Surgeon of the Third, who was to be married to one of Virginia's fair daughters, and Captain T. W. Gary, of same
regiment, who was to act as best man. Dr. Evans was a
native South Carolinian and a brother of Brigadier General
N. G. Evans, of Manassas fame. While still a young man, he
was considered one of the finest surgeons and practitioners in
the army. He was kind and considerate to his patients, punc-
tual and faithful in his duties, and withal a dignified, refined
gentleman. Such confidence had the soldiers in his skill and
competency, that none felt uneasy when their lives or limb
were left to his careful handling. Both officers rejoined us
a few days.

We reached Ringold on the evening of the 19th of Septe

ber, and marched during the night in the direction of the day's battlefield. About midnight we crossed over the sluggish stream of Chickamauga, at Alexander's Bridge, and bivouaced near Hood's Division, already encamped. Chickamauga! how little known of before, but what memories its name is to awaken for centuries afterwards! What a death struggle was to take place along its borders between the blue and the gray, where brother was to meet brother—where the soldiers of the South were to meet their kinsmen of the Northwest! In the long, long ago, before the days of fiction and romance of the white man in the New World, in the golden days of legend of the forest dwellers, when the red man chanted the glorious deeds of his ancestors during his death song to the ears of his children, this touching story has come down from generation to generation, until it reached the ears of their destroyers, the pale faces of to-day:

Away in the dim distant past a tribe of Indians, driven from their ancestral hunting grounds in the far North, came South and pitched their wigwams along the banks of the "river of the great bend," the Tennessee. They prospered, multiplied, and expanded, until their tents covered the mountain sides and plains below. The braves of the hill men hunted and sported with their brethren of the valley. Their children fished, hunted, played, fought, and gamboled in mimic warfare as brothers along the sparkling streamlets that rise in the mountain ridges, their sparkling waters leaping and jumping through the gorges and glens and flowing away to the "great river." All was peace and happiness; the tomahawk of war had long since been buried, and the pipe of peace smoked around their camp fires after every successful hunting expedition. But dissentions arose—distrust and embittered feelings took the place of brotherly love. The men of the mountains became arrayed against their brethren of the plains, and they in turn became the sworn enemies of the dwellers of the cliffs. The war hatchet was dug up and the pipe of peace no longer passed in brotherly love at the council meeting. Their bodies were decked in the paint of war, and the once peaceful and happy people forsook their hunting grounds and entered upon the war path.

Early on an autumn day, when the mountains and valleys were clothed in golden yellow, the warriors of the dissenting

factions met along the banks of the little stream, and across its
turbid waters waged a bitter battle from early morn until the
"sun was dipping behind the palisades of Look-Out Mountain"—no quarters given and none asked. It was a war of
extermination. The blood of friend and foe mingled in the
stream until its waters were said to be red with the life-
blood of the struggling combatants. At the close of the fierce
combat the few that survived made a peace and covenant, and
then and there declared that for all time the slugglish stream
should be called Chickamauga, the "river of blood." Such is
the legend of the great battleground and the river from whence
it takes its name.

General Buckner had come down from East Tennessee with
his three divisions, Stewart's, Hindman's, and Preston's, and
had joined General Bragg some time before our arrival, making General Bragg's organized army forty-three thousand
eight hundred and sixty-six strong. He was further reinforced by eleven thousand five hundred from General Joseph
E. Johnston's army in Mississippi and five thousand under
General Longstreet, making a total of sixty thousand three
hundred and thirty-six, less casualties of the 18th and 19th of
one thousand one hundred and twenty-four; so as to numbers
on the morning of the 20th, Bragg had of all arms fifty-nine
thousand two hundred and forty-two; while the Federal commander claimed only sixty thousand three hundred and sixty-
six, but at least five thousand more on detached duty and non-
combatants, such as surgeons, commissaries, quartermasters,
teamsters, guards, etc. Bragg's rolls covered all men in his
army. Rosecraus was far superior in artillery and cavalry, as
all of the batteries belonging to Longstreet's corps, or that
were to attend him in the campaign of the West, were far
back in South Carolina, making what speed possible on the
clumsy and cumbersome railroads of that day. So it was with
Wofford's and Bryan's Brigades, of McLaw's Division, Jenkins'
and one of Hood's, as well as all of the subsistence and ordnance
trains. The artillery assigned to General Longstreet by
General Lee consisted of Ashland's and Bedford's (Virginia),
Brooks' (South Carolina), and Madison's (Louisiana) batteries
of light artillery, and two Virginia batteries of position, all
under the command of Colonel Alexander.

As for transportation, the soldiers carried all they possessed.

on their backs, with four days of cooked rations all the time.
Generally one or two pieces of light utensils were carried by
each company, in which all the bread and meat were cooked
during the night.

Our quartermasters gathered up what they could of teams
and wagons from the refuse of Bragg's trains to make a semblance of subsistence transportation barely sufficient to gather
in the supplies. It was here that the abilities of our chiefs of
quartermaster and commissary departments were tested to the
utmost. Captains Peck and Shell, of our brigade, showed
themselves equal to the occasion, and Captain Lowrance, of
the Subsistence Department, could always be able to furnish
us with plenty of corn meal from the surrounding country.

The sun, on the morning of the 20th, rose in unusual splen-
dor, and cast its rays and shadows in sparkling brilliancy over
the mountains and plains of North Georgia. The leaves of
the trees and shrubbery, in their golden garb of yellow, shown
out bright and beautiful in their early autumnal dress—quite
in contrast with the bloody scenes to be enacted before the
close of day. My older brother, a private in my company,
spoke warmly of the beautiful Indian summer morning and
the sublime scenery round about, and wondered if all of us
would ever see the golden orb of day rise again in its magnifi-
cence. Little did he think that even then the hour hand on
the dial plate of destiny was pointing to the minute of "high
noon," when fate was to take him by the hand and lead him
away. It was his turn in the detail to go to the rear during
the night to cook rations for the company, and had he done so,
he would have missed the battle, as the details did not return
in time to become participants in the engagement that commenced early in the morning. He had asked permission to
exchange duties with a comrade, as he wished to be near me
should a battle ensue during the time. Contrary to regulations, I granted the request. Now the question naturally arises,
had he gone on his regular duties would the circumstances
have been different? The soldier is generally a believer in
the doctrine of predestination in the abstract, and it is well he
is so, for otherwise many soldiers would run away from battle.
But as it is, he consoles himself with the theories of the old
doggerel quartet, which reads something like this:—

"He who fights and runs away,
May live to fight another day;
But he who is in battle slain,
Will ne'er live to fight again."

Longstreet's troops had recently been newly uniformed, consisting of a dark-blue round jacket, closely fitting, with light-blue trousers, which made a line of Confederates resemble that of the enemy, the only difference being the "cut" of the garments—the Federals wearing a loose blouse instead of a tight-fitting jacket. The uniforms of the Eastern troops made quite a contrast with the tattered and torn home-made jeans of their Western brethren.

General Bragg had divided his army into two wings—the right commanded by Lieutenant General Leonidas Polk (a Bishop of the M. E. Church, and afterwards killed in the battles around Atlanta,) and the left commanded by that grand chieftain (Lee's "Old War Horse" and commander of his right), Lieutenant General James Longstreet. Under his guidance were Preston's Division on extreme left, Hindman's next, with Stewart's on extreme right of left wing, all of Major General Buckner's corps. Between Hindman and Stewart was Bushrod Johnson's new formed division. In reserve were Hood's three brigades, with Kershaw's and Humphries', all under Major General Hood, standing near the center and in rear of the wing.

The right wing stood as follows: General Pat Cleburn's Division on right of Stewart, with Breckenridge's on the extreme right of the infantry, under the command of Lieutenant General D. H. Hill, with Cheatham's Division of Polk's Corps to the left and rear of Cleburn as support, with General Walker's Corps acting as reserve. Two divisions of Forrest's Cavalry, one dismounted, were on the right of Breckenridge, to guard that flank, while far out to the left of Longstreet were two brigades of Wheeler's Cavalry. The extreme left of the army, Preston's Division, rested on Chickamauga Creek, the right thrown well forward towards the foot hills of Mission Ridge.

In the alignment of the two wings it was found that Longstreet's right overlapped Polk's left, and fully one-half mile in front, so it became necessary to bend Stewart's Division back to join to Cleburn's left, thereby leaving space between Bush-

rod Johnson and Stewart for Hood to place his three brigades
on the firing line.

Longstreet having no artillery, he was forced to engage all
of the thirty pieces of Buckner's. In front of Longstreet lay a
part of the Twentieth Corps, Davis' and Sheridan's Divisions,
under Major General McCook, and part of the Twenty-first
Corps, under the command of General Walker. On our right,
facing Polk, was the distinguished Union General, George H.
Thomas, with four divisions of his own corps, the Fourteenth,
Johnson's Division of the Twentieth, and Van Cleve's of the
Twenty-first Corps.

General Thomas was a native Virginian, but being an officer
in the United States Army at the time of the secession of his
State, he preferred to remain and follow the flag of subjugation, rather than, like the most of his brother officers of
Southern birth, enter into the service of his native land and
battle for justice, liberty, and States Rights. He and General Hunt, of South Carolina, who so ably commanded the
artillery of General Meade at Gettysburg, were two of the most
illustrious of Southern renegades.

In the center of Rosecrans' Army were two divisions, Woods'
and Palmer's, under Major General Crittenden, posted along
the eastern slope of Mission Ridge, with orders to support
either or both wings of the army, as occasions demanded.

General Gordon Granger, with three brigades of infantry
and one division of cavalry, guarded the Union left and rear
and the gaps leading to Chattanooga, and was to act as general
reserve for the army and lay well back and to the left of Bran-
nan's Division that was supporting the front line of General
Thomas.

The bulk of the Union cavalry, under General Mitchell, was
two miles distant on our left, guarding the ford over Chickamauga at Crawfish Springs. The enemy's artillery, consisting of two hundred and forty-six pieces, was posted along the
ridges in our front, giving exceptional positions to shell and
grape an advancing column.

Bragg had only two hundred pieces, but as his battle line
occupied lower ground than that of the enemy, there was little
opportunity to do effective work with his cannon.

The ground was well adapted by nature for a battlefield, and
as the attacking party always has the advantage of manoeuver

and assault in an open field, each commander was anxious to get his blow in first. So had not Bragg commenced the battle as early as he did, we would most assuredly have had the whole Federal Army upon our hands before the day was much older.

Kershaw's Brigade, commanded by General Kershaw, stood from right to left in the following order: Fifteenth Regiment on the right, commanded by Lieutenant Colonel Joseph Gist; Second Regiment, Colonel James D. Kennedy; Third, Colonel James D. Nance; Third Battalion, by Captain Robert H. Jennings; Eighth, Colonel John W. Henagan; Seventh, Colonel Elbert Bland.

CHAPTER XXII

The Battle of Chickamauga.

As I have already said, this was a lovely country—a picturesque valley nestling down among the spurs cf the mountain, with the now classic Chickamauga winding its serpentine way along with a sluggish flow. It was also a lovely day; nature was at her best, with the fields and woods autumn tinged—the whole country rimmed in the golden hue of the Southern summer. The battling ground chosen, or rather say selected by fate, on which the fierce passions of men were to decide the fortunes of armies and the destiny of a nation, was rolling, undulating, with fields of growing grain or brown stubble, broken by woods and ravines, while in our front rose the blue tinted sides of Mission Ridge.

Both commanders were early in the saddle, their armies more evenly matched in numbers and able Lieutenants than ever before, each willing and anxious to try conclusions with the other—both confident of success and watchful of the mistakes and blunders of their opponent, ready to take advantage of the least opportunity that in any way would lead to success. The armies on either side were equally determined and confident, feeling their invincibility and the superiority of their respective commanders. Those of the North felt that it was impossible for the beaten Confederates to stand for a moment, with any hope of triumph, before that mighty machine of armed force

that had been successfully rolling from the Ohio to the confines
of Georgia.   On the other hand, the Army of Tennessee felt
that, with the aid from Joe Johnston, with Buckner, and the
flower of Lee's Army to strengthen their ranks, no army on
earth could stay them on the battlefield.

The plan of battle was to swing the whole army forward in a
wheel, Preston's Division on Longstreets extreme left being
the pivot, the right wing to break the enemy's lines and
uncover the McFarland and Rossville Gaps, thus capturing the
enemy's lines of communication to Chattanooga.

The Union Army was well protected by two lines of earthworks and log obstructions, with field batteries at every
salient, or scattered along the front lines at every elevation,
supported by the pieces of position on the ridges in rear.

The Confederate commander made no secret of his plan of
battle, for it had been formulated three days before, and his
manoeuvers on the 18th and 19th indicated his plan of operations.   Early in the morning Bragg saluted his adversary with
thirty pieces of artillery from his right wing, and the Federal
commander was not slow in acknowledging the salutation.
The thunder of these guns echoed along the mountain sides
and up and down the valleys with thrilling effect.   Soon the
ridges in our front were one blaze of fire as the infantry began
their movements for attack, and the smoke from the enemy's
guns was a signal for our batteries along the whole line.

The attack on the right was not as prompt as the commander
in chief had expected, so he rode in that direction and gave
positive orders for the battle to begin.   General D. H. Hill
now ordered up that paladin of State craft, the gallant Kentuckian and opponent of Lincoln for the Presidency, General
John C. Breckenridge, and put him to the assault on the
enemy's extreme left.   But one of his brigade commanders
being killed early in the engagement, and the other brigades
becoming somewhat disorganized by the tangled underbrush,
they made but little headway against the enemy's works.
Then the fighting Irishman, the Wild Hun of the South, General Pat Cleburn, came in with his division on Breckenridge's
left, and with whoop and yell he fell with reckless ferocity
upon the enemy's entrenchments.   The four-gun battery of
the Washington (Louisiana) Artillery following the column of
assault, contended successfully with the superior metal of the

three batteries of the enemy. The attack was so stubborn and
relentless that the enemy was forced back on his second line,
and caused General Thomas to call up Negley's Division from
his reserves to support his left against the furious assaults of
Breckenridge and Cleburn. But after somewhat expending
their strength in the first charge against the enemy's works,
and Federal reinforcements of infantry and artillery coming up,
both Confederate divisions were gradually being forced back
to their original positions. Deshler's Brigade, under that
prince of Southern statesmen, Roger Q. Mills, supported by a
part of Cheatham's Division, took up Cleburn's battle, while
the division under General States R. Gist (of South Carolina),
with Liddell's, of Walker's Corps, went to the relief of Breckenridge. Gist's old Brigade (South Carolina) struck the angle
of the enemy's breastworks, and received a galling fire from
enfilading lines. But the other brigades of Gist's coming up
and Liddell's Division pushing its way through the shattered
and disorganized ranks of Breckenridge, they made successful
advance, pressing the enemy back and beyond the Chattanooga
Road.

Thomas was again reduced to the necessity of calling for
reinforcements, and so important was it thought that this
ground should be held, that the Union commander promised
support, even to the extent of the whole army, if necessary.

But eleven o'clock had come and no material advantage had
been gained on the right. The reinforcements of Thomas having succeeded in checking the advance of Gist and Liddell, the
Old War Horse on the left became impatient, and sent word to
Bragg, "My troops can break the lines, if you care to hav-
them broken." What sublime confidence did Lee's old commander of the First Corps have in the powers of his faithful
troops! But General Bragg, it seems, against all military rules
or precedent, and in violation of the first principles of army
ethics, had already sent orders to Longstreet's subalterns,
directly and not through the Lieutenant General's headquarters, as it should have been done, to commence the attack.
General Stewart, with his division of Longstreet's right, was
at that moment making successful battle against the left of the
Twentieth and right of Twenty-first Corps. This attack so
near to Thomas' right, caused that astute commander to begin
to be as apprehensive of his right as he had been of his left

flank, and asked for support in that quarter. Longstreet now ordered up the gallant Texan, General Hood, with his three brigades, with Kershaw's and Humphreys in close support. Hood unmercifully assailed the column in his front, but was as unmercifully slaughte·ed, himself falling desperately wounded. Benning's Brigade was thrown in confusion, but at this juncture Kershaw and Humphreys moved their brigades upon the firing line and commenced the advance. In front of these two brigades was a broad expanse of cultivated ground, now in stubble. Beyond this field was a wooded declivity rising still farther away to a ridge called Pea Ridge, on which the enemy was posted. Our columns were under a terrific fire of shells as they advanced through the open field, and as they neared the timbered ridge they were met by a galling tempest of grape and canister. The woods and underbrush shielded the enemy from view.

Law now commanding Hood's Division, reformed his lines and assaulted and took the enemy's first lines of entrenchments. Kershaw marched in rear of the brigade, giving commands in that clear, metalic sound that inspired confidence in his troops. At the foot of the declivity, or where the ground begun to rise towards the enemy's lines, was a rail fence, and at this obstruction and clearing of it away, Kershaw met a galling fire from the Federal sharpshooters, but not a gun had been fired as yet by our brigade. But Humphreys was in it hot and heavy. As we began our advance up the gentle slope, the enemy poured volley after volley into us from its line of battle posted behind the log breastworks. Now the battle with us raged in earnest.

Bushrod Johnson entered the lists with his division, and routed the enemy in his front, taking the first line of breastworks without much difficulty. Hindman's Division followed Johnson, but his left and rear was assailed by a formidable force of mounted infantry which threw Manigault's (South Carolina) Brigade on his extreme left in disorder, the brigade being seriously rattled. But Twiggs' Brigade, from Preston's pivotal Division, came to the succor of Manigault and succeeded in restoring the line, and the advance continued. Kershaw had advanced to within forty paces of the enemy's line, and it seemed for a time that his troops would be annihilated. Colonel Bland, then Major Hood, commanding the

18

Seventh, were killed. Lieutenant Colonel Hoole, of the Eighth, was killed. Colonel Gist, commanding the Fifteenth, and Captain Jennings, commanding the Third Battalion, were dangerously wounded, while many others of the line officers had fallen, and men were being mown down like grain before a sickle.

General Kershaw ordered his men to fall back to the little ravine a hundred paces in rear, and here they made a temporary breastwork of the torn down fence and posted themselves behind it. They had not long to wait before a long line of blue was seen advancing from the crest of the hill. The enemy, no doubt, took our backward movement as a retreat, and advanced with a confident mien, all unconscious of our presence behind the rail obstruction. Kershaw, with his steel-gray eyes glancing up and down his lines, and then at the advancing line of blue, gave the command repeatedly to "Hold your fire." When within a very short distance of our column the startling command rang out above the din of battle on our right and left, "Fire!" Then a deafening volley rolled out along the whole line. The enemy halted and wavered, their men falling in groups, then fled to their entrenchments, Kershaw closely pursuing.

From the firing of the first gun away to the right the battle became one of extreme bitterness, the Federals standing with unusual gallantry by their guns in the vain hope that as the day wore on they could successfully withstand, if not entirely repel, the desperate assaults of Bragg until night would give them cover to withdraw.

The left wing was successful, and had driven the Federal lines back at right angles on Thomas' right. The Federal General, Gordon Granger, rests his title to fame by the bold movement he now made. Thomas was holding Polk in steady battle on our right, when General Granger noticed the Twentieth Corps was being forced back, and the firing becoming dangerously near in the Federal's rear. General Granger, without any orders whatever, left his position in rear of Thomas and marched to the rescue of McCook, now seeking shelter along the slopes of Mission Ridge, but too late to retrieve losses—only soon enough to save the Federal Army from rout and total disaster.

But the turning point came when Longstreet ordered up a

battalion of heavy field pieces, near the angle made by the bending back of the enemy's right, and began infilading the lines of Thomas, as well as Crittenden's and McCook's. Before this tornado of shot and shell nothing could stand. But with extraordinary tenacity of Thomas and the valor of his men he held his own for a while longer.

Kershaw was clinging to his enemy like grim death from eleven o'clock until late in the evening—his men worn and fagged, hungry and almost dying of thirst, while the ammunition was being gradually exhausted and no relief in sight. Hindman (Johnson on the left) had driven the enemy back on Snodgrass Hill, where Granger's reserves were aiding them in making the last grand struggle. Snodgrass Hill was thought to be the key to the situation on our left, as was Horse Shoe Bend on the right, but both were rough and hard keys to handle. Kershaw had driven all before him from the first line of works, and only a weak fire was coming from the second line. All that was needed now to complete the advance was a concentrated push along the whole line, but the density of the smoke settling in the woods, the roar of battle drowning all commands, and the exhaustion and deflection of the rank and file made this move impossible.

But just before the sun began dipping behind the mountains on our left, a long line of gray, with glittering bayonets, was seen coming down the slope in our rear. It was General Gracie, with his Alabama Brigade of Preston's Division, coming to reinforce our broken ranks and push the battle forward. This gallant brigade was one thousand one hundred strong and it was said this was their first baptism of fire and blood. General Gracie was a fine specimen of physical manhood and a finished looking officer, and rode at the head of his column. Reaching Kershaw, he dismounted, placed the reins of his horse over his arm, and ordered his men to the battle. The enemy could not withstand the onslaught of these fresh troops, and gave way, pursued down the little dell in rear by the Alabamians. The broken lines formed on the reserves that were holding Snodgrass Hill, and made an aggressive attack upon Gracie, forcing him back on the opposite hill.

Twigg's Brigade, of the same division, came in on the left and gave him such support as to enable him to hold his new line.

The fire of Longstreet's batteries from the angle down Thomas' lines, forced that General to begin withdrawing his troops from their entrenchments, preparatory to retreat. This movement being noticed by the commanding General, Liddell's Division on the extreme right was again ordered to the attack, but with no better success than in the morning. The enemy had for some time been withdrawing his trains and broken ranks through the gaps of the mountain in the direction of Chattanooga, leaving nothing in front of the left wing but the reserves of Granger and those of Crittenden. These held their ground gallantly around Snodgrass Hill, but it was a self-evident fact to all the officers, as well as the troops, that the battle was irretrievably lost, and they were only fighting for time, the time that retreat could be safely made under cover of darkness. But before the sun was fairly set, that great army was in full retreat. But long before this it was known to the brilliant Union commander that fate had played him false—that destiny was pointing to his everlasting overthrow. He knew, too, that the latter part of the battle, while brief and desperate, the luried cloud of battle settling all around his dead and dying, a spectre had even then arisen as from the earth, and pointing his bony fingers at the field of carnage, whispering in his ear that dreaded word, "Lost!"

As night closed in upon the bloody scenes of the day, the Federal Army, that in the morning had stood proud and defiant along the crests and gorges of the mountain ridges, was now a struggling mass of beaten and fleeing fugatives, or groups groping their way through the darkness towards the passes that led to Chattanooga.

Of all the great Captains of that day, Longstreet was the guiding genius of Chickamauga. It was his masterful mind that rose equal to the emergency, grasped and directed the storm of battle. It was by the unparalleled courage of the troops of Hood, Humphreys, and Kershaw, and the temporary command under Longstreet, throwing themselves athwart the path of the great colossus of the North, that checked him and drove him back over the mountains to the strongholds around Chattanooga. And it is no violent assumption to say that had the troops on the right under Polk supported the battle with as fiery zeal as those on the left under Longstreet, the Union Army would have been utterly destroyed and a possible differeut ending to the campaign, if not in final, results might have been confidently expected.

The work of the soldier was not done with the coming of night. The woods along the slopes where the battle had raged fiercest had caught fire and the flames were nearing the wounded and the dead. Their calls and piteous wails demanded immediate assistance. Soldiers in groups and by ones and twos scoured the battlefield in front and rear, gathering up first the wounded then the dead. The former were removed to the field infirmaries, the latter to the new city to be built for them—the city of the dead. The builders were already at work on their last dwelling places, scooping out shallow graves with bayonets, knives, and such tools that were at hand. Many pathetic pectacles were witnessed of brother burying brother. My brother and five other members of the company were laid side by side, wrapped only in their blankets, in the manner of the Red Men in the legend who fought and died here in the long, long ago. Here we left them "in all their glory" amid the sacred stillness that now reigned over the once stormy battlefield, where but a short while before the tread of struggling legions, the thunder of cannon, and the roar of infantry mingled in systematic confusion. But now the awful silence and quietude that pervades the field after battle--where lay the dreamless sleepers of friend and foe, victor and vanquished, the blue and the gray, with none to sing their requiems—nothing heard save the plaintive notes of the night bird or the faint murmurs of grief of the comrades who are placing the sleepers in their shallow beds! But what is death to the soldier? It is the passing of a comrade perhaps one day or hour in advance to the river with the Pole Ferryman.

Bragg, out of a total of fifty-nine thousand two hundred and forty-two, lost seventeen thousand eight hundred. Rosecran's total was sixty thousand eight hundred and sixty-seven (exclusive of the losses on the 18th and 19th). His loss on the 20th was sixteen thousand five hundred and fifty. The greater loss of the Confederates can be accounted for when it is remembered that they were the assaulting party—the enemy's superior position, formidable entrenchments, and greater amount of artillery.

The Battle of Chickamauga was one of the most sanguinary

of the war, when the number of troops engaged and the time
in actual combat are taken into consideration. In the matter
of losses it stands as the fifth greatest battle of the war. History gives no authentic record of greater casualties in battle in
the different organizations, many of the regiments losing from
fifty to fifty-seven per cent. of their numbers, while some
reached as high as sixty-eight per cent. When it is remembered that usually one is killed out right to every five that are
wounded, some idea of the dreadful mortality on the field can
be formed.

CHAPTER XXIII

Notes of the Battle--Pathetic Scenes--Sketches of Officers.

The Seventh Regiment was particularly unfortunate in the
loss of her brilliant officers. Colonel Bland and Lieutenant
Colonel Hood both being killed, that regiment was left without a field officer. Lieutenant Colonel Joseph Gist, of the
Fifteenth, being permanently disabled, and Major William Gist
being soon afterwards killed, the Fifteenth was almost in the
same condition of the Seventh. So also was the Third Battalion. Captain Robert Jennings, commanding the battalion
as senior Captain, lost his arm here, and was permanently
retired, leaving Captain Whitner in command. Major Dan
Miller had received a disabling wound in some of the former
battles and never returned. Colonel Rice returning soon after
this battle, he likewise received a wound from which he never
sufficiently recovered for active service, so the Third Battalion
was thereafter commanded by a Captain, Captain Whitner
commanding until his death one year later. The Eighth Regiment met an irreparable loss in the death of Lieutenant Colonel Hoole. No officer in the brigade had a more soldierly
bearing, high attainments, and knightly qualities than Colonel
Hoole, and not only the regiment, but the whole brigade felt
his loss. He was one of those officers whose fine appearance
caused men to stop and look at him twice before passing. The
many fine officers, Captains as well as Lieutenants, that were

killed or wounded here made a death and disabled roll, from the effects of which the brigade never fully recovered. Then the whole army mourned the supposed death of the gallant and dashing Texan, General Hood, but he lived to yet write his name in indellible letters on the roll of fame among the many officers of distinction in the Army of Tennessee.

In our first general advance in the morning, as the regiment reached the brow of the hill, just before striking the enemy's breastworks, my company and the other color company, being crowded together by the pressure of the flanks on either side, became for the moment a tangled, disorganized mass. A sudden discharge of grape from the enemy's batteries, as well as from their sharpshooters posted behind trees, threw us in greater confusion, and many men were shot down unexpectedly. A Sergeant in my company, T. C. Nunamaker, received a fearful wound in the abdomen. Catching my hand while falling, he begged to be carried off. "Oh! for God's sake, don't leave me here to bleed to death or have my life trampled out! Do have me carried off!" But the laws of war are inexorable, and none could leave the ranks to care for the wounded, and those whose duty it was to attend to such matters were unfortunately too often far in the rear, seeking places of safety for themselves, to give much thought or concern to the bleeding soldiers. Before our lines were properly adjusted, the gallant Sergeant was beyond the aid of anyone. He had died from internal hemorrhage. The searchers of the battlefied, those gatherers of the wounded and dead, witness many novel and pathetic scenes.

Louis Spillers, a private in my company, a poor, quiet, and unassuming fellow, who had left a wife and little children at home when he donned the uniform of gray, had his thigh broken, just to the left of where the Sergeant fell. Spillers was as "brave as the bravest," and made no noise when he received the fatal wound. As the command swept forward down the little dell, he was of course left behind. Dragging himself along to the shade of a small tree, he sought shelter behind its trunk, protecting his person as well as he could from the bullets of the enemy posted on the ridge in front, and waited developments. When the litter-bearers found him late at night, he was leaning against the tree, calmly puffing away at his clay pipe. When asked why he did not call for assistance, he replied: "Oh, no; I thought my turn would come after awhile to be cared for, so I just concluded to quietly wait and try and smoke away some of my misery." Before morning he was dead. One might ask the question, What did such men of the South have to fight for—no negroes, no property, not even a home that they could call their own? What was it that caused them to make such sacrifices—to even give their lives to the cause? It was a principle, and as dear to the poorest of the poor as to him who counted his broad acres by the thousands and his slaves by the hundreds. Of such mettle were made the soldiers of the South—unyielding, unconquerable, invincible !

An old man in Captain Watts' Company, from Laurens, Uncle Johny Owens, a veteran of the Florida War, and one who gave much merriment to the soldiers by his frequent comparisons of war, "fighting Indians" and the one "fighting Yankees," was found on the slope, just in front of the enemy's breastworks, leaning against a tree, resting on his left knee, his loaded rifle across the other. In his right hand, between his forefinger and thumb, in the act of being placed upon the nipple of the gun, was a percussion cap. His frame was rigid, cold, and stiff, while his glossy eyes seemed to be peering in the front as looking for a lurking foe. He was stone dead, a bullet having pierced his heart, not leaving the least sign of the twitching of a muscle to tell of the shock he had received. He had fought his last battle, fired his last gun, and was now waiting for the last great drum-beat.

A story is told at the expense of Major Stackhouse, afterwards the Colonel of the Eighth, during this battle. I cannot vouch for its truthfulness, but give it as it was given to me by Captain Harllee, of the same regiment. The Eighth was being particularly hard-pressed, and had it not been for the unflinching stoicism of the officers and the valor of the men, the ranks not yet recruited from the results of the battle at Gettysburg, the little band would have been forced to yield. Major Stackhouse was in command of the right wing of the regiment, and all who knew the old farmer soldier knew him to be one of the most stubborn fighters in the army, and at the same time a "Methodist of the Methodists." He was moreover a pure Christian gentleman and a churchman of the straightest sect. There was no cant superstitions or affectation in his make-up,

Lieut. James N. Martin,
Co. E. 3d S. C. Regiment.
Col. James D. Nance,
3d S. C. Regiment.
Page 153.

Maj. Wm. D. Peck,
Quarter Master of Kerswaw's
Division. Page 162.
David E. Ewart,
Major and Surgeon,
3d S. C. Regiment.

and what he said he meant.   It was doubtful if he ever had an
evil thought, and while his manners might have been at times
blunt, he was always sincere and his language chosen and
chaste, with the possible exception during battle.   The time of
which I speak, the enemy was making a furious assault on the
right wing of the Eighth, and as the Major would gently rise
to his knees and see the enemy so stubbornly contesting the
ground, he would call out to the men, "There they are, boys,
give them hell!" Then in an under tone he would say, "May
God, forgive me for that!"   Still the Yankees did not yield,
and again and again he shouted louder and louder, "Boys,
give it to them; give them hell!" with his usual undertone,
"May God, forgive me for that," etc.   But they began closing
on the right and the center, and his left was about to give
way; the old soldier could stand it no longer.   Springing to
his feet, his tall form towering above all around him, he
shouted at the top of his voice, "Give them hell; give them
hell, I tell you, boys; give them hell, G— — — souls" The
Eighth must have given them what was wanting, or they
received it from somewhere, for after this outburst they scampered back behind the ridge.

   Years after this, while Major Stackhouse was in Congress,
and much discussion going on about the old Bible version of
hell and the new version hades, some of his colleagues twitted
the Major about the matter and asked him whether he was
wanting the Eighth to give the Union soldiers the new version
or the old.   With a twinkle in his eye, the Major answered
"Well, boys, on all ordinary occasions the new version will
answer the purposes, but to drive a wagon out of a stall or the
Yankees from your front, the old version is the best."

   Major Hard, who was killed here, was one of the
finest officers in the brigade and the youngest, at that
time, of all the field officers.   He was handsome, brilliant,
and brave.   He was one of the original officers of the
Seventh; was re-elected at the reorganization in May, 1862,
and rose, by promotion, to Major, and at the resignation of
Colonel Aiken would have been, according to seniority, Lieutenant Colonel.   Whether he ever received this rank or not,
I cannot remember.   I regret my inability to get a sketch of
his life.

   But the Rupert of the brigade was Colonel Bland, of the

Seventh. I do not think he ever received his commission as full Colonel, but commanded the regiment as Lieutenant Colonel, with few exceptions, from the battle of Sharpsburg until his death. Colonel Aiken received a wound at Sharpsburg from which he never fully recovered until after the war. Colonel Aiken was a moulder of the minds of men ; could hold them together and guide them as few men could in Kershaw's Brigade, but Bland was the ideal soldier and a fighter "par excellence." He had the gift of inspiring in his men that lofty courage that he himself possessed. His form was fault-less—tall, erect, and well developed, his eyes penetrating rather than piercing, his voice strong and commanding. His was a noble, generous soul, cool and brave almost to rashness. He was idolized by his troops and beloved as a comrade and commander. Under the guise of apparent sternness, there was a gentle flow of humor. To illustrate this, I will relate a little circumstance that occurred after the battle of Chancellors-ville to show the direction his humor at times took. Colonel Bland was a bearer of orders to General Hooker across the Rappahannock, under a flag of truce. At the opposite bank he was met by officers and a crowd of curious onlookers, who plied the Colonel with irrelevant questions. On his coat collar he wore the two stars of his rank, Lieutenant Colonel. One of the young Federal officers made some remark about Bland's stars, and said, "I can't understand your Confederate ranks; some officers have bars and some stars. I see you have two stars; are you a Brigadier General?"

"No, sir," said Bland, straightening himself up to his full height; "but I ought to be. If I was in your army I would have been a Major General, and in command of your army." Then with a merry chuckle added, "Perhaps then you would not have gotten such a d—n bad whipping at Chancellors-ville." Then all hands laughed.

COLONEL ELBERT BLAND, SEVENTH REGIMENT.

Elbert Bland was born in Edgefield County, S. C., and attended the common schools until early manhood, when choosing medicine as a profession, he attended the Medical College of New York, where he graduated with distinction. Ardently ambitious, he remained sometime after graduation, in order to perfect himself in his chosen profession. Shortly after his graduation, war broke out between the States and Mexico, and he was offered and accepted the position of Assistant Surgeon of the Palmetto Regiment, Colonel P. M. Butler commanding. By this fortunate occurrence he was enabled to greatly enlarge his knowledge of surgery. At the close of the war he came home, well equipped for the future. Shortly after his return from the war he was happily married to Miss Rebecca Griffin, a daughter of Hon. N. L. Griffin, of Edgefield. Settling in his native county, he entered at once into a lucrative practice, and at the beginning of the late war was enjoying one of the largest country practices in the State. When the mutterings of war began he was one of the first to show signs of activity, and when Gregg's Regiment went to the coast in defense of his native State, he was appointed Surgeon of that Regiment. Having had some experience already as a Surgeon in the Mexican War, he determined to enter the more active service, and in connection with Thos. G. Bacon, raised the Ninety-Six Riflemen, which afterwards formed part of the Seventh South Carolina Regiment. Bacon was elected Captain and Bland First Lieutenant. Upon organizing the regiment, Bacon was elected Colonel of the regiment and Bland was to be Captain.

Whilst very little active service was seen during the first year of the war, still sufficient evidence was given of Bland's ability as a commander of the men, and upon the reorganization of the regiment, Captain Bland was elected Lieutenant Colonel. From this time until September 20th, 1863, his fortunes were those of the Seventh Regiment. He was conspicuous on nearly every battlefield in Virginia, and was twice wounded—at Savage Station, seriously in the arm, from which he never recovered, and painfully in the thigh at Gettysburg. At the sanguinary battle of Chickamauga. on September 20th, 1863, whilst in command of his regiment, and in the moment of victory, he fell mortally wounded, living only about two hours.

No knightlier soul than his ever flashed a sabre in the cause he loved so well, and like Marshall Nay, he was one of the bravest of the brave. He sleeps quietly in the little cemetery of his native town, and a few years ago, upon the death-bed of his wife, her request was that his grave and coffin should be opened at her death, and that she should be placed upon his bosom, which was done, and there they sleep.   May they rest in peace.

LIEUTENANT COLONEL HOOLE, EIGHTH REGIMENT.

Axalla John Hoole was of English decent, his grandfather, Joseph Hoole, having emigrated from York, England, about the close of the Revolutionary War, and settled at Georgetown, S. C.

James C. Hoole, the father of A. J. Hoole, was a soldier of the war of 1812.   He removed to Darlington District and married Elizabeth Stanley, by whom he had five children, the third being the subject of this sketch.

Axalla John Hoole was born near Darlington Court House, S. C., October 12th, 1822.   His father died when he was quite small, leaving a large family and but little property, but his mother was a woman of great energy, and succeeded in giving him as good an education as could be obtained at St. John's Academy, Darlington Court House.   Upon the completion of the academic course, at the age of eighteen, he taught school for twelve years, after which he followed the occupation of farming.

While a young man he joined the Darlington Riflemen, and after serving in various capacities, he was elected Captain about 1854 or 1855.   He was an enthusiastic advocate of States Rights, and during the excitement attending the admission of Kansas as a State, he went out there to oppose the Abolitionists.   He married Elizabeth G. Brunson, March 20th, 1856, and left the same day for Kansas.   Taking an active part in Kansas politics and the "Kansas War," he was elected Probate Judge of Douglas County by the pro-slavery party, under the regime of Governor Walker.

He returned to Darlington December 5th, 1857, and shortly afterwards was re-elected Captain of the Darlington Riflemen. At a meeting of the Riflemen, held in April, 1861, on the Academy green, he called for volunteers, and every man in the company volunteered, except one.   The company went to Charleston April 15th, 1861, and after remaining a short while, returned as far as Florence, where they were mustered in as Company A, Eighth S. C. V.

The Eigth Regiment left Florence for Virginia June 2d, 1861.   At the expiration of the period of enlistment, the regiment was reorganized, and Captain Hoole was elected Lieutenant Colonel, in which capacity he served until he was killed at the battle of Chickamauga, September 20th, 1863.

He was buried at the Brunson graveyard, near Darlington.

COLONEL E. T. STACKHOUSE, EIGHTH REGIMENT.

As I have made some mention of Major Stackhouse, he being promoted to Lieutenant Colonel, and afterwards Colonel of the Eighth, I will take this opportunity of giving the readers a very brief sketch of the life of this sterling farmer, patriot, soldier, and statesman, who, I am glad to say, survived the war for many years.

Colonel E. T. Stackhouse was born in Marion County, of this State, the 27th of March, 1824, and died in the City of Washington, D. C., June 14th, 1892. He was educated in the country schools, having never enjoyed the advantages of a collegiate course. He married Miss Anna Fore, who preceded him to the grave by only a few months. Seven children was the result of this union. In youth and early manhood Colonel Stackhouse was noted for his strict integrity and sterling qualities, his love of truth and right being his predominating trait. As he grew in manhood he grew in moral worth—the better known, the more beloved.

His chosen occupation was that of farming, and he was ever proud of the distinction of being called one of the "horny-handed sons of toil." In the neighborhood in which he was born and bred he was an exemplar of all that was progressive and enobling.

In April, 1861, Colonel Stackhouse was among the very first to answer the call of his country, and entered the service as Captain in the Eighth South Carolina Regiment. By the casualties of war, he was promoted to Major, Lieutenant Colonel, and Colonel, and led the old Eighth, the regiment he loved so well, in some of the most sanguinary engagements of the war. All that Colonel Stackhouse was in civil life he was that, and more if possible, in the life of a soldier. In battle he was calm, collected, and brave; in camp or on the march he was sociable, moral—a Christian gentleman. As a tactician and disciplinarian, Colonel Stackhouse could not be called an exemplar soldier, as viewed in the light of the regular army; but as an officer of volunteers he had those elements in him to

cause men to take on that same unflinching courage, indom-
inable spirit, and bold daring that actuated him in danger and
battle. He had not that sternness of command nor niceties
nor notion of superiority that made machines of men, but he
had that peculiar faculty of endowing his soldiers with confidence and a willingness to follow where he led.

He represented his county for three terms in the State Legislature, and was President of the State Alliance. He was
among the first to advocate college agricultural training for
the youth of the land, and was largely instrumental in the
establishment of Clemson College, and became one of its first
trustees.

He was elected, without opposition, to the Fifty-first Con-
grees, and died while in the discharge of his duties at Washington.

CHAPTER XXIV

In Front of Chattanooga.

Early on the morning of the 22d we were ordered forward
towards Chattanooga, the right wing having gone the day before. On nearing the city, we were shelled by batteries posted
on the heights along the way and from the breastworks and
forts around the city. It was during one of the heavy engagements between our advanced skirmish lines and the rear
guard of the enemy that one of the negro cooks, by some
means, got lost between the lines, and as a heavy firing began,
bullets flying by him in every direction, he rushed towards the
rear, and raising his hands in an entreating position, cried out,
"Stop, white folks, stop! In the name of God Almighty,
stop and argy!"

In moving along, near the city we came to a great sink in
the ground, caused by nature's upheaval at some remote
period, covering an acre or two of space. It seemed to have
been a feeding place for hogs from time immemorial, for corn
cobs covered the earth for a foot or more in depth. In this
place some of our troops were posted to avoid the shells, the
enemy having an exact range of this position. They began

throwing shells right and left and bursting them just over our heads, the fragments flying in every direction. At every discharge, and before the shell reached us, the men would cling to the sides of the slooping sink, or burrow deeper in the cobs, until they had their bodies almost covered. A little man of my company, while a good soldier, had a perfect aversion to cannon shot, and as a shell would burst just overhead, his body was seen to scringe, tremble, and go still deeper among the cobs. Some mischievous comrade took advantage of his position, seized a good sound cob, then just as a shell bursted overhead, the trembling little fellow all flattened out, he struck him a stunning blow on the back. Such a yell as he set up was scarcely ever heard. Throwing the cobs in every direction, he cried out, "Oh! I am killed; I am killed! Ambulance corps! Ambulance corps!" But the laugh of the men soon convinced him his wound was more imaginary than real, so he turned over and commenced to burrow again like a mole.

Rosecrans having withdrawn his entire force within the fortifications around Chattanooga, our troops were placed in camp, surrounding the enemy in a semi-circle, and began to fortify. Kershaw's Brigade was stationed around a large dwelling in a grove, just in front of Chattanooga, and something over a mile distant from the city, but in plain view. We had very pleasant quarters in the large grove surrounding the house, and, in fact, some took possession of the porches and outhouses. This, I think, is the point Grant stormed a few months afterwards, and broke through the lines of Bragg. We had built very substantial breastworks, and our troops would have thought themselves safe and secure against the charge of Grant's whole army behind such works.

If those who are unfamiliar with the life of the soldier imagines it is one long funeral procession, without any breaks of humor, they are away off from the real facts. The soldier is much the same as the schoolboy. He must have some vent through which the ebullition of good feelings can blow off, else the machinery bursts.

While encamped around this house, a cruel joke was played upon Captain—well we will call him Jones; that was not his name, however, but near enough to it to answer our purpose. Now this Captain Jones, as we call him, was engaged to be married to one of the fairest flowers in the Palmetto State, a perfect queen among beauties—cultured, vivacious, and belonging to one of the oldest families in that Commonwealth of Blue Bloods. The many moves and changes during the last month or two considerably interrupted our communications and mail facilities, and Jones had not received the expected letters. He became restless, petulant, and cross, and to use the homely phrase, "he was all torn up." Instead of the "human sympathy" and the "one touch of nature," making the whole world akin, that philosophers and sentimentalists talk about, it should be "one sight of man's misery"—makes the whole world "wish him more miserable." It was through such feelings that induced Captain I. N. Martin, our commissary, with Mack Blair and others, to enter into a conspiracy to torture Jones with all he could stand. Blair had a lady cousin living near the home of Jones' fiancee, with whom he corresponded, and it was through this channel that the train was laid to blow up Jones while said Jones was in the piazza engaged in a deeply interesting game of chess. Martin was to be in the piazza watching the game, when Blair was to enter reading a letter. Then something like the following colloquy took place :

"Well, Mack, what is the news from home?"

"Nothing very interesting," replies Blair. Then, as a sudden recollection strikes him, "Oh, yes, there is to be a big wedding at Old Dr. Blanks."

"You don't say so?" (The game of chess stands still.) "And who is to be married, pray?" innocently enquires Martin.

"Why, it will surprise you as much as it did me, I suppose and I would not believe it, only Cousin Sallie says she is to be bride's maid." (Jones ceases to play and listens intently.

"It is nobody else than Mr. ——— and Miss "Blank."

Now, this Miss "Blank" is Jones' intended. Jones is paralyzed. His face turns livid, then pale, now green! He motionless, his eyes staring vacantly on the chessboard. Then with a mighty exertion Jones kicked the board aside and sprang to his feet. Shaking his trembling finger in the face Blair, his whole frame convulsed with emotion, his very on fire, he hissed between his teeth : "That's an infernal I don't care whose Cousin Sallie wrote it."

Jones was nearly crazed for the balance of the day. He whistled and sang strange melodies while walking aimlessly about. He read and re-read the many love missives received long ago. Some he tore into fragments; others he carefully replaced in his knapsack.

But those evil geniuses were still at work for further torture, or at least to gloat over Jones' misery. It was arranged to formally bury him, allegorically. At night, while Jones was asleep, or trying to sleep on the piazza, a procession was formed, headed by Major Maffet, who was to act as the priest, and I must say he acted the part like a cardinal. We had a little rehearsal of the part each was to play, and those who "couldn't hold in" from laughing were ruled out, for it was expected that Jones would cut some frightful antics as the ceremony proceeded. I was not allowed to accompany the procession, as it was decided I could not "hold in," and under no condition was there to be a laugh or even a smile; but I took up position behind the balusters and watched events as the shadows were cast before. Major Maffet was dressed in a long dark overcoat, to represent the priestly gown, with a miter on his head, carrying Hardee's Tactics, from which to read the burial service. All had in their hands a bayonet, from which burned a tallow candle, in place of tapers. The procession marched up the steps in single file, all bearing themselves with the greatest solemnity and sombre dignity, followed by the sexton, with a frying-pan as a shovel, and took their places around the supposed corpse. Maffett began the duties by alluding to that part of the service where "it is allotted that all men shall die," etc., waving his hand in due form to the sexton as he repeated the words, "Earth to earth and dust to dust," the sexton following the motions with the frying pan.

I must say, in all truthfulness, that in all my life I never saw a graver or more solemn set of faces than those of the would-be mourning procession. Captain Wright appeared as if he was looking into his own grave, and the others appeared equally as sorrowful. Major Maffett gave out in clear, distinct tones the familiar lines of—

> "Solemn strikes the funeral chime,
> Notes of our departing time."

Well, such grotesque antics as Jones did cut up was perfectly dreadful. He laughed, he mimicked the priest, kicked at the mourners, and once tried to grab the tactics. The Major and his assistants pitched the tune on a high key. Captain Wright braced it with loud, strong bass, while Martin and Sim Pratt came in on the home stretch with tenor and alto that shook the rafters in the house. Then all dispersed as silently and sorrowfully as they had come.

In a few days Jones got a letter setting all things straight. Martin and Blair confessed their conspiracy against his peace of mind, and matters progressed favorably thereafter between Jones and Miss "Blank," but Jones confessed afterwards that he carried for a long time "bad, wicked blood in his heart."

But soldiers have their tragedies as well as their comedies in camp. It was here we lost our old friend, Jim George, the shallow-pated wit—the man who found us the flour on the Potomac, and who floundered about in the river "for three hours," as he said, on that bitter cold night at Yorktown. It was also told of Jim, that during the first battle he was loading and shooting at the wounded enemy for all his gun was worth, and when remonstrated with by his Captain, Chesley Herbert, telling Jim he "should not kill them," Jim indignantly asked, "What in the hell did we come to the war for, if not to kill Yankees?" But this, I think, is only a joke at Jim's expense. Nevertheless, he was a good solider, of the harmless kind, and a good, jolly fellow withal, taking it as a pleasure to do a friend a kindness.

As I have said, however, Jim was a great boaster and blusterer, glorying in the marvelous and dangerous. Had he lived in the heroic age, I have no doubt he would have regaled the ears of his listeners with blood curdling stories of his battles with giants, his fights with dragons and winged serpents. He claimed to possess a charm. He wore an amulet around his neck to protect him against the "bullets of lead, of copper, or of brass" of his enemies, through which, he said, nothing could penetrate but the mystic "balls of silver," the same with which "witch rabbits" are killed. He would fill his pockets, after battle, with spent and battered bullets, and exhibit them as specimens of his art in the catching of bullets on "the fly."

He professed to be a very dangerous and blood-thirsty individual, but his comrades only laughed at his idiosyncrasies, knowing him as they did as being one of the best and most harmless soldiers in the army. He often boasted, "No Yankee will ever kill me, but our own men will," his companions little dreaming how prophetic his words would prove.

One night while Jim, in company with some companions, were on a "foraging expedition," they came to a farm house on Missionary Ridge and ordered supper. A cavalryman was there, also, waiting to be served. A negro servant attending to the table gave some real or imaginary affront, and the soldiers, in a spirit of jest, pretended as if they were going to take the negro out and flog him. Now Jim, as well as the cavalryman, thought the midnight revelers were in earnest; and Jim was in high glee at the prospect of a little adventure. But nothing was further from the thoughts of the soldiers than doing harm to the negro. When they had him in the yard the cavalryman came on the porch, and in an authoritative manner, ordered the negro turned loose.

This was a time Jim thought that he could get in some of his bullying, so going up on the steps where the cavalryman stood, jesticulating with his finger, said, "When we get through with the negro we will give you some of the same."

In an instant the strange soldier's pistol was whipped out— a flash, a report, and Jim George fell dead at his feet, a victim to his own swagger and an innocent jest of his companions. So dumbfounded were the innocent "foragers," that they allowed the cavalryman to ride away unmolested and. unquestioned.

The bones of the unfortunate Jim lie buried on the top of Missionary Ridge, and the name of his slayer remains a mystery to this day.

While in Tennessee our diet was somewhat changed. In the East, flour, with beef and bacon, was issued to the troops; but here we got nothing but corn meal, with a little beef and half ration of bacon. The troops were required to keep four days' rations cooked on hand all the time. Of the meal we made "cart wheels," "dog heads," "ash cakes," and last, but not least, we had "cush." Now corn bread is not a very great delicacy at best, but when four days' old, and green with mold, it is anything but palatable. But the soldiers got around this in the way "cush" was manipulated. Now it has been said "if you want soldiers to fight well, you must feed them

well ;'' but this is still a mooted question, and I have known
some of the soldiers of the South to give pretty strong battle
when rather underfed than overfed.

For the benefit of those Spanish-American soldiers of the
late war, who had nothing to vary their diet of ham and eggs,
steak, pork, and potatoes, buscuit, light bread, coffee, and
iced teas, but only such light goods as canned tomatoes, green
corn, beans, salmon, and fresh fish, I will tell them how to
make "cush." You will not find this word in the dictionaries
of the day, but it was in the soldier's vocabulary, now obsolete. Chip up bacon in fine particles, place in an oven and fry
to a crisp. Fill the oven one-third or one-half full of branch
water, then take the stale corn bread, the more moldy the better, rub into fine crumbs, mix and bring the whole to a boil,
gently stirring with a forked stick. When cold, eat with
fingers and to prevent waste or to avoid carrying it on the
march, eat the four days' rations at one sitting. This dish
will aid in getting clear of all gestion of meat, and prevent
bread from getting old. A pot of "cush" is a dish "fit for a
king," and men who will not fight on it would not fight if
penned.

The forest and farms around abounded in sheep and hogs.
In fact, Tennessee and North Georgia were not the worst
places in the South in which to live through a campaign. We
had strict orders to protect all private property and molest
nothing outside of camp requirements, but the men would
forage at night, bring in a sheep or hog, divide up, and by the
immutable law of camps it was always proper to hang a
choice piece of mutton or pork at the door of the officers' tent.
This helped to soothe the conscience of the men and pave the
way to immunity from punishment. The stereotyped orders
were issued every night for "Captains to keep their men in
camp," but the orders were as often disregarded as obeyed.
It was one of those cases where orders are more regarded "in
the breach than in the observance." Officers winked at it, if
not actually countenancing the practice, of "foraging for
something to eat." Then again the old argument presented
itself, "If we don't take it the Yankees will," so there you were.

Most of the soldiers took the opportunity of visiting Lookout Mountain and feasting their eyes upon the finest scenery of
the South. While they had crossed and recrossed the Blue

Ridge and the many ranges of lesser note in Virginia, Maryland, and Pennsylvania—had gazed with wonder and admiration at the windings of the Potomac and Shenandoah from the Heights of Maryland overlooking Harper's Ferry—yet all these were nothing as compared to the view from Lookout Mountain. Standing on its brow, we could see the beautiful blue waters of the Tennessee flowing apparently at our feet, but in reality a mile or two distant. Beyond lay the city of Chattanooga, nestling down in the bend of the river, while away in the distance occasional glimpses of the stream could be had as it wound in and out around the hills and mountains that lined its either side, until the great river looked no larger than a mountain brooklet. From the highest peak of Lookout Mountain we catch faint streaks of far away Alabama; on the right, North Carolina; to the north, Tennessee; and to the south and east were Georgia and our own dear South Carolina. From this place many of our soldiers cast the last lingering look at the land they loved so well. On the plateau of the mountain was a beautiful lake of several acres in extent, surrounded by lovely little villas and summer houses, these all hurriedly deserted by the necessities of war—the furniture and fixtures left all in place as the owners took their hastened departure. In one house we visited was left a handsome piano, on which those who could perform gave the soldiers delightful music.

There was a roadway winding around the base of the mountain and gradually up its slopes to the plateau above, where wagons and other vehicles passed to the top. Most of the soldiers who wished to visit this beautiful and historic place passed up this road way, but there was another route—just a foot-path—up its precipitous sides, which had to be climbed hundreds of feet, perpendicularly, by means of ladders fastened to its sides. After going up one ladder, say fifty or seventy-five feet, we would come to a little offset in the mountain side, just wide enough to get a foot-hold, before taking another ladder. Some of the boldest climbers took this route to reach the summit, but after climbing the first ladder and looking back towards the gorge below, I concluded it was safer and more pleasant to take the "longer way round." It certainly takes a man of stout heart and strong nerves to climb those ladders up to the "lands of the sky."

The scenery in and around Chattanooga and Lookout Mountain is grand, far beyond pen picturing. The surroundings had a kind of buoyancy even to the spirits of the badly clad and badly fed soldiers, which caused their stale bread and "cush" to be eaten with a relish. The mountain homes seemed veritable "castles in the air." Looking from the top of Lookout Mountain—its position, its surroundings, its natural fortresses—this would have made an old Feudal lord die of envy. Autumn is now at hand, with its glorious sunsets, its gorgeous coloring of the leaves and bushes away to the right on Missionary Ridge, the magnificent purple draperies along the river sides that rise and fall to our right and left, its blue waters dwindling away until they meet the deeper blue of the sky—are all beautiful beyond description. Lovely though this scenery may be in autumn, and its deeper coloring of green in the summer, how dazzled must be the looker on in beholding it in its tender, blushing mantle of spring?

For quite a time rumors came of Burnside's advance through East Tennessee and of Longstreet's detachment from the army to meet him. The troops were kept in constant expectation, with the regulation "four days" cooked rations on hand. It is not our purpose to criticise the acts of Generals, or the schemes and plans of the Southern Government, but future historical critics will not differ as to the ultimate results of the East Tennessee move. That Longstreet's advance to East Tennessee was without results, if not totally disastrous, all will agree. To divide an army in the face of an enemy, is dangerous at best, and, with few exceptions, has been avoided by Generals and commanders of all time. Lee could afford it, because he was LEE and had a JACKSON to execute the movements, but on occasions when the enemy in front are more numerous and commanded by the most able and astute Generals of the time, the movement is hazardous in the extreme. Lee and his Lieutenants had already "robbed the cradle and the grave" to replenish their ranks, and what real benefit would accrue to the South had Longstreet captured the whole of Burnside's Army, when the North had many armies to replace it? The critics of the future will judge the movement as ill-timed and fraught with little good and much ill to the Confederacy. However, it was so ordered, and no alternate was left the officers and soldiers but to obey.

On the 9th of October President Davis came out to Chatta-nooga to give matters his personal attention and seek, if possi-ble, some "scape-grace" upon which to saddle the blame for not reaping greater fruits of the battle, and to vindicate the conduct of his commander in chief.

General Bragg had already preferred charges against Lieu-tenant General Polk, commander of the right wing of the army, for his tardiness in opening the battle of the 20th, and General Hindman was relieved of the command of his division for alleged misconduct prior to that time. Many changes were proposed and made in the corps and division command-ers, as well as plans discussed for the future operations of the army. All agreed that it should be aggressive.

Major General Cheatham was temporarily placed in com-mand of Polk's Corps after the downfall of that General, and he himself soon afterwards superseded by Lieutenant General Hardee. President Davis had thought of placing Pemberton, who had capitulated to Grant at Vicksburg, but who had been exchanged, in command of the corps; but the officers and troops demurred at this, and public opinion was so outspoken, that Mr. Davis was forced to abandon the idea. It was, there-fore, given to Hardee. For some offense given by Major Genaral D. H. Hill, who commanded the right of the right wing on the 20th, he was relieved of his command and his connection with the Army of Tennessee. Major General Buckner, commanding the divisions on the left of Longstreet's wing, also came under the ban of official displeasure and was given an indefinite leave of absence. There was wrangling, too, among the Brigadiers in Hood's Division, Jenkins, Law, and Robertson. Jenkins being a new addition to the division, was senior officer, and commanded the division in Hood's absence by virtue of his rank. Law had been in the division since its formation, and after Hood's disabilities from wounds, commanded very acceptably the balance of the days at Gettys-burg. For this and other meritorious conduct, he thought the command should be given to him as senior in point of service with the division. Robertson had some personal diffi-culty with General Longstreet, which afterwards resulted in a call for a court-martial. The advanced ideas and undisguised views of Longstreet himself were considered with suspicion by both the President and the General commanding the army, and had it not been for the high prestige and his brilliant achievements in the East, the unbounded love and devotion of his troops, the loyalty and confidence of General Lee in the high military ability of the old War Horse, his commander of the First Corps, in all probability his official head would have fallen in the basket. But President Davis was strong in his prejudices and convictions, and as usual, tenacious in his friendship and confidence towards his favorites. Bragg, in President Davis' estimation at least, was vindicated, but at the expense of his subalterns, and was, therefore, retained in command in the face of overwhelming discontent among the Generals and the pressing demands of public opinion for his recall from the command of the army.

General Lee in the meantime had sought to relieve the pressure against Bragg as much as possible by making a demonstration in force against Meade, forcing the Federal Army back behind Bull Run, thereby preventing a further reinforcement of Rosecrans from the Army of the Potomac.

I digress thus far from the thread of my story, that the reader may better understand the conditions confronting our army—the morale and *esprit de corps* of the officers and troops composing it.

On the 19th of October General Rosecrans was superseded by Major General George B. Thomas, in command of the Union Army, with Grant, who was rapidly climbing to the zenith of this renown, marching to his relief as commander of the department.

A considerable commotion was caused in camp about the last of October by the news of a large body of Union soldiers making a demonstration against our left flank and rear. It seems that a body of troops had embarked on board pontoon and flat boats in Chattanooga, and during the night had floated eight miles down the river and there were joined by a similar body marching over land on the north side. This formidable array was crossed over to the south side and moved in the direction of our rear and our line of communication under cover of the hills and mountain ridges. Jenkins' and McLaw's Divisions were ordered to intercept them and drive them off. A night attack was ordered, but by some misunderstanding or disobedience of orders, this movement on the part of the Confederates miscarried, and was abandoned; not, however, until General Bratton, of Jenkins' old Brigade, came up and attacked the rear guard with such vigor that the enemy was glad enough to get away, leaving their wounded and dead upon the field. No further movements were made against the army until after our removal to East Tennessee.

About the first of November orders were issued for the transfer of Longstreet to begin, and on the 5th and 6th the greater part of his army was embarked on hastily constructed trains at Tyner's Station, some five or six miles out on the E. T. & K. R. R. The horses, artillery, and wagon trains took the dirt road to Sweetwater, in the Sweetwater Valley, one of the most fertile regions in East Tennessee.

Longstreet's command consisted of Kershaw's (South Carolina), Bryan's and Wofford's (Georgia), and Humphreys' (Mississippi) Brigades, under Major General McLaws; Anderson's (Georgia), Jenkins' (South Carolina), Law's (Alabama), Robertson's (Arkansas and Texas), and Benning's (Georgia) Brigades, under Brigadier General M. Jenkins, commanding division; two batteries of artillery, under General Alexander; and four brigades of cavalry, under Major General Wheeler.

General Hood had been so desperately wounded at Chickamauga, that it was thought he could never return to the army; but he had won a glorious name, the prestige of which the war department thought of too much value to be lost, but to be used afterwards so disastrously in the campaign through Middle Tennessee. General Hood was, no doubt, an able, resolute, and indefatigable commander, although meteoric, something on the order of Charles, the "Madman of the North;" but his experience did not warrant the department in placing him in the command of an expedition to unde.take the impossible—the defeat of an overwhelming army, behind breastworks, in the heart of its own country.

The movement of Longstreet to East Tennessee and Hood through Middle Tennessee was but the commencement of a series of blunders on the part of our war department that culminated eventually in the South's downfall. But it is not our province to speculate in the rosy fields of "might-have-been," but to record facts.

General Longstreet had of all arms fifteen thousand men, including teamsters, guards, medical and ambulance corps. General Burnside had an army of twenty-five thousand men

and one hundred pieces of artillery, and this was the army
Longstreet was expected to capture or destroy.

General Grant was marching from Mississippi with a large
portion of his victorious troops of the Vicksburg campaign to
reinforce Rosecrans, Sherman coming down through Tennessee, and Meade was sending reinforcements from the East, all
to swell the defeated ranks of Rosecrans. With the knowledge of all these facts, the department was preparing to further
reduce the forces of Bragg by sending Longstreet up in East
Tennessee, with soldiers badly clad, worse equipped, and with
the poorest apology of camp equipage, for an active and progressive campaign.

Both governments were greatly displeased with the results
of the battle of Chickamauga—the Federals at their army failing to come up to their expectations and gaining a victory,
instead of a disastrous defeat; the Confederates at their commanders in not following up their success and reaping greater
results. Under such circumstances, there must be some one
on whom to place the blame. General Rosecrans censured
General McCook and General Crittenden, commanders of the
Twentieth and Twenty-first Corps, and these two able soldiers
were relieved of their commands, while General Rosecrans
himself was severely censured by the department in Washing
ton, and soon afterwards relieved of his command.

The regiments of the brigade were now all short of fiel
officers—the Seventh and Battalion with none, and the Eight
and Fifteenth in charge of Majors. However, Colonel W. (
Rice joined us on the way to East Tennessee and took co
mand of his battalion.

After a stay of a week in the beautiful Valley of Sw
water, we were moved to London, the railroad crossing of
Tennessee River, the railroad bridge having been burned
the enemy. The country in East Tennessee was greatl
vided in sentiment, some for the Union cause and some fo
Confederate cause. Rumors of outrages and doings of de
adoes were rife, and the soldiers were somewhat dubio
going far into the country, for fear of running up a
bushwhackers, of which the country was said to be full.

While one train with the Third was being pulled ov
East Tennessee Railroad towards Sweetwater by a
engineer over a track long unused, and cars out of rep

occurrence took place which might have ended more seriously than it did under the circumstances. The train, composed of box cars, one company inside and one on top, was running along at a good, lively rate. A stampede took place among the troops on top, who began jumping right and left down a steep embankment and running with all their speed to the woods in the distance. It was just after daylight, and those inside the cars not knowing what the trouble was, and a great many on the top being roused from their slumbers and seeing the others leaping in great disorber, and hearing the word "bushwhackers" being called out, threw their blankets aside and jumped likewise. Soon the cars were almost empty, those above and within all thinking danger was somewhere, but invisible. Just then a train of passenger cars, containing General McLaws, General Kershaw, their staffs, and others, rounded the cut in our rear, and was running at break-neck speed into the freight train in front. Those in the passenger cars seeing those from the train in front running for dear life's sake for the woods, began to climb through windows and off of the platforms, the engineers and firemen on both trains leaping like the men. So we had the spectacle of one train running into another and neither under control, although the levers had been reversed. In a moment the rear train plunged into the front one, piling up three or four cars on their ends. Fortunately, only one or two were hurt by jumping and none by the collision. It seems almost miraculous to think of two car loads of soldiers jumping from trains at full speed and on a high embankment and a great many from top, and so few getting hurt.

General Longstreet's plan of campaign was to move up the east side of the Holston, or, as it is now called, the Tennessee River, pass through Marysville, cross the river in the vicinity of Knoxville with his infantry, the cavalry to take possession of the heights above and opposite the city, thus cutting off the retreat of the Federals in front of London, and capture the garrison in the city of Knoxville. But he had no trains to move his pontoon bridge, nor horses to pull it. So he was forced to make a virtue of necessity and cross the river just above the little hamlet of London in the face of the enemy. On the night of the 12th the boats and bridge equipment were carried to the river, the boats launched and manned by a detachment of Jenkins' South Carolina Brigade, under the command of the gallant Captain Foster. This small band of men pushed their boats across the river under a heavy fire of the enemy's pickets, succeeded in driving off the enemy, and took possession of the opposite side. The boats were soon joined together and the bridge laid. The troops then began to cross rapidly and push their way out far in advance. By morning the greater part of the army was on the west side of the river.

General Wheeler, with his cavalry, started simultaneously with the infantry, but on the east side, with the view of taking possession of the heights around Knoxville, which he partly accomplished after several severe engagements with the Union cavalry, in which the young Confederate cavalier came off victorious.

The next morning after our crossing the enemy showed some disposition to attack our lines, but did no more than drive in our skirmishers, and then began to fall slowly back. Longstreet remained near the river constructing some defensive earthworks to protect the bridge, and to allow the supply train, which had been out on a foraging expedition, time to come up. By his not making as rapid advance as was expected, the enemy again, on the 14th, returned to feel our lines and to learn the whereabouts of his foe.

On the morning of the 15th, just at daylight, we took up our line of march through a blinding mist or fog, our skirmishers not being able to see an object fifty paces in front. Our line of advance was along the dirt road, on the west side of the little mountain range, a spur of the clinch, while the main body of the enemy kept close to the railroad, on the east side, and between the mountain range and the river, traversing a narrow valley, which gave him strong positions for defensive battle. The mountain was crossed in several places by dull roads and bridle paths, and it was the intention of the commanding General to take possession of these passes and turn the enemy's flank, or to move around the head of the mountain, where the two roads followed by the armies came together on converging lines, then to either close him in between the mountain and the river and give battle, or fall upon his rear and crush him. Some few miles out Jenkins' skirmishers came upon those of the enemy and a running fight took place, the Federals retreating through the mountain gap to the east side.

Jenkins kept up his advance (not following the enemy, however, over the mountain), with Alexander's Battalion of Artillery, while McLaws followed closely, with Leydon's Battery as a support. Thus the march was continued all day, taking up camp at night far in advance of the enemy on the other side of the mountain. Jenkins was ordered at midnight, with a part of his command, to take possession of a gap in the mountain, and at daylight throw himself across the line of the enemy's retreat. But for some unforeseen circumstance, or treachery or ignorance in Jenkins' guide, he failed in his undertaking, and the enemy passed in safety during the night beyond our lines to a place of comparative security.

Early next morning the army was in motion, but instead of an enemy in our front we found a park of eighty wagons, well laden with supplies of provisions, camp equipage, tools, etc., deserted by the retreating column. The horses had been cut loose, still this capture was a very serviceable acquisition to the outfit of the army, especially in entrenching tools. Jenkins followed close on the heels of the retreating army, occasionally coming to a severe brush with the enemy's rear guard, using every exertion to force Burnside to battle until McLaws, with Hart's Brigade of Cavalry, could reach Cambell's Station, the point where the two converging roads meet. McLaws marched nearly all day in full line of battle, Kershaw being on the left of the main thoroughfare and under a continual skirmish fire. But all too late. The wily foe had escaped the net once more and passed over and beyond the road crossing, and formed line of battle on high ground in rear. Longstreet still had hopes of striking the enemy a crushing blow before reaching Knoxville, and all he desired and all that was necessary to that end was that he should stand and give battle. The attitude of the Union Army looked favorable towards the consummation of the Confederate leader's plan. Our troops had been marching all the forenoon in one long line of battle, near a mile in length, over ditches, gullies, and fences; through briars, brambles, and undergrowth; then again through wide expanse of cultivated fields, all the while under a galling fire from the enemy's batteries and sharpshooters, and they felt somewhat jaded and worn out when they came upon their bristling bayonets, ready for combat. A great number of our men were barefooted, some with shoes partly worn out, clothes ragged and torn, not an overcoat or extra garment among the line officers or men throughout the army, as all surplus baggage had been left in Virginia. But when the battle was about to show up the soldiers were on hand, ready and willing as of old, to plunge headlong into the fray. McLaws was on the left wing and Jenkins on the right.

Preparation for a general engagement was made. McLaws was ordered to throw forward, Wofford on his extreme left, supported by cavalry, while Jenkins was to send two of his brigades, under General Law, far to the right, on the flank and rear of the enemy's left. Law was first to make the attack on the enemy's flank, then the columns in front were to advance and make direct assault. But the "best laid plans of mice and men oft' gang aglee." Law missed his line of direction—failed to come upon the enemy's flank, night was upon us, and it must be remembered that all these movements took time, thus giving the Union Army an opportunity, under the sable curtains of night, to "fold their tents and gently steal away."

General Longstreet, in his book written nearly thirty years after the occurrence of Cambell's Station, severely criticises General Law, who commanded the two flanking brigades, and in withering and scathing terms directly charges him with th loss of a great victory. He quotes one of his staff officers a saying that it was the common camp rumor that General La had made the remark "that he could have made a successf attack, but that Jenkins would have reaped the credit of hence he delayed until the enemy got out of the way." T is unjust and ungenerous to a gallant and faithful officer, c too, who had, by his many and heavy blows in battle, ad largely to the immortal fame of Longstreet himself. ? there was a laudable ambition and rivalry among all off and men in the Confederate Army, there can be no questi an ambition to outstrip all others in heroic actions, deeds, and self-sacrificing, but jealously never. A treachery, as General Longstreet clearly intimates in th of General Law, why the poorest, ragged, starved, or n soldier in the South would not have sold his country o panions for the wealth of the Indies, nor would he have essarily sacrificed a life of a comrade for the greatest place on this continent, or the fairest crown of Europe. It must be remembered in this connection that there were personal differences between the corps commander and General Law at times, and with one of his division commanders, all during our Western campaign. That General Law was obstinate, petulant, and chafed under restraint, is true, but this is only natural in a volunteer army, and must be expected. And had General Longstreet, so rigid a disciplinarian as he was, but a breath of suspicion at the time of disobedience, lack of courage, or unfaithfulness in his subaltern, General Law would have been put under immediate arrest, and a court-martial ordered. The old General, in several places in his memoirs, makes uncomplimentary remarks and insinuations against some of his old compatriots in arms, but these should not be taken seriously. It will be remembered by all the old Confederates in this connection that during the period just succeeding the war mighty social convulsions took place in the South—political upheavals, whereby one party was as bitter against the other as during the mighty struggle of the North against the South, and that General Longstreet, unfortunately for his name as a civilian, aligned himself along with the party whom the whites of the South acknowledged as antagonistic to their welfare and interest. This roused the ire of all his old army associates, and many of his former friends now began to hurl poisoned and fiery shafts at the old "War Horse" of the South, and no place so vulnerable as his army record. This, of course, was resented by him, and a deadly feud of long standing sprang up between Generals Longstreet, Mahone, and a few others, who joined him on the one side, and the whole army of "Codfederate Brigadiers" on the other. This accounts, in a large measure, for many of Longstreet's strictures upon the conduct of officers of the army, and, no doubt, a mere after thought or the weird imaginations of an old and disappointed politico-persecuted man.

No, No! The officers and men of the Confederate Army were patriots of diamond purity, and all would have willingly died a martyr's death that the Confederacy might live.

CHAPTER XXV

Around Knoxville---The Siege and Storming of Fort Sanders.

After the fiasco at Cambell's Station, the enemy retired behind his entrenched position in the suburbs of Knoxville. Longstreet followed rapidly, with McLaws in front, in line of battle, but all hopes of encountering the enemy before he reached his fortified position around the city had vanished. We reached the rolling hillsides just outside of the city limits about noon on the 17th, and found the enemy's dismounted cavalry, acting as sharpshooters, posted on the heights in front and between the railroad and the river, well protected by rail piles along the crest of the hill.

Colonel Nance was ordered with the Third South Carolina Regiment to dislodge those on the hill, near the railroad, by marching over and beyond the road and taking them in flank, which was successfully done by making a sudden dash from a piece of woodland over an open field and gaining the embankment of the railroad immediately on the right flank of the enemy's sharpshooters. But scarcely had the Third got in position than it found itself assailed on its left and rear by an unseen enemy concealed in the woods. Here Colonel Nance was forced to sacrifice one of his most gallant officers, Lieutenant Allen, of Company D. Seeing his critical and untenable position, he ordered the Lieutenant, who was standing near him, to report his condition to General Kershaw and ask for instruction. This was a hazardous undertaking in the extreme, but Lieutenant Allen undertook it with rare courage and promptness. Back across the open field he sped, while the whole fire of the sharpshooters was directed towards him instead of to our troops behind the embankment. All saw and felt that the brave officer was lost as soon as he got beyond the cover of the railroad, and turned their heads from the sickening scene. But Allen did not hesitate or falter, but kept on to the fulfilment of his desperate mission, while hundreds of bullets flew around him in every direction—over his head, under his feet, before, and behind—until at last the fatal messenger laid him low, a heroic martyr to the stern duties of war. Colonel Nance seeing the hopelessness of his attack, ordered a retreat. Then the whole regiment had to run the same gauntlet in which young Allen lost his life. Away across the open corn field the troops fled in one wild pell mell, every man for himself, while the bullets hummed and whistled through our scattered ranks, but luckily only a few were shot.

Jenkins' Division came up late in the day and took position on McLaws' left, then with the cavalry commenced the investment of the city on the west side of the Holston or Tennessee River. To advance McLaws' lines to a favorable position, it was first necessary to dislodge the sharpshooters on the hill tops between the river and the railroad. General Kershaw was ordered to take the works in front by direct assault. The Third was on the extreme left of the brigade, next to the railroad, while the Second, Seventh, Eighth, and Third Battalion were in the center, with the Fifteenth, under Major Gist, between the dirt road on which we had traveled and the river on extreme right. The Third had to assault the same troops and position that they had failed to dislodge some hours before.

Major William Wallace was in command of the skirmishers. The heavy siege pieces at Fort Sanders had been hammering away at us all day, as well as the many field batteries that bristled along the epaulments around Knoxville. The skirmishers were ordered forward, the battle line to closely follow; but as Colonel Wallace was in front and could see the whole field, I will allow him to give his version of the engagement.

"We were stationed on a high hill," says Colonel Wallace, "west of said town, which descended gradually some two hundred yards, then rose to a smaller hill nearer to Knoxville. Between these two hills was a smooth valley, the middle of which was distinctly marked by a line running north and south by different crops which had been planted on opposite sides of it. Brigade skirmishers were ordered to advance towards Knoxville and drive in the enemy's pickets. I was in command of the left wing, and drove the enemy from my front, across the creek, which was beyond the smaller hill. On reaching the creek and finding our skirmishers on my

20

right, did not advance over the hill. I returned to my original position where I found them. Soon afterwards the skirmish line was again ordered forward to the line in the valley above described, and to lie down. Just then I heard a yell behind me and saw the Third South Carolina advancing rapidly towards the smaller hill. I did not order my skirmishers to lie down, but as soon as the regiment was abreast of me I advanced and drove the enemy again across the creek. On hearing firing on the west of the hill, I closed up my skirmishers and advanced south towards the crest of the hill. I found a regiment of Union sharpshooters lying behind a breastwork of rails and firing on the Third, which was within forty yards of them. As soon as the enemy saw us on their flank, they threw up their hands and surrendered. The Third had lost forty men up to this time."

Colonel Wallace tells also of how a Federal soldier, who had surrendered, was in the act of shooting him, but was prevented from doing so by the muzzle of a rifle being thrust in his face by a member of Company E, W. W. Riser, afterwards Sheriff of Newberry County. Colonel Nance was much gratified at the able assistance rendered him by Colonel Wallace, and made special and favorable mention of him in his report.

The Second, Seventh, Eighth, and Third Battalion swept across the plain like a hurricane, driving everything before them right in the teeth of the deadly fire of Fort Sanders, but the Third and Fifteenth Regiments were unusually unfortunate in their positions, owing to the strength of the works in their front. The Fifteenth got, in some way, hedged in between the road and river, and could make little progress in the face of the many obstacles that confronted them. Their young commander, Major William Gist, son of ex-Governor Gist, becoming somewhat nettled at the progress his troops were making, threw aside all prudence and care, recklessly dashed in front of his column, determined to ride at its head in the assault that was coming, but fell dead at the very moment of victory. How many hundreds, nay thousands, of brave and useful officers and men of the South wantonly threw away their lives in the attempt to rouse their companions to extra exertions and greater deeds of valor.

The Third fought for a few moments almost muzzle to muzzle, with nothing but a few rails, hastily piled, between

assailants and the assailed.　At this juncture another gallant
act was performed by Captain Winthrop, of Alexander's Battery.　Sitting on his horse in our rear, watching the battle as
it ebbed and flowed, and seeing the deadly throes in which
the Third was writhing, only a few feet separating them from
the enemy, by some sudden impulse or emotion put spurs to
his horse and dashed headlong through our ranks, over the
breastworks, and fell desperately wounded in the ranks of the
Federals, just as their lines gave way or surrendered.　This
was only one of the many heroic and nerve-straining acts witnessed by the soldiers that followed the flag of Kershaw,
McLaws, and Longstreet.

Colonel Rice, of the Battalion, was so seriously wounded
that he never returned to active duty in the field.　Major
Miller, in a former battle, had been permanently disabled, but
no other field promotions were ever made, so the gallant little
Battalion was commanded in future by senior Captains.

By morning of the 19th of November the enemy had retired
within the walls of Knoxville, and the investment of the city
completed.　During the nights our sharpshooters were advanced a little distance at a time until they were under the
very walls of the city, and there entrenched themselves in rifle
pits.　The troops began building works to protect against
attacks, and laying parallels, so that every few nights we
advanced a little nearer the city.

Jenkins, with three brigades and a part of the cavalry,
stretched around the city on the north and to the river on the
opposite side of us.　A pontoon bridge was laid across the
river below the city, and Law, with two brigades of Jenkins'
Division and a battery of our best artillery, crossed the Holston River and took possession of some heights that were
thought to command the city on the south side.　Burnside
had also some strong works on the south of the Holston,
strongly guarded by infantry, dismounted cavalry, and some
of their best rifled pieces of artillery.　This force was just
opposite the city, having easy access thereto by a military
bridge and a pontoon bridge.　Burnside had twelve thousand
regular troops in his outer trenches, several thousand recent
volunteers from Tennessee in his inner lines, with fifty-one
pieces of artillery in place, ready for action, in Knoxville
alone.　Longstreet had between fifteen and seventeen thou-

sand, after some reinforcements had reached him, and **three**
battalions of artillery, inclusive of the horse artillery.

Night and day the work of entrenchment went bravely on
in both armies, each working in plain view of the other, without any disposition to disturb the operations of either by
shelling from the forts in our front or from our works in the
rear. Each commander seemed willing and disposed to give
his opponent an open field and a fair fight. No advantage was
asked and none taken on either side, and the coming contest
appeared to be one between the hot blood of the South in
assault and the dogged determination of the North in resistance—valor, impetuosity, dash, impulsive courage against
cool, calculating, determined resistance. Greeks of the South
were preparing to meet Greeks of the North—the passionate
Ionian was about to measure swords with the stern Dorian,
then of a necessity "comes the tug of war."

On the 22d, McLaws reporting as being ready for the
assault, he was ordered to prepare for it on the night of the
23d. But a report coming to the commanding General that a
large body of the enemy's cavalry was moving upon our rear
from near Kinston, General Wheeler, with his troopers, was
detached from the army to look after them, and did not return
until the 26th, having frightened the enemy away in the meantime. The officers of McLaws' assaulting column protested
against the night attack, preferring daylight for such important
tant work, which in the end was granted.

The night of the 24th the enemy made a sally, attacking
Wofford's front; but was soon repulsed and driven back within
his lines. Longstreet now awaited the reinforcement that was
approaching with all speed. Jones' Brigade of Cavalry, from
Southwest Virginia, came up on the 28th, while Bushrod
Johnston, with his own Brigade of Tennessee Infantry and
Gracie's Brigade of Alabamians, was near at hand and moving
with all haste. The infantry and artillery promised from Virginia were more than one hundred miles away, and could not
reach us in time to take part in the pending attack. General
Bragg, commanding the Army of Tennessee after his disastrous defeat at Missionary Ridge, in front of Chattanooga, was
at the head of the war department, and ordered Longstreet to
assault Knoxville at once.

Orders were given and preparations made to commence the

attack on Fort Sanders at early dawn on the 29th by the brigades of McLaws. Fort Sanders, the key to Burnside's position, was a formidable fortress, covering several acres of ground, built by the Confederates when in possession of Knoxville, and called by them "Fort London," but named "Fort Sanders" by the Federals, in honor of the brave commander who fell in wresting it from the Confederates. The enemy had greatly strengthened it after Longstreet's advent in East Tennessee. It was surrounded by a deep and wide moat, from the bottom of which to the top of the fort was from eighteen to twenty feet. In front of the moat for several hundred yards was felled timber, which formed an almost impassable abattis, while wire netting was stretched from stump to stump and around the fort. The creek that ran between our lines and the enemy's had been dammed in several places, forcing the water back to the depth of four to five feet. The fort was lined on three sides with the heaviest of field and siege pieces, and crowded to its utmost capacity with infantry. This fort was on an acute angle of the line of entrenchments. From the right and left ran the outer or first line of breastworks, manned by infantry, and at every salient position cannons were mounted, completely encircling the entire city.

In the early gray of the morning Longstreet had marshalled his forces for the combat, while the troops in Fort Sanders slept all unconscious of the near approaching storm cloud, which was to burst over their heads. The artillery was all in position, the gunners standing by their guns, lanyard in hand, awaiting the final order to begin the attack. The armies were separated by a long, shallow vale—that to our left, in front of Jenkins, was pierced by a small stream, but obstructed by dams at intervals, until the water was in places waist deep. But the men floundered through the water to the opposite side and stood shivering in their wet garments, while the cool air of the November morning chilled their whole frames. All along the whole line the men stood silent and motionless, awaiting the sound of the signal gun.

Wofford, with his Georgians, and Humphrey, with his Mississippians, were to lead the forlorn hope in the assault on Fort Sanders, supported by Bryan's (Georgia) Brigade and one regiment of Mississippians. Kershaw stood to the right of the fort and Anderson, of Jenkins' Division, on the left, supported

by the other two brigades then present of Jenkins'. The
battle was to focus around the fort until that was taken
or silenced, then Kershaw was to storm the works on
the right, carry them, charge the second line of entrenchment, in which were posted the reserves and recent Tennessee
recruits. Jenkins, with Anderson's Brigade on his right and
next to McLaws, was to act as a brace to the assaulting column until the fort was taken, then by a sudden dash take the
entrenchments to the left of the fort, wheel and sweep the line
towards the north, and clear the way for Jenkins' other
brigades.

The expectant calm before the great storm was now at
hand. The men stood silent, grim, and determined, awaiting
the coming crash! The crash came with the thunder of the
signal gun from Alexander's Battery. Longstreet then
saluted his enemy with the roar of twenty guns, the shells
shrieking and crashing in and around Fort Sanders. Burnside
answered the salutation with a welcome of fifty guns from the
fort and angles along the entrenchments. Salvos after salvos
sounded deep and loud from the cannon's mouth, and echoed
and re-echoed up and down the valleys of the Holston. After
the early morning compliments had continued ten or fifteen
minutes, the infantry began to make ready for the bloody fray.
Wofford commenced the advance on the northwest angle of the
fort, Humphrey the South. Not a yell was to be given, not
a gun to be fired, save only those by the sharpshooters. The
dread fortress was to be taken by cold steel alone. Not a
gun was loaded in the three brigades. As the mist of the
morning and the smoke of the enemy's guns lifted for a moment, the slow and steady steps of the "forlorn hope" could
be seen marching towards the death trap—over fallen trees and
spreading branches, through the cold waters of the creek, the
brave men marched in the face of the belching cannon, raking
the field right and left. Our sharpshooters gave the cannoneers a telling fire, and as the enemy's infantry in the fort rose
above the parapets to deliver their volley, they were met by
volleys from our sharpshooters in the pits, now in rear of the
assaulting columns, and firing over their heads. When near
the fort the troops found yet a more serious obstruction in the
way of stout wires stretched across their line of approach.
This, however, was overcome and passed, and the assailants

soon found themselves on the crest of the twelve foot abyss that surrounded Fort Sanders. Some jumped into the moat and began climbing up upon the shoulders of their companions. The enemy threw hand bombs over the wall to burst in the ditch. Still the men struggled to reach the top, some succeeding only to fall in the fort. Scaling ladders were now called for, but none were at hand. Anderson had moved up on Wofford's left, but finding the fort yet uncovered, instead of charging the entrenchment, as ordered, he changed his direction towards the fort, and soon his brigade was tangled in wild confusion with those of Worfford and Humphrey, gazing at the helpless mass of struggling humanity in the great gulf below.

Kershaw's men stood at extreme tension watching and waiting the result of the struggle around the fort. Never perhaps were their nerves so strung up as the few moments they awaited in suspense the success or reverse of the assaulting column, bending every effort to catch the first command of "forward." All but a handful of the enemy had left the fort, and victory here seemed assured, and in that event the result of Kershaw's onslaught on the right and Jenkins' South Carolinians and Benning's Georgians on the left would have been beyond the range of conjecture. Just at this supreme moment Major Goggans, of McLaws' staff, who had been at the fort and took in the worst phases of the situation, rode to General Longstreet and reported the fortress impregnable without axes and scaling ladders. Under this misapprehension, General Longstreet gave the fatal order for the assaulting columns to retire, and all the support back to their entrenchments. Thus was one of the most glorious victories of the war lost by the ill judgment of one man. General Longstreet bitterly regretted giving this order so hastily, but pleads in extinuation his utmost confidence in Major Goggans, his class-mate at West Point.

In the twenty minutes of the assault Longstreet lost in his three brigades, Wofford's, Humphrey's, and Anderson's, eight hundred and twenty-two; Burnside, six hundred and seventy-three. During the campaign Longstreet lost twelve hundred and ninety-six. During the campaign Burnside lost fourteen hundred and eighty-one.

Kershaw's Brigade lost many gallant officers and men dur-

ing the sanguinary struggles around Knoxville, and it must be
confessed in sorrow and regret, all to no purpose. Not that
the commanding general was wanting in ability, military training, or tactical knowledge; nor the soldiers in courage, daring,
and self-denials. None of these were lacking, for the officers
and men of the line performed deeds of prowess that have
never been excelled by any soldiers on the planet, while in
skill or fearlessness the regimental brigade and division commanders were equal to Ney, Murat, St. Cyr, or any of the host
of great commanders of the Napoleonic era. But in the first
place the Confederate forces were too weak, poorly equipped
in all those essentials that are so requisite to an invading army.

MAJOR WILLIAM M. GIST.

Major William M. Gist was a son of Governor W. H. Gist,
the Governor just preceding Secession, and Mrs. Mary E.
Gist; born in Union County in 1840. He was educated in the
common schools of Union and York Counties and by private
tutors, until January, 1854. He then went to school at Glenn
Springs to Rev. C. S. Beard for six months. His health failing, he returned to his home, and in January, 1855, entered
the Mt. Zion College, at Winnsboro, Fairfield County, taught
by Hon. J. W. Hudson, and spent one year at that institution.
He next entered the South Carolina College, in January, 1856,
and graduated in the class of '59. The class which Major
Gist was in at the time, the Junior, did not participate in the
great "college rebellion" of March 28th, 1858. Through that
rebellion one hundred and eleven of the students were sus-
pended for six months.

When the first alarm of war was sounded, Major Gist re —
sponded promptly, with the same chivalric spirit that was s▬▬
characteristic of his whole life. He joined, as a private▬▬
Captain Gadberry's Company, from Union, and left for Char▬▬
leston on January 12, 1861, the company forming a part c▬▬
Colonel Maxey Gregg's First Six Months' Volunteers, an▬ ◢
remained with the command until their term of service e▬▬
pired. A vacancy occurring, Colonel Gregg appointed him h▬▬.
Sergeant Major.

After the fall of Sumter a part of Colonel Gregg's Regimer▬▬
was disbanded, and Major Gist returned to Union and bega▬▬
at once organizing a company for the Confederate Stat▬▬

Army. He was elected Captain of the company and was
joined to the Fifteenth Regiment, then collecting at camp
near Columbia for drill and instruction. He served as Captain
until the death of Colonel DeSaussure, then was promoted to
Major. There being no officer senior to him, his way was
open to the Colonelcy of his regiment at the time of his death.

Major Gist was a young man of rare qualities—open, frank,
generous, and brave. He commanded the respect and esteem
of all. Just verging into mature manhood as the toscin of war
sounded, he had no opportunity to display his great qualities
as a civilian, but as a soldier he was all that the most exacting
could desire. He was beloved by his men, and they appreciated his worth. He was kind and affectionate to all, and
showed favoritism or privileges to none. It was through that
ungovernable impulse that permeates the body and flows
through the hot Southern blood that he so recklessly threw
his life away, leading his men to the charge. In a moment
of hesitancy among his troops, he felt the supreme responsibility of leadership, placed himself where danger was greatest, bullets falling thick and fast; thus by the inspiration of
his own individual courage, he hoped to carry his men with
him to success, or to meet a fate like his own.

LIEUTENANT COLONEL W. G. RICE.

Lieutenant Colonel W. G. Rice was born in Union County,
S. C., on December 9th, 1831. He was the fourth son of
R. S. Rice and Agnes B. Rice, nee Morgan, and resided in the
upper portion of the county, near Broad River. His family
removed to the lower section of the county, near Goshen Hill,
when the son was ten years old, and he attended the schools
of the surrounding country until fourteen years of age, when
he was sent to the Methodist Conference School, at Cokesbury. He remained a pupil here until October, 1848, then he
entered the South Carolina College. graduating from that
institution with the class of '51. He engaged in planting for
one year at his original home, then began the study of law in
the office of Judge T. N. Dawkins, but did not prosecute the
study to graduation.

In March following he married Miss Sarah E. Sims, of
Broad River, of which union eleven children were born, seven
of whom are living. The year of his marriage he moved to

Laurens County, near Waterloo, where we find him surrounded by "peace and plenty" until the outbreak of the Civil War. In October, 1861, he raised a volunteer company, and later, together with three other companies from Laurens County, formed a battalion, and tendered the .command to George S. James, who had resigned from the United States Army. Major James assumed command at Camp Hampton in December. During the early months of 1862 three other companies united with the battalion, and Major James was promoted to Lieutenant Colonel, and Captain W. G. Rice being senior Captain, was made Major.

During the month of April following, a reorganization took place, and Lieutenant Colonel James and Major Rice were re-elected to their former positions by exactly the same vote. Major Rice being detailed on court martial on James' Island, did not accompany his battalion to Virginia, but joined it soon thereafter, near Richmond.

The battalion marched with the brigade (Drayton's) from Gordonsville to second battle of Manassas, but was not actively engaged. At the battle of Crompton's Gap, Md., Colonel Rice was severely wounded, Colonel James killed, and the battalion almost torn to pieces. Colonel Rice was left for dead upon the field, and when he gained consciousness he was within the enemy's line, and only by exerci-ing the greatest caution, he regained the Confederate camp. By Colonel Rice's prudence at this battle in ordering a retreat to a more sheltered position, the battalion was saved from utter destruction, but suffering himself almost a fatal wound. He was sent across the Potomac, and next day to Shepherdstown. Returning from leave of absence occasioned by the desperate nature of his wound, he found that he had been promoted to Lieutenant Colonel, and that his battalion and the Fifteenth Regiment made a part of Kershaw's Brigade, this being in December, 1862. Colonel Rice led his command through the battles of Fredericksburg and Chancellorsville without incident of special interest (vide sketch of battalion).

Returning from an enjoyable leave of absence, he found his command at Chambersburg, Pa. Three days later he commanded the battalion at the bloody battle of Gettysburg. Again Colonel Rice is absent on sick leave, and regains the army just as Longstreet was crossing the Holston. Four day afterwards he was given one company from each of the five regiments to reinforce his battalion, and ordered to feel for and drive the enemy from the position which they held. This proved to be a fortified camp and the enemy in strong line of battle. In the engagement that followed, Colonel Rice was again so severely wounded as to render him unfit for service thereafter.

After this he returned home to the prosecution of his life-work, farming. He removed to Abbeville, now Greenwood County, December, 1869, where he may now be found, as he says, "in the enjoyment of a reasonable degree of health and strength, surrounded by friends and relatives."

JULIUS ZOBEL.

To show with what devotion and fidelity the private soldier of the Southland served the cause he espoused, I will relate as an example the act of Julius Zobel, who fell so dangerously wounded before Knoxville. This is not an isolated case, for hundreds and thousands were tempted like Zobel, but turned away with scorn and contempt. But Julius Zobel was an exception in that he was not a native born, but a blue-eyed, fair-haired son of the "Fatherland." He had not been in this "Land of the free and home of the brave" long enough to comprehend all its blessings, he being under twenty-one years of age, and not yet naturalized. He was a mechanic in the railroad shops, near Newberry, when the first call for volunteers was made. He laid aside his tools and promptly joined Company E (Captain Nance), of the Third South Carolina, called "Quitman Rifles."

He had a smooth, pleasant face, a good eye, and the yellow hair of his countrymen. His nature was all sunshine, geniality, and many a joke he practiced upon his comrades, taking all in good humor those passed upon him. One day, as a comrade had been "indulging" too freely, another accosted him with—

"Turn away your head, your breath is awful. What is the matter with you?"

Zobel, in his broad German brogue, answered for his companion. "Led 'em alone, dare been nodden to madder mid Mattis, only somding crawled in him and died."

He lost his leg at Knoxville and fell in the enemy's hands

after Longstreet withdrew, and was sent North with the other wounded. While in the loathsome prison pen, enduring all the sufferings, hardships, and horrors of the Federal "Bastile," he was visited by the German Consul, and on learning that he had not been naturalized, the Consul offered him his liberty if he would take the oath of allegiance to the North.

Zobel flashed up as with a powder burst, and spoke like the true soldier that he was. "What! Desert my comrades; betray the country I have sworn to defend; leave the flag under whose folds I have lost all but life? No, no! Let me die a thousand deaths in this hell hole first!"

He is living to-day in Columbia, an expert mechanic in the service of the Southern Railroad, earning an honest living by the sweat of his brow, with a clear conscience, a faithful heart, and surrounded by a devoted family.

That the campaign against Knoxville was a failure, cannot be wondered at under the circumstances. In the first place Longstreet's forces were too weak—the two thousand reinforcements to come from Virginia dwindled down to a few regiments of cavalry and a battery or two. The men were badly furnished and equipped—a great number being barefoot and thinly clad. Hundreds would gather at the slaughter pens daily and cut from the warm beef hides strips large enough to make into moccasins, and thus shod, marched miles upon miles in the blinding snow and sleet. All overcoats and heavy clothing had been left in Virginia, and it is a fact too well known to be denied among the soldiers of the South that baggage once left or sent to the rear never came to the front again.

Longstreet did not have the support he had the right to expect from his superiors and those in authority at Richmond. He had barely sufficient transportation to convey the actual necessaries of camp equippage, and this had to be used daily in gathering supplies from the surrounding country for man and beast. He had no tools for entrenching purposes, only such as he captured from the enemy, and expected to cross deep and unfordable rivers without a pontoon train. With the dead of winter now upon him, his troops had no shelter to protect them from the biting winds of the mountains or the blinding snow storms from overhead save only much-worn blankets and

thin tent flys five by six feet square, one to the man. This
was the condition in which the commanding General found
himself and troops, in a strange and hostile country, completely cut off from railroad connection with the outside world.
Did the men murmur or complain? Not a bit of it. Had
they grown disheartened and demoralized by their defeat at
Knoxville, or had they lost their old-time confidence in themselves and their General? On the contrary, as difficulties and
dangers gathered around their old chieftain, they clung to
him, if possible, with greater tenacity and a more determined
zeal. It seemed as if every soldier in the old First Corps
was proud of the opportunity to suffer for his country—never
a groan or pang, but that he felt compensated with the
thought that he was doing his all in the service of his country
—and to suffer for his native land, his home, and family, was
a duty and a pleasure.

The soldiers of the whole South had long since learned by
experience on the fields of Virginia, Maryland, and Pennsylvania, along the valleys of Kentucky, the mountains and
gorges of Tennessee, and the swamps of the Mississippi, that
war was only "civilized barbarism," and to endure uncom-
plaining was the highest attributes of a soldier. Civilization
during the long centuries yet to come may witness, perhaps,
as brave, unselfish, unyielding, and patriotic bands of heroes
as those who constituted the Confederate Army, but God in
His wisdom has never yet created their equals, and, perhaps,
never will create their superiors.

CHAPTER XXVI

The Siege of Knoxville Raised---Battle of Bean
Station---Winter Quarters.

On the night of the 4th of December preparations were
made to raise the siege around Knoxville and vacate the fortifications built around the city after a fortnight's stay in the
trenches. The wagons had begun moving the day before,
with part of the artillery, and early in the night the troops

north and west of the city took up the line of march towards
Rutledge, followed by McLaws on the right.

Kershaw being on the extreme right of the army and next
to the river on the South, could not move until the troops on
the left were well under way, thus leaving us in position until
near midnight. Lieutenant Colonel Rutherford commanded the
rear guard of skirmishers, deployed several hundred yards on
either side of the road. Our march was extremely fatiguing,
the roads being muddy and badly cut up by the trains in our
front. The weather was cold and bleaky; the night so dark
that the troops could scarcely see their way, but all night long
they floundered through the mud and slough—over passes and
along narrow defiles, between the mountain and the river to
their right—the troops trudged along, the greater portion
of whom were thinly clad, some with shoes badly worn,
others with none. Two brigades of cavalry were left near the
city until daylight to watch the movements of the enemy.
The next day we met General Ranson with his infantry division and some artillery on his long march from Virginia to reinforce Longstreet, but too late to be of any material service to
the commanding General. Bragg's orders had been imperative, "to assault Knoxville and not to await the reinforcement."

Burnside did not attempt to follow us closely, as he was
rather skeptical about leaving his strong positions around
Knoxville with the chances of meeting Longstreet in open
field. But strong Federal forces were on a rapid march to
relieve the pressure against Knoxville—one column from the
West and ten thousand men under Sherman were coming up
from Chattanooga, and were now at London, on the Tennessee.

Longstreet continued the march to Rodgersville, some fifty
or sixty miles northeast of Knoxville, on the west bank of the
Holston, and here rested for several days. It was the impression of the troops that they would remain here for a length of
time, and they began building winter quarters. But Burnside
feeling the brace of strong reinforcements nearing him, moved
out from Knoxville a large detachment in our rear to near
Bean Station (or Cross Roads), the one leading from Knoxville by way of Rutledge, the other from the eastern side of
the Holston and over the mountain on the western side at
Bean's Gap. Longstreet determined to retrace his steps, strike

Burnside a stunning blow, and, if possible, to capture his advance forces at Bean Station.

Here I will digress a few moments from my narrative to relate an incident that took place while encamped near Rodgersville, an incident that will ever remain fresh in the memory of all of the old First Division who witnessed it. It is with feelings of sorrow at this distant day to even recall it to mind, and it is with pain that I record it. But as I have undertaken to give a faithful and true story of the army life of the First Brigade, this harrowing scene becomes a part of its history. It was near the middle of the month. The sun had long since dropped out of sight behind the blue peaks of the distant Cumberland. All is still in camp; the soldiers, after their many hardships and fatiguing marches, rest, and soon all in sound slumber. Even the very voices of nature seemed hushed and frozen in the gloomy silence of the night. All is quiet, save in one lonely tent, apart some distance from the rest, before which walks a silent sentinel, as if he, too, feels the chilling effects of the sombre stillness. Murmurings soft and low in the one lighted tent are all that break the oppressive death-like silence. In the back ground the great forest trees of the mountain stand mute and motionless, not even a nod of their stately heads to a passing breeze, while far away to the south could be seen an occasional picket fire, making the surrounding objects appear like moving, grotesque phantoms. The heavens above were all bedecked with shimmering stars, pouring down upon the sleeping Valley of the Holston a cold and trembling light.

In the lonely tent sits a soldier, who is spending his last night on earth; by his side sits his little son, who has come far away over the mountains to spend the last moments with his father and see him die—not to die like a soldier wishes for death, but as a felon and outcast, the ignominious death at the stake. An occasional sob escapes the lips of the lad, but no sigh or tears of grief from the condemned. He is holding converse with his Maker, for to His throne alone must he now appeal for pardon. Hope on earth had gone. He had no friend at court, no one to plead his cause before those who had power to order a reprieve. He must die. The doomed man was an ignorant mountaineer, belonging to one of the regiments from North Georgia or Tennessee, and in an ill-fated moment he allowed his longings for home to overcome his sense of duty, and deserted his colors—fled to his mountain home and sought to shelter himself near his wife and little ones in the dark recesses and gorges thereabout. He was followed, caught, returned to his command, courtmartialed, and sentenced to death—time, to-morrow.

During the days and nights that passed since the dread sentence had been read to him, he lay upon his rude couch in the guard tent all indifferent to his environments, and on the march he moved along with the guard in silence, gazing abstractedly at the blue vaults of heaven or the star-strewn, limitless space. That far away future now to him so near— that future which no vision can comtemplate nor mortal mind comprehend - is soon to be unfolded. Little heed was paid to the comforting words of his sympathetic comrades in arms, who bid him hope, for the condemned man felt inwardly and was keenly conscious of the fact that he had been caught upon the crest of a great wave of destiny, soon to be swept away by its receding force to darkness, despair, death. "Fate had played him falsely."

To witness death, to see the torn and mangled remains of friends and comrades, are but incidents in the life of a soldier, While all dread it, few fear it. Yet it is upon the field of battle that it is expected—amid the din and smoke, the shouts of his comrades, the rattle of musketry, and the cannon's roar. There is the soldier's glory, his haven, his expected end; and of all deaths, that upon the battlefield, surrounded by victorious companions and waving banners, the triumphant shouts of comrades, is the least painful.

The grounds selected for the carrying out of the court's sentence were on a broad plateau, gently sloping towards the center on three sides. So well were the grounds and surroundings adapted to the end in view, that it seemed as if nature had anticipated the purposes of man.

By 9 o'clock the troops of the division were in motion, all under the command of Colonel James D. Nance, of the Third South Carolina, marching for the field of death. Kershaw's Brigade took the lead, and formed on the left of the hollow square, Wofford's on the right, with Bryan's doubling on the two, while Humphrey's closed the space at the west end of the square.

A detail of thirty men were made to do the firing, fifteen guns being loaded with powder and ball, the others with powder alone, this arrangement being made, perhaps, with a view to ease the qualms of conscience, should any of the guards have scruples of shedding the blood of a former comrade in arms. None could know positively who held the death-dealing guns. An opening was made at the lower end and the first platoon of guards entered with arms reversed, then the band playing the "Dead March," followed by the condemned and his son, the second platoon bringing up the rear. The cortege marched around the whole front of the lined-up troops, keeping step to the slow and dismal sounds of the "Dead March." The prisoner walked with the firm and steady step of a Sagamore, or an Indian brave marching and singing his death chants, to the place of his execution. His son was equally as courageous and self-possessed, not a tremor or faltering in either. At times the father and son would speak in low, soft tones to each other, giving and receiving, perhaps, the last messages, the last farewells on earth, the soldier-outcast being now under the very shadow of death.

After making the entire circuit of the square, the condemned was conducted to the open space at the eastern side, where a rude stake had been driven in the ground. To this he boldly walked, calmly kneeling in front, allowing himself to be bandaged and pinioned thereto. The guards had formed in double ranks, fifteen paces in front, his faithful son standing some distance to his right, calm, unmoved, and defiant, even in the face of all the terrors going on before him. The officer in charge gives the command, "ready," thirty hammers spring back; "aim," the pieces rise to the shoulders; then, and then only, the tension broke, and the unfortunate man, instead of the officer, cried out in a loud, metallic voice, "fire." The report of the thirty rifles rang out on the stillness of the morning; the man at the stake gives a convulsive shudder, his head falls listlessly on his breast, blood gushes out in streams, and in a moment all is still. The deserter has escaped.

The authorities at Washington had grown tired of Burnside's failure to either crush Longstreet or drive him out of East Tennessee, and had sent General Foster to relieve him, the latter General bringing with him the standing orders, "Crush or drive out Longstreet." How well General Foster

21

succeeded will be related further on. In obedience to the department's special orders, General Longstreet had, several days previous, sent Wheeler's Cavalry back to General Johnston, now commanding Bragg's Army. Our troops had heard the confirmation of the report of General Bragg's desperate battle at Missionary Ridge—his disastrous defeat, his withdrawal to Dalton, and his subsequent relinquishment of command of the Army of Tennessee. This had no effect upon our troops, no more so than the news of the fall of Vicksburg just after Lee's bloody repulse at Gettysburg. The soldiers of the Eastern Army had unbounded confidence in themselves and their commander, and felt that so long as they stood together they were invincible.

The enemy had fortified a position at Bean's Station, in a narrow valley between the Holston River and the Clinch Mountains, the valley being about two miles in breadth. This force Longstreet determined to capture, and his plans were admirably adapted to bring about the result. To the right of the enemy was the river; to their left, a rugged mountain spur, passable at only a few points. Part of our cavalry was to pass down the western side of the mountain, close the gaps in rear, the infantry to engage the enemy in front until the other portion of the cavalry could move down the east bank of the river, cross over, and get in the enemy's rear, thus cutting off all retreat. This part of the Valley of the Holston had been pretty well ravaged to supply the Federal Army, and our troops, with never more than a day's rations on hand at a time, had to be put on short rations, until our subsistence trains could gather in a supply and the neighborhood mills could grind a few days' rations ahead. Old soldiers know what "short rations" mean—next to no rations at all.

General Longstreet says of the morale of his army at this time: "The men were brave, steady, patient. Occasionally they called pretty loudly for parched corn, but always in a bright, merry mood. There was never a time we did not have corn enough, and plenty of wood with which to keep us warm and parch our corn. At this distance it seems as almost incredible that we got along as we did, but all were then so healthy and strong that we did not feel severely our really great hardship. Our serious trouble was in the matter of shoes and clothing."

Early on the morning of the 14th the troops were put in motion and marched rapidly down the almost impassable thoroughfare. Bushrod Johnston's Division being in the front, followed by McLaws'—Kershaw's Brigade in the lead. Part of Jenkins' Division was acting as escort for supply trains in the surrounding country, and that Division did not join the army for several days. Late in the day of the 15th we came in sight of the enemy's breastworks. The Federal artillery opened a furious fusilade upon the troops, coming down the road with their rifled guns and field mortars. Bushrod Johnston had filed to the left of the road and gotten out of range, but the screaming shells kept up a continual whiz through the ranks of Kershaw. The men hurried along the road to seek shelter under a bluff in our front, along the base of which ran a small streamlet. The greater portion of the brigade was here huddled together in a jam, to avoid the shells flying overhead. The enemy must have had presage of our position, for they began throwing shells up in the air from their mortars and dropping them down upon us, but most fell beyond, while a great many exploded in the air. We could see the shells on their downward flight, and the men pushed still closer together and nearer the cliff. Here the soldier witnessed one of those incidents so often seen in army life that makes him feel that at times his life is protected by a hand of some hidden, unseen power. His escape from death so often appears miraculous that the soldier feels from first to last that he is but "in the hollow of His hand," and learns to trust all to chance and Providence.

As a shell from a mortar came tumbling over and over, just above the heads of this mass of humanity, a shout went up from those farther back, "Look out! Look out! There comes a shell." Lower and lower it came, all feeling their hopelessness of escape, should the shell explode in their midst. Some tried to push backwards; others, forward, while a great many crowded around and under an ambulance, to which was hitched an old broken down horse, standing perfectly still and indifferent, and all oblivious to his surroundings. The men gritted their teeth, shrugged their shoulders, and waited in death-like suspense the falling of the fatal messenger—that peculiar, whirling, hissing sound growing nearer and more distinct every second. But instead of falling among the men, it fell directly upon the head of the old horse, severing it almost from the body, but failed to explode. The jam was so great that some had difficulty in clearing themselves from the falling horse. Who of us are prepared to say whether this was mere chance, or that the bo't was guided and directed by an invisible hand?

Bushrod Johnston had formed on the left of the road; Kershaw marching over the crest of the hill in our front, and putting his brigade in line of battle on a broad plateau and along the foot hills of the mountains on the right. Here the troops were halted, to wait the coming up of the rest of the division and Jenkins' two brigades. The cannonading of the enemy was especially severe during our halt, and General Kershaw had to frequently shift his regiments to avoid the terrific force of the enemy's shells. It was not the intention of the commanding General to bring on a general engagement here until he heard from his cavalry beyond the river and those to the west of the mountain. The cavalry had been sent to cut off retreat and close the mountain passes, and the infantry was to press moderately in front, in order to hold the enemy in position.

Just before sunset, however, a general advance was made. One of Kershaw's regiments was climbing along the mountain side, endeavoring to gain the enemy's left, and as our skirmishers became hotly engaged, the movements of the regiment on the side of the mountain were discovered, and the enemy began to retire. Now orders were given to press them hard. The rattle of Bushrod Johnston's rifles on our left told of a pretty stiff fight he was having. As the long row of bristling bayonets of Kershaw's men debouched upon the plain in front of the enemy's works, nothing could be seen but one mass of blue, making way to the rear in great confusion. Our artillery was now brought up and put in action, our infantry continuing to press forward, sometimes at double-quick.

We passed over the enemy's entrenchments without firing a gun. Night having set in, and General Longstreet hearing from his cavalry that all in the enemy's rear was safe, ordered a halt for the night, thinking the game would keep until morning. During the night, however, by some misunderstanding of orders, the commander of the cavalry withdrew from the mountain passes, and the enemy taking advantage of this outlet so unexpectedly offered, made his escape under cover of darkness. Here we had another truthful verification of the oft' quoted aphorism of Burns, about "the best laid plans of mice and men."

This last attempt of Longstreet to bring the enemy to an engagement outside of Knoxville proving abortive, the commanding General determined to close the campaign for the season, and to put his troops in as comfortable winter quarters as possible. This was found on the right or east bank of the Holston, near Morristown and the little hamlet of Russellville. The brigade crossed the Holston about the 17th of December, in a little flat boat, holding about two companies at a time, the boat being put backwards and forwards by means of a stout rope, the men pulling with their hands. A blinding sleet was falling, covering the rope continually with a sheet of ice, almost freezing the hands of the thinly clad and barefooted soldiers. But there was no murmuring nor complaint—all were as jolly and good-natured as if on a picnic excursion. Hardship had become a pleasure and sufferings, patriotism. There were no sickness, no straggling, nor feelings of self-constraint.

General Longstreet speaks thus of his army after he had established his camps and the subsistence trains began to forage in the rich valleys of the French Broad and Chucky Rivers and along the banks of Mossy Creek: .

"With all the plentitude of provisions, and many things, which, at the time, seemed luxuries, we were not quite happy. Tattered blankets, garments, shoes (the later going some gone) opened ways on all sides for piercing winter blasts. There were some hand looms in the country from which we occasionally picked up a piece of cloth, and here and there we received other comforts—some from kind, some from unwilling hands, which could nevertheless spare them. For shoes, we were obliged to resort to raw-hides, from beef cattle, as temporary protection from the frozen ground. Then we found soldiers who could tan the hides of our beeves, some who could make shoes, some who could make shoe pegs, some who could make shoe lasts, so that it came about that the hides passed rapidly from the beeves to the feet of the soldiers in the form of comfortable shoes."

We took up very comfortable quarters, in the way that comfort goes with a soldier—cut off from the outside world.   Only a few officers had the old army fly tents; the soldiers were each supplied, or rather had supplied themselves upon the battlefield of the enemy with small tent flies, about five by six feet, so arranged with buttons and button holes that two being buttoned together and stretched over a pole would make the sides or roof and the third would close the end, making a tent about six feet long, five feet wide, and four feet high, in which three or four men could sleep very comfortably.   In the bitter weather great roaring fires were built in front during the night, and to which the soldier, by long habit, or a kind of intuition, would stretch his feet, when the cold would become unbearable under his thread-bare blanket.

But notwithstanding all these disadvantages, the men of Kershaw's Brigade were bent on having a good time in East Tennessee.   They foraged during the day for apples, chickens, butter, or whatever they could find to eat.   Some of sporting proclivities would purchase a lot of chicken roosters and then fight, regiment against regiment, and seemed to enjoy as much seeing a fight between a shanghai and a dunghill, as a match between gaved Spanish games.

Many formed the acquaintance of ladies in the surrounding country, and they, too, Union as well as Southern, being cut off like ourselves—their husbands and brothers being either in the Northern or Southern Army—seemed determined on having a good time also.   Dancing parties were frequent, and the ladies of Southern sympathies gave the officers and soldiers royal dinners.

In this connection, I will relate an anecdote told on our gallant Lieutenant Colonel Rutherford, of the Third, by a friend of his.

When the Third South Carolina Regiment of Infantry was in East Tennessee, in the month of January, 1864, not only did the soldiers find it difficult to get enough to eat, but their supply of shoes and clothing ran pretty low.   Those who had extra pants or jackets helped their needy friends.   Lieutenant Colonel Rutherford had turned over his extra pair of pants to some one, which left him the pair he wore each day as his only stock on hand in the pants line.   Heavy snows fell.   The regiment was encamped very near a pleasant residence, where a bevy of pretty girls lived.   After an acquaintance of some-

time, a snow-balling was indulged in. It was observed that
Colonel Rutherford used his every endeavor to constantly face
the girls, who were pelting him pretty liberally on all sides.
After awhile he slipped up and fell, but in his fall his face was
downward, when lo! the girls discovered that he had a hole in
his pants. Too good-natured to appear to see his predicament,
no notice was seemingly taken of his misfortune; but as the
officers were about going off to bed that night, the married
lady said to him:

"Colonel, lay your pants on the chair at your room door to-
night, and you will find them there again in the morning.
We hope you won't mind a patch."

The Colonel, who was always so gallant in actual battle,
and could not bear to turn his back to the Federal soldiers,
was just as unwilling to turn his back to snow-balls, who happened to be Confederate lasses, and the reason therefor,
although never told, was discovered by them.

The weather had gotten down to two degrees below zero,
the ground frozen as hard as brick-bats, and the winds whistled gaily through our tattered tents, our teeth beating tattoo
and our limbs shivering from the effects of our scanty clothing
and shoes. But our wagons were gathering in supplies from
the rich valleys of the French Broad and the Nollachuckey,
and while we suffered from cold, we generally had provisions
sufficient for our want. By the middle of January we had to
temporarily break up camp to meet the enemy, who had left
Knoxville with the greater part of the army, and was marching up on the right banks of the French Broad to near Dan-
dridge. General Foster seeing the penalty put upon General
Burnside for not driving out Longstreet from East Tennessee,
the former undertook to accomplish in this bitter weather
what the latter had failed to do in comparative good season.
Our cavalry, with Jenkins' Division, headed direct towards the
moving column of the enemy, while McLaws' Division marched
in the direction of Strawberry Plains, with a view to cutting
off the enemy and forcing him to battle in an open field. But
General Granger, in command of the Federal column, was too
glad to cross the French Broad and beat a hasty retreat to
Knoxville. We returned to our old camps, and waited, like
Micawber, "for something to turn up."

By some disagreement or want of confidence in General

McLaws by the commanding General, he was relieved of his command, and General Kershaw being the senior Brigadier General of the division, was placed in command. What the differences were between General Longstreet and his Major General were never exactly understood by the soldiers. While General McLaws may have been a brave soldier and was well beloved by officers and men, still he was wanting in those elements to make a successful General of volunteer troops—dash, discipline, and promptness in action.

General Longstreet had bent all his energies to the repairing of the railroad through East Tennesse and Virginia, and as soon as this was accomplished, a limited number of soldiers were furloughed for twenty-one days. A large lot of shoes and clothing was sent us from Richmond, and this helped to make camp life more enjoyable. Not all the men by any means could be spared by furlough even for this brief period, for we had an active and vigilant foe in our front. Most of the men drew their furloughs by lot, those who had been from home the longest taking their chances by drawing from a hat, "furlough" or "no furlough."

While in winter quarters, during the spasm of chicken fighting, a difficulty occurred between Lieutenant A and Private B, of the Third, both good friends, and no better soldiers were ever upon a battlefield. These are not the initials of their names, but will answer the purpose at hand, and that purpose is to show the far-reaching results of the courtmartial that followed, and a decision reached under difficulties, that the most learned jurist might feel proud of.

I will say for the benefit of those not learned in the law of army regulations, that for an officer to strike a private he is cashiered, and for a private to strike an officer the penalty is either death or long imprisonment with ball and chain attachments.

Now it appeared to the officers who composed the courtmartial, Captain Herbert. Lieutenant Garlington, and the writer of this (all parties of the Third), that Lieutenant A had knocked Private B down. The officer appeared in his own defense, and gave in extenuation of his crime, that Private B had hit his (Liutenant A's) chicken a stunning blow on the head while they were ' petting'' them between rounds. Now that decision of the courtmartial astonished our Colonel as much as the men who were parties to the combat themselves. Now it read something like this—time, dress parade:

"Whereas, Lieutenant A, of Company ———, Third South Carolina, did strike Private B, of same company and regiment, with his fist in the face, that he should receive the severest of punishment; but, whereas, Private B did strike the game chicken in the hands of Lieutenant A, without cause or provocation, therefore both are equally guilty of a crime and misdemeanor, and should be privately reprimanded by the Colonel commanding."

Such a laugh as was set up, notwithstanding the grave countenance of the Colonel, was never heard on ordinary occasions.

CHAPTER XXVII

In Winter Quarters, 1863 and 1864---Re-enlistment.

Christmas came as usual to the soldiers as to the rest of the world, and if Longstreet's men did not have as "merry and happy" a Christmas as those at home, and in the armies outside, they had at least a cheerful one. Hid away in the dark and mysterious recesses of the houses of many old Unionists, was yet a plentitude of "moon-shine," and this the soldiers drew out, either by stealth or the eloquent pleadings of a faded Confederate bill. Poultry abounded in the far away sections of the country, not yet ravaged by either army, which it was a pleasure to those fixtures of the army called "foragers" to hunt up. The brotherhood of "foragers" was a peculiar institute, and some men take as naturally to it as the duck to water. They have an eye to business, as well as pleasure, and the life of a "forager" becomes almost an art. They have a peculiar talent, developed by long practice of nosing out, hunting up, and running to quarry anything in the way of "eatables or drinkables." During the most stringent times in a country that had been over-run for years by both armies, some men could find provisions and delicacies, and were never known to be without "one drink left" in their canteens for a needy comrade, who had the proper credentials, the Confederate "shin-plaster." These foragers had the instinct (or acqui.ed it) and the gifts of a "knight of the road" of worming out of the good house-wife little dainties, cold meats, and stale bread, and if there was one drop of the "oh be joyful" in the house, these men of peculiar intellect would be sure to get it. So with such an acquisition to the army, and in such a country as East Tennessee, the soldiers did not suffer on that cold Christmas day. Bright and cheerful fires burned before every tent, over which hung a turkey, a chicken, or a choice slice of Tennessee pork, or, perhaps, better still, a big, fat sausage, with which the smoke-houses along the valleys of the French Broad were filled.

It was my misfortune, or rather good fortune, to be doing picket duty on the Holston on that day. Here I had an adventure rather out of the regular order in a soldier's life, one more suited to the character of Don Quixotte. I, as commandant of the post, had strict orders not to allow anyone to cross the river, as "beyond the Alps lie Italy," beyond the Holston lay the enemy. But soldiers, like other men, have their trials. While on duty here a buxom, bouncing, rosy cheeked mountain lass came up, with a sack of corn on her shoulder, and demanded the boat in order that she might cross over to a mill and exchange her corn for meal. This, of course, I had to reluctantly deny, hower gallantly disposed I might otherwise have been. The lass asked me, with some feeling of scorn, "Is the boat yours?" to which I was forced to answer in the negative. She protested that she would not go back and get a permit or pass from anyone on earth; that the boat was not mine, and she had as much right to its use as anyone, and that no one should prevent her from getting bread for her family, and that "you have no business here at best," arguments that were hard to controvert in the face of a firey young "diamond in the rough." So to compromise matters and allow chivalry to take, for the time being, the place of duty, I agreed to ferry her over myself. She placed her corn in the middle of the little boat, planting herself erect in the prow; I took the stern. The weather was freezing cold, the wind strong, and the waves rolled high, the little boat rocking to and fro, while I battled with the strong current of the river.

: or twice she cast disdainful glances at my feeble and
:iated form, but at last, in a melting tone, she said: "If
can't put the boat over, get up and give me the oar."
taunt made me strong, and the buxom mountain girl was
at the mill.   While awaiting the coming of the old miller,
cluded to take a stroll over the hill in search of further
nture.   There I found, at a nice old-fashioned farm house,
'y of the prettiest young ladies it had been my pleasure to
in a long while—buoyant, vivacious, cultured, and loyal
e core.   They did not wait very long to tell me that they
"Rebels to the bone."   They invited me and any of my
ds that I chose to come over the next day and take dinner
them, an invitation I was not loath nor slow to accept.
nountain acquaintance was rowed back over the Holston
ie season, without any of the parting scenes that fiction
;ht in, and the next day, armed with pass-ports, my
ds and myself were at the old farm house early.   My
)anions were Colonel Rutherford, Dr. James Evans, Lieu-
nt Hugh Farley, Captains Nance, Gary, and Watts, with
itant Pope as our chaperone.   Words fail me here in giv-
ι description of the dinner, as well as of the handsome
ιg ladies that our young hostess had invited from the sur-
ding country to help us celebrate.
)w will any reader of this question the fact that Long-
:t's men suffered any great hardships, isolated as they were
. the outside world?   This is but a sample of our suffer-
We had night parties at the houses of the high and the
dinners in season and out of season, and not an enemy
ide of the walls of Knoxville.   Did we feel the cold?   Did
'rozen ground cut our feet through our raw-hide mocca-
?   Did any of the soldiers long for home or the opening of
ιext campaign?   Bah!
was during our stay in winter quarters, March, 1864,
the term of our second enlistment expired.   The troops
volunteered for twelve months at the commencement of
war; this expiring just before the seven days' battle around
ımond, a re-enlistment and reorganization was ordered in
ipring of 1862 for two more years, making the term of
ihaw's Brigade equal with other troops that had enlisted
'three years or the war."   By an Act of Congress, in
, all men between the ages of eighteen and thirty-five

service. This brought out the expression of Gran[
authorities in Washington, that "Lee had robbed tl
and the grave." Our re-enlistment was only a f
change in officers or organization. Some few failed t
tarily re-enlist, not with any view to quit the army, l
had grown weary of the hard marches of the infantr
and wished to join the cavalry. However, when the
came for re-enlistment the troops were called out i
regiments and a call made by the Colonel to all w
willing to enlist for the war to step two paces to t
All, with the very fewest exceptions, stepped proudl
front. Of course, none were permitted to leave his
for the cavalry, as that branch of the service was yet
its full quoto, its ranks had in no discernable deg
depleted by the casualties of war. It seemed that
favored our troopers, for battle as they would, no
scarcely ever wounded, and a less number killed.
soldiers were furloughed, through wounds, by the th
and artillerymen by the hundreds, after every great b;
the cavalryman was denied this luxury, and his only
furlough was a short leave of absence to replace a
horse that had fallen by the wayside. Their rank;
loughed men in this line were usually quite full.

As for returning to their homes, no soldier, howeve
his station, either in the army or socially at home, wc
dared to leave the service had a discharge been off

after said farms, manage the negroes, and collect the government taxes or tithes. These tithes were one-tenth of all that was raised on a plantation—cotton, corn, oats, peas, wheat, potatoes, sorghum, etc.—to be delivered to a government agent. generally a disabled soldier, and by him forwarded to the army.

During the winter most of the vacancies in company and field officers were filled by promotion, according to rank. In most cases, the office of Third Lieutenant was left to the choice of the men in pursuance to the old Democratic principle, "government by the will of the people." Non-commissioned officers usually went up by seniority, where competent, the same as the commissioned officers.

All these vacancies were occasioned by the casualties of war during the Pennsylvania, Chickamauga, and Knoxville campaigns. The Seventh, Fifteenth, and Third Battalion were without field officers. Captain Huggins was placed in command of the Seventh, and Captain Whiter, the Third Battalion. No promotions could be made in the latter, as Major Miller and Colonel Rice had not resigned, although both were disabled for active service in consequence of wounds.

There was considerable wrangling in the Fifteenth over the promotion to the Colonelcy. Captain F. S. Lewie, of Lexington, claimed it by seniority of rank, being senior Captain in the regiment. Captain J. B. Davis, of Fairfield, claimed it under an Act of the Confederate Congress in regard to the rank of old United States officers entering the Confederate service—that the officers of the old army should hold their grade and rank in the Confederate Army, the same as before their joining the South, irrespective of the date of these commissions issued by the war department. Or, in other words, a Lieutenant in the United States Army should not be given a commission over a Captain, or a Captain, over a Major, Lieutenant Colonel, or Colonel, etc., in the Southern Army. As all the old army officers entering the service of the South at different periods, and all wanted a Generalship, so this mode of ranking was adopted. as promising greater harmony and better results. Captain Davis had been a Captain in the State service, having commanded a company in Gregg's six months' troops around Charleston. And. furthermore, Davis was a West Pointer—a good disciplinarian, brave, resolute, and an all round good officer. Still Lewie was his peer in every respect, with the exception of early military training. Both were graduates of medical colleges—well educated, cultured, and both high-toned gentlemen of the "Old School." But Lewie was subject to serious attacks of a certain disease, which frequently incapacitated him for duty, and on marches he was often unable to walk, and had to be hauled for days in the ambulance. Then Lewie's patriotism was greater than his ambition, and he was willing to serve in any position for the good of the service and for the sake of harmony. Captain Lewie thus voluntarily yielded his just claims to the Colonelcy to Captain Davis, and accepted the position of Lieutenant Colonel, places both filled to the end.

COLONEL J. B. DAVIS.

Colonel J. B. Davis was born in Fairfield County, of Scotch-Irish decent, about the year 1835. He received his early education in the schools of the country, at Mount Zion Academy, at Winnsboro, in same county. Afterwards he was admitted to the United States Military School, at West Point, but after remaining for two years, resigned and commenced the study of medicine. He graduated some years before the war, and entered upon the practice of his profession in the western part of the county. He was elected Captain of the first company raised in Fairfield, and served in Gregg's first six months' volunteers in Charleston. After the fall of Sumter, his company, with several others, disbanded.

Returning home, he organized a company for the Confederate service, was elected Captain, and joined the Fifteenth Regiment, then forming in Columbia under Colonel De-Saussure. He was in all the battles of the Maryland campaign, in the brigade under General Drayton, and in all the great battles with Kershaw's Brigade. In the winter of 1863 he was made Colonel of the Fifteenth, and served with his regiment until the surrender. On several occasions he was in command of the brigade, as senior Colonel present. He was in command at Cold Harbor after the death of Colonel Keitt. Colonel Davis was one among the best tacticians in the command; had a soldierly appearance—tall, well-developed, a commanding voice, and an all round good officer.

He returned home after the war and began the practice of medicine, and continues it to the present.

COLONEL F. S. LEWIE.

Colonel F. S. Lewie was born in Lexington County, in 1830, and received his early training there. He attended the High School at Monticello, in Fairfield County. He taught school for awhile, then began the study of medicine. He attended the "College of Physicians and Surgeons" in Paris, France, for two years, returning a short while before the breaking out of hostilities between the North and South.

At the outbreak of the war he joined Captain Gibbs' Company, and was made Orderly Sergeant. He served with that company, under Colonel Gregg, in the campaign against Sumter. His company did not disband when the fort fell, but followed Gregg to Virginia. At the expiration of their term of enlistment he returned to Lexington County, raised a company, and joined the Fifteenth. He was in most of the battles in which that regiment was engaged. Was promoted to Lieutenant Colonel, and in 1864 was elected to the State Senate from Lexington. He refused to leave his regiment, and did not accept the honor conferred upon him by the people of his county. While with his regiment in South Carolina, early in the spring of 1865, he was granted a few days' furlough to visit his home, at which smallpox had broken out, but was captured by Sherman's raiders before reaching home. He was parolled in North Carolina.

He was elected to the Legislature in 1866, serving until reconstruction. He died in 1877.

There was never a Major appointed afterwards in the Fifteenth.

About the last of January we had another little battle scare, but it failed to materialize. General Longstreet had ordered a pontoon bridge from Richmond, and had determined upon a decent upon Knoxville. But the authorities at Washington having learned of our preparation to make another advance, ordered General Thomas to reinforce General Foster with his corps, take command in person, and to drive Longstreet "beyond the confines of East Tennessee." The enemy's cavalry was thrown forward, and part of Longstreet's command having been ordered East, the movement was abandoned; the inclemency of the weather, if no other cause, was

sufficient to delay operations. Foster being greatly reinforced, and Longstreet's forces reduced by a part of his cavalry going to join Johnston in Georgia, and a brigade of
infantry ordered to reinforce Lee, the commanding General
determined to retire higher up the Holston, behind a mountain chain, near Bull's Gap.

On the 22d of February we quit our winter quarters, and
took up our march towards Bull's Gap, and after a few days
of severe marching we were again snugly encamped behind a
spur of the mountain, jutting out from the Holston and on to
the Nolachucky River. A vote of thanks from the Confederate States Congress was here read to the troops :

"Thanking Lieutenant General James Longstreet and the
officers and men of his command for their patriotic services
and brilliant achievements in the present war, sharing as they
have the arduous fatigues and privations of many campaigns
in Virginia, Maryland, Pennsylvania, Georgia, and Tennessee," etc.

CHAPTER XXVIII

In Camp on the Holston, East Tennessee.
Return to Virginia.

While Longstreet's Corps had done some of the most stubborn fighting, and the results, as far as victories in battle were
concerned, were all that could be expected, still it seemed,
from some faults of the Generals commanding departments, or
the war department in Richmond, that the fruits of such victories were not what the country or General Longstreet expected. To merely hold our own, in the face of such overwhelming numbers, while great armies were springing up all
over the North, was not the true policy of the South, as General Longstreet saw and felt it. We should go forward and
gain every inch of ground lost in the last campaign, make all
that was possible out of our partial successes, drive the enemy
out of our country wherever he had a foothold, otherwise the
South would slowly but surely crumble away. So much had
been expected of Longstreet's Corps in East Tennessee, and so

little lasting advantage gained, that bickering among the officers began. Brigadier Generals were jealous of Major Generals, and even some became jealous or dissatisfied with General Longstreet himself. Crimination and recrimination were indulged in; censures and charges were made and denied, and on the whole the army began to be in rather a bad plight for the campaign just commencing. Had it not been for the unparalleled patriotism and devotion to their cause, the undaunted courage of the rank and file of the army, little results could have been expected. But as soon as the war cry was heard and the officers and men had sniffed the fumes of the coming battle, all jealousies and animosities were thrown aside, and each and every one vied with the other as to who could show the greatest prowess in battle, could withstand the greatest endurance on marches and in the camp.

General Law, who commanded an Alabama Brigade, had been arrested and courtmartialed for failing to support General Jenkins at a critical moment, when Burnside was about to be entrapped, just before reaching Knoxville. It was claimed by his superiors that had Law closed up the gaps, as he had been ordered, a great victory would have been gained, but it was rumored that Law said "he knew this well enough, and could have routed the enemy, but Jenkins would have had the credit," so that he sacrificed his men, endangered the army, and lost an opportunity for brilliant achievements through jealousy of a brother officer. Much correspondence ensued between General Longstreet and President Davis, and as usual with the latter, he interfered, and had not the Wilderness campaign commenced so soon, serious trouble would have been the result between General Lee and General Longstreet on one side, and President Davis and the war department on the other. But General Law never returned to our army, and left with any but an ennobling reputation.

General Robertson, commanding Hood's old Texas Brigade, was arrested for indulging in mutinous conversation with his subaltern officers, claiming, it was said, that should General Longstreet give him certain orders (while in camp around Lookout Mountain), he would not recognize them, unless written, and then only under protest. He was relieved by General Gregg.

General McLaws was relieved of his command from a want

22

of confidence in General Longstreet, and more especially for
his inactivity and tardiness at the assaults on Fort Sanders, at
Knoxville. On ordinary occasions, General McLaws was
active and vigilant enough—his courage could not be doubted.
He and the troops under him had added largely to the name
and fame of the Army of Northen Virginia. He had officers
and men under him who were the "flower of chivalry" of the
South, and were really the "Old Guard" of Lee's Army.
McLaws was a graduate of West Point, and had seen service
in Mexico and on the plains of the West. But General Mc
Laws was not the man for the times—not the man to command
such troops as he had—was not the officer to lead in an active
vigorous campaign, where all depended on alertness and dash
He was too cautious, and as such, too slow. The two Georgia
brigades, a Mississippi brigade, and a South Carolina brigade
composed mostly of the first volunteers from their respective
States, needed as a commander a hotspur like our own J. B
Kershaw. While the army watched with sorrow and regret
the departure of our old and faithful General, one who had
been with us through so many scenes of trials, harships, and
bloodshed, whose name had been so identified with that o
our own as to be almost a part of it, still none could deny
that the change was better for the service and the Con
federacy.

One great trouble with the organization of our army was
that too many old and incompetent officers of the old regula
army commanded it. And the one idea that seemed to haun
the President was that none but those who had passed through
the great corridors and halls of West Point could command
armies or men—that civilians without military training were
unfit for the work at hand—furthermore, he had favorites
that no failures or want of confidence by the men could
shake his faith in as to ability and Generalship. What th
army needed was young blood—no old army fossils to com
mand the hot-blooded, dashing, enthusiastic volunteers, who
could do more in their impetuosity with the bayonet in a few
moments than in days and months of manœuvering, planning
and fighting battles by rules or conducting campaigns by fol
lowing the precedent of great commanders, but now obsolete

When the gallant Joe Kershaw took the command and
began to feel his way for his Major General's spurs, the divis

ion took on new life. While the brigade was loath to give him up, still they were proud of their little "Brigadier," who had yet to carve out a name for himself on the pillars of fame, and write his achievements high up on the pages of history in the campaign that was soon to begin.

It seems from cotemporaneous history that President Davis was halting between two opinions, either to have Longstreet retire by way of the mountains and relieve the pressure against Johnston, now in command of Bragg's Army, or to unite with Lee and defend the approaches to Richmond.

A counsel of war was held in Richmond between the President, General Bragg as the military advisor of his Excellency, General Lee, and General Longstreet, to form some plan by which Grant might be checked or foiled in the general grand advance he was preparing to make along the whole line. The Federal armies of Mississippi and Alabama had concentrated in front of General Johnston and were gradually pressing him back into Georgia.

Grant had been made commander in chief of all the armies of the North, with headquarters with General Meade, in front of Lee, and he was bending all his energies, his strategies, and boldness in his preparations to strike Lee a fatal blow.

At this juncture Longstreet came forward with a plan—bold in its conception; still bolder in its execution, had it been adopted—that might have changed the face, if not the fate, of the Confederacy. It was to strip all the forts and garrisons in South Carolina and Georgia, form an army of twenty-five thousand men, place them under Beauregard at Charleston, board the train for Greenville, S. C.; then by the overland route through the mountain passes of North Carolina, and by way of Aberdeen, Va.; then to make his way for Kentucky; Longstreet to follow in Beauregard's wake or between him and the Federal Army, and by a shorter line, join Beauregard at some convenient point in Kentucky; Johnston to flank Sherman and march by way of Middle Tennessee, the whole to avoid battle until a grand junction was formed by all the armies, somewhere near the Ohio River; then along the Louisville Railroad, the sole route of transportation of supplies for the Federal Army, fight a great battle, and, if victorious, penetrate into Ohio, thereby withdrawing Sherman from his intended "march to the sea," relieving Lee by weakening Grant, as that General would be forced to succor the armies forming to meet Beauregard.

This, to an observer at this late hour, seems to have been the only practical plan by which the downfall of the Confederacy could have been averted. However, the President and his cabinet decided to continue the old tactics of dodging from place to place, meeting the hard, stubborn blows of the enemy, only waiting the time, when the South, by mere attrition, would wear itself out.

About the 10th of April, 1864, we were ordered to strike tents and prepare to move on Bristol, from thence to be transported to Virginia. All felt as if we were returning to our old home, to the brothers we had left after the bloody Gettysburg campaign, to fight our way back by way of Chickamauga and East Tennessee. We stopped for several days at Chancellorsville, and here had the pleasure of visiting the home of the great Jefferson. From thence, down to near Gordonsville.

The 29th of April, 1864, was a gala day for the troops of Longstreet's Corps, at camp near Gordonsville. They were to be reviewed and inspected by their old and beloved commander, General R. E. Lee. Everything possible that could add to our looks and appearances was done to make an acceptable display before our commander in chief. Guns were burnished and rubbed up, cartridge boxes and belts polished, and the brass buttons and buckles made to look as bright as new. Our clothes were patched and brushed up, so far as was in our power, boots and shoes greased, the tattered and torn old hats were given here and there "a lick and a promise," and on the whole I must say we presented not a bad-looking body of soldiers. Out a mile or two was a very large old field, of perhaps one hundred acres or more, in which we formed in double columns. The artillery stationed on the flank fired thirteen guns, the salute to the commander in chief, and as the old warrior rode out into the opening, shouts went up that fairly shook the earth. Hats and caps flew high in the air, flags dipped and waved to and fro, while the drums and fifes struck up "Hail to the Chief." General Lee lifted his hat modestly from his head in recognition of the honor done him, and we know the old commander's heart swelled with emotion at this outburst of enthusiasm by his old troops on his appearance. If he had had any doubts before as to the loyalty of his troops, this old "Rebel yell" must have soon dispelled them. After taking his position, near the centre of the columns, the command was broken in columns of companies and marched by him, each giving a salute as it passed. It took several hours to pass in review, Kershaw leading with his division, Jenkins following. The line was again formed, when General Lee and staff, with Longstreet and his staff, rode around the troops and gave them critical inspection. No doubt Lee was then thinking of the bloody day that was soon to come, and how well these brave, battle-scarred veterans would sustain the proud prestige they had won.

Returning to our camp, we were put under regular discipline—drilling, surgeon's call-guards, etc. We were being put in active fighting trim and the troops closely kept in camp. All were now expecting every moment the summons to the battlefield. None doubted the purpose for which we were brought back to Virginia, and how well Longstreet's Corps sustained its name and reputation the Wilderness and Spottsylvania soon showed. Our ranks had been largely recruited by the return of furloughed men, and young men attaining eighteen years of age. After several months of comparative rest in our quarters in East Tennessee, nothing but one week of strict camp discipline was required to put us in the best of fighting order. We had arrived at our present camp about the last week of April, having rested several days at Charlottsville.

General Lee's Army was a day's, or more, march to the north and east of us, on the west bank of the Rapidan River. It was composed of the Second Corps, under Lieutenant General Ewell, with seventeen thousand and ninety-three men; Third Corps, under Lieutenant General A. P. Hill, with twenty-two thousand one hundred and ninety-nine; unattached commands, one thousand one hundred and twenty-five; cavalry, eight thousand seven hundred and twenty-seven; artillery, four thousand eight hundred and fifty-four; while Longstreet had about ten thousand; putting the entire strength of Lee's Army, of all arms, at sixty-three thousand nine hundred and ninety-eight.

General Grant had, as heretofore mentioned, been made commander in chief of all the Union armies, while General Lee held the same position in the Confederate service. Grant had taken up his headquarters with the Army of the Potomac, giving the direction of this army his personal attention, retaining, however, General George S. Meade as its immediate commander.

Grant had divided his army into three corps—Second, under Major General W. S. Hancock; Fifth, Major General G. K. Warren; Sixth, Major General John Sedgwick—all in camp near Culpepper Court House, while a separate corps, under Major General A. E. Burnside, was stationed near the railroad crossing on the Rappahannock River.

Lee's Army was divided as follows: Rodes', Johnston's, and Early's Divisions, under Lieutenant General Ewell, Second Corps; R. H. Anderson's, Heath's, and Wilcox's Divisions, under Lieutenant General A. P. Hill, Third Corps.

Longstreet had no Major Generals under him as yet. He had two divisions. McLaws' old Division, under Brigadier General Kershaw, and Hood's, commanded by Brigadier General Fields. The division had been led through the East Tennessee campaign by General Jenkins, of South Carolina. Also a part of a division under General Bushrod Johnston, of the Army of the West.

Grant had in actual numbers of all arms, equipped and ready for battle, one hundred and sixteen thousand eight hundred and eighty-six men. He had forty-nine thousand one hundred and ninety-one more infantry and artillery than Lee and three thousand six hundred and ninety-seven more cavalry. He had but a fraction less than double the forces of the latter. With this disparity of numbers, and growing greater every day, Lee successfully combatted Grant for almost a year without a rest of a week from battle somewhere along his lines. Lee had no reinforcements to call up, and no recruits to strengthen his ranks, while Grant had at his call an army of two million to draw from at will, and always had at his immediate disposal as many troops as he could handle in one field. He not only outnumbered Lee, but he was far better equipped in arms, subsistence, transportation, and cavalry and artillery horses. He had in his medical, subsistence, and quartermaster departments alone nineteen thousand one hundred and eighty-three, independent of his one hundred and sixteen thousand eight hundred and eighty-six, ready for the field, which he called non-combatants. While these figures and facts are foreign to the "History of Kershaw's Brigade," still I give them as matters of general history, that the reader may better understand the herculean undertaking that confronted Longstreet when he joined his forces with those of Lee's. And as this was to be the deciding campaign of the war, it will be better understood by giving the strength and environment of each army. The Second South Carolina Regiment was commanded by Lieutenant Colonel Gaillard; the Third, by Colonel Jas. D. Nance; the Seventh, by Captain Jerry Goggans; the Eighth, by Colonel Henagan; the Fifteenth, by Colonel J. B. Davis; the Third Battalion, by Captain Whiter. The brigade was commanded by Colonel J. D. Kennedy, as senior Colonel.

Thus stood the command on the morning of the 4th of May, but by the shock of battle two days later all was changed. Scarcely a commander of a regiment or brigade remained. The two military giants of the nineteenth century were about to face each other, and put to the test the talents, tactics, and courage of their respective antagonists. Both had been successful beyond all precedent, and both considered themselves invincible in the field. Grant had tact and tenacity, with an overwhelming army behind him. Lee had talent, impetuosity, and boldness, with an army of patriots at his command, who had never known defeat, and considered themselves superior in courage and endurance to any body of men on earth. Well might the clash of arms in the Wilderness of these mighty giants cause the civilized world to watch and wonder. Lee stood like a lion in the path—his capital behind him, his army at bay—while Grant, with equal pugnacity, sought to crush him by sheer force of overwhelming numbers.

CHAPTER XXIX

Battle of the Wilderness.

At midnight, on the 3rd of May, Grant put this mighty force of his in motion—the greatest body of men moving to combat that had ever been assembled on the continent. On the 4th his army crossed the Rapidan, at Germania and Ely's Fords, and began moving out towards the turn-pike, leading from Orange Court House by way of the Wilderness to Fredericksburg.

On the 5th Ewell had a smart engagement on the turn-pike, while Heath's and Wilcox's Divisions, of Hill's Corps, had met successfully a heavy force under Hancock, on the plank road—two roads running parallel and about one mile distant. Both armies closed the battle at night fall, each holding his own field. However, the enemy strongly entrenched in front, while Hill's troops, from some cause unexplainable, failed to take this precaution, and had it not been for the timely arrival of Longstreet at a critical moment, might have been fatal to Lee's Army.

On the morning of the 5th we had orders to march. Foragers coming in the night before reported heavy firing in the direction of the Rapidan, which proved to be the cavalry engagement checking Grant at the river fords. All felt after these reports, and our orders to march, that the campaign had opened. All day we marched along unused roads—through fields and thickets, taking every near cut possible. Scarcely stopping for a moment to even rest, we found ourselves, at 5 o'clock in the evening, twenty-eight miles from our starting point. Men were too tired and worn out to pitch tents, and hearing the orders "to be ready to move at midnight," the troops stretched themselves upon the ground to get such comfort and rest as was possible. Promptly at midnight we began to move again, and such a march, and under such conditions, was never before experienced by the troops. Along blind roads, overgrown by underbrush, through fields that had lain fallow for years, now studded with bushes and briars, and the

Capt. Chesley W. Herbert,
Co. C, 3d S. C. Regiment.

Capt. Theodore F. Malloy,
Co. C, 8th S. C. Regiment.

Capt. John W. Wofford,
Co. K, 3d S. C. Regiment.

Capt. John Hampden Brooks,
Co. G, 7th S. C. Regiment.

night being exceedingly dark, the men floundered and fell as they marched. But the needs were too urgent to be slack in the march now, so the men struggled with nature in their endeavor to keep in ranks. Sometimes the head of the column would lose its way, and during the time it was hunting its way back to the lost bridle path, was about the only rest we got. The men were already worn out by their forced march of the day before, and now they had to exert all their strength to its utmost to keep up. About daylight we struck the plank road leading from Orange Court House to Fredericksburg, and into this we turned and marched down with a swinging step. Kershaw's Brigade was leading, followed by Humphreys' and Wofford's, with Bryan bringing up the rear. The Second South Carolina was in front, then the Third, Seventh, Fifteenth, Third Battalion, and Eighth on extreme right, the brigade marching left in front.

After marching some two miles or more down the plank road at a rapid gait, passing Hill's field infirmary, where the wounded of the day before were being cared for, we heard a sharp firing in our immediate front. Longstreet's artillery was far in the rear, floundering along through the blind roads as the infantry had done the night before. Our wagons and subsistence supplies had not been since dawn of the 5th, although this made little difference to the men, as Longstreet's Corps always marched with three days' rations in their haversacks, with enough cooking utensils on their backs to meet immediate wants. So they were never thrown off their base for want of food. The cartridge boxes were filled with forty rounds, with twenty more in their pockets, and all ready for the fray.

As soon as the musketry firing was heard, we hastened our steps, and as we reached the brow of a small elevation in the ground, orders were given to deploy across the road. Colonel Gaillard, with the Second, formed on the left of the road, while the Third, under Colonel Nance, formed on the right, with the other regiments taking their places on the right of the Third in their order of march. Field's Division was forming rapidly on the left of the plank road, but as yet did not reach it, thus the Second was for the time being detached to fill up. The Mississippians, under Humphreys, had already left the plank road in our rear, and so had Wofford, with his Georgians, and were making their way as best they could through this tangled morass of the Wilderness, to form line of battle on Kershaw's right. The task was difficult in the extreme, but the men were equal to the occasion. Bryan's Georgia Brigade filed off to the right, in rear, as reserves.

The line had not yet formed before a perfect hail of bullets came flying overhead and through our ranks, but not a man moved, only to allow the stampeded troops of Heath's and Wilcox's to pass to the rear. It seems that these troops had fought the day before, and lay upon the battlefield with the impression that they would be relieved before day. They had not reformed their lines, nor replenished their ammunition boxes, nor made any pretention towards protecting their front by any kind of works. The enemy, who had likewise occupied their ground of the day before, had reformed their lines, strengthened their position by breastworks—all this within two hundred yards of the unsuspecting Confederates. This fault lay in a misunderstanding of orders, or upon the strong presumption that Longstreet would be up before the hour of combat. Hancock had ordered his advance at sunrise, and after a feeble defense by Heath's and Wilcox's skirmish line, the enemy burst upon the unsuspecting Confederates, while some were cooking a hasty meal, others still asleep--all unprepared for this thunderbolt that fell in their midst. While forming his lines of battle, and while bullets were flying all around, General Kershaw came dashing down in front of his column, his eyes flashing fire, sitting his horse like a centaur —that superb style as Joe Kershaw only could—and said in passing us, "Now, my old brigade. I expect you to do your duty." In all my long experience, in war and peace, I never saw such a picture as Kershaw and his war-horse made in riding down in front of his troops at the Wilderness. It seemed an inspiration to every man in line, especially his old brigade, who knew too well that their conduct to-day would either win or lose him his Major General's spurs, and right royally did he gain them. The columns were not yet in proper order, but the needs so pressing to check the advance of the enemy, that a forward movement was ordered, and the lines formed up as the troops marched.

The second moved forward on the left of the plank road, in support of a battery stationed there, and which was drawing a

tremendous fire upon the troops on both sides of the road.
Down the gentle slope the brigade marched, over and under
the tangled shrubbery and dwarf sapplings, while a withering
fire was being poured into them by as yet an unseen enemy.
Men fell here and there, officers urging on their commands
and ordering them to "hold their fire." When near the
lower end of the declivity, the shock came. Just in front of
us, and not forty yards away, lay the enemy. The long line
of blue could be seen under the ascending smoke of thousands
of rifles; the red flashes of their guns seemed to blaze in our
very faces. Now the battle was on in earnest. The roar of
Kershaw's guns mingled with those of the enemy. Longstreet
had met his old antagonist of Round Top, Hancock, the Northern hero, of Gettysburg. The roar of the small arms, mingled with the thunder of the cannon that Longstreet had
brought forward, echoed and re-echoed up and down the little
valley, but never to die away, for new troops were being put
rapidly in action to the right and left of us. Men rolled and
writhed in their last death struggle; wounded men groped
their way to the rear, being blinded by the stifling smoke.
All commands were drowned in this terrible din of battle—the
earth and elements shook and trembled with the deadly shock
of combat. Regiments were left without commanders; companies, without officers. The gallant Colonel Gaillard, of the
Second, had fallen. The intrepid young Colonel of the Third,
J. D. Nance, had already died in the lead of his regiment.
The commander of the Seventh, Captain Goggans, was
wounded. Colonel John D. Kennedy, commanding the
brigade, had left the field, disabled from further service for
the day.

Still the battle rolled on. It seemed for a time as if the
whole Federal Army was upon us—so thick and fast came the
death-dealing missiles. Our ranks were being decimated by
the wounded and the dead, the little valley in the Wilderness
becoming a veritable "Valley of Hennom." The enemy held
their position with a tenacity, born of desperation, while the
confederates pressed them with that old-time Southern vigor
and valor that no amount of courage could withstand. Both
armies stood at extreme tension, and the cord must soon snap
one way or the other, or it seemed as all would be annihilated.
Longstreet seeing the desperate struggle in which Kershaw

and Humphreys, on the right, and Hood's old Texans, on the left, were now engaged, sought to relieve the pressure by a flank movement with such troops as he had at his disposal. R. H. Anderson's Division, of Hill's Corps, had reported to him during the time Kershaw was in such deadly throes of battle. Four brigades, Wofford's, of Kershaw's, and G. T. Anderson's, Mahone's, and Davis', of Anderson's Division, were ordered around on our right, to strike the left of Hancock But during this manœuver the enemy gradually withdrew from our front, and Kershaw's Brigade was relieved by Bratton's South Carolina Brigade. I quote here from Colonel Wallace, of the Second.

"Kershaw's Division formed line in the midst of this confusion, like cool and well-trained veterans as they were, checked the enemy, and soon drove them back. The Second Regiment was on the left of the plank road, near a battery of artillery, and although completely flanked at one time by the giving away of the troops on the right, gallantly stood their ground, though suffering terribly; they and the battery, keeping up a well-directed fire, to the right oblique, until the enemy gave way. General Lee now appeared on our left, leading Hood's Texas Brigade. We joined our brigade on the right of the plank road, and again advanced to the attack. * * * We were relieved by Jenkins' Brigade, under command of that able and efficient officer, General Bratton, and ordered to the rear and rest. We had scarcely thrown ourselves upon the ground, when General Bratton requested that a regiment be sent him to fill a gap in the lines, which the enemy had discovered and were preparing to break through. I was ordered to take the Second Regiment and report to him. A staff officer showed me the gap, when I double quicked to it, just in time, as the enemy were within forty yards of it. As we reached the point we poured a well-directed volley into them, killing a large number, and putting the rest to flight. General Bratton witnessed the conduct of the regiment on this occasion and spoke of it in the highest terms."

But, meanwhile, Longstreet's flanking columns were steadily making their way around the enemy's left. At ten o'clock the final crash came. Like an avalanche from a mountain side, Wofford, Mahone, Anderson, and Davis rushed upon the enemy's exposed flank, doubling up Hancock's left upon his center, putting all to flight and confusion. . In vain did the Federal commander try to bring order out of confusion, but at this critical moment Wadsworth, his leading Division General, fell mortally wounded. Thus being left without a commander, his whole division gave way, having, with Stephen's Division, been holding Fields in desperate battle. The whole of Hancock's troops to the right of the plank road was swept across it by the sudden onslaught of the flanking column, only to be impeded by the meeting and mixing with Wadsworth's and Stephen's retreating divisions.

At this moment a sad and most regretable occurrence took place, that, in a measure, somewhat nullified the fruits of one of the greatest victories of the war. One of Mahone's regiments, gaining the plank road in advance of the other portion of the flanking column, and seeing Wadsworth giving such steady battle to Fields, rushed over and beyond the road and assailed his right, which soon gave way. Generals Longstreet, Kershaw, and Jenkins, with their staffs, came riding down the plank road, just as the Virginia Regiment beyond the road was returning to join its brigade. The other regiments coming up at this moment, and seeing through the dense smoke what they considered an advancing foe, fired upon the returning regiment just as General Longstreet and party rode between. General Jenkins fell dead, Longstreet badly wounded. Captain Doby, of Kershaw's staff, also was killed, together with several couriers killed and wounded.

This unfortunate occurrence put a check to a vigorous pursuit of the flying enemy, partly by the fall of the corps commander and the frightful loss in brigade and regimental commanders, to say nothing of the officers of the line. Captain Doby was one of the most dashing, fearless, and accomplished officers that South Carolina had furnished during the war. The entire brigade had witnessed his undaunted valor on so many battlefields, especially at Mayree's Hill and Zoar Church, that it was with the greatest sorrow they heard of his death. Captain Doby had seemed to live a charmed life while riding through safely the storms upon storms of the enemy's battles, that it made it doubly sad to think of his dying at the hands of his mistaken friends. On this same plank road, only a few miles distant, General Jackson lost his life one year before, under similar circumstances, and at the

hands of the same troops.   Had it not been for the coolness of
General Kershaw in riding out to where he heard Jenkins'
rifles clicking to return the fire, and called out, ''Friends,'' it
would be difficult to tell what might have been the result.

To show the light in which the actions of Kershaw's
Brigade were held in thus throwing itself between Lee and
impending disaster at this critical moment, and stemming the
tide of battle singlehanded and alone, until his lines were
formed, I will quote an extract from an unprejudiced and
impartial eye witness, Captain J. F. J. Caldwell, who in his
''History of McGowan's Brigade'' pays this glowing but just
tribute to Kershaw and his men.   In speaking of the surprise
and confusion in which a part of Hill's Corps was thrown, he
says:

''We were now informed that Longstreet was near at hand,
with twenty-five thousand fresh men.   This was good matter
to rally on.   We were marched to the plank road by special
order of General Hill; but just as we were crossing it, we
received orders to return to the left.   We saw General Longstreet riding down the road towards us, followed by his column
of troops.   The firing of the enemy, of late rather scattering
now became fierce and incessant, and we could hear a reply to
it from outside.   Kershaw's South Carolina Brigade, o
McLaws' (afterwards Kershaw's) Division, had met them
The fire on both sides of the road increased to a continuous
roar.   Kershaw's Brigade was extended across the road, and
received the grand charge of the Federals.   Members of that
Brigade have told me that the enemy rushed upon them at the
double-quick, huzzahing loudly.   The woods were filled with
Confederate fugitives.   Three brigades of Wilcox's Division
and all of Heath's were driven more or less rapidly, crowding
together in hopeless disorder, and only to be wondered at
when any of them attempted to make a stand.   Yet Kershaw's
Brigade bore themselves with illustrious gallantry.   Some of
the regiments had not only to deploy under fire, but when
they were formed, to force their way through crowds of flying
men, and re-established their lines.   They met Grant's
legions, opened a cool and murderous fire upon them, and
continued it so steadily and resolutely, that the latter were
compelled to give back.   Here I honestly believe the Army of
Northern Virginia was saved!   The brigade sustained a heavy

loss, beginning with many patient, gallant spirits in the ranks and culminating in Nance, Gaillard, and Doby.''

No further pursuit being made by Kershaw's Brigade during the day, it was allowed to rest after its day and night march and the bloody and trying ordeal of the morning. Friends were hunting out friends among the dead and wounded. The litter-bearers were looking after those too badly wounded to make their way to the rear.

Dr. Salmond had established his brigade hospital near where the battle had begun in the morning, and to this haven of the wounded those who were able to walk were making their way. In the rear of a battlefield are scenes too sickening for sensitive eyes and ears. Here you see men, with leg shattered, pulling themselves to the rear by the strength of their arms alone, or exerting themselves to the utmost to get to some place where they will be partially sheltered from the hail of bullets falling all around; men, with arms swinging helplessly by their sides, aiding some comrade worse crippled than themselves; others on the ground appealing for help, but are forced to remain on the field amid all the carnage going on around them, helpless and almost hopeless, until the battle is over, and, if still alive, await their turn from the litter-bearers. The bravest and best men dread to die, and the halo that surrounds death upon the battlefield is but scant consolation to the wounded soldier, and he clings to life with that same tenacity after he has fallen, as the man of the world in "piping times of peace.''

Just in rear of where Colonel Nance fell, I saw one of the saddest sights I almost ever witnessed. A soldier from Company C, Third South Carolina, a young soldier just verging into manhood, had been shot in the first advance, the bullet severing the great artery of the thigh. The young man seeing his danger of bleeding to death before succor could possibly reach him, had struggled behind a small sapling. Bracing himself against it, he undertook deliberative measures for saving his life. Tying a handkerchief above the wound, placing a small stone underneath and just over the artery, and putting a stick between the handkerchief and his leg, he began to tighten by twisting the stick around. But too late; life had fled, leaving both hands clasping the stick, his eyes glassy and fixed.

The next day was devoted to the burying of the dead and gathering such rest as was possible. It was my misfortune to be wounded near the close of the engagement, in a few feet of where lay the lamented Colonel Nance. The regiment in some way became doubled up somewhat on the center, perhaps in giving way for the Second to come in, and here lay the dead in greater numbers than it was ever my fortune to see, not even before the stone wall at Fredericksburg.

In rear of this the surgeons had stretched their great hospital tents, over which the yellow flag floated. The surgeons and assistant surgeons never get their meed of praise in summing up the "news of the battle." The latter follow close upon the line of battle and give such temporary relief to the bleeding soldiers as will enable them to reach the field hospital. The yellow flag does not always protect the surgeons and their assistants, as shells scream and burst overhead as the tide of battle rolls backward and forward. Not a moment of rest or sleep do these faithful servants of the army get until every wound is dressed and the hundred of arms and legs amputated, with that skill and caution for which the army surgeons are so proverbially noted. With the same dispatch are those, who are able to be moved, bundled off to some city hospital in the rear.

In a large fly-tent, near the roadside, lay dying the Northern millionaire, General Wadsworth. The Confederates had been as careful of his wants and respectful to his station as if he had been one of their own Generals. I went in to look at the General who could command more ready gold than the Confederate States had in its treasury. His hat had been placed over his face, and as I raised it, his heavy breathing, his eyes closed, his cold, clamy face showed that the end was near. There lay dying the multi-millionaire in an enemy's country, not a friend near to hear his last farewell or sooth his last moments by a friendly touch on the pallid brow. Still he, like all soldiers on either side, died for what he thought was right.

> "He fails not, who stakes his all, ... -
> Upon the right, and dares to fall ;
> What, though the living bless or blame
> For him, the long success of fame."

Hospital trains had been run up to the nearest railroad

station in the rear, bringing those ministering angels of mercy, the "Citizens' Relief Corps," composed of the best matrons and maidens of Richmond, led by the old men of the city. They brought crutches by the hundreds and bandages by the bolt. Every delicacy that the South afforded these noble dames of Virginia had at the disposal of the wounded soldiers. How many thousands of Confederate soldiers have cause to bless these noble women of Virginia. They were the spartan mothers and sisters of the South.

COLONEL JAMES D. NANCE.

I do not think I would be accused of being partial in saying that Colonel Nance was the best all round soldier in Kershaw's Brigade, none excepted. I have no allusion to the man, but the soldier alone. Neither do I refer to qualities of courage, for all were brave, but to efficiency. First to recommend him was his military education and training. He was a thorough tactician and disciplinarian, and was only equaled in this respect by General Connor. In battle he was ever cool and collected—he was vigilant, aggressive, and brave. Never for a moment was he thrown off his base or lost his head under the most trying emergencies. His evolution in changing the front of his regiment from columns of fours to a line of battle on Mayree's Hill, under a galling fire from artillery and musketry, won the admiration of all who witnessed it. Socially, he had the manners of a woman—quiet, unassuming, tender of heart, and of refined feelings. On duty—the march or in battle—he was strict and exacting, almost to sternness. He never sought comfort or the welfare of himself—the interest, the safety, the well being of his men seemed to be his ruling aim and ambition.

I append a short sketch of Colonel Nance taken from Dr. Barksdale's book, "Eminent and Representative Men of the Carolinas :"

"Colonel James Drayton Nance, the subject of this sketch, was born in Newberry, S. C., October 10th, 1837, and was the son of Drayton and Lucy (Williams) Nance. He received his school education at Newberry, and was graduated from the Citadel Military Academy, at Charleston. In 1859 he was admitted to the bar and began the practice of law at New-

"When the State seceded from the Union, December, 1860, and volunteers for her defense were called for, he was unani- mously elected Captain of "The Quitman Rifles," an infantry company formed at Newberry, and afterwards incorporated into the Third Regiment, South Carolina Volunteers. With his company he was mustered into the Confederate service at Columbia in April, 1861, and was in command of the company at the first battle of Manassas and in the Peninsula campaign in Virginia.

"On May 16th, 1862, upon the reorganization of the Third Regiment, he was chosen its Colonel, a position which he filled until his death. As Colonel, he commanded the regi- ment in the various battles around Richmond, June and July 1862, Second Manassas, Maryland Heights, Sharpsburg Fredericksburg (where he was severely wounded), Gettys burg, Chickamauga, Knoxville, and the Wilderness, where on the 6th of May, 1864, he was instantly killed. His body was brought home and interred at Newberry with fitting honors He was a brave, brilliant young officer, possessing the confi dence and high regard of his command in an extraordinary degree, and had he lived, would have risen to higher rank and honor. His valuable services and splended qualities and achievements in battle and in council were noted and appreci ated, as evidenced by the fact that at the time of his death a commission of Brigadier General had been decided upon as his just due for meritorious conduct.

"At the age of seventeen he professed religion and united with the Baptist Church at Newberry, and from that time to his death was distinguished for his Christian consistency."

LIEUTENANT COLONEL FRANKLIN GAILLARD.

Lieutenant Colonel Franklin Gaillard is not known to fame by his military record alone, but was known and admired al over the State as the writer of the fiery editorials in the "Carolinian," a paper published in Columbia during the day just preceding Secession, and noted for its ardent State Right sentiment. These eloquent, forcible, and fearless discussion of the questions of the day by young Gaillard was a potent factor in shaping the course of public sentiment and rousing the people to duty and action, from the Mountains to the Sea Through the columns of this paper, then the leading one in the State, he paved the way and prepared the people for the great struggle soon to take place, stimulating them to an enthusiasm almost boundless.

He was in after years as fearless and bold with the sword as he had been with the pen. He was not the man to turn his back upon his countrymen, whose war-like passions he had aroused, when the time for action came. He led them to the fray—a paladin with the pen, a Bayard with the sword. He was an accomplished gentleman, a brave soldier, a trusted and impartial officer, a peer of any in Kershaw's Brigade.

Colonel Gaillard was born in 1829, in the village of Pineville, in the present County of Berkeley. In his early childhood his father, Thomas Gaillard, removed to Alabama. But not long thereafter Franklin returned to this State, to the home of his uncle, David Gaillard, of Fairfield County. Here he attended the Mount Zion Academy, in Winnsboro. under the distinguished administration of J. W. Hudson. In the fall of 1846 he entered the South Carolina College, and graduated with honor in the class of 1849, being valedictorian of the class. Shortly after graduation, in company with friends and relatives from this State and Alabama, he went to California in search of the "yellow metal," the find of which, at that time, was electrifying the young men throughout the States.

After two or three years of indifferent success, he returned to this State once more, making his home with his uncle, in Winnsboro. In 1853 (or thereabout) he became the proprietor of the "Winnsboro Register," and continued to conduct this journal, as editor and proprietor, until 1857, when he was called to Columbia as editor of the "Carolinian," then owned by Dr. Robert W. Gibbes, of Richland, and was filling that position at the time of the call to arms, in 1861, when he entered the service in Captain Casson's Company, as a Lieutenant, and became a member of the renowned Second Regiment.

In March, 1853, he was married to Miss Catherine C. Porcher, of Charleston, but this union was terminated in a few years by the death of the wife. Colonel Gaillard left two children, one son and one daughter, who still survive, the son a distinguished physician, of Texas, and the daughter the wife of Preston S. Brooks, son of the famous statesman of that name, now of Tennessee.

Colonel Gaillard was a descendant of a French Huguenot emigrant, who, with many others, settled in this State after the Revocation of the Edict of Nantes in 1685.

CHAPTER XXX

Brock's Cross Road and Spottsylvania to North Anna.

Having been wounded in the last assault, I insert here Adjutant Y. J. Pope's description of the operations of Kershaw's Brigade from the Wilderness to North Anna River, covering a period of perhaps two weeks of incessant fighting. The corps had been put under the command of Major General R. H. Anderson, known throughout the army as "Fighting Dick Anderson." His division had been assigned to Longstreet's Corps in the place of Pickett's, now on detached service. Colonel Hennegan, of the Eighth, commanded the brigade as senior Colonel.

NORTH ANNA RIVER, VIRGINIA.

How many times, as soldiers, have we crossed this stream, and little did we imagine in crossing that on its banks we would be called upon to meet the enemy. "Man proposes, but God disposes." In may, 1864, after the battles of the Wilderness, Brock's Road, and Spottsylvania—stop a minute and think of these battles—don't you recall how, on that midnight of the 5th day of May, 1864, the order came, "Form your regiments," and then the order came to march? Through the woods we went. The stars shown so brightly. The hooting of the owls was our only music. The young Colonel at the head of his regiment would sing, in his quiet way, snatches of the hymns he had heard the village choir sing so often and so sweetly, and then "Hear me Norma." His mind was clear; he had made up his determination to face the day of battle, with a calm confidence in the power of the God he trusted and in the wisdom of His decrees. The Adjutant rode silently by his side. At length daylight appears. We have at last struck in our march the plank road. The sun begins to rise, when

HISTORY OF KERSHAW'S BRIGADE.   357

all of a sudden we hear the roll of musketry.   The armies are
at work.   General Lee has ridden up the plank road with his
First Lieutenant, the tried, brave old soldier, Longstreet.

Nance has fallen, pierced by five balls, but we knew it not.
Every band is full.   Presently, our four companies came up,
so gallantly they looked as they came.   Promptly filling up
the broken line, we now move forward once more, never to
fall back.   We have Nance's body.   The wild flowers around
about him look so beautiful and sweet, and some of them are
plucked by his friend to send to his sister, Mrs. Baxter

But go back to the fight.   It rages wildly all around.
Presently, a crash comes from the right.   It is Longstreet at
the head of the flanking column, and then Hancock is swept
from the field in front.   Joy is upon us.   Hastily Longstreet
rides to the front.   Then a volley and he falls, not dead, but
so shattered that it will be months before we see him again.
Then comes the peerless chieftain, Lee, and he orders the pursuing columns to halt.   A line of hastily constructed field-
works arise.   A shout—such a shout rolls from right to left of
Lee's lines.   It has a meaning, and that meaning is that
Grant's advance is baffled!   But the Federal commander is not
to be shut off.   If he cannot advance one way, he will another.
Hence, the parallel lines are started—the farther he stretches
to our right, we must stretch also.

So now comes the affair at Brock's Road, on the 8th of May,
1864.   As before remarked, Grant commenced his attempt at
a flank movement, by means of an extension of his columns
parallel to ours, hoping to meet some opening through which
he might pour a torrent of armed men.   Early in the morning
of the 8th of May, 1864, we are aroused and begin our march.
Soon we see an old Virginia gentleman, bareheaded and without his shoes, riding in haste towards us.   He reports that our
cavalry are holding the enemy back on Brock's Road, but that
the Federal infantry are seen to be forming for the attack,
and, of course, our cavalry cannot stand such a pressure.
General Kershaw orders us forward in double quick.   Still we
are not then.   Then it was that a gallant cavalryman rushes
to us and said, "Run for our rail piles; the Federal infantry
will reach them first, if you don't run."   Our men sprang forward as if by magic.   We occupy the rail piles in time to see
a column, a gallant column, moving towards us, about sixty

yards away. Fire, deadening fire, is poured into that column by our men. A gallant Federal officer rides just in rear, directing the movement. "Pick that officer off of his horse," is the command given to two or three of our cool marksmen. He falls. The column staggers and then falls back. Once more they come to time. We are better prepared for them.

Right here let me state a funny occurrence. Sim Price observed old man John Duckett, in the excitement, shooting his rifle high over the heads of the Yankees. This was too much for Sim Price, and he said, "Good God, John Duckett, are you shooting at the moon?"

Here is the gallant J. E. B. Stuart, Lieutenant General, commanding the cavalry of the Army of Northern Virginia, with hat off, waiving it in an enthusiastic cheering of the gallant men of the old Third. Well he may, for the line they held on that day was that adopted by General Lee for the famous Spottsylvania battle.

Just prior to the battle of Spottsylvania Court House, which was fought on the 12th of May, 1864, sharpshooters were posted in trees in the woods, and kept up a pretty constant fusilade when any head showed itself. It is recalled that when Major R. P. Todd returned to our command an officer, eager to hear from his home in South Carolina, entered a little fly-tent with Todd, and presently one of these sharpshooters put a ball through this tent, between the heads of the two. Maybe they didn't move quickly. Here it was, that lest a night attack might be made, one-third of the men were kept in the trenches all the time, day and night. One of these nights, possibly the 11th of May, a staff officer stole quietly where the Colonel and Adjutant were lying and whispered, "It is thought that the enemy have gotten betwixt our out-posts and the breastworks and intend to make a night attack. So awaken the soldiers and put every man in the trenches." The Colonel went to one end of the line and the Adjutant to the other, and soon had our trenches manned. The Colonel was observed full of laughter, and when questioned, stated that on going to the left wing of the regiment to awaken the men, he came across a soldier with some small branches kin-dled into a blaze, making himself a cup of coffee. He spoke to the soldier, saying:

"Who is that?"

The soldier replied, not recognizing the Colonel's voice: "Who in the h—l are you?"

The Colonel said: "Don't you know the Yankees are between the pickets and the breastworks, and will soon attack our whole line?"

He reported the man at these words, saying: "The Jesus Christ, Colonel!" rolling as he spoke, and he never stopped rolling until he fell into the pit at the works. Never was a revolution in sentiment and action more quickly wrought than on this occasion with this soldier.

It is needless to speak of the battle of Spottsylvania Court House, except to remark that here our comrades of McGowan's Brigade showed of what stuff they were made, and by their gallantry and stubborn fighting, saved the day for General Lee.

Soon after this battle General Grant, though baffled by its result, renewed his effort to reach Richmond. By a rapid march, General Lee was before Grant's columns at the North Anna River. Here we hoped the enemy would attack us. On the South side of this river, on the road leading to Hanover Junction, good heavy works had been completed, while a fort of inferior proportions on the North side was intended to protect the bridge across the river from raiding parties of the enemy. To our surprise, when the part of our army that was designed to cross the river at this point, had crossed over, the Third Regiment, James' Battalion, and the Seventh Regiment were left behind about this fort. We had no idea that anything serious was intended; but after awhile it leaked out that General Lee needed some time to complete a line of works from one point of the river to another on the same stream, on the South side, and that it was intended that the bare handful of men with us were intended to hold the approach to the bridge in face of the tens of thousands of Grant's Army in our front. Trying to realize the task assigned us, positions were assigned the different forces with us. It was seen that the Seventh Regiment, when stretched to the left of the fort, could not occupy, even by a thin line, the territory near them. We were promised the co-operation of artillery just on the other side of the river. Presently the attack opened on the right and center, but this attack we repulsed. Again the same points were assailed, with a like result. Then the attack

was made on our left, and although the Seventh Regiment did
its whole duty, gradually our left was seen to give way. This
emboldened the enemy to press our right and center again,
but they were firm. It was manifest now that the enemy
would soon be in our rear, and as the sun was sinking to rest
in the West, we made a bold dash to cross the river in our
rear, bringing down upon us the enemy's artillery fire of shot
and shell, as well as musketry. It looked hard to tell which
way across the river was best—whether by way of the bridge,
or to wade across. It was said our Lieutenant Colonel, who
was on foot when reaching the opposite bank, and finding his
boots full of water, said to a soldier: "Tom, give me your
hand." "No, no, Major," was the reply; "this is no time for
giving hands." The ascent of the long hill on the South side
was made under the heavy fire of the enemy. When at its
height, a stuttering soldier proposed to a comrade to lay down
and let him get behind him. Of course the proposition was
declined without thanks. When we reformed at the top of
the hill, there was quite a fund of jokes told. Amongst
others, the one last stated, Tom Paysinger said: "Nels., if I
had been there, I would have killed myself laughing." Whereupon, the stutterer said: "T-T-Tom Paysinger, I saw a heap
of men down there, but not one that laughed."

War has its humorous as well as its serious side, and many
a joke was cracked in battle, or if not mentioned then, the
joke was told soon afterwards. It is recalled just here that in
this battle an officer, who had escaped being wounded up to
that time, was painfully wounded. When being borne on the
way to the rear on a stretcher, he was heard to exclaim: "Oh!
that I had been a good man. Oh! that I had listened to my
mother." When he returned to the army, many a laugh was
had at his expense when these expressions would be reported.
But the officer got even with one of his tormentors, who was
one of the bearers of the litter upon which the officer was borne
away, for while this young man was at his best in imitating
the words and tone of the wounded man, he was suddenly
arrested by the words: "Yes, I remember when a shell burst
pretty close you forgot me, and dropped your end of the litter." The laugh was turned. All this, however, was in
perfect good humor.

It has been shown how Kershaw's South Carolina Brigade closed the breach in Lee's Army on the 6th of May, and turned disaster into a glorious victory, and as the 12th of May, at "Bloody Angle," near Spottsylvania Court house, will go down in history as one among the most memorable battles of all time, I wish to show how another gallant South Carolina Brigade (McGowan's) withstood the shock of the greater portion of Grant's Army, and saved Lee's Army from disaster during the greater part of one day.   This account is also taken from Captain Caldwell's "History of McGowan's Brigade." Being an active participant, he is well qualified to give a truthful version, and I give in his own language his graphic description of the battle of the "Bloody Angle."

HISTORY OF MCGOWAN'S BRIGADE.

Reaching the summit of an open hill, where stood a little old house, and its surrounding naked orchard, we were fronted and ordered forward on the left of the road. * * * Now we entered the battle.   There were two lines of works before us; the first or inner line, from a hundred and fifty to two hundred yards in front of us; the second or outer line, perhaps a hundred yards beyond it, and parallel to it.   There were troops in the outer line, but in the inner one only what appeared to be masses without organization.   The enemy were firing in front of the extreme right of the brigade, and their balls came obliquely down our line; but we could not discover, on account of the woods about the point of firing, under what circumstances the battle was held.   There was a good deal of doubt as to how far we were to go, or in what direction. * * * The truth is, the road by which we had come was not at all straight, which made the right of the line front much farther north than the rest, and the fire was too hot for us to wait for the long loose column to close up, so as to make an entirely orderly advance.   More than this, there was a death struggle ahead, which must be met instantly.   We advanced at a double-quick, cheering loudly, and entered the inner works. Whether by order or tacit understanding, we halted here, except the Twelfth Regiment, which was the right of the brigade.   That moved at once to the outer line, and threw itself with its wanted impetuosity into the heart of the battle. * * * The brigade advanced upon the works.   About the time we

reached the inner lines, General McGowan was wounded by a
minie ball in the arm, and forced to quit the field. Colonel
Brockman, senior Colonel present, was also wounded, and
Colonel Brown, of the Fourteenth Regiment, assumed command then or a little later. The four regiments, the First,
Thirteenth, Fourteenth, and Rifles (the Twelfth had passed on
to the outer line), closed up and arranged their lines. Soon
the order was given to advance to the outer liue. We did so
with a cheer and a double-quick, plunging through mud knee
deep and getting in as best we could. Here, however, lay
Harris' Mississippi Brigade. We were ordered to close to the
right. We moved by the flank, up the works, under the
fatally accurate firing of the enemy, and ranged ourselves
along the entrenchments. The sight we encountered was not
calculated to encourage us The trenches dug on the inner
side were almost filled with water. Dead men lay on the surface of the ground and in the pools of water. The wounded
bled, stretched, and groaued, or huddled in every attitude of
pain. The water was crimson with blood. Abandoned knap-
sacks, guns, and accourtrements, with ammunition boxes,
were scattered all around. In the rear disabled caissons stood
and limbers of guns. The rain poured heavily, and an incessant fire was kept upon us from front and flank. The enemy
still held the works on the right of the angle, and fired across
the traverses. Nor were these foes easily seen. They barely
raised their heads above the logs at the moment of firing. It
was plainly a question of bravery and endurance now.

We entered upon the task with all our might. Some fired
at the line lying in our front on the edge of the ridge before
described; others kept down the enemy lodged in the traverses
on the right. At one or two places Confederates and Federals were only separated by the works, and the latter not a
few times reached their guns over and fired right down upon
the heads of the former. So continued the painfully unvary-
ing battle for more than two hours. At the end of that time a
rumor arose that the enemy was desirous to come in and surrender. Colonel Brown gives the following in his official
report: "About two o'clock P. M. the firing ceased along the
line, and I observed the enemy, standing up in our front, their
colors flying and arms pointing upwards. I called to them to
lay down their arms and come in. An officer answered that

he was waiting our surrender—that we had raised a white flag, whereupon he had ceased firing. I replied, 'I command here,' and if any flag had been raised it was without authority, and unless he came in, firing would be resumed. He begged a conference, which was granted, and a subordinate officer advanced near the breastwork and informed me that a white flag was flying on my right. He was informed that unless his commander surrendered, the firing would be continued. He started back to his lines, and failing to exhibit his flag of truce, was shot down midway between the lines, which was not more than twenty yards at this point. The firing again commenced with unabating fury." * * * The firing was astonishingly accurate all along the line. No man could raise his shoulders above the works without danger of immediate death. Some of the enemy lay against our works in front. I saw several of them jump over and surrender during the relaxation of the firing. An ensign of a Federal regiment came right up to us during the "peace negotiations" and demanded our surrender. Lieutenant Carlisle, of the Thirteenth Regiment, replied that we would not surrender. Then the ensign insisted, as he had come under a false impression, he should be allowed to return to his command. Lieutenant Carlisle, pleased with his composure, consented. But as he went away a man from another part of the line shot him through the face, and he came and jumped over to us. This was the place to test individual courage. Some ordinarily good soldiers did next to nothing, while others excelled themselves. The question became pretty plainly, whether one was willing to meet death, not merely to run the chances of it. There was no further cessation of fire, after the pause before described. Every now and then a regular volley would be hurled at us from what we supposed a fresh line of Federals, but it would gradually tone down to the slow, particular, fatal firing of the siege. The prisoners who ran into us now and then informed us that Grant's whole energies were directed against this point. They represented the wood on the other side as filled with dead, wounded fighters, and skulkers. We were told that if we would hold the place till dark, we would be relieved. Dark came, but no relief. The water became a deeper crimson, the corpses grew more numerous. Every tree about us, for thirty feet from the ground, was barked by balls. Just

before night a tree six or eight inches in diameter, just behind
the works, was cut down by the bullets of the enemy. We
noticed at the same time a large oak hacked and torn in such a
manner never before seen. Some predicted its fall before morning, but the most of us considered that out of the question.
But about 10 o'clock it did fall forward on our works, wounding some men and startling a great many more. An officer,
who afterwards measured this tree, informed me that it was
twenty-two inches in diameter. This was entirely the work
of rifle balls. Midnight came, still no relief; no cessation of
the firing. Numbers of the troops sank, overpowered, into
the muddy trenches and slept soundly. The rain continued.
Just before daylight we were ordered, in a whisper, which was
passed along the line, to slowly and noiselessly retire from the
works. * * * Day dawned, and the evacuation was
complete.

*   *   *   *   *   *   *

Thus ended one of the most stubbornly contested battles of
the war, if not of the century. The whole army, from one
end to the other, sung the praises of the gallant South Carolinians, who, by their deeds of valor, made immortal the
"Bloody Angle."

CHAPTER XXXI

From North Anna to Cold Harbor---Joined by the Twentieth South Carolina.

It was while entrenched south of North Anna that our
troops heard of the death of our great cavalry leader, General
J. E. B. Stuart, who fell mortally wounded at Yellow Tavern,
on May the 18th. If the death of Jackson was a blow to the
army and the South, the death of Stuart was equally so. He
was the Murat of the Southern Army, equally admired and
beloved by the infantry as the cavalry. The body of the
army always felt safe when the bugle of Stuart could be
heard on the flank or front, and universal sadness was thrown
around the Army of Northern Virginia, as well as the whole

South, by his death. It was conceded by the North, as well as the South, that Stuart was the finest type of cavalry leader in either army. Longstreet badly wounded, Stuart and Jenkins dead, certainly gave the prospects of the campaign just opening anything but an assuring outlook.

TWENTIETH SOUTH CAROLINA REGIMENT.

About this time our brigade was reinforced by the Twentieth South Carolina Regiment, one of the finest bodies of men that South Carolina had furnished during the war. It was between one thousand and one thousand two hundred strong,. led by the "silver-tongued orator," Lawrence M. Keitt. It was quite an acceptable acquisition to our brigade, since our ranks had been depleted by near one thousand since the 6th of May. They were as healthy, well clad, and well fed body of troops as anybody would wish to see, and much good-humored badgering was indulged in at their expense by Kershaw's "web feet." From their enormous strength in numbers, in comparison to our "corporal guards" of companies, the old soldiers called them "The Twentieth Army Corps." I here give a short sketch of the regiment prior to its connection with the brigade.

The Twentieth Regiment was organized under the call for twelve thousand additional troops from South Carolina, in 1862. along with the Seventeenth, Eighteenth, and Nineteenth, Holcomb Legion, and other regiments. The companies composing the Twentieth assembled at the race course, in Charleston. S. C., in the fall of 1862. The companies had already organized in the respective counties, and elected officers, and after assembling in Charleston and organizing the regiment, elected the following field officers:

Colonel—L. M. Keitt.

Lieutenant Colonel—O. M. Dansler.

Major—S. M. Boykin.

Adjutant--John Wilson.

Quartermaster—John P. Kinard.

Commissary— ——— Brock.

Surgeon—Dr. Salley.

Assistant Surgeon—Dr. Barton.

Chaplain—Rev. W. W. Duncan.

Company A, Anderson and Pickens—Captain Partlow.

Company B, Orangeburg—Captain McMichael.

Company C, Lexington—Captain Leaphart.

Company D, Orangeburg—Captain Danley.

Company E, Laurens—Captain Cowen.

Company F, Newberry—Captain Kinard.

Company G, Sumter—Captain Moseley.

Company H, Orangeburg and Lexington—Captain Ruff.

Company I, Orangeburg and Lexington—Captain Gunter.

Company K, Lexington—Captain Harmon.

Captain Jno. P. Kinard, of Company F, was made Quartermaster, and First Lieutenant Jno. M. Kinard was promoted to Captain.

A singularity of one of the companies, I, was that it had twenty-eight members by the name of Gunter. The Captain and all three Lieutenants and seven non-commissioned officers were of the name of Gunter, and it is needless to add that it was called the Gunter Company.

Colonel Keitt, acting as Brigadier General while in Charleston, the entire management of the regiment was left to Lieutenant Colonel Dansler. He was a fine officer, a good tactician, and thorough disciplinarian. A courteous gentleman, kind and sociable to all, he was greatly beloved by officers and men, and it was with feelings of universal regret the regiment was forced to give him up, he having resigned in the spring of 1864, to accept the position of Colonel of the Twenty-Second Regiment.

The regiment remained at the race course for several months, for drill and instruction. In February, 1863, they were moved to the west end of James' Island, near Secessionville, for guard and picket duty. After this, they were transferred to Sullivan's Island, and quartered in the old Moultrie House and cottages adjacent. Four companies were ordered to Battery Marshall, on the east side of the Island, to assist in the management of the siege guns at that point.

On the 7th of May the Federal gunboats crossed the bar and made an attack upon Forts Sumter, Moultrie, and the batteries on Morris' Island. Here the regiment was subjected to a heavy cannonading from the three hundred pounders from the Federal ironclads. Colonel Dansler, however, moved the regiment to the east, in the sandhills, thus avoiding the direct fire of the enemy. One of the ironclads was sunk and others badly crippled, drawing off after dark. In December eight companies were moved over to Mt. Pleasant and two to Kinloch's Landing.

During the memorable siege of Morris' Island, the Twentieth did its turn at picketing on that island, going over after dark in a steamer and returning before day.

On the night of the 30th July, 1863, while the regiment was returning from Morris' Island, the tide being low, the steamer Sumter, on which the regiment was being transported, was forced to take the main ocean channel. It was the duty of those on garrison duty at Fort Sumter to signal Moultrie and the shore batteries of the movements of the transport steamer. For some cause or other Sumter failed to give the signals, and Moultrie being aware that there was a steamer in the harbor and no signals up, opened upon the ill-fated steamer with all her guns, thinking it one of the enemy's ironclads. This was a signal for the shore batteries to open their guns, and in a few moments shells came crashing through the decks and cabins of the crowded steamer from all sides. This created a panic among the troops, and had it not been for the self-possession and coolness of the captain of the steamer, the loss of life would have been appalling. The captain turned his boat and beached it as soon as possible, not, however, before the men began leaping over the sides of the vessel in one grand pellmell. The dark waves of unknown death were below them, while the shells shrieked and burst through the steamer. There was but little choice for the panic stricken men. Fortunately the waters here were shallow enough for the men to touch bottom and wade out, some to Fort Johnson, some to Fort Sumter, while others remained in the shallows until relieved by small boats from shore. The regiment lost sixteen men, either killed or drowned.

On the 16th or 18th of May, 1864, the regiment was ordered to Virginia, and reached Richmond about the twenty-second, and was ordered to join Kershaw's Brigade, reaching it about the 28th of May, near South Anna River.

After the resignation of Lieutenant Colonel Dansler, Major Boykin was promoted to that position, and Captain Partlow made Major. By the death of Colonel Keitt, Boykin and Partlow were raised in regular grade, and Captain McMichael made Major. Lieutenant Colonel Partlow was wounded at

Deep Bottom soon after this, and did not return to duty until near the close of the war. Colonel Boykin and Major Mc-Michael were both captured at Cedar Creek, and neither returned until after peace was declared. The regiment was commanded during the remainder of the service, with short exceptions, by Captain Leaphart.

Colonel Keitt being senior Colonel now in the brigade, was placed in command. It was unfortunate for Colonel Keitt and his command, being transferred to our army just at the moment it was in one of the most active and vigorous campaigns of the war. The men were ill-prepared to meet the requirements expected of soldiers, to undergo forced marches in the burning heat of summer, to accustom themselves so suddenly to the scant and badly-prepared food, night pickets in the open, in face of the enemy, and all the hardships incident to a soldier's life in the field. These troops had seen but little of real service, having only done garrison duty around Charleston, quartered in barracks or good tents, while now they had to take the field, with no advantage of the veterans, in the way of supplies and in accommodations, and with none of their experience and strength of endurance. They had all the courage of the veteran troops, but lacked acclimation. Their company discipline was well enough, and had excellent company and field officers, but were sadly deficient in regimental and brigade drill. It is doubtful if either their commander or any of their field officers had ever been in brigade drill or executed a manœuver in a larger body than a regiment. Like all new troops in the field, they had over-loaded themselves with baggage, and being thus overloaded, straggling was universal in the regiment, until they became enured to the fatigues and hardships of the march. Had they come out two or three months earlier, and taken on the ways and customs of the soldier in the field, it would have been much better. Still they deserve the highest degree of praise for their self-denials, their endurance, and fortitude in the march and in battle. The necessity of the occasion caused them to learn rapidly the intricacies in the life of the veteran, and their action in battle in a few days after their arrival, stamped them as a gallant body of men.

On the night of the 31st of May orders came to prepare to march. Grant had withdrawn from our front, and was still rolling along on Lee's right. Both armies were now moving in the direction of Cold Harbor, where McClellan, two years before, had tried to stay the flight of his troops and to check the victorious march of Jackson, Hill, and Longstreet. Now Grant was tempting fate by moving his beaten troops to this ill-fated field, there to try conclusions with McClellan's old antagonist.

The Federals were moving with rapid gait to this strategic point, but Lee having the inner line, was first on the field. It must be borne in mind that since the 4th of May the army had been idle scarcely a day. From that day to the 1st of June it had been one continual battle. If the infantry was not engaged, it was the artillery that kept hammering away, while Stuart's Cavalry hovered around the flanks and rear of the enemy, ready at a moment to swoop like an eagle upon his prey. We were continually under arms, either on a forced march night and day, checking the enemy here, baffling him there, driving back his advance lines, or assaulting his skirmishers. At night the sound of the enemy's drums mingled with that of our own, while the crack of the rifles in the sharpshooters' pits was almost continuous. Early on the morning of June 1st Kershaw's Brigade was aroused and put on the march at a rapid pace in a southeasterly direction.

When nearing the old battlefield of Cold Harbor the men began to snuff the scent of battle. Cartridge boxes were examined, guns unslung, and bayonets fixed, while the ranks were being rapidly closed up. After some delay and confusion, a line of battle was formed along an old roadway. Colonel Keitt had never before handled such a body of troops in the open field, and his pressing orders to find the enemy only added perplexity to his other difficulties. Every man in ranks knew that he was being led by one of the most gifted and gallant men in the South, but every old soldier felt and saw at a glance his inexperience and want of self-control. Colonel Keitt showed no want of aggressiveness and boldness, but he was preparing for battle like in the days of Alva or Turenne, and to cut his way through like a storm center.

As soon as the line was formed the order of advance was given, with never so much as a skirmish line in front. Keitt led his men like a knight of old—mounted upon his superb iron-gray, and looked the embodiment of the true chevalier

24

that he was.   Never before in our experience had the brigade
been led in deliberate battle by its commander on horseback,
and it was perhaps Colonel Keitt's want of experience that
induced him to take this fatal step.   Across a large old field
the brigade swept towards a densely timbered piece of oak-
land, studded with undergrowth, crowding and swaying in
irregular lines, the enemy's skirmishers pounding away at us
as we advanced.   Colonel Keitt was a fine target for the sharpshooters, and fell before the troops reached the timber, a
martyr to the inexorable laws of the army rank.   Into the
dark recessess of the woods the troops plunged, creeping and
crowding their way through the tangled mass of undergrowth,
groups seeking shelter behind the larger trees, while the firing
was going on from both sides.   The enemy meeting our
advance in a solid regular column, our broken and disorganized ranks could not cope with them.   Some of the regimental
officers seeing the disadvantage at which our troops were fighting, ordered a withdrawal to the old roadway in our rear.
The dense smoke settling in the woods, shielded our retreat
and we returned to our starting point without further molestation than the whizzing of the enemy's bullets overhead.   The
lines were reformed, and Colonel Davis, of the Fifteenth,
assumed command (or perhaps Colonel Henagan).

Colonel William Wallace, of the Second, in speaking of this
affair, says:

"Our brigade, under the command of the lamented Colonel
Keitt, was sent out to reconnoitre, and came upon the enemy
in large force, strongly entrenched.   Keitt was killed, and the
brigade suffered severely.   A few skirmishers thrown out
would have accomplished the object of a reconnoissance, and
would have saved the loss of many brave men.   Our troops
finding the enemy entrenched, fell back and began to fortify.
Soon our line was established, and the usual skirmishing and
sharpshooting commenced.   That same evening, being on the
extreme left of Kershaw's Division, I received orders to hasten
with the Second Regiment to General Kershaw's headquarters.
I found the General in a good deal of excitement.   He informed me that our lines had been broken on the right of his
division, and directed me to hasten there, and if I found a
regiment of the enemy flanking his position, to charge them.
I hurried to the point indicated, found that our troops to the

extent of a brigade and a half had been driven from their
works, and the enemy in possession of them. I determined to
charge, however, and succeeded in driving them from their
position, with but little loss. Our regiment numbered one
hundred and twenty-seven men. The enemy driven out consisted of the Forty-eighth and One Hundred and Twelfth New
York. We captured the colors of the Forty-eighth, took some
prisoners, and killed many while making their escape from the
trenches. We lost in this charge one of our most efficient
officers, Captain Ralph Elliott, a brother of General Stephen
Elliott. He was a brave soldier and a most estimable gentleman.''

Our lines were formed at right angles to that on which we
had fought that day, and the soldiers were ordered to fortify.
The Second and Third on the left were on an incline leading to
a ravine in front of a thicket; the Fifteenth and Twentieth, on
the right of the Third, were on the brow of a plateau; in front
was the broad old field, through which we had marched to the
first advance; the Third Battalion, Eighth, and Seventh, on
extreme right, were on the plateau and fronted by a thicket of
tall pines.

As nearly all regimental commanders had been killed since
the 6th of May, I will give them as they existed on the 1st of
June, three weeks later:

Second—Major Wm. Wallace.

Third—Lieutenant Colonel W. D. Rutherford.

Seventh—Captain James Mitchel.

Eighth—Major E. S. Stackhouse.

Twentieth—Lieutenal Colonel S. M. Boykin.

Third Battalion—Captain Whitener.

Brigade Commander—Colonel James Henagan.

Grant stretched his lines across our front and began approaching our works with his formidable parallels. He would
erect one line of breastworks, then under cover of night, another a hundred or two yards nearer us; thus by the third of
June our lines were not one hundred yards apart in places.
Our pickets and those of the enemy were between the lines
down in their pits, with some brush in front to shield them
while on the look out. The least shadow or moving of the
branches would be sure to bring a rifle ball singing dangerously near one's head—if he escaped it at all. The service in

the pits here for two weeks was the most enormous and fatiguing of any in the service—four men being in a pit for twenty-
four hours in the broiling sun during the day, without any
protection whatever, and the pit was so small that one could
neither sit erect nor lie down.

Early on the morning of the 3rd of June, just three days
after our fiasco at Cold Harbor, Grant moved his forces for the
assault. This was to be the culmination of his plan to break
through Lee's lines or to change his plans of campaign and
settle down to a regular siege. Away to our right the battle
commenced. Heavy shelling on both sides. Then the musketry began to roll along in a regular wave, coming nearer
and nearer as new columns moved to the assault. Now it
reaches our front, and the enemy moves steadily upon our
works. The cheering on our right told of the repulse by our
forces, and had a discouraging effect upon the Federal troops
moving against us. As soon as their skirmish line made its
appearance, followed by three lines of battle, our pickets in
front of us were relieved, but many fell before gaining our
breastworks, and those who were not killed had to lie during
the day between the most murderous fire in the history of the
war, and sad to say, few survived. When near us the first
line came with a rush at charge bayonets, and our officers had
great difficulty in restraining the men from opening fire too
soon. But when close enough, the word "fire" was given,
and the men behind the works raised deliberately, resting
their guns upon the works, and fired volley after volley into
the rushing but disorganized ranks of the enemy. The first
line reeled and attempted to fly the field, but were met by the
next column, which had el the retreating troops with the
bayonet, butts of guns, and officers' sword, until the greater
number were turned to the second assault. All this while our
sharpshooters and men behind our works were pouring a galling fire into the tangled mass of advancing and retreating
troops. The double column, like the first, came with a shout,
a huzzah, and a charge. But our men had by this time re-
loaded their pieces, and were only too eager awaiting the command "fire." But when it did come the result was telling—
men failing on top of men, rear rank pushing forward the first
rank, only to be swept away like chaff. Our batteries on the
hills in rear and those mounted on our infantry line were rak-

ing the field, the former with shell and solid shot, the latter
with grape and canister. Smoke settling on the ground,
soon rendered objects in front scarcely visible, but the steady
lashing of the enemy's guns and the hail of bullets over our
heads and against our works told plainly enough that the
enemy were standing to their work with desperate courage, or
were held in hand with a powerful grasp of discipline. The
third line of assault had now mingled with the first two, and
all lying stretched upon the ground and hidden by the dense
smoke, caused the greater number of our bullets to fly over
their heads. Our elevated position and the necessity of rising
above the works to fire, rendered our breastworks of little real.
advantage; conside.ing, too, the disparity of numbers, then
three lines against our one, and a very weak line at that. The
loud Rebel yell heard far to our right told us to be of good
cheer, they were holding their own, and repulsing every
assault. The conflict in front of Breckenridge's Dvision was
the bloodiest, with the possible exception of that of Mayree's
Hill, in front of Fredericksburg, and the "Bloody Angle," of
ty during the war. Negro troops were huddled together and
forced to the charge by white troops—the poor, deluded, unfortunate beings plied with liquor until all their sensibilities
were so deadened that death had no horrors. Grant must
ve learned early in the day the impossibility of breaking
's line by direct charge, for by twelve o'clock the firing
ed.

his last assault of Grant's thoroughly convinced the hero
Vicksburg and Missionary Ridge of the impossibility of
cing Lee's lines by direct advances. He could not sur-
him at any point, or catch him off his guard, for Lee
every foot of the ground too well, having fought all over
two years. It was estimated and confirmed aftewards by
l reports, that Grant had lost sixty thous:nd men from
ssing of the Rapidan to the end of the 3rd of June, just
days—more men than Lee had in the commencement of
npaign. Grant had become wiser the more familiar he
with Lee and his veterans, and now began to put in
tics—that of stretching out his lines so as to weaken
nd let attrition do the work that shells, balls, and the
had failed to accomplish. The end showed the wis-
he plan.

The two regiments on the left of the brigade did not suffer so greatly as the others, being protected somewhat by the timber and underbrush in their front. The enemy's dead lay in our front unburied until Grant's further move to the right, then it became our duty to perform those rites.

COLONEL LAWRENCE MASSILLON KEITT.

Colonel Lawrence Massillon Keitt was the second son of George and Mary Magdalene Wannamaker Keitt. He was born on the 4th day of October, 1824, in St. Matthews Parish, Orangeburg District, S. C. He received his early education at Asbury Academy, a flourishing institution near the place of his birth.

In his thirteenth year he entered Mt. Zion College at Winnsboro, Fairfield County, where he spent one year in preparation for the South Carolina College, which he entered in his fourteenth year, graduating third in his class. He read law in Attorney General Bailey's office in Charleston, S. C., and was admitted to the bar as soon as he was of legal age. He opened a law office at Orangeburg, the county seat.

At the first vacancy he was elected a member to the Lower House of the General Assembly of the State, in which body he served until his election to the Lower House of Congress in 1853. He served in that body until December, 1860, when he resigned his seat and returned to South Carolina on the eve of the secession of his State from the Union. He was a leading Secessionist and was elected a member of the Secession Convention. That body after passing the Ordinance of Secession elected him a delegate to the Provisional Congress of the Confederate States, which met at Montgomery, Ala. He was a very active member. On the adjournment of the Provisional Government of the Confederate States he returned to South Carolina and raised the Twentieth Regiment of South Carolina Volunteers and went into the Confederate Army. His command was ordered to Charleston. He served with his command on James' Island, Sullivan's Island, Morris' Island, and in Charleston in all the important engagements. He was in command of Morris' Island twenty-seven days and nights during its awful bombardment. When ordered to evacuate the island he did so, bringing off everything without the loss of a man. He was the last person to leave the island. General Beauregard in his report to the War Department said it was one of the greatest retreats in the annals of warfare.

The latter part of May, 1864, he left Charleston with his command and joined General Lee's Army thirteen miles from Richmond.   He carried about sixteen hundred men in his regiment to Virginia.   It was called the "Twentieth Army Corps." He was assigned to Kershaw's Brigade and put in command of the brigade.   On the first day of June, 1864, while leading the brigade, mounted on a grey horse, against a powerful force of the enemy he was shot through the liver and fell mortally wounded.   He died on the 2d of June, 1864.   By his request his remains were brought to South Carolina and laid by the side of his father in the graveyard at Tabernacle Church. Thus passed away one of South Carolina's brightest jewels.

CHAPTER XXXII

From Cold Harbor to Petersburg.

The field in the front at Cold Harbor where those deadly assaults had been made beggars description.   Men lay in places like hogs in a pen—some side by side, across each other, some two deep, while others with their legs lying across the head and body of their dead comrades.   Calls all night long could be heard coming from the wounded and dying, and one could not sleep for the sickening sound "W—a - t—e—r" ever sounding and echoing in his ears.   Ever and anon a heart-rending wail as coming from some lost spirit disturbed the hushed stilness of the night.   There were always incentives for some of the bolder spirits, whose love of adventure or love of gain impelled them, to visit the battlefield before the burial detail had reached it, as many crisp five-dollar greenbacks or even hundred-dollar interest-bearing United States bonds could be found in the pockets of the fallen Federal either as a part of his wages or the proceeds of his bounty.   The Federal Government was very lavish in giving recruits this bounty as an inducement to fill the depleted ranks of "Grant the Butcher." Tom Paysinger, of the Third, who had been detailed as a scout to General Longstreet, was a master hand at foraging up the battlefield.   Whether to gain information or to replenish his purse is not known, but be that as it may, the night after the battle he crept quietly through our lines and in the stillness and darkness he made his way among the dead and wounded, searching the pockets of those he found.   He came upon one who was lying face downward and whom he took to be beyond the pale of resistance, and proceeded to rifle his pockets.   After gathering a few trifles he began crawling on his hands and knees towards another victim.   When about ten steps distant the wounded Federal, for such it proved to be, raised himself on his elbow, grasped the gun that was lying beside him, but unknown to Paysinger, and called out, "You d—n grave robber, take that," and bang! went a shot at his retreating form.   He then quietly resumed his recumbent position.   The bullet struck Paysinger in the thigh and ranging upwards lodged in his hip, causing him to be a cripple for several long months.   It is needless to say Paysinger left the field. He said afterwards he "would have turned and cut the rascal's throat, but he was afraid he was only 'possuming' and might brain him with the butt of his gun."

We remained in our position for several days and were greatly annoyed by the shells thrown by mortars or cannon mounted as such, which were continually bursting overhead or dropping in our works.   The sharpshooters with globe-sighted rifles would watch through the brush in front of their rifle pits and as soon as a head was thoughtlessly raised either from our pits, which were now not more than fifty yards apart, or our breastwork, "crack!" went a rifle, a dull thud, and one of our men lay dead.   It is astonishing how apt soldiers are in avoiding danger or warding it off, and what obstacles they can overcome, what work they can accomplish and with so few and ill assortment of tools when the necessity arises.   To guard against the shells that were continually dropping in our midst or outside of our works, the soldiers began burrowing like rabbits in rear of our earthworks and building covered ways from their breastwork to the ground below.   In a few days men could go the length of a regiment without being exposed in the least, crawling along the tunnels all dug with bayonets, knives, and a few worn-out shovels.   At some of these angles the passer-by would be exposed, and in going from one opening to another, only taking the fraction of a second to accomplish, a bullet would come whizzing from some unseen source, either to the right or left. As soon as one of these openings under a covered way would be darkened by some one passing, away a bullet would come singing in the aperture, generally striking the soldier passing through. So annoying and dangerous had the practice become of shooting in our works from an unseen source that a detail of ten or twenty men was sent out under Lieutenant D. J. Griffith, of the Fifteenth, to see if the concealed enemy might not be located and an end put to the annoyance. Griffith and his men crept along cautiously in the underbrush, while some of our men would wave a blanket across the exposed places in the breastwork to draw the Federal fire, while Griffith and his detail kept a sharp lookout. It was not long before they discovered the hidden "Yank" perched in the top of a tall gum tree, his rifle resting in the fork of a limb. Griffith got as close as he well could without danger of being detected by some one under the tree. When all was ready they sighted their rifles at the fellow up the tree and waited his next fire. When it did come I expect that Yankee and his comrades below were the worst surprised of any throughout the war; for no sooner had his gun flashed than ten rifles rang out in answer and the fellow fell headlong to the ground, a distance of fifty feet or more. Beating the air with his hands and feet, grasping at everything within sight or reach, his body rolling and tumbling among the limbs of the tree, his head at times up, at others down, till at last he strikes the earth, and with a terrible rebound in the soft spongy needles Mr. "Yank" lies still, while Griffith and his men take to their heels. It was not known positively whether he was killed or not, but one thing Lieutenant Griffith and his men were sure of—one Yankee, at least, had been given a long ride in midair.

After Grant's repulse at Cold Harbor he gave up all hopes of reaching Richmond by direct assault and began his memorable change of base. Crossing the James River at night he undertook the capture of Petersburg by surprise. It appears from contemporaneous history that owing to some inexcusable blunders on our part Grant came very near accomplishing his designs.

To better understand the campaign around Petersburg it is necessary to take the reader back a little way. Sim~~ultaneous~~

with Grant's advance on the Rapidan an army of thirty thousand under the Union General B. F. Butler was making its way up the James River and threatening Petersburg. It was well known that Richmond would be no longer tenable should the latter place fall. Beauaegard was commanding all of North Carolina and Virginia on the south side of the James River, but his forces were so small and so widely scattered that they promised little protection. When Lee and his veterans were holding back Grant and the Union Army at the Wilderness, Brocks Cross Roads, and Spottsylvania C. H., Beauregard with a handful of veterans and a few State troops was "bottling up Butler" on the James. What Kershaw had been to Lee at the Wilderness, McGowan at Spottsylvania, General Hagood was to General Beauregard on the south side around Petersburg. General Beauregard does not hesitate to acknowledge what obligations he was under to the brave General Hagood and his gallant band of South Carolinians at the most critical moments during the campaign, and it is unquestioned that had not General Hagood come up at this opportune moment, Petersburg would have fallen a year before it did.

General Beauregard fought some splendid battles on the south side, and if they had not been overshadowed by the magnitude of Lee's from the Wilderness to the James, they would have ranked in all probability as among the greatest of the war. But from one cause and then another during the whole campaign Beauregard was robbed of his legitimate fruits of battle.

The low, swampy nature of the country below Richmond, especially between the James and the Chickahominy, prevented Lee's scouts from detecting the movements of Grant's Army for some days after the movement began. Grant had established his headquarters at Wilcox's Landing, on the James, and had all his forces in motion on the south of the river by the 13th of June, while Lee was yet north of the Chickahominy.

General Beauregard and the gallant troops under him deserve the highest praise for their conduct in successfully giving Butler battle, while Petersburg was in such imminent peril, and Lee still miles and miles away. It is scarcely credible to believe with what small force the plucky little Creole held back such an overwhelming army.

When Grant made his first crossing of the James and began the movement against Petersburg, General Beauregard had only Wise's Brigade of infantry, twenty-two pieces of artillery, two regiments of cavalry under General Dearing, and a few regiments of local militia.

Grant had ordered the Eighteenth Corps (Smith's) by way of the White House to Bermuda Hundreds, and this corps had crossed the narrow neck of land between the James and the Appomattox, crossing the latter river on a pontoon bridge, and was at the moment firing on Petersburg with a force under his command of twenty-two thousand, with nothing between General Smith and Petersburg but Beauregard's two thousand men of all arms. Kant's Cavalry and one division of negro troops, under Hinks, had joined their forces with Smith after coming to the south side. Hancock's and Warren's Corps crossed the Chickahominy at Long Bridge and the James at Wilcox's Landing, and with Grant at the head, all were pushing on to Petersburg. Wright (Sixth) and Burnside (Ninth) crossed by way of Jones' Bridge and the James and Appomattox on pontoon bridges, pushing their way rapidly, as the nature of the ground permitted, in the direction of Petersburg. Beauregard in the meantime had been reinforced by his own troops, they having been transferred temporarily to Lee, at Spottsylvania Court House.

Hoke's Division reached Petersburg at twelve o'clock, on the 15th of June. Hagood's Brigade, of that division, being transported by rail from the little town of Chester, reached the city about night. Bushrod Johnson's Brigade was ordered up from Bermuda on the 16th. Beauregard being thus reinforced, had ten thousand troops of all arms on the morning of the 16th, with which to face Meade's Army, consisting of Hancock's, Smith's, and Burnside's Corps, aggregating sixty-six thousand men. Meade made desperate and continuous efforts to break through this weak line of gray, but without effect Only one division of Federals gained any permanent advantage. Warren, with four divisions, now reinforced Meade, bringing the Federal Army up to ninety thousand, with no help for Beauregard yet in sight. From noon until late at night of the 17th the force of this entire column was hurled against the Confederate lines, without any appreciable advantage, with the exception of one division before alluded to. Lee

was still north of the James with his entire army, and undecided as to Grant's future movements.   He was yet in doubt
whether Grant had designs directly against the Capital, or was
endeavoring to cut his communications by the capture of
Petersburg.   Beauregard had kept General Lee and the war
department thoroughly advised of his peril and of the overwhelming numbers in his front, but it was not until midnight
of the 17th that the Confederate commander determined to
change his base and cross to the south side of the James.   It
was at that hour that Kershaw's Brigade received its orders to
move at once.   For the last few days the army had been gradually working its way towards the James River, and was now
encamped near Rice's Station.   From the manner in which we
were urged forward, it was evident that our troops somewhere
were in imminent peril.   The march started as a forced one,
but before daylight it had gotten almost to a run.   All the
regiments stood the great strain without flinching, with the
exception of the Twentieth.   The "Old Twentieth Army
Corps," as that regiment was now called, could not stand
what the old veterans did, and fell by the way side.   It was
not for want of patriotism or courage, but simply a want of
seasoning.   Fully half of the "Corps" fell out.   When we
reached Petersburg, about sunrise, we found only Wise's
Brigade and several regiments of old men and boys, hastily
gotten together to defend their city, until the regulars came
up.   They had been fighting in the ranks, these gray-beards
and half-grown boys, for three days, and to their credit be it
said, "they weathered the storm" like their kinsmen in Wise's
Brigade, and showed as much courage and endurance as the
best of veterans.   On the streets were ladies of every walk in
life, some waving banners and handkerchiefs, some clapping
their hands and giving words of cheer as the soldiers came by
with their swinging step, their clothes looking as if they had
just swum the river.   Were the ladies refugeeing—getting
out of harm's way?   Not a bit of it.   They looked equally as
determined and defiant as their brothers and fathers in ranks—
each and all seemed to envy the soldier his rifle.   If Richmond
had become famous through the courage and loyalty of her
daughters, Petersburg was equally entitled to share the glories
of her older sister, Richmond.

Kershaw's Brigade relieved that of General Wise, taking

position on extreme right, resting its right on the Jerusalem plank road, and extending towards the left over the hill and across open fields. Wise had some hastily constructed works, with rifle pits in front. These later had to be relieved under a heavy fire from the enemy's battle line. As the other brigades of the division came up, they took position on the left. Fields' Division and R. H. Anderson's, now of this corps, did not come up for some hours yet. General Anderson, in the absence of General Longstreet, commanded the corps as senior Major General. Before our division lines were properly adjusted, Warren's whole corps made a mad rush upon the works, now manned by a thin skirmish line, and seemed determined to drive us from our entrenchments by sheer weight of numbers. But Kershaw displayed no inclination to yield, until the other portions of our corps came upon the field. After some hours of stubborn fighting, and failing to dislodge us, the enemy withdrew to strengthen and straighten their lines and bring them more in harmony with ours. About four o'clock in the afternoon Meade organized a strong column of assault, composed of the Second, Fifth, and the Ninth Army Corps. and commanded in person, holding one corps in reserve. The artillery of the four corps was put in position, and a destructive fire was opened upon us by fifty pieces of the best field artillery. The infantry then commenced the storming of our works, but Field's Division had come up and was on the line. General Lee had given strength to our position by his presence, coming upon the field about eleven o'clock, and gave personal direction to the movements of the troops. The battle raged furiously until nightfall, but with no better results on the enemy's side than had attended him for the last three days —a total repulse at every point. By noon the next day Lee's whole force south of the James was within the entrenched lines of the city, and all felt perfectly safe and secure. Our casualties were light in comparison to the fighting done during the day, but the enemy was not only defeated, but badly demoralized.

Kershaw and Fields, of Lee's Army, with ten thousand under General Beauregard, making a total of twenty thousand, successfully combatted Grant's whole army, estimated by the Federals themselves as being ninety thousand. These are some figures that might well be taken in considera-

tion when deeds of prowess and Southern valor are being
summed up.

————

Grant seemed determined to completely invest Petersburg on
the south side by continually pushing his lines farther to the
left, lengthening our lines and thereby weakening them.   On
the 21st of June the Second and Sixth Corps of the Federal
Army moved on to the west of the Jerusalem plank road, while
the Fifth was to take up position on the east side.   In the manœuver, or by some misunderstanding, the Fifth Corps became
separated from those of the other divisions, thereby leaving a
gap of about a division intervening.   General Lee seeing this
opportunity to strike the enemy a blow, and as A. P. Hill was
then coming up, he ordered him to push his force forward and
attack the enemy in flank.   Moving his troops forward with
that despatch that ever attended the Third Corps of our army,
it struck the enemy a stunning blow in the flank and rear,
driving them back in great disorder, capturing several thous-
and prisoners and a battery or two of artillery.   The enemy
continued to give way until they came upon their strong entrenched position; then Hill retired and took his place on the
line.   Again Grant started his cavalry out on raids to capture
and destroy the railroads leading into Petersburg and Richmond, the route by which the entire army of Lee had to look
for supplies.   But at Reams' Station Hampton met the larger
body of the enemy's cavalry and after a hard fought battle, in
which he utterly routed the enemy, he captured his entire
wagon train and all his artillery.   A short time after this
Grant sent Hancock, one of the ablest Generals in the Federal Army, (a true, thorough gentleman, and as brave as the
bravest, and one whom the South in after years had the pleasure of showing its gratitude and admiration for those qualities
so rare in many of the Federal commanders, by voting for him
for President of the United States) with a large body of cavalry
to destroy the Weldon Road at all hazard and to so possess it
that its use to our army would be at an end.   After another
hard battle, in which the enemy lost five thousand men, Hancock succeeded in his mission and captured and retained the
road.   The only link now between the capital and the other
sections of the South on which the subsistence of the army depended was that by Danville, Va.   This was a military road

mpleted by the government in anticipation of those very
ents that had now transpired. Another road on which the
vernment was bending all its energies to complete, but failed
· want of time, was a road running from Columbia to
igusta, Ga. This was to be one of the main arteries of the
uth in case Charleston should fail to hold out and the junc-
n of the roads at Branchville fall in the hands of the enemy.
r lines of transportation, already somewhat circumscribed,
re beginning to grow less and less. Only one road leading
uth by way of Danville, and should the road to Augusta,
., via Columbia and Branchville, be cut the South or the
mies of the West and that of the East would be isolated.
gloomy as our situation looked, there was no want of con-
ence in the officers and the troops. The rank and file of the
uth had never considered a condition of failure. They felt
eir cause to be sacred, that they were fighting for rights and
inciples for which all brave people will make every sacrifice
maintain, that the bravery of a people like that which the
uth had shown to the world, the spirits that animated them,
e undaunted courage by which the greatest battles had been
ught and victories gained against unprecedented numbers,
l this under such circumstances and under such leadership—
e South could not fail. Momentary losses, temporary re-
rses might prolong the struggle, but to change the ultimate
sults, never. And at the North there were loud and wide-
read murmurings, no longer confined to the anti-abolitionist
d pro slavery party, but it came from statesmen the highest
the land, it came from the fathers and mothers whose sons
d fallen like autumn leaves from the Rapidan to the Appo-
attox. The cries and wails of the thousands of orphans went
to high Heaven pleading for those fathers who had left them
fill the unsatiate maw of cruel, relentless war. The tears of
ousands and thousands of widows throughout the length and
eadth of the Union fell like scalding waters upon the souls
the men who were responsible for this holocaust. Their
ices and murmuring, though like Rachael's "weeping for
r children and would not be comforted," all this to appease
e Moloch of war and to gratify the ambition of fanatics. The
ople, too, of the North, who had to bear all this burden,
re sorely pressed and afflicted at seeing their hard earned
asures or hoarded wealth, the fruits of their labor, the re-

sult of their toil of a lifetime, going to feed this army of over
two millions of men, to pay the bounties of thousands of mer-
cenaries of the old countries and the unwilling freedmen soldiers of the South. All this only to humble a proud people
and rob them of their inherent rights, bequeathed to them by
the ancestry of the North and South. How was it with the
South? Not a tear, not a murmur. The mothers, with that
Spartan spirit, buckled on the armor of their sons with pride
and courage, and with the Spartan injunction, bade them "come
home with your shield, or on it." The fathers, like the Scot-
tish Chieftain, if he lost his first born, would put forward his
next, and say, "Another one for Hector." Their store-
houses, their barns, and graneries were thrown open, and
with lavish hands bade the soldiers come and take—come and
buy without money and without price. Even the poor docile
slave, for whom some would pretend these billions of treasure
were given and oceans of blood spilled, toiled on in peace and
contentment, willing to make any and every sacrifice, and toil
day and night, for the interest and advancement of his
master's welfare. He was as proud of his master's achievements, of our victories, and was even as willing to throw his
body in this bloody vortex as if the cause had been his own.
The women of the South, from the old and bending grand-
mothers, who sat in the corner, with their needles flying
steady and fast, to the aristocratic and pampered daughter of
wealth, toiled early and toiled late with hands and bodies that
never before knew or felt the effects of work—all this that the
soldier in the trenches might be clothed and fed—not alone for
members of their families, but for the soldiers all, especially
those who were strangers among us—those who had left their
homes beyond the Potomac and the Tennessee. The good
housewife stripped her household to send blankets and bedding
to the needy soldiers. The wheel and loom could be heard in
almost every household from the early morn until late at night
going to give not comforts, but necessities of life, to the boys
in the trenches. All ranks were leveled, and the South was
as one band of brothers and sisters. All formality and restraint were laid aside, and no such thing as stranger known.
The doors were thrown open to the soldiers wherever and
whenever they chose to enter; the board was always spread,
and a ready welcome extended. On the march, when homes

were to be passed, or along the sidewalks in cities, the ladies
set the bread to baking and would stand for hours in the door-
way or at some convenient window to cut and hand out slice
after slice to the hungry soldiers as long as a loaf was left or a
soldier found.

With such a people to contend, with such heroes to face in
the field, was it any wonder that the North began to despair
of ever conquering the South? There was but one way by
which the Northern leaders saw possible to defeat such a
nation of "hereditary madmen in war." It was by continually wearing them away by attrition. Every man killed in
the South was one man nearer the end. It mattered not what
the cost might be—if two or a dozen soldiers fell, if a dozen
households were put in mourning, and widows and orphans
were made by the score—the sacrifice must be made and endured. The North had found in Grant a fit weapon by which
to give the blow—a man who could calmly see the slaughter of
thousands to gain an end, if by so doing the end in view could
be expedited. The absence of all feelings of humanity, the
coolness and indifference with which he looked upon his dead,
his calmness in viewing the slaughter as it was going on,
gained for him the appellation of "Grant, the Butcher."
Grant saw, too, the odds and obstacles with which he had to
contend and overcome when he wrote these memorable words,
"Lee has robbed the cradle and the grave." Not odds in
numbers and materials, but in courage, in endurance, in the
sublime sacrifice the South was making in men and treasure.
Scarcely an able-bodied man in the South—nay, not one who
could be of service—who was not either in the trenches, in
the ranks of the soldiers, or working in some manner for the
service. All from sixteen to fifty were now in actual service,
while all between fourteen and sixteen and from fifty to sixty
were guarding forts, railroads, or Federal prisoners. These
prisoners had been scattered all over the South, and began to
be unwieldy. The Federals under the policy of beating the
South by depleting their ranks without battle in the field had
long since refused the exchange of prisoners. They had, by
offers of enticing bounties, called from the shores of the Old
Country thousands of poor emigrants, who would enlist merely
for the money there was in it. Thousands and thousands of
prisoners captured could not speak a word of English. They

had whole brigades of Irish and Dutch, while the Swedes, Poles, Austrians, as well as Italians, were scattered in the ranks throughout the army. In the capturing of a batch of prisoners, to a stranger who would question them, it would seem more like we were fighting the armies of Europe than our kinsmen of the North. In fact, I believe if the real truth of it was known, the greater part of the Federal Army in the closing days of the Confederacy was either foreigners or sons of foreigners.

Were there ever before such people as those of the Southland? Were there ever such patriotic fathers, such Christian mothers, such brave and heroic sons and daughters? Does it look possible at this late day that a cause so just and righteous could fail, with such men and women to defend it? It is enough to cause the skeptic to smile at the faith of those who believe in God's interference in human affairs and in the efficacy of prayers. The cause of the South was just and right, and no brave men would have submitted without first staking their all upon the issue of cruel, bloody war. Impartial history will thus record the verdict.

CHAPTER XXXIII

In the Trenches Around Petersburg.

As soon as General Lee's Army was all up and his lines established, we began to fortify in earnest. The breastworks that were built now were of a different order to the temporary ones in the Wilderness and at Cold Harbor. As it was known now that a regular siege had begun, our breastworks were built proportionately strong. Our lines were moved to the left to allow a battery to occupy the brow of a hill on our right, Kershaw's Brigade occupying both slopes of the hills, a ravine cutting it in two. Field pieces were mounted at intervals along the line with the infantry, every angle covered by one or more cannon. The enemy commenced shelling us from mortars from the very beginning of our work, and kept it up night and day as long as we remained in the trenches. The day after Kershaw took position Grant began pressing our picket line and running his parallels nearer and nearer our works. It was said that Grant won his laurels in the West with picks and shovels instead of rifles and cannon, but here it looked as if he intended to use both to an advantage. As soon as he had his lines located, he opened a fusilade upon Petersburg, throwing shells into the city from his long-ranged guns, without intermission. It was in the immediate front of the right of the brigade and the battery on the hill that the enemy's mine was laid that occasioned the "Battle of the Crater" a month afterwards. Before we had finished our works, several night assaults were made upon us, notably the one up the ravine that separated the Second and Third on the night of the 21st of June. It was easily repulsed, however, with little loss on our side, the enemy firing too high. What annoyed the soldiers more than anything else was the continual dropping of shells in our works or behind them. We could hear the report of the mortars, and by watching overhead we could see the shell descending, and no one could tell exactly where it was going to strike and no chance for dodging. As every old soldier knows, card playing was the national vice, if vice it could be called, and almost all participated in it, but mostly for amusement, as the soldiers scarcely ever had money to hazard at cards. While a quartet was indulging in this pastime in the trenches, some one yelled, "Lookout, there comes a shell!" Looking up the disciples of the "Ten Spots" saw a shell coming down right over their heads. Nothing could be done but to stretch themselves at full length and await developments. They were not long in suspense, for the shell dropped right upon the oilcloth on which they had been playing. There it lay sizzing and spluttering as the fuse burned lower and lower, the men holding their breath all the while, the other troops scattering right and left. The thing could not last; the tension broke, when one of the card-players seized the shell in his hands and threw it out of the works, just before exploding. It was the belief in the brigade that those men did not play cards again for more than thirty days.

Another annoyance was the enemy's sharpshooters, armed with globe-sighted rifles. These guns had a telescope on top of the barrel, and objects at a distance could be distinctly seen. Brush screened their rifle pits, and while they could see

plainly any object above our works, we could not see them.
A head uncautiously raised above the line, would be sure to
get a bullet in or near it.

About one hundred yards in our rear, up the ravine, was a
good spring of water.   The men could reach this in safety by
going down the breastworks in a stooping posture, then up the
ravine to the spring.   A recruit in the Second Regiment had
gone to this spring and was returning.   When about twenty
paces from the works he undertook, through a spirit of adventure, or to save a few steps, to run diagonally across the field
to his regiment.   It was his last.   When about midway he
was caught by a bullet from the enemy's picket, and only
lived long enough to call out, "Oh, mother!"   Many lost
their lives here by recklessness or want of caution.

After remaining in the trenches about two weeks, Kershaw's
Brigade was relieved by a part of Hoke's Division and retired
to some vacant lots in the city in good supporting distance of
the front line.   We were not out of reach of the shells by any
means; they kept up a continual screaming overhead, bursting
in the city.   The soldiers got passes to visit the town on little
shopping excursions, notwithstanding the continual bursting
of the shells in the city.   The citizens of Petersburg, white
and black, women and children, like the citizens of Charleston, soon became accustomed to the shelling, and as long as
one did not drop in their immediate vicinity, little attention
was paid to it.   One night after a furious bombardment the
cry was heard, "The city is on fire; the city is on fire."   A
lurid glare shot up out of the very heart of the city, casting
a dim light over the buildings and the camps near about.
Fire bells began ringing. and the old men rushing like mad to
fight the fire.   As soon as the enemy discovered that the city
was on fire, they concentrated all their efforts to the burning
buildings.   Shells came shrieking from every elevated position
on the enemy's lines, and fell like "showers of meteors on a
frolic."   Higher and higher the flames rose until great molten-
like tongues seemed to lick the very clouds.   The old men
mounted the ladder like boys, and soon the tops of the surrounding buildings were lined with determined spirits, and the
battle against the flames began in earnest.   We could see
their forms against the dark back-ground, running hither and
thither, fighting with all the power and energy of the brave

and fearless men they were. They paid no heed to the screaming, shrieking, bursting shells all around, but battled bravely to save the city. After the burning of several contiguous buildings, the flames were gotten under control, and eventually the fire was extinguished. I have seen many battles, but never more heroism displayed than by the old citizens and boys that night in Petersburg. The soldiers were not allowed to leave their camp, and all the citizens of military age were away in the army, so the old men and boys had to fight this fire single-handed and alone, and amid a perfect storm of shot and shell.

Grant had been daily reinforced by recruits and forces from the West. Butler had received a large reinforcement from Banks, on the lower Mississippi, and was gradually working his way up to Richmond. A great number of these troops, to judge from the prisoners we captured, were foreigners; many could not speak a word of English. Kershaw was ordered to reinforce the troops on the north side, and on the 13th of July we crossed the James on a pontoon bridge, near Chaffin's Bluff, after an all night's march over brush, briars, through field and bog, and took position on a high ridge running out from the river. In front of us was a vast swamp of heavy timber and underbrush, called Deep Bottom. Beyond Deep Bottom the enemy had approached and entrenched, being supported by gun boats in the James. This position it was determined to surprise and take by assault. Early at night the brigade was moved out in this swamp, along a dull road that ran along its edge, and advanced in the direction of the enemy. No attempt of assault was ever more dreaded or looked on with such apprehension, save, perhaps, our charge on the works at Knoxville, than this night charge at Deep Bottom. When near the enemy's position, we formed line of battle, while it was so dark in the dense woods that an object ten feet away could not be distinguished. We had to take and give commands in whispers, for fear the enemy would discover our presence. We moved forward gradually, a few steps at a time, each step a little nearer the enemy, who lay asleep behind their works. We had advanced, perhaps, two hundred yards, and as yet had encountered none of the enemy's pickets or videttes, showing how securely they felt in regard to a night attack. While halting to

which had to be done every few paces, Colonel Rutherford
and myself were reconnoitering in front, and discovered a
white object a few feet away. The men saw it, too, and
thought it a sheep. The Colonel advanced and gave it a
slight jab with his sword. In a moment a white blanket was
thrown off, and there lay, as nicely coiled up as little pigs, two
of the Yankee sentinels. They threw up their hands in a
dazed kind of way, and to our whispered threats and uplifted
swords, uttered some unintelligible jargon. We soon saw they
did not understand a word of English. So it was we captured
almost their entire picket line, composed of foreigners of
Banks' Army, of Louisiana. Just then, on our right, whether
from friend or foe, I never learned, several discharges of rifles
alarmed both armies. It was too late then to practice secrecy,
so the command "charge" was given. With a tremendous
yell, we dashed through the tangled, matted mass of undergrowth, on towards the enemy's line. Aroused thus suddenly
from their sleep, they made no other resistance than to fire a
few shots over our head, leaving the breastworks in haste.
Some lay still, others ran a few rods in the rear, and remained
until captured, while the greater part scampered away towards
their gun boats.

Colonel Henagan, of the Eighth, being in command of the
brigade, ordered breastworks to be thrown up on the opposite
side of an old road, in which the enemy lay and which they
had partly fortified. The next day, about 3 o'clock, the
enemy opened upon us a heavy fusilade with their siege
mortars and guns from their gun boats and ironclads in the
James. These were three hundred-pounders, guns we had
never before been accustomed to. Great trees a foot and a
half in diameter were snapped off like pipe-stems. The peculiar frying noise made in going through the air and their enormous size caused the troops to give them the name of "camp
kettles." They passed through our earthworks like going
hrough mole hills. The enemy advanced in line of battle,
and a considerable battle ensued, but we were holding our
own, when some watchers that Colonel Henagan had ordered
in the tops of tall trees to watch the progress of the enemy,
gave the warning that a large body of cavalry was advancing
around our left and was gaining our rear. Colonel Henagan
gave the command "retreat," but the great "camp kettles"

coming with such rapidity and regularity, our retreat through this wilderness of shrubbery and tangled undergrowth would have ended in a rout had not our retreat been impeded by this swamp morass.   We reached the fortification, however, on the bluff, the enemy being well satisfied with our evacuation of the position so near their camp.

The brigade, with the exception of marching and counter-marching, relieving other troops and being relieved, did no further service than occupying the lines until the 6th of August.   The brigade boarded the train on that day at Chester for destination at that time unknown.

About the first of July the enemy, commanded by General Burnside, undertook to blow up a portion of our lines by tunneling under the works at a convenient point suitable for assault, and attempted to take our troops by surprise.   The point selected was that portion of the line first held by Kershaw's Brigade, near Cemetery Hill, and in front of Taylor's Creek, near Petersburg.   The continual night assaults on us at that point and the steady advance of their lines were to gain as much distance as possible.   From the base of the hill at Taylor's Creek they began digging a tunnel one hundred and seventy yards long, and at its terminus were two laterals, dug in a concave towards our works, of thirty-seven feet each.   In these laterals were placed eight hundred pounds of powder, with fuse by which all could be exploded at once.

General Beauregard, who commanded at this point, had been apprised of this undertaking, and at first had sunk counter-mines.   But this was abandoned, and preparations were made to meet the emergency with arms.   At this point and near the "Crater," as it was afterwards called, were stationed Colquit's (Ga.), Gracie's (Ala.), and Elliott's (S. C.) Brigades.   Elliott's was posted immediately over it with Pegram's Battery.   Rear lines had been established by which the troops could take cover, and reinforcements kept under arms night and day, so that when the explosion did take place, it would find the Confederates prepared.   Batteries were placed at convenient places to bear upon the line and the place of explosion.

On the morning of the 30th of July, everything being in readiness, the fuse was placed, and at 3.30 o'clock the light was applied.   Before this terrible "Crater," soon to be a holocaust

of human beings, were massed Ledlie's, Potter's, Wilcox's, and
Ferrero's Divisions, supported by Ames'. In the front was
Ferrero's Division of negro troops, drunk and reeling from the
effects of liquor furnished them by the wagon loads. This
body of twenty-three thousand men were all under the imme
diate command of Major General Ord. On the left of Burn
side, Warren concentrated ten thousand men, while the Eigh
teenth Corps, with that many more, were in the rear to ai
and support the movement—the whole being forty-three thou
sand men, with eight thousand pounds of gun-powder to fire
spring the mine. General Sheridan, with his cavalry, was t
make a demonstration in our front and against the roads lead
ing to Petersburg. Hancock, too, was to take a part, if a
things proved successful—fifty thousand men were to make
bold dash for the capture of the city. Immediateiy over th
mine was Elliott's Brigade, consisting of the Seventeenth
Twenty-sixth, Twenty-third, Twenty-second, and Eighteent
South Carolina Regiments. At 3.30 o'clock the fuse wa
lighted, and while the Confederates, all unconscious of th
impending danger, lay asleep, this grand aggregation of me
of Grant's Army waited with bated breath and anxious eye th
fearful explosion that eight thousand pounds of powder, und
a great hill, were to make. Time went on, seconds in t
minutes. The nerves of the assaulters were, no doubt, a
extreme tension. Four o'clock came, still all was still an
silent. The Federal commanders held their watches in han
and watched the tiny steel hands tick the seconds away. Th
streaks of day came peeping up over the hills and cast shadow
high overhead. The fuse had failed! A call was made for
volunteer to go down into the mine and relight the fuse.
Lieutenant and Sergeant bravely step forward and offered t
undertake the perilous mission. They reach the mouth of th
tunnel and peer in. All was dark, silent, sombre, and stil
Along they grope their way with a small lantern in the
hands. They reach the barrel of powder placed at the junc
tion of the main and the laterals. The fuse had ceased t
burn. Hurriedly they pass along to the other barrels. Ex
pecting every moment to be brown into space, they find all a
the first, out. The thousands massed near the entrance an
along Taylor's Creek, watched with fevered excitement th
return of the brave men who had thus placed their lives i

such jeopardy for a cause they, perhaps, felt no interest. Quickly they placed new fuse, lit them, and quickly left the gruesome pit. Scarcely had they reached a place of safety than an explosion like a volcano shook the earth, while the country round about was lit up with a great flash. The earth trembled and swayed—great heaps of earth went flying in the air, carrying with it men, guns, and ammunition. Cannon and carriages were scattered in every direction, while the sleeping men were thrown high in the air.

But here I will allow Colonel F. W. McMaster, an eye witness, who commanded Elliott's Brigade after the fall of that General, to tell the story of the "Battle of the Crater" in his own words. I copy his account, by permission, from an article published in one of the newspapers of the State.

BY COLONEL F. W. McMASTER.

In order to understand an account of the battle of the "Crater," a short sketch of our fortifications should be given.

Elliott's Brigade extended from a little branch that separated it from Ransom's Brigade on the north, ran three hundred and fifty yards, joining Wise's Brigade on the south. Captain Pegram's Virginia Battery had four guns arranged in a half circle on the top of the hill, and was separated from the Eighteenth and Twenty-second South Carolina Regiments by a bank called trench cavalier.

The Federal lines ran parallel to the Confederate. The nearest point of Pegram's Battery to the Federal lines was eighty yards; the rest of the lines was about two hundred yards apart. The line called gorge line was immediately behind the battery, and was the general passage for the troops. The embankment called trench cavalier was immediately in rear of the artillery and was constructed for the infantry in case the battery should be taken by a successful assault.

The general line for the infantry, which has been spoken of as a wonderful feat of engineering, was constructed under peculiar circumstances. Beauregard had been driven from the original lines made for the defense of Petersburg, and apprehensive that the enemy, which numbered ten to one, would get into the city, directed his engineer, Colonel Harris, to stake a new line. This place was reached by General Hancock's troops at dark on the third day's fighting, and our men were ordered to make a breastwork. Fortifications without spades or shovels was rather a difficult feat to perform, but our noble soldiers went to work with bayonets and tin cups, and in one night threw up a bank three feet high—high enough to cause Hancock to delay his attack. In the next ten days' time the ditches were enlarged until they were eight feet high and eight feet wide, with a banquette of eighteen inches high from which the soldiers could shoot over the breastwork.

Five or six traverses were built perpendicularly from the main trench to the rear, so as to protect Pegram's guns from the enfilading fire of the big guns on the Federal lines a mile to the north. Besides these traverses there were narrow ditches five or six feet deep which led to the sinks.

The only safe way to Petersburg, a mile off, was to go down to the spring branch which passed under our lines at the foot of the hill, then go to the left through the covered way to Petersburg, or to take the covered way which was half way down the hill to Elliott's headquarters.

At this point a ravine or more properly a swale ran up the hill parallel to our breastworks. It was near Elliott's headquarters where Mahone's troops went in from the covered way and formed in battle array.

The soldiers slept in the main trench. At times of heavy rains the lower part of the trench ran a foot deep in water. The officers slept in burrows dug in the sides of the rear ditches. There were traverses, narrow ditches, cross ditches and a few mounds over officers' dens, so that there is no wonder that one of the Federal officers said the quarters reminded him of the catacombs of Rome.

An ordinary mortal would not select such a place for a three months' summer residence.

About ten days after the battle, and while I was acting Brigadier General and occupying General Elliott's headquarters, a distinguished Major General visited me and requested me to go over the lines with him. I gladly complied with the request. He asked me where the men rested at night. I pointed out the floor of the ditch. He said, "But where do the officers sleep?" We happened then to be in the narrow ditch in front of my quarters, and I pointed it out to him. He replied, in language not altogether suitable for a Sunday School teacher, that he would desert before he would submit to such hardships.

THE "CRATER."

The explosion took place at 4.45 A. M.   The "Crater" made
by eight thousand pounds of gun powder was one hundred and
thirty-five feet long, ninety-seven feet broad and thirty feet
deep.   Two hundred and seventy-eight men were buried in
the debris—Eighteenth Regiment, eighty-two; Twenty-second,
one hundred and seventy, and Pegram's Battery, twenty-two
men.

To add to the terror of the scene the enemy with one hundred and sixty-four cannon and mortars began a bombardment
much greater than Fort Sumter or battery were ever subjected
to.   Elliott's Brigade near the "Crater" was panic stricken,
and more than one hundred men of the Eighteenth Regiment
covered with dirt rushed down.   Two or three noble soldiers
asked me for muskets.   Some climbed the counterscarpe and
made their way for Petersburg.   Numbers of the Seventeenth
joined the procession.   I saw one soldier scratching at the
counterscape of the ditch like a scared cat.   A staunch Lieutenant of Company E. without hat or coat or shoes ran for dear
life way down into Ransom's trenches.   When he came to con-
ciousness he cried out, "What! old Morse running!" and
immediately returned to his place in line.

The same consternation existed in the Federal line.   As
they saw the masses descending they broke ranks, and it took
a few minutes to restore order.

FEDERAL CHARGE.

About fifteen minutes after the explosion General Ledlie's
Corps advanced in line.   The cheval-de-frise was destroyed for
fifty yards.   Soon after General Wilcox's Corps came in line
and bore to Ledlie's left.   Then Potter's Corps followed by
flanks and was ordered to the right of Ledlie's troops.

The pall of smoke was so great that we could not see the
enemy until they were in a few feet of our works, and a lively
fusillade was opened by the Seventeenth Regiment on the north
side of the "Crater."   I saw Starling Hutto, of Company H,
a boy of sixteen, on the top of the breastworks, firing his
musket at the enemy a few yards off with the coolness of a
veteran.   As soon as I reached him I dragged him down by
his coat tail and ordered him to shoot from the banquette.   On
the south of the "Crater" a few men under Major Shield, of

the Twenty-second, and Captain R. E. White, with the Twenty-third Regiment, had a hot time in repelling the enemy.

Adjutant Sims and Captain Floyd, of the Eighteenth Regiment, with about thirty men, were cut off in the gorge line. They held the line for a few minutes. Adjutant Sims was killed and Captain Floyd and his men fell back into some of the cross ditches and took their chances with the Seventeenth

It was half an hour before the Federals filled the "Crater," the gorge line and a small space of the northern part of the works not injured by the explosion. All this time the Federals rarely shot a gun on the north of the "Crater."

Major J. C. Coit, who commanded Wright's Battery and Pegram's battery, had come up to look after the condition of the latter. He concluded that two officers and twenty men were destroyed. Subsequently he discovered that one man had gone to the spring before the explosion, that four men were saved by a casemate and captured.

Colonel Coit says he took twenty-five minutes to come from his quarters and go to Wright's Battery, and thinks it was the first gun shot on the Federal side. Testimony taken in the court of inquiry indicate the time at 5.30 A. M.

GENERAL STEPHEN ELLIOTT.

General Stephen Elliott, the hero of Fort Sumter, a fine gentleman and a superb officer, came up soon after the explosion. He was dressed in a new uniform, and looked like a game cock. He surveyed the scene for a few minutes; he disappeared and in a short time he came up to me accompanied by Colonel A. R. Smith, of the Twenty-sixth, with a few men, who were working their way through the crowd. He said to me: "Colonel, I'm going to charge those Yankees out of the "Crater;" you follow Smith with your regiment."

He immediately climbed the counterscrape. The gallant Smith followed, and about half a dozen men followed. And in less than five minutes he was shot from the "Crater" through his shoulder. I believe it was the first ball shot that day from the northern side of the "Crater." He was immediately pulled down into the ditch, and with the utmost coolness, and no exhibition of pain turned the command over to me, the next ranking officer. Colonels Benbow and Wallace were both absent on furlough.

I immediately ordered John Phillips, a brave soldier of Com-
any I, to go around the "Crater" to inform the commanding
fficer of the serious wounding of General Elliott, and to
nquire as to the condition of the brigade on the south side.
Major Shield replied that Colonel Fleming and Adjutant
Inattlebaum, with more than half the Twenty-second, were
uried up, but with the remainder of his men and with the
Twenty-third, under Captain White, and a part of Wise's
rigade we had driven the Yankees back, and intended to keep
hem back.

Being satisfied that the object of the mine was to make a
gap in our line by which General Meade could rush his troops
to the rear, I ordered Colonel Smith to take his Regiment, and
Captain Crawford with three of my largest Companies, Com-
anies K, E and B, containing nearly as many men as Smith's,
to proceed by Elliott's headquarters up the ravine to a place
immediately in rear of the "Crater"—to make the men lie
down—and if the enemy attempted to rush down to resist them
to the last extremity. This was near 6 o'clock A. M., and
the enemy had not made any advace on the North side of the
"Crater."

By this time the "Crater" was packed with men. I counted
fourteen beautiful banners. I saw four or five officers waiving
words and pointing towards Petersburg, and I supposed they
were preparing for a charge to the crest of the hill.

ELLIOTT'S BRIGADE.

The line and strength of the Brigade from left to right was
as follows: Twenty-sixth Regiment, two hundred and fifty
men; Seventeenth, four hundred; Eighteenth, three hundred
and fifty; Twenty-second, three hundred; Twenty-third, two
hundred. In all one thousand and five hundred men, a full
estimate.

BENBOW'S REGIMENT.

The first severe attack of the enemy was on the South of
the "Crater," which was defended by a part of the Twenty-
second under Major Shedd, and Benbow's Twenty-third under
Captain White. The enemy attacked with fury. Our men
fought nobly, but were driven down their ditch. Wise's
brigade then joined in, and our men rushed back and recovered the lost space. About this time they shot Colonel Wright,

leading the Thirteenth Minnesota regiment, and then the
Federals slacked their efforts and bore to their right, and mul-
titudes of them climbed the "Crater" and went to the rear of
it and filled the gorge line and every vacant space on the
North side.   No serious aggressive attack was made on the
Twenty-third Regiment during the rest of the day.   The
principal reason I suppose was the direct line to Cemetery Hill
was through the Seventeenth Regiment.   Every Federal officer was directed over and over again to rush to the crest of
the hill.

SEVENTEENTH REGIMENT.

The Federals being checked on the South of the "Crater"
charged Company A, the extreme right Company, next to
the "Crater."   Captain W. H. Edwards was absent sick, and
a few of the men were covered with dirt by the explosion and
were consequently demoralized.   Private Hoke was ordered to
surrender—declared he never would surrender to a Yankee.
He clubbed his musket and knocked down four of his assailants, and was bayoneted.   There were five men killed in
Company A.   Company F was the next attacked, and private
John Caldwell shot one man and brained two with the butt of
his musket.   Lieutenant Samuel Lowry, a fine young man of
twenty years, and four privates were killed.   Company D
surrendered in a traverse, and twenty-seven men were killed.
Had the splendid Lieutenant W. G. Stevenson been present
the result would have been different.   Fourteen out of twenty-
seven of these men died in prison of scurvy at Elmira, N. Y.
Private J. S. Hogan, of Company D, leaped the traverse.   He
joined in Mahone's charge, and after the fight was sickened
by the carnage; went to the spring to revive himself, then
went into the charge under General Sanders.   After the battle
he procured enough coffee and sugar to last him a month.
This young rebel seemed to have a furor for fighting and
robbing Yankees.   At the battle of Fort Steadman he manned
a cannon which was turned on the enemy, and in the retreat
from Petersburg he was in every battle.   He was always on
the picket line, by choice, where he could kill, wound or capture the enemy.   He feasted well while the other soldiers fed
on parched corn, and surrendered at **Appomattox** with his
haversack filled with provisions.

Company C, the next Company, had fourteen men killed. Its Captain, William Dunovant, was only eighteen years of age, and as fine a Captain as was in Lee's Army. Lieutenant C. Pratt, a fine officer not more than twenty-five years old, was killed. The command devolved on Sergeant T. J. La-Motte. G and H had two each; I, three; K, five; and B, one; F, five.

The Federals had the advantage over the Seventeenth because there were some elevated points near the "Crater" they could shoot from. After being driven down about fifty yards there was an angle in the ditch, and Sergeant LaMotte built a barricade, which stopped the advance. A good part of the fighting was done by two men on each side at a time—the rest being cut off from view.

LOOKING AFTER SMITH'S MEN.

About 6:30 I went down a narrow ditch to see if Smith and his men were properly located to keep the enemy from going down to the ravine before I got back. I saw there was a vacant space in our trench. I hustled in and saw two muskets poked around an angle, as I got in the muskets were fired and harmlessly imbedded the balls in the breastworks. I immediately concluded that it was not very safe for the commander being on the extreme right of his men and went lower down. In a short time I again went in a ditch a little lower down the hill, anxious about the weak point on our line. I was smoking a pipe with a long tie-tie stem. As I returned I observed a rush down the line. As I got in the ditch the bowl of the pipe was knocked off. A big brawny fellow cried out, "Hold on men! the Colonel can't fight without his pipe!" He wheeled around, stopped the men until he picked up the bowl and restored it to me. I wish I knew the name of this kind-hearted old soldier.

The principal fighting was done by the head of the column. A few game fellows attempted to cross the breastworks. A Captain Sims and a negro officer were bayoneted close together on our breastworks, but hundreds of the enemy for hours stuck like glue to our outer bank.

A LONG AND LAZY FIGHT.

The sun was oppressively hot. There was very little musketry, the cannonading had closed; it was after 7 o'clock, and the soldiers on both sides, as there was not much shooting going on, seemed to resort to devices to pass the time. I saw Captain Steele throwing bayonets over a traverse. I saw Lamotte on one knee on the ground, and asked what he was doing. He whispered, "I'm trying to get the drop on a fellow on the other side." They would throw clods of clay at each other over the bank. As an Irishman threw over a lump of clay I heard him say, "Tak thart, Johnny." We all wished that Beauregard had supplied us with hand grenades, for the battle had simmered down to a little row in the trenches.

THE BATTLE THAT CONQUERED MEADE.

At 8.10 A. M. Ferrero's four thousand three hundred negroes rushed over and reached the right flank of the Seventeenth. This horde of barbarians added greatly to the thousands of white men that packed themselves to the safe side of the breastworks. Thousands rushed down the hill side. Ransom's Twenty-sixth and Twenty-fifth Regiments were crazy to get hold of the negroes. "Niggers" had been scarce around there during the morning, now they were packed in an acre of ground and in close range. The firing was great all down the hill side, but when it got down to the branch the musketry was terrific, and Wright's Battery two hundred yards off poured in its shells. About half past 8 o'clock, at the height of the battle, there was a landslide amongst the negroes. Colonel Carr says two thousand negroes rushed back and lifted him from his feet and swept him to the rear. General Delavan Bates, who was shot through the face, said at that time that Ransom's Brigade was reported to occupy those lines.

When the battle was at its highest the Seventeenth was forced down its line about thirty yards. Lieutenant Colonel Fleming, of Ransom's Forty-ninth Regiment, came up to me and pointed out a good place to build another barricade. I requested him to build it with his own men, as mine were almost exhausted by the labors of the day. He cheerfully assented, stepped on a banquette to get around me, and was shot in the neck and dropped at my feet.

At this moment of time an aide of General Bushrod Johnson told me that the General requested me to come out to Elliott's headquarters. I immediately proceeded to the place, and

General Mahone came up. I was introduced to him, and suggested to him when his men came in to form them on Smith's men who were lying down in the ravine. A few minutes afterwards, by order of General Johnson, Captain Steele brought out the remnant of the Seventeenth Regiment, and they marched in the ravine back of Mahone's men.

MAHONE'S CHARGE.

By this time General Mahone's Brigade of Virginians, eight hundred men strong, was coming in one by one, and were formed a few steps to the left and a little in advance of Smith's and Crawford's men. I was standing with General Johnson, close to Elliott's headquarters, and could see everything that transpired in the ravine. It took Mahone so long to arrange his men I was apprehensive that the enemy would make a charge before he was ready. A few Federal officers began to climb out of the main ditch until they numbered perhaps twenty-five men. General Mahone was on the extreme right; it seemed to me busy with some men—I have heard since they were some Georgians. Captain Girardey had gone to Colonel Weisinger, who was worried with the delay, and told him General Mahone was anxious to take some of the Georgians with him. But the threatening attitude of the enemy precipitated the charge.

The noble old Roman, Colonel Weisinger, cried out "Forward!" and eight hundred brave Virginians sprung to their feet and rushed two hundred yards up the hill. It had not the precision of a West Point drill, but it exhibited the pluck of Grecians at Thermopylae. The men disappeared irregularly as they reached the numerous ditches that led to the main ditch until all were hid from view. The firing was not very great for the bayonet and butt of the muskets did more damage than the barrel. If any one desires a graphic description of a hand to hand fight I beg him to read the graphic detailed account given by Mr. Bernard in his "War Talks of Confederate Veterans."

In a few minutes the enemy in the ditches up to fifty yards of the "Crater" were killed or captured. The whole battlefield of three acres of ground became suddenly quiet comparatively.

Mahone in an hour's time sent in the Georgia Brigade, under

26

General Wright.   There was such a heavy fire from the
"Crater" the brigade was forced to oblique to the left and
banked on Mahone's men.   In a few minutes after they landed
at the foot of the "Crater" in their second charge.

Sanders' Alabama Brigade came up at this time.   Besides
his Alabamians were Elliott's Brigade and Clingman's Sixty-
first North Carolina.   The charge was made about one o'clock
P. M., and the Federal artillery poured all its fire on the
"Crater" for some minutes, slaughtering many of their own
men.   At this charge Lieutenant Colonel Culp, who was absent
at the explosion, being a member of a courtmartial, came up
and took charge of the Seventeenth in the ravine, where Captain
Steele had them.   In the charge of the "Crater" under Sanders
were Colonel Culp, Colonel Smith and Lieutenant Colonel
J. H. Hudson with the Twenty-sixth, and a large number of
privates, especially from the Seventeenth Regiment, which also
had a good many in Mahone's charge.

A good many of the Twenty-third joined in the charge, and
Private W. H. Dunlap, Company C, Twenty-third Regiment,
now of Columbia, was the first man who got in the "Crater"
on the south side.

While the men were piled up around the "Crater" Adjutant
Fant heard some Alabama soldiers picking out the fine banners
within, and he was lucky to get two of them.   He laid them
down, and in a minute they were spirited away.

A little incident recited by Honorable George Clark Sanders,
Adjutant General, illustrates how true politeness smoothes the
wrinkled brow of war.   He says that he saw a fine looking
Federal officer making his way out of the "Crater" with much
pain, using two reversed muskets for crutches, seeing one leg
was shot off.   He said I'm very sorry to see you in so much
pain.   The soldier replied the pain occurred at Spottsylvania a
year ago.   This is a wooden leg shot off to-day—then gave his
name as General Bartlett, but Colonel Sanders kindly helped
him out.

The horrors of war are sometimes relieved with incidents
which amuse us.   Adjutant Fant tells an amusing incident of
Joe Free, a member of Company B.   The Adjutant had gone
in the afternoon to the wagon yard to be refreshed after the
labors of the day.   There was a group of men reciting incidents.   The Adjutant overheard Free say he had gone into an

officer's den for a few minutes to shade his head from the heat
of the sun, as he was suffering from an intense headache, and
as he began to creep out he saw the trench full of negroes. He
dodged back again. Joe says he was scared almost to death,
and that he "prayed until great drops of sweat poured down
my face." The Adjutant knew that his education was defec-
tive and said, "What did you say, Joe?" "I said Lord have
mercy on me! and keep them damned niggers from killing
me !"

It was an earnest and effective prayer, for Mahone's men in
an hour afterwards released him.

In a recent letter received from Captain E. A. Crawford, he
says the enemy formed three times to charge, but we gave them
a well directed volley each time and sent them into the rear
line in our trench. When Mahone came in and formed my
three companies charged with him. Colonel Smith told me
they charged four times. Cusack Moore, a very intelligent
private of Company K, said they charged five times. After
the charge Captain Crawford requested General Mahone to
give him permission to report to his regiment, and he ordered
him to report to General Sanders, and he joined in that charge
with his men. Company K had fifty-three men, Captain
Cherry; Company E, forty, and Captain Burley, Company B,
twenty-five; in all, one hundred and eighteen men.

Lieutenant Colonel Culp was a member of a military court
doing duty in Petersburg at the time of the explosion, and
could not get back until he reported to me at Elliott's headquarters. I made some extracts from his letter recently received: "I recollect well that in the charge (the final one)
which we made that model soldier and Christian gentleman,
Sergeant Williams, of Company K, was killed, and that one of
the Crowders, of Company B, was killed in elbow touch of me
after we got into the works. These casualties, I think, well
established the fact that Companies K and B were with me in
the charge, and, as far as I know now, at least a portion of all
the companies were with me. I recollect that poor Fant was
with us very distinctly, and that he rendered very efficient
service after we got to the "Crater" in ferreting out hidden
Federals, who had taken shelter there, and who, for the most
part, seemed very loath to leave their hiding places. I feel
quite confident that Capt. Crawford was also there, but there

is nothing that I can recall at this late day to fasten the fact of his presence on my mind, except that he was always ready for duty, however perilous it might be, and I am sure his company was there, in part at least. So, too, this will apply to all of the officers of our regiment whose duty it was to be there on that occasion, and who were not unavoidably kept away. In the charge that we made we were to be supported by the Sixty-first North Carolina. They were on our left, and I suppose entered the works entirely to the left of the "Crater," for I am sure that our regiment, small as it was, covered the "Crater," and when I reached the old line with my command we found ourselves in the very midst of the old fort, which, I may say, had been blown to atoms in the early morning. When we arrived the Federals began, in some instances, to surrender to us voluntarily, others, as before intimated, had to be pulled out of their hiding places. And with these prisoners we captured quite a number of colors, probably as many as a dozen, certainly not less than eight or ten. I was so occupied in trying to clear the trenches of the enemy that I gave no attention to these colors after they fell into the hands of our men, and afterwards learned, to my sorrow, that they had fallen into hands which were not entitled to them. Suffice it to say that few, if any of them, could be found. After perfect quiet had been restored, and we were thus robbed of these significant trophies of our triumph at which we felt quite a keen disappointment, it is pleasing to me to say that I think that every man of our regiment who was present acted his part nobly in the performance of the hazardous duty assigned us on that memorable occasion. * * * You gave me the order to make the final charge already referred to."

THE ARTILLERY.

The Confederates only had twenty-six cannon, and only three of them were conspicuous. The Federals had one hundred and sixty-four cannon and mortars. They fired five thousand and seventy-five rounds. They had only one man killed and two wounded.

General Hunt and others spoke slightingly of our guns, with two exceptions, Wright's Battery and Davenport's, which is mentioned as the two-gun battery. General Hunt the day before had accurately prepared to silence all these guns, except the Davenport Battery. General Hunt said he expected a company of infantry would take us in fifteen minutes after Pegram's Battery was gone. But the Wright Battery was a complete surprise. It was constructed just behind Ransom's Brigade, about one hundred yards. General Hunt never could locate the place, and shot at short range above five hundred shells doing no damage, but honeycombing the surrounding ground.

Wright's Battery was in five hundred yards of the "Crater," and Colonel Coit informed me he shot about six hundred rounds of shell and shrapnel at short range.

In my opinion it did more damage than all our guns put together. Its concealed location gave it a great advantage over all other guns.

Davidson's Battery had only one gun, which only could shoot in one line. But it created more anxiety amongst the enemy than any other. The infantry officers constantly alluded to its destructive power, and they dug a trench to guard against its fire. Major Hampton Gibbes commanded it until he was wounded, and then Captain D. N. Walker for the rest of the day did his duty nobly, and no doubt killed many Federals. General Warren was ordered to capture this gun about 8.30, but at 8.45 he was ordered to do nothing "but reconnoitre." This was before Mahone came up.

The most interesting of our guns were the two coehorns of Major John C. Haskell, because all of his shells were emptied into the "Crater," which was packed with men. General Mahone says: "In the meantime Colonel Haskell, a brilliant officer of our artillery, hunting a place where he could strike a blow at our adversary, presented himself for any service which I could advise. There were two coehorn mortars in the depression already referred to, and I suggested to him that he could serve them. I would have them taken up to the outside of the "Crater," at which place he could employ himself until one o'clock, as perhaps no such opportunity had ever occurred or would be likely to occur for effective employment of these little implements of war. Colonel Haskell adopted the suggestion, and the mortars being removed to a ditch within a few feet of the "Crater," they were quickly at work emptying *their contents upon the crowded mass of men in this horrible pit."*

Lieutenant Bowley, a Federal officer, says: "A mortar battery also opened on us. After a few shots they got our range so well that the shells fell directly among us. Many of them did not explode at all, but a few burst directly over us and cut the men down cruelly." He also speaks of a few Indians from Michigan. "Some of them were mortally wounded, and, drawing their blouses over their faces, they chanted a death song and died—four of them in a group."

A FEAST AFTER A FAMINE.

About 3 o'clock p. m. absolute quietness prevailed over the battlefield where the carnage of war rioted a few hours before. My Orderly, M. C. Heath, a boy of sixteen, who now is a distinguished physician of Lexington, Ky., came to me at Elliott's headquarters and told me that the Lieutenant Colonel and Adjutant sent their compliments and requested me to come to dinner at my den in the trench. I went, and had to step over the dead bodies—all negroes. A narrow ditch led to a plaza six feet square, where a half dozen men, in fine weather, could sit on campstools. On the breastworks hung a dead negro. In the ditch I had to step over another dead negro. As I got to my plaza I saw two more negroes badly wounded in a cell two feet deeper than the plaza where I slept. One of the negroes was resting his bloody head on a fine copy of Paley's philosophy, which I came across in my wanderings. Heath's big basket was well stored with good viands, and we ate with the ferocity of starving men, regaling ourselves with the incidents of battle, without any expressions of sorrow for our friends, Colonel David Fleming and Adjutant Quattlebaum, who a few yards above were entombed in our old sleeping place in the "Crater" which we occupied as our quarters until they succeeded us ten days before, or any lamentations for the hundreds of dead and dying on the hillside around.

The joy of the glorious victory drowned out all sentiments of grief for a season, and it seemed a weird holiday.

A BLUNDER IN BEAUREGARD'S BOOK.

Mr. Barnard, in his interesting article on the "Crater," criticises a remarkable paragraph in Colonel Roman's work, "basing his statements made by General Bushrod Johnson and Colonel McMaster." The only objection to my statement was I said Mahone's charge was at 10 o'clock a. m.

The paragraph is as follows:

"Such was the situation.. The Federals unable to advance and fearing to retreat, when, at 10 o'clock, General Mahone arrived with a part of his men, who had laid down in the shallow ravine to the rear of Elliott's salient held by the forces under Colonel Smith, there to await the remainder of the Division, but a movement having occurred among the Federals, which seemed to menace an advance, General Mahone then forwarded his Brigade with the Sixty-first North Carolina, of Hoke's Division, which had now also come up. The Twenty-fifth and Forty-ninth North Carolina, and the Seventeenth South Carolina, all under Smith, which were formed on Mahone's left, likewise formed in the "Crater" movement, and three-fourths of the gorge line was carried with that part of the trench on the left of the "Crater" occupied by the Federals. Many of the latter, white and black, abandoned the breach and fled under a scourging flank fire of Wise's Brigade."

This is confusion worse confounded. It is difficult to find a paragraph containing so many blunders as the report of General Johnson to Colonel Roman.

The Sixty-first North Carolina of Hoke's Brigade was not present during the day, except at Sander's charge two hours afterwards. The Twenty-fifth and Forty-ninth North Carolina were not present at all, but remained in their trench on the front line.

Smith's men on the extreme right did not as a body go into Mahone's charge. Captain Crawford with one hundred and eighteen men did charge with Mahone. In fact he commanded his own men separate from Smith, although he was close by.

Colonel Roman's account taken from General Johnson's statement is unintelligible.

TIME OF MAHONE'S CHARGE.

I dislike to differ with Mr. Bernard, who has been so courteous to me, and with my friend, Colonel Venable, for we literally carried muskets side by side as privates in dear old Captain Casson's company, the Governor's Guards, in Colonel Kershaw's Regiment, at the first battle of Manassas, and I shot thirteen times at Ellsworth's Zouaves. Venable was knocked down with a spent ball and I only had a bloody mouth. And

the rainy night which followed the battle we sheltered ourselves under the same oilcloth. But I can't help thinking of
these gentlemen as being like all Virginians, which is illus-
trated by a remark of a great Massachusetts man, old John
Adams, in answering some opponent, said: "Virginians
are all fine fellows. The only objection I have to you is, in
Virginia every goose is a swan."

Colonel Venable says: "I am confident the charge of the
Virginians [was made before 9 o'clock a. m." Mr. Bernard
says, in speaking of the time: "Mahone's Brigade left the
plank road and took to the covered way." "It is now half-
past 8 o'clock." In a note he says: "Probably between 8.15
and 8.30." "At the angle where the enemy could see a moving column with ease the men were ordered to run quickly by,
one man at a time, which was done for the double purpose of
concealing the approach of a body of troops and of lessening
the danger of passing rifle balls at these points."

It took Mahone's Brigade, above eight hundred men, to
walk at least five hundred yards down this covered way and
gulch, one by one, occassionally interrupted by wounded men
going to the rear, at least twenty minutes. At a very low
estimate it took them half an hour to form in the ravine, to
listen to two short speeches, and the parley between Weisinger
and Girardey. With the most liberal allowance this will bring
the charge at 9.15 A. M., but it took more time than that.

Captain Whitner investigated the time of the charge in less
than a month after the battle. I extract the following, page
795, 40th "War of Rebellion:" "There is a great diversity of
opinion as to the time the first charge was made by General
Mahone * * * But one officer of the division spoke with certainty, Colonel McMaster, Seventeenth South Carolina Volunteers. His written statement is enclosed." Unluckily the paper
was "not found." But there is no doubt I repeatedly said it
was about ten o'clock A. M.

General Mahone took no note of the time, but says: "According to the records the charge must have been before nine
o'clock. General Burnside in his report fixes the time of the
charge and recapture of our works at 8.45 A. M." 40th "War
of Rebellion," page 528. He is badly mistaken. General
Burnside says: "The enemy regained a portion of his line on
'he right. This was about 8.45 A. M., but not all the colored

James Evans,
    Major and Surgeon,
        3d S. C. Regiment. (Page 564.)

Capt. D. A. Dickert,
    Co. H, 3d S. C. Regiment.
        (Age 15 years when he first
            entered service.)

Capt. L. P. Foster,
    Co. K, 3d S. C. Regiment.
        (Page 192.)

J. E. Tuesdale,
    Co. G, 2d S. C. Regiment.

troops retired. Some held pits from behind which they had
advanced severely checking the enemy until they were nearly
all killed."

"At 9.15 I received, with regret, a peremptory order from
the General commanding to withdraw my troops from the
enemy's lines."

Now this battle indicated as at 8.45 was a continuation
of the one that many officers said was about half-past eight
o'clock. And both Mahone and Mr. Bernard were mistaken
in stating that the great firing and retreat of soldiers was the
result of the Virginian's charge, whereas at this time Mahone's
Brigade was at the Jerusalem plank road. Moreover, when
Mahone did come up his eight hundred men could not create
one-fourth of the reverberation of the Seventeenth Regiment,
Ransom's Brigade, and the thousands of the enemy. Besides
Mahone's men's fighting was confined to the ditches, and they
used mostly the butts and bayonets instead of the barrels of
their muskets. No it was the fire of Elliott's men, Ransom's
men, the torrent of shells of Wright's Battery and the enemy,
Ord's men, and the four thousand negroes, all of them in an
area of one hundred yards. The part of the line spoken of by
Generals Delavan Bates and Turner and others as the Confederate line were mere rifles pits which the Confederates held
until they had perfected the main line, and then gave up the
pits. They were in the hollow, where the branch passes
through to the breastworks.

Now the tumultuous outburst of musketry. Federal and
Confederate, and the landslide of the Federals, was beyond
doubt before I went out to Elliott's headquarters on the order
of General Johnson.

For two hours before this Meade had been urging Burnside
to rush to the crest of the hill until General B. was irritated
beyond measure, and replied to a dispatch: "Were it not insubordination I would say that the latter remark was unofficer
like and ungentlemanly." Before this time Grant, Meade and
Ord had given up hope. They had agreed to withdraw, hence
the positive order "to withdraw my troops from the enemy's
line at 9.15.

Now this must have been before Mahone came up, for there
is *no allusion to a charge* by any Federal General at the court
of inquiry. With the 8.30 charge made at the hollow, there

was a synchronous movement made by General Warren on the south of the "Crater," but at 8.45 he was informed that it was intended alone for a reconnoissance of the two-gun battery.

At 9.15 General Warren sends dispatch: "Just before receiving your dispatch to assault the battery on the left of the "Crater" occupied by General Burnside the enemy drove his troops out of the place and I think now hold it. I can find no one who for certainty knows, or seems willing to admit, but I think I saw a Rebel flag in it just now, and shots coming from it this way. I am, therefore, if this (be) true no more able to take this battery now than I was this time yesterday. All our advantages are lost."

The advantages certainly were not lost on account of Mahone's men, but on account of the losses two hundred yards down the hill, of which he had doubtless been advised. He saw what he thought was a "Rebel flag," but for a half an hour he had heard of the terrific castigation inflicted on the Federals down the hill.

But here is something from the court of inquiry that approximates the time of Mahone's charge.

General Griffen, of Potter's Ninth Corps, in reply to the question by the court: "When the troops retired from the "Crater" was it compulsory from the enemy's operations, or by orders from your commanders?" Answer. "Partly both. We retired because we had orders. At the same time a column of troops came up to attack the 'Crater,' and we retired instead of stopping to fight. This force of the enemy came out of a ravine, and we did not see them till they appeared on the rising ground."

"What was the force that came out to attack you? The force that was exposed in the open?" Answer. "five or six hundred soldiers were all that we could see. I did not see either the right or left of the line. I saw the center of the line as it appeared to me. It was a good line of battle. Probably if we had not been under orders to evacuate we should have fought them, and tried to hold our position, but according to the orders we withdrew."

General Hartranft, of Ninth Corps, says in answer to the question "Driven out?" "They were driven out the same time, the same time I had passed the word to retire. It was a simultaneous thing. When they saw the assaulting column within probably one hundred feet of the works I passed the word as well as it could be passed for everybody to retire. And I left myself at that time. General Griffen and myself were together at that time. The order to retire we had endorsed to the effect that we thought we could not withdraw the troops that were there on account of the enfilading fire over the ground between our rifle pits and the "Crater" without losing a great portion of them, that ground being enfiladed with artillery and infantry fire. They had at that time brought their infantry down along their pits on both sides of the "Crater," so that their sharpshooters had good range, and were in good position. Accordingly we requested that our lines should open with artillery and infantry, bearing on the right and left of the "Crater," under which fire we would be able to withdraw a greater portion of our troops, and, in fact, everyone that could get away. While we were in waiting for the approach of that endorsement and the opening of the fire, this assaulting column of the enemy came up and we concluded— General Griffin and myself—that there was no use in holding it any longer, and so we retired."

This proves beyond doubt that Mahone's charge was after 9.15. It probably took Burnside some minutes to receive this order and some minutes for him and Griffin to send it down the line, and to send orders to the artillery to open on their flanks to protect them. This would bring Mahone's charge to 9.30 or 9.45.

SMITH AND CRAWFORD SAVE PETERSBURG.

I ordered Smith to take his regiment, the Twenty-sixth, and Crawford with Companies K, E, and B, to lie down in the ravine. Every General was ordered to charge to the crest. Had the enemy gotten beyond Smith's line fifty yards they could have marched in the covered way to Petersburg; not a cannon or a gun intervened. General Potter says his men charged two hundred yards beyond the "Crater," when they were driven back. Colonel Thomas said he led a charge which was not successful; he went three or four hundred yards and was driven back. General Griffin says he went about two hundred yards and was driven back. Colonel Russell says he went about fifty yards towards Cemetery Hill and "was driven back by two to four hundred infantry, which rose up from a little ravine and charged us." Some officer said he went five hundred yards beyond the "Crater." There was the greatest confusion about distances. General Russell is about right when he said he went about fifty yards behind the "Crater." When they talk of two or three hundred yards they must mean outside the breastworks towards Ransom's Brigade.

From the character of our breastworks, or rather our cross ditches, it was impracticable to charge down the rear of our breastworks. The only chance of reaching Petersburg was through the "Crater" to the rear. Smith and Crawford, whose combined commands did not exceed two hundred and fifty men, forced them back. Had either Potter, Russell, Thomas, or Griffin charged down one hundred yards farther than they did, the great victory would have been won, and Beauregard and Lee would have been deprived of the great honor of being victors of the great battle of the "Crater."

ELLIOTT'S BRIGADE.

After the explosion, with less than one thousand two hundred men, and with the co-operation of Wright's Battery and Davenport's Battery, and a few men of Wise's Brigade, resisted nine thousand of the enemy from five to eight o'clock. Then four thousand five hundred blacks rushed over, and the Forty-ninth and Twenty-fifth North Carolina, Elliott's Brigade, welcomed them to hospitable graves at 9 o'clock A. M.

At about 9.30 A. M. old Virginia—that never tires in good works—with eight hundred heroes rushed into the trench of the Seventeenth and slaughtered hundreds of whites and blacks, with decided preference for the Ethiopeans.

Captain Geo. B. Lake, of Company B, Twenty-second South Carolina, who was himself buried beneath the debris, and afterwards captured, gives a graphic description of his experience and the scenes around the famous "Crater." He says in a newspaper article:

BY CAPTAIN GEORGE B. LAKE.

The evening before the mine was sprung, or possibly two evenings before, Colonel David Fleming, in command of the Twenty-second South Carolina Regiment—I don't know whether by command of General Stephen Elliott or not—ordered me to move my company, Company B, Twenty-second South Carolina, into the rear line, immediately in rear of Pegram's four guns. I had in my company one officer, Lieutenant W. J. Lake, of Newberry, S. C., and thirty-four enlisted men. This rear line was so constructed that I could fire over Pegram's men on the attacking enemy.

The enemy in our front had two lines of works. He had more men in his line nearest our works than we had in his front. From this nearest line he tunnelled to and under Pegram's salient, and deposited in a magazine prepared for it not less than four tons of powder, some of their officers say it was six tons. We knew the enemy were mining, and we sunk a shaft on each side of the four-gun battery, ten feet or more deep, and then extended the tunnel some distance to our front. We were on a high hill, however, and the enemy five hundred and ten feet in our front, where they began their work, consequently their mine was far under the shaft we sunk. At night when everything was still, we could hear the enemy's miners at work. While war means kill, the idea of being blown into eternity without any warning was anything but pleasant.

THAT TERRIBLE SATURDAY MORNING.

On that terrible Saturday morning, July 30, 1864, before day had yet dawned, after the enemy had massed a large number of troops in front of our guns, the fuse which was to ignite the mine was fired. The enemy waited fully an hour, but there was one explanation, the fuse had gone out. A brave Federal officer, whose name I do not know, volunteered to enter the tunnel and fire it again, which he did.

A minute later there was a report which was heard for miles, and the earth trembled for miles around. A "Crater" a hundred and thirty feet long, ninety-seven feet in breadth, thirty feet deep, was blown out. Of the brave artillery company, twenty-two officers and men were killed and wounded, most of them killed. Hundreds of tons of earth thrown back on the rear line, in which my command

A WHOLE COMPANY BURIED.

was the greatest loss suffered by any command on either side in the war, myself, my only Lieutenant, W. J.

Lake, and thirty-four enlisted men were all buried, and of
that little band thirty-one were killed. Lieutenant Lake and
myself and three enlisted men were taken out of the ground
two hours after the explosion by some brave New Yorkers.
These men worked like beavers, a portion of the time under
perpetual fire.

BURIED THIRTY FEET DEEP.

Colonel Dave Fleming and his Adjutant, Dick Quattlebaum,
were also in the rear line, only a few feet to my left, and were
buried thirty feet deep; their bodies are still there. I do not
know how many of the Federal troops stormed the works, but
I do know the Confederates captured from them nineteen flags.
The attacking columns were composed of white men and
negroes; sober men and men who were drunk; brave men and
cowards.

One of the latter was an officer high in command. I have
lost his name, if I ever knew it. He asked me how many
lines of works we had between the "Crater" and Petersburg,
when I replied, "Three." He asked me if they were all
manned. I said, "Yes." He then said, "Don't you know
that I know you are telling a d—d lie?" I said to him.
"Don't you know that I am not going to give you information
that will be of any service to you?" He then threatened to
have me shot, and I believe but that for the interference of a
Federal officer he would have done so.

DEATH TO ADVANCE AND DEATH TO RETREAT.

I had just seen several of our officers and men killed with
bayonets after they had surrendered, when the enemy, who
had gone through the "Crater" towards Petersburg, had been
repulsed, and fell back in the "Crater" for protection. There
was not room in the "Crater" for another man. It was death
to go forward or death to retreat to their own lines. It is said
there were three thousand Yankees in and around the
"Crater," besides those in portions of our works adjacent
thereto.

Then the Coshorn mortars of the brave Major Haskell and
other commanders of batteries turned loose their shells on the
"Crater." The firing was rapid and accurate. Some of these
mortars were brought up as near as fifty yards to the "Crater."

Such a scene has never before nor never will be witnessed again. The Yankees at the same time were using one hundred and forty pieces of cannon against our works occupied by Confederate troops.

Elliott's Brigade in the day's fight lost two hundred and seventy-eight officers and men. Major General B. R. Johnson's Division, Elliott's Brigade included, lost in the day, nine hundred and thirty-two officers and men. This was the most of the Confederate loss.

FEDERAL TOTAL LOSS OVER FIVE THOUSAND.

While the enemy acknowledged a loss of from five to six thousand men—and that I am sure is far below their real loss— I make another quotation from Major General B. R. Johnson's official report:

"It is believed that for each buried companion they have taken a tenfold vengeance on the enemy, and have taught them a lesson that will be remembered as long as the history of our wrongs and this great revolution endures."

Virginians, Georgians, North Carolinians, South Carolinians and others who may have fought at the "Crater," none of you have the right to claim deeds of more conspicuous daring over your Confederate brethren engaged that day. Every man acted well his part.

What about the four cannons blown up? you ask. One piece fell about half way between the opposing armies, another fell in front of our lines, not so near, however, to the enemy, a third was thrown from the carriage and was standing on end, half buried in the ground inside the "Crater," the fourth was still attached to the carriage, but turned bottom side up, the wheels in the air, and turned against our own men when the enemy captured it. That day, however, they all fell into the hands of the Confederates, except the one thrown so near the enemy's works, and in time we regained that also.

CAPTAIN LAKE A PRISONER.

Before the fighting was over the Yankee officer who could curse a prisoner so gallantly ordered two soldiers to take charge and carry me to their lines, no doubt believing that the Confederates would succeed in recapturing the "Crater." We had to cross a plain five hundred and ten feet wide that was being raked by rifle balls, cannon shot and shell, grape and canister. It was not a very inviting place to go, but still not a great deal worse than Haskell's mortar shells that were raining in the center. I had the pleasure of seeing one of my guards die. The other conducted me safely to General Patrick's head-quarters. Patrick was the Yankee provost marshall.

When I was placed under guard near his quarters he sent a staff officer to the front to learn the result of the battle.

After a short absence he galloped up to General Patrick and yelled out "We have whipped them !"

Patrick said: "I want no foolishness, sir !"

The staff officer then said: "General, if you want the truth, they have whipped us like hell.

CHAPTER XXXIV

Leaves the Trenches in the Shenandoah Valley.

To relieve the tension that oppressed both Richmond and Petersburg, General Lee determined to dispatch a force to the Valley to drive the enemy therefrom, to guard against a flank movement around the north and west of Richmond, and to threaten Washington with an invasion of the North. The Second Corps of the army was ordered Northwest. General Ewell being too enfeebled by age and wounds, had been re-lieved of his command in the field and placed in the command of Henrico County. This embraced Richmond and its defen-sive, the inner lines, which were guarded and manned by re-serves and State troops. General Early, now a Lieutenant General, was placed in command of the expedition. Why or what the particular reason a corps commander was thus placed in command of a department and a separate army, when there were full Generals occupying inferior positions, was never known. Unless we take it that Early was a Virginian, better informed on the typography of the country, and being better acquainted with her leading citizens, that he would find in them greater aid and assistance than would a stranger. The department had hopes of an uprising in the "Pan Handle" of

Maryland in recruits from all over the States. The prestige of Early's name might bring them out. Early was a brave and skillful General. Being a graduate of West Point, he was well versed in the tactical arts of war; was watchful and vigilant, and under a superior he was second to none as a commander. But his Valley campaign—whether from failures of the troops or subaltern officers, I cannot say—but results show that it was a failure. There could be no fault found with his plans, nor the rapidity of his movements, for his partial successes show what might have been accomplished if faithfully carried out. Still, on the whole, his campaign in the Valley was detrimental, rather than beneficial, to our cause. Early had already made a dash through the Valley and pushed his lines beyond the Potomac, while his cavalry had even penetrated the confines of Washington itself. It was said at the time, by both Northern and Southern military critics, that had he not wavered or faultered at the critical moment, he could have easily captured the city. No doubt his orders were different—that only a demonstration was intended—and had he attempted to exceed his orders and failed, he would have received and deserved the censure of the authorities. The bane of the South's civic government was that the Executive and his military advisors kept the commanders of armies too much under their own leading strings, and not allowing them enough latitude to be governed by circumstances—to ride in on the flow tide of success when an opportunity offered. But the greatest achievements, the greatest of victories, that history records are where Generals broke away from all precedent and took advantage of the success of the hour, that could not have been foreseen nor anticipated by those who were at a distance. Be that as it may, Early had gone his length, and now, the last of July, was retreating up the Valley.

Kershaw, with his division, was ordered to join him, and on the 6th of August the troops embarked at Chester Station and were transported to Mitchel Station, on the Richmond and Mannassas Railroad, not far from Culpepper. On the 12th the troops marched by Flint Hill, crossed the Blue Ridge, and camped near the ancient little hamlet of Front Royal. The next day we were moved about one mile distant to a large spring, near the banks of the beautiful and now classic Shenandoah. How strange to the troops of the far South to see

27

this large river running in the opposite direction from all our
accustomed ideas of the flow of rivers—that water seeks its
level and will therefore run South, or towards the coast.   But
here the stream rises in the south and runs due north towards
the Potomac.   After long and fatiguing marches, the soldiers
here enjoyed a luxury long since denied them on account of
their never ceasing activity.   The delight of a bath, and in
the pure, clear waters of the Shenandoah, was a luxury indeed.
On the 17th of August the march was again resumed, and we
reached Winchester, Va., on the next day.   Remaining two
days near the old city which had become so dear to the hearts
of all the old soldiers through the hospitality and kindness of
her truly loyal people, and being the place, too, of much of
our enjoyment and pleasure while camping near it two years
before, we left on the 21st, going in the direction of Charleston.

On nearing the latter place we found the enemy in force,
and had to push our way forward by heavy skirmishing.   When
within two miles of Charlestown, we halted and went into
camp, and threw our pickets beyond the town on the north.
On the 25th we moved through the city and took the Harper
Ferry Road, two miles beyond.   Here we took up camp, and
were in close proximity to the enemy, who lay in camp near
us.   A heavy skirmish line was thrown out about half a mile
in our front.   Lieutenant Colonel Maffett of the Third. but
commanding the Seventh, was deployed in a large old field as
support.   We were encamped in line of battle in a beautiful
grove overlooking and in full view of our skirmishers.

The enemy seemed to display little activity.   Now and then
a solitary horseman could be seen galloping away in the direction of his camp.

The want of alertness on the part of the enemy threw our
pickets off their guard.   Colonel Maffett was lounging under
the shade of a tree in the rear of the skirmish line, with a few
of the reserves, while those on the picket line lay at convenient
distances, some with their coats off, others lying under the
shade of trees or in the corners of a fence, all unconscious of
an approaching enemy.   The Federals had surveyed the field,
and seeing our pickets so lax, and in such bad order for defense, undertook to surprise them.   With a body of cavalry,
concealed by the forest in their front, they made their way,

under cover of a ravine, until within a short distance of the
unsuspecting pickets. Then, with a shout and a volley, they
dashed upon the line and over it, capturing nearly all, made
their way to the rear, and there captured Lieutenant Colonel
Maffett and many of his reserves.

Commotion struck our camp. Drums beat, men called to
arms, line of battle formed, and an advance at double-quick
was made through the old field, in the direction of our unfortunate friends. But all too late. The surprise had been complete and the captured prisoners had been hurried to the rear.
Colonel Maffett's horse, which was grazing near the scene of
the skirmish, galloped through the enemy's disorganized lines,
some trying to head him off, others to capture him, but he
galloped defiantly on to camp. The enemy amused themselves
by throwing a few shells into our lines.

The horse of Colonel Maffett was carried home by his faithful body servant, Harry, where both lived to a ripe old age.
Not so with the unfortunate master. Reared in the lap of
luxury, being an only son of a wealthy father and accustomed
to all the ease and comforts that wealth and affluence could
give, he could not endure the rigor and hardships of a Northern prison, his genial spirits gave way, his constitution and
health fouled him, and after many months of incarceration he
died of brain fever. But through it all he bore himself like a
true son of the South. He never complained, nor was his
proud spirit broken by imprisonment, but it chafed under confinement and forced obedience to prison rule and discipline.
The Confederacy lost no more patriotic, more self-sacrificing
soldier than Lieutenant Colonel Robert Clayton Maffett.

On the 27th we marched to Princeton, and remained until
the 31st, picketing on the Opequan River, then returned to
Charlestown. On the day before, the Third Regiment went
out on the Opequan, being in hearing of the church bells and
in sight of the spires of Washington. What an anomaly! The
Federals besieging the Confederate capital, and the Confederates in sight of Washington.

From Charlestown we were moved back to Winchester and
went into camp for a few days. So far Early's demonstration
had been a failure. Either to capture Washington or weaken
Grant, for day in and day out, he kept pegging away at Petersburg and the approaches to it and Richmond. These

seemed to be the objective points, and which eventually caused
the downfall of the two places.   The enemy in our front had
moved up to Berryville, a small hamlet about eight miles from
Winchester, and on the 30th of September we were ordered
out to attack the plan.   The Federals had fortified across the
turnpike and had batteries placed at every commanding point.
In front of this fortification was a large old field, through
which we had to advance.   The Brigade was formed in line of
battle in some timber at the edge of the opening and ordered
forward.   The frowning redoubts lined with cannon and their
formidable breastwork, behind which bristled the bright bayonets, were anything but objects to tempt the men as they advanced to the charge.   As soon as we entered the opening the
shells came plunging through our ranks, or digging up the
earth in front.   But the Brigade marched in good order, not a
shot being fired, the enemy all the while giving us volley after
volley.   The men began to clamor for a charge, so much so
that when we were about half way through the old field the
command came "charge."   Then a yell and a rush, each man
carrying his gun in the most convenient position, and doing all
in his power to reach the work first.   The angle in front of
the Third was nearer than the line in front of the other Regiments.   Just before we reached the works the enemy fled to a
grove in rear under an incline and began firing on our troops,
who had now reached the work and began to fire from the
opposite side.   The firing in this way became general all along
the line.   The Artillery had withdrawn to the heights in rear
and opened upon us a tremendous fire at short range.   The
enemy could be seen from our elevated position moving around
our right through a thicket of pines, and some one called out
to the troops immediately on the right of the Third Regiment,
"The enemy are flanking us."   This caused a momentary
panic, and some of the Brigade left the captured work and
began running to the rear.   Colonel Rutherford ordered some
of his officers to go down the line and get the demoralized
troops to return to the ranks, which was accomplished without
much delay.

The enemy in front began slackening their fire, which
caused some of the men to leap over the works and advance to
the brow of a hill just in front of us to get a better view.   The
enemy rallied and began pouring a heavy fire into the bold

spirits who had advanced beyond the lines, wounding quite a number. General Kershaw, with a brigade of the division, crossed over the turn-pike and began a counter-move on the enemy's right, which caused such panic, that in a few minutes their whole line withdrew beyond the little town. Acting Assistant General Pope, on the brigade staff, received a painful wound in the cheek, but outside of a sprinkling throughout the brigade of wounded, our loss was slight.

That night the enemy was reinforced, and about 9 o'clock next day there was a general advance. The enemy had changed his direction, and now was approaching parallel to the turn-pike. I was in command of the brigade skirmishers during the night, posted in a large old field on left of the turn-pike. Just as a detail, commanded by an officer of the Twentieth, came to relieve me, the enemy was seen advancing through a forest beyond the old field. The officer, not being familiar with the skirmish tactics, and never being on a skirmish line during action before, asked me to retain the command and also my line of skirmishers and conduct the retreat, which I did. The brigade at that time was on the retreat, and this double skirmish line covered and protected the rear. If there is any sport or amusement at all in battle, it is while on skirmish line, when the enemy is pressing you. On a skirmish line, usually, the men are posted about ten paces apart and several hundred yards in front of the main line of battle, to receive or give the first shock of battle. In our case the line was doubled, making it very strong, as strong, in fact, as some of the lines of General Lee's at that time holding Petersburg. When the enemy's skirmishers struck the opening our line opened upon them, driving them helter-skelter back into the woods. I ordered an advance, as the orders were to hold the enemy in check as long as possible to give our main line and wagon train time to get out of the way. We kept up the fire as we advanced, until we came upon the enemy posted behind trees; then, in our turn, gave way into the opening. Then the enemy advanced, so forward and backward the two lines advanced and receded, until by the support of the enemy's line of battle we were driven across the turn-pike, where we assembled and followed in rear of the brigade. There is nothing in this world that is more exciting, more nerve stirring to a soldier, than to participate in a battle line of skirmishers, when you have a fair field and open fight. There it takes nerve and pluck, however, it is allowed each skirmisher to take whatever protection he can in the way of tree or stump. Then on the advance you do not know when to expect an enemy to spring from behind a tree, stump, or bush, take aim and fire. It resembles somewhat the order of Indian warfare, for on a skirmish line "all is fair in war."

We returned without further molestation to the vicinity of Winchester, the enemy not feeling disposed to press us. It was never understood whose fault it was that a general engagement did not take place, for Early had marched and began the attack, and pressed the enemy from his first line of works, then the next day the enemy showed a bold front and was making every demonstration as if to attack us.

General Kershaw having been promoted to Major General, General James Connor was sent to command the brigade. He was formerly Colonel of the Twenty-second North Carolina Regiment, promoted to Brigadier, and commanded McGowan's Brigade after the battle of Spottsylvania Court House. After the return of General McGowan, he was assigned to the command of Laws' Brigade, and about the 6th or 7th of September reached us and relieved Colonel Henagan, of the Eighth, who had so faithfully led the old First Brigade since the battle of the Wilderness.

While in camp near Winchester, the Eighth Regiment, under Colonel Henagan, was sent out on picket on the Berryville road. In the morning before day General Sheridan, with a large force of cavalry, made a cautious advance and captured the videttes of the Eighth, which Colonel Henagan had posted in front. and passing between the regiment and the brigade, made a sudden dash upon their rear, capturing all of the regiment, with Colonel Henagan, except two companies commanded by the gallant Captain T. F. Malloy. These two companies had been thrown out on the right, and by tact and a bold front Captain Malloy saved these two companies and brought them safely into camp. The whole brigade mourned the loss of this gallant portion of their comrades. Colonel Henagan, like Colonel Maffett, sank under the ill treatment and neglect in a Northern prison and died there.

COL. J. W. HENAGAN.

Col. J. W. Henagan was born November 22nd, 1822, in Marlboro County, S. C. Was the son of E. L. Henagan and wife, Ann McInnis. His father was a Scotch-Irishman. His mother Scotch. Was educated at Academy in Bennettsville and Parnassus. Was elected Sheriff of Marlboro County in October, 1852, and went into office February, 1853. In 1860 was elected to the Legislature. Was re-elected to the Legislature in 1863.

Prior to the war was prominent in militia service, serving consecutively as Captain, Colonel and Brigadier General. In March, 1861, volunteered, and in April became Lieutenant Colonel of Eighth Regiment South Carolina Volunteers and went with the Regiment to Virginia. Was in battle of Bull Run or First Manassas. In 1862 he became by election Colonel of the Eighth South Carolina Volunteers and served in that capacity until his capture near Winchester in the fall of 1864 when he was sent a prisoner to Johnson's Island, Ohio. Here he died a prisoner of war, April 22, 1865.

No Regiment of the Confederacy saw harder service or was engaged in more battles than the Eighth South Carolina of Kershaw's Brigade and no officer of that Brigade bore himself with more conspicuous gallantry than Colonel Henagan. He was always at his post and ready to go forward when so ordered. There was little or no fear in him to move into battle, and he was always sure, during the thickest of the fight, cheering on his men to victory.

Colonel Henagan, as a citizen of the County, was as generous as brave. His purse was open to the needs of the poor. Did not know how or could not refuse the appeals to charity. He was the eldest son of a large family. When about twenty years old his father died and left on his shoulders the responsibility of maintaining and educating several younger brothers and sisters. He never swerved from this duty, but like the man that he was, did his work nobly. He was a dutiful son, a kind brother, a friend to all. He knew no deception, had no respect for the sycophant. Loved his country. A friend to be relied on. Was a farmer by profession. A good politician. Was a very quiet man, but always expressed his views firmly and candidly when called upon.

COLONEL ROBERT CLAYTON MAFFETT.

Colonel Robert Clayton Maffett was born in Newberry County, about the year 1836. Was the only son of Captain James Maffett, long time a member of the General Assembly of South Carolina. At the breaking out of the war Colonel Maffett was Colonel of the Thirty-ninth Regiment of State Militia. From this regiment two companies were formed in answer to the first call for volunteers. One of these companies elected him Captain, which afterwards became Company C, Third South Carolina Regiment. His company was one of the few that reorganized before the expiration of the term of the first twelve months' enlistment, and again elected Colonel Maffett as its Captain. After a thirty days' furlough, just before the seven days' battle, he returned with his company and became senior Captain in command. He soon became Major by the death of Lieutenant Colonel Garlington, Major Rutherford being promoted to Lieutenant Colonel. After the death of Colonel Nance, 6th of May, he became Lieutenant Colonel. He participated in nearly all the great battles in which the regiment was engaged, and was often in command. He was several times wounded, but not severely. At the time of his capture he was in command of the Seventh Regiment. Colonel Maffett was conspicuous for his fine soldierly appearance, being a perfect type of an ideal soldier.

He was loved and admired by the men as few officers of his station were. In camp he was the perfect gentleman, kind and indulgent to his men, and in battle he was cool, collected, and gallant. He died in prison only a short while before the close of the war, leaving a wife and one daughter of tender age.

CHAPTER XXXV

Reminiscences of the Valley.

Y. J. Pope, Adjutant of the Third South Carolina, but then acting as Assistant Adjutant General on General Connor's Staff, gives me here a very ludicrous and amusing account of a "Fox hunt in the valley." A hunt without the hounds or

without the fox.   No man in Kershaw's Brigade was a greater
lover of sport or amusement of any kind than Adjutant Pope.
In all our big snow "festivals," where hundreds would engage
in the contest of snow-balling, Adjutant Pope always took a
leading part.   It was this spirit of sport and his mingling with
the common soldier, while off duty, that endeared Pope so
much to the troop.   With his sword and sash he could act the
martinet, but when those were laid aside Adjutant Pope was
one of the "boys," and engaged a "boat" with them as much
as any one in the "Cross Anchors," a company noted for its
love of fun.

Says, Adjutant Pope, now a staid Judge on the Supreme
Court Bench.

"The Third South Carolina Infantry had been placed on
pickets in front of Early in September, 1864.   The point at
which picket were posted were at two fords on the Opequan
River, Captain Dickert, with his company, was posted at some
distance from the place where the other portion of the Regiment was posted to cover one of the fords.   I can see now the
work laid cut for Captain Dickert, ought to have been assigned
to the Cavalry for a company of Infantry, say a half mile from
the Regiment, might have been surrounded too quickly for the
company to be retired or to receive assistance from the Regiment.   Well, as it was, no harm came of it for the company
held the ford unassailable.   A company of the Regiment was
placed at a ford on the highway as it crossed the river.   While
a few officers were enjoying a nice supper here comes an
order to call in the companies on picket and to follow the Regiment with all possible speed towards Winchester, to which
latter place the army of Early had already gone.   Guides were
sent to us, and our Regiment had marched by country road
until we struck the turnpike.   The march was necessarily
rapid lest the Regiment might be assailed by overwhelming
numbers of the enemy.   The soldiers did not fancy this rapid
marching.

To our surprise and horrow, after we had reached the turn-
pike road, and several miles from our destination, the soldiers
set up an imitation of barking, just as if a lot of hounds in
close pursuit of a fresh jumped fox.   Now any one at all
familiar with the characteristic of the soldier know imitation is
his weak point, one yell, all yell, one sing, all sing, if one is

merry, all are merry. We were near the enemy, and the
Colonel knew the necessity of silence, and caution Colonel
Rutherford was, of course indignant at this outburst of good
humor in the dark watches of the night, and the enemy at our
heels or flank. He sent back orders by me (Pope) to pass
down the lines and order silence. But "bow-wow," "bow,"
"bow-wow," "yelp, yelp," and every conceivable imitation of
the fox hound rent the air. One company on receiving the
orders to stop this barking would cease, but others would take
it up. "Bow-wow," "toot," "toot," "yah-oon," "yah-oon,"
dogs barking, men hollowing, some blowing through their
hands to imitate the winding of the huntman's horn. "Stop
this noise," "cease your barking," "silence," still the chase
continued. "Go it, Lead," catch him, Frail," "Old Drive
close to him," "hurah Brink," "talk to him old boys." The
valley fairly rung, with this chase. Officers even could not
refrain from joining in the encouragement to the excited dogs
as the noise would rise and swell and echoe through the distant mountain gorges to reverberate up and down the valley—at
last wore out by their ceaseless barking and yelling, the noise
finally died out, much to the satisfaction of the Colonel commanding, myself and the officers who were trying to stop it.
As mortified as I was at my inability to execute the orders of
Colonel Rutherford, still I never laughed so much in my life
at this ebullition of good feelings of the men, after all their
toils and trials, especially as I would hear some one in the line
call out as if in the last throes of exhaustion, "Go on old dog,"
"now you are on him," "talk to him, old Ranger.' What the
Yankees thought of this fox chase at night in the valley, or
what their intentions might have been is not known, but they
would have been mighty fools to have tackled a lot of old
"Confeds" out on a lark at night."

The negro cooks of the army were a class unique in many
ways. While he was a slave, he had far more freedom than
his master, in fact had liberties that his master's master did
not possess. It was the first time in the South's history that
a negro could roam at will, far and wide, without a pass. He
could ride his dead master's horse from Virginia to Louisiana
without molestation. On the march the country was his, and
so long as he was not in the way of moving bodies of troops,
the highways were open to him. He was never jostled or

pushed aside by stragglers, and received uniform kindness and consideration from all. The negro was conscious of this consideration, and never took advantage of his peculiar station to intrude upon any of the rights or prerogatives exclusively the soldier's. He could go to the rear when danger threatened, or to the front when it was over. No negro ever deserted, and the fewest number ever captured. His master might fall upon the field, or in the hands of the enemy, but the servant was always safe. While the negro had no predilection for war in its realities, and was conspicuous by his absence during the raging of the battles, still he was among the first upon the field when it was over, looking after the dead and wounded. At the field hospitals and infirmaries, he was indispensable, obeying all, serving all, without question or complaint. His first solicitude after battle was of his master's fate—if dead, he sought him upon the field; if wounded, he was soon at his side. No mother could nurse a child with greater tenderness and devotion than the dark-skinned son of the South did his master.

At the breaking out of the war almost every mess had a negro cook, one of the mess furnishing the cook, the others paying a proportional share for hire; but as the stringency of the Subsistence Department began to grow oppressive, as the war wore on, many of these negroes were sent home. There was no provision made by the department for his keep, except among the officers of the higher grade; so the mess had to share their rations with the cook, or depend upon his ability as a "forager." In the later years of the war the country occupied by the armies became so devastated that little was left for the "forager." Among the officers, it was different. They were allowed two rations (only in times of scarcity they had to take the privates' fare). This they were required to pay for at pay day, and hence could afford to keep a servant. Be it said to the credit of the soldiers of the South, and to their servants as well, that during my four years and more of service I never heard of, even during times of the greatest scarcity, a mess denying the cook an equal share of the scanty supply, or a servant ever found stealing a soldier's rations. There was a mutual feeling of kindness and honesty between the two. If all the noble, generous and loyal acts of the negroes of the army could be recorded, it would fill no insignificant volume.

There was as much cast among the negroes, in fact more, as among the soldiers. In times of peace and at home, the negro based his claims of cast upon the wealth of his master. But in the army, rank of his master overshadowed wealth. The servant of a Brigadier felt royal as compared to that of a Colonel, and the servant of a Colonel, or even a Major, was far ahead, in superiority and importance, to those belonging to the privates and line officers. The negro is naturally a hero worshiper. He gloried in his master's fame, and while it might often be different, in point of facts, still to the negro his master was "the bravest of the brave."

As great "foragers" as they were, they never ventured far in front while on the advance, nor lingered too dangerously in the rear on the retreat. They hated the "Yankee" and had a fear of capture. One day while we were camped near Charlestown an officer's cook wandered too far away in the wrong direction and ran up on the Federal pickets. Jack had captured some old cast-off clothes, some garden greens and an old dominicker rooster. Not having the remotest idea of the topography of the country, he very naturally walked into the enemy's pickets. He was halted, brought in and questioned. The Federals felt proud of their capture, and sought to conciliate Jack with honeyed words and great promises. But Jack would have none of it.

"Well, look er here," said Jack, looking suspiciously around at the soldiers; "who you people be, nohow?"

"We are Federal soldiers," answered the picket.

"Well, well, is you dem?"

"Dem who?" asked the now thoroughly aroused Federal.

"Why dem Yankees, ob course—dem dat cotched Mars Clayt."

The Federal admitted they were "Yankees," but that now Jack had no master, that he was free.

"Is dat so?" Then scratching his head musingly, Jack said at last, "I don know 'bout dat—what you gwine do wid me, anyhow; what yer want?"

He was told that he must go as a prisoner to headquarters first, and then dealt with as contrabands of war.

"Great God Almighty! white folks, don't talk dat er way." The negro had now become thoroughly frightened, and with a sudden impulse he threw the chicken at the soldier's feet, saying, "Boss, ders a rooster, but here is me," then with the speed of a startled deer Jack "hit the wind," to use a vulgarism of the army.

"Halt! halt!,'—bang, whiz, came from the sentinel, the whole picket force at Jack's heels. But the faithful negro for the time excelled himself in running, and left the Federals far behind. He came in camp puffing, snorting, and blowing like a porpoise. "Great God Almighty! good people, talk er 'bout patter-rollers, day ain't in it. If dis nigger didn't run ter night, den don't talk." Then Jack recounted his night's experience, much to the amusement of the listening soldiers.

Occasionally a negro who had served a year or two with his young master in the army, would be sent home for another field of usefulness, and his place taken by one from the plantation. While a negro is a great coward, he glories in the pomp and glitter of war, when others do the fighting. He loves to tell of the dangers (not sufferings) undergone, the blood and carnage, but above all, how the cannon roared round and about him.

A young negro belonging to an officer in one of the regiments was sent home, and his place as cook was filled by Uncle Cage, a venerable looking old negro, who held the distinguished post of "exhorter" in the neighborhood. His "sister's chile" had filled Uncle Cage's head with stories of war— of the bloodshed on the battlefield, the roar of cannon, and the screaming of shells over that haven of the negro cooks, the wagon yards—but to all the blood and thunder stories of his "sister's chile" Uncle Cage only shook his head and chuckled, "Dey may kill me, but dey can't skeer dis nigger." Among the other stories he had listened to was that of a negro having his head shot off by a cannon ball. Sometime after Uncle Cage's installation as cook the enemy made a demonstration as if to advance. A few shells came over our camp, one bursting in the neighborhood of Uncle Cage, while he was preparing the morning meal for his mess.

Some of the negroes and more prudent non-combattants began to hunt for the wagon yard, but Uncle Cage remained at his post. He was just saying:

"Dese yer young niggers ain't no account; dey's skeered of dere own shad—"

"Boom, boom," a report, and a shell explodes right over his head, throwing fragments all around.

Uncle Cage made for the rear, calling out as he ran, "Oh, dem cussed Yankees! You want er kill er nudder nigger, don't you?" Seeing the men laughing as he passed by in such haste, he yelled back defiantly, "You can laff, if you want to, but ole mars ain't got no niggers to fling away.

———

"Red tape" prevailed to an alarming extent in the War Department, and occasionally a paroxyism of this disease would break out among some of the officers of the army, especially among the staff, "West Pointers," or officers of temporary high command—Adjutant Pope gives his experience, with one of those afflicted functionaries, "Where as Adjutant of the Third South Carolina," says he, "I had remained as such from May, 1862, till about the 1st of September, 1864, an order came from brigade headquarters, for me to enter upon the responsibilities of acting Assistant Adjutant General of Kershaw's Brigade. When General Connor was disabled soon after, and the Senior Colonel of the brigade, present for duty, the gallant William D. Rutherford, received his death-wound, General Kershaw, commanding division, sent the Assistant Adjutant General of the division, (a staff officer), Major James M. Goggans, to command the brigade. About the 17th of October there came a delegation to brigade headquarters, to learn, if possible, whether there could be obtained a leave of absence for a soldier, whose wife was dead, leaving a family of children to be provided for.

I was a sympathetic man, and appreciated the sad condition of the poor soldier, who had left his all to serve his country, and now had at home, a house full of motherless children. I said "wait till I see the brigade commander," and went to Major Goggans, relating the circumstances, and was assured of his approval of the application for leave of absence in question. This news, the spokesman of the delegation, gladly carried back to the anxiously awaiting group. Soon papers were brought to headquarters, signed by all the officers below. When the papers were carried by me to the brigade commander for his approval, it raised a storm, so to speak, in the breast of the newly appointed, but temporary Chieftain. "Why do you bring me this paper to sign this time of day?" it being in the afternoon. "Do you not know that all papers are considered at nine o'clock A. M?" In future, and as long as I am in command of the Brigade, I want it understood that under no considerations and circumstances, I wish papers to be signed, brought to me before or after nine o'clock A. M. The faces of the officers composing the delegation, when the news was brought to them, plainly expressed their disgust; they felt, at the idea, that no grief, however great, would be considered by the self-exalted Chief; except as the clock struck nine in the morning.

Circumstances and occurrences of this kind were so rare and exceptional, that I record the facts given by Judge Pope, to expose an exception to the general rule of gentlemanly deportment of one officer to another, so universal throughout the army. The kindness, sympathy and respect that superiors showed to subalterns and privates became almost a proverb. While in a reminiscent mood, I will give a story of two young officers as given by the writer of the above. He claims to have been an eye witness and fully competent to give a true recital. It is needless to say that the writer of these memoirs was one of the participants, and as to the story itself, he has only a faint recollection, but the sequel which he will give is vivid enough, even after the lapse of a third of a century. Judge Pope writes, "It is needless to say that the Third South Carolina Regiment had a half-score or more young officers, whose conduct in battle had something to do with giving prestige to the regiment, whose jolly good nature, their almost unparallel reciprocal love of officers and men, helped to give tone and recognition to it, their buoyancy of spirits, their respect for superiors and kindness and indulgence to their inferiors, endeared them to all—the whole command seemed to embibe of their spirit of fun, mischief and frolic." Captains L. W. Gary, John W. Watts, John K. Nance, Lieutenants Farley and Wofford, Adjutant Pope and others, whom it may be improper to mention here, (and I hope I will not be considered egotistical or self praise, to include myself), were a gay set. Their temperatures and habits, in some instances, were as wide as the poles, but there was a kind of affinity, a congeniality of spirits between them, that they were more like brothers in reality than brothers in arms, and all might be considered a "chip of the old block." Nor would our dearly beloved, kind, generous hearted Colonel Rutherford, when off duty, feel himself too much exalted to take a "spin with the boys" when occasions and circumstances admitted. Many, many have been the jolly carousals these jolly knights enjoyed while passing through some town or city. The confinement and restrictions of camp life induced them, when off duty and in some city, to long for a "loosening of the bit" and an ebullition of their youthful spirits.

Judge Pope, continuing, says: "In the spring of 1864 Longstreet's soldiers were ordeced from East Tennessee, to join Lee in Virginia, and it follows that there ·was joy in the camp among the soldiers, for who does not love Virginia? In route the command was halted in Lynchburg, and what was more natural for the fun-loving, jovial members of the old brigade, after being isolated so long, cut off from civilization as it seemed to them, shut up in the gorges of the mountains, than to long for a breath of fresh air—to wish for the society and enjoy the hospitality of the fair ladies of old Virginia, especially the quaint old city of Lynchburg. With such feelings, two handsome and gallant Captains of the Third Regiment applied for and obtained leave of absence for the day. I will call this jolly couple John and Gus. To say that these two young Captains—one of the right and the other of the left color company—were birds rare, would scarce express it. They were both in their 'teens,' and small of statue withal. They were two of the youngest, as well as the smallest, officers in the brigade. Notwithstanding their age and build, they would not hesitate to take a 'bout' with the strongest and the largest. As one would say to the other, 'When your wind fails you, I will leg him.' Now, these two knights, out on a lark and lookout for adventure, did not hesitate to shie their castors in the ring and cross lances the first opportunity presented. No doubt, after being a while with the famous Sancho Pauza at the wine skins, they could see as many objects, changed through enchantment, as the Master Dan Quixotte did, and demanded a challenge from them. In walking up a side street in the city, they, as by enchantment, saw walking just in front of them, a burly, stout built man, dressed out in the finest broad cloth coat. What a sight for a soldier to see! a broad cloth coat!" and he a young man of the army age. Ye gods was it possible. Did their eyes deceive them, or had they forgotten this was a Sabbath day, and the city guard was accustomed to wear his Sunday clothes. There were a set of semi-soldiers in some cities known as "city guards," whose duties consisted of examining soldier's furloughs and passes in cities and on trains. Their soft places and fine clothes were poison to the regular soldiers, and between whom, a friendly and good natured feud existed. There was another set that was an abomination to both, the gambler, who, by money or false papers, exempted themselves. Richmond was their city of refuge, but now and then one would venture out into a neighboring town.

"'Come out of that coat; can't wear that in the city to-day,' was the first salutation the jolly knights gave the fine dressed devotee of the blue cloth.

"'What, do you wish to insult me?' indignantly replied the man, turning and glaring at the two officers with the ferocity of a tiger.

"'Oh, no,' says John, 'we want that coat;' and instinctively the young Captains lay hands upon the garment that gave so much offense.

"'Hands off me, you cowardly young ruffians!'

"'Oh, come out of that coat,' replied the jolly couple.

"'Rip, rip,' went the coat; 'biff, biff,' went the non-combattant's fist. Right and left he struck from the shoulders, to be replied to with equal energy by the fists of the young men.

"'Rip, rip,' goes the coat, 'bang, biff,' goes the fists. Down in the street, over in the gutter, kicks and blows, still 'rip, rip,' goes the coat.

"'Help!' cries the non-combatant.

"'Yes,' cries Gus, 'help with the coat John.'

"The noise gathered the crowd. With the crowd came Lieutenant H. L. Farley. The burly frame of Farley soon separated the fighters. The gambler seeing his hopelessness in the face of so much odds, rose to his feet, and made a dash for liberty, leaving in the hands of each of the boys a tail of the much prized coat, all 'tattered and torn.' The gambler made quite a ludicrous picture, streaking it through town with his coat-tails off."

This is Pope's story, but I will here tell the sequel which was not near so amusing to me.

Sometime afterwards, the writer and participant in the fray

28

of the "coat-tail" was slightly wounded, and was sent (
Lynchburg to the hospital, formerly a Catholic college, if
am not mistaken. After being there for a time with m
wounded brother officers (this was a hospital for officers alone
I became sufficiently convalescent to feel like a stroll throug
the city.   I felt a little tender, lest I might meet unexpectedl
my unknown antagonist and erstwhile hostile enemy; but on
night I accepted the invitation of a tall, robust-built Capta:
from Tennessee (a room-mate, and also convalescent from
slight wound) to take a stroll. Being quite small, friendles
and alone, I did not object to this herculean chaparon
After tiring of the stroll, we sauntered into a soldier's chea
restaurant and called for plates. While we were waiting tt
pleasure of "mine host," the tread of footsteps and men
laughter of a crowd of jolly roisters met our ears, and :
walked some soldiers in the garb of "city police," and with tt
crowd was my man of the "long coat-tail." My heart san
into the bottom of my boots, my speech failed me, and I s
stupified, staring into space. Should he recognize me, the
what? My thought ran quick and fast. I never once e:
pected help from my old Tennesseean. As we were onl
"transient" acquaintances, I did not think of the brotherhoc
of the soldier in this emergency. The man of the "long coat
approached our table and raised my hat, which, either b
habit or force of circumstances, I will not say, I had the mc
ment before pulled down over my eyes.

"Hey, my fine young man, I think I know you. Are't
you the chap that tore my coat sometime ago? Answer me
sir," giving me a vigorous shake on the shoulder. "You ar
the very d—n young ruffian that did it, and I am going t
give you such a thrashing as you will not forget."

I have never yet fully decided what answer I was going t
make—whether I was going to say yes, and ask his pardon
with the risk of a thrashing, or deny it—for just at that momen
the "tall sycamore of the Holston" reached out with his fis
and dealt my assailant a blow sufficient to have felled an ox o
the Sweetwater. Sending the man reeling across the room
the blood squirting and splattering, he said:

"Gentlemen, I came here with this boy, and whoever whip
him has first got to walk my log, and that is what few peopl
can do."

The old "sycamore" from Tennessee looked to me at that precious moment as tall as a church steeple, and fully as large around. In all my whole life never was a man's presence so agreeble and his services so acceptable. It gave me a confidence in myself I never felt before nor since. His manly features and giant-like powers acted like inspiration upon me, and I felt for the time like a Goliah myself, and rose to my feet to join in the fray. But my good deliverer pushed me back and said:

"Stand aside, young man, I have tickets for both in here," and with that he began to wield his mighty blows first here and then there—first one and then another went staggering across the room, until the crowd gathered outside and put an end to the frolic. No explanations were given and none asked. Taking me by the arm, the big Captain led me away, saying, after we had gone some little distance:

"Young man, that was a narrow escape. you made, and it was lucky I was on hand."

He spoke with so much candor and logic, that I did not have the heart nor disposition to doubt or contradict it.

I would be willing to qualify before a grand jury to my dying day that I had had a close call.

CHAPTER XXXVI

Leaves the Valley---Return to Early---Second Valley Campaign.

On the 15th of September we began our return to Lee, marching about six miles south of Middleton. The next day we took up the march again to within fifteen miles of Luray Court House, then to within eleven miles of Sperryville, on the turn-pike, between the two points. Virginia or that part of it is blessed for her good roads on the main thoroughfares. The road from Staunton to the Potomac is one of the finest in America, being laid with cobble stones the entire length, upwards of one hundred and twenty-five miles. Then the road engineers did one thing that should immortalize them, that is in going around hills instead of over them, as in our

State.   Those engineers of old worked on the theory that the
distance around a hill was no greater than over it, and much
better for travel.

Over the Blue Ridge at Thornton Gap and to within five
miles of Woodville, reaching Culpepper at three o'clock P. M.,
the 9th, our ears were greeted with the distant roar of artillery, which proved to be our artillery firing at a scouting party
of United States cavalry.   On through Culpepper we marched,
to within one mile of Rapidan Station, our starting point of
near two months before.   And what a fruitless march—over
the mountains, dusty roads, through briars and thickets, and
heat almost unbearable—fighting and skirmishing, with
nightly picketing, over rivers and mountain sides, losing
officers, and many, too, being field officers captured.   While
in camp here we heard of Early's disaster in the Valley, which
cast a damper over all the troops.   It seems that as soon as
Sheridan heard of our detachment from Early's command he
planned and perfected a surprise, defeating him in the action
that followed, and was then driving him out of the Valley.
Could we have been stopped at this point and returned to
Early, which we had to do later, it would have saved the
division many miles of marching, and perhaps further discomfiture of Early and his men.   But reports had to be made to
the war department.

Orders came for our return while we were continuing our
march to Gordonsville, which place we reached on the 23rd of
September, at 4 o'clock, having been on the continuous march
for exactly fifty days.   On the morning of the 24th we received the orders to return to the relief of Early, and at daylight, in a blinding rain, we commenced to retrace our steps,
consoling ourselves with the motto, "Do your duty, therein all
honor lies," passing through Barboursville and Standardville,
a neat little village nestled among the hills, and crossed the
mountain at Swift Run Gap.   We camped about one mile of
the delightful Shenandoah, which, by crossing and recrossing
its clear, blue-tinged waters and camping on its banks so often,
had become near and dear to all of us, and nothing was more
delightful than to take a plunge beneath its waters.   But most
often we had to take the water with clothes and shoes on in
the dead of winter, still the name of the Shenandoah had
become classic to our ears.

This report had been made over and over again, until it became threadbare; but a cavalry officer thought it a feather in his cap to report his defeat or repulse by, "We met their infantry." We made a junction with Early near Brown's Gap, on the 26th, and camped at night with orders to be prepared to march at daylight. The troops of Early's were in a dependent mood, but soon their spirits revived at the sight of Kershaw's Division. We moved forward in the direction of Harrisonburg, our duty being to guard the two roads leading thereto. Early sent the other part of the army to the left and forward of us, and in this order we marched on to Waynsboro. Reaching there next day, the enemy's cavalry scattered when our troops came in sight. We began, on October 1st, moving in the direction of the turn-pike, leading from Winchester to Staunton, striking near Harrisonburg on the 6th.

The situation of Early had become so critical, the orders so imperative to join him as soon as possible, that we took up the march next morning at a forced speed, going twelve miles before a halt, a feat never before excelled by any body of troops during the war. When within two miles of Port Republic, a little beyond its two roads leading off from that place, one to Brown's Gap, we encountered the enemy's cavalry. Here they made an attack upon our brigade, but were repulsed at first fire from the infantry rifles. There was one thing demonstrated during this war, that whatever might have been accomplished in days of old, the cavalry on either side could not stand the fire of the infantry. And it seemed that they had a kind of intuition of the fact whenever the infantry was in their front. Nothing better as an excuse did a cavalry commander wish, when met with a repulse, than to report, "We were driving them along nicely until we came upon the enemy's infantry, then we had to give way."

We began the forward movement down the Valley on the 7th, the enemy slowly giving way as we advanced. We passed through those picturesque little cities of the Valley, Harrisonburg, New Market, and Woodstock, marching a day or two and then remaining in camp that length of time to give rest to the troops, after their long march. It must be remembered we had been two months cut off from the outside world —no railroad nearer than Staunton, the men being often short of rations and barefooted and badly clad; scarcely any mail was received during these two months, and seldom a paper ever made its appearance in camp. We only knew that Lee was holding his own. We reached and passed through Strausburg on the 13th. In the afternoon of this day, while we were on the march, but at the time laying by the side of the turn-pike, the enemy tried to capture some of our artillery. We had heard firing all day in our front, but thought this the effects of the enemy's sullen withdrawal. While resting by the road side, the enemy made a spirited attack upon the troops in front. We were hurriedly rushed forward, put in line of battle, advanced through an uneven piece of ground, and met the enemy posted behind a hill in front. They opened upon us at close range, killing and wounding quite a number, but as soon as our brigade made the first fire, they fled to a brick wall, running at an angle from the turn-pike. General Connor fell at the first fire, badly wounded in the knee, from the effects of which he lost his leg, and never returned, only to bid his brigade farewell in the pine regions of North Carolina. Colonel Rutherford being next in command, advanced the troops to the top of the hill and halted. In going out in front to reconnoitre in the direction of the stone wall, a party of the enemy, who had concealed themselves behind it, rose and fired, mortally wounding the gallant and much beloved Colonel. A charge was made, and the enemy fled to a thicket of pine timber and made their escape. This was a bloody little battle for the brigade, and some of its loss was irreparable. We halted after driving the enemy away, and at night withdrew to Fisher's Hill and camped for the night. Fisher's Hill is a kind of bluff reaching out from the Massanutten Mountain on our right; at its base ran Cedar Creek. It is a place of great natural strength. In the presence of some of his friends Colonel Rutherford passed away that night, at one o'clock, and his remains were carried to his home by Captain Jno. K. Nance. General Connor had his leg amputated. The brigade was without a field officer of higher grade than Major, and such officer being too inexperienced in the handling of so large a number of men, Major James Goggans, of the division staff, was ordered to its command. While some staff officers may be as competent to handle troops in the field as the commanders themselves, still in our case it was a lamentable failure. Major Goggans was a good staff officer, a graduate of West Point, but he was too old and inexperienced to command troops of such vigor and enthusiasm as the South Carolinians who composed Kershaw's Brigade.

We remained a short time on Fisher's Hill, throwing up some slight fortifications. Kershaw's Brigade was encamped in a piece of woods on the left of the turn-pike as you go north.

COLONEL WILLIAM DRAYTON RUTHERFORD.

Colonel William Drayton Rutherford was the son of Dr. Thomas B. Rutherford and Mrs. Laura Adams Rutherford, his wife. He was born on the 21st of September, 1837, in Newberry District, South Carolina. By his father he was a descendant of Virginians, as well as of that sturdy and patriotic stock of Germans who settled what was known as the "Fork." By his mother he was a descendant of the New England Adams family—what a splendid boy and man he was! He was educated in the best schools in our State, and spent sometime abroad. At the sound of arms he volunteered and was made Adjutant of the Third South Carolina Infantry. At the reorganization of the regiment, in May, 1862, he was elected Major of his regiment. When Lieutenant Colonel B. Conway Garlington was killed at Savage Station, June 29th, 1862, Rutherford became Lieutenant Colonel of his regiment. When Colonel James D. Nance fell in the battle of the Wilderness, on the 6th day of May, 1864, he became Colonel of the Third South Carolina Regiment. He was a gallant officer and fell in the front of his regiment at Strausburg, Va., on the 13th of October, 1864.

He married the beautiful and accomplished Miss Sallie H. Fair, only daughter of Colonol Simeon Fair, in March, 1862, and the only child of this union was "the daughter of the regiment," Kate Stewart Rutherford, who is now Mrs. George Johnstone.

Colonel Rutherford was in the battles of First Manassas, Williamsburg, Savage Station, Malvern Hill, First Fredericksburg (12th December, 1862, where he was badly wounded), Knoxville, Wilderness, Brock's Road (and other battles about Spottsylvania), North Anna Bridge, Second Cold Harbor, Deep Bottom, Berryville, and Strausburg.

He was a delight to his friends; by reason of his rare intelligence, warm heart, and generous impulses; to his family, because he was always so considerate of them, so affectionate, and so brimfull of courtesy; but to his enemies (and he never made any except among the viceous), he was uncompromisingly fierce.

I will state here that General James Connor had been in command of the brigade for about two or three months, Colonel Kennedy, the senior officer of the brigade, being absent on account of wounds received at the Wilderness. There is no question but what General Connor was one of the best officers that South Carolina furnished during the war. But he was not liked by the officers of the line or the men. He was too rigid in his discipline for volunteers. The soldiers had become accustomed to the ways and customs of Kershaw and the officers under him, so the stringent measures General Connor took to prevent straggling and foraging or any minor misdemeanor was not calculated to gain the love of the men. All, however, had the utmost confidence in his courage and ability, and were willing to follow where he led. Still he was not our own Joseph Kershaw. Below I give a short sketch of his life.

GENERAL JAMES CONNOR.

General James Connor, son of the late Henry Connor, was born in Charleston, S. C., 1st of September, 1829. Graduated at the South Carolina College, 1849, same class with L. Wyatt Aiken, Theo G. Barker, C. H. Simonton, and W. H. Wallace (Judge). Read law with J. L. Pettigrew. Admitted to the bar in 1852. Practiced in Charleston. Appointed United States District Attorney for South Carolina in 1856, Hon A. G. Magrath then District Judge. As District Attorney, prosecuted Captain Carrie, of the "Wanderer," who had brought a cargo of Africans to the State; also prosecuted T. J. Mackey for participation in Walker's filibustering expedition. Always justified the expectations of his friends in their high opinion of his talents and marked ability in all contingencies. Resigned as District Attorney in December, 1860. Was on the committee with Judge Magrath and W. F. Colcock, charged to urge the Legislature to call a convention of the people to consider the necessity of immediate Secession, and upon the passage of the Secession Ordinance, prepared for active service in the army. But upon the formation of the Confederate States Government, he was appointed Confederate States of America. District Attorney for South Carolina, but declined. Went into the service as Captain of the Montgomery Guards, and, in May, 1861, was chosen Captain of the Washington Light Infantry, Hampton Legion. In July, 1861, he became Major, and in June, 1863, was appointed Colonel of the Twenty-second North Carolina Volunteers. Being disabled for field duty, temporarily, was detailed as one of the judges of the military court of the Second Army Corps. With rank of Colonel, June, 1864, was commissioned Brigadier General, and by assignment commanded McGowan's and Laws' Brigades. Subsequently, as Acting Major General, commanded McGowan's, Laws', and Bushrod Johnson's Brigades. On return of McGowan to duty, was assigned permanently to command of Kershaw's Brigade.

He engaged in the following battles: Fort Sumter, First Manassas, Yorktown, New Stone Point, West Point, Seven Pines, Mechanicsville, Chancellorsville, Riddle's Shop, Darby's Farm, Fossil's Mill, Petersburg, Jerusalem, Plank Road, Reams' Station, Winchester, Port Republic, and Cedar Run. Severely wounded in leg at Mechanicsville and again at Cedar Run, October 12th, 1864. Leg amputated.

Returning to Charleston after the war, he resumed law practice with W. D. Portier. Was counsel for the South Carolina Railway. In 1878 was Receiver of the Georgia and Carolina Railway. Was candidate for Lieutenaut Governor in 1870. Elected Attorney General in 1876, resigned in 1877. Was at one time since the war M. W. G. M. of the Grand Lodge of Masons in this State.

One of the most distinguished looking and fearless officers of the Twentieth South Carolina Regiment was killed here, Captain John M. Kinard. Captain Kinard was one of the finest line officers in the command—a good disciplinarian and tactician, and a noble-hearted, kind-hearted gentleman of the "Old School." He was rather of a taciturn bend, and a man of great modesty, but it took only a glimpse at the man to tell

of what mould and mettle he was made.   I give a short sketch
of his life.

CAPTAIN JOHN MARTIN KINARD.

Captain John Martin Kinard was born July 5, 1833, in the
section of Newberry County known as the Dutch Fork, a settlement of German emigrants, lying a few miles west of Poma-
ria.   In 1838 his father, General Henry H. Kinard, was elected
Sheriff of Newberry County, and moved with his family to
the court house town of Newberry.   Here Captain Kinard attended school until he was about seventeen years old, when
he went to Winnsboro, S. C., to attend the famous Mount
Zion Academy.   He entered South Carolina College in 1852,
but left before finishing his college course to engage in farming, a calling for which he had had a passionate longing from
his boyhood days.   Having married Mary Alabama, the
daughter of Dr. P. B. Ruff, he settled on his grandfather's
plantation now known as Kinards.   While living here his
wife died, and a few years afterwards he married Lavinia
Elizabeth, the daughter of Dr. William Rook.

When the State called her sons to her defense, he answered
promptly, and enlisted as First Lieutenant in a company commanded by his uncle, John P. Kinard.   His company was a
part of the Twentieth Regiment, Colonel Lawrence Keitt, and
was known as Company F.   During the first years of the war
he was engaged with h s company in the defense of Charleston
Harbor, rising to the rank of Captain on the resignation of his
uncle.

While serving with his regiment in Virginia, to which place
it had been moved in 1864, Captain Kinard came home on
furlough.   Very soon, however, he set out for the front again,
and was detailed for duty in the trenches around Richmond.
While engaged here he made repeated efforts to be restored to
his old company, and joined them with a glad heart in October, 1864.   On the 13th of October, a few days after his
return, he warned his faithful negro body-guard, Ham Nance,
to keep near, as he expected some hot fighting soon.   And it
came.   The next day the enemy was met near Strausburg, and
Captain Kinard fell, with a bullet in his heart.   He died the
death of the happy warrior, fighting as our Anglo-Saxon forefathers fought, in the midst of his kinsmen and friends.   Ham

ce bore his body from the field, and never left it until he
rned it to his home in Newberry.

aptain Kinard left three children. By his first wife, a
ghter, Alice, now the wife of Elbert H. Aull, Esq.; by his
nd wife, two sons, John M. Kinard, Commandant of the
1 M. Kinard Camp, Sons of Veterans, and James P.
ard.

CHAPTER XXXVII

ttle of Cedar Creek or Fisher's Hill, 19th October, 1864.

fter the retreat of the enemy across Cedar Creek, on the
1, the brigade returned to Fisher's Hill, and encamped in
autiful grove. It was now expected that we would have a
;, sweet rest—a rest so much needed and devoutly wished
after two months of incessant marching and fighting.
foragers now struck out right and left over the mountains
ither side to hunt up all the little delicacies these moun-
homes so abounded in—good fresh butter-milk, golden
er—the like can be found nowhere else in the South save
he valleys of Virginia—apple butter, fruits of all kinds,
occasionally these foragers would run upon a keg of good
mountain corn, apple jack, or peach brandy—a "nectar
ng for the gods," when steeped in bright. yellow honey.
se men were called "foragers" from their habit of going
ugh the country, while the army was on the march or in
p, buying up little necessaries and "wet goods," and
iging them into camp to sell or share with their mess-
es. It mattered not how long the march, how tired they
e, when we halted for the night's camp, while others
ild drop, exhausted, too tired to even put up their tents or
k a supper, these foragers would overcome every obstacle,
ib mountains, and wade rivers in search of something to
or drink, and be back in camp before day. In every regi-
it and in almost every company you could find these
igers, who were great stragglers, dropping in the rear or
iking to the right or left among the farm houses in search

of honey, butter, bread, or liquors of some kind. Some of these foragers in the brigade were never known to be without whiskey during the whole war. Where, how, or, when they got it was as a sealed book to the others. These foragers, too, when out on one of their raids, were never very particular whether the owner of the meat or spring house, or even the cellar, was present or not, should they suspicion or learn from outside parties that these places contained that for which they were looking. If at night, they would not disturb the old man, but while some would watch, others would be depredating upon his pig pen, chicken roast, or milk house. It was astonishing what a change in the morals of men army life occasioned. Someone has said, "A rogue in the army, a rogue at home;" but this I deny. Sometimes that same devilish, school-boy spirit that actuates the truant to filch fruit or melons from orchards of others, while he had abundance at home, caused the soldier oftentimes to make "raids," as they called these nocturnal visits to the farm houses outlying the army's track. I have known men who at home was as honorable, honest, upright, and who would scorn a dishonest act, turn out to be veteran foragers, and rob and steal anything they could get their hands on from the citizens, friend or foe alike. They become to look upon all as "fish for a soldier's net." I remember the first night on Fisher's Hill, after fighting and marching all day, two of my men crossed over the Massanutton Mountain and down in the Luray Valley, a distance of ten miles or more, and came back before day with as unique a load of plunder as I ever saw. While in some of the mountain gorges they came upon a "spring house" a few hundred feet from the little cabin, nestled and hid in one of those impenetrable caves, where the owner, no doubt, thought himself safe from all the outside world. They had little difficulty in gaining an entrance, but all was dark, so kneeling down and examining the trough they found jars of pure sweet milk, with the rich, yellow cream swimming on top. This, of course, they could not carry, so they drank their fill. While searching around for anything else that was portable, they found a lot of butter in a churn, and to their astonishment, a ten-gallon keg of peach brandy. Now they were in the plight of the man who "when it rained mush had no spoon." They had only their canteens, but there was no

nnel to pour through. But the mother of invention, as
sual, came to their assistance. They poured out the milk in
ie jars, filled two for each, and returned over the mountain
ith a jar of brandy under each arm. The next morning I
und, to my surprise, hanging to the pole of my tent, my
:nteen filled with the choicest brandy. Whiskey sold for
1.oo per drink, so their four jars of brandy added something
) their month's pay. As a Captain of a company, I could
ot give leave of absence, nor could I excuse any who left
amp against orders or without permission. So I had it
nderstood that should any of my men wish to undertake a
)raging expedition, not to ask my permission, but go; and if
hey did not get caught by outside guards, I would not report
or punish them, but if they got caught, not to expect any
ivors or mercy at my hands. While I never countenanced
.or upheld foraging, unless it was done legitimately and the
rticles paid for, still when a choice piece of mutton or pork,
. mess tin of honey, or canteen of brandy was hanging on my
ifle pole in the morning, I only. did what I enjoined on the
nen, "say nothing and ask no question." And so it was
rith nearly all the Captains in the army. And be it said to
he credit of the Southern troops, pilfering or thieving was
lmost an unknown act while camping in our own country.
t was only done in the mountains of Virginia or East Tennes-
ee, where the citizens were generally our enemies, and who
rere willing to give aid and comfort to the Federals, while to
he Southern troops they often denied the smallest favors, and
efused to take our money.

On the night of the 18th of October we received orders to
)repare for marching at midnight. No drums were to be
)eaten, nor noise of any kind made. From this we knew an
.dvance was to be made, as Gordon's Division had orders to
narch soon after nightfall. The most profound secrecy, the
:bsence of all noise, from rattling of canteens or tin cups, were
:njoined upon the men. They were to noiselessly make their
vay over the spur of the Massanutton Mountain, which here
)utted out in a bold promontory, dividing the Shennandoah and
he Luray Valleys, and strike the enemy in the flank away to
)ur right. The other divisions were to be in readiness to
ttack as the roll of battle reached their front or right. The
:nemy was posted on an almost impregnable position on the

bluff overlooking Cedar Creek, while in their rear was a
plateau of several miles in extent.   The enemy's breastw
were built of strong timbers, with earth thrown against t
with a deep trench on the inside, being deeper from the
tom of the trench to the top of the works than the heigl
the soldiers when standing.   Thus a step of three or fou:
was built for the troops to stand on and fire.   The breastw
wound in 'and out with the creek, some places juttin;
almost to the very brink; at others, several hundred yar
the rear; a level piece of bottom land intervening.   This
and plateau were some fifty feet or more above the level o
creek, and gave elegant position for batteries.   In front o:
breastwork, and from forty to fifty feet in breadth, wa
abattis constructed of pine trees, the needles stripped.
limbs cut and pointed five to ten feet from the trunks.   T
were packed and stacked side by side and on top of each o
being almost impossible for a single man even to pick his
through, and next to impossible for a line of battle to
over.   All along the entire length of the fortifications
built great redoubts of earthwork in the form of squares,
earth being of sufficient tickness to turn any of our can
balls, while all around was a ditch from twelve to fifteen
deep—only one opening in the rear large enough to admi:
teams drawing the batteries.   Field pieces were poste
each angle, the infantry, when needed, filled the space
tween.   These forts were built about two hundred ;
apart, others being built in front of the main line.   T:
believe was the most completely fortified position by na
as well as by hand, of any line occupied during the war,
had the troops not been taken by surprise and stood
ground, a regiment strung out could have kept an arm
bay.

General Gordon's troops left camp earlier than did
shaw's, beginning their winding march at single file ar
the mountain side, over the great promontory, down in
plain below, through brush and undergrowth, along dull t:
catching and pulling themselves along by the bushes
vines that covered the rough borders and ledges of the m
tain.   Sometime after midnight Kershaw moved out acros
turn-pike in the direction of the river, the Second South (
lina in front, under Captain McCulcheon; then the T:

under Major Todd; then the Eighth, Twentieth, Fifteenth, and the Seventh. The James' or Third Battalion having some months before been organized into brigade sharpshooters, adding two companies to it, preceded the brigade, and was to charge the fords and capture the pickets. When near the river the brigade was halted, and scouting parties sent ahead to see how the land lay. A picked body moved cautiously along in front, and when all was in readiness, a charge was made—a flash, a report or two, and the enemy's out post at this point was ours. As we were feeling our way along the dull road that led to this ford, one poor fellow, who had been foremost in the assault on the pickets, was carried by us on a litter. Nothing but a low, deep groan was heard, which told too plainly that his last battle had been fought. The river crossed, the brigade continued in columns of fours, moving rapidly forward that all would be in readiness by the time Gordon's guns opened to announce that he was in position and ready.

Now our line of battle was formed, and never before or since was the brigade called in action with so few officers. Not a Colonel, nothing higher than a Major, in the entire brigade, the brigade itself being commanded by a staff officer, who had never so much as commanded a company before. At the close of the day there were but few officers in the command of the rank of Captain even.

Just at the beginning of dawn we heard the guns of Gordon belching forth far to our right. The cannon corps of the enemy roused up from their slumbers and met the attack with grape and cannister, but Gordon was too close upon them, the assault so sudden, that the troops gave way. Nearer and nearer came the roll of battle as each succeeding brigade wa put in action. We were moving forward in double-quick to reach the line of the enemy's breastworks by the time the brigade on our right became engaged. Now the thunder of their guns is upon us; the brigade on our right plunges through the thicket and throw themselves upon the abattis in front of the works and pick their way over them. All of our brigade was not in line, as a part was cut off by an angle in Cedar Creek, but the Second and Third charged through an open field in front of the enemy's line. As we emerged from a thicket into the open we could see the enemy in great com-

motion, but soon the works were filled with half-dressed troops
and they opened a galling fire upon us. The distance was too
great in this open space to take the works by a regular advance in line of battle, so the men began to call for orders to
"charge." Whether the order was given or not, the troops
with one impulse sprang forward. When in a small swale or
depression in the ground, near the center of the field, the
abattis was discovered in front of the works. Seeing the impossibility to make their way through it under such a fire, the
troops halted and returned the fire. Those behind the works
would raise their bare heads above the trenches, fire away,
regardless of aim or direction, then fall to the bottom to re-
load. This did not continue long, for all down the line from
our extreme right the line gave way, and was pushed back to
the rear and towards our left, our troops mounting their works
and following them as they fled in wild disorder. "Over the
works, cross over," was the command now given, and we
closed in with a dash to the abattis—over it and down in the
trenches—before the enemy realized their position. Such a
sight as met our eyes as we mounted their works was not often
seen. For a mile or more in every direction towards the rear
was a vast plain or broken plateau, with not a tree or shrub in
sight. Tents whitened the field from one end to the other for
a hundred paces in rear of the line, while the country behind
was one living sea of men and horses—all fleeing for life and
safety. Men, shoeless and hatless, went flying like mad to
the rear, some with and some without their guns. Here was
a deserted battery, the horses unhitched from the guns; the
caissons were going like the wind, the drivers laying the lash
all the while. Cannoneers mounted the unhitched horses
barebacked, and were straining every nerve to keep apace
with caissons in front. Here and there loose horses galloped
at will, some bridleless, others with traces whipping their
flanks to a foam. Such confusion, such a panic, was never
witnessed before by the troops. Our cannoneers got their
guns in position, and enlivened the scene by throwing shell,
grape. and cannister into the flying fugitives. Some of the
captured guns were turned and opened upon the former owners. Down to our left we could see men leaving the trenches,
while others huddled close up to the side of the wall, displaying
a white flag. Our ranks soon became almost as much disor-

ganized as those of the enemy. The smoking breakfast, just ready for the table, stood temptingly inviting, while the opened tents displayed a scene almost enchanting to the eyes of the Southern soldier, in the way of costly blankets, overcoats, dress uniforms, hats, caps, boots, and shoes all thrown in wild confusion over the face of the earth. Now and then a suttler's tent displayed all the luxuries and dainties a soldier'a heart could wish for. All this fabulous wealth of provisions and clothing looked to the half-fed, half-clothed Confederates like the wealth of the Indies. The soldiers broke over all order and discipline for a moment or two and helped themselves. But their wants were few, or at least that of which they could carry, so they grab a slice of bacon, a piece of bread, a blanket, or an overcoat, and were soon in line again following up the enemy. There was no attempt of alignment until we had left the breastworks, then a partial line of battle was formed and the pursuit taken up. Major Todd, of the Third, having received a wound just as we crossed the works, the command of the regiment devolved on the writer. The angle of the creek cutting off that portion of the brigade that was in rear, left the Second and Third detached, nor could we see or hear of a brigade commander. The troops on our right had advanced several hundred yards, moving at right angle to us, and were engaging the enemy, a portion that had made a stand on the crest of a hill, around an old farm house. Not knowing what to do or where to go, and no orders, I accepted Napoleon's advice to the lost soldier, "When a soldier is lost and does not know where to go, always go to where you hear the heaviest firing." So I advanced the regiment and joined it on the left of a Georgia brigade. Before long the enemy was on the run again, our troops pouring volley after volley into them as they fled over stone fences, hedges, around farm houses, trying in every conceivable way to shun the bullets of the "dreaded gray-backs." I looked in the rear. What a sight! Here came stragglers, who looked like half the army, laden with every imaginable kind of plunder—some with an eye to comfort, had loaded themselves with new tent cloths, nice blankets, overcoats, or pants, while others, who looked more to actual gain in dollars and cents, had invaded the suttler's tents and were fairly laden down with such articles as they could find readiest sale for. I saw one man with a stack

29

of wool hats on his head, one pressed in the other, until it reached more than an arm's length above his head. Frying-pans were enviable utensils in the army, and tin cups—these articles would be picked up by the first who came along, to be thrown aside when other goods more tempting would meet their sight.

After getting the various brigades in as much order as possible, a general forward movement was made, the enemy making only feeble attempts at a stand, until we came upon a stone fence, or rather a road hedged on either side by a stone fence, running parallel to our line of battle. Here we were halted to better form our columns. But the halt was fatal—fatal to our great victory, fatal to our army, and who can say not fatal to our cause. Such a planned battle, such complete success, such a total rout of the enemy was never before experienced—all to be lost either by a fatal blunder or the greed of the soldier for spoils. Only a small per cent. comparatively was engaged in the plundering, but enough to weaken our ranks. It was late in the day. The sharpshooters (Third Battalion) had been thrown out in a cornfield several hundred yards in our front. The men lay in the road behind the stone fence without a dream of the enemy ever being able to rally and make an advance. Some were inspecting their captured plunder; others sound asleep, after our five miles' chase. The sun was slowly sinking in the west. Oh, what a glorious victory! Men in their imagination were writing letters home, telling of our brilliant achievements—thirty pieces of artillery captured, whole wagon trains of ordnance, from ten to twenty thousand stands of small arms, horses and wagons, with all of Sheridan's tents and camp equippage—all was ours, and the enemy in full retreat!

But the scenes are soon to be shifted. Sheridan had been to Winchester, twenty miles away. He hears the firing of guns in the direction of Fisher's Hill, mounts his black charger with none to accompany him but an orderly, he leaves the streets of Winchester. Louder and louder the guns roar, faster and faster his faithful steed leaps over the stones in the road, plunging the steel rowels into the foaming sides. When he is near enough to hear the deep, rolling volleys of musketry, accompanied by the dreaded Rebel yell, he knew his troops were retreating from the sound he hears.   A few more leaps, and he comes face to face with his panic stricken troops.   The road was crowded, the woods and fields on either side one vast swarm of fleeing fugatives.   A few of the faithful were still holding the Confederates at bay, while the mass were seeking safety in flight.   His sword springs from its scabbard, and waving it over his head, he calls in a loud voice, "Turn, boys, turn; we are going back."   The sound of his voice was electrical.   Men halt, some fall, others turn to go back, while a few continue their mad flight.   A partial line is formed, Sheridan knowing the effect of a show of forward movement, pushes his handful of men back to meet the others still on the run.   They fall in.   Others who have passed the line in their rush, return, and in a few moments this wild, seething, surging, panic stricken mass had turned, and in well formed lines, were now approaching the cornfield and woods in which our pickets and skirmishers lay, all unconscious of the mighty change—a change the presence of one man effected in the morale of the routed troops.   They rush upon our sharpshooters, capturing nearly the whole line, killing Captain Whitner, the commander, and either capturing or wounding nearly all the commissioned officers.   Before we knew it, or even expected it, the enemy was in our front, advancing in line of battle.   The men hadn't time to raise a gun before the bullets came whizzing over our heads, or battering against the stone wall.   We noticed away to our right the lines give way.   Still Kershaw's Brigade held their position, and beat back the enemy in our front.   But in the woods on our left some troops who were stationed there, on seeing the break in the line beyond us, gave way also.   Someone raised the cry and it was caught up and hurried along like all omens of ill luck, that "the cavalry is surrounding us."   In a moment our whole line was in one wild confusion, like "pandemonium broke loose."   If it was a rout in the morning, it was a stampede now.   None halted to listen to orders or commands. Like a monster wave struck by the head land, it rolls back, carrying everything before it by its own force and power, or drawing all within its wake.   Our battle line is forced from the stone fence.   We passed over one small elevation, down through a vale, and when half way up the next incline, Adjutant Pope, who was upon the staff of our brigade commander, met the fleeing troops and made a masterly effort to stem the tide by getting some of the troops in line. Around him was formed a nucleus, and the line began to lengthen on either side, until we had a very fair battle line when the enemy reached the brow of the hill we had just passed We met them with a stunning volley, that caused the line to reel and stagger back over the crest. Our lines were growing stronger each moment. Pope was bending all his energies to make Kershaw's Brigade solid, and was in a fair way to succeed. The troops that had passed, seeing a stand being made, returned, and kept up the fire. It was now hoped that the other portion of the line would act likewise and come to our assistance, and we further knew that each moment we delayed the enemy would allow that much time for our wagon train and artillery to escape. But just as all felt that we were holding our own, Adjutant Pope fell, badly wounded by a minnie ball through the eye, which caused him to leave the field. Then seeing no prospects of succor on our right or left, the enemy gradually passing and getting in our rear, the last great wave rolls away, the men break and fly, every man for himself, without officers or orders—they scatter to the rear. The enemy kept close to our heels, just as we were rising one hill their batteries would be placed on the one behind, then grape and cannister would sweep the field. There were no thickets, no ravines, no fences to shield or protect us. Everything seemed to have been swept from off the face of the earth, with the exception of a lone farm house here and there. Every man appeared to be making for the stone bridge that spanned the creek at Stransburg. But for the bold, manly stand made by Y. J. Pope, with a portion of Kershaw's Brigade (the brigade commander was seldom seen during the day), the entire wagon train and hundreds more of our troops would have been lost, for at that distance we could hear wagons, cannons, and caissons crossing the stone bridge at a mad gallop. But in the rush some wagons interlocked and were overturned midway the bridge, and completely blocked the only crossing for miles above and below. Teamsters and wagoners leave their charge and rush to the rear. In the small space of one or two hundred yards stood deserted ambulances, wagons, and packs of artillery mules and horses, tangled and still hitched, rearing and kicking like mad, using all their strength to unloosen themselves from the matted mass of vehicles, animals, and men, for the stock had caught up the spirit of the panic, and were eager to keep up the race. As by intuition, the flying soldiers felt that the roadway would be blocked at the bridge over Cedar Creek, so they crossed the turn-pike and bore to the left in order to reach the fords above. As I reached the pike, and just before entering a thicket beyond, I glanced over my shoulder toward the rear. One glance was enough! On the hill beyond the enemy was placing batteries, the infantry in squads and singly blazing away as rapidly as they could load and fire, the grape and cannister falling and rattling upon the ground like walnuts thrown from a basket. The whole vast plain in front and rear was dotted with men running for life's sake, while over and among this struggling mass the bullets fell like hail. How any escaped was a wonder to the men themselves. The solid shot and shell came bouncing along, as the boys would laughingly say afterwards, "like a bob-tailed dog in high oats '—striking the earth, perhaps, just behind you, rebound, go over your head, strike again, then onward, much like the bounding of rubber balls. One ball, I remember, came whizzin.' in the rear, and I heard it strike, then rebound, to strike again just under or so near my uplifted foot that I felt the peculiar sensation of the concussion, rise again, and strike a man twenty paces in my front, tearing away his thigh, and on to another, hitting him square in the back and tearing him into pieces. I could only shrug my shoulders, close my eyes, and pull to the rear stronger and faster.

The sun had now set. A squadron of the enemy's cavalry came at headlong speed down the pike; the clatter of the horses hoofs upon the hard-bedded stones added to the panic, and caused many who had not reached the roadway to fall and surrender. About one hundred and fifty of the Third Regiment had kept close at my heels (or I had kept near their front, I can't say which is the correct explanation), with a goodly number of Georgians and Mississippians, who had taken refuge in a thicket for a moment's breathing spell, joining our ranks, and away we continued our race. We commenced to bend our way gradually back towards the stone bridge. But before we neared it sufficiently to distinguish friend from foe, we heard the cavalry sobering our men, cursing, commanding, and yelling, that we halted for a moment to listen and consult. In the dim twilight we could distinguish some men about one hundred yards in front moving to and fro. Whether they were friends, and like ourselves, trying to escape the cavalry in turn and creep by and over the bridge, or whether they were a skirmish line of the enemy, we could not determine. The Captain of a Georgia regiment (I think his name was Brooks), with four or five men, volunteered to go forward and investigate. I heard the command "halt," and then a parley, so I ordered the men to turn towards the river. The command came after us to "halt, halt," but we only redoubled our speed, while "bang, bang," roared their guns, the bullets raining thick and fast over our head. I never saw or heard of my new found friends again, and expect they, like many captured that day, next enjoyed freedom after Lee and Johnston had surrendered. When we reached the river it was undecided whether we could cross or not. So one of my men, a good swimmer, laid off his accoutrement and undertook to test the depth. In he plunged, and was soon out of sight in the blue waters. As he arose he called out, "Great God! don't come in here if you don't want to be drowned. This river has got no bottom." Our only alternative was to go still higher and cross above the intersection of the north and south prongs of the Shenandoah, where it was fordable. This we did, and our ranks augmented considerable as we proceeded up the banks of the stream, especially when we had placed the last barrier between us and the enemy. We had representatives of every regiment in Early's Army, I think, in our crowd, for we had no regiment, as it naturally follows that a man lost at night, with a relentless foe at his heels, will seek company.

We returned each man to his old quarters, and as the night wore on more continued to come in singly, by twos, and by the half dozens, until by midnight the greater portion of the army, who had not been captured or lost in battle, had found rest at their old quarters. But such a confusion! The officers were lost from their companies—the Colonels from their regiments, while the Generals wandered about without staff and without commands. The officers were as much dazed and lost in confusion as the privates in the ranks. For days the men recounted their experiences, their dangers, their hair-breadth escapes, the exciting chase during that memorable rout in the

morning and the stampede in the evening, and all had to
laugh. Some few took to the mountains and roamed for days
before finding an opportunity to return; others lay in thickets
or along the river banks, waiting until all was still and quiet,
then seek some crossing. Hundreds crowded near the stone
bridge (the Federal pickets were posted some yards distance),
and took advantage of the darkness to cross over under the
very nose of the enemy. One man of the Fifteenth came face
to face with one of the videttes, when a hand to hand encounter took place—a fight in the dark to the very death—but
others coming to the relief of their comrade beat the Confederate to insensibility and left him for dead. Yet he crawled to
cover and lay concealed for a day and night, then rejoined his
regiment in a sickening plight.

A man in my company, Frank Boozer, was struck by a
glancing bullet on the scalp and fell, as was thought, dead.
There he lay, while hundreds and hundreds trampled over
him, and it was near day when he gained consciousness and
made his way for the mountain to the right. There he wandered along its sides, through its glens and gorges, now dodging a farm house or concealing himself in some little cave,
until the enemy passed, for it was known that the mountains
and hills on either side were scoured for the fugitives.

Captain Vance, of the Second, with a friend, Myer Moses,
had captured a horse, and they were making their way
through the thickets, Moses in front, with Vance in rear, the
darkness almost of midnight on them. They came upon a
squad of Federal pickets. They saw their plight in a moment,
but Moses was keen-witted and sharp-tongued, and pretended
that he was a Yankee, and demanded their surrender. When
told that they were Federals, he seemed overjoyed, and urged
them to "come on and let's catch all those d—n Rebels."
But when they asked him a few questions he gave himself
away. He was asked:

"What command do you belong to?"

"Eighty-seventh New York," Moses answered, without
hesitation.

"What brigade?" "What division?" etc. "We have no
such commands in this army. Dismount, you are our prisoners."

But Captain Vance was gone, for at the very outset of the

parley he slid off behind and quietly made his escape. In such emergencies it was no part of valor to "stand by your friend," for in that case both were lost, while otherwise one was saved.

What was the cause of our panic, or who was to blame, none ever knew. The blame was always laid at "somebody else's" door. However disastrous to our army and our cause was this stampede—the many good men lost (killed and captured) in this senseless rout—yet I must say in all candor, that no occasion throughout the war gave the men so much food for fun, ridicule, and badgering as this panic. Not one man but what could not tell something amusing or ridiculous on his neighbor, and even on himself. The scenes of that day were the "stock in trade" during the remainder of the war for laughter. It looked so ridiculous. so foolish, so uncalled for to see twenty thousand men running wildly over each other, as it were, from their shadows, for there was nothing in our rear but a straggling line of Federals, which one good brigade could have put to rout.

Both Colonel Boykin and Lieutenant Colonel McMichael, of the Twentieth, were captured and never returned to the service, not being parolled until after the surrender. The Twentieth was commanded by Major Leaphart until the close.

As Adjutant Pope never returned in consequence of his wounds, I will give a few facts as to his life. No officer in the army was parted with with greater reluctance than Adjutant Pope.

ADJUTANT YOUNG JOHN POPE.

Y. J. Pope was born in the town of Newberry, S. C., on the 10th of April, 1841. Was the son of Thomas Herbert Pope and Harriett Neville Pope, his wife. He was educated in the Male Academy, at Newberry, and spent six years at Furman University, Greenville, S. C., from which institution he graduated in August, 1860. After studying law under his uncle, Chief Justice O'Neall, he entered the Confederate Army on April 13th, 1861, as First Sergeant in Company E, of Third South Carolina Regiment of Infantry. He participated in the battles of First Manassas and Williamsburg while in his company. In May, 1862, he was made Adjutant of the Third South Carolina Regiment, and as such participated in the battles of Savage Station, Malvern Hill, Maryland Heights, Sharpsburg, First Fredericksburg (where he was slightly wounded), Chancellorsville, Gettysburg (where he received three wounds), Chickamauga (where he was severely wounded), Wilderness, Brock's Road and other battles around Spottsylvania Court House, North Anna River Bridge, Second Cold Harbor, Berryville (where he was shot through the mouth). Strausburg, and Cedar Creek, on the 19th of October, 1864, where he lost his left eye, which was totally destroyed by a minnie bullet.

Since the war he has been elected Mayor of his native town at five elections. He was elected by the Legislature District Judge of Newberry, in December, 1865, and served as such until June, 1868, when Radicals abolished that office. He was elected to the House of Representatives of his State in the year 1877, and was by the Joint Assembly of the Legislature elected Associate Counsel for the State to test the legality of State bonds, when more than two million dollars were saved the State. He was elected State Senator in 1888, and served until he was elected Attorney General of the State, in 1890. He served in this office until the 3rd of December, 1891, when he was elected Associate Justice of Supreme Court of the State, and on the 30th of January, 1896, he was unanimously re-elected Associate Justice of the Supreme Court of South Carolina.

On the 3rd of December, 1874, he married Mrs. Sallie H. F. Rutherford. By this union there were two daughters, Mary Butler Pope and Neville Pope. The former died in October, 1893, and left a wound which has never healed.

During a part of the year 1864 Adjutant Pope served on the brigade staff as Assistant Adjutant General, and was acting in this capacity when he received the wound that incapacitated him from further service in the field.

———

Lieutenant U. B. Whites, formerly of my company, but later in command of Company G, Third Battalion, writes a very entertaining sketch of prison life, which I very willingly give space to, so that the uninitiated may have some idea of prison life, and the pleasure of being called "fresh fish" by the old prison "rats." Lieutenant Whites was a gallant soldier and a splendid officer. He was what is called in common parlance "dead game" in battle and out.   He is a commercial man, and at present a member of the South Carolina colony of Atlanta, Ga.

HOW IT FEELS TO BE TAKEN A PRISONER OF WAR.

After being flushed with the most signal victory of more than half a day's fighting, and while gloating over the brilliant success and planning and scheming future glories, and after having captured a great number of Federal soldiers, together with a large number of field pieces, and then in turn to be captured yourself, especially after having boasted and affirmed oftentimes that you never would be taken a prisoner unless sick or wounded, is exceedingly humiliating, to say the least of it, and the feelings of such an one can better be imagined than described.   Yet such was the exact condition of the writer on the evening of October 19th, :864, at the battle of Strausburg, or as it is known at the present day among the veterans, "Early's Stampede."

It is proper to note here that the writer was a line officer belonging to Company H, Third Regiment South Carolina Volunteers, but several months previous had been assigned to command a company of "picked" men made from the various companies and regiments of the old brigade (Kershaw's), and this company was assigned to duty in the Third Battalion. This battalion was to do the skirmishing and sharpshooting for the brigade.   This explanation is necessary in order that the reader may better understand my position and place when captured.

Late in the afternoon of this exciting day General Phil Sheridan succeeded in rallying his routed columns and led the attack on our line   Our skirmish line was in excellent condition.   We had no trouble in effectually resisting and driving back the enemy's skirmish line.   When within short range of our rifles we opened fire, and for nearly half an hour held them in check, while they fairly rained lead into our ranks. The command "retreat" was given, and we retired, firing. During the retreat brave Captain Whitener was killed.   I rallied the remnant of my company in rear of the Third South Carolina.   General Kershaw rode rapidly up to where I had rallied what few men I had left and enquired for Captain Whitener.   I replied, "He is killed, General."   He then ordered me to take what few I had and could gather and double-quick to a point on the extreme left of his division. When I arrived at the point designated, which was in thick woods, to my horror I found the place literally alive with Yankees. I had double-quicked right into the midst of the "blue bellies." "Surrender," came in tones of thunder. I stood amazed, astonished beyond conception. "Surrender," again came the command. There was absolutely no alternative. There was no chance to fight and less chance to run. My brave boys and I were prisoners of war. This was one of the consequences of war that I had never figured upon, and was wholly unprepared for it. I said to the officer who demanded my sword that I would rather give him my right arm. He preferred the sword and got one—I had two, having captured one that morning. Just then an unusual incident occurred.

"Hello, Lieutenant Whites, my old friend, I am glad to see you."

I looked and recognized a Federal Sergeant, whom I had befriended while en route with him and many other Federal prisoners from East Tennessee to Richmond. I replied:

"My dear fellow, I know, under the circumstances, you will excuse me when I tell you that I am truly sorry that I cannot return the compliment."

I was ordered to the rear under guard of one soldier. I was turned over to the provost guard. My other sword was demanded. Of course I gave it up without a word. My emotions were too intense for utterance. I was a disarmed, helpless prisoner of war. My feelings can better be described by relating an incident which occurred later on. After Lee's surrender, a few uncompromising, unconquered Confederates attempted to make their way to Johnston's Army in North Carolina. The way was full of obstacles, and one of the party, nearly overcome, sat with his elbows on his knees and his face in his hands, when a comrade accosted him with—

"Hello, John, what is the matter with you?"

"O, I was just thinking," replied John.

"Well, what in the world were you thinking so deeply about that you were lost to every other environment?"

"Well, Jim, to tell you the truth, I was thinking I wished I was a woman."

"Wish you were a woman! Great Scotts, John, are you gone crazy? A brave soldier like you wishing to be a woman!"

"Now, Jim, I'll tell you the truth; if I were a woman I could just cry as much as I pleased, and no one would think that I was a fool."

I felt very much like John. I wished I was a woman, so that I could cry as much as I pleased.

That night all the prisoners were marched to General Sheridan's headquarters, where we went into camp without supper. Some said their prayers, while others cursed the Yankees inaudibly, of course. Next morning we were lined up and counted. Eleven hundred Confederates answered at Sheridan's roll call. It looked like Kershaw's whole Brigade was there, though there were many Georgians among us. Sheridan then inspected the prisoners, and at his personal instance —shame be it said to his memory—we were all robbed of our good blankets and dirty, worn out ones given in their stead.

After the inspection by Sheridan, we began the march (we knew not where to) under a heavy guard—a whole regiment of infantry to guard eleven hundred prisoners. This guard was old soldiers, who knew how to treat a prisoner. They were kind to us. Nothing of special interest occurred on this day. We arrived at Winchester about sundown. We got some rations, ate supper, lay down to sleep, when we were hurriedly aroused and ordered to "fall in line quickly," "fall in," "fall in."

"What is the trouble?" I ventured to ask.

"Mosby! Mosby is coming."

The name of Mosby was a holy terror to the Federals in that part of Virginia. Silently we prayed that Mosby might make a dash and rescue us. All night long we vainly listened for the clatter of the hoops of Mosby's troopers. But, alas! Mosby did not come. The rumor was false. We took up the night march under double guard. A line of cavalry was placed outside the already heavy infantry guard. The night was dark and drizzly—a good night to escape, had not the guard been so heavy. There were two infantry guards to every four prisoners, besides the outer cavalry guard. The hope of an escape was a forlorn one, but I made the attempt and succeeded in passing both guards, but in my ecstacy I foolishly ran in the dark, and ran right squarely against a plank fence with so much force as to attract the attention of a cavalryman, who was soon at my side and escorted me back with a "d—n you, stay in your place." Several prisoners more fortunate than myself did succeed in making their escape in the darkness.

The guards had kindly informed us that at Harper's Ferry we would be searched and relieved of all valuables, and if we had a knife or anything that we desired to retain, they would keep it for us until after the search. This promise they sacredly kept. The search, or robbery as I call it, was very. rigid. Like vandals, they searched every pocket and relieved us of all money, pocket-books, knives, keys, and every other thing, except our tobacco. I beat them a little, notwithstanding their rigid search. I had a five-dollar greenback note inside of my sock at the bottom of my boot. This they failed to find.

From Harper's Ferry to Baltimore, the trip was by rail at night. The guard had now been greatly reduced, only eight to each coach. They had got plenty of whiskey for themselves and for all who wanted it. We were having a jolly good time. At this point, knowing that we were in a friendly part of Maryland, I conceived the idea of making a dash for the guns of the guard, uncoupling the rear coaches, put on the brakes, and make our escape across the Potomac. This plan was quietly communicated to all the prisoners in this the rear coach. All agreed to the plan, except Lieutenant Colonel McMichael, of the Twentieth South Carolina Regiment. He protested so strongly that the plan was abandoned. The trip from this on to Fort Delaware was without incident or special interest.

On our arrival at Fort Delaware we were again subjected to a rigid examination and search, and what few trinklets the kind guards saved for us at Harper's Ferry, were now taken away from us. I, however, saved my five-dollar greenback note, which was safely esconced inside my sock at the bottom of my foot. Here officers and privates were separated and registered, each as to command, rank, and state. The heavy gates swung open with a doleful noise. We marched in amid the shouts of the old prisoners, "fresh fish," "fresh fish." I wanted to fight right then and there. I did not want to be guyed. I wanted sympathy, not guying. "Fresh fish" was the greeting all new arrivals received, and I being an apt scholar, soon learned to shout "fresh fish" as loud as a Texas cowboy.

The heavy prison gates closed around with a dull sepulchra[1] sound, and prison life began in earnest, with Brigadier General Schoeff master of ceremonies. The prison was in the shape of an oblong square, with the "shacks" or "divisions" on the long side and at the short sides or ends. At the other long side was built a plank fence twelve or fifteen feet high. This fence separated the officers and privates. Near the top of this fence was erected a three-foot walk, from which the strictest guard was kept over both "pens" day and night. Fifteen feet from this plank fence on either side was the "dead line." Any prisoner crossing the "dead line" was shot without being halted. There was not an officer shot during my eight months' sojourn there, but it was a frequent occurrence to hear the sharp report of a guard's rifle, and we knew that some poor, unfortunate Confederate soldier had been murdered. The cowardly guards were always on the lookout for any semblance of an excuse to shoot a "d—n Rebel."

There was a rigid censorship placed over all mail matter being sent from or received at the "pen." All letters were read before being mailed, and all being received were subjected to the same vigilant censorship. They were all opened and read by an official to see that they contained nothing "contraband of war." Money was "contraband." Only such newspapers as suited the fastidious taste of General Schoeff were permitted to come inside the "pen." The officers and privates were supposed to be strictly "incommunicado," but even these found means of communication. The open, spacious courts on both sides of the separating fence, on fair days, were always thronged with men taking exercise. A short note—a small piece of coal was the "mail coach"— the twine was the "air line"—the note securely tied to the piece of coal, and at an opportune moment, when the guard's face was in a favorable direction, the "mail" passed over the "dead line" into the other pen, and vice versa. This line kept up a regular business, but was never detected.

A large majority of prisoners (officers) had some acquaintance, friend, or relative in Baltimore, New York, or other

Northern cities, who would gladly furnish money or clothing to them. Provisions were not permissible under the rules and regulations of the prison authorities. Baltimore, especially, and New York did much toward relieving the burdens of prison life. Such inestimable ladies as Mrs. Mary Howard, of Baltimore, and Mrs. Anna Hoffman, of New York, deserve an everlasting monument of eternal gratitude for the great and good service rendered the unfortunate Confederate prisoners. These philanthropic ladies, with hundreds of other sympathizing men and women of the North, kept many of us furnished with money and clothing. The money itself we were not permitted to have. In its stead the prison officials issued the amounts of money on bits of parchment in denominations of five cents, ten cents, twenty-five cents, fifty cents, and one dollar peices. This was the prison currency. The prison name for it was "sheepskin." The prison officials would not allow us to have the "cold cash," lest we should enter into a combination and bribe an important guard, thereby effecting an escape. The "sheepskin" answered every other purpose for trade. We had a suttler who was a suttler right. He was a real, genuine, down-east Yankee. He loved money ("sheepskins" were money to him), and he would furnish us with anything we wanted for plenty "sheepskins." He would even furnish whiskey "on the sly," which was positively prohibited by the prison regulations. He had only to go to headquarters at the close of the day and have his "sheepskins" cashed in genuine greenbacks, and he went away happy and serene, to dream of more "sheepskins."

The amusements and diversions of prison life are wonderful to contemplate. They were numerous and varied. A man could find anything to suit his inclinations. Of all the many diversions, gaming was probably the most prominent, and stands at the head of the list. By common consent, it seemed that a certain part of the open court was set aside for gaming purposes. It made no difference how severe the weather was, these gaming tables were always in full blast. A man could amuse himself with any game at cards that he desired. There were "farrow bank," "chuck a luck," "brag," "euchre," "draw poker," "straight poker," "seven up," "five . . . most prominent of all, a French game, pronoun . . . Delaware "vang-tu-aug," meaning twenty-one were games for "sheepskins"—bets, five cents; limit, ten cents. All were conducted on a high plane of honor. If a dealer or player was detected in attempting anything that was unclean, he was tried in court, convicted, and punished.

There were courts and debating societies; classes in French, Spanish, and Greek. There were Bible students and students in the arts and sciences prosecuting their varied studies. The gutta-percha ring-makers were quite numerous, and it was really astonishing to see the quality of the work turned out, being handsomely engraved and inlaid with silver. There were diversion and amusement for everybody and every class of men, except croakers and grumblers. They had no lot, parcel, or place, and such characters were not permitted to indulge in their evil forebodings. They had to be men, and real live men, too. The reader may desire to know whence all the books, cards, materials, etc.. came. I answer, from the Yankee suttler, for "sheepskins."

It must be said to the credit of the Federal prison officials, that the sanitary and hygienic arrangements were as near perfect as man could well make them. These officials were exceedingly jealous of the health of the place. In fact, it was often thought they were unnecessarily strict in enforcing their hygienic rules. Everything had to be thoroughly clean. Cleanliness was compulsory. A laundry machine was furnished, and a kind of laundrying was accomplished. Blankets were required to be dusted and sunned regularly. Every few weeks the whole army of prisoners were turned out into the cold, and there remained until the "shacks" were thoroughly white-washed, both inside and outside. This work was performed by "galvanized Yankees." A "galvanized Yankee" was a Confederate prisoner who had "swallowed the yellow pup," i. e., had taken the oath of allegiance to the United States Government. These men were looked upon even by the Federal officers as a contemptible set, and were required to do all kinds of menial service.

The water was good and plentiful. There could be no just criticism along this line. I am constrained to believe that it was owing to these stringent health laws that the percentage of sickness was so very small. Of course, I can only speak of the officers in Fort Delaware.

The prison fare is the most difficult, as well as unpleasant, part of prison life of which to treat. However, I will give the simple facts, and allow the reader to draw his own conclusions as to the justice and necessity for such treatment. To say that the fare was entirely insufficient, is putting it mildly, and would not be more than might be expected under similar circumstances and conditions; but the reader will more fully understand the situation when this insufficiency is exemplified by the facts which follow. Think of being compelled to live on two ounces of meat and six ounces of bread per day. Yet this was a prison ration for us towards the close of the war. This was totally inadequate to appease hunger. Men who had no other means of procuring something to eat were nearly starved to death. They stalked about listlessly, gaunt looking, with sunken cheeks and glaring eyes, which reminded one of a hungry ravenous beast. Hungry, hungry all the time. On lying down at night, many, instead of breathing prayers of thankfulness for bountiful supplies, would lie down invoking the most severe curses of God upon the heads of the whole Federal contingent, from President Lincoln down to the lowest private. Hunger makes men desperate and reckless. The last six or eight months of the war the fare was much worse than at any time previous. It was at this period that the Federal administration was retaliating, as they claimed, for the treatment their prisoners were receiving at Andersonville, Ga.

This inhuman condition of affairs was absolutely brought about by the United States Government itself by positively refusing time and again an exchange of prisoners, and it can not escape the just odium and stigma of the inhuman treatment, the untold suffering, and agonies of both the Confederate and Union prisoners of war.

As already observed, there were not a great number of officers who suffered so intensely, but there were some, who, like nearly all the privates, had no friends or acquaintances in the North to render any assistance, and they suffered greatly. Of course, we endeavored to relieve one another as far as we could. Often have I and others given our entire day's ration from the mess hall to some brother officer less fortunate than ourselves. I have seen an officer peal an apple, throw the pealing upon the ground, and immediately an unfortunate one would pick it up and ravenously devour it. There were a great many wharf rats burrowing under the plank walks which traversed the open court of the prison. These rodents are much larger than our common barn rats, and they were eagerly sought by the starving officers. There was a general warfare declared on the wharf rat in prison. When these rats were taken and being prepared, the odor arising therefrom was certainly tempting to a hungry man, and when ready they were eaten with a keen relish. The rats did not require any of Lee's and Perin's Worcester sauce to make them palatable, or to give them zest. This will give the reader some idea of the straits to which some of the Confederate officers, and nearly all the privates, in prison at Fort Delaware were reduced to by gaunt hunger.

I must here chronicle an event which I desire to go down in history. After being in prison and being hungry for about two months, I received a letter, addressed in a lady's handwriting, to "Lieut. U. B. White, Division 28, Fort Delaware," and postmarked "Baltimore, Md." My surprise was great, but on opening it and finding the writer's name to be "Mrs. Mary Howard, of Lexington Avenue, Baltimore," my surprise was unbounded. I knew no such person as Mrs. Mary Howard, and, in fact, at that time I did not know a soul in Baltimore. I felt sure that there must be some mistake about it. I read and re-read that letter. I scrutinized and examined the address again and again. It was plain, except that the final "s" in my name was wanting, which was and is, to my mind, a very natural and correct omission. Mrs. Howard said in her letter that she had been informed that I was a prisoner of war and that I was in Division Twenty-eight, Fort Delaware, and that I was in need of both money and clothing, and that if this was true she would be glad to relieve my wants. I immediately answered that letter. I said to Mrs. Howard that her information was only too true, which I very much regretted. From that time my hunger was appeased and my nakedness clad. Thirty-five years have elapsed since Mrs. Mary Howard wrote that letter, and to-day it is as much of a mystery to me as it was on the day I received it—by whom or by what means or device Mrs. Howard ever found out who I was, or what my condition and circumstances were, I will never know. She and I corresponded regularly during the balance of my prison life, and for sometime after the war when I returned to South Carolina, and yet that mystery was never explained. Mrs. Mary Howard! Grand, noble, heroic, Christian woman! "She hath done what she could." Through her agency and her means and her efforts she not only assisted and relieved me, but hundreds of other poor, helpless Confederate prisoners. To-day she is reaping her sublime reward, where there are no suffering, hungry, starving prisoners to relieve. God bless her descendants!

When General Lee surrendered we refused to believe it, notwithstanding the prison was flooded with various newspapers announcing the fact, and the nearby cities were illuminated, the big guns were belching forth their terrific thunder in joy of the event. However, the truth gradually dawned upon us, and we were forced to realize what we at first thought impossible—that Lee would be forced to surrender. A few days later we were all ordered into line, and officially notified of General Lee's surrender. The futility of further resistance was emphasized, and we were urgently requested to take the oath of Allegiance to the United States Government. This was "a bitter pill," "the yellow pup," to swallow, and a very few solemnly complied. The great majority still had a forlorn hope. Generals Johnston, Kirby Smith, Mosby, and others were still in the field, and it seemed to be a tacit understanding, that we would never take the oath of allegiance as long as one Confederate officer contended in the field.

Finally, when there was no disguising the fact that General Johnston and all others had honorably surrendered—that all was lost—on the 19th day of June, 1865, the last batch of officers in prison took the oath of allegiance to the United States Government, bade farewell to Fort Delaware, and inscribed on its walls, on its fences, in books, and divisions the French quotation, "Font est perdeu l'honeur"—All is lost but honor.

> "A prison! Heavens, I loath the hated name,
> Famine's metropolis, the sink of shame,
> A nauseous sepulchre, whose craving womb
> Hourly inters poor mortals in its tomb;
> By ev'ry plague and ev'ry ill possessed,
> Ev'n purgatory itself to thee's a jest;
> Emblem of hell, nursery of vice,
> Thou crawling university of lice;
> When wretches numberless to ease their pains,

With smoke and all delude their pensive chains.
How shall I avoid thee? or with what spell
Dissolve the enchantment of thy magic cell?
Ev'n Fox himself can't boast so many martyrs,
As yearly fall within thy wretched quarters.
Money I've none, and debts I cannot pay,
Un'ess my vermin will those debts defray.
Not scolding wife, nor inquisition's worse;
Thou'rt ev'ry mischief crammed into one curse."

CHAPTER XXXVIII.

Leave the Valley for the Last Time---October 20th to December 31st, 1864.

The retreat from Fisher's Hill to New Market will never be forgotten by those who participated therein as long as they live. To recapitulate the movements of the last thirty-six hours and reflect upon what had been accomplished, it seems beyond human endurance. No retreat in history, even the famous retreat of Xenophon, while of greater duration and under different circumstances, still it did not equal that of Early during the same length of time. From midnight of the 18th the troops were in line, crossing the river some miles in the distance before daylight, storms and takes the enemy's lines by nine o'clock, incessant fighting for five or six miles (either fighting or on the run), then a stampede of the same distance, then back across the river and to camp, a two hours' halt, a forced march of thirty-five miles—making over fifty miles in all—without eating or drinking, only as could be "caught up" on the march or run. Up the valley this routed, disorganized rabble (it could not be called an army) marched, every man as he saw fit, here a General at the head of a few squads called regiments, or a Colonel or Captain with a few men at his heels, some with colors and some without; here a Colonel without a man, there a score or two of men without a commissioned officer. A great number had abandoned their arms and accoutrements, others their scanty baggage. Some regiments had lost their whole supply trains that hauled their cooking utensils and provisions. Then we could see artillerymen with

othing but a few jaded horses, their cannons and caissons left
1 the general upheaval and wreck at the Stone Bridge, or on
ae field of battle; Quartermasters, with their teamsters riding
r leading their horses, their wagons abandoned or over run by
thers in the mad rush to escape across the bridge before it
vas blocked. Along the road loose horses roamed at will,
vhile the sides of the pike were strewn with discarded blankets,
ent flies. oilcloths and clothing, the men being forced to free
hemselves of all surplus incumbrances in order to keep up
vith the moving mass. At one place we passed General Early,
itting on his horse by the roadside, viewing the motley crowd
s it passed by. He looked sour and haggard. You could see
y the expression of his face the great weight upon his mind,
.is deep disappointment, his unspoken disappointment. What
vas yesterday a proud, well-disciplined army that had accom-
lished during the first part of the day all, or more, that even
he most sanguine General could have expected —crossed rivers,
ulled themselves over the mountains, assaulted and surprised
n enemy who lay in feeling security behind almost impregna-
le fortifications, routed and driven them from the field, cap-
uring almost the whole camp equipage with twenty field
ieces—now before him poured, the same victorious army,
eaten, stampeded, without order or discipline. all the fruits of
ictory and his own camp equipage gone, his wagon trains
bandoned, the men without arms, his cannoneers without can-
onry and every color trailing in the dust. And what caused
:? The sudden change from victory to defeat. It was not
he want of Generalship, for General Early had wisely planned.
t was not for lack of courage of the troops, for that morning
hey had displayed valor and over come obstacles which
vould have baffled and dismayed less bold spirits. Was it for
he superior gallantry of the enemy's troops or the superior
jeneralship of their adversary? The latter was awry, and the
ormer had been routed from their entrenchments by the bayo-
et of the Confederates. Sheridan did not even hope to stop
ur victorious march, only to check it sufficiently to enable
.im to save the remnant of his army. A feeble advance, a
anic strikes our army, and all is lost, while no individual,
fficer, brigade, or regiment could be held responsible. It
hows that once a panic strikes an army all discipline is lost,
nd nothing but time will restore it. For nearly one hundred

years historians have been framing reasons and causes of Napoleon's Waterloo, but they are as far from the real cause to-day as they were the night of the rout.   It will ever remain the same sad mystery of Early at Cedar Creek.   Men are, in some respects, like the animal, and especially in large bodies. A man, when left alone to reason and think for himself, and be forced to depend upon his own resources, will often act differently than when one of a great number.   The "loss of a head" is contageous.   One will commit a foolish act, and others will follow, but cannot tell why.   Otherwise quiet and unobtrusive men, when influenced by the frenzy of an excited mob, will commit violence which in their better moments their hearts would revolt and their consciences rebel against.   A soldier in battle will leave his ranks and fly to the rear with no other reason than that he "saw others doing the same, and followed.

The stampede of Early was uncalled for, unnecessary, and disgraceful, and I willingly assume my share of the blame and shame.   My only title to fame rests upon my leading the Third South Carolina Regiment in the grandest stampede of the Southern Army, the greatest since Waterloo, and I hope to be forgiven for saying with pardonable pride that I led them remarkably well to the rear for a boy of eighteen.   A General could not have done better.

We passed the little towns and villages of the Valley, the ladies coming to their doors and looking on the retreat in silence.   Were we ashamed?   Don't ask the pointed question, gentle reader, for the soldiers felt as if they could turn and brain every Federal soldier in the army with the butt of his rifle.   But not a reproach, not a murmur from those self-sacrificing, patriotic women of the Valley.   They were silent, but sad—their experience during the time the enemy occupied the Valley before told them they had nothing to expect but insult and injury, for their bold, proud Virginia blood would not suffer them to bend the knee in silent submission.   Their sons and husbands had all given themselves to the service of their country, while rapine and the torch had already done its work too thoroughly to fear it much now or dread its consequences. But the presence alone of a foreign foe on their threshold was the bitterness of gall.

On reaching New Market, men were gathered together in

regiments and assigned to camping grounds, as well as the disorganized state of the army would allow. All night long the stragglers kept coming in, and did so for several days. We were suffering for something to eat more than anything else. Rations of corn were issued, and this was parched and eaten, or beaten up, when parched, and a decoction which the soldiers called "coffee" was made and drunk

The troops remained in camp until the last of October, then began their march to rejoin Lee. The campaign of Early in the Valley had been a failure, if measured by the fruits of victory. If, however, to keep the enemy from occupying the Valley, or from coming down on the north or rear of Richmond was the object, then it had accomplished its purpose, but at a heavy loss and a fearful sacrifice of life. We arrived at Richmond early in November, and began building winter quarters about seven miles from the city, on the extreme left of the army. Everything north of the James continued quiet along our lines for a month or more, but we could hear the deep baying of cannon continually, away to our right, in the direction of Petersburg.

When we had about finished our huts we were moved out of them and further to the right, in quarters that Hoke's Division had built. These were the most comfortable quarters we occupied during the war. They consisted of log huts twelve by fourteen, thoroughly chinked with mud and straw, some covered with dirt, others with split boards. We had splendid breastworks in front of us, built up with logs on the inside and a bank of earth from six to eight feet in depth on the outside, a ditch of three or four feet beyond and an escarpment inside. At salients along the line forts for the artillery were built, but not now manned, and in front of our lines and around our forts mines or torpedoes were sunk, which would explode by tramping on the earth above them.

At these mines were little sticks about three feet long stuck in the ground with a piece of blue flannel tied to the end to attract the attention of our pickets going out. But hundreds of white sticks, exactly like those above the mines, were stuck into the earth every three feet for a distance of forty feet all around, but these were marked red instead of blue. This was so that the enemy, in case of a charge, or spies coming in at night, could not distinguish harmless stakes from those of the torpedo. We picketed in front and had to pass through where these stakes were posted single file, along little paths winding in and out among them. The men were led out and in by guides and cautioned against touching any, for fear of mistake and being blown up. It is needless to say these instructions were carried out to the letter and no mistake ever made. On several occasions, even before we had our first quarters completed, a report would come occasionally that the enemy was approaching or quartered near our front, and out we would go to meet them, but invariably it proved to be a false alarm or the enemy had retired. Once in December the enemy made a demonstration to our right, and we were called out at night to support the line where the attack was made. After a few rounds of shelling and a few bullets flying over our heads (no harm being done), at daylight we returned to our camp. Our lines had been so extended that to man our works along our front we had not more than one man to every six feet. Still with our breastworks so complete and the protection beyond the line, it is doubtful whether the enemy could have made much headway against us. All the timber and debris in our front for more than one thousand yards had been felled or cleared away.

The ladies of Richmond had promised the soldiers a great Christmas dinner on Christmas day, but from some cause or other our dinner did not materialize. But the soldiers fared very well. Boxes from home were now in order, and almost every day a box or two from kind and loving friends would come in to cheer and comfort them. Then, too, the blockaders at Wilmington and Charleston would escape the Argus eyes of the fleet and bring in a cargo of shoes, cloth, sugar, coffee, etc. Even with all our watchfulness and the vigilance of the enemy on the James, that indefatigable and tireless Jew, with an eye to business, would get into Richmond with loads of delicacies, and this the soldier managed to buy with his "Confederate graybacks." They were drawing now at the rate of seventeen dollars per month, worth at that time about one dollar in gold or one dollar and seventy cents in greenbacks. The Jews in all countries and in all times seemed to fill a peculiar sphere of usefulness. They were not much of fighters, but they were great "getters." They would undergo any hardships or risks for gain, and while our government

may not have openly countenanced their traffic, still it was
thought they "winked" at it. I do know there were a lot of
Jews in Richmond who could go in and out of our lines at
will. Sometimes they were caught, first by one army and
then by another, and their goods or money confiscated, still
they kept up their blockade running. I was informed by one
of General Gary's staff officers since the war, that while they
were doing outpost duty on the lower James, Jews came in
daily with passports from the authorities at Richmond, author-
izing them to pass the lines. On many occasions they claimed
they were robbed by our pickets. Once this officer allowed
two Jews to pass out of the lines, with orders to pass the
pickets, but soon they returned, saying they were robbed.
General Gary, who could not tolerate such treachery, had the
men called up and the Jews pointed out the men who had
plundered them. But the men stoutly denied the charge, and
each supported the other in his denials, until a search was
ordered, but nothing was found. They cursed the "lieing
Jew" and threatened that the next time they attempted to pass
they would leave them in the woods with "key holes through
them." "While at the same time," continued the officer, "I
and so was General Gary satisfied these same men had robbed
them."

We were now again under our old commander, Lieutenant
General Longstreet. He had recently returned to the army,
convalescent from his severe wound at the Wilderness, and
was placed in command of the north side. Scarcely had he
assumed command, and prior to our arrival, before he was attacked by General Butler, with twenty thousand men. He
defeated him, sustaining little loss, with Fields' and Hokes'
Divisions, and Gary's Cavalry. Butler lost between one
thousand two hundred and one thousand five hundred men.
The year was slowly drawing to a close, with little percepti-
ble advantage to the South. It is true that Grant, the idol
and ideal of the North, had thrown his legions against the
veterans of Lee with a recklessness never before experienced,
and with a loss almost irreparable, still the prospects of the
Confederacy were anything but encouraging. Yet the child-
ike faith and confidence of the Confederate privates in their
cause and in their superiors, that disaster and defeat never
troubled them nor caused them worry or uneasiness. General

Hood had gone on his wild goose chase through Middle Tennessee, had met with defeat and ruin at Franklin and Nashville; Sherman was on his unresisted march through Georgia, laying waste fields, devastating homes with a vandalism unknown in civilized warfare, and was now nearing the sea; while the remnant of Hood's Army was seeking shelter and safety through the mountains of North Georgia. Still Lee, with his torn and tattered veterans, stood like a wall of granite before Richmond and Petersburg. What a .halo of glory should surround the heads of all who constituted the Army of Lee or followed the fortunes of Longstreet, Hill, Ewell, and Early. At Chickamauga, Chattanooga, East Tennessee, Wilderness, or wherever the plumes of their chieftains waved or their swords flashed amid the din of battle, victory had ever perched upon their banners. It was only when away from the inspiration and prestige of Longstreet did the troops of Kershaw fail or falter, and only then to follow in the wake of others who had yielded.

Owing to the casualties in battle during the last few months and the disasters of the two Valley campaigns, many changes in the personnel of the companies and regiments necessarily took place, once we got fairly settled in camp.

Brigadier General Kershaw had been made Major General in place of General McLaws soon after the battle of the Wilderness. His Aid-de-Camp, Lieutenant Doby, having been killed on that day, I. M. Davis. Adjutant of the Fifteenth was placed upon the personnel staff of the Major General.

Colonel John D. Kennedy, of the Second, having recovered from the wounds received on the 6th of May, was promoted in place of General Connor to the position of Brigadier General.

The Colonel and Lieutenant Colonel of the Twentieth both being captured on the 19th of October, Lieutenant Colonel F. S. Lewie, of the Fifteenth, was assigned temporarily to the command of the Twentieth. Captain G. Leaphart, senior Captain, was afterwards promoted to Major, and commanded the "Twentieth Army Corps" until the close of the war.

Lieutenant Colonel Stackhouse was made Colonel of the Eighth after the death of Henagan, and either Captain McLucas or Captain T. F. Malloy was promoted to Major (I am not positive on this point). Captain Rogers was also one

f the senior Captains, and I think he, too, acted for a part of
he time as one of the field officers.

The Third Battalion was commanded by one of the Cap-
ains for the remainder of the war, Colonel Rice and Major
filler both being permanently disabled for field service, but
till retained their rank and office.

There being no Colonel or Lieutenant Colonel of the
eventh, and Major Goggans having resigned soon after the
Vilderness battle, Captain Thomas Huggins was raised to the
ank of Colonel. I do not remember whether any other field
fficers of this regiment were ever appointed, but I think not.
Lieutenant John R. Carwile, who had been acting Adjutant
f the Seventh for a long time, was now assigned to duty on
he brigade staff.

Captain William Wallace was promoted to Colonel of the
econd, with Captain T. D. Graham and B. F. Clyburn,
Lieutenant Colonel and Major respectively.

Colonel Rutherford, of the Third, having been killed on the
3th of October, and Lieutenant Colonel Maffett, captured a
hort while before, Captain R. P. Todd was made Major, then
aised to the rank of Lieutenant Colonel, and Captain J. K. G.
Tance, Major.

Many new Captains and Lieutenants were made, to fill the
acancies occasioned by the above changes and deaths in bat-
e, but I have not the space to mention them.

———

Our last Brigadier General, J. D. Kennedy, was a very good
fficer, however, his kindness of heart, his sympathetic na-
ure, his indulgent disposition caused him to be rather lax in
iscipline. There was quite a contrast in the rigidity of Gen-
ral Connor's discipline and the good, easy "go as you please"
f General Kennedy. But the latter had the entire confidence
f the troops, and was dearly loved by both officers and men.
Ie was quite sociable, courteous, and kind to all. The men
ad been in service so long, understood their duties so well,
aat it was not considered a necessity to have a martinet for a
ommander. General Kennedy's greatest claim to distinction
ras his good looks. He certainly was one of the finest look-
ng officers in the army. I fear little contradiction when I say
eneral Kennedy and Major W. D. Peck, of the Quartermas-
er Department, were two of the finest looking men that South

Carolina gave to the war.   I give a short sketch of General
Kennedy.

GENERAL JOHN D. KENNEDY.

General John D. Kennedy was born in Camden, South Carolina, January 5th, 1840, the son of Anthony M. and Sarah
Doby Kennedy.   His mother was the grand-daughter of
Abraham Belton, a pioneer settler of Camden and a patriot soldier in the Revolution.   His father was born in Scotland, having emigrated to the United States about the year 1830, at
which time he settled in Kershaw County, S. C., where he
married.   (He has been engaged in planting and merchandising
for many years.   Two sons and two daughters were the issue of
this marriage.)   General Kennedy obtained his early scholastic
training in the Camden schools, and in 1855, at the age of fifteen, entered the South Carolina College at Columbia.   He
entered the law office of Major W. Z. Leitner soon after, and
was admitted to practice in January, 1861, and in April of that
year joined the Confederate Army as Captain of Company E,
Second South Carolina Regiment, under the command of Colonel J. B. Kershaw.   In 1862 he was made Colonel of the Second South Carolina Regiment, and in 1864 was promoted to
the rank of Brigadier General, and held that position to the
close of the war, having surrendered with General Johnston at
Greensboro, North Carolina, in 1865.   General Kennedy was
six times wounded, and fifteen times was hit by spent balls.
At the close of the war he resumed his practice of law at Camden, but abandoned it soon after and turned his attention to
farming.   In 1877 he once more returned to the bar, and has
since been actively and prominently engaged in his practice.
In 1876 he was a member of the State Democratic Executive
Committee, and was its chairman in 1878.   In December, 1865,
he was elected to Congress, defeating Colonel C. W. Dudley,
but did not take his seat, as he refused to take the iron clad
oath.   In 1878-9 he represented his county in the Legislature,
and was Chairman of the Committee on Privileges and Elections.   He was elected Lieutenant Governor of the State in
1880, and in 1882 was a prominent candidate for Governor, but
Colonel Hugh Thompson received the nomination over General
Bratton and himself.   He was elected Grand Master of the
Grand Lodge A. F. M. of South Carolina in 1881, and served

two years. As a member of the National Democratic Convention in 1876, he cast his vote for Tilden and Hendricks, and in 1884 was Presidential Elector at large on the Democratic ticket. President Cleveland sent him as Consul General to Shanghai, China, in 1886. In 1890 he was Chairman of the State Advisory Committee, of the straightout Democratic party. In early life he was married to Miss Elizabeth Cunningham, who died in 1876. In 1882 Miss Harriet Boykin became his wife.

The above is taken from Cyclopædia of Eminent and Representative Men of the Carolinas of the Nineteenth Century.

Notes on General Kennedy's life, furnished by one of his soldiers:

He was born at Camden, S. C., January 5th, 1840. While in his 'teens he became a member of the Camden Light Infantry, of which J. B. Kershaw was Captain; elected First Lieutenant in 1860. Upon the secession of South Carolina, December 20th, 1860, Captain Kershaw was elected Colonel of the Second South Carolina Volunteers, and Lieutenant Kennedy was chosen Captain of the Camden Volunteers, a company composed of members of the Camden Light Infantry and those who united with them for service in the field. This company became Company E, Second South Carolina Volunteers, was ordered to Charleston April 8th, 1861, and witnessed from their position on Morris Island the siege of Fort Sumter, April 12th, 1861. The Second Regiment formed part of the First Brigade, commanded by General M. L. Bonham, of the Army of the Potomac, as the Confederate Army in Northern Virginia was then called. In the spring of 1862 the troops who had volunteered for twelve months reorganized for the war, the Second South Carolina Volunteers being, I believe, the first body of men in the army to do so. At reorganization Captain Kennedy was elected Colonel, in which capacity he served until 1864, when he was promoted to the command of the brigade, which he held until the close of the war. In 1862 the name of the army was changed to the Army of Northern Virginia, the Federals having called theirs the Army of the Potomac. The Second was engaged in every battle fought by the army in Virginia, from the first Manassas to Petersburg, except Second Manassas, and was also in battle of Chickamauga, battles around Knoxville, Averysboro, and Bentonville, and surrendered at Greensboro April 27th, 1865. General Kennedy was in every battle in which his command was engaged, and was wounded six times and struck fifteen times. He died in Camden, S. C., April 14th, 1896.

COLONEL R. P. TODD.

Colonel R. P. Todd was born in Laurens County, about the year 1838. Graduated at a literary college (I think the South Carolina), read law, and entered upon the practice of his profession a year or two before the beginning of hostilities. At the first call by the State for twelve months' volunteers, Colonel Todd enlisted in the "Laurens Briars," afterwards Company G, Third South Carolina Regiment, and was elected Captain. He took his company with him into the Confederate service, and at the reorganization in 1862, was again elected Captain. Was made Major in 1864 and Lieutenant Colonel in the early part of 1865. He was in most of the great battles in which the regiment was engaged, and was several times severely wounded. He surrendered at Greensboro, N. C.

After the war he again took up the practice of law and continued it until his death, which took place several years ago. He represented his county in the Senate of the State for one term.

Soon after the close of the war he married Miss Mary Farley, sister of General Hugh L. Farley, formerly Adjutant and Inspector General of South Carolina, and of Captain William Farley, one of the riders of General Stuart, and a famous character in John Estin Cook's historical romances.

Colonel Todd was a good officer, gallant soldier, and loyal and kind to his men. He was a man of brilliant attainments and one of the most gifted and fluent speakers in the brigade.

The writer regrets his inability to get a more enlarged sketch of this dashing officer, talented lawyer, and perfect gentleman.

CAPTAIN JOHN K. NANCE.

Captain John K. Nance was one of the most jovial, fun-loving, light-hearted souls in the Third Regiment. He was all sunshine, and this genial, buoyant disposition seemed to be always caught up and reflected by all who came about him. He was truly a "lover of his fellow-men," and was never so happy as when surrounded by jolly companions and spirits like his own. He was a great lover of outdoor sports, and no game or camp amusement was ever complete without this rollicksome, good-natured knight of the playground.

He was born in Laurens County, in 1839. Graduated from Due West College and soon afterwards joined the "Quitman Rifles," Company E, of the Third Regiment, then being organized by his kinsman, Colonel James D. Nance. He was first Orderly Sergeant of the company, but was soon elected Lieutenant. At the reorganization of his company, in 1862, he was elected First Lieutenant, and on James D. Nance being made Colonel of the Third, he was promoted to Captain. Many times during the service he was called upon to command the regiment, and in the latter part of 1864 or the first of 1865 he was promoted to Major.

Captain John K. Nance was one of the best officers upon the drillground in the regiment, and had few equals as such in the brigade. He was a splendid disciplinarian and tactician, and could boast of one of the finest companies in the service. His company, as well as himself, was all that could be desired upon the battlefield.

In 1864 he married Miss Dolly, daughter of Dr. Thomas B. Rutherford, and sister of the lamented Colonel W. D. Rutherford. After the war he was engaged in planting in Newberry County. He was three times elected Auditor of the county. He was a leading spirit among the Democrats during the days of reconstruction, and lent all energies and talents to the great upheaval in politics in 1876 that brought about the overflow of the negro party and gave the government to the whites of the State. He died about 1884, leaving a widow and several children.

COLONEL WILLIAM WALLACE.

Colonel William Wallace, of the Second South Carolina Regiment, was undoubtedly the Murat of the Old First Brigade. His soldierly qualities, his dashing courage, and the prestige that surrounds his name as a commander, especially upon the skirmish line, forcibly recalls that impetuous prince, the Roland of Napoleon's Army. Upon the battle line he was brave almost to rashness, and never seemed to be more in his element or at ease than amidst the booming cannon, the roar of musketry, or the whirl of combat. Colonel Wallace was a soldier born and a leader of men. He depended not so

much upon tactics or discipline, but more upon the cool, stern
courage that was in himself and his men.

His life as a soldier and civilian has been fortunate and brilliant, in which glory and promotion followed hand in hand.
A comrade gives a few facts in his life.

Colonel William Wallace was born in Columbia, S. C.,
November 16th, 1824, and was graduated at the South Carolina College in 1844. He then studied law under Chancellor
James J. Caldwell. Was admitted to the bar in 1846, and
began the practice of law at Columbia, in which he continued,
with the exception of his military service, giving attention
also to his planting interests.

At the beginning of the Confederate War he held the rank
of General in the State Militia. At the call for troops, ordered
out the Twenty-third Regiment, State Troops, and was the
first man of the Regiment to volunteer. He was elected Captain of the "Columbia Grays," afterwards Company C of the
Second South Carolina Volunteer Infantry, Colonel Kershaw
commanding. After the reduction of Fort Sumter, with his
company and three others of the Second, he volunteered for
service in Virginia, and about a month after their arrival in
Virginia the regiment was filled up with South Carolinians.
He was promoted to Major in 1863, to Lieutenant Colonel
after the battle of the Wilderness, and to Colonel after the battle of Bentonville.

He had the honor of participating in the capture of Fort
Sumter and the battles of Blackburn's Ford, First Manassas,
Williamsburg, Savage Station, Malvern Hill, Sharpsburg,
Fredericksburg, Chancellorsville, Gettysburg, Chattanooga,
Knoxville, Wilderness, Spottsylvania Court House, Second
Cold Harbor, the defense of Petersburg until the winter of
1864-1865, and the campaign in the Carolinas, including the
battles of Averysboro and Bentonville.

During the desperate struggle at Second Cold Harbor, in
June, 1864, with the Second Regiment alone, he recaptured
our breastworks on Kershaw's right and Hoke's left, from
which two of our brigades had been driven. The enemy
driven out consisted of the Forty-eighth and One hundred and
Twelfth New York, each numbering one thousand men, while
the Second numbered only one hundred and twenty-six men
all told. So rapid was the assault that the color bearer of the

Forty-eighth New York, with his colors, was captured and sent to General Kershaw, who was at his proper position some distance in rear of his division.

During his service Colonel Wallace was twice wounded—in the foot, at Charlestown, W. Va., and in the arm, at Gettysburg. After the conclusion of hostilities he returned to his home and the care of his plantation. Previous to the war he had an honorable career in the Legislature, and immediately afterwards he was a member of the Convention of 1865 and of the Legislature next following, and was elected to the State Senate for four years, in 1881. From 1891 to 1894 he was engaged in the correction of the indexes of the records of the Secretary of State's office, and in 1894 was appointed postmaster of Columbia by President Cleveland.

By his marriage, in 1848, to Victoria C., daughter of Dr. John McLemore, of Florida, Colonel Wallace has five children living, Andrew, William, Bruce, Edward Barton. and Margaret. After the death of his first wife he married, in 1876, Mrs. Fannie C. Mobley, nee Means.

CAPTAIN JOHN HAMPDEN BROOKS.

John Hampden Brooks was Captain of Company G, Seventh South Carolina Regiment, from its entry into State service to the end of its twelve months' enlistment. At the reorganization of the regiment he declined re-election, and served for a short time as Aid-de-Camp on General Kershaw's staff. At this time, upon recommendation of Generals Kershaw and Jos. E. Johnston, he raised another company of Partisan Rangers, and was independent for awhile. Upon invitation, he joined Nelson's Seventh South Carolina Battalion, Hagood's Brigade, and served with this command (save a brief interval) to the end of the war. He was in the first battle of Manassas and in Bentonville, the last great battle of the war. At Battery Wagner his company was on picket duty the night of the first assault, and it was by his order that the first gun was fired in that memorable siege, and one of his men was the first Confederate killed. At the battle of Drewry's Bluff, Va., Captain Brooks was three times wounded, and lost sixty-eight out of the seventy-five men carried into action, twenty-five being left dead upon the field. Upon recovery from his wounds he returned to his command, but was soon detached,

31

by request of General Beauregard and order of General Lee, to organize a foreign battalion from the Federal prisoners at Florence, S. C., with distinct promise of promotion. This battalion was organized and mustered into Confederate service at Summerville, S. C., as Brooks' Battalion, and in December, 1864, Captain Brooks took a part of the command to Savannah (then being invested by General Sherman) and they served a short time on the line of defense. In consequence of bad behavior and mutiny, however, they were soon returned to prison. Captain Brooks was now placed in command of all unattached troops in the city of Charleston, but he became tired of inactivity, at his own request was relieved, and upon invitation of his old company, ignoring his promotion, he returned to its command.

Captain Brooks was born at Edgefield Court House and was educated at Mt. Zion, Winnsboro, and the South Carolina College. His father, Colonel Whitfield Brooks, was an ardent nullifier, and named his son, John Hampden, in honor of that illustrious English patriot. That Captain Brooks should have displayed soldierly qualities was but natural, as these were his by inheritance. His grandfather, Colonel Z. S. Brooks, was a Lieutenant in the patriotic army of the Revolutionary War, and his grandmother a daughter of Captain Jas. Butler, killed in the "Cloud's Creek massacre." His brothers, Captain Preston S. and Whitfield B. Brooks, were members of the Palmetto Regiment in the Mexican War; the latter mortally wounded at Cherubusco and promoted to a Lieutenant in the Twelfth Regulars for gallantry in action.

Captain Brooks is the sole survivor of the first Captains of the Seventh Regiment, and resides at Roselands, the old family homestead, formerly in Edgefield, but now Greenwood County.

CAPTAIN ANDREW HARLLEE.

Captain Andrew Harllee, of Company I, Eighth South Carolina Regiment, when a boy went with a number of the best young men of the State to Kansas Territory, in 1856, and saw his first service with the Missourians in the border troubles in that Territory, and took part in several severe engagements at Lawrence, Topeka, and Ossawattonic Creek with the Abolition and Free State forces, under old John Brown and Colonel

Jim Law; the Southern or pro-slavery forces being under
General David R. Atchison and Colonels Stingfellow and
Marshall. After remaining in Kansas a year, he returned to
his home and commenced the study of law at Marion Court
House, but after a short time was appointed to a position in
the Interior Department at Washington by the Hon. Thos. A.
Hendrix, under whom he served as a clerk in a land office
while in Kansas. This position in the Interior Department
he held at the time of the secession of the State, and was the
recipient of the first dispatch in Washington announcing the
withdrawal of South Carolina from the Union, which was sent
him by his uncle, General W. W. Harllee, then Lieutenant
Governor and a member of the Secession Convention. He at
once began preparations for his departure from Washington
for Charleston, but was notified from Charleston to remain
until the Commissioners appointed by the Convention to proceed to Washington and endeavor to treat with the authorities
should arrive, which he did, and was appointed their Secretary. The Commission consisted of Senator Robert W. Barnwell, General James H. Adams, and Honorable James L. Orr.
After many fruitless efforts, they finally got an audience with
President Buchanan, who refused to treat with them in any
manner whatever, and Mr. Harllee was directed to proceed at
once to Charleston, the bearer of dispatches from the Commissioners to the Convention still in session, and after delivering
the same he reported to Governor Pickens for duty. The
Governor appointed him Assistant Quartermaster, with the
rank of Captain, and he discharged the duties of that office
around Charleston until the fall of Fort Sumter.

Anxious for service at the front, he resigned from the
Quartermaster Department and enlisted as a private in Company I, Eighth South Carolina Regiment, and fought through
the battles of Bull Run and Manassas with a musket. General
Bonham, in command of the brigade, detailed him for scouting
duty in and near Alexandria and Washington, and he had
many thrilling adventures and narrow escapes in the discharge
of those duties. In October, 1861, Lieutenant R. H. Rogers,
of his company, resigned, and Private Harllee was elected
Second Lieutenant in his stead. At the reorganization of the
regiment and companies, in April, 1862, he was elected Captain of his company, which he commanded to the surrender.

He was several times severely wounded, and bears upon his person visible evidences of the battle-scarred veteran. He was regarded by all his comrades as a daring and intrepid officer.

He lives upon his plantation, near Little Rock, where he was born and reared, is a bachelor, a professional farmer, and one of the leading citizens of his section of the State.

CAPTAIN WILLIAM D. CARMICHAEL.

Captain William D. Carmichael volunteered in 1861, and assisted in raising Company I, Eighth South Carolina Regiment, and was elected Second Lieutenant at reorganization. In April, 1862, he assisted Captain Stackhouse in raising Company L for the same regiment, and was elected First Lieutenant of that company, and upon the promotion of Captain Stackhouse to Major, he was promoted Captain of Company L and commanded it to the surrender.

He was three times wounded, twice severely, and was one of the most gallant and trusted officers of that gallant regiment. After the war he settled on his plantation, near Little Rock, married, and has lived there ever since, raising a large family of children, and is one of the most successful farmers of that progressive section. He is one of the foremost citizens of Marion County.

CAPTAIN DUNCAN MCINTYRE.

Captain Duncan McIntyre, of Company H, Eighth South Carolina Regiment, Kershaw's Brigade, was born at Marion S. C., on August 30th, 1836. Was prepared for college at Mount Zion Institute, at Winnsboro, S. C. Entered Freshman Class of South Carolina College, December, 1853.

Married Julia R., daughter of General William Evans, December, 1858. Commenced life as a planter on the west side of Pee Dee River, in Marion County, January 1st, 1860.

On secession of the State, he volunteered for service in the Jeffries' Creek Company. Was elected First Lieutenant of the company, Captain R. G. Singletary having been elected as commander. On Governor Pickens' first call for troops the company offered its services and was assigned to the Eighth South Carolina Regiment, Colonel E. B. C. Cash commanding. The company was ordered to Charleston on fall of Fort Sumter, where it remained until the last of May, when it was ordered to Florence, S. C., where, about the 1st of June, it was mustered into Confederate service by General Geo. Evans, and immediately ordered to Virginia to form a part of Bonham's Brigade.

Captain McIntyre was with the regiment at the first battle of Manassas or Bull Run, and with the exception of two short leaves of absence from sickness and from wounds, was with the regiment in nearly all of its campaigns and important skirmishes and battles, Williamsburg, battles around Richmond, Va., Maryland Heights, Sharpsburg, Fredericksburg, Chancellorsville, Wilderness, Spottsylvania Court House, and all of the battles against Grant up to the investment of Petersburg, Va. He was with the regiment and Longstreet's Corps in the campaign in Tennessee.

In the Tennessee campaign he commanded the Eighth Regiment at the battle of Ream's Station, and when the Second, Eighth, and Third Battalion, under the command of the gallant Colonel Gaillard, of the Second, made a daring and successful attack (at night) on the picket line of the enemy, the Eighth was on the right and first to dislodge the enemy and occupy the pits.

Captain McIntyre was twice wounded—first, in the chest at the battle of Fredericksburg, Va., and second time, severely in the thigh at Deep Bottom, Va.

COLONEL WILLIAM DRAYTON RUTHERFORD.

When Colonel William Drayton Rutherford fell in battle at Strasburg, Virginia, on the 13th of October, 1864, he was but a little more than twenty-seven years of age, having been born in Newberry, S. C., on the 23rd day of September, 1837.

The life thus destroyed was brimful of hope, for he was gifted with a rare intelligence, and possessed of an affectionate nature, with a deep sympathy for his fellow men and a patriotism which could only terminate with his own life. His father, Dr. Thomas B. Rutherford, was a grandson of Colonel Robert Rutherford, of Revolutionary fame, and his mother, Mrs. Laura Adams Rutherford, was a direct descendant of the Adams family of patriots who fought for their country in the State of Massachusetts.

The boyhood of Colonel Rutherford was spent on the plan-

tation of his father, in Newberry County.   Here was laid the
foundation of his splendid physical nature, and his mind as
well.   While not beyond the height of five feet and ten inches,
and with not an ounce of spare flesh, physically he was all
bone and muscle, and was the embodiment of manly beauty.
His early training was secured in the Male Academies of
Greenville and Newberry.   At the age of sixteen years he
entered the Citadel Academy in Charleston, S. C.   It was at
this school he first exhibited the remarkable power arising
from his ability to concentrate every faculty of his mind to the
accomplishment of a single purpose, for, by reason of his fond-
ness for out door sports and reading, he had fallen in stand
amongst the lowest members of a large class, but, conceiving
that some persons thought he could do no better, by a determined effort to master all the branches of study in an incredible space of time he was placed among the first ten members of
his class.   Military discipline was too restrictive for him,
hence he left the Citadel Academy and entered the Sophomore
Class of the South Carolina College at Columbia, S. C.   In a
few months after entering this college he was advanced from
the Sophomore Class to that of the Junior.   However, he
never took his degree, for owing to a so-called college rebellion, he left college.   Afterwards he regretted his step.   Not
content with the advantages he had already enjoyed, he went
to Germany to complete his education, but the war between
the States caused him to return to America.   He espoused
with heart and soul the cause of his native State.   Before
going to Germany he had been admitted to the practice of the
law.   Chief Justice John Belton O'Neall expressed himself as
delighted with young Rutherford's examination for the bar,
and predicted for him a brilliant career as a lawyer.

He was made Adjutant of the Third South Carolina Regiment of Infantry, and so thoroughly did he perform his duties
as a soldier, and so delighted were his comrades in arms with
his courage and generous nature, that he was elected, without
opposition, on 16th of May, 1862, Major of his regiment, and
on the 29th of June, 1862, he became Lieutenant Colonel, and
on the 6th of May, 1864, he was promoted to the Colonelcy of
his regiment.   General James Connor was so much delighted
with him as an officer that he recommended him for promotion to Brigadier General.   When this gallant officer fell in

the front of his regiment, there was naught but sorrow for his untimely end.

In March, 1862, he married the beautiful and accomplished Miss Sallie Fair, only daughter of Colonel Simeon Fair, of Newberry. The only child of this union was Kate Stewart Rutherford. who was known as the "daughter of the regiment." Kate is now the wife of the Honorable George Johnstone.

CHAPTER XXXIX

Peace Conference---State Troops---Women of the South.

The civilized world, especially the Monarchies of Europe, which at first viewed with satisfaction this eruption in the great Republic across the waters, now anxiously watched them in their mad fury, tearing to tatters the fabric of Democratic government. This government, since its withdrawal from the Old World influence, had grown great and strong, and was now a powerful nation—a standing menace to their interest and power. But they began to look with alarm on the spectacle of these two brothers—brothers in blood, in aims, ambition, and future expectations, only an imaginary line separating them—with 'glaring eyes, their hands at each others throat, neither willing to submit or yield as long as there was a vestige of vitality in either. Even the most considerate and thoughtful of the North began to contemplate the wreck and ruin of their common country, and stood aghast at the rivers of blood that had flown, the widows and orphans made, and the treasures expended. They now began to wish for a call to halt. This useless slaughter caused a shudder to run through every thinking man when he contemplated of the havoc yet to come. The two armies were getting nearer and nearer together, one adding strength as the other grew weaker —the South getting more desperate and more determined to sacrifice all, as they saw the ground slipping inch by inch beneath their feet; the North becoming more confident with each succeeding day. It began to look like a war of extermi-

nation of American manhood. The best and bravest of the
North had fallen in the early years of the war, while the bulk
of the army now was composed of the lowest type of foreigners,
who had been tempted to our shores by the large bounties paid
by the Union Government. Taking their cue from their
native comrades in arms, they now tried to outdo them in
vandalizing, having been taught that they were wreaking
vengeance upon the aristocracy and ruining the slave-holders
of the South. The flower of the South's chivalry had also
fallen upon the field and in the trenches, and now youths and
old men were taking the places of soldiers who had died in the
"Bloody Angles" and the tangled Wilderness.

A talk of peace began once more, but the men of the South
were determined to yield nothing as long as a rifle could be
raised. Nothing but their unrestricted independence would
satisfy them. The man who could call nothing his own but
what was on his back was as much determined on his country's independence as those who were the possessors of broad
acres and scores of negroes.

Congressman Boyce, of South Carolina, began to call for a
peace conference in the Confederate Congress. Montgomery
Blair, the father of General Frank P. Blair, then commanding
a corps in Sherman's Army, begged the North to halt and
listen to reason—to stop the fratricidal war. Generals, soldiers, statesmen, and civilians all felt that it had gone on long
enough. Some held a faint hope that peace could be secured
without further effusion of blood. A peace conference was
called at Hampton Roads, near the mouth of the Potomac.
President Lincoln and Secretary of State William H. Seward,
on the part of the North, and Vice-President Stephens, Honorable R. T. M. Hunter, and Judge Campbell, on the part of
the South, attended. Lincoln demanded an "unconditional
surrender" of the army—emancipation of the slaves and a
return to our former places in the Union. Mr. Stephens and
his colleagues knew too well the sentiment of the Southern
people to even discuss such a course. Not a soldier in ranks
would have dared to return and face the women of the South
with such a peace and on such terms as long as there was the
shadow of an organized army in the field.

General Ord, of the Union Army, a humane and Christian
gentleman, wrote and sought an interview with General

Longstreet. He wished that General to use his influence
with General Lee and the officers of the army to meet General
Grant, and with their wives mingling with the wives of the
respective Generals, talk over the matter in a friendly manner,
and see if some plan could not be framed whereby peace could
be secured honorable to all parties. All had had glory enough
and blood sufficient had been shed to gratify the most savage
and fanatical. These officers or the most of them had been
old school-mates at West Point, had been brother officers in
the old army, their wives had mingled in pleasant, social inter-
course at the army posts, and they could aid as only women
can aid, in a friendly way, to bring back an era of good feelings. General Ord further intimated that President Lincoln
would not turn a deaf ear to a reasonable proposition for compensation for the slaves. General Longstreet accepted the
overtures with good grace, but with a dignity fitting his position. He could not, while in the field and in the face of the
enemy, with his superior present, enter into negotiations for a
surrender of his army, or to listen to terms of peace. He
returned and counseled Lee. Urged him to meet Grant, and
as commander-in-chief of all the armies in the South, that he
had a wide latitude, that the people were looking to him to
end the war, and would be satisfied with any concessions he
would recommend. That the politicians had had their say,
now let the soldiers terminate the strife which politicians had
begun. That Napoleon while in Italy, against all precedent
and without the knowledge of the civil department, had
entered into negotiations with the enemy, made peace, and
while distasteful to the authorities, they were too polite to
refuse the terms. But General Lee was too much a soldier to
consider any act outside of his special prerogatives. He,
however, was pleased with the idea, and wrote General Grant,
asking an interview looking towards negotiations of peace.
But General Grant, from his high ideals of the duty and
dignity of a soldier, refused, claiming that the prerogatives of
peace or war were left with the civil, not the military arm of
the service. So it all ended in smoke.

General Lee began making preparations to make still greater
efforts and greater sacrifices. He had been hampered, as well
as many others of our great commanders, by the quixotic and
blundering interference of the authorities at Richmond, and

had become accustomed to it.   There can be no question at this late day that the end, as it did come, had long since dawned upon the great mind of Lee, and it must have been with bitterness that he was forced to sarcifice so many brave and patriotic men for a shadow, while the substance could never be reached.   His only duty now was to prolong the struggle and sacrifice as few men as possible.

General Bragg, that star of ill omen to the Confederacy, was taken out of the War Department in Richmond and sent to Wilmington, N. C., and that brilliant, gallant Kentuckian, General John C. Breckenridge, was placed in his stead as Secretary of War.   General Breckenridge had been the favorite of a great portion of the Southern people in their choice of Presidential candidates against Lincoln, and his place in the cabinet of Mr. Davis gave hope and confidence to the entire South.

General Lee, no doubt acting on his own good judgment, and to the greatest delight of the army, placed General Joseph E. Johnston at the head of the few scattered and disorganized bands that were following on the flanks of Sherman. Some few troops that could be spared from the trenches were to be sent to South Carolina to swell, as far as possible, the army to oppose Sherman.

Governor Brown had called out a great part of the Georgia State Troops, consisting of old men and boys, to the relief of General Hardee, who was moving in the front of Sherman, and a great many of this number crossed over with General Hardee to the eastern side of the Savannah, and remained faithful to the end.   Governor McGrath, of South Carolina, too, had called out every man capable of bearing arms from fifteen to sixty, and placed them by regiments under Beauregard and Johnston.   The forts along the coast in great numbers were abandoned, and the troops thus gathered together did excellent service.   North Carolina brought forward her reserves as the enemy neared her border, all determined to unite in a mighty effort to drive back this ruthless invader.

In this imperfect history of the times of which I write, I cannot resist at this place to render a deserved tribute to the noble women of the South, more especially of South Carolina. It was with difficulty that the soldiers going to the army from their homes after the expiration of their furloughs, or going

to their homes when wounded or sick, procured a night's
lodging in Richmond, for it must be remembered that that
city was already crowded with civilians, officers of the department, surgeons of the hospitals, and officials of every kind.
The hotels and private residences were always full. Scarcely
a private house of any pretentions whatever, that did not have
some sick or wounded soldier partaking of the hospitalities of
the citizens, who could better care for the patient than could
be had in hospitals. Then, again, the entire army had to
pass through the city either going to or from home, and the
railroad facilities and the crowded conditions of both freight
and passenger cars rendered it almost obligatory on the soldiers to remain in the city over night. And it must be remembered, too, that the homes of hundreds and thousands of
soldiers from Tennessee, Maryland, Kentucky, Mississippi,
and all from the Trans-Mississippi were in the hands of the
enemy, and the soldiers were forbidden the pleasure of returning home, unless clandestinely. In that case they ran the
risk of being shot by some bush-whacker or "stay outs," who
avoided the conscript officer on one side and recruiting officer
on the other. In these border States there was a perpetual
feud between these bush-whackers and the soldiers. It was
almost invariably the case that where these "lay outs" or
"hide outs" congregated, they sympathized with the North,
otherwise they would be in the ranks of the Confederacy.
Then, again, Richmond had been changed in a day from the
capital of a commonwealth to the capital of a nation. So it
was always crowded and little or no accommodation for the
private soldier, and even if he could get quarters at a hotel his
depleted purse was in such condition that he could not afford
the expense. Nor was he willing to give a month's wages for
a night's lodging. A night's lodging cost five dollars for supper, five for breakfast, and five for a bed, and if the soldiers
were any ways bibulously inclined and wished an "eye
opener" in the morning or a "night cap" at supper time, that
was five dollars additional for each drink. Under such circumstances the ladies of South Carolina, by private contribu-
tions alone, rented the old "Exchange Hotel" and furnished
it from their own means or private resources. They kept also
a store room where they kept socks for the soldiers, knit by
the hands of the young ladies of the State; blankets, shirts,

and under clothing, from the cloth spun, woven, and made up
by the ladies at home and shipped to Richmond to Colonel
McMaster and a staff of the purest and best women of the
land.   Only such work as washing and scrubbing was done by
negro servants, all the other was done by the ladies themselves.   Too much praise cannot be given to Colonel McMaster for his indefatigable exertions, his tireless rounds of duty,
to make the soldiers comfortable.   The ladies were never too
tired, night nor day, to go to the aid of the hungry and
broken down soldiers.   Hundreds and thousands were fed and
lodged without money and without price.   Car loads of the
little comforts and necessities of life were shared out to the
passing soldiers whenever their wants required it.   Never a
day or night passed without soldiers being entertained or
clothing distributed.   One night only was as long as a soldier
was allowed to enjoy their hospitality, unless in cases of emergency.   The officers of the army, whenever able, were required
to pay a nominal sum for lodging.   Better beds and conveni-
ences were furnished them, but if they were willing to take
private's "fare," they paid private's "fee," which was gratui-
tous.   As a general rule, however, the officers kept apart
from the men, for the officer who pushed himself in the private's quarters was looked upon as penurious and mean.   It
was only in times of the greatest necessity that a Southern
officer wished to appear thus.   If the Southern soldier was
poor, he was always proud.   This hotel was called the "South
Carolina Soldiers' Home," and most of the other States inside
the lines had similar institutions.   In every home throughout
the whole South could be heard the old "hand spinning
wheel" humming away until far in the night, as the dainty
damsel danced backwards and forwards, keeping step to the
music of her own voice and the hum of the wheel.   The old
women sat in the corners and carded away with the hand-card,
making great heaps of rolls, to be laid carefully and evenly
upon the floor or the wheel.   Great chuncks of pine, called
"lite'ood," were regularly thrown into the great fire place
until the whole scene was lit up as by an incandescent lamp.
What happiness, what bliss, and how light the toil, when it
was known that the goods woven were to warm and comfort
young "massa" in the army.   The ladies of the "big house"
were not idle while these scenes of activity were going on at

the "quarter." Broaches were reeled into "hanks" of "six cuts" each, to be "sized," "warped," and made ready for the loom. Then the little "treadle wheel" that turned with a pedal made baskets of spools for the "filling." By an ingenious method, known only to the regularly initiated Southern housewife, the thread was put upon the loom, and then the music of the weaver's beam went merrily along with its monotonous "bang," "bang," as yard after yard of beautiful jeans, linsey, or homspuns of every kind were turned out to clothe the soldier boys, whose government was without the means or opportunity to furnish them. Does it look possible at this late day that almost the entire Southern Army was clothed by cloth carded, spun, and woven by hand, and mostly by the white ladies of the South?

Hats and caps were made at home from the colored jeans. Beautiful hats were made out of straw, and so adapt had the makers become in utilizing home commodities, that ladies' hats were made out of wheat, oat, and rice straw. Splendid and serviceable house shoes were made from the products of the loom, the cobbler only putting on the soles. Good, warm, and tidy gloves were knit for the soldier from their home-raised fleece and with a single bone from the turkey wing. While the soldiers may have, at times, suffered for shoes and provisions, still they were fairly well clothed by the industry and patriotism of the women, and for blankets, the finest of beds were stripped to be sent voluntarily to the camps and army. As for tents, we had no need to manufacture them, for they were invariably captured from the enemy. Think of going through an army of sixty or seventy thousand men, all comfortably housed, and all through capture upon the battlefield. As for cooking utensils, nothing more nor better were wanted by the soldiers than a tin cup and frying-pan.

Salt was an article of great scarcity in the South. Coming over from Liverpool in ante bellum times as ballast, made it so cheap that little attention was given to the salt industry, and most of our best salt mines were in the hands of the enemy. But the Southern people were equal to any emergency. Men were put along the sea coast and erected great vats into which was put the salt sea water, and by a system of co-operation nice, fine salt was made. Farmers, too, that had the old-time "smoke" or meat houses with dirt floors, dug up the earth in the house and filtered water through it, getting a dark, salty brine, which answered exceedingly well the purpose of curing their meats.

All taxes, as I said before, were paid in "kind," and the tenth of all the meat raised at home was sent to the army, and with the few cattle they could gather, was sufficient to feed the troops. There were no skulking spirits among the people. They gave as willingly and cheerfully now as they did at the opening of the war. The people were honest in their dealings with the government, and as cheerful in their gifts to the cause as the Israelites of old in their "free will offerings" to the Lord. There were no drones among them, no secretion or dishonest division. The widows, with houses filled with orphans, gave of their scanty crops and hard labor as freely as those who owned large plantations and scores of slaves. In fact, it was noticeable that the poorer class were more patriotic and more cheerful givers, if such could be possible, than the wealthy class.

Negroes were drafted to go upon the coast to work in salt mills or to work upon the fortifications. This duty they performed with remarkable willingness, until, perhaps, some Federal gunboat got their range and dropped a few shells among them. Then no persuasion nor threat could induce them to remain, and numbers of them would strike out for home and often get lost and wander for days, half starved, through the swamps of the lower country, being afraid to show themselves to the whites for fear of being "taken up" and sent back. Many were the adventures and hair-breath escapes these dusty fugitives had, and could tell them in wonderful yarns to the younger generation at home. It may be that the negro, under mental excitement, or stimulated with strong drink, could be induced to show remarkable traits of bravery, but to take him cool and away from any excitement, he is slow at exposing himself to bodily dangers, and will never make a soldier in the field.

CHAPTER XL

Opening of 1865---Gloomy Outlook---Prison Pens--Return to South Carolina of Kershaw's Brigade.

The opening of the year 1865 looked gloomy enough for the cause of the Confederacy. The hopes of foreign intervention had long since been looked upon as an ignisfatuus and a delusion, while our maritime power had been swept from the seas. All the ports, with the exception of Charleston, S. C., and Wilmington, N. C., were now in the hands of the Federals. Fort Fisher, the Gibralter of the South, that guarded the inlet of Cape Fear River, was taken by land and naval forces, under General Terry and Admiral Porter. Forts Sumter and Moultrie, at the Charleston Harbor, continued to hold out for a while longer. The year before the "Alabama," an iron-clad of the Confederates, was sunk off the coast of France. Then followed the "Albemarle" and the "Florida." The ram "Tennessee" had to strike her colors on the 5th of August, in Mobile Bay. Then all the forts that protected the bay were either blown up or evacuated, leaving the Entrance to Mobile Bay open to the fleet of the Federals.

Sherman was recuperating his army around Savannah, and was preparing a farther advance now northward after his successful march to the sea. At Savannah he was met by a formidable fleet of iron-clads and men of war, which were to accompany him by sailing along the coast in every direction. These were to form a junction with another army at Newburn, N. C.

Another matter that caused the South to despond of any other solution of the war than the bloody end that soon followed, was the re-election of Abraham Lincoln as President of the United States. The South felt that as long as he was at the head of the nation nothing but an unconditional surrender of our armies and the emancipation of the slaves would suffice this great emancipator. To this the South could not nor

would not accede as long as there were rifles in the field and
men to wield them.   A great problem now presented itself to
the Confederate authorities for solution, but who could cut the
Gordion knot?   The South had taken during the war two
hundred and seventy thousand prisoners, as against two hundred and twenty-two thousand taken by the Federals, leaving
in excess to the credit of the South near fifty thousand.   For
a time several feeble attempts had been made for an equitable
exchange of prisoners, but this did not suit the policy of the
North.   Men at the North were no object, and to guard this
great swarm of prisoners in the South it took an army out of
the field, and the great number of Southern soldiers in Northern prisons took quite another army from the service.   In addition to the difficulty of supplying our own army and people
with the necessities of life, we were put to the strain of feeding one hundred thousand or more of Federal prisoners.
Every inducement was offered the North to grant some cortel
of exchange or some method agreed upon to alienate the sufferings of these unfortunates confined in the prison pens in the
North and South.   The North was offered the privilege of
feeding and clothing their own prisoners, to furnish medical
aid and assistance to their sick.   But this was rejected in the
face of the overwhelming sentiments of the fathers, mothers,
sisters, and brothers of those who were suffering and dying
like flies in the Southern pens.   Thousands and thousands of
petitions were circulated, with strings of signatures from all
classes in the Union, urging Congress to come in some way to
the relief of their people.   But a deaf ear was turned to all entreaties, this being a war measure, and no suffering could be
too great when the good of the service required it.   Taking it
from a military point of view, this was the better policy, shock-
ing as it was to humanity.

At one time it was considered in the Confederate Congress
the propriety of turning loose and sending home as early as
practicable these thousands of prisoners, trusting alone to their
honor the observance of the parole.   It was thought by the
majority that the indiscriminate mingling and mixing of these
fanitical agitators with the peaceable slaves in the country
might incite insurrection and a bloody social war break out
should the prisoners be released at the prison pens.   Under all
the varying circumstances the South was still busily engaged

in mobilizing these prisoners in certain quarters, to protect them as far as possible from liberation by raiding parties. At Andersonville, Ga., there were twenty-two thousand; at Florence, S. C., two thousand; Salisbury, N. C., ten thousand; several hundred in Columbia, and detached numbers scattered along at various points on the railroads, at such places where convenient quarters could be secured and properly guarded. Quite a large number were at Bell Isle, on the James River, as well as at the Liby Prison, in Richmond. These prisoners were sometimes guarded by the State militia and disabled veterans. Those at Florence were guarded by boy companies, under command of Colonel Williams, the former commander of the Third South Carolina. The stockades, as the prison pens were called, consisted of tall pine trees set into the ground some six or eight feet, standing upright and adjoining. The space thus enclosed covered several acres or as much more as there were prisoners or troops to guard them. The stockade fence was about fifteen feet above the level of the ground, with a walk way three feet from the top, on which the guards watched. There was a "dead line" some fifteen or twenty paces from the inside of the wall, over which no prisoner was allowed to cross, on penalty of being shot. And to prevent any collision between the prisoners and the guard, none were permitted to speak to the sentinels under any circumstances. To better carry out these orders, the soldier who detected a prisoner speaking to a guard and shot him, a thirty days' furlough was given as an acknowledgment of his faithful observance of orders. On more occasions than one the prisoners in their attempt to draw inexperienced guards into a conversation, and perhaps offer a bribe, met their death instantly. Inside the enclosure some of the prisoners huddled under little tents or blankets, but the greater number burrowed under the ground like moles or prairie dogs. Numbers made their escape by tunnelling under the wall.

When Sherman began his march through Georgia, the major portion at Andersonville were removed to Salisbury, N. C., where a great national cemetery was set apart after the war, and kept under the authority of the war department, containing thousands of graves—monuments to the sufferings and death of these unfortunate people—a sacrifice to what their government called a "military necessity." Our prison-

32

ers were scattered in like manner at Camp Chase, in Ohio; Fort Johnston, in Lake Michigan; Fort Delaware, in the Delaware River; and many other places, subject to greater sufferings and hardships than the Federal prisoners in our hands.

The Government of the South had nothing to do but accept the conditions imposed upon the sufferers by the authorities in Washington.

In January, 1865, rumors were rife in camp of the transfer of some of the South Carolina troops to their own State to help swell the little band that was at that time fighting on the flanks and front of Sherman. Of course it was not possible that all could be spared from Lee, but it had become a certain fact, if judged from the rumors in camp, that some at least were to be transferred. So when orders came for Kershaw's Brigade to break camp and march to Richmond, all were over-joyed. Outside of the fact that we were to be again on our "native heath" and fight the invader on our own soil, the soldiers of Kershaw's Brigade felt not a little complimented at being selected as the brigade to be placed at such a post of honor. It is a settled feeling among all troops and a pardon-able pride, too, that their organization, let it be company, regiment, brigade, or even division or corps, is superior to any other like organization in bravery, discipline, or any soldierly attainments. Troops of different States claim superiority over those of their sister States, while the same rivalry exists be-tween organizations of the same State. So when it was learned for a certainty that the old First Brigade was to be transferred to South Carolina, all felt a keen pride in being thus selected, and now stamped it as a settled fact, that which they had always claimed, "the best troops from the State." The State furnished the best to the Confederacy, and a logical conclusion would be "Kershaw's Brigade was the best of the service." Thus our troops prided themselves. Under such feelings and enthusiasm, it is little wonder that they were anxious to meet Sherman, and had circumstances permitted and a battle fought in South Carolina, these troops would have come up to the expectations of their countrymen.

But here I will state a fact that all who read history of this war will be compelled to admit, and that is, the department at Richmond had no settled or determined policy in regard to the actions of the army at the South. It would appear from read-

ing cotemporary history that Mr. Davis and his cabinet acted
like Micawber, and "waited for something to turn up." His
continual intermeddling with the plans of the Generals in the
field, the dogged tenacity with which he held to his policies,
his refusals to allow commanders to formulate their own plans
of campaigns, forced upon Congress the necessity of putting
one at the head of all the armies whom the Generals, soldiers,
as well as the country at large, had entire confidence. General
Lee filled this position to the perfect satisfaction of all, still his
modesty or a morbid dislike to appear dictatorial, his timidity
in the presence of his superiors, often permitted matters to go
counter to his own views. It appears, too, that when General
Sherman allowed Hood to pass unmolested to his right, and
he began tearing up the railroads in his rear, it was a move so
different to all rules of war, that it took the authorities with
surprise. Then when he began his memorable march through
the very heart of Georgia—Hood with a great army in his
rear, in his front the sea—the South stood stupified and bewildered at this stupendous undertaking. It was thought by the
army and the people that some direful blow would be struck
Sherman when he was well under way in Georgia, and when
too far from his base in the rear, and not far enough advanced
to reach the fleet that was to meet him in his front.

How, when, or by whom this blow was to be struck, none
even ventured an opinion, but that the authorities had Sherman's overthrow in view, all felt satisfied and convinced. But
as events have shown since, it seems that our authorities in
Richmond and the commanders in the field were as much at
sea as the soldiers and people themselves. It was the purpose
of General Beauregard to collect out all the militia of Governor
Clark of Mississippi, of Governor Watts of Alabama, Governor
Brown of Georgia, and of Governor Bonham of South Carolina
to the southern part of Georgia, there, as Sherman approached, to reinforce General Hardee with all these State
troops and reserves, under General Cobb, which numbered in all about eight thousand, and hold him in check
until Hood came upon Sherman's rear, or forced him to
retire. Of course it was expected, as a matter of fact, that
Hood would be successful against the hastily concentrated
army of Thomas, and Sherman would be forced to return for
the protection of Kentucky and Ohio. But in military mat-

ters, as in others, too much must not be taken for granted,
and where great events hinge on so many minor details, it is
not suprising that there should be miscarriages. Hood was
totally defeated and routed in Tennessee. The Governors of
the sister States, on false principles of safety and obsolete
statistics, refused to permit the State troops to leave the borders of their respective States, leaving nothing before Sherman
but the handful of wornout veterans of Hardee and the few
State troops of Georgia, to be beaten in detail as Sherman
passed through the State. The women and children of our
State were in the same frenzied condition at this time as those
of Georgia had been when the Federals commenced their
march from Atlanta. In fact, more so, for they had watched
with bated breath the march of the vandals across the Savannah—the smoke of the burning homesteads, the wreck and
ruin of their sister State—left little hope of lieneucy or mercy
at the hands of the enemy, while all their strength and depend-
ence in the way of manhood were either in the trenches with
Lee or with the reserves along the borders of the State. Companies were formed everywhere of boys and old men to help
beat back the mighty annaconda that was now menacing with
its coils our common country. These were quite unique
organizations, the State troops of the South. The grand-
fathers and grandsons stood side by side in the ranks; the
fathers and sons had either fallen at the front or far away in a
distant State, fighting for the Southland.

The people of this day and generation and those who are to
come afterwards, will never understand how was it possible
for the women of the South to remain at their homes all alone,
with the helpless little children clustering around their knees,
while all that had the semblance of manhood had gone to the
front. Yet with all this, a merciless, heartless, and vengeful
foe stood at their threshold, with the sword in one hand and
the torch in the other. Not only thus confronted, they were
at the mercy of four or five millions of negro slaves, waiting
for freedom, as only a people could after two centuries of slavery. The enemy was ready and willing to excite these
otherwise harmless, peaceful, and contented negroes to insurrection and wholesale butchery. But be it said to the everlasting credit and honor of the brave women of the South, that
they never uttered a reproach, a murmur, or a regret at the

conditions in which circumstances had placed them. But the negro, faithful to his instincts, remained true, and outside of an occasional outburst of enthusiasm at their newly found freedom, continuel loyal to the end to these old masters, and looked with as much sorrow and abhorence upon this wanton destruction of the old homestead, around which clustered so many bright and happy memories, as if they had been of the same bone and the same flesh of their masters. Notwithstanding the numberless attempts by Federal soldiers now spread over an area of fifty miles to excite the negro to such frenzy that they might insult and outrage the delicate sensibilities of the women of the South, still not a single instance of such acts has been recorded.

Such were the feelings and condition of the country when Kershaw's Brigade, now under General Kennedy, boarded the train in Richmond, in January, 1865. We came by way of Charlotte and landed in Columbia about nightfall. The strictest orders were given not to allow any of the troops to leave or stop over, however near their homes they passed, or how long they had been absent. In fact, most of the younger men did not relish the idea of being seen by our lovely women just at that time, for our disastrous valley campaign and the close investiture of Richmond by Grant—the still closer blockade of our ports—left them almost destitute in the way of shoes and clothing. The single railroad leading from our State to the capital had about all it could do to haul provisions and forage for the army, so it was difficult to get clothing from home. We were a rather ragged lot, while the uniforms of the officers looked shabby from the dust and mud of the valley and the trenches around Richmond. Our few brief months in winter quarters had not added much, if any, to our appearance. By some "underground" road, Captain Jno. K. Nance, of the Third, had procured a spick and span new uniform, and when this dashing young officer was clad in his Confederate gray, he stood second to none in the army in the way of "fine looking." New officers did not always "throw off the old and on with the new" as soon as a new uniform was bought, but kept the new one, for a while at least, for "State occasions." These "occasions" consisted in visiting the towns and cities near camp or in transit from one army to another. An officer clad in a new uniform on ordinary occa-

sions, when other soldiers were only in their "fighting garments," looked as much out of place as the stranger did at the
wedding feast "without the wedding garments." But the
day of our departure from Richmond Captain Nance rigged
himself out in the pomp and regulations of war, his bright
new buttons flashing in the sunlight, his crimson sash tied
naughtily around his waist, his sword dangling at his side, he
looked the "beheld of all beholders" as the troops marched
with a light and steady step along the stone-paved streets of
Richmond.   He had married a year or so before the beautiful
and accomplished sister of our lamented Colonel, and had telegraphed her to meet him at Columbia on our arrival.   He
dared not trust these innoculate garments to the dirty and
besmeared walls of a box car, so he discarded the new on our
entrance to the train and dressed in his old as a traveling suit.
All the way during our trip he teased his brother officers and
twitted them with being so "shabbily dressed," while he
would be such a "beaw ideal" in his new uniform when he
met his wife.   He had never met his wife since his honey-
moon a year before, and then only with a twenty-one days'
furlough, so it can be well imagined with what anticipations
he looked forward to the meeting of his wife.   He was so
happy in his expectations that all seemed to take on some of
his pleasant surroundings, and shared with him his delight in
the expected meeting of his young wife.   He would look out
of the car door and hail a comrade in the next car with,
"Watch me when we reach Columbia, will you," while the
comrade would send back a lot of good-natured railery.   It
was an undisputed fact, that Captain Nance was a great favorite among officers and men, and while all were giving him a
friendly badgering, everyone was glad to see him in such a
happy mood.   He had given his new suit in charge of his
body servant, Jess, with special injunction to guard it with his
life.   Now Jess was devoted to his master, and was as proud
of him as the "squires" of old were of the knights.   Jess, to
doubly secure this "cloth of gold" so dear to the heart of his
master, folded the suit nicely and put it in his knap-sack and
the knap-sack under his head, while he slept the sleep of the
just in the far corner of the box car.   When we reached Charlotte Captain Nance concluded to rig himself out, as this was
to be our last place of stoppage until Columbia was reached,

and should his wife meet him there, then he would be ready. So he orders water and towel, and behind the car he began preparations for dressing, all the while bantering the boys about his suit.

At last he was ready to receive the treasured gray. He called out to his man Jess, "Bring out the uniform."

Jess goes into the car. He fumbles, he hunts—knap-sacks thrown aside, guns and accourtrements dashed in every direction—the knap-sack is found, hastily opened, and searched, but no uniform! The more impatient and more determined to find the missing clothes, the idea began more forcibly to impress Jess that he might have slept on the way. So engrossed was he in the search for the missing suit, that he failed to hear the orders from his master to—

"Hurry up! If you don't soon bring on that coat I'll frail you out. You think I can wait out here naked and freeze?"

But still the hunt goes on, haver-sacks once again thrown aside, knap-sacks overhauled for the third time, while beads of perspiration begin to drop from the brow of Jess. The real facts began to dawn more surely upon him. Then Jess spoke, or I might say gave a wail—

"Marse John, 'fore God in heaven, if some grand rascal ain't done stole your clothes." His great white eyes shone out from the dark recesses of the car like moons in a bright sky.

Nance was speechless. Raising himself in a more erect position, he only managed to say: "Jess, don't tell me that uniform is gone. Don't! Go dig your grave, nigger, for if you black imp of Satan has gone to sleep and let some scoundrel steal my clotes, then you die."

Such a laugh, such a shout as was set up from one end of the train to the other was never heard before or since of the "Lone Pine Tree State." All of us thought at first, and very naturally, too, that it was only a practical joke being played upon the Captain, and that all would be right in the end. But not so. What became of that uniform forever remained a mystery. If the party who committed the theft had seen or knew the anguish of the victim for one-half hour, his conscience would have smote him to his grave.

But all is well that ends well." His wife failed to reach him in time, so he wore the faded and tattered garments, as momentous of the Valley, through all the tangled swamps and morasses of the Saltkahatchie, the Edisto, and the Santee with as much pride as if clothed in the finest robes of a king.

We remained at Branchville for several days, and from thence we were transported by rail to Charleston and took up quarters on the "Mall." The citizens hailed us with delight and treated us with the greatest hospitality. The greater number of the best-to-do citizens had left the city, and all that lived on the bay and in reach of the enemies guns had moved to safer quarters in the city or refugeed in the up country. But every house stood open to us. Flags and handkerchiefs waved from the windows and housetops, and all was bustle and commotion, notwithstanding the continual booming of cannon at Sumter and on Sullivan's Island. Every minute or two a shell would go whizzing overhead or crashing through the brick walls of the buildings. Soldiers were parading the streets, citizens going about their business, while all the little stores and shops were in full blast, the same as if the "Swamp Angle" was not sending continually shells into the city. The people had become accustomed to it and paid little attention to the flying shells.

On one occasion, while a bridal ceremony was being performed in one of the palatial residences in the city, the room filled with happy guests, a shell came crashing into the apartment, bursting among the happy bridal party, killing one of the principals and wounding several of the guests.

While I and several other officers were eating breakfast at one of the hotels, a great noise was heard in the upper portion of the building, giving quite a shock to all. Someone asked the colored waiter, "What was that noise?" "Only a shell bursting in one of the upper rooms," was the reply.

Women and children walked leisurely to market or about their daily vocations, the shells roaring overhead, with no more excitement or concern than had it only been a fourth of July celebration.

Even the negroes, usually so timid and excitable, paid but momentary attention to the dangers.

The Confederates had abandoned the greater part of Morris' Island, and great batteries had been erected on it by General *Gillmore*, with the avowed purpose of burning the city. Some weeks before this he had erected a battery in the marshes of

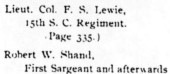

Lieut. Col. F. S. Lewie,
  15th S. C. Regiment.
  (Page 335.)

Robert W. Shand,
  First Sargeant and afterwards
    Lieut. 2d S. C. Regiment.

Capt. Duncan McIntyre,
  Co. H, 8th S. C. Regiment.
  (Page 484.

D. H. Crawford,
  Private 2d S. C. Regiment.

the island and a special gun cast that could throw shells five miles, the greatest range of a cannon in that day. The gun was named the "Swamp Angel" and much was expected of it, but it did no other execution than the killing of a few civilians and destroying a few dwellings. The citizens were too brave and patriotic to desert their homes as long as a soldier remained on the islands or in the forts. The gallant defenders of Sumter, after a month of the most terrific cannonading the world had ever seen, were still at their guns, while the fort itself was one mass of ruins, the whole now being a huge pile of stone, brick, and masonry. Fort Moultrie, made famous by its heroic defense of Charleston in the days of the Revolution, and by Jasper leaping the sides of the fort and replenishing the flag over its ramparts, still floated the stars and bars from its battlements. All around the water front of Charleston bristled great guns, with ready and willing hands to man them. These "worthy sons of noble sires," who had, by their unflinching courage, sent back the British fleet, sinking and colors lowered, were now ready to emulate their daring example—either to send the fleet of Gillmore to the bottom, or die at their post. No wonder the people of South Carolina felt so secure and determined when such soldiers defended her borders.

The city guards patrolled the streets of Charleston to prevent the soldier from leaving their camps without permits, and between these two branches of the service a bitter feud always existed. The first night we were in the city some of the soldiers, on the verbal permission of their Captains, were taking in the city. Leaving their arms at camp, they were caught "hors de combat," as it were, and locked up in the city guardhouse over night. The next morning I went to look for my absentees, and away up in the top story of the lower station house I saw them, their heads reaching out of the "ten of diamonds" and begging to be released. After much red tape, I had them turned out, and this incident only added to the ill will of the two parties. After the soldiers began to congregate and recount their grievances as they thought, they used the city guards pretty roughly the remainder of our stay. But the most of all these differences were in the nature of "fun," as the soldiers termed it, and only to give spice to the soldier's life.

There were two young Captains in the Third, who, both together, would only make one good man, physically. So small in statue were they that on some previous occasion they had agreed to "whip the first man they ever met that they thought small enough to tackle." This personage they had never as yet met, but walking down King street they entered a little saloon kept by a Jew. The Jew could scarcely see over the counter, so low was he, but otherwise well developed. On seeing the little Jew, the two young officers eyed each other and said one gleefully:

"John, here's our man."

"Yes, yes," said D, "You tackle him in front and I'll leg him in rear. By all that's sacred, we can say we whipped one man, at least."

So telling the little Jew of their agreement, and that they thought he was the man they were looking for, ordered him out to take his medicine like a little man. The Jew took it good humoredly and told the officers he was their friend and did not care to fight them, etc. But the officers persisted so, to "humor them" "and to show friendship for the young men," said he would "accommodate them." At that the Jew struck out with his right on John's jaw, hitting the ceiling with the little officer. Then with his left he put one in the pit of D.'s stomach, lifting him clear of the floor and dropping him across a lot of barrels. Then John was ready by this time to receive a "header" under the chin, piling him on top of D. The boys crawled out as he was preparing to finish up the two in fine style, but—

"Hold on! hold on! young man, cried both in a breath. "we are not mad; we are only in fun; don't strike any more."

"All right," said the Jew, "if you are satisfied I am. Come let's have a drink."

So all three took a friendly sip, and as the two wiser, if not stronger, young men left the shop, one said to the other:

"We'll have to get a smaller man yet before we can say we whipped anybody."

"You are right," said the other; "I was never worse mistaken in all my life in the size of the man, or he grew faster after he began to fight than anything I ever saw. He stretched out all over, like a bladder being blown up."

They found out afterwards that the Jew was a professional

boxer, and was giving lessons to the young men of the city.

The soldiers seemed to be getting rather demoralized by the influences of the city, and were moved over the Ashley River and encamped about four miles of the city, in a great pine forest, near the sea. This was a great sight for many, for as much travelling as the troops had done during the last four years, this was their first close quarters to the ocean, and many had never before witnessed the great rolling waters of the sea. Oysters were plentiful, and negroes on the plantation brought out boat loads for the soldiers, and gave them out for a little tobacco or a small amount of Confederate "shin-plasters." These were about the only articles they had seen in a long time that they could buy with a "shin-plaster" (fractional currency), as almost every other comodity was worth from one dollar up. Great fires were built at night, and eight or ten bushels of the sweet, juicy bivalves were poured over the heap, to be eaten as the shells would pop by the heat.

From this place, after a week's sojourn, we were carried by rail to the Saltkahatchie River, at the crossing of the Charleston and Savannah Railroad.

CHAPTER XLI

On the Saltkahatchie. February, 1865.

When we reached our destination on the Saltkahatchie, we were met by our old commander of Virginia and Tennessee, Major General McLaws, from whom we had been separated for more than a year. The soldiers were glad to see him, and met him with a rousing cheer, while the old veteran was equally delighted to see us. It was like the meeting of father and absent children, for General McLaws was kind and indulgent to his men, even if not a very successful General. After being relieved of his command in East Tennessee and succeeded by General Kershaw, he had commanded the post at Augusta, Ga., to which place he returned after the close of hostilities and remained until his death. He was the greater part of the time postmaster of the city of Augusta. There being few occupations that the old West Pointers of the South could fill, they generally accepted any office in the gift of the government that would insure them an honest livelihood.

General McLaws was facing two corps of Sherman's Army at this place with some few veterans, State troops, and reserves. Sherman had been quiet for some time, recruiting his army with negroes from the great plantations along the coast, and resting up his army for his march through the State. Negroes flocked to his army by the thousands, and were formed into regiments and brigades, officered by white men. Even our own Generals and some of our statesmen at this time and before were urging Congress to enlist the negroes, but the majority were opposed to the movement. To show how confident were our leaders even at this late day of the Confederacy, I will quote from Wm. Porcher Miles, then in the Confederate Congress, in reply to General Beauregard urging the enlistment of the slaves. It must be understood that at this time Lee had all he could do to hold his own against Grant, growing weaker and weaker as the days rolled by, while Grant was being reinforced from all over the United States. Lee had the solitary railroad by which to subsist his army. Sherman had laid waste Georgia and was now on the eve of marching through South Carolina. The Army of the Trans-Mississippi was hopelessly cut off from the rest of the Confederacy. The Mississippi River was impassable, to say nothing of the Federal pickets that lined its banks and the gunboats that patrolled its waters, so much so that one of our Generals is said to have made the report "that if a bird was dressed up in Confederate gray, it could not cross the Mississippi." Hood's Army was a mere skeleton of its former self—his men, some furloughed, others returned to their home without leave, so disheartened were they after the disastrous defeat in Tennessee. Still all these conditions being known and understood by the authorities, they were yet hopeful. Says Mr. Miles in Congress:

"I cannot bring my mind to the conviction that arming our slaves will add to our military strength, while the prospective and inevitable evils resulting from such measures make me shrink back from such a step. This can be when only on the very brink of the brink of the precipice of ruin."

From such language from a Confederate Congressman, dark as the day looked on February 4th, 1865, the date of the

letter, the people did not seem to feel that they were on the
"brink of the precipice." Continuing, Mr. Miles goes on in
a hopeful strain:

"But I do not estimate him [speaking of Grant] as a soldier
likely to decide the fate of battle. We have on our rolls this
side of the Mississippi four hundred and one thousand men,
one hundred and seventy-five thousand effective and present.
We can easily keep in the field an effective force of two hundred thousand. These are as many as we can well feed and
clothe, and these are sufficient to prevent subjugation or the
overrunning of our territory."

How a man so well informed and familiar with the forego-
ing facts could hope for ultimate results, is hard to comprehend by people of this day and generation. It was the plan
of General Beauregard to concentrate all the available troops
in North and South Carolina on the Saltkahatchie, to keep
Sherman at bay until Dick Taylor, with the remnant of Hood's
Army, could come up, then fall back to the Edisto, where
swamps are wide and difficult of passage, allow Sherman to
cross over two of his corps, fall upon them with all the force
possible, destroy or beat them back upon the center, then
assail his flanks, and so double him up as to make extrication
next to impossible. But in case of failure here, to retire
upon Branchville or Columbia, put up the strongest fortifications possible, withdraw all the troops from Charleston, Wilmington, and in the other cities, put in all the State troops
that were available from the three States, push forward as
many veterans as Lee could temporarily spare from the
trenches, barely leaving a skirmish line behind the works
around Richmond and Petersburg, then as Sherman approached, fall upon him with all the concentrated force and
crush him in the very heart of the State, or to so cripple him
as to make a forward movement for a length of time impossible; while the railroads in his rear being all destroyed, his
means of supplies would be cut off, and nothing left but retreat. Then, in that event, the whole of Beauregard's troops
to be rushed on to Lee, and with the combined army assault
the left flank of Grant and drive him back on the James.
That the soldiers in the ranks and the subaltern officers felt
that some kind of movement like this was contemplated, there
can be no doubt. It was this feeling that gave them the con-

fidence in the face of overwhelming numbers, and nerved them to greater efforts in time of battle. It was this sense of confidence the soldiers had in the heads of departments and in the commanding Generals that gave the inspiration to the breaten army of Hood that induced these barefoot men to march half way across the continent to place themselves in battle lines across the pathway of Sherman. It was this confidence in the wisdom of our rulers, the genius of the commanders, the stoicism of the soldiers, and above all, the justness of our cause and the helping hand of the Omnipotent, that influenced the women of the South to bear and indure the insults of the Federal soldiers, and view with unconcern the ruin of their homes and the desecration of their country. From the standpoint of the present, this would have been the only possible plan whereby any hopes of ultimate success were possible. But to the people of this day and time, the accomplishment of such an undertaking with the forces and obstacles to be overcome looks rather far-fetched, especially when we reflect that Johnston, with fifty or sixty thousand of the best troops in the service, had failed to check Sherman among the mountain passes of North Georgia, or even to prevent his successful advance to the very walls of Atlanta. That General Beauregard, with his handful of regular troops and a contingent of boys and old men, could accomplish what General Johnston, with a well equipped army of veterans, failed in, was simply a blind faith in the occult influence of Providence.

But it seems as if the department at Richmond had lost its head, and had no settled policy. Telegrams were being continually sent to the Generals in the field to "Crush the enemy," "You must fight a great battle," "Either destroy him or so cripple his efforts to reach Grant, that reinforcements would be taken from Lee's front," "Why don't you fight?" etc. These were the encouraging messages Generals Beauregard and Hardee were receiving, but where were the troops to accomplish such work? Generals from every direction were calling for aid—to be reinforced, or that the enemy was making advances, without means to stop him. The answer to all these calls were the same, in substance at least, as that given by Napoleon to the request of Ney of Waterloo, when that marshal called upon the Emperor for reinforcements, "Where does he expect me to get them? Make them?" It seems that the people, with the exception of the privates in the field and the women and children at home, had become panic stricken.

On the 3rd of February General Sherman began crossing the Saltkahatchie at places between Broxton's and Rivers' Bridges (and above the latter), and was moving by easy stages in the direction of Branchville. It was not conclusively known whether Sherman, on reaching that place, would turn towards Augusta or in the direction of Charleston, or continue his march to Columbia. President Davis having declined the proposition of General Beauregard to evacuate all the cities on the coast and make a stand on the Edisto, declined also a like proposition to fight the great battle at either Branchville or Columbia, without offering any better policy himself. The only alternative the latter had was to keep out of Sherman's way as well as possible and to allow him to continue laying waste the entire center of the State. His only encouragements were dispatches from the President to "Turn and Crash Sherman," "Call on the Governors," "Bring out the militia," etc.

Sherman's columns of advance consisted of four great parolled lines, with a corps on each. His extreme right was made up of the Seventeenth Corps, under General Frank P. Blair, the Fifteenth next, under General Jno. A. Logan, the two being the right wing of the army, commanded by General Howard. The left wing, under General Slocum, consisted of the Fourteenth Corps, on extreme left, General Jeff. C. Davis commanding; the next, the Twentieth, under General A. S. Williams, the whole numbering sixty thousand. The cavalry, numbering four thousand additional, was on either flank.

To meet this formidable array, Beauregard had under his immediate command Hardee, with thirteen thousand seven hundred (three thousand being State militia); around Augusta and on the march in Georgia and upper South Carolina was the remnant of Hood's Army—Steven D. Lee, with three thousand three hundred and fifty; Dick Cheatham, with two thousand five hundred.

Stewart's Corps was far back in Georgia, and too far away to give any hopes of meeting Beauregard in this State. It consisted of Loring's Division, one thousand eight hundred and eighty-seven; Wathals' Division, one thousand and thirty-six; French's Division, one thousand five hundred and nineteen.

It must not be forgotton that the number under Hardee included the troops in and around Charleston, and all the cities and towns in the State where soldiers were stationed.

General Wheeler, in command of several brigades of cavalry, now reduced to a mere skeleton organization, was hovering around the enemy's flanks and in front between Branchville and Augusta.

Just prior to the evacuation of Columbia, General Beauregard applied to the war department for the promotion of General Wade Hampton to Lieutenant General, to take precedence over Major General Wheeler, now in command of all the cavalry in this army. He further asked that he be assigned to the command of the cavalry of his department, all of which was granted. Generals Hampton and Butler were both at home at the time, the former on furlough, the latter recruiting and mounting his troops. These two Generals being natives of the State, and General Hampton so familiar with the topography of the country through which the army had to pass, General Beauregard thought him a desirable officer for the post. Furthermore, Wheeler's Cavalry had become thoroughly demoralized and undisciplined. From their long, continual retreats the cavalry had become to look upon "retreat" as the regular and national order. Acting on the principle that all which was left in their wake of private property would be appropriated by the enemy, they fell with ruthless hands upon whatsoever property their eyes took a fancy to, consoling themselves with the reasoning "that if we don't take it, the enemy will." So audacious had become the raids of Wheeler's command that citizens had little choice between the two evils, "Wheeler's Cavalry or the Federals." The name of "Wheeler's men" became a reproach and a by-word, and remains so to this day with the descendants of those who felt the scourge of these moving armies.

These are matters that are foreign to the subject or to the "History of Kershaw's Brigade," but as the greater part of the soldiers of South Carolina were away during the march through their State and ignorant of the movements of the armies, I write for their information, and the concluding part of this work will be rather a history of the whole army than of one brigade.

CHAPTER XLII

March Through South Carolina, February and March, 1865.

When Sherman put this mighty machine of war in motion, Kershaw's Brigade was hurried back to Charleston and up to George's Station, then to the bridge on the Edisto. Raiding parties were out in every direction, destroying bridges and railroads, and as the Southern Army had no pontoon corps nor any methods of crossing the deep, sluggish streams in their rear but by bridges, it can be seen that the cutting of one bridge alone might be fatal to the army. It was discovered early in the march that Sherman did not intend to turn to the right or the left, but continue on a direct line, with Columbia as the center of operations. We were removed from the Edisto back to Charleston, and up the Northeastern Railroad to St. Stephen's, on the Santee. It was feared a raiding party from Georgetown would come up the Santee and cut the bridge, thereby isolating the army Hardee had in Charleston and vicinity. Slowly Sherman "dragged his weary length along." On the 13th of February the corps of General Blair reached Kingsville and drove our pickets away from the bridge over the Congaree.

On the 15th of February the advance column of the Twentieth Corps came in sight of Columbia. All the bridges leading thereto were burned and the Southern troops witdrawn to the eastern side. Frank Blair's Corps left the road leading to Columbia at Hopkin's, and kept a direct line for Camden. Another corps, the Fifteenth, crossed the Broad at Columbia, while the Fourteenth and Twentieth were to cross at Freshley's and Alston. Orders had been given to evacuate Charleston, and all the troops under General McLaws, at Four Hole Swamp, and along the coast were to rendezvous at St. Stephen's, on the Santee, and either make a junction with the Western Army at Chester, S. C., or if not possible, to continue to Chesterfield or Cheraw. The plan of the campaign was now

33

to concentrate all the forces of Hood's State Troops and Hardee's at some point in upper South Carolina or in North Carolina, and make one more desperate stand, and by united action crash and overthrow Sherman's Army, thereby relieving Lee.

On the morning of the 16th of February the enemy, without any warning whatever, began shelling the city of Columbia, filled with women and children. Now it must be remembered that this was not for the purpose of crossing the river, 'for one of Sherman's corps had already crossed below the city and two others above. One shell passed through the hotel in which General Beauregard was at the time, others struck the State House, while many fell throughout the city. General Hampton withdrew his small force of cavalry early on the morning of the 17th, and the Mayor of the city met an officer of the Federal Army under a flag of truce and tendered him the surrender of the city, and claimed protection for its inhabitants. This was promised.

All during the day thousands of the enemy poured into the city, General Sherman entering about midday. Generals Davis' and Williams' Corps crossed the Saluda and continued up on the western bank of Broad River, one crossing ten, the other twenty-five miles above Columbia. The people of Columbia had hopes of a peaceful occupation of the city, but during the day and along towards nightfall, the threatening attitude of the soldiers, their ominous words, threats of vengeance, were too pretentious for the people to misunderstand or to expect mercy. These signs, threats, and mutterings were but the the prelude to that which was to follow.

About 9 o'clock P. M. the alarm of fire was given and the dread sound of the fire bells, mingled with the hum and roar of ten thousand voices and the tread of as many troops hurrying to and fro on their cursed mission, could be heard by the now thoroughly frightened populace. The people, with blanched countenances, set features, looked in mute silence into the faces of each other. All knew and felt, but dared not even to themselves to whisper, the unmistakable truth. Now another alarm, another fire bell mingles its sound with the general chorus of discord, shouts of the soldiery, the frightened cries of the people—yells of the drunken troops all a seathing, maddening turbulance in the crowded streets. A

lurid glare shoots up above the housetops, then the cracking
and roaring of the dread elements told but too plainly that the
beautiful city was soon to be wrapped in flames. The sack
and pillage had begun!

Few men being in the city, the women, with rare heroism,
sought to save some little necessities of life, only to see it
struck to the floor or snatched from their hands and scattered
in the streets. Here would be a lone woman hugging an
infant to her breast, with a few strips of clothing hanging on
her arms; helpless orphans lugging an old trunk or chest, now
containing all they could call their own—these would be
snatched away, broken open, contents rifled by the drunken
soldiers, or if not valuable, trampled under foot.

Soldiers, with axes and hammers, rushed from house to
house, breaking in doors, smashing trunks, boxes, bureaus,
and robbing them of all that was valuable, then leaving the
house in flames. Helpless women, screaming children, babes
in the arms, invalids on beds, jolted and jostled against the
surging mob—none to help, none to advise—these defenseless
sufferers rushed aimlessly about, their sole purpose being to
avoid the flames and seek a place of safety. The fires originated principally in the southern section of the city, and as
the fire eat its way up, the howling throng followed, driving
the innocent and helpless ahead.

As the night wore on, the drunken soldiers, first made in-
toxicated by the wine in private cellars or the liquors in the
government buildings, now became beastly drunk in their
glee at the sight of the destruction they had wrought. The
women and children followed the dark background of that
part of the city not yet in flames. The Federal officers, instead of offering assistance or a helping hand to the ruined and
distressed people, added insult to injury by joining in with the
private soldiers in the plundering of the city, insulting the
women and adding fuel to the flame.

All night long did the flames rage, leap, and lick the clouds
as one block of buildings after another fell—food for the de-
vouring elements. This drunken orgies was kept up until their
craven hearts were fully satisfied. A few squares in the northeastern part of the city were left, also several churches, and
into these the women and children were huddled and packed,
and had to remain for days and some for weeks, almost on the

verge of starvation. The Federal commander, through the boundless dictates of his sympathetic heart, after destroying all that fire and rapine could reach, left the starving thousands a few rations each of the plunder he had robbed of the planters in the country.

No vehicles nor horses were left in the city's limits—the bridges burned that lead across the river to the west. To the east, Blair's Corps was laying waste everything in their pathway, while above and below the city, for a distance of fifty miles, Sherman had swept the country as bare as if a blight had fallen upon it. How the people of Columbia subsisted during the time they were penned in the city churches and the few buildings left, will ever remain a mystery, and to none so much as the sufferers themselves.

Grains of corn were eagerly picked up in the streets as they dropped from the wagons, and the women and children of the lower class and the negroes flocked to the deserted camps to gather up the crumbs left by the soldiers or the grains trampled under foot of the horses.

Every house in a stretch of fifty miles was entered and insults and indignities offered the defenseless women which would have shamed the savage Turk. Ladies were forced to disclose, at the point of the pistol or the sabre, the hiding-place of their little valuables. Some were forced to cook meals and wait upon the hell hounds, while they regaled themselves upon the choice viands or medicinal wines of the planters' wives. But be it known to their immortal honor, that it was only on the most rare occasions that these proud dames of the South could, either by threat or brutal treatment, be forced to yield to their insolent demands. With the orders from the soldiers to "prepare a meal" or "disclose the whereabouts of their money or valuables," came the threat, "We will burn your house if you do not." But almost invariably came the quick response, "Burn it, burn it, you cowardly wretches, and kill me, if you wish, and all of us, but I will never soil my hands by waiting upon a cowardly Yankee, nor tell you the place of concealment—find it if you can." The soldiers would question the negroes to find out if there were any watches, silver plate, or money belonging to the household; if so, they would, by a system of inquisition, attempt to force the women to give it up, but in vain.

A woman, Mrs. Miller, the wife of a neighbor of mine, had her husband's gold watch in her bosom, and refused to give it up when demanded, even when a cocked pistol was at her head. The vandal struck her a stunning blow with the butt end of the pistol—all in vain. The brave heroine held to the heirloom, and stoutly resisted all entreaties and threats.

Two old people living near me, brother and maiden sister, named Loner, both pass three scores, were asked to give their money. They had none. But one of the ruffians threw a fire brand under the bed, saying:

"I will put it out if you will tell me where you keep your money; you have it, for I've been so informed."

"Let it burn," answered the old women. "Do you think to frighten or intimidate me by burning my house that I will tell what I choose to conceal? Do you think I care so much for my house and its belongings? No, no; you mistake the women of the South. You will never conquer her people by making war upon defenseless women. Let the house go up in flames, and my ashes mingle with its ashes, but I will remain true to myself, my country, and my God."

Soon all that was left of the once happy home was a heap of ashes. Will God, in His wisdom, ever have cause to again create such women as those of the Southland? Or were there ever conditions in the world's history that required the presence of such noble martyrdom as was displayed by the women of the South during the Civil War?

But a Nemesis in this case, as in many others, was lurking near. Bands of Confederates and scouts had scattered themselves on the flanks and rear of the enemy; old men and boys and disabled veterans were lying in wait in many thickets and out of the way places, ready to pounce upon the unsuspecting freebooters and give to them their just deserts. Was it any wonder that so many hundreds, nay thousands, of these Goths failed to answer to Sherman's last roll call? Before the sun was many hours older, after the burning of the Loner homestead, the dreaded "bushwhackers" were on the trail of the vandals.

For years afterwards people, from curiosity, came to look at a heap of human bones in a thicket near, bleached by winter's rain and summer's sun, while some of the older men, pointing to the ghostly relics, would say, "Those are the remains of

Sherman's houseburners." And such were the scenes from the Saltkahatchie to the Cape Fear. Who were to blame?

Sherman now directs his march towards Winnsboro and Chester, still in the four great parols, burning and plundering as they go. It seems that in their march through Georgia they were only whetting their appetites for a full gorge of vandalism in South Carolina. After their carnival of ruin in Columbia the Federals, like the tiger, which, with the taste of blood, grows more ravenous, they became more destructive the more destruction they saw. Great clouds of black smoke rose up over the whole country and darkened the sky overhead, while at night the heavens were lit up by the glare of the burning buildings. The railroad tracks were torn up and bridges burned, the iron being laid across heaps of burning ties, then when at red heat, were wrapped around trees and telegraph posts—these last through pure wontonness, as no army was in their rear that could ever use them again.

While that part of Sherman's Army was crossing Broad River at Alston and Freshley's, and the other near Ridgeway, General Hampton wrote General Beauregard to concentrate all his forces at or near the latter place by shipping Hardee and all forces under him at once by railroad—Stephenson's Division of Western men, now with Hampton and all the cavalry to fall upon the Fifteenth Corps, under Blair, and crush it before the other portions of the army could reach it. He argued that the enemy was marching so wide apart, the country so hilly, and the roads in Fairfield County almost impassable, that one wing of the army could be crushed before the other could reach it. But General Beauregard telegraphed him, "The time is past for that move. While it could have been done at the Edisto or Branchville, it is too late now."

On the night of the 17th and morning of the 18th Charleston was evacuated. Before the commencement of the retirement, orders were given by General Beauregard to General Hardee to withdraw the troops in the following order, but General Hardee being sick at this time, the execution of the order devolved upon General McLaws: One brigade of Wright's Division, in St. Paul's Parish, to move by railroad to Monk's Corner, then march by Sandy Run to the Santee; the other portion of Wright's Division to move by Summerville to St. Stephen's. The trrops in Christ Church Parish to go

by steamer to St. Stephen's. The troops from James' Island
to move out by Ashley's Ferry and follow the Northeastern
railroad, to be followed in turn by all the troops in the city.
McLaws was to withdraw from Sherman's front at Branchville
and follow on to St. Stephen's. After all the troops were
here congregated, the line of march was taken up in the direction of Cheraw. Away to our left we could see the clouds of
smoke rise as houses went up in flames, while forest fires
swept the country far and wide. It was not fully understood
to what point Sherman was making, until he reached Winnsboro. Here he turned the course of direction by turning to
the right, crossing the Catawba at Pea's Ferry and Rocky
Mount, the right wing under General Howard, at Pea's; the
left, under General Slocum, at Rocky Mount, all marching to
form a junction again at Cheraw. Sherman did not dare to
trust himself far in the interior for any length of time, but was
marching to meet the fleet that had left him at Savannah and
the troops under Schofield, at Newbern, N. C. This is the
reason he turns his course towards the sea coast. Raiding
parties, under Kilpatrick, were sent out in the direction of
Darlington and Lancaster, burning and plundering at will.

About this time Fort Fisher and all the works at the mouth
of the Cape Fear River fell into the hands of the enemy.
Wilmington surrendered and General Bragg, who was in command there, retreated to Goldsboro.

How, in the face of all these facts, could it be possible for
Generals to deceive themselves or to deceive others, or how
President Davis could have such delusive hopes, is now impos-
sible to comprehend. On February 22nd, after the fall of
Wilmington, the Army of Sherman was on the border of
North Carolina, while Hood's was straggling through the
upper part of this State, with no protection of forming a junc-
tion with Beauregard. President Davis wrote on that day:

"General Beauregard: I have directed General J. E. Johnston to assume command of the Southern Army and assign
you to duty with him. Together, I feel assured you will beat
back Sherman."

To add one man, even if a great commander, would add but
little strength to any army, already exausted beyond the hope
of recuperation, still "You will beat Sherman back!" the President writes. I for one cannot see how a General could receive

such an order at such time in any other spirit than ridicule. President Davis, even after the fall of Richmond and the battle of Bettonville fought, where Johnston tried once more to "beat back Sherman" and failed—after all the circumstances and conditions were given to him in detail—said, "The struggle could be still carried on to a successful issue by bringing out all our latest resources; that we could even cross the Mississippi River, join forces with Kirby Smith, and prolong the war indefinitely." Was there ever such blind faith or dogged tenacity of purpose? Did Mr. Davis and our Generals really believe there was still a chance for a successful issue at this late day, or was it the knowledge of the disposition of the troops whom they knew would rather suffer death than defeat.

It must, within all reason, have been the latter, for no great commander cognizant of all the facts could have been so blind. Even while the Confederate troops were overwhelmed by numbers, communications cut on all sides, all out posts and the borders hemmed in one small compass, some of our soldiers entered a publishing house in Raleigh, destroyed all the type, broke the presses, and demolished the building—all this because the editor of the paper advised the giving up of the contest! Did the soldiers of the South believe as yet that they were beaten? Circumstances and their surly moods say not. Well might a commander or executive have apprehensions of his personal safety should he counsel submission as long as there was a soldier left to raise a rifle or draw a lanyard. I ask again was there ever before such troops as those of the South? Will there ever be again?

Kershaw's Brigade, now attached to Hardee's Corps, reached Cheraw about the first of March, but the enemy's advance was at Chesterfield, causing Hardee to continue his march by Rockinham on to Fayetteville, N. C., near which place the two armies, that is the one under Hampton and the other under Hardee, came together. Hardee having recovered from his indisposition, relieved General McLaws, the latter returning to Augusta, Ga. Kershaw's Brigade was soon after put in Wathal's Division.

On the 22nd of February General Jos. E. Johnston, who was then living at Lincolnton, N. C., was called from his retirement and placed in command of all the troops in North and South Carolina and Georgia. Although the army was

nothing more than detachments, and widely separated and
greatly disorganized when he reached them, still they hailed
with delight the appointment of their former faithful old commander. His one great aim was the convergence of the various armies to one point in front of the enemy and strike a blow
at either one or more of his columns, either at Fayetteville or
at the crossing of the Cape Fear River. Hardee had been
racing with Sherman to reach Cheraw and cross the PeeDee
before Sherman could come up. He only accomplished this
after many forced marches by "the skin of his teeth," to use a
homely expression. He crossed the PeeDee one day ahead of
the enemy, burning the bridge behind him, after moving all
the stones that were possible. The right wing, under General
Howard, crossed the Pee Dee at Cheraw, while the left, under
Slocum, crossed higher up, at Sneedsboro. Hampton was
forced to make a long detour up the PeeDee and cross at the
fords along the many little islands in that stream.

On the 8th of March General Bragg, with Hoke's Division,
reinforced by a division under D. H. Hill, of Johnston's command, numbering in all about two thousand, attacked three
divisions under General Cox, at Kiniston, defeating him with
much loss, capturing one thousand five hundred prisoners and
three pieces of artillery.

During the campaign our cavalry was not idle on the flanks
or front of Sherman, but on the contrary, was ever on the
alert, striking the enemy wherever possible. General Butler
intercepted and defeated a body of Federals on their way to
destroy the railroad at Florence, at or near Mount Elan.
General Wheeler, also, at Homesboro, came up with the
enemy, and after a spirited brush, drove the enemy from the
field, capturing a number of prisoners. Again, near Rockinham, the same officer put the enemy to rout. General Kilpatrick had taken up camp on the road leading to Fayetteville,
and commanding that road which was necessary for the concentration of our troops. In the night General Hampton,
after thoroughly reconnoitering the position, surrounded the
camp of Kilpatrick, and at daybreak, on the 10th, fell like a
hurricane upon the sleeping enemy. The wildest confusion
prevailed; friend could not be distinguished from foe. Shooting and saber slashing were heard in every direction, while
such of the enemy who could mounted their horses and rode at

break-neck speed, leaving their camp and camp equippage, their artillery and wagon trains. The enemy was so laden with stolen booty, captured in the Carolinas and Georgia, that this great treasure was too great a temptation to the already demoralized cavalry. So, instead of following up their victory, they went to gathering the spoils. Hundreds of horses were captured, but these ran off by our troops forcing all the artillery captured to be abandoned, after cutting the wheels to pieces. But the long train of wagons, laden with supplies, was a good addition to our depleted resources. A great number of the enemy were killed and wounded, with five hundred prisoners, besides recapturing one hundred and fifty of our own troops taken in former battles.

General Johnston now ordered the troops of General Bragg who had come up from Kiniston and the Western troops, under Stuart, Cheatham, and Lee, as well as a part of Hardee's, to concentrate at Smithfield. The bulk of Hardee's Corps, of which Kershaw's Brigade was a part, withdrew from Cheraw in the direction of Goldsboro, and at Averysboro the enemy came up with Hardee, and by the overpowering weight of numbers forced the Confederates from their position. The density of the pine forest was such, that after a few fires, the smoke settled among the undergrowth and under the treetops in such quantity that a foe could not be seen even a short distance away. The level condition of the country prevented our artillery from getting in any of its work, and a flank movement by the Federals could be so easily made, unnoticed, that Hardee was forced to retire in the direction of Smithfield and to an elevation.

General Johnston having learned that the enemy was marching in the direction of Glodsboro, instead of Raleigh, and that the right wing was a day's advance of the left, ordered a concentration of his troops near the little hamlet of Bentonville, situated near the junction of the roads, one leading to Raleigh and the other to Goldsboro, and there fall upon the one wing of the army and defeat it before the other came up. This was not so difficult in contemplation as in the perforance, under the present condition of the troops and the topography of the country. General Johnston was misled by the maps at hand, finding afterwards that the Federal General, Howard, was much nearer Bentonville than was General Hardee. But General Hampton put General Butler's Division of Cavalry in front of this whole force, behind some hastily constructed breastworks, and was to keep Slocum at bay until the troops had all gotten in position.

General Hardee began moving early on the morning of the 19th, and on reaching Bentonville we now, for the first time, came up with all the other troops of the army. Hoke's Division lead off to take position and stood on both sides of a dull road leading through the thickets. Batteries were placed on his right. Next to the artillery was posted the Army of Tennessee, its right thrown forward. Before Hardee could get in position the enemy attacked with the utmost vigor, so much so that General Bragg, who was commanding in person at this point, asked for reinforcements. General Hardee, moving by at this juncture, ordered McLaws' Old Division to the aid of Hoke. But the almost impenetrable thicket prevented hasty movement, and the smoke in front, overhead and the rear, with bullets passing over the heads of Hoke's men, made it impossible for these unacquainted with the disposition of the troops to know whether it was friend or foe in our front. The troops became greatly entangled and some of the officers demoralized. Some troops on our right, by mistaking the head of direction, began to face one way, while Kershaw's Brigade was facing another. But after much manœuvering, McLaw's got the troops disentangled and moved upon the line, and after several rounds at close range, the enemy retreated. Hardee was then ordered to charge with his wing of the army, composed of troops under Stuart and a division under Taliaferro, while Bragg was to follow by brigades from right to left. The firing was now confusing, our troops advancing in different direction, and the sound of our guns and cannon echoing and reverberating through the dense forest, made it appear as if we were surrounded by a simultaneous fire. But finding our way the best we could by the whizzing of the bullets, we rushed up to the enemy's first line of entrenchments, which they had abandoned without an effort, and took position behind the second line of works. After firing a round or two, the Confederates raised the old Rebel yell and went for their second line with a rush. Here General Hardee led his men in person, charging at their head on horseback. The troops carried everything before them; the enemy in double columns and favorably entrenched, was glad to take cover in the thicket in the rear. On the extreme left our troops were less successful, being held in check by strong breastworks and a dense thicket between the enemy and the troops of General Bragg. After sweeping the enemy from the field, General Hardee found it necessary to halt and reform his line and during this interval the enemy made an unsuccessful assault upon the troops of General Stuart. After nightfall and after all the killed and wounded had been removed from the field, General Johnston moved the troops back to the line occupied in the morning and threw up fortifications. Here we remained until the 21st; McLaws was detached and placed on the left of Hoke; the cavalry deployed as skirmishers to our left. There was a considerable gap between our extreme left and the main body of cavalry, and this break the writer commanded with a heavy line of skirmishers. Late in the day the enemy made a spirited attack upon us, so much so that General McLaws sent two companies of boys, formerly of Fizer's Brigade of Georgia Militia. The boys were all between sixteen and eighteen, and a finer body of young men I never saw. He also sent a regiment of North Carolina Militia, consisting of old men from fifty to sixty, and as these old men were coming up on line the enemy were giving us a rattling fire from their sharpshooters. The old men could not be induced to come up, however. The Colonel, a venerable old gray-beard, riding a white horse, as soon as the bullets began to pelt the pines in his front, leaped from his horse and took refuge behind a large tree. I went to him and tried every inducement to get him to move up his men on a line with us, but all he would do was to grasp me by the hand and try to jerk me down beside him. "Lie down, young man," said he, "or by God you'll be shot to pieces. Lie down!" The old militiaman I saw was too old for war, and was "not built that way." But when I returned to the skirmish line, on which were my own brigade skirmishers, reinforced by the two boy companies, the young men were fighting with a glee and abandon I never saw equalled. I am sorry to record that several of these promising young men, who had left their homes so far behind, were killed and many wounded.

This ended the battle of Bentonville, and we might say the war. The sun of the Confederacy, notwithstanding the hopes of our Generals, the determination of the troops, and the prayers of the people, was fast sinking in the west. The glorious rising on the plains of Manassas had gone down among the pine barriers of North Carolina. The last stroke had been given, and destiny seemed to be against us. For hundreds of miles had the defeated troops of Hood marched barefooted and footsore to the relief of their comrades of the East, and had now gained a shallow victory. They had crossed three States to mingle their blood with those of their friends who had fought with dogged resistence every step that Sherman had made. But their spirits were not broken. They were still ready to try conclusions with the enemy whenever our leaders gave the signal for battle. The South could not be conquered by defeat—to conquer it, it must be crushed. The tattered battle flags waved as triumphantly over the heads of the shattered ranks of the battle-scared veterans here in the pine barriers as it ever did on the banks of the Rapidan.

It is sad to chronicle that on this last day, in a battle of the cavalry, in which the infantry had to take a part, the gallant son of the brave General Hardee fell at the head of his column as the Eighth Texas Cavalry was making a desperate charge.

In the battle of Bentonville the Confederates had fourteen thousand infantry and cavalry. The cavalry being mostly on the flanks, and General Wheeler on the north side of Mill Creek, could not participate in the battle in consequence of the swolen stream. The Federal Army had thirty-five thousand engaged on the 19th and seventy thousand in line on the 20th. The loss on the Confederate side was one hundred and eighty killed, one thousand two hundred and twenty wounded, and five hundred and fifteen missing. The enemy's losses in killed and wounded far exceeded the Confederates, besides the Confederates captured nine hundred prisoners.

On the night of the 21st the army began its retreat, crossing Mill Creek on the morning of the 22ud, just in time to see the enemy approach the bridge as our last troops had crossed.

On the 23rd General Sherman marched his army to Goldsboro, there uniting with General Schofield. It was the intention of General Lee that as soon as General Sherman had approached near enough, to abandon the trenches at Petersburg, and, with the combined armies, turn and fall upon his front, flank, and rear.

CHAPTER XLIII

From Smithfield to Greensboro---The Surrender.

The army took up quarters for a while around Smithfield. The troops were as jolly and full of life as they ever were in their lives. Horse racing now was the order of the day. Out in a large old field, every day thousands of soldiers and civilians, with a sprinkling of the fair ladies of the surrounding country, would congregate to witness the excitement of the race course. Here horses from Kentucky, Tennessee, Georgia, and North and South Carolina tried each others mettle. They were not the thoroughbreds of the course, but cavalry horses, artillery horses, horses of Generals, Colonels, and the staff—horses of all breeds and kinds, all sizes and description—stood at the head of the track and champed their bits with eagerness, impatient to get away. Confederate money by the handfuls changed owners every day. It was here that Governor Zeb Vance, of North Carolina, visited us, and was a greater favorite with the soldiers than any man in civil life. It was here, too, our old disabled commander, General James Connor, came to bid us an affectionate farewell. General Kennedy formed the brigade into a hollow square to receive our old General. He entered the square on horseback, accompanied by General Kennedy and staff. He had come to bid us farewell, and spoke to us in feeling terms. He recounted our many deeds of valor upon the field, our sufferings in camp and upon the march, and especially our supreme heroism and devotion in standing so loyally to our colors in this the dark hour of our country's cause. He spoke of his great reluctance to leave us; how he had watched with sympathy and affection our wanderings, our battles, and our victories, and then envoking Heaven's blessings upon us, he said in pathetic tones, "Comrades, I bid you an affectionate farewell," and rode away.

While in camp here there was a feeble attempt made to reorganize and consolidate the brigade by putting the smaller companies together and making one regiment out of two. As these changes took place so near the end, the soldiers never really realizing a change had been made, I will do no more than make a passing allusion to it, as part of this history. The only effect these changes had was the throwing out of some of our best and bravest officers (there not being places for all), but as a matter of fact this was to their advantage, as they escaped the humiliation of surrender, and returned home a few days earlier than the rest of the army.

After passing through South Carolina and venting its spleen on the Secession State, the Federal Army, like a great forest fire, sweeping over vast areas, stops of its own accord by finding nothing to feed upon. The vandalism of the Union Army in North Carolina was confined mostly to the burning of the great turpentine forests. They had burned and laid waste the ancestral homes of lower South Carolina, left in ashes the beautiful capital of the State, wrecked and ruined the magnificent residences and plantations of the central and upper part of the country, leaving in their wake one vast sheet of ruin and desolation, so that when they met the pine barrens of North Carolina, their appetites for pillage, plunder, and destruction seems to have been glutted.

It was the boast of the Federal commander and published with delight in all the Northern newspapers, that "where his army went along a crow could not pass over without taking its rations along." Then, too, this very country was to feed and support, while in transit to these horrors almost the whole of Johnston's and the greater part of Lee's Army. All these, in squads or singly, were fed along the way from house to house wherever they could beg a little meal or corn, with a morsel of meat or molasses. A great number of negro troops also passed through this country on their way to the coast to be disbanded. But the noble women of South Carolina never turned a hungry soldier from their doors as long as there was a mouthful in the house to eat.

Another terror now alarmed the people—the news of a great raid, under Stoneman, being on its way through North Carolina and upper South Carolina, coming across the country from East Tennessee, laying waste everything in its track. General Sherman had concentrated his whole army at Goldsboro, and was lying idle in camp, preparatory to his next great move to connect with Grant. He had at his command the right wing, under General Howard, twenty-eight thousand eight hundred and thirty-four; its left wing, under General Slocum, twenty-eight thousand and sixty-three. General Schofield had come up from Newbern with twenty-six thousand three hundred and ninety-two and constituted the center, besides five thousand six hundred and fifty-nine cavalry, under Kilpatrick, and ninety-one pieces of artillery. General Johnston had encamped his army between two roads, one leading to Raleigh, the other to Weldon. The Confederate Government, after the evacuation of Richmond, had now established its quarters at Danville, Va., awaiting the next turn of the wheel. Lee had fallen back from Petersburg; while Johnston, before Sherman, was awaiting the move of that General to fall back still nearer to his illustrious chieftain. The government and all the armies were now hedged in the smallest compass. Still our leaders were apparently hopeful and difiant, the troops willing to stand by them to the last.

On the 10th of April President Davis and a part of his cabinet left Danville on his way to Greensboro. Even at this late day President Davis was urging the concentration of the troops under General Walker, the scattered troops at Salisbury and Greensboro, and those under Johnston at same place on the Yadkin, and crush Sherman, and then it is supposed to turn on Grant. All this with less than twenty thousand men!

The last conference of the great men of the Confederacy met at Greensboro, on the 13th of April, 1865. Those present were President Davis, Messrs. Benjamin, Secretary of State; Mallory, of the Navy; Reagin, Postmaster General; Breckinridge, Secretary of War, and General Johnston. The army had been falling back daily through Raleigh, and was now encamped near Greensboro. President Davis still clung to the delusion that by pressing the conscript act and bringing out all absentees, they could yet prolong the struggle, even if they had to cross the Mississippi and join with Kirby Smith. General Johnston urged in his and General Beauregard's name its utter impracticability, and informed the President plainly and positively that it was useless to continue the struggle—that they had as well abandon all hope of any other issue than that which they could gain through the Federal authorities, and besought Mr. Davis to open negotiations looking to peace—that he was yet the executive and head of the Confederate Government; that he was the proper one to commence such negotiations. This Mr. Davis refused, saying the Federal authorities would refuse to treat with him. Then General Johnston proposed doing so in his own name. This was agreed to, and a letter written by Mr. Mallory, he being the best penman in the group, and signed and sent by General Johnston to General Sherman. The letter recapitulated the results in the army in the last few days, changing the status of the two armies and the needless amount of bloodshed and devastation of property that the continuance of the struggle would produce, and asked for a conference looking to an armistice in the armies until the civil government could settle upon terms of peace. The letter was sent to General Hampton, and by him to the Federal commander the next day. General Sherman acknowledged the receipt of the letter on the 14th, and it reached General Johnston on the 16th, agreeing to a cessation of hostilities until further notice. General Sherman expressed in his letter a great desire to spare the people of North Carolina the devastation and destruction the passing of his army through the State would necessitate. When it began to be noised about in the camp that the army was about to be surrendered, the soldiers became greatly excited. The thought of grounding their arms to an enemy never before entered their minds, and when the news came of a surrender the greatest apprehension and dread seized all. So different the end to their expectation. None could even think of the future without a shudder. Some anticipated a term in Federal prisons; others, the higher officers, a military trial; others thought of their private property and their arms. Even in a prison camp, where our soldiers would be kept confined under a Federal guard, all was mystery and uncertainty. The wives and helpless children, left in the rear to the mercy of the negroes (now for the first time known to be free), agitated the minds of not a few. Men began to leave the army by twos and by squads. Guards were placed on all roads and around camps, and the strictest orders were given against leaving the army without leave. Cavalrymen in great numbers had

34

mounted their horses and rode away. General Sherman sent guards to all fords and bridges to examine all the paroles of the troops of Lee now swarming through the country.

General Johnston met General Sherman at Durham, on the 17th of April, at the house of Mr. Bennett, but after a long and tedious controversy, nothing was agreed upon. A second meeting took place at the same house next day, at which General Breckinridge was unofficially present, when terms of an armistice were agreed to until the department at Washington could be heard from. President Davis had already gone South with such of his cabinet as chose to follow him, the whole settlement of difficulties now devolving upon General Johnston alone.

But just as all negotiations were progressing finely the news came of President Lincoln's assassination, throwing the whole of the Federal Army in a frenzy of excitement. While the troops of the South may not have given their assent to such measures, yet they rejoiced secretly in their hearts that the great agitator, emancipator—the cause of all our woes—was laid low. To him and him alone all looked upon as being the originator, schemer, and consummater of all the ills the South had suffered. However the hearts of the Southern people may have changed in the thirty years that have passed, or how sadly they deplored his death, even in a decade afterwards, I but voice the sentiment of the South at the time when I say they hated Lincoln with all the venom of their souls, and his untimely taking off by the hands of the assassin partly consoled them for all they had suffered.

Orders came from General Sherman to General Johnston to the effect that part of their agreement was rejected by the Washington Authority, and notifying the latter that the truce would be called off in forty-eight hours. This occasioned a third meeting between the two commanders to make such changes that were required by the authorities. On the 26th General Johnston sent a communication to General Sherman requesting a meeting at same place for further conference. This was agreed to and the meeting took place, where such terms were agreed upon and signed as was thought to be in accordance with the wishes of the Washington Government. Rolls were made out in duplicate of all the officers and soldiers, and on the 2nd of May the troops marched out, stacked their

arms, were given paroles, and slowly turned away and commenced their homeward journey.

A military chest, containing $39,000, had been received
from the Government in Richmond and divided out among the
soldiers, being $1.29 apiece. All the wagon and artillery
horses and wagons, also, were loaned to the soldiers and
divided by lot. A few days' rations had been issued, and
with this and the clothes on their back, this remnant of a once
grand army bent their steps towards their desolate homes. It
was found advisable to move by different routs and in such
numbers as was most agreeable and convenient. Once away
from the confines of the army, they took by-ways and cross
country roads, avoiding as much as possible the track of the
late army. The troops of Kershaw's Brigade, on reaching the
borders of their State, each sought for himself the easiest and
nearest path home. The Western Army made their way, the
most of them at least, to Washington, Ga., where there was
yet railroad communication a part of the way through Georgia.

And now, gentle reader, my task is done—my pen laid
aside, after days and days of earnest toil to give a faithful and
correct account of your daring, your endurance, your patriotism, and your fidelity to the cause you had espoused. Your
aims have been of the highest, your performances ideal, and
while you were unsuccessful, still your deeds of daring will
live in history as long as civilization lasts. While your cherished hopes ended in a dream, still your aspirations have been
of the loftiest, and your acts will be copied by generations yet
unborn, as a fitting pattern for all brave men. You have
fought in all the great battles of the East, from the trenches
of Petersburg to the rugged heights of Round Top. Your
blood mingled with that of your comrades of the West, from
Chickamauga to the storming of Fort London. You combatted the march of Sherman from the Saltkahatchie to the close,
and stacked your arms more as conquering heroes than beaten
foes. You have nothing to regret but the results—no hope
but the continued prosperity of a reunited people. This heritage of valor left to posterity as a memorial of Southern manhood to the Southern cause will be cherished by your descendants for all time, and when new generations come on and read
the histories of the great Civil War, and recall to their minds

the fortitude, the chivalry, and the glories of the troops engaged, Kershaw's Brigade will have a bright page in the book of their remembrance.

CHAPTER XLIV

Retrospect.

It would be supposed that the writer, who had fought by the side of nearly all. and who had visited battlefields where troops from every State had fallen, could form an idea of "Which were the best troops from the South?" The South has furnished a type of the true soldier that will last as a copy for all time. She had few regulars, and her volunteer troops were brought into service without preparation or without the knowledge of tactical drill, but in stoicism, heroism, and martyrdom they excelled the world

I give in these pages a brief synopsis of the characteristics of the troops from different States, and while this is the view of the author alone, still I feel assured that the great mass of the old soldiers will admit its correctness. To the question, "Which were the best troops from the South?" there would be as many answers and as much differences of opinions as there were States in the Confederacy, or organizations in the field, as each soldier was conscientious in his belief that those from his own State were the best in the army, his brigade the best in the division, his regiment the best in the brigade, and his own company the best in the regiment. This is a pardonable pride of the soldier, and is as it should be to make an army great. Where all, individually and collectively, were as good or better than any who ever before faced an enemy upon a battlefield, there really are no "best."

But soldiers from different States, all of the same nationality and of the same lineage. from habits, temperaments, and environments, had different characteristics upon the field of battle. From an impartial standpoint, I give my opinion thus:

The Virginians were the cavaliers of the South, high-toned, high-bred, each individual soldier inspired by that lofty idea of loyalty of the cavalier. They were the ideal soldiers in an open field and a fair fight. They were the men to sweep a battle line that fronts them from the field by their chivalrous and steady courage. Virginia, the mother of Presidents, of great men, and noble women, the soldier of that State felt in honor bound to sustain the name and glory of their commonwealth. As a matter of fact, the Virginians, as a rule, with exceptions enough to establish the rule, being one of the oldest of the sister States, her wealth, her many old and great institutions of learning, were better educated than the mass of soldiers from the other States. They were soldiers from pride and patriotism, and courageous from "general principles." In an open, fair field, and a square and even fight, no enemy could stand before their determined advance and steady fire. They were not the impulsive, reckless, head-strong soldiers in a desperate charge as were those from some other Southern States, but cool, collected, steady, and determined under fire. They were of the same mettle and mould as their kinsmen who stood with Wellington at Waterloo.

The North Carolinians were the "Old Guard" of the Confederacy. They had little enthusiasm, but were the greatest "stickers" and "stayers" on a battle line of any troops from the South. They fought equally as well in thicket or tangled morass as behind entrenchments. To use an army expression, "The North Carolinians were there to stay." It was a jocular remark, common during the war, that the reason the North Carolina troops were so hard to drive from a position was "they had so much tar on their heels that they could not run." They were obstinate, tenacious, and brave.

South Carolinians took on in a great measure the inspirations of some of their French Huguenot ancestors and the indomitable courage of their Scotch and German forefathers of the Revolution. They were impulsive, impetuous, and recklessly brave in battle, and were the men to storm breastworks and rush to the cannon's mouth at the head of a "forlorn hope." They possibly might not stay as long in a stubbornly contested battle as some from other States, but would often accomplish as much in a few minutes by the mad fury of their assault as some others would accomplish in as many hours. They were the Ironsides of the South, and each individual felt that he had a holy mission to fulfill. There were no obstacles they could not surmount, no position they would not assail. Enthusiasm and self-confidence were the fort of South Carolinians, and it was for them to raise the Rebel yell and keep it up while the storm of battle raged fierce and furious. They were the first to raise the banner of revolt, and right royally did they sustain it as long as it floated over the Southland.

What is said of the South Carolinians can be truthfully said of Georgians. People of the same blood, and kindred in all that makes them one, they could be with propriety one and the same people. The Georgians would charge a breastwork or storm a battery with the same light-heartedness as they went to their husking bees or corn-shucking, all in a frolick. To illustrate their manner of fighting, I will quote from a Northern journal, published just after the seven days' battles around Richmond, a conversation between Major D., of the —— New York, and a civilian of the North. The Major was boasting in a noisy manner of the courage, daring, and superiority of the Northern soldiers over those of the South. "Well, why was it," asked the civilian, "if you were so superior in every essential to the Rebels, that you got such an everlasting licking around Richmond?" "Licking, h—l," said the wounded Major, "who could fight such people? Indians! Worse than an Appache. Just as we would get in line of battle and ready for an advance, a little Georgia Colonel, in his shirt sleeves and copperas breeches, would pop out into a corn field at the head of his regiment, and shout at the top of his voice, 'Charge!' Man alive! here would come the devils like a whirl-wind— over ditches, gullies, fences, and fields; shouting, yelling, whooping, that makes the cold chills run up your back—flash their glittering bayonets in our very faces, and break our lines to pieces before you could say 'boo.' Do you call that fighting? It was murder." No more need be said of the Georgians.

Little Florida did not have many troops in the field, but little as she was, she was as brave as the best. Her troops, like those of Georgia and South Carolina, were impulsive, impetuous, and rapid in battle. They were few in numbers, but legions in the fray.

The Alabamians and Mississippians came of pioneer stock, and like their ancestry, were inured to hardships and dangers

from childhood; they made strong, hardy, brave soldiers. Indifferent to danger, they were less careful of their lives than
some from the older States. They were fine marksmen; with
a steady nerve and bold hearts, they won, like Charles Martel,
with their hammer-like blows. They were the fanatical Sara-
ceus of the South; while nothing could stand before the broad
scimeters of the former, so nothing could stand in the way of
the rifle and bayonet of the latter.

The Louisianians were the Frenchmen of the South. Of
small statue, they were the best marchers in the army. Like
their ancestors in the days of the "Merry Monard," and their
cousins in the days of the "Great Napoleon," they loved glory
and their country. Light-hearted and gay in camp, they
were equally light-hearted and gay in battle. Their slogan
was, "Our cause and our country." The Louisianians were
grand in battle, companionable in camp, and all round soldiers
in every respect.

The Texan, unlike the name of Texan immediately after
the war, when that country was the city of refuge for every
murderer and cut-throat of the land, were gallant, chivalrous,
and gentlemanly soldiers. Descendants of bold and adventurous spirits from every State in the South, they were equally
bold and daring in battle, and scorned the very word of fear or
danger. Hood's old Texas Brigade shared honors with the
old Stonewall Brigade in endurance, courage, and obstinacy in
action. The soldiers of Texas were tenacious, aggressive,
and bold beyond any of their brethren of the South.

The Tennesseeans, true to the instincts of their "back
woods" progenitors, were kind-hearted, independent, and
brim-ful of courage. Driven from their homes and firesides
by a hostile foe, they became a "storm center" in battle.
They were combative and pugnacious, and defeat had no effect
upon their order, and they were ever ready to turn and strike
a foe or charge a battery. Their courage at Chickamauga is
distinguished by showing the greatest per cent. of killed and
wounded in battle that has ever been recorded, the charge of
the Light Brigade not excepted, being over forty-nine per
cent.

What is said of the Tennesseeans is equally true of the
Arkansans. Of a common stock and ancestry, they inherited
all the virtues and courage of their forefathers. The Con-

federacy had no better soldiers than the Arkansans—fearless, brave, and oftentimes courageous beyond prudence.

The border States' soldiers, Missourians, Kentuckians, and Marylanders, were the free lance of the South. They joined the fortunes of the South with the purest motives and fought with the highest ideals. Under Forrest and Morgan and the other great riders of the West, they will ever be the soldiers of story, song, and romance. Their troops added no little lustre to the constellation of the South's great heroes, and when the true history of the great Civil War shall be written, they will be remembered. Indomitable in spirits, unconquerable and unyielding in battle, they will ever stand as monuments to the courage of the Southern Army.

THE MAGNITUDE OF THE WAR—ITS LOSSES IN KILLED AND DIED.

What were the Confederate losses during the war? Where are the Confederate dead? Which State lost the most soldiers in proportion to the number furnished the war? These are questions which will perhaps be often asked, but never answered. It can never be known, only approximately. The cars containing the Confederate archives were left unguarded and unprotected at Greensboro on its way from Richmond, until General Beauregard noticed papers from the car floating up and down the railroad track, and had a guard placed over them and sent to Charlotte. There was a like occurrence at this place, no protection and no guard, until General Johnston had them turned over to the Federal authorities for safe keeping. Consequently, the Confederate rolls on file in Washington are quite incomplete, and the loss impossible to ever be made good.

The Federal authorities commenced immediately after the war to collect their dead in suitable cemeteries, and the work of permanently marking their graves continued systematically until the Federal loss in the war can be very accurately estimated. There are seventy-five public cemeteries for the burial of the Federal soldiers, in which are buried three hundred and sixty thousand two hundred and seven; of these, one hundred and thirty-nine thousand four hundred and ninety-six are marked unknown. There were thirty-three thousand five hundred and twenty negro soldiers buried in the cemeteries,

and more than fifty thousand Union dead never accounted for.
A great number of these fell by the wayside during "Sherman's march to the sea;" lost by "Sherman's rear guard,"
called by the Federal soldiers "Confederate bushwhackers."

The rolls of the Confederate dead in the archives at Washington, given by States, are very unsatisfactory and necessarily incomplete. Only two States can even approximate their
loss. But as this is the record in Washington, I give it.

	Killed.	Died of Wounds.	Died of Disease.
Virginia	5,328	2,519	6,947
North Carolina	14,522	5,151	20,602
South Carolina	9,187	3,725	4,700
Georgia	5,553	1,716	3,702
Florida	793	506	1,047
Alabama	552	190	724
Mississippi	5,807	2,651	6,807
Louisiana	2,612	858	3,059
Texas	1,348	1,241	1,260
Arkansas	2,165	915	3,872
Tennessee	2,115	874	3,425
Regulars	1,007	468	1,040
Border States	1,959	672	1,142
Totals	52,954	21,570	59,297

In the above it will be seen that North Carolina, which may
be considered approximately correct, lost more than any other
State. Virginia furnished as many, if not more, troops than
North Carolina, still her losses are one-third less, according to
the statistics in Washington. This is far from being correct.
Alabama's dead are almost eliminated from the rolls, while it
is reasonable to suppose that she lost as many as South Carolina, Mississippi, or Georgia. South Carolina furnished more
troops in proportion to her male white population than any
State in the South, being forty-five thousand to August, 1862,
and eight thousand reserves. It is supposed by competent
statisticians that the South lost in killed and died of wounds,
ninety-four thousand; and lost by disease, one hundred and
twenty-five thousand.

In some of the principal battles throughout the war, there
were killed out right, not including those died of wounds —

First Manassas	387	Gettysburg	3,530
Wilson's Creek	279	Chickamauga	2,380
Fort Donelson	466	Missionary Ridge	381

Pea Ridge	360	Sabine Cross Roads	350
Shiloh	1,723	Wilderness	1,630
Seven Pines	980	Atlanta Campaign	3,147
Seven Days Battles	3,286	Spottsylvania	1,310
Second Manassas	1,553	Drury's Bluff	355
Sharpsburg	1,512	Cold Harbor	960
Corinth	1,200	Atlanta, July 22, 1864	1,500
Perryville	510	Winchester	286
Fredericksburg	596	Cedar Creek	339
Murfreesboro	1,794	Franklin	1,750
Chancellorsville	1,665	Nashville	360
Champion Hill	380	Bentonville	289
Vicksburg Siege	875	Five Forks	350

There were many other battles, some of greater magnitude than the above, which are not here given. There are generally five wounded to one killed, and nearly one-third of the wounded die of their wounds, thus a pretty fair estimate of the various battles can be had. There were more men killed and wounded at Gettysburg than on any field of battle during the war, but it must be born in mind that its duration was three days. General Longstreet. who should be considered a judge, says that there were more men killed and wounded on the battlefield at Sharpsburg (or Antietam), for the length of the engagement and men engaged, than any during this century. The Union losses on the fields mentioned above exceeded those of the Confederates by thirteen thousand five hundred in killed and died of wounds.

There were twenty-five regular prison pens at the North, at which twenty-six thousand seven hundred and seventy-six Confederate prisoners died, tabulated as follows:

PRISONS.	No. Deaths.	PRISONS.	No. Deaths.
Alton. Ill	1,613	Hart's Is., N. Y. Harbor	230
Camp Butler, Ill.	816	Johnson s Island, Ohio	270
Camp Chase. Ohio	2,108	Knoxville, Tenn	138
Camp Douglass, Ill	3,750	Little Rock, Ark	220
Camp Horton, Ind	1,765	Nashville, Tenn.	561
Camp Randall, Wis.	137	New Orleans, La	329
Chester. Penn	213	Point Lookout, Md	3,446
David's Is , N. Y. Harbor	178	Richmond, Va	175
Elmira, N. Y.	2,960	Rock Island, Ill	1,922
Fort Delaware, Del	2,502	St. Louis, Mo.	589
Fort Warren, Bos'n H'b'r	13	Ship Island, Miss.	162
Frederick, Md	226	Washington, D C	457
Gettysburg, Penn	210		

War is an expensive pastime for nations, not alone in the loss of lives and destruction of public and private property, but the expenditures in actual cash—gold and silver—is simply appalling. It is claimed by close students of historical data, those who have given the subject careful study, that forty million of human beings lose their lives during every century by war alone. Extravagant as this estimate may seem, any-one who will carefully examine the records of the great con-flicts of our own century will readily be convinced that there are not as much extravagance in the claim as a cursory glance at the figures would indicate. Europe alone loses between eighteen and twenty million, as estimated by the most skillful statisticians. Since the time of the legendary Trojan War (three thousand years), it is supposed by good authority that one billion two hundred thousand of human beings have lost their lives by the hazzard of war, not all in actual battle alone, but by wounds and diseases incident to a soldier's life, in addi-tion to those fallen upon the field.

In the wars of Europe during the first half of this century two million and a half of soldiers lost their lives in battle, and the country was impoverished to the extent of six billions eight hundred and fifty millions of dollars, while three millions of soldiers have perished in war since 1850. England's na-tional debt was increased by the war of 1792 to nearly one billion and a half, and during the Napoleonic wars to the amount of one billion six hundred thousand dollars.

During the last seventy years Russia has expended for war measures the sum of one billion six hundred and seventy mil-lion dollars, and lost seven hundred thousand soldiers. It cost England, France, and Russia, in the crimson war of little more than a year's duration, one billion five hundred million dollars, and five hundred thousand lives lost by the four com-bined nations engaged.

But all this loss, in some cases lasting for years, is but a bagatelle in comparison to the loss in men and treasure during the four years of our Civil War.

According to the records in Washington, the North spent, for the equipment and support of its armies during the four years of actual hostilities, four billion eight hundred million in money, outside of the millions expended in the maintenance of its armies during the days of Reconstruction, and lost four

hundred and ten thousand two hundred and fifty-seven men.
The war cost the South, in actual money on a gold basis,
two billion three hundred million, to say nothing of the tax in
kind paid by the farmers of the South for the support of the
army.   The destruction and loss in public and private property, outside of the slaves, is simply appalling.   The approximate loss in soldiers is computed at two hundred and nineteen
thousand.

The actual cost of the war on both sides, in dollars and
cents, and the many millions paid to soldiers as pensions since
the war, would be a sum sufficient to have paid for all the
negroes in the South several times over, and paid the national
debt and perhaps the debts of most of the Southern States at
the commencement of the war.

This enormous loss in blood and treasure on the part of the
South was not spent in the attempts at conquest, the subver-
sion of the Union, or the protection of the slave property, but
simply the maintenance of a single principle—the principle of
States Rights, guaranteed by the Federal Constitution.

THE CONFEDERATE DEAD—THE BATTLEFIELDS OF THE CIVIL WAR—THE TWO CIVILIZATIONS.

The North has gathered up the bones of the greater part of
her vast armies of the dead, commencing the task immediately
after the war, and interred them in her vast national cemeteries.   At the head of each is an imperishable head-stone, on
which is inscribed the name of the dead soldier, where a record
has been kept, otherwise it is simply marked "unknown."
The North was the victor; she was great, powerful, and rolling
in wealth; she could do this, as was right and just.

But where are the South's dead?   Echo answers from every
hill and dale, from every home where orphan and widow weep
and mourn, "Where?"   The South was the vanquished,
stricken in spirits, and ruined in possessions; her dead lie scattered along every battle ground from Cemetery Ridge and the
Round Top at Gettysburg, to the Gulf and far beyond the
Father of Waters.   One inscription on the head-stones would
answer for nearly all, and marked "unknown."   One monument would suffice for all the army of the dead, and an appro-
priate inscription would be a slight paraphrase of old Simoni-
des on the shaft e.ected to the memory of the heroes of
Thermopylae—

"Go, stranger, and to Southland tell
That here, obeying her behest, we fell."

The names of the great majority have already been forgotten, only within a circumscribed circle are they remembered, and even from this they will soon have passed into oblivion. But their deeds are recorded in the hearts of their countrymen in letters everlasting, and their fame as brave and untarnished soldiers will be remembered as long as civilization admires and glories in the great deeds of a great people. Even some of the great battle grounds upon which the South immortalized itself and made the American people great will soon be lost to memory, and will live only in song and story. Yet there are others which, through the magnificent tribute the North has paid to her dead, will be remembered for all time.

Looking backwards through the lapse of years since 1861, over some of the great battlefields of the Civil War, we see striking contrasts. On some, where once went carnage and death hand in hand, we now see blooming fields of growing grain, broad acres of briar and brush, while others, a magnificent "city of the dead." Under the shadow of the Round Top at Gettysburg, where the earth trembled beneath the shock of six hundred belching cannon, where trampling legions spread themselves along the base, over crest and through the gorges of the mountain, are now costly parks, with towering monuments—records of the wonderful deeds of the dead giants, friend and foe.

Around the Capital of the "Lost Cause," where once stood forts and battlements, with frowning cannon at each salient, great rows of bristling bayonets capping the walls of the long winding ramparts, with men on either side standing grim and silent, equally ready and willing to consecrate the ground with the blood of his enemy or his own, are now level fields of grain, with here and there patches of undergrowth and briars. Nothing now remains to conjure the passer-by that here was once encamped two of the mightiest armies of earth, and battles fought that astounded civilization.

On the plains of Manassas, where on two different occasions the opposing armies met, where the tide of battle surged and rolled back, where the banners of the now vanquished waved in triumph from every section of the field, the now victors fleeing in wild confusion, beaten, routed, their colors trailing in the dust of shame and defeat, now all to mark this historic battle ground is a broken slab or column, erected to individuals, defaced by time and relic seekers, and hidden among the briars and brush.

From the crest and along the sides of Missionary Ridge, and from the cloud-kissed top of Lookout Mountain, to Chickamauga, where the flash of cannon lit up the valley and plain below, where swept the armies of the blue and the gray in alternate victory and defeat, where the battle-cry of the victorious mingled with the defiant shouts of the vanquished, where the cold steel of bayonets met, and where brother's gun flashed in the face of brother, where the tread of contending armies shook the sides and gorges of the mountain passes, are now costly granite roadways leading to God's Acre, where are buried the dead of the then two nations, and around whose border runs the "River of Death" of legend, Chickamauga. Over this hallowed ground floats the flag of a reunited country, where the brother wearing the uniform of the victor sleeps by the side of the one wearing the uniform of the vanquished. Along the broad avenues stand lofty monuments or delicately chiseled marble, erected by the members of the sisterhood of States, each representing the loyalty and courage of her respective sons, and where annually meet the representatives of the Frozen North with those of the Sunny South, and in one grand chorus rehearse the death chants of her fallen braves, whose heroism made the name of the nation great. To-day there stands a monument crowned with laurels and immortelles, erected by the State to the fallen sons of the "Dark and Bloody Ground," who died facing each other, one wearing the blue, the other the gray, and on its sides are inscribed: "As we are united in life, and they in death, let one monument perpetuate their deeds, and one people, forgetful of all aspirations, forever hold in grateful remembrance all the glories of that terrible conflict, which made all men free and retaining every star in the Nation's flag."

The great conflict was unavoidable; under the conditions, it was irresistable. It was but the accomplishment, by human agencies, the will of the Divine. Its causes were like paths running on converging lines, that eventually must meet and cross at the angle, notwithstanding their distances apart or length. From the foundation of the government these two

converging lines commenced. Two conflicting civilizations
came into existence with the establishment of the American
Union—the one founded on the sovereignty of the States and
the continuance of slavery was espoused by the hot-blooded
citizens of the South; the other, upon the literal construction
of the Declaration of Independence, that "all men are created
free and equal," and the supremacy of the general government over States Rights, and this was the slogan of the cool,
calculating, but equally brave people of the North. The
converging lines commenced in antagonism and increased in
bitterness as they neared the vertex. The vertex was 1861.
At this point it was too late to make concessions. There was
no room for conciliation or compromise, then the only recourse
left is what all brave people accepts—the arbitrament of the
sword.

The South sought her just rights by a withdrawal from the
"Unholy Alliance." The North sought to sustain the supremacy and integrity of the Union by coercing the "Erring
Sisters" with force of arms. The South met force with force,
and as a natural sequence, she staked her all. The North
grew more embittered as the combat of battles rolled along the
border and the tread of a million soldiers shook the two nations
to their centers. First, it was determined that the Union
should be preserved, even at the expense of the South's cherished institution; then, as the contest grew fiercer and more
unequaled, that the institution itself should die with the re-
establishment of the Union. Both played for big stakes – one
for her billions of slave property, the other for the forty or
more stars in her constellation. Both put forward her mightiest men of war. Legions were mustered, martialed, and
thrown in the field, with an earnestness and rapidity never
before witnessed in the annals of warfare. Each chose her
best Captains to lead her armies to battle, upon the issue of
which depended the fate of two nations. The Southern
legions were led by the Lees, Johnstons, Beauregards, Jack-
sons, Stuarts, Longstreets, and other great Lieutenants; the
North were equally fortunate in her Grants, Shermans,
Thomases, Sheridans, and Meads. In courage, ability, and
military sagacity, neither had just grounds to claim superiority
over the other. In the endurance of troops, heroism, and
unselfish devotion to their country's cause, the North and

South each found foemen worthy of their steel. Both claimed justice and the Almighty on their side. Battles were fought, that in the magnitude of the slaughter, in proportion to the troops engaged, has never been equalled since the days of recorded history; Generalship displayed that compared favorably with that of the "Madman of the North," the Great Frederick, or even to that of the military prodigy of all time —Napoleon himself. The result of the struggle is but another truth of the maxim of the latter, that "The Almighty is on the side of the greatest cannon."

I close my labors with an extract from a speech of one of the Southern Governors at Chickamauga at the dedication of a monument to the dead heroes from the State.

"A famous poem represents an imaginary midnight review of Napoleon's Army. The skeleton of a drummer boy arises from the grave, and with his bony fingers beats a long, loud reveille. At the sound the legions of the dead Emperor come from their graves from every quarter where they fell. From Paris, from Toulon, from Rivoli, from Lodi, from Hohenlinden, from Wagram, from Austerlitz, from the cloud clapped summit of the Alps, from the shadows of the Pyramids, from the snows of Moscow, from Waterloo, they gather in one vast array with Ney, McDonald, Masenna, Duroc, Kleber, Murat, Soult, and other marshals in command. Forming, they silently pass in melancholy procession before the Emperor, and are dispersed with 'France' as the pass word and 'St. Helena' as the challenge.'

"Imagine the resurrection of the two great armies of the Civil War. We see them arising from Gettysburg, from the Wilderness, from Shiloh, from Missionary Ridge, from Stone River, from Chickamauga—yea, from a hundred fields—and passing with their great commanders in review before the martyred President. In their faces there is no disappointment, no sorrow, no anguish, but they beam with light and hope and joy. With them there is no 'St. Helena,' no 'Exile,' and they are dispersed with 'Union' as a challenge and 'Reconciliation' as a pass word."

APPENDIX

I have in this appendix endeavored to give a complete roll of all the members who belonged to Kershaw's Brigade. I have taken it just as it stands in the office of the State Historian in Columbia. The work of completing the rolls of the Confederate soldiers from this State was first commenced by the late General H. L. Farley and finished by Colonel John P. Thomas, to whose courtesy I am indebted for the use of his office and archives while completing these rolls. There may be some inaccuracies in the spelling of names or in the names themselves, but this could not be avoided after the lapse of so many years. Then, again, the copy sent to the State Historian was often illegible, causing the same names to appear different and different names to look the same. But I have followed the records in the office in Columbia, and am not responsible for any mistakes, omissions, or inaccuracies.

In the list of officers there will appear some seeming irregularities and inaccuracies, but this is accounted for by the fact that the duplicate rolls were those taken from the companies' muster rolls when first enlisted in the Confederate service, and little or no record kept of promotions. Thus we will see Captains and Lieutenants in these rolls marked as non-commissioned officers. This was occasioned by those officers being promoted during the continuance of the war, and no record kept of such promotions.

ROLL OF SECOND SOUTH CAROLINA VOLUNTEER REGIMENT.

Field and Staff.

COLONELS: Kershaw, J. B., Jones, E. P., Kennedy, Jno. D., Wallace, Wm.

LIEUTENANT COLONELS: Goodwin, A. D., Gaillard, Frank, Graham, J. D.

MAJORS: Casson, W. H., Clyburn, B., Leaphart, G.

ADJUTANTS: Sill, E. C., Goodwin, A. D., McNeil, A.

ASSISTANT QUARTERMASTERS: Wood, W. S., Peck, W. D.

ASSISTANT COMMISSARY SERGEANT: Villipugue, J. J.

SURGEON: Salmond, F.

ASSISTANT SURGEONS: Nott, J. H., Maxwell, A.

CHAPLAINS: McGruder, A. I., Smith, ——.

35

COMPANY "A."

CAPTAINS: Casson, W. H., Shelton, M. A., Gaillard, F., Leaphart, S.,
L., Maddy, M. M.   FIRST LIEUTENANT: Shuler, P. H. B.   SECOND LIEU-
TENANTS: Brown, R., Myers. W. M., Eggleston, D. B.   SERGEANTS:
West, W. H., Reid, J. C., Bryant, J. F., Livingston, J. B., Cooper, G. F.,
Gilbert, J. G., Wells, J. F., McTurious, E. C., Joiner, B., DuBose, J.
CORPORALS: Sulaff, W. C., Bruns, G., Newman, R., Rowan, S. W.,
Mack, J. M., Goodwin, C. T.
PRIVATES: Atta, T. M., Andre, Geo., Anderson, M. J., Anderson, Geo.,
Andrews, T. P., Blackwell, Jas., Bryant, B. F., Brown, C. K., Brown,
Jessie, Baker, J. L., Burns, L., Benjamin, T., Banks, C. C., Casson, J.
H., Cavis, J. W., Canning, Thos., Clowdy, ——, Cannon, M., Calais, W.
J., Cooper, J. W., DuBose, J. B., Durin, Thos., Deckerson, Geo., Dwight,
W. M., Emlyn, H. N., Field, G. R., Forde, Edwin, Griffin, J. W.,
Gasoue, W., Gibson, J., Graham, J., Graham, Thos., Glass, W. G., Hall,
J. R., Hoeffir, Chas, Hartnett, M., Hinton, S. P., Hinkle, E., Howard,
W. P., Hays, A. G., Hall, J. W., Hennies W., Holmes, C. R., Hollis,
M., Hollis, Carles, Howell, O. F., Hutchinson, B. B., Halsey, M. P.,
Johnson, D. B., Joiner, P. H., Kelly, James, Kind, Wm., Kelly, J. G.,
Kindman, J. D., Loomis, H. H., Ladd, P. B., Lee, Isom, Lindsey, S. J.,
Landrum, A. P., Leaphart, J. E., Landrum, L. M., Magillan, C., McGee,
Alex., McFie, Joseph, Mathews, Jno., McDonald, D. J., McCarter, W.
E., McCully, W. H., Miller, R. L., Mitchell, D., Marsh, J. A., Murphy,
Geo., Myers, John, Maw, R. E., Martin, E. R., Marsh, Thos., Martin,
Saml., Newman, J. M., Neuffer, C. E., Nott, Carles, Norton, R., Nott,
W. J., Pritchard, D., Pelfry, I., Roberts, I. D., Roberts, J. F., Radcliff,
L. J., Rentiers, J. G., Roach, W. J., Rose, J. C., Rulland, C. L., Randolph,
W. J., Reilly, W. I., Stubbs, W. G., Stubbs, J. D., Starling, W. D., Star-
ling, R., Starling, Jno., Smith, B., Smith, Richard, Stokes, E. R., Thurs-
ton, J., Taylor, H., Vaughn, B., Williams, Jno., Winchester, J. M., Win-
chester, J.

COMPANY "B."

CAPTAINS: Hoke, A. D., Pulliam, R. C., Cagle, J. W.   FIRST LIEU-
TENANTS: Isaacs, A., Holland, Wm.   SECOND LIEUTENANTS: Elford,
Geo. E.   SERGEANTS: Price, W. P., Watson, Wm. C., Dyer, G. B., Clyde,
S. C., Pool, R. W., Pickle, O. A., Moore, T. H. L., Stall, Thos., Sud-
with, Peter F., Jones, Jno. M., Towns, John M., Bacon, Randolph.
CORPORALS: Harris, Frank E., Jennings, Jno. A., West, L. M., Ingram.
H. G., Roberts, J. M., Shumate, W. T.
PRIVATES: Anderson, G. T., Allen, D., Beacham, E. F., Bowen, O. E.,
Brown, H. C., Bacon, A., Baldwin, Jas., Baldwin, W. W., Baldwin, E.,
Blakely, R. L., Bramlett, R. H., Bramlett, Joseph, Barbary, Wm., Car-
son, Joseph M., Carson, John, Carson, C. H., Carpenter, S. J., Carpen-
ter, J. F., Cureton, A. H., Chandler, W. G., Coxe, F., Cooper, M., Cox,
J. A., Cox, Wm. F., Dyer, G. W., Dyer, J. N., Diver, W. S., Diver, J. E.,
Diver, R. F., D'Oyle, C. W., Duncan, A. S., Duncan, W. H., Duncan, J.
M., Duncan, Robert, Donaldson, Thos. R., Davis, Saml., Dauthit, S. J.,
Foster, A. A., Goodlett, F. M., Goodlett, L. M., Goodlett, J. H., Good-
lett, J. Y., Garmany, W. H., Grogan, T. R., Gibson, S. K., Gibson, J.,
Gosett, I. P., Gibreath, W. W., Gibreath, L. P., Goldsmith, W. H.,
Gwin, R. A., Harris, R. A., Hawkins, L. P., Henning, N. P., Hirch, G.
W., Hill, J. W., Hudson, W. A., Huff, P. D., Huff, P. W., Holland, D.
W., Holland, A. J., Holland, Jno., Irvin, D. P., Ingram, W. P., Jones.
E. P., Jones, E. T., Jones, B., Johnson, I. T., Kilburn, T. C., Kirkland,
P., Long, W. D., Long, S. F., Mauldin, Jas., McKay, R. W., Miller, J.
P., Miller, W. S., Markley, H. C., Markley, Jno., Markley, Charles,
Morgan, W. N., Moore, E., Moore, Lewis M., Moore, John, Moore, J.
T., Mills, J., Payne, J., Parkins, G. W., Parkins, J. D., Pickett, J. H.,

Price, J. M., Poore, J. W., Pool, Cartery Y., Poor, G. B., Rowley, E. F., S., Roe, H. D., Rice, J. H., Ramsey, W. H., Smith, L. R., Scrugg, W. L. M. A., Shumate, J. S., Shumate, R. Y. H., Shumate, L. J., Sullivan, J. N., Smyer, M. A., Sinder, J., Salmons, J. M., Turpin, W. P., Tracy, Fred. S., Thompson, W. D., Thornley, J. L., Turner, J. L., West, R. W., Wisnant, W. F., Wisnant, Alex., Whitmire, Wm., Walton, D. S., Williams, G. W., Watson, P. D., Watson, W. W., Watkins, Lynn, Yeargin, J. O.

COMPANY "C."

CAPTAINS: Wallace, Wm., Lorick, S., Vinson, A. P. FIRST LIEUTENANTS: Wood, W. S., Bell, J. C., Peck, W. D., Wallace, E., Youmans, O. J., Scott, J. T., McGregor, W. C., Stenhouse, E. SERGEANTS: Myers, Jno. A., Howie, Wm., Radcliff, L. J., Beck, Chas, J., Shand, R. W., Clarkson, I. O. H., Bell, Jacob, Hill, Wm., Medlin, N., Corrall, Jno., Edwards, J. G., Bell, E. H. CORPORALS: McCullough, Jno., Owens, Peter, Garner, Thos., Robertson, R. D., Lee, J. W. G., Osment, J. R., Davis, H., Freeman, R. G., Loomis, T. D.

PRIVATES: Ballard, J. N., Boyer, Thomas, Busard, Sam., Boyle, J. C., Brown, S., Brice, Robert, Campbell, James, Campbell, J. M., Copeland, J., Cook, F., Chestnut, ——, Chambers, E. R., Cupps, C. M., Douglass, Jno., Dougherty, J., Dickens, H. C., Davis, R. A., Flaherty, M., Freeman, Wm., Glaze, Jno., Garner, Wm., Goodwin, E. M., Gruber, Jno., Gruber, S., Goins, Henry, Gunnell, J. S., Gunnel, W. H., Grier, J., Heminnis, M., Hurst, J. P., Harrison, B., Hauleely, Henry, Hendricks, Jno., Hunt, J., Hammett, H. B., Hamilton, D., Isbell, Walter, King, W. H., Kallestrane, M. H., Lee, U., Lee, L. W., Lee, A. J., Leach, C., Lochlier, ——, Martin, J. M., Martin, Joel, Martin, C. B., Martin, Daniel, Martin, Saml., Manville, A. T., Medlin, C., McPherson, S., McPherson, W., McPherson, Jno., McGregor, P. C., Murrell, W. S., Medlin, P., Perry, J., Perry, C., Palmer, W. R., Pearson, Robt., Poag, R. F., Ramsay, J., Robertson, F. L., Ransom, Wm., Scarborough, Wm., Scott, J. R., Sheely, W. C., Sharp, G. W., Stubblefield, W. H., Tate, I. O., Vinson, Wm., Wailes, R., Wilson, K., Walker, C. A., Williamson, W. I., Woolen, James, Zesterfelt, F.

COMPANY "D."

CAPTAINS: Richardson, Jno. S., Bartlett, L. W., Graham, I. D. FIRST LIEUTENANTS: Wilder, J. D., Wilder, W. W., Jacob, I. SECOND LIEUTENANTS: Durant, T. M., Pelot, W. L., Rembert, L. M. THIRD LIEUTENANTS: Nettles, J. H., Gardner, H. W. SERGEANTS: Gayle, I. P., Nettles, J. D., Hodge, J. W., Brennan, J. P., Bowman, S. J., McQueen, W. A., Pringle, S. M. CORPORALS: Wilson, S. T., Thompson, R. M., Gardner, A., Reams, H. M., Miller, J. I., Cole, S. R.

PRIVATES: Ard, J. P., Alsobrooks, J. E., Alsobrooks, Bog., Baker, W. T., Beard, D., Beck, I. S., Bradford, J. F., Brogdon, J. D., Brogdon, T. M., Brown, F. H., Brown, H. J., Browning, T. S., Brumby, G. S., Brunson, W. E., Brunson, W. J., Ballard, W. R., Blight, J., Burkett, I. L., Burkett, T. H., Brunson, I. R., Brown, S. J., Bird, J. P., Bass, S. C., Blanding, O., Britton, J. J., Caraway, P. T., Clyburn, B., Cook, W. H., Davis, J. L., DeLorme, W. M., DeLorme, T. M., DeLorme, C., Dennis, John W., Dennis, J. M., Dennis, S. M., Dennis, R. E., Dennis, E. E., Dougherty, J., Dalrymple, S., Eubanks, A., Flowers, S. F., Flowers, T. E., Felder, W. E., Fowler, A., Freman, I. H., Gallagher, P. B., Garden, H. R., Green, H. D., Graham, J. A., Gibson, H., Grooms, A., Haynsworth, J. H., Haynsworth, M. E., Hodge, I. B., Hodge, W. T., Holladay, D. J., Holladay, T. J., Huggins, W. H., Ives, J. E., Jenkins, W. W., Jackson, J. H., Jones, C. H., Jones, E. C., Jones, P. H., Kavanagh, T. D., Kelly, H. T., Kinney, Jno., Lesesne, J. I., London, Peter, Lynam, T. M.

Lucas. A. P.. Mellett, J. Y.. McLaurin, J. C.. McNeal, W. M.. Moses. M.
B.. McKagan. G. P.. Moses. H. C., Moses, Perry. Moses, Perry, Mul-
drow. I. R.. Myers. R. C.. Norton, J. J.. Newman, S. I., O'Neil, W. J..
Prv. J. C.. Pool. W. M.. Patterson. J. S.. Ramsay. W. M., Redford, J. B..
Richardson. G. Rhame. J. F. Ross. D. J.. Rodgers. I.. Shaw, J. H., Scott.
J.. Sledge. W. A.. Smith. F. H.. Smith. T. J.. Thompson. W. T.. Trouble-
field. A. D.. Troublefield. T. J. Troublefield. W. B.. Vaughn, F. O..
Watts. W. D.. Wheeler. C. O.. Wilson. C. A.. Wilson. T. D.. Witler. O..
Wedckind. H.. Wilder. Saml.. Wilder. J.. Frazer. J. B.. Gilbert, J. C. T..
Kirkland. I. G.. McCoy. W. P.. Myers. J. B.. Richburg. J. B.. Sims. E.
R.. Wells. J. A., Wilson, Robt.. Hartley, T. J.

COMPANY "E."

CAPTAINS: Kennedy. Jno. D.. Leitner. Wm. S. LIEUTENANTS: Dun-
lop. Josp. D.. Sill. E. E.. Drakeford. Jos. J.. DePass, W. J.. McKain,
Jno. J.. Riddle. James M. SERGEANTS: Dutton. W. C.. Pegues, R. H..
Hodgon. H. F.. McKalgen. H. G.. Ryan. D. R.. Gerald. R. L.. Nettles,
Hiram. CORPORALS: Niles. A.. Boswell. J. P.. Perry. J. A.. Honnet. B..
Devine. F. G.. Gardiner. E.. Polk. J. W.
PRIVATES: Allen. W. R.. Ancrum. Thos. J.. Sr.. Arrants. J. H.. Ar-
rants. W. T.. Arrants. R. H.. Arrants. J. R.. Barnes. J. B.. Barnes. S.
Y.. Frown. John. Brown. Jas. R.. Baum. Marcus. Buchanan. W. L..
Baker. M.. Reaver. Jno. R.. Barrett. E.. ... ington. J.. Burchfield. E. C.
Bowen. A.. Bowen. W.. Baer. B. M.. Boykin. ... Campell. Alex.. Cook,
M.. Cook. J.. Cook. John. Cook. Joseph. Croft. J.. Coker. R.. Crump. T.
M.. Crick. P. Cunningham. J. S.. Cooper. J. C.. Cooper. J. D.. Cren-
shaw. W. J.. Davis. J. T.. DeBruhl. ——. Dunlap. E. R.. Dunlap. C. J..
Durant. I. A.. Dawkins. W. B.. Doby. A. E.. Delton. B. Z.. Evans. D..
Evans. G.. Elkins. E. E.. Francis. Jno.. Freeman. J.. Freeman. M.. Ful-
lerton. G. F.. Ford. A.. Gardner. T. B.. Gibson. H. B.. Graham. D.. Gra-
ham. I. T.. Goens. E.. Howell. M.. Haile. J. S.. Harrison. B.. Heath. B.
D.. Hinson. J. E.. Jeffers. L.. Enks. E. W.. Johnson. W. E.. Kendrick,
James Kelly. B. E.. Kelly. D. H.. Kirkland. R. R.. Kirkley. R.. King. G..
Legroul. J. M.. Leitner. B. F.. Love. Wm.. Love. L. W.. Lawrence. E.
H.. Middleton. D. P.. Munroe. G.. Munroe. J.. Munroe. Alex.. Munroe.
Jno.. Michie. Jno. P.. Murchison. A. A.. Moroh. L. C.. Moore. Levi.
Maddox. Tom. McDaniel. L. Miller. J. A.. McCown. J.. McMillan. J..
McKain Wm.. McIntosh. T. R.. Means. S. B.. McRea. D.. Nelson. G..
Nettles. W. N.. Nettles. J. T. Nettles. J. E.. Nettles. Joseph S.. Pegue.
C. J.. Pickett. J.. Page. T. W.. Prichard. D.. Proctor. R. W.. Pennington.
R. A.. Pierson. P. J.. Ryan. P. H.. Rembert. T. M.. Scarborough. H. G..
Scarborough. L. W.. Scott. Jno.. Strawbridge. B. R.. Small. R. E..
Smith. Jno. Stokes. W.. Smith. Geo.. Smyth. J.. Team. J.. Tidwell. D..
Turner. W.. Vaughn. Lewis. Wethersbee. J. A.. Wethersbee. T. C.
Waner. J. O.. Watts. Wm.. Wilson. Roland. Wilson. T. R.. Wilson. J.
S.. Winder. J. R.. Witherspoon. I. M.. Wood. J. Mc.. Wood. Jno..
Wood. Pinckney. Wells. D. E.. Wright. W. H.

COMPANY "F."

CAPTAINS: Perryman. W. W.. McDowell. G. W.. Vance. W. Cal.
LIEUTENANTS: Fouche. ——. Maxwell. J. C.. McNeil. A.. Parks. J. T.,
Adams. J. J.. Koon. S. A.. Lunbecker. W. A.. Appleton W. L.. Connor,
G. W.. Johnson. W. A. SERGEANTS: Moore. A. W.. Fuller. H. F.
Smith. J. W.. Bond. S. Lewis. Brooks. Chas. E.. Seaborn. ——.
PRIVATES: Anderson. J. W.. Anderson. James. Bailey. W. H.. Benson.
V. S.. Blake. A. W.. Burrell. W. J.. Butler. Jno.. Brooks. Stanmore.
Boozer. S. P.. Boozer. William. Benson. Thos.. Brownlee. J. A.. Barratt,
Jno. G.. Bell. Wm. S.. Bell. Wm. F.. Carr. Jno. L.. Chaney. Willis,
Chaney. J. S.. Chaney. R. E.. Chaney. Ransom. Cheatham. J. T.. Cheat-

ham, Jno., Crews, C. W., Crews, M. A., Carter, V. C., Creswell, I. D., Creswell, P., Caldwell, G. R., Chipley, W. W., Chipley, T. W., Cobb, C. A., Calvert, J. H., Crawford, H. Henry, Cason, Richard, Cason, J. F., Day, M., Davis, Dr. Frank, Davis, Jno. F. H., Deal, S. C., Douglass, W. W., Ellis, A. B., Fisher, C. D., Fouche, Jno., Fouche, Ben., Fuller, P. M., Fennel, J. L., Gilmer, Robt. P., Gilmer, Wm., Gillam, J. M., Griffin, V., Griffin, G. W., Grant, W. H., Grant, Jno., Goodwin, Jno., Hancock, W. H., Harris, G. M., Heffernan, J. L., Hearst, T. J., Hughey, J. E., Hughey, Fred. T., Hughey, N., Hodges, J. W., Harris, T., Hutchison, Soule, Hutchison, Jno. W., Hutchison, R. F., Henderson, W. E., Hunter, W. C., Henderson, J. T., Ingraham, M. S., Jackson, C., Johnson, F. P., Johnson, Saml., Johnson, J. W., Johnson, D. Q., Johnson, G. W., Jones, J. R., Johnson, J. W., Jones, C. C., Jones, Thomas, Jones, Willie, Jester, Benj., Lomax, W. G., Lenard, V. A., Lenard, J. J., Meriwether, W. N., Moreen, Jno. A., Milford, J. T., Marshall, G. W., McKellar, L. W., McKellar, G. W., McKellar, J. R., McCord, D. W., McNeill, H. B., McKensie, Jno., Major, R. W., Major, J. M., Moore, J. R., Moore, Robt., Moore, Henry, McCrary, B., Malone, A., Malone, Jno., Partlow, Jno. E., Powers, J. W., Pinson, A., Pinson, T. R., Pinson, Jno. V., Parks, Wm., Pelot, Dr. J. M., Rampey, G. W., Rampey, S. D., Reynolds, B., Reynolds, A. D., Reynolds, Jno. M., Roderick, W. F., Riley, E. C., Rykard, T. J., Riley, W. N., Rykard, L. H., Robertson, Jno., Ross, T. M., Ross, Jno., Ross, G. F., Ross, Wiley, Reed, J. S., Saddler, J. H., Saddler, Willis, Shadrick, W. S., Shepard, E. Y., Shepard, J. S., Selby, E. C., Selleck, C. W., Smith, R. G., Smith, T. N., Seal, J. R., Silk, Jas., Turner, J. S., Townsend, J. F., Turner, Ira, Teddards, D. F., Vance, J. C., Watson, G. McB., Waller, W. W., Waller, C. A. C., Walker, W L., Wiss, E., Younge, J. C.

COMPANY "G."

CAPTAINS: Haile, C. C., Clyburn, T. J. LIEUTENANTS: Cantley, T. R., Jones, W. J. SERGEANTS: Cunningham, J. P., Tuesdale, J. E., Benton, F. J., Cauthen, A. J. CORPORALS: West, W. S., Coats, D. W., Jones, B. N., Williams, R. H., Jones, S. D., Kirkland, B. M.

PRIVATES: Alexander, J. H. R., Baskin, J. C. J., Blackburn, B. J., Blackwell, J. A., Boone, J., Boone, W., Boone, J. W., Bruce, J. H., Bowers, G. M., Baskin, C. E., Baskin, R. C., Bird, W. L., Blackmon, J. E., Blackmon, W. N., Belk, J. M., Cauthen, J. S., Coats, H. J., Coats, G. H., Copeland, W. W., Crawford, S., Chaney, B., Clark, J. W., Croxton, J. Q., Cook, J. E., Cook, T., Cato, A. D., Coon, S. S., Dixon, B. S., Dixon, F. L., Downs, A. J., Dixon, G. L., Davis, H. G., Deas, H., Dumm, J. W., Falkinberry, J. W., Falkinberry, W. J., Fletcher, D. G., Falkenberry, J., Fail, J., Gaftin, J. E., Gardner, R. C., Gray, W., Graham, J., Gaskin, D., Gaskin, J., Hall, J. D., Holly, J., Howie, E. P., Howie, S. D., Hough, N., Hough, J., Hough, W. P., Haile, G. W., Hunter, W. J., Johnson, W., Johnson, W. M., Johnson, A. A., Knight, J. A., Knox, W. L., Kelly, M. P., Kirby, J., Kirkland, R. R., Knight, W. A., Love, McD. R., Mahaffy, W. W., Martin, J. S., Martin, W. H., Marshall, W. S., Marshall, J. S., Mosely, C., Mosely, F., Murchison, J. J., McLure, J., McDowell, J. E. C., McKav, H. C., Mahaffy, O. C., Mason, T. E., McMahan, A. W., Marshall, W. D., Marshall, W. H., Mason, L. R., Nelson, T. J., Patterson, R. B., Patterson, W. W., Perry, T. J., Peach, W., Parker, B., Phaile, J., Powers, W. T., Philipps, W. P., Redick, R., Reaver, D. R., Robertson, L. D., Robertson, E. H., Roe, J., Ray, D., Raysor, J. C., Rasey, B., Stover, D. G., Sheorn, Morris D., Sheorn, James, Sowell, J. A., Suggs, Wm., Sutton, E., Small, A. J., Trantham, W. D., Tuesdel, W. J., Tuesdel, B., Tuesdel, W. M., Tuesdel, H., Tuesdel, J. T., West, J. A., West, T. G., West, S., West, W. M., Williams, Jno., Williams, J. N., Williams, C. D., Wilkerson, J., Whitehead, S., Young, C. P., Young, G. W., Young, J. N., Young, W. C., Young, W. J.

COMPANY "H."

CAPTAINS: McManus, A., Clyburn, B. R. LIEUTENANTS: Perry, A. M., Welsh, S. J., Brasington, G. C., Reeves, T. J., Hinson, M. R. SERGEANTS: Perry, J. F., Gardener, S. C., Kennington, W. R., Williams, D. A., McKay, Dr. J. F., Ingram, I. N., Moody, J. J., Love, M. C., Sowells, W. S. CORPORALS: Baker, A. J., Small, J. M., Johnson, G. D., Johnson, D. G., Small, J. M., Douglass, S. A., Kelly, B. L., Cook, J. C., McHorton, W., Williams, T. E., Hilton, R. F., Bolling, R. A.

PRIVATES: Adkins, W. C., Baker, J. J. T., Baker, W., Bailey, J. D., Bailey, Jno., Bell, W. T., Bunnett, G. W., Bowers, N. H., Bowers, W. J., Brasington, W. M., Blackman, B., Bridges, P. H., Caston, W. J., Cato, R. E., Cauthen, G. L., Cauthen, L. D., Craige, W. M., Cauthen, J. M., Deas, A., Ellis, G. W., Ellis, W. W., Funderburk, W. B., Funderburk, J. C., Faulkenberry, J. T., Gardener, C. L., Gardener, S., Gardener, W. W., Gregory, W. T., Gregory, Willis, Harris, G. T., Harris, J. K., Harrell, D., Hilkon, T., Hinson, E., Hinson, W. L., Horton, A. J., Hough, M. J., Horton, W. C., Horton, J. B., Horton, J. T., Harvel, D. B., Jones, B. R., Johnson, J. D., Johnson, F. M., Johnson, D. T., Kennington, B. R., Kennington, R. W., Kennington, G. W., Kennington, J., Kennington, N., Kennington, R., Kennington, R., Jr., Kennington, W. J., Kennington, S. L., Knight, E. R., Lucas, M., Lowery, R. J., Lowery, W. W., Minor, L., Lyles, W. J., Lynn, W. T., Lathan, J. T., Lucas, J. R., Love, V. H., McManus, W. H., McManus, C. W., McManus, W. A., McManus, G. B., Neal, W. M., Perry, B. C., Phifer, W. T., Phillips, A., Phillips, J., Phillips, H. S., Phillips, A. L., Reaves, T. C., Robertson, W. U. R., Robertson, V. A., Reaves, J. J., Short, J. G., Small, J. M., Small, W. F., Sowell, S. F., Snipes, A., Sowell, A., Sodd, W., Swetty, A. M., Woeng, W. D., Welsh, T. J., Wilkinson, H. W., Williams, C. H., Williams, D. A., Williams, J. F., Williams, W. J., Wilson, G. B., Wright, W., Williams, A. M., Witherspoon, J. B.

COMPANY "I."

CAPTAINS: Cuthbert, G. B., Elliott, R. E., Fishburn, Robt. LIEUTENANTS: Holmes, C. R., Brownfield, T. S., Webb, L. S., Robinson, S., Derby, W. J., Brailsford, A. M., Bissell, W. S., Daniel, W. L. SERGEANTS: Wright, J. E., Lalane, G. M., Hanahan, H. D. CORPORALS: Boyd, J. B., Gaillard, T. E., DeSausure, E., Duttard, J. E., Bellinger, E. W., Mathews, O. D., Miller, R. S.

PRIVATES: Vincent, A. M., Artes, P. F., Bedon, H. D., Bellinger, J., Bellinger, C. C. P., Bird, J. B., Brownfield, R. I., Brailford, D. W., Brisbane, W., Bull, C. S., Baynord, E. M., Calder, S. C., Chaplain, D. J., Chaplain, E. A., Claney, T. D., Crawford, J. A., Cambell, J. E., Carr, J. T., Colcock, C. J., Davis, W. C., Dwight, C. S., Dyer, G. B., DeCavadene, F., Dupont, A., Elliott, W. S., Fludd, W. R., Farman, C. M., Gadsden, T. S., Galliard, T. G., Girardeau, G. M., Glover, J. B., Godfrey, W., Goodwin, J. J., Green, W. G., Hanckel, J. S., Hane, W. C., Harllee, J., Harllee, W. S., Harllee, P., Jackson, A., Jacobs, H. R., Kerrison, C., Kerrison, E., Larrisey, O., Lawton, W. M., Lawton, J. C., Miller, J. C., Mackey, J. J., Mackey, W. A., Mathews, P. F., Miller, A. B., Miller, P. G., Mills, E. J., Moses, J. L., Moses, P., Mortimer, Le. B., Munnerlyn, J. K., Mitchell, F. G., Myers, S. C., Montgomery, ——, McCoy, H. A., McLean, M. M., Pinckney, S. G., Palmer, J. J., Pinckney, H., Palmer, G., Palmer, K. L., People, H. M., Pendergrass, M. G., Prentiss, O. D., Prentiss, C. B., Ruffin, E., Ruffin, C., Raysor, J. C., Reeder, T. H., Rice, L. L., Rivers, R. H., Rivers, W., Roumillat, A. J. A., Royal, J. P., Sanders, A. C., Sanders, J. B., Shipman, B. M., Screven, R. H., Seabrook, J. C., Scott, M. O., Shoolbred, J., Shoolbred, R. G., Smith, G. McB., Stocker, T. M., Strobhart, James, Thompson, T. S., Tillinghast, E. L., Trapier, E. S., Walker, W. A., Walker, W. J., Wescoat, W. P., Wescoat, T. M., Wickenberg, A. V., Zealy, J. E.

COMPANY "K."

CAPTAINS: Rhett, A. B., Moorer, J. F., Webb, J., Dutart, J. E. LIEUTENANTS: Elliott, W., Dwight, W. M., Lamotte, C. O., Edwards, D., Bradley, T. W. SERGEANTS: Fickling, W. W., Gilbert, S. C., Webb, J. J., Phillips, S. R., Fell, T. D., Hamilton, J., Phillips, L. R., Goldsmith, A. A., Moorer, R. G., Burrows, F. A., Williams, D. F., Wayne, R., Ferriera, F. C., O'Neill, E. F., Simmonds, J. R. CORPORALS: Purse, E. L., Lawson, P. A., Calvitt, W. L., Rushe, F. R., Sheller, D. A., Sparkman, A. J., Murphy, M., Plunkett, J., O'Neill, E. F., Heirs, G. S., Wooley A., Ackis, R. W., Autibus, G., Lord, R.

PRIVATES: Anderson, Wm., Allgood, J. F., Ackison, R. W., Allgood, J. L., Adams, D. A., Appleby, C. E., Baily, J., Barrett, R., Blatz, J. B., Brum, H., Brown, R. M., Brown, W., Brady, J., Buckner, J., Buckner, A., Buckner, J. A., Buckner, A. H., Burrows, F. A., Bruning, H., Ballentine, J. C., Byard, D. E., Bartlett, S. C., Bartlett, F. C., Buag, W., Braswell, T. T., Bell, C. W., Bell, W. P., Bull, C. J., Bull, E. E., Bazile, J. E., Bishop, J. S., Blume, C. C., Benson, J. N., Bailey, J., Bruce, J. H., Calvitt, W. T., Campsen, B., Casey, W. T., Conway, P., Cartigan, J. M., Cole, C., Cotchett, A. H., Creckins, A., Castills, M., Coward, R. M., Craige, W. S., Copeland, W. J., Deagen, P., Daly, F. R., Dillon, J. F., Dinkle, J., Dorum, W. D., Doran, J., Douglass, C. M., Day, M., Duncan, W. M., Estill, W., Elle, A., Tarrell, J. F., Ferria, F. C., Fisher, W. S., Fant, T. R., Furt, W., Fleming, A. H., Froysell, J. D., Gammon, J. E., Gammon, E. M., Goldsmith, A. A., Gibbs, W. H., Grubbs, W. L., Green, W. H., Grenaker, J. A., Griffeth, A., Gruber, J., Hammond, C. S., Hoys, T., Hibbard, F. C., Happoldd, D., Hoeffer, C. M., Haganes, H. C., Harris, J., Hendricks, J. A., Hendricks, M., Hunt, H. D., Hunt, J. H., Hunt, R., Hunter, T. T., Haigler, E. N., Haigler, W. L., Heirs, J. A., Howard, R. P., Hough, H. J., Heirs, G., Harley, J. M., Harley, P., Jones, G. T., Jones, D. H., Joseph, A. H., Jowers, J. P., Johnson, W. G., Kerney, G., Kelly, J. G., Kunney, A. A., Kennedy, J., Kennedy, H. R., Kennedy, J. A., Lavell, A. J., Lawson, T. A., Lonergan, J. D., Maher, E., Marshall, W., McCollum, E., Meylick, F. W., Meyleick, W., McKensie, A., McLure, A., Meyers, A. C., Murphy, M., Martin, W., McGellom, B., Martin, A., Moorer, R. A., Mitchel, D. H., Mitchel, F. G., Musgrove, W. W., Martin, J., Neill, R. T., Noll, C., Nicklus, J., Nevek, R. F., Nesmith, E. C., Nix, J. B., O'Neill, J., Oppenhimer, E. H., Oppenheimer, H. H., Platt, W. W., Philipps, L. R., Prace, A., Purse, E., Purse, W. G., Page, J. J., Plunkett, J., Pearson J. H., Payne, J. F., Richardson, C. O., Ryan, T. A., Randolph, L. A., Robinson, S. L., Reentz, J. W., Righter, J. A., Reid, J. W., Reeves, J. P., Rushe, F. D., Schmitt, T., Scott, W., Shepard, D. H., Sammonds, J. R., Sporkman, A. J., Sellick, C. H., Street, E., Summers, E., Sutherland, J. F., Sherer, J. R., Sandifer, J., Shuler, S. N., Spillers, W. F., Schmitt, R., Smith, J. C., Simons, J. R., Smith, O. A. C., Thompson, M. N., Timmonds, G. C., Turner, J. W., Taylor, C. M., Turner, C., Welmer, M. W., Wallace, J. L., Walsh, P., Wilkins, J. R., Wilkins, T. K., Willis, J. V., Watts, W. D., Williams, T. A., Weeks, T. S., Wolley, A., Wolly, H. A., Williman, W. H., Yates, M. J., Youngblood, J., Zimmerman, U. A., Zeigler, J. B. E.

ROLL OF THIRD SOUTH CAROLINA VOLUNTEER REGIMENT.

Field and Staff.

COLONELS: Williams, James H., Nance, James D., Rutherford, W. D., Moffett, R. C.
LIEUTENANT COLONELS: Foster, B. B., Garlington, B. C., Todd, R. P.
MAJORS: Baxter, James M., Nance, J. K. G.
ADJUTANTS: Rutherford, W. D., Pope, Y. J.

SERGEANT MAJORS: Williams, J. W., Simpson, O. A., Garlington, J. D.
QUARTERMASTERS: McGowan, Jno. G. (Captain), Shell, G. W. (Captain).
COMMISSARIES: Hunt, J. H. (Captain), Lowrance, R. N. (Captain).
SURGEONS: Ewart, D. E., Evans, James.
ASSISTANT SURGEONS: Dorroah, Jno. F., Drummond, ——, Brown, Thomas.

COMPANY "A."

CAPTAINS: Garlington, B. C., Hance, W. W., Richardson, R. E. LIEUTENANTS: Gunnels, G. M., Arnold, J. W., Garlington, H. L., Hollingsworth, J., Hudgens. W. J., Mosely, Jno. W., Shell. G. W., Shell, Henry D., Simpson, C. A., Fleming, H. F. SERGEANTS: Simpson. T. N., Robertson, V. B., Wilson, T. J., Teague, A. W., Motte, Robert P., Garlington, Jno., Jr., McDowells, Newman, Griffin, W. D., Jones, P. C., Gunnels, W. M. CORPORALS: Mosely, R. H., Sullivan, W. P., Martin, R. J., Richardson, S. F., West, E., Atwood, I. L., Richardson, W. M. PRIVATES: Anderson, D. A., Anderson, W. J., Allison, T. W., Anderson, W. Y., Allison, W. I., Adams, Jno. S., Atwood, W. M., Ballew, J. B., Ballew, B. F., Bass, John, Beard, W. F., Boyd, W. T., Black, W. E., Ball, J. S., Bolt, T. W., Bolt, W. T., Bolt, Pink, Bolt, John L., Bolt, H., Bradford, W. A., Bright, Jno. M., Beasley, B. H., Cason, W. B., Clark, J. Q. A., Campton, L. D., Crasy, J. B., Chappell, W. T., Day, N. T., Day, John, Davenport, T. J., Donaldson, W. M., Davis, J. J., Donnon, J. M., Evans, Wm., Elmore, ——, Fleming, J. O. C., Finley, C. G., Finley, J. M., Finley, J. R., Franks, N. D., Franks, C. M., Franks, T. B., Franks, J. W. W., Gray, Duff, Gary, J. D., Going, Wm., Garrett, W. H., Garlington, S. D., Hall, J. F., Hance, Theodore, Ham, James E., Harrison, P. M., Harrison, J. A., Hill, L. C., Hellams, D. L., Henderson, W. H., Henderson, Lee A., Hix, E. M., Hawkins, J. B., Hix, W. P., Hix, Willis, Hix, C. E., Hudgens, J. M., Hudgens, J. H., Hudgens, W. H., Hudgens, J. B., Irby, G. M., Irby, A. G., Jennings, A., Jennings, R., Jenerette, Wm., Jones, B. F., Kirk, C. E., Lovelace, J. H., Monroe, W., Medlock, J. T., McKnight, H. W., McDowell, Baker, McCollough, J. L., Milan, Jno. A., Milan, W. W., Milan, M. F., McAbee, A., McAbee, ——, McAbee, ——, Metts, J. A., Miller, Harry, Neal, S. H., Nolan, Jno., Oliver, S. A., Odell, L. M., Parks, John M., Pinson, W. V., Pinson W. S., Pinson, M. A., Pope, D. Y., Ramage, Frank, Robertson, Z., Robertson, A., Rodgers, W. S., Simpson, B. C., Simpson, R. W., Simpson, J. D., Simpson, O. F., Sullivan, M. A., Sullivan, J. M., Smith, P., Shell, Frank, Simmons, S. P., Sharp, A. L., Speke, S. A., Teague, Thomas J., Teague, M. M., Templeton, J. L., Templeton, P., Templeton, S. P., Templeton, W. A., Tribble, M. P., Tribble, J. C. C., Tobin, Thos. A., Todd, S. F., Vance, S. F., Vaughan, Jno., Winebrenner, George, Williams, Jno., Williams, W. A., Wilson, J. M., West, S. W. West, Joseph, Wilbanks, John S., Woods, Harvey, Willis, E. R., Young, Martin J., Young, Robert H.

COMPANY "B."

CAPTAINS: Davidson, Samuel N., Gary, Thomas W., Connor, Thompson. LIEUTENANTS: Hunter, W. P., Lipscomb, T. J., Buzhardt, M. P., Davenport, C. S., Pulley, S. W. SERGEANTS: Summer, M. B., Reeder, J. R. C., Moffett, R. D., Clark, J. F., Spears, L. M., Copeland, J. A., Peterson, W. G., Livingston, A. J., Smith, J. D., Bradley, E. P., Tribble, A. K. CORPORALS: Davis, T. M., Gary, Jno. C., Dean, Julius, Lark, Dennis, Chalmers, Joseph H., Anderson, W. A., Wallace, W. W., Spears, A. S., Perkins, H. S., Gibson, B. W., Workman, Robt., Stephens, P. J., Suber, Mid.

PRIVATES: Brooks, E. A., Burton, Kay, Butler, J. C., Bishop, W. F., Bishop, Jno., Bailey, A. W., Brown, D., Brown, J. A., Butler, E. A., Butler, J. N., Butler, B. R., Butler, D. M., Cannon, Isaac P., Crooks, L. T., Crooks, J. A. B., Chalmers, E. P., Craddock, D. F., Craddock, S., Chupp, J. G., Cole, John, Campell, Jno. B., Cleland, J. P., Clark, E. G., Connor, Robt., Clamp, D. L., Chappells, J. B., Davenport, H., Davenport, W. P., Davenport, E. W., Dalrymple, John, Davis, A. P., Davis, D. P., Davis, J. T., Dumas, J. H., Davenport, J. C., Floyd, Jno. S., Floyd, J. N., Gary, J. W., Gary, M. H., Gary, C. M., Gary, Jessie, Griffin, S. B., Griffin, W. B., Grimes, W. M., Grimes, T. A., Gibson, M., Gibson, W. W., Golding, James W., Golding, Jno. F., Galloway, Jno., Graham, T. J., Greer, R. P., Hopkins, G. T., Harp, David, Harmon, W. C., Harmon, H. T., Jones, J. S. B., Johnson, W., Johnson, W. R., James, W. A., King, W. H., Keller, W. J., Lank, J. W., Lyles, I. E., Livingston, H., Livingston, E., Longshore, E. C., Longshore, A. J., McKettrick, J. W., Middleton, J. H., Moates, J. L., Moates, F., Montgomery, G. B., McEllunny, R. N., Neel, J. M., Neel, T. M., Pitt, J. M., Pitt, W., Pitt, J., Pitt, D., Pitt, A. N., Reeder, A. M., Richey, E., Robertson, S. J., Reid, W. W., Reeder, W., Spruel, J. S., Spruel, W. F., Stewart, J. P., Senn, D. R., Satterwhite, R. S., Scurry, J. R., Sterling, G. P., Saddler, G. W., Suber, G. A., Suber, A., Thrift, C., Thrift, G. W., Templeton, R. W., Willinghan, W. W., Workman, J. A., Workman, J. M., Workman, H., Workman, P., Whitman, J. C., White, G. F., Wells, G. F., Waldrop, W. W., Williams, B.

COMPANY "C."

CAPTAINS: Moffett, R. C., Herbert, C. W. LIEUTENANTS: Moffett, D. S., Wilson, Jno. C., Culbreath, Joseph, Speake, J. L., Piester, ——. SERGEANTS: Kibler, A. A., Moffett, T. J., Cromer, E. P., Wilson, T. R., Long, G. F., Fellers, J. B. CORPORALS: Young, N. H., Boozer, D. W., Fulmer, J. B., Bowers, J. S., Sites, George, Kelly, James M., Paysinger, S. S.

PRIVATES: Adams, W. H., Albritton, Joseph, Banks, James C., Baird, Henry, Baughn, Henry, Bouknight, F., Blair, T. S., Blair, J. P., Boland, S. D., Boland, James M., Boozer, C. P., Boozer, S. D., Boulware, I. H., Boyd, G. M., Cannon, H. D., Calmes, Jno. T., Calmes, Wash., Carmichael, J. D., Counts, W. F., Cromer, A. B., Crosson, H. S. N., Crosson, D. A., Crouch, Jacob, Crouch, Wade, Davenport, Wm., Davenport, J. M., Davis, Jno., Duncal, J. W., Dominick, D. W. S., Elmore, J. A., Enlow, Nathan, Ferguson, G., Fellers, J. P., Fellers, S. H., Folk, H. S., Frost, Eli, Gallman, D. F., Gallman, Henry G., Gallman, J. J., George, James M., George, N. B., George, L. O., Griffeth, G. W., Gruber, I. H., Grimes, Thos., Guise, Albert, Hair, J. B., Hartman, J. M., Hawkins, P. M., Hawkins, J. M., Hawkins, E. P., Hendricks, J. E., Herbert, J. W., Hussa, Carwile, Halfacre, D. N., Huff, Andrew, Kelly, J. H., Kelly, Y. S., Kelly, W. J., Kinard, Levi, Kibler, Levi, Kibler, I. M., Kibler, J. H., Kibler, H. C., Lane, G. G., Lane, W. R., Lester, Alen, Lester, Alfred, Lester, Charles, Long, A. J., Long, M. J., Long, L. W., Livingston, J. M., McGraw, P. T., McGraw, B. F., McCracken, L. C., McCracken, Jno., McNealus, Jno., Mansel, R. J., Moffett, R. D., Martin, Allen, Moon, Frank, Morris, S., Nates, J. C., Neill, J. B., Neill, J. Calvin, Neill, J. Spencer, Nelson, J. G., Paysinger, H. M., Paysinger, T. M., Pugh, Wm., Pugh, H., Quattlebaum, I. E., Quattlebaum, D. B., Rankin, A. J., Rankin, G. W., Rawls, S. Sanders, Reagen, James B., Reagen, H. W., Reagen Jno. W. Reid, Newt., Reid, J. P., Richardson, D., Rikard, J. A., Rikard, J. W., Kinard, L. C., Sease, N. A., Sease, J. Luke, Shepard, Jno. R., Seigman, Jesse E., Spence, Sam'l, Spence, Jno. D., Sligh, J. W., Sligh, D. P., Stillwell, J. T., Stockman, J. Q. A., Stribbling, J. M., Stockman, Jno. C., Stuart, W., Stuart, C. T., Sultan, R. J., Thompson, T. J., Whites, J. D., Werts, M., Whites, G. J., Werts, Andrew, Werts, Jno. A., Wilson, Wm., Willingham, Hav.

COMPANY "D."

CAPTAINS: Fergerson, Thos. B., Walker, F. N. LIEUTENANTS: Bobo, Y. J., Abernathy, C. P., Moore, J. P., Floyd, N. P., Ray, P. John, Walker, J. Henry, Allen, Wade, Gordon, F. M., Bobo, Hiram. SERGEANTS: Campell, Levi, Allen, Garland, Floyd. Chance, M., Ray, Hosea, Roy, Robt. Y., Ducker, H. W., Davis, M. M. CORPORALS: Abernathy, J. D. C., Hill, T. F. C., Dillard, Geo. M., Fergerson, Jno. W., Welburn, Robt. C.

PRIVATES: Allen, B. R., Bobo, J. P., Bardine, T. C., Barrett, J, Browning, Hosea, Carson, John, Cathcart, H. P., Cooper, J., Dodd, W. T., Cooper, T. M., Fergerson, H. T., Floyd, A. F., Floyd, J. M., Farmer, W., Fergerson, E., Franklin, Y. F., Farrow, A. T., Finger, Mark. Graham, Isaac. Graham, J. F., Gentry, J. W., Gentry. E., Huckaby, P., Hill, B. M., Hollis, P. W., Hembree, C. B., Andrew, ——, Jackson, Drewy, Graham, A., Kelly, Wm., Kelly, M., Lamb, Thomas, Lamb, Robert, Lynch, W. E., Lynch, A., Lynch, John, Lynch, B. S., Murphy, R. C., Myers, J. D., McCravy, A. F., McCravy, R. S., McCravy, Sam., Murray, Peter, Murray, F. H., Nix, Stephen, McMillen, Wm., Ramsay, Robt., Ramsay, P., Mullens, Wm., Pruitt, E. A., Pope, C., Poole, Robt., Smith, Caspar, Smith, Wm., Stephens, M., Stephens, J. F., Shands, Anthony. Shands, Frank, Stone, T. B., Shands, A. B., Shands, Saml., Pruitt, John, Sexton, J. W., Tinsley, J. L., Tinsley, A. R., Tinsley, J. P., Taylor, W. B., Varner, Andrew, Varner, M. S., Varner, J. W., Vaugh, Jas., Williams, C. M., Williams, J. D., Workman, H., Wesson, Frank. Woodbanks, Thomas. Woodbanks, Jno., Lynch, Pink. Ray, Thos., Poole, Robt.

COMPANY "E."

CAPTAINS: Nance. J. D., Nance, Jno. K. G., Wright, Robt. H. LIEUTENANTS: Bailey, E. S., Moorman, Thos. S., Hair, Jno. S., Hentz. D. J., Haltiwanger, Richard, Martin, J. N., James, B. S., Langford. P. B., Weir, Robt. L., Cofield, Jas. E. SERGEANTS: Pope, Y. J., Lake, T. H., Boyd, C. F., Chapman, S. B., Ruff, Jno. S., Kingore, A. J., Buzzard. B. S., Reid, H. C., Hood, Wm., Duncan, T. S., Rutherford, W. D., Paysinger, T. M., Thompson, W. H., Ramage, D. B., Leavell, R. A., Horris, T. J., Glymph, L. P., Sloan, T. G., Matts, Jno., Harris, J. R.

PRIVATES: Abrams, J. N., Abrams, J. K., Abrams, C. R., Atchison, S. L., Atkins, R. W., Assman, H. M., Brantly, H., Bernhart, H. C., Blatts, W. H., Bell, Jno. F., Bruce, J. D., Boazman, W. W., Boazman, Grant, Bramlett, A. W., Boozer, D. C., Boozer, E. P., Boyd, M. P., Burgess, C. H., Brown, T. C., Brown, J. E., Blackburn, James, Bailey, A. Wm., Butler, J. C., Canedy, A. B., Clend, M. P., Caldwell. J. E. Collins, A. P., Clamp, G., Cameron, J. S., Cameron, J. P., Cromer, S. D., Davis, J. H., Davis, Jas., Davis, Jno., Derick, S. S., Duckett, Jno. G., Duckett, J. C., Duckett, J., Duckett, G. T., Facir, W. Y., Fair, Robt., Facir, G. A., Foot, M., Gary, J. N., Glasgow, L. K., Graham, C. P., Gallman, H., Harris, M. M., Hargrove, P. H., Hiller, S. J., Hiller, G. E., Haltin, Wm., Haltin, R., Johnson, J. A., Johnson, W., Kelly, I. J., Keom, G., Keney, G., Keitler, J. N., Lindsey, J., Lovelace, B. H., Lake, T. W., Lake, E. G., Lee, W., Lindsey, W. R., Marshall, J. R., Mayes, J. B., McCrey, S. T., McCaughrin, S. T., McMillen, W. J., Miller, J. W., Mathis, J. M., Marshall, J. L., Metts, W., Metts, McD., Metts, W. G., Murtishaw, S. W., Nance, A. D., O'Dell, I. N., Pratt, S., Price, S., Pope, B. H., Pope, W. H., Pope, T. H., Pope, H., Reid, J. M., Reid, W. W., Renwick, H., Ruff, J. H., Ruff, W. W., Ruff, J. M. H., Ruff, R. S., Rodlesperger, T., Rice, J., Riser, J. W., Riser, W. W., Riser, Joe, Ruff, M., Sligh, T. W., Sloan, E. P., Sligh, G., Sligh, W. C., Suber, W. H., Suber, G. B., Souter, F. A., Summer, F. M., Schumpert, B., Schumpert, P. L., Sawyer, F. A., Sultsbacer, W., Stribling, M., Scurry, D. V., Tarrant, W. T., Tribble, J. R., Turnipseed, J. O., Wheeler, D. B., Wright,

J. M., Witt, M. H., Wilson, T. R., Wilson, C., Wood, S. J., Wingard, H. S., Wideman, S., Wilson, J. W., Willingham, W. P., Weir, T. W., Willingham, ——, Zoblel, J., Hornsby, J. D., Harris, J. Y.

COMPANY "F."

CAPTAIN: Walker, T. LIEUTENANTS: McGowan, H. L., Williams, J. G., Loaman, S. SERGEANTS: East, I. H. L., Hill, J. C., Neil, W. W., Bailey, W. F., Gray, W. S., Madden, J., Wells, B. W.

PRIVATES: Alston, F. V., Andrews, H. A., Andrews, T., Ballew, R., Bryson, H. H., Byson, R., Boyd, W. M. J., Boyd, W., Bryson, H. J., Bryson, J. E., Byson, J. A., Burrill, B., Burrill, W., Byson, J. G., Boseman, L. J., Bale, A., Cannon, J. L., Cole, J., Conner, J. B., Coleman, O. A., Cook, M. C., Crisp, J. T., Crim, S. J., Cannon, L. A., Dogan, W. S., Dalrymple, T. E. J., Donald, T. P., Darnell, W. R., Davenport, W. R., Dobbins, J., Franklin, H. G., Franklin, J. N., Franklin, N., Feets, J., Fowler, P. O., Fuller, J. C., Fuller, J. N., Fuller, W., Furguson, J. W., Goodlett, S. P., Grant, M., Garlington, J. D., Hollingworth, J., Hitt, H., Hitt, B., Hitt, E., Jones, W., Johnson, H. S., Johnson, W. R., Johnson, Miller, Langey, B. P., Lindsay, J., Lindsay, A., Lowe, W. W., Lowe, P. W., Lake, J., Lake, Y., Madden, A., Madden, S. C., Madden, D. N., Madden, J. H., Madden, J., Martin, L., McGowan, J. S., McDowell, W., McGee, J., McCoy, A., McClure, D., McClure, W., McGowan, S., McWilliams, I., Mauldin, J., Monroe, W. E., Monroe, J. W., Morgan, J. C., Moore, H., Moore, E., Moore, G., Nabors, W. A., Nichols, R. M., Nichols, T. D., Nichols, J., Nelson, A., Nelson, M., Neely, W., Nixon, W., O'Neal, J. B., Puckett, R., Pirvem, J. H., Pierce, C. E., Pills, J., Propes, M., Reid, M., Riddle, T. R., Riddle, J. S., Sadler, G. M., Shirley, J., Smith, T. M., Sincher, T., Sparks, S., Vance, W. A., Waldrop, T. M., Walker, J. P., Winn, J., Wilbur, J. Q., Waldrop, E., Wilson, C., Watson, S.

COMPANY "G."

CAPTAIN: Todd, R. P. LIEUTENANTS: Burnside, A. W., Barksdale, J. A., Watts, J. W. SERGEANTS: Wright, A. Y., Garlington, J. D., Winn, W. C., Sanford, B. W., Farley, H. L. CORPORALS: Owengs, A. S., Brownlee, D. J. G., McCarley, T. A., Patton, M. P., Thompson, A. G. H., Templeton, D. C.

PRIVATES: Avery, T. M., Avery, F. H., Adams, W. A., Ball, W. H., Ball, H. P., Barksdale, A., Barksdale, T. B., Barksdale, M. S., Branks, C. B., Brooks, L. R., Brooks, W. J., Bendle, R. T., Byrant, R. F., Blackaby, J. L., Burns, B. F., Burns, J. H., Brownlee, J. R., Brumlett, C., Childress, D., Childress, W. A., Cook, Geo., Curry, J. A., Curry, T. R., Curry, W. L., Curry, J. F., Crisp, J., Coleman, J. D., Chisney, W., Chisney, J. N., Chisney, N., Chisney, R. J., Chisney, G., Craig, J., Chick, W., Coley, R. B., Dorroh, J. A., Dorroh, J. R., Dorroh, J. W., Dial, J., Edwards, L. L., Edwards, M., Evins, H. C., Fairbairn, E. J., Fairbairn, J. A., Fairbairn, J. D., Franks, B. T., Franks, S., Franklin, W., Fleming, M. Fuller, J., Grumbles, R. P., Garrett, H. M., Harris, R. T., Hellams, J. T., Hellams, R. V., Hellams, W. R., Hellams, R. T. Hellams, W. H., Henderson, T. Y., Henry, I. F., Henry, S. P., Hill, D. S., Higgins, R. J., Higgins, R. J., Higgins, J. B., Hunter, J. P., Hobby, J. A., Jones, E., Knight, J., Knight, R. S., Lamb, W., Lanford, J. M., Landford, P., Lindsey, E. E., Lanford, E. L., McNeely, A. Y., Martin, J. A., Martin, B. A., Martin, M. P., Martin, M. G., Martin, J., Martin, J. A., Morgan, W. B., Morris, W. H., McClentock, W. A., Maddox, J., Madden, W. B., Motes, S. C., Owens, H. Y., Owens, W. C., Owens, M. B., Owens, S. D., Owens, J., O'Gwalt, W. D., Paysinger, T., Power, J. D., Poole, F. F., Robertson, R., Rodgers, A. M., Roland, A., Starms, T. A., Simpson, W. W., Simpson, A., Simpson, S., Stoddard, D. F., Stod-

dard, J. F., Stoddard, D. C., Stoddard, A. R., Stewart, J. C., Summers,
W. W., Smith, R., Shockley, J. W., Stone, E., Shesly, E., Templeton,
J. P., Thackston, E. R., Thackston, S. R., Thompson, I. G., Thompson,
W., Thompson, A. Y., Thompson, W. F., Townsend, J., Vonodore, J.,
Wadell, A. J., Wadell, J. T., Wine, A. W., Wilson, T. C., Witte, J. B.,
H., White, J. K., Workman, J. M., Wofford, B. H.

COMPANY "H."

CAPTAINS: Nunnamaker, D., Summer, J. C., Swygert, G. A., Dickert,
D. A. LIEUTENANTS: Epting, J. H., Nunnamaker, S., White, U. B.,
Fulmer, A. P., Huffman, J. SERGEANTS: Hipp, A. J., Derrick, F. W.,
Kesler, W. A., Swindler, W. C., Werts, A. A., Haltiwanger, J. S.,
Wheeler, S., Kempson, L. C. CORPORALS: Weed, T. C., Busby, W. A.,
Stoudemire, J. A. W., Mayer, J. A., Counts, W. J., Werts, W. W.,
Guise, A.

PRIVATES: Adams, M., Addy, J. M., Burrett, J., Burkett, H., Boozer,
L., Boozer, B. F., Boozer, D. T., Bedenbaugh, L., Bundric, T. J., Busby,
J. L., Busby, L., Busby, W., Cannon, J. J., Caughman, L., Chapman, H.
H., Chapman, D., Chapman, B. F., Cook, J. S., Comerlander, M. Cor-
ley, F., Dawkins, J. D., Dickert, J. O., Dickert, B. F., Dickert, C. P.,
Dominick, H., Dreher, D. J., Dreher, J., Derrick, A., Ellisor, C. G., Elli-
sor, G. M., Ellisor, G. P., Ellisor, J. T., Enlow, B., Epting, J., Fulmer,
H. J., Fulmer, G. W., Fulmer, J. E., Frost, E., Folk, S. H., Farr, J.,
Feugle, J. N., Fort, H. A., Green, W. T., Gibson, A., Guise, N. A.,
Geiger, W. D., George, J., Gortman, M., Hanriter, J. H., Haltiwanger, J.
L., Haltiwanger, A. K., Hartman, S., Hobbs, L. P., Hipp, W. W., Hipp,
J. M., Hipp, J. J., Hiller, G., Jacob, W. A., Kelly, B., Kinard, J. J.,
Kunkle, H. L., Koon, G. W., Long, H. M., Long, D. S., Long, D. P.,
Long, G. A., Long, J. H., Long, G., Long, J., Lake, T., Lake, E. J., Liv-
ingstone, J., Livingstone, S., Livingstone, M., Lester, G., Lever, C.,
Mayer, A. B., Miller, A. B., Miller, J., Miller, L., Monts, J. W., Monts,
T., Monts, N., Monts, F., Monts, J., Martin, A., Metts, T., Nunnamaker,
T. C., Rucker, W., Russell, L. F., Rikard, L., Riser, R. E., Summer, J.
G., Summer, W., Summer, P., Summer, J. B., Summer, J. K., Summer,
A. J., Stoudemire, G. W., Stoudemire, R. T., Smith, S. H., Smith, J. A.,
Shealy, P. H., Schwarts, G., Schwarts, H. C., Sease, A. M., Slice, G. N.,
Slice, R., Setzler, W., Setzler, J. T., Spillers, L., Stuck, G. M., Stuck,
M. C., Swetingburg, D. R., Suber, A., Thompson, P., Wilson, H. C.,
Wilson, A. A., Werts, A., Werts, W. A., Werts, J., Werts, W. A.,
Werts, I., Weed, W., Wheeler, L. B., Youngener, G. W., Yonce, J.,
Yonce, W.

COMPANY "I."

CAPTAINS: Jones, B. S., Langston, D. M. H., Pitts, T. H., Johnson,
J. S. LIEUTENANTS: Harris, N. S., West, S. L., Byrd, W. B., Belk, W.
B., Duckett, T. J. SERGEANTS: Henry, D. L., Williams, E., McLang-
ston, G., Byrd, A. B., Copeland, D. T., Berkley, T., Adair, J. W. COR-
PORALS: Maylan, P., Blakely, M., Goodwin, R., Butler, P. M., Blakely,
W.

PRIVATES: Arnant, ——, Atrams, R., Anderson, J., Anderson, W.,
Anderson, M., Byrd, G., Byrd, J. D., Beasley, G., Bell, J. L., Bell, J. E.,
Blakely, E. T., Blakely, M. P., Richmond, ——, Boyce, C. B., Brown, J.,
Bearden, T., Compton, E., Canady, J. W., Craige, G., Cannon, H.,
Casey, C. C., Campbell, P., Dillard, G. W., Donnon, G. M., Donnon,
W., Duval, C. W., Davis, W., Ferguson, J. G., Ferguson, C. C., Foster,
J. F. M., Gordon, M., Graham, D., Hill, S., Holland, J. G., Holland, R.
R., Hollingsworth, F., Hollingsworth, J., Hanby, J. W., Harris, F., Hol-
land, W., Hewett, F. M., Hemkapeeler, C., Hipps, R., Hipps, C. M.,
Hirter, M., Huskey, W., Henry, J. E., Huckabee, J., Jones, A., Jones, R.

F., James, Z., Johnson, R. C., Jacks, I., King, A. A., Langston, J. T., Lyles, P., McKelvy, J., Maddox. W. C., McInown, M. M., Meeks, T., Mars. N., McDowell, J. T. B., McMakin, G., Merton, G., Newman, T. D., Neal, S. H., Owens, T., Oxner, J. T., Prather, G., Prather, N. C., Powell, A., Powell, R., Potter, M., Pearson J. P., Philson, S. P., Philips, A. N., Ramage, J. W., Ray, W., Reynolds, M., Suber. M., Suber, M., Stokes, T., Stokes, W., Sneed, C., Simpson, J. M., Snook. W. M., Smith, J. C., Taylor, W. J., Taylor. H. S., Templeton, A., Templeton, H., Templeton, J., Talleson, J., Talleson. J., Todd, N. C., Todd, S. A., Thaxton, Z. A., Willard, J., Young, G. R., Zeigler, ——.

COMPANY "K."

Captains: Kennedy, B., Lanford, S. M., Foster. L. P., Young, W. H., Cunningham, J. H., Roebuck, J. P. Lieutenants: Wofford, J. W., Wofford. J. Y., Bearden, W., Layton, A. B., Thomas. W., Smith, R. M., Sergeants: Bray, D. S., Wofford. W. B., Thomas. J. A., Varner, C. P., McArthur, J. N., Jentry, J. L. Corporals: Vise, James S., Nesbitt, W. A., Smith, W. A., Davis, A. F., James. G. W., Lanford, F. M., Pettitt, N. H., Roundtree. J. R., Smith, A. S., West, T. H., Bass, J. B. C.

Privates: Bass, G. W., Beason, B. S., Beason, B., Bishop, J. W., Beard, J. C., Brewton, I., Brice, D., Birch, F. C., Bearden, W. S., Barnett, W. H., Bearden. G., Cook, N., Cunningham, H. W., Chunmey, G. W., Chunmey. J., Drummond, R. A., Elmore. J. H., Foster. J. A., Gwinn, C. T., Gwinn, D., Gwinn, M., Gwin, J., Harmon. T. P., Harmon, J., Harmon. W., Havener, J. P., Hyatt, G. T., Hyatt. J., Hamby, J. H., Hill. L., Johnson. J. A., Lanham S. W. T., Lawrence, W., Lancaster, W. H., Marco. J. J., Mattox. P., Mayes, S. S., Mayes. D. W., Mayes, W. J., Meadows. T. M., Meadows, T. S., McAbee. W., McAbee. J., McDonald. J. E., McArther. J., Pearson, J. W., Petty. T., Petty. P., Pettis, B. F., Pearson. H., Roundtree. J. S., Riddle, J. M., Riddle. T., Rogers. M., Rogers. J., Rogers, E., Rogers W., Rogers. G., Roebuck, B. F., Roebuck. J., Roebuck. W., Sammonds, G., Shackleford. J. L., Stribblan. A. C., Stribland. S., Stribland, J., Shands. B. A., Shands. S., Stallions. J., Smith .B. M., Smith. S., Smith, E. F., Smith. Robt., Smith, W. P., Sherbutt. W. T., Sherbutt, S. Z., Sherbutt. A. T., Slater. Jno., Story. G. H., Storey. D. G., Story, J. S., Thomas. T. S., Thomas, L. P., Thomas. W., Thomas. M., Turner. J., Vehorn. W. J., Vaughan. L., Vaughan. J., Varner. R., Williams. R. M., Wofford. B., Wofford. W. T., Wofford. J. H., Wofford, W. A., West. T. J., West. G. W., West. E. M., West. H., Wingo. H. A., White. R. B., Westmoreland. S. B., Wright, W. M., Woodruff. R., Zimmerman. T. H.

ROLL OF SEVENTH SOUTH CAROLINA VOLUNTEER REGIMENT.

Field and Staff.

Colonels: Bacon, T. G., Aiken, D. W., Bland. Elbert.
Lieutenant Colonel: Fair, R. A.
Majors: Seibels, E., Hard, J. S.
Adjutant: Sill, T. M.
Quartermaster: Lovelace. B. F.
Commissary Sergeant: Smith, Fred.
Surgeons: Dozier, ——, Spence, W. F., Horton, O. R.
Assistant Surgeons: Carlisle, R. C., Stallworth, A.
Chaplain: Carlisle, J. M.

COMPANY "A."

CAPTAINS: Bland, Elbert, Harrison, S. LIEUTENANTS: Bland, J. A., Wenner, M. B. SERGEANTS: Addison, H. W., Bert, A. W., Smiles, N. G., Connels, J. R., Gregory, R. CORPORALS: Cogburn, R. M., Mathis, C. A., Regan, B. G., Fair, W. B., Hill, T. T., Butler, E. S. PRIVATES: Aultman, Jno., Aultman, J., Burton, T., Boatwright, B., Boyce, W. G., Broadwets, T. A., Brown, J. J., Brown, J. C., Bryant, H. G., Barnett, W. H., Carpenter, J., Cogburn, B. J., Cogburn, W. H., Crawford, W., Courtney, J. G., Casar, E. H., Casar, C. G. D., Casar, J. L., Carson, H., Cushman, C. B., Daily, R. J., Day, J. S., Davis, E. G., Day, J. S., DeLoach, J., Dunagant, J., Easley, J., Edison, W. M., Elsman, J. E., Fair, J. E., Glover, A., Glover, R. J., Gomillian, L., Gray, H. C., Green, J., Green, M., Hagood, J. V., Walsenback, L., Horn, J. S., Johnson, L. S., Johnson, D. F., Johnson, D. W., Jones, S. A., Jones, F. A., Kirksey, W. H., Legg, E. W., Littleton, L. W., Libeschutts, M., Long, W. R., Lott, G. H., Lovelace, G. C., Miles, C. L., Miles, A., Miles, S., Mims, R. S., Mims, W. D., Mobley, G. S., Mobley, S. C., McDaniels, F. S., McGeires, Charley, Nichholson, J. A., Perin, J. D., Powell, R., Prescott, H. H., Prescott, S. J., Radford, J. A., Radford, A., Raney, D. D., Randall, F. E., Riddle, S., Robertson, J. F., Rodgers, C. E., Ryon, S. D., Salter, G. F., Salter, J. R., Samuel, W., Smith, W. J., Smith, D. W., Smith, F. L., Sheppard, S., Stevenson, T., Sweringer, R., Swearinger, A. S., Snelgrove, J. F., Toney, Ed., Turner, H. R., Walker, P. E., Whitlock, W., Whitlock, G. W., Whitman, S., Weathelsy, L., Williams, G. D., Williams, R. R., Williams, W. B. F., Williams, D. S., Willing, R., Willing, J., Woolsey, J. D., Wright, W. M., Wright, J. H.

COMPANY "B."

CAPTAINS: Mattison, G. M., Hodges, W. L., Hudgens, T. A., Townsend, J. A. LIEUTENANTS: Clinkscales, E. B., Townsend, I. F., Hodges, J. F., Klugh, P. D., Hodges, J. R., Callahan, S. W., Hodges, W. C. C. SERGEANTS: McGee, J. S., Riley, W., Agnew, J. A., Henderson, J. W., Franklin, T., Stevenson, F. A., Rolinson, C. CORPORALS: Norris, E. B., Sitton, J. Y., Mathis, J., McGee, A. C., Dolan, F., Tribble, D. A., Dunn, R. H., Brown, J. N., Pruitt, F. V. PRIVATES: Armstrong, J. C., Armstrong, W. C., Austin, J. H., Ashley, J. S., Anderson, J. C., Alguny, H. H., Ashley, W. S., Allen, A., Bowles, I. W., Bowle, H. W., Bowle, E. B., Bowen, S. M., Bowen, J. O., Barmore, W. C., Bailey, J. M., Brownlee, J. R., Bramyon, T. M., Bell, F. M., Bryant, H., Coleman, T. J., Calvert, J. M., Cochran, R. M., Carpenter, T. J., Cromer, A. F., Callahan, M., Callahan, W. N., Coleman, J. T., Clark, H. B., Cowen, J. W., Davis, S. J., Davis, I. W., Davis, T., Davis, W. Y., Davis, J. A., Deal, M. L., Donald, J. L., Drennan, L. O., Duncan, W. P., Duncan, J. B., Duncan, D., Ellison, S., Graham, J. M., Graham, B. C., Graham, E. C., Griffen, J., Gilmore, J. W., Grimes, W. B., Hemphill, R. R., Hinton, A., Hughes, H. H., Hawthorn, H. B., Hawthorn, C., Hawthorn, L., Hodges, C. R., Harris, J. N., Harris, W. M., Kay, W. A., Killingworth, W. P., Kirly, B., Latimer, S. N., Lindsay, A. B. C. Long, G. W. M., Long, H. J. S., Lovelace, R., Martin, J. R., McAdams, R. V., McAdams, W. N., McAdams, A. J., McDowell, W. N., McCown, J., McWhorter, J. R., McGee, J. M., Moore, T., Moore, R., Moseley, W. L., Nabors, A., Owens, S., Owens, V., Owens, W., Owens, D. B., Peeler, J. W., Pratt, T. W., Pratt, W. A., Pruitt, J. J., Pruitt, W. A., Robinson, R. A., Strickland, W. A., Sharp, M. C., Simpson, J. H., Stone, J. E., Stone, R. P., Seawright, J. B., Straborn, R., Shirley, G., Seawright, R. W., Smith, R. N., Taylor, J., Timms, J. T., Vandiver, E. W., Wakefield, J. A., Ware, W. A., Ware, R. A., Waddell, G. H., Webb, J., Weir, W. A., Whitelock, F., Wilson, J. S., Wilson, J. L., Wilson, John S., Williamson, J. A., Williams, J. F., Williams, G., Young, J. V., Young, L. J., Young, I. B., Young, J. C.

COMPANY "C."

CAPTAINS: Bradley, P. H., Cothran, W. E., Palmer, N. H., Lyons, John. LIEUTENANTS: Thayler, A. T., McClain, T. E., Childs, T. M., Calhoun, J. S., Rodgers, T. A. SERGEANTS: Hearst, J. W., Edmonds, S. F., Corley, J. A., Gray, T. C., Bradley, T. C., Quarles, T. P., Robinson, J. P., Martin, J. C., Newby, E. G., Willis, J., Brown, J. S. CORPORALS: Pennal, C. D., Lyon, J. F., Joy, D. W., Weed, R., Walker, W.

PRIVATES: Adamson, J. L., Aiken, A. M., Ansley, J. A., Bosdell, I. S., Bosdell, S. E., Boisworth, J., Bouchilson, T. M., Baker, W., Benson, W., Bradley. W., Bradley. J. E., Bellot. J. E., Blackwell. J., Berdashaw, W. J., Butler, W., Belcher, J. C., Bond. I. C., Burns, M., Brugh, T. J., Barksdale, W., Barksdale. J., Barksdale. B. B., Barksdale, T. W., Banks, G. M., Banks. W. W., Banks. C. C., Barksdale. G. T., Belcher, H. C., Corroll. V., Chamberlain, W., Childs. T. W., Cook, W., Cook, F. L., Connor. A. P., Crose, W. M., Cook. T. W., Childs, T. C., Calhoun, E., Davis. P., Devlin. J. A., Devlin. W. P., Derracort. W. G., Drennan. D. H., Dowtin, D. W., Elkins, W., Eunis, G., Edmonds, W. F., Edwards, W. W., Edmonds. T. J., Finley. J. C., Gillebeau. J. C. Gillebeau, P. D., Hill, J. W., Harris. S. N., Holloway. J. L., Harrison. J., Knox, S., Kennedy. J. M., Kennedy, W. P., Link, J. J., Link, S. C., Link, W. T., Lyon, J. E., Lyon. L. W., Leak. T. N., Lyon, R. N., Lands, W., Ligon. T. C., Lamonds, J. F. A., LeRoy, J. N., Martin. G. W., Martin. P. C., McKettrick. J., McClinton. J., McQuerns. J. A., McKinney. W. W., McKinney, J., McKelvey. W. H., McCaslan. G. D., Morrow. W. R., Morrow. J. A., McClain, R., Noble. E. P., McGowan, O., New. F., Noble. J. S., O'Neill, P., Palmer, W. O., Pennal. J. E., Paris, H., Rodgers, M. J., Robinson, P. H., Russell. J. R., Reagan. Y. P., Seigler, J. A., Sibert. J. H., Shoemaker, A. M., Scott. C., Tennant, G. C., Tennant. P., Turnage. J., Traylor. A. A., Wells, W. H., Wideman. J. J., Wilson, J. L., Willis. W. W., Willis, J. P., Wideman. C. A., Zimmerman, D. R., Zimmerman. J. H.

COMPANY "D."

CAPTAINS: Hester, S. J., Allen, T. W. LIEUTENANTS: Owen, J. T., Carlisle, J. C., Power, E. F., Carlisle, R. H., Prince. H. M., Cunningham. J. R., McGee, M. M. SERGEANTS: Kennedy, J. T., Allen, J. B., Hester. J. J., Clark, A. D., Gibert, J. S., McCurne, W. L., Clinkscales. L. C. CORPORALS: Norwood. O. A., Bowen. L. M., Boyd, D., Barnes, A. J.

PRIVATES: Alewine, J. H., Allen. J. B., Allen, S., Burress. W., Bell, J. H., Bass, J., Black. J. P., Boyd, R. P., Brooks, R. H., Brooks. J. M., Bowen. L., Bowen. W., Burton. R. H., Barnes. J., Barnes, W., Basken, J. F., Beaty, W., Caldwell. E., Cowen. H. F., Cromer. H., Cunningham, J. D., Clark, A. D., Campbell. W. H., Campbell. M. B., Calhoun, J. C., Calhoun, W. N., Carmbe. J., Clinkscales, W. R., Davis. B. A., Danelly, J., Dunlop. W., Edwards. E. E., Edwards. F., Freeman. H., Freeman. R. V., Fleming. W., Frisk, J., Hogan, J., Hogan. W. A., Hall, Tuck, Hall, A., Hall. H., Harkness. W. B., Haddon, S. P., Hill. J. A., Huckabee, J. P., Hester, J. J., Hutchinson. B. F., Hodges, W. A., Hunter, T., Johnson, G. W., Jones. C. C., Kennedy, L. D., Kennedy, I., Kennedy. J. T., Kay. W. A., Longbridge, W. S., Longbridge, L. L., Latimer, W. A., McCurrie, M. C., McCurrie. W., Mauldin, A., Mauldin. H., McDaniel, ——, Morrow, W. R., Martin. H., Melford, C., Moore. T. A., McComb, J. F., McAdams. S. T., Newby, J. N., Norwood. O. H., Oliver. P. E., Presly, R. A., Powell, J. W., Russell, W. H., Ritchie, W., Ritchie, J. A., Starks. J. S. H., Sanders, J. W., Sanders, J., Shaw, J. A., Shaw. J. C., Shoemaker. A. M., Scott, J. E., Scott. J. J., Stevenson, J. E., Speers, E. H., Taylor, E. M., Taylor, M. T., Watts, A., Williams, B. W., Wilson, J.

COMPANY "E."

CAPTAINS: Denny, D., Mitchell, J. LIEUTENANTS: Rutland, W. A., Daniel, J. M., Pinson, J., Denny, J. W. SERGEANTS: Roach, J. C. H., Suddath, J. B., Denny, A. W., Coleman, M. W., Mitchel, E. CORPORALS: Powe, J., Smith, L. A., McGee, U. R., Padgett, E.
PRIVATES: Black, H., Black, J., Black, X., Crouch, W., Crouch, T. B., Crouch, H., Crouch, J. L., Crouch, R., Crouch, M., Crout, Q., Corley, J. M., Corley, J., Corley, F., Cooner, W. E., Chapman, J., Cash, R. F., Denny, G. W., Denny, J. O., Denny, J. M., Derrick, J., Dougalss, J., Douglass, W., Etheredge, W., Etheredge, W., Etheredge, N., Etheredge, H. C. Etheredge, G. M., Edwards, J., Geiger, J., Geiger, D., Goodwin, W., Goff, J., Hughes, C. W., Inabinett, J., Little, W., Lott, L., Marony, A., Mitchell, P., Mitchell, W. A., Mitchell, J., Murich, J., Merchant, J. W., McCorty, D. D. W., McLendon, I., Parson, R., Penson, J. R., Powe, J. R., Padgett, E., Ridlehoover, W., Rodgers, F., Ramage, J. C., Ridgell, W., Ridgels, J., Ridgers, D., Story, ——. Smith, G. W., Smith, L. L., Smith, J. H., Smith, W. W., Shealy, J., Sheeley, A., Sheely, A., Samples, W. E., Saulter, J., Thompson, J., Thompson, J., Vansant, J. T., Vansant, H., Venters, W., Watson, M. B., Watson, J. L., Watson, N., Walker, R., Whittle, W., White, L., Yarbrough, J., Yarbrough, M.

COMPANY " F."

CAPTAINS: Harde, J. S., Harden, J. E., Brooks, W. D., McKibbin, Mc. LIEUTENANTS: Jennings, T. A., Greggs, J. B., Sentell, J. L., Baker, G. W., Wise, L. W., Hard, B. W. SERGEANTS: Matthensy, N. O., Gullege, T., Davis, J., Howard, H. H., Cobh, R. CORPORALS: Stevens, H. M., Rearden, W. E., Athenson, G. E., Odom, M., Readen, R. W.
PRIVATES: Athenson, J. L., Aulmond, J. R., Autmond, T., Archer, W. B., Baggate, E., Beck, W., Brown, J., Brown, J., Brown, M., Bagwell, L. B., Brwer, G. A., Brooks, G., Bland, L., Brooks, R., Cawall, W., Corten, J. A., Cashman, R., Cash, W., Cochran, G., Corley, J., Clark, H., Donold, R., Dickens, E., Davis, B., Duncan, J., Duncan, R., Davis, J., Duncan, B., Ellis, W., Friday, P. A., Faulklan, T., Faulkner, W. P., Franklan, A., Fagin P., German W., Galledge, H., Galledge, Wm., Gissus, J., Henderson, C. R., Hall, J. C., Hamonett, W. P., Hatcher, W., Hawistow, S., Jackson, J., Jackson, J., Jackson, D. L., Johnson, E., Johnson, A. L., Kirksey, W. J., Key, J. A., Lacks, W., Lispard, W., Littleton, L., Lawrence, W., Lesnard, E., Maddox, J., Maddox, G., Maddox, J., Maddox, M., Medlock, B., Maddox, B., McKee, G. W., Myers, W., McGee, J. W., McKenzie, W., Mathews, M., Mathis, M., McKennie, M., McGee, J., New, J., New, E., New, J., Overstreet, J., Price, J. D., Platt, G. W., Parker, A., Prescott, L., Perden, G., Parker, J., Pruce, T., Radford, S., Ramsey, J. A., Ramsey, M., Rannold, E., Sharpton, B., Smith, W., Seigler, E., Stringfield, E., Seigler, A. S., Serger, W. B., Serger, B. F., Seitzes, J., Tarner, H., Tollison, T. P., Taylor, J. A., Taylor, B. F., Wade, H., West, W. A., Wicker, A., Walker, W.

COMPANY "G."

CAPTAINS: Brooks, J. H., Clark, W. E., Kemp, J. W., Williams, J. C. LIEUTENANTS: Edson, J. W., King, H. C., Strothers, G. J., Strothers, R. C. SERGEANTS: Youngblood, R. S., Calbreath, H. C., Griffen, J. W., Ouzts, M., Rambo, J. C., Clarey, R. C., Durst, T. W., Wrighlet, J. K., Calesman, D., Williams, C. T.
PRIVATES: Adams, S., Adams, H. W., Actoin, J. S., Actons, W. J., Atom, R., Attaway, S. C. Attaway, T., Bagwell, W., Boom, B. F., Boulware, J. S., Branson, T. N., Brooks, J. S., Brooks, L., Bryan, A. M., Bryan, R. C., Burkhalter, M. R., Burnett, J. L., Burnett, H., Clark, G.,

Clark, V., Clary, W. M., Coleman, J. S., Croach. D. H., Crawford, W. A., Dees, H. C., Dogen, H. C., Dogin, W., Dorn, D., Dorn, H., Duffy, J., Duffy, J., Edison, W. A., Edison, L.. Foosher, B., Fell, J., Gasperson, J. B., Gentry, J. W., Grant, J. W. D., Gragary, J., Griffeth, A. B., Griffeth, M. A., Haltiwanger, G., Hamilton, G. W., Hamilton, J. P., Hargrove, A., Hardy, M., Heard, Wm., Holloway, D. P., Holloway, R. C., Hollingsworth, J. A., Hudson, J. W., Jay, J., Jay, J., King, W. D., King, A. P., Koon, L., Lamb, B., May, J. A., Mannous, W. A., Neil, J. W., Neil, M. W., Odum, W. L., Ouzts, F., Ouzts, W. H., Palmer, W. C., Procter, J. M., Quattlebaum, J. A., Reaves, G. E., Rhodes, J. B., Reley, J. M., Roton, J., Rushton, J. M., Rushton, W. M., Rushton, W. M., Rushton, D., Seatel, J. R., Smith, J. W., Smith, L. R., Smith, G., Stalworth, A. C., Steadman, J. C., Steadman, H., Steifle, H. C., Stevens, B. T.. Stevens, R., Tompkins, J., Townsend. F. A., Turner, R. P., Turner, G. W., Turner, S., Turner, G., Turner, Wm., Walker, E. P., Walton, ——, Wallington, W. J., Wheeler, Wm., Whatley, J. P., Willingham, J., Williams. H. Williams, P., William, T. H., William, M. P.. Williams, W., Worter, L., Wright, J. H., Wright, W. H., Youngblood, D., Youngblood, Wm.

COMPANY "H."

CAPTAINS: Goggans, J. E. LIEUTENANTS: Bouknight, J. R., McCelvey, J. C., Bouknight, A. P., Huiet, H. SERGEANTS: McDaniel, J. C., Whittle, M. A., Watson, J. H., Ruston, W. CORPORALS: Huiet, J., Wyse, A. L., Sample, B. F., Jennings, G.
PRIVATES: Barnes, H., Bedenbaugh, J. T., Bedenbaugh, L., Bedenbaugh, J.. Bouknight, A. S., Bouknight S. J., Bouknight, N., Buzzard, J. C., Charles, P., Duffie, J., Duffie, P., Duncan, A., Duncan, V., Faland, ——, Gunter, R., Goff, Z., Gibson, J., Gibson, W., Harris, W., Harris, S., Henson, D., Henson, J., Inabinet. I., Leppard, G., Leppard, J., Livingstone, P., Matthews, E., Miller, J. Merchant, T., Mitchell, M., Martin. G., Padgett, E., Parmer, D. K., Rotten, J., Rushton, D., Rushton, H., Rushton, J., Sadler. J., Sadler, W., Smith, B., Spann, W., Spann, P., Shealy, M. W., Watson, W., Wise, J., Wise, W., Whittle, M., Wright, B. W.

COMPANY "I."

CAPTAIN: Prescott, W. T. LIEUTENANTS: Nixon, J. P., Roper, B., Blocker. S. B. SERGEANTS: Morgan, G. W., Holmes, W. J., Holmes, W. L., Brunson, R. V., Holson, Wm. CORPORALS: Crafton, T. M., Middleton, R. H., Mathis, J. A., Brunson, S. T., McKee, J. S., Griffis, J. N., Parkman, S., McDaniel, J.
PRIVATES: Anderson, E. J., Burt, A. H., Barkley, E. N., Bartley, J. W., Brigs, A. J., Brigs, H., Brigs, J., Bussey, W. N., Bussey, J. A., Broadwater, N. A., Broadwater, S., Brooks, R., Colloham, M., Garvett, W. A., Hammond, C., Holmes, S., Holmes, L. E., Jennings, W., Middleton, W. E., Matthis, W. H., Menererether, N., Morgan, E., McGee, T. W., Oham, R., Prince, J., Prince, D., Parkman, J. P., Parkman, S., Pressley, T. N.. Patterson, T. H., Price, A. J., Parkman, N., Prescott, H. H., Shafton, J. S., Shafton. B. F., Shanall, J., Percy, J. H., Thernman, J. W.. Thernman, T. B., Thomas, T. B., Bruse, J. W., Wood, H., Wood, J., Whitlock, ——, Whitaker, N., Wesman, C. L., Whitlock, W.

COMPANY "K."

CAPTAIN: Burees, J. F. LIEUTENANTS: Talbert, J. L., Berry, J. M., Chetham, J. W. SERGEANTS: Culbreath, O. T., Martin, W. N., Reynolds, W. M., Lamer, L. W., Burress, C. M. CORPORALS: Reynolds, J. W., Shibley, L. D., White, W. G., Williams, T. R.

36

PRIVATES: Adams, B. O., Blake, J. E., Carthledge, T. A., Crafton, T. M., Coleman, W. L., Coleman, G. R., Culbreth, J., Deal, A., Devore, C. L., Franks, J. A., Hammonds, C. T., Harrison, C. H., Henderson, J. T., Henderson, J. E., Holmes, W. L., Holmes, H. J., Howell, H., Lamer, T. B., Lamer, O. W., Limbecher, C. H., Lockridge, J. L., Mayson, J. H., Quarles, H. M., Reynolds, J. C., Reynolds, E. W., Rountree, T. J., Rush, T. P., Stalmaker, G. I., Stalmaker, J. R., Stalmaker, J. W., Timmerman, G. H., Williams, J. R., Wood, W. B., Yeldell, W. H.

COMPANY "L."

CAPTAINS: White, W. C., Litchfield, J. L., Litchfield, G. S. LIEUTENANTS: Beaty, T. W., Petman, S., Cooper, T. B., Newton, K. M., Grissett, J. D., Reves, J. W. SERGEANTS: Waid, G. W., Nercen, J. W., Floyd, A., Johnson, J. M., Anderson, ——, Gregary, T. H., Granger, J., Prince, J. L., Rabon, D., Johnson, C. L., Anderson, D. R. CORPORAL: Green, S. F.

PRIVATES: Barnhill, W. H., Barnhill, H., Cooper, L., Cooper, R., Creaven, W. H., Creach, C., Chesnut, D. M. W., Cork, M. C., Cox, P. V., Cox, G. W., Dussenberry, J.,H., Dussenberry, N. G., Edge, D. M., Edge, W., Faulk, G., Floyd, W., Faulk, L., Faulk, J. L., Foreland, N., Fund, G., Grattely, J., Granger, J., Granger, W., Granger, F., Graddy, N., Graham, D., Graham, D. N., Gore, F., Grant, J. E., Hacks, ——, Harden, A. J., Harden, W. H., Hardwick, ——, Howell, ——, Harden, C. B., Hamilton, W. H., Hamilton, ——, Holland, W., Jenkins, Wm., Jewreth, ——, Jones, J., Jordan, J. T., Jordan, J., Johnson, T., Johnson, J. J., James, ——, Jenningham, D., King, J. J., King, J. D., King, G. W., Lilly, D., Murry, J. T., Murry, E. H., Misham, T. K., McKnot, Wm. R., Martin, B. W., Norris, J. K., Oliver, J. M., Powell, L., Perkins, ——, Parker, A. D., Parker, H. H., Powell, F. L., Powell, J. M., Roberts, J. T., Rhenark, J. C., Stalvey, C. M., Stalvey, J. J., Squers, J., Smith, Wm., Savris, A., Sessions, O., Sengleton, M. J., Vaught, S., Vereen, J. T., Watts, ——, Wade, K.

ROLL OF EIGHTH SOUTH CAROLINA VOLUNTEER REGIMENT.

Field and Staff.

COLONELS: Cash, E. B. C., Henagan, Jno. W., Stackhouse, E. T.
LIEUTENANT COLONELS: Hoole, A., McLeod, ——.
ADJUTANTS: Lucas, Thomas E., Ingliss, Wm. C., Mullins, W. S., Weatherly, C. M.
QUARTERMASTERS: McClenigan, Jno., Henagan, J. M., Hunagan, J. M.
COMMISSARIES: Cawley, J. H., Griffen, E. M.
SURGEONS: Wallace, W. D., David, W. J., Pearce, J. F., Coit, D.
ASSISTANT SURGEONS: Dunlop, R. J., Dudley, T. E., Murdock, Byron. Henson, J. B., McIver, Hansford, Bristow, C. D.
COMMISSARY SERGEANTS: McCown, R. A., Coker, C. W.
ORDERLY SERGEANT: Tyler, H. A.

COMPANY "A."

CAPTAINS: Hoole, A. J., Muldrow, J. H., Odum, Wm., Odum, E., Rodgers, E., Rouse, J. J., Bryant, Jas. T., Goodson, J. T., Hudson, J. E. LIEUTENANTS: Reynolds, W. C., Gardner, E. M., Bruce, C. A., Large, James F., Farmer, S. P., Branch B., Morris, J. B.
PRIVATES: Reddick, W. H., Bryant, James, J., Boone, L. F., Blackburn, Wade, Bradshaw, J., Beck, W. D., Bass, Jesse, Blackman, John, Bradstraw, M., Beasley, O., Barns, Robt., Carter, W. R., Cox, B. F.,

Clemens, J., Dennis, Thomas A., Ervin, J. R., Flowers, C., Florence, T. D., Farmer, G. B., Garrison, J., Gorman, C., Goodson, J., Gudgen, J. I. B., Goodson, A., Gray, R., James, J. C., Gardner, C. D., Jordan, Wm. A., Gardner, P. T., Hill, W. M., Hill, B., Hill, E. T., Johnson, William, Johnson, Peter, Johnson, Robert, Langston, Jno. F., Langston, Ira D., Law, Frank, Large, N., Morrell, H., Morrell, W. E., Morrell, Isaac, Muller, J., Maye, R. F., Neal, Jno., Neal, J., Odom, J. S., Odom, S. J., Outlaw, James, Outlaw, John, Privett, E., Reynolds, E. J., Reddeck, W., Reddick, A., Stokes, J. F., Stokes, A. D., Sandesbery, J. H., Privett, W. B., Eligah, ——, Stakes, A. D., Stokes, J. H., Sandbarry, J. H., Severence, R. E., Stewart, A. C., Stewart, Hardey, Smith, S., Sexton, Thomas, Scott, W., Wingate, W. Z., Williams, W., Wadford, N., Woods, S. J.

COMPANY "B."

CAPTAINS: Hough, M. J., Powell R. T. LIEUTENANTS: Parker, G. A., Thurman, M. T., Turnage, P. A., Sellers, D., Johnson, C. B., Hough, J. M., Moore, P. A., White, J. F., Chapman, H. C., Courtney, W. R. SERGEANTS: Jones, J., Rivers, W. F., Douglass, W., Rivers, W. F., Douglass, J. B., Sellers, R. C., Evans, B. F., Kite, B., Hammock, J. E., CORPORALS: Rivers, W. B., Rashing, J. P., Sellers, P. A., Herst, L., Campbell, J. A., Hancock, R. F. M.

PRIVATES: Anderson, B., Adams, B. F., Brown, V. F., Brown, D., Boon, E., Loon, C., Boon, A., Beaver, M., Brock, C., Boon, W. B., Cassadlay, A. J., Courtney, O., Courtney, J., Courtney, J. P., Cross, H., Cross, P., Chapman, A., Davis, F., Deas, T. A., Driggers, J., Dixon, R., Funderburk, H. W., Funderburk, J. B., Gaskins, J. B., Horn, J. D., Horn, J. W., Harp, W. C., Hancock, J. T., Hicks, J., Johnson, W. B., Johnson, T. B., Jordon, J. W., Lisenly, S., Lear, B. F., Lewis, T. H., McBride, J. A., McPriest, P., Massey, B. F., McKey, D. A., McCrany, D. A., Melton, J., Melton, A., Melton, W., Moore, H., McDuffie, J, McLean, J. W., McLean, D. A., McNair, ——, McManus, R., McNair, N. C., Nelson, M., Nelson, H., Price, H., Polson, J., Rivers, F., Rogers, P., Sellers, J. D., Sellers, W. B., Sellers, W. R., Sellers, H. J., Sillivan, T., Sillivan, S., Sweatt, W., Sweatt, S., Stricklen, H., Teed, T. B., Tarnage, D., Threatt, J. W., Threatt, W., Threatt, T., Threatt, H., Terry, J., Timmons, W., Tadlock, W., White, H., Whittaker, J. W., Wilkerson, J., West, J. S., McNair, N.

COMPANY "C."

CAPTAINS: Coit, W. H., Powe, T. E., Malloy, S. G. LIEUTENANTS: Gillespie, G. S., McIver, D. W., Evans, R. E., Hurst, L. SERGEANTS: Strother, J., Gayle, H. A., Crail, C. W., Crail, T. P., Stancel, J., Smith, W. P., McCallman, J. C., White, B. S., Coit, J. T., Grimsley, S. B., Sellers, J., McIver, H. CORPORALS: Malloy, C. A., Godfrey, W. R., Callens, J., Sellers, S.

PRIVATES: Adams, W., Adams, J., Bevil, J., Buchanan, J. A., Braddock, R., Clark, J., Cadien, B. F., Coker, H., Coker, M., Chapman, W. G., Chapman, A. G., Craig, J., Crawford, F. D., Campbell, D. A., DeLorne, T. W., Dickson, S. G., Douglas, A., Douglas, M. A., Ellerbe, A. W., Emanuel, E., Freeman, J., Freeman, W., Gardner, J. N., Gaskin, J. D., Goodwin, J., Grimsley, W., Grady, J. A., Goodwin, D., Grant, H. P., Grant, H., Grant, A., Graves, S., Hicks, W. H., Hayes, A. A., Haggins, A., Inglis, W. C., Inglas, L. S., Inglas, P., Knight, W. W., Lang, J., Link, J. A., Lisendy, W., Linton, J. H., Lee, H., McBride, F., McLean, J. K., McColl, W., Murphy, C. W., McIver, F. M., Mahon, J., McDuffie, F. J., McMillan, J. D., Malloy, J. H., Murray, J. C., McIntosh, J. W., Melton, H., Moore, H., Melton, E. H., McRa, D., Mash, ——, Melton, W., *Nichols*, W. P., Odom, D. P., Odom, J., Petter, L. L., Pinchman, H.

C., Powell, A. H. C., Poston, H. C., Poston, W., Purvis, W., Purvis, L.
D., Poston, J., Quick, B., Rainwaters, W. T., Richards, J. G., Roberson,
G., Spencer, S. H., Sellers, H., Smith. S. S., Sweatt, T., Stacey, O.,
Spencer, T. D., Sellers W. P., Smith. T., Smith. J., Turnage. T. D.,
Turner, W. W., White. D., White, J., Wright, J., Wallace, J. C.

COMPANY "D."

CAPTAINS: Miller, J. S., Miller, R. P., Spofferd, P. F. LIEUTENANTS:
Blakeney, H., Timmons, J. J., Paker, L. C., Kirkley, W. P., Lowry, J.
H. SERGEANTS: Jackson, H. H., Baker, A. J., Gatlim, J. B., Jackson,
A., Wesh, S. CORPORALS: Hendrick, J. H., King, E. T., Lee, J. C.,
Sowell, W. H.
PRIVATES: Adams, J. J., Carter, S. H., Carter. G. W., Calege, J.,
Crain, J. A., Crowley, B. D., Crowley, T. W., Dees, T. M., Dees, W.,
Foster, S., Griffith, J., Gandy, E., Gandy, W. H., Gibson, A., Handcock,
J. P., Handcock, J. J., Handcock, J. J., Handcock, J. T., Handcock, R. F.,
Handcock, J. L., Hudrick, R., Hudrick, J. L., Horn, L., Horn, J., Horn,
M., Horton, G. W. Horton, S., Holly, P. W., Hough, J. T., Hough, J. E.,
Jordan. H. S., Jordan, J., Jordan, A., Key, A., Key, J. A., Knight. J. H.,
Knight, J. R., Knight, J. A., Knight, W. H., Knight, T. J., Knighton, J.
T., Kibbie. J., Lowery, J., Lowery, W., Love, J. J., Mangum, J. C., Man-
gum, W. P., Myers, J., Miller, J. T., McMillan, T. E., McMair, D. D.,
McManus, M. B., McLauchlin, D. A., C   r, J. T., Ogburn, L., Philips,
E., Philips. A., Philips, C., Plyler, A., Face   , Rollins, B. F., Rollins,
G. W., Rollins, J., Rollins, J. C. Robinson, G., Robinson. S., Sinclair, J.,
Sinclair. J. A., Stricklin, J., Stricklin, M., Stricklin, M., Small, C.,
Threatt, J. S., Threatt. J., Threatt, R., Therrill, L., Terry J., Talbert, O.
W., Talbert. W. S., Thratt. J. A., Watson, M., Watson, E., Watts, J. J.,
Williams, B. B.

COMPANY "E."

CAPTAINS: Young, J. D., Joy, W. D. LIEUTENANTS: Westhimes, H.,
Hewitt, T. M., Halford, J. J. SERGEANTS: Athenson, S. R., Ward, R.
H., Hollyman, M. W., Miller, T. J. CORPORALS: Philips, J. R., Moody,
E. T., Moon, W. W., Morris, T. E.
PRIVATES: Allen, R. M., Anderson, T. J., Anderson, W. D., Alford,
R. H., Askin, J. A. J., Anderson, C., Anderson, J. F., Anderson, W. H.,
Anderson, W. T., Anderson, G., Anderson, J. M., Barfield, M., Bristow,
C. C., Bristow, J. N., Barefoot, D. R., Brookington, E. S., Byrd, J. E.,
Carter, W. A., Carter, G., Carter, H. M., Carter, N. S. J., Carter, H.,
Carter, R. M., Carter, S. B., Coward, W., Cook, T. J., Courtney, S. J.,
Connor, E. J., Connor, G., Chandler, T. A., Cone, R., Danels, E.,
DaBase, A. E., Doralds, M. H., Evington, G., Elliott, A. J., Graham,
C. S., Gilchrist, J., Gee, S., Gardner, J. D., Gardner, C., Ganniginn, D.,
Hill, E. F., Hill, J. J., Hill, B., Hill, H., Hill, J., Hill, R. M., Hill., I. T.,
Howall, W. H., Hollan, J. S., Hollan, S. S., Hamphury, S. S., Ham-
phury, R. F., Hane, H. W., Hane, A. J., Hane, H. A. W., Hane, W.,
Hatchell, I., Hatchell, C. A., Hatchell, L., Hancock, H., Hollyman, A.,
Halford, J. M., Hix, T., Hase, G. N., Hickson, J. S., Jackson, T., Jones,
R. M., Jordan, P. A., Kerth, J. H., Kirby, S. J., Kirby, H., Kent, J. L.,
Lockhart, J. C., Lockhart, R. C., Lockhart, G. R., Lockhart, W. J., Mc-
Coy, C. D., McCoy, I. G., McCoy, J. J., McCoy, S., McCoy, J., McGee,
J. M., McGee, W., McKnight, W., Moore, J. G., Moore, J. D., McGill,
J. F., McGill, J., Morris, M. E., Morris, H., Morris, J. L., Matthews,
W. A., McKessick, W. J., Nettles, L. F., Nettles, G. T., Nettles, R. C.,
Norwood, J. F., Philips, J. R., Philips, L. A., Price, J. A., Price, G. P.,
Pool A. A., Pawley, J. H., Plummer, C. H., Powers, M. J., Powers, A.
D., Powers, W., Rollins, R. D. F., Rice, D. H., Rogers, M. D., Single-
tary, C., Smoot, W. B., Smoot, W. L., Snipes, M., Timmons, W. H.,

Timmons, W. B., Truitt, J. E., Turner, J. C., Ward, J. W., Ward, R. H., Ward, C. E., Ward, J. J., Witherspoon, S. B., Windham, J. R., Windham, I., Windham, J. H., Wooten, S., Wittington, J. W., Wadford, N., Wadford, G. W., Winburn, S., Young, W. W.

COMPANY "F."

CAPTAINS: Evans, W. H., Howle, T. E., McIver, J. K., Bass, J. E. LIEUTENANTS: McIver, J. J., Kelly H., James, W. E., Ferguson, J. W., Griffin, P. E., Griffin, E. M., Rhodes, J. T., James, R. E., Coker, W. C., Smoot, J., Rhodes, W. B., Williams, J. A., Williams, A. L., Howle, J. F., Evans, C. D., Bearly, J. M., Wilson, I. D., Carter, W. P. CORPORALS: Parrott, A. W., Hearon, G. W., Bruce, C. A., Harroll, L. B., Parrott, B. M.
PRIVATES: Alexander, A., Atkinson, W. K., Bacot, T. W., Bass, J. C., Bass, B., Bass, J. B., Baswell, L. T., Bozeman, B. C., Bozeman, J. W., Bozeman, P. W., Bozeman, J, Bozeman, H., Bozeman, W., Brown, W., Byrd, D. M., Coltins, A., Colvin, J. R., Cook, D. B., Davis, J. M., Dixon, A. P., Dixon. J. E., Elliott, W. A., Ervin, E. M., Fraser, J. G., Fort, J. E., Flowers, J., Garland, W. H., Galloway, A., Galloway, W. M., Galloway, W. L., Galloway, M., Galloway, G. W., Gullege, A., Gullege, J. L., Gatlin, H., Hale, J. O., Halliburton, J. J., Halliburton, R. J., Harrall, J. M., Harris, D. J., Hazelton, J., Higgins, R. D., Hurst, S., Jenks, M., Jenks, G., Jordon, A., King, T. F., Kelly, T., Lawson, J. T., Lee, J. T., Lewis, W., McCown, R., McIntosh, J. H., McKenzie, W. W., Marco, M., Mazing, W. H., Mixon, J., Martin, W., Nettles, R. F., Outlaw, B., Outlaw, J., Parrott, J. R., Peoples, R. H., Price, A. J., Privett, J. H., Privett, J. H., Rhodes, J. D., Rhodes, F. E., Rhodes, R. B., Smith, A., Smith, J. S. M., Skinner, B., Shumaker, S., Stukey, A. F., Suggs, R. B., Stokes, R., Tallevasb, H. P., Thomas, J. M., Thomas. R. C., Tyler, H., Thomlinson, ——, Wallace, G., Wordham, A. E., Wilk, J., Wilson, P.

COMPANY "G."

CAPTAIN: Harrington, J. W. LIEUTENANTS: Townsend. C. F., Parker, John, Weatherly C. M. SERGEANTS: Dudley, T. F., Lester, I. B., Murdock, John T., Odum, L., Crosland, W. A. CORPORALS: Easterling, Thomas, Townsend. H. E., Cook, John A., Tatum, R. J., Gillespie, O. H., Douglas, H. J.
PRIVATES: Adams, E., Adams, H. A., Adams, J. T., Andrews, S. D., Briston, C. D., Briston, E. D., Bullard. Henry, Bundy, William, Butler, William, Butler, E., Campbell, J., Caulk, D., Cook, T. A. M., Cowen, L. M., Crosland, Samuel, Connor, R. D. T., Cooper, Wm. C., Cooper, V. H., David, E. C., David, R. J., David, J. H., Dudley, James, Drigger, Jesse, Drigger, J. G., David, A. I., Easterling, A. A., Easterling, R. C., Easterling, J. K., Easterling, W. T., Easterling, Elijah, Edens, T. W., Emanuel, C. L., Fletcher, J. D., Gibson, W. L., Grant, J. S., Graham, H. C., Gillespie, S. J., Harvel, John, Henagen, James M., Heyward, Isham, Hinson, J. B., Hinson, P. H., Huckabee, J. L., James, J. H., Hambrick, J., Irby, W. W., Jackson. I. A. L., Jackson. Enos, Johnson, N. D., Johnson, H. I., Johnson, D., Laviner, G. W., Laviner, D., Long, H. A., Lyles, J. R., Miller. J. M., Munnerlyn. C. T., Miller, Henry, McCollum, J. H., McIntosh. N. H., McIntosh. A., McQueen. J., McIrmis, S. J., McKenzie. A., Odum, Josiah, Odum, S. W., Odum, P. W., Parker, H., Prince. John T., Potter, Sol., Privatt, Evander, Pearson, R. C., Roscoe, John, Roscoe, G. W., Rowe, J. H., Roundtree. M., Skipper, J., Snead, Israel, Stanton, Noah, Stanton, J. A., Stanton, Milton, Thomas, C. J., Thomas, J. M., Thomas. R. D., Thornwell, C. A., Williams, David, Wright, D. G., Wright, F. E., Wright, G. W., Webster, H. D., Webster, T. M., Webster, H., Sutherland, T. A.

COMPANY "H."

CAPTAINS: Singletary, B. L., McIntire, Duncan. LIEUTENANTS: Myers, M. G., Brunson, J. B., Culpepper, George, McPherson, P. E., Gregg, Walter, Cooper, R. D. SERGEANTS: Gregg, Smith A., Gregg, McF., Moore, B., Gregg, John W., Mathews, Frank, Hughes, G. W., Godbold, D., Colston, G.. Stone, W. C. P., Armfield, A. L., McWhite, E.

PRIVATES: Altman, J., Bartley, J. G., Barthy, Charles, Barthy, E., Bellflower, H., Bragton, J. J., Balley, John, Broach, G. W., Cain, S. G., Cain, K. S., Cain, J. J., Cain, R. M., Cain, Church, Cain, J. Coon, Cain, J. H., Cox, J. T., Cooper, Brunson, Cooper, Witherspoon, Christmas, Jarrett, Davis. J. G., Deas, Simeon, Eagerton, H., Finklen, John, Flowers, W. D., Guy, J. H., Graham, J. M., Hampton, Thomas, Hampton, George, Hutchinson, George. Hutchinson, W. C., Hutchinson, Samuel, Hunter, D., Harrall, E.. Harrall, N. W., Harrall, W. T., Hyman, Benjamin, Hughes, R. S., Holland, J. S., Holland. George, Hodges, Barney, Kennedy, Alfred, Kennedy Andrew, Kersey, E.. Lewellyn, J. B., Leach, Julius, McKissick, A. G., McKissick, M.. Myers, William, McWhite, A. A., Myers, A. A., Pearce, R. H., Prosser, Michael, Rodgers, C. Rodgers. M., Roy, A., Stephenson, A., Stone, F. F.. Williams, H., Williams, Thomas. Williams, R. L., Williams, S. B.. Weatherford, W. S., Weatherford, Benjamin, Gregg, S. J., Gregg, S. E., Howard, Tillman, Powers, Jonas.

COMPANY "I."

CAPTAINS: Stackhouse, E. T., Harllee. A. T. LIEUTENANTS: Cook. H., B.. Ross, J. N., Rodgers, R. H.. Carmichael, W. D.. Stafford. D. C., Cusack, G. W. SERGEANTS: McClenagham. H. H., Harllee, Peter S., Pearce, J. F., Ayers. E. S., McDuffie. D. Q.. Harllee, R. A.. Gregg, A. Stuart, Jenkins. R. W. CORPORALS: Woodrow, J. E.. Huggins. Geo. W., Harelson, Joel, Sparkman, Levi, Cusack. S. C.. DeBarry. Edmond. Robbins. J. B.. Fenaghan, James. Rodgers. E.. Carmichael. Alex.. Brigman. A.. Butler. J. A.. Butler, Silas W.

PRIVATES: Bigham, W. H.. Bullock, Joel, Benton. Joel, Benton. G. W., Baker. John, Cox, G. B.. Cribb. Levi. Collin, E. H.. Crawford. H. W.. Cottingham. Stewart. Cottingham, Thomas F.. Cohen, David, Cohen. Isaac. Dove. J. W.. Dove, H. G.. Ellen, E. J.. Elvington, Dennis. Fryer, A. J.. Freeman, Joseph, Gaddy. R. M.. Gaddy. W. D.. Gregg, T. C., Harralson. M. J.. Harralson. E. P.. Herring. E. B.. Hinton. J. W., Jones. J.. James. Robert. Loyd, Henry, Llewellyn. B. F.. Mace. James C.. Meekins. P. B.. Morgan. W. C.. Miller. W. H.. Myers, John E.. Moody. John B.. Murphy. J. C.. McCall. L. A.. McRae, James, Owens, D. R.. Owens. S. S.. Sparkman, G. R.. Snipes. Michael. Smalley. Isaiah. Turner. John C.. Watson. John R.. Watson. Quinn, Woodrow. W. J., Whitner, J. N.. Woodberry. W. D.

COMPANY "K."

CAPTAINS: McLeod. D. M. D.. Manning. Frank. Rodgers. Ben. A. LIEUTENANTS: McQueen. S. F.. McLucas. John D.. Hearsey. Geo. R., Rodgers, W. T.. Peterkin. J. A.. Alfred, J. M. I.. McQuage, J. J., Smith, J. W.. Alford. M. N.. McCall. H. D.. Willis. Eli. Smith. W. D.. McRae, Frank. McLucas. Hugh. McKinnon. C.. Gunter. John. Calhoun. J. C, McLaurin. L. A.. Edens. J. A.. McCall. C.. Covington. J. T.. Alford. N. A.. Hargroves. David. Bruce. J. D.

PRIVATES: Allen. E.. Barrington. H.. Bruce, T. R.. Bundy. W. R.. Cottingham. C.. Covington. E. T.. Covingion. J. T.. Crowey. R. C. Crowley. William, Cape. Thomas. Curtin, ——. Clark, J., Drake, Ansel, Davis. C.. Driggers. R. S.. Dupre. Thomas J.. Edens, Joseph. Edens, T.

H., English, William, Emanuel, J. M., Easterling, Lewis, Easterling, David, Freeman, L. D., Freeman, Benjamin, Fletcher, W. R., Greggard, J. W., Graham, E., Groomes, F., Gunter, John, Hargrove, James, Hargrove, D. T., Harvel, Tristam, Hathcock, W., Hayes, J. J., Hayes, Robt. W., Hasken, John W., Huckabee, John, Huckabee, John W., Hodges, Thomas C., Ivey, H. W., Ivey, Levi, Jones, John C., Jones, Martin, Jacobs, Robert, Jacobs, J. Frost, Jackson, John C., John, Daniel C., Joy, W. H., Kirby, H., McCall, C., McCall, Alex., McCall, John T., McRae, A. D., McRae, John D., McRae, John C., McDaniel, J. R., McLucas, A. C., McLaurin, John F., McLeod, M., McPherson, Malcolm, McPhearson, Angus, Matherson, Hugh, Manship, John, Rodgers, C., Rodgers, F. A., Roscoe, Daniel, Smith, W. D., Stubbs, Lucius, Sparks, George, Satvis, A. S., Staunton, A. A., Webster, Wm. R., Williams, Lazarus, Woodley, Alex., Weatherly, A. W.

COMPANY "L."

CAPTAINS: Stackhouse, E. T., Carmichael, W. D. LIEUTENANTS: Higgins, W. D., Clark, G. W. SERGEANTS: Carmichael, D. D., Ayers, E. S., Rodgers, E., Manning, Eli, Murchison, Duncan. CORPORALS: Carmichael, Alex., Page, J. N., Roberts, J. H., Barfield, Thompson.

PRIVATES: Alford, Robert, H., Alford, Artemus, Alford, W. McD., Ammonds, J. D., Ayers, D. D., Barfield, R. Tally, Barfield, M., Barfield, H., Bethea, J. Frank, Bethea, H. P., Bridgeman, A. P., Byrd, H. G., Carmichael, A., Carmichael, D. C., Cottingham, C., Candy, S., Clark, R. Knox, Crawley, W. C., Coward, H., Cook, John, Harper, J. M., Herring, Samuel, Huckabee, John, Hicks, John C., Huggens, W. E., Huggens, D., Hunt, J. E., Herring, E. B., Irwin, I. R., Jackson, Robert, Jackson, M., Jackson, N., Lane, Samuel, Lane, E., McPhane, D., McRae, Colin, McRae, N., McRae, Roderick, McRae, Franklin, McGill, Colin, McLaurin, D., Morgan, W. C., McGill, David, Owens, S. I., Page, D. N., Page, D. P., Rogers, Thompson, Rogers, John F., Rogers, William D., Rogers, E. B., Rogers, L. B., Sarris, John, Turner, John C., Turberville, Calvin, Waters, John W., Watson, John R., Watson, Quinn, Watson, Lindsay.

COMPANY "M."

CAPTAINS: Howie, Thomas E., Coker, William C. LIEUTENANTS: Howie, James F., Rhodes, W. B., Galloway, W. L., Smoot, J., Galloway, George. SERGEANTS: Brearly, James W., Halliburton, Robert, Garland, W. H., Mixon, J. CORPORALS: Mozingo, W. H., Philips, J. C., McKenzie, W. W., Harrell, L. W., Mozingo, E., Howle, R. F.

PRIVATES: Alexander, H., Atkinson, Wiley, Byrd, D. M., Byrd, G. F., Bozeman, Peter, Beasley, Burton, Beasley, Ira, Bruce, C. A., Coker, C. W., Collins, E., Flowers, William, Galloway, Abram, Galloway, Nathan, Gainey, Isaiah, Gainey, Peter, Gulledge, Alex., Goodson, Robert, Halliburton, J. J., Harris, D. J., Hill, William T., Hill, William M., Hill, Nelson, Hudson, Jesse, Hall, David, Jenks, Mark, Jenks, Thomas, Jenks, G. W., Kirven, M. L., King, J. B., King, C. R., Lewis, Zach., McCown, J. M., McCown, J. J., McPherson, Robert, McKissick, ——. Moore William H., Mathews, William, Mozingo, William, Morrell, Peter, Northcoat, ——. Norwood, James, Peebles, W. D., Peebles, Robert, Privett, J. Hamilton, Privett, J. Henry, Privett, John H., Parrott, Pinkney, Parrott, Benj. M., Plummer, William, Rhodes, John J., Rhodes, John B., Skinner, Benj., Smith, J. S. M., Smith, Bryant, Suggs, A. T., Suggs, R. Rush, Thomas, J. M., Williams, David, Wright, Jonathan, Wright, Thomas L., Wright, J. B. C., Wilson, Peter, Wilson, Joseph, Woodman, A. Edward, Smith, Alex., Matuse, William, Colvin, John, Dixon, James, Bass, J. C.

ROLL OF FIFTEENTH SOUTH CAROLINA VOLUNTEER REGIMENT.

Field and Staff.

COLONELS: DeSaussure, W. D., Davis, J. B.
LIEUTENANT COLONELS: Gist, J. F., Lewie, S. F.
MAJOR: Gist, Wm. M.
ADJUTANT: Davis, J. M.
ASSISTANT QUARTERMASTER: Middleton, J. S.
ASSISTANT COMMISSARY SERGEANT: Kirkland, J. M.
SURGEON: James, J. A.
ASSISTANT SURGEON: Wallace, A., McCullum, H. B.
SERGEANT MAJOR: Giles, C. H.
QUARTERMASTER SERGEANT: Price, J. R.
ORDNANCE SERGEANT: Boyd, R. W.
HOSPITAL STEWARD: Maurice, R. F.

COMPANY "A."

CAPTAIN: Radcliffe, Thos. W. LIEUTENANTS: Beard, Henry, Brown, Pressley, Shields, Wm. SERGEANTS: Black, J. E., Campbell, J. S., Cathcart, J. N., O'Neale, Richard, Beard, T. A., Zealy, R. F. CORPORALS: Pollock, T. M., Long, S. S., Hutchison, J. H., Bruns, J. Henry.

PRIVATES: Anderson, W. C., Assman, W. J., Asbury, W. E., Anderson, Richard, Brown, Ira B., Baum, M. H., Branham, R. T., Beckwith, Wm. H., Boscheen, Charley, Blankenstine, Jacob, Bedell, Allen, Bynum, Ben, Beckwith, L. R., Brown, Fred. J., Beck, Robt. C., Brown, J. H., Burrows, DeS., Beckham, W. M., Bass, Toland, Crawford, D. H., Capers, Geo. R., Clarkson, E. McC., Crawford, Daniel, Davis, John, Dougal, C. H., Dixon, S. W., Dreisden, Julius, DeSaussure, W. D., Ehelers, Geo., Emlyn, H. N., Edwards, J. G., Frazee, P. F., Fritz, J. A., Gibson, F. A., Glbenwrath, J. F., Grieshaber, Fritze, Gardener, C. H., Glaze, Wm., Green, M. B., Gandy, J. H., Graham, Wm., Geiger, J. G., Gunther, Jno., Gaither, J. W., Goodwin, G. W., Howel, D. B., Henrick, Lewis, Hardie, J. W., Howell, O. F., Johnson, C. P., Johnson, J. R., Isaacs, J. H., James, Joeseph, Kaigler, J. A., Killian, Jno. H., Keenan, Roland A., Levin, G. W., Ledingham, W. J., Lesher, Wm., Lumsden, J. L., McCammon, G., McCammon, ——, Morgan, Isaac C., McGorvan, Jno., McKenzie, Frank L., McCoy, John M., Milling, James, Orchard, Henry Pearson, A. W., Price, J. R., Puryear, R. T., Poppe, Julius, Parker, Wm. E., Perry, G. H., Pollock, B. C., Peixotto, S. C., Pope, F. M., Radcliffe, C. C., Reynolds, Jno. H., Roberts, W. H., Row, Louis, Rawley, Jno., Reed, R. C., Stark, A., Smith, J. C., Smith, Warren, Scott, John M., Stork, A., Stork, J. J., Stork, W. H., Schnider, Henry, Scott, W. H., Schultze, George, Stewart, Edmond, Starling, T. J., Toumey, Tim. J., Templeton, I. G., Templeton, Wm. A., Templeton, W. L., Townsend, J. V., Veal, J. M., Wells, Jacob H., Walker, T. P., Walsh, P. H., Wade, T. H., Wade, Geo. McD., Wallace, A., Yates, Joseph.

COMPANY "B."

CAPTAINS: Gist, Wm. H., Sheldon, S. H. LIEUTENANTS: Rogers, J. Rice, Barnett, Wm. R., Huckabee, ——, McWhirter, ——, Smith, W. M., Yarborough, P. P. SERGEANTS: Giles, C. H., West, John I., Haselwood, Hosea, Bailey, W. P. H., Bobo, Barham, Williams, J. H. CORPORALS: Hughes, J. A., Lowe, M. V., Lancaster, W. A., Young, I. H., Williams, Gordon.

PRIVATES: Abernathy, John, Anderson, Thomas, Barrett, T. Lyles, Barrett, Alonzo, Barnett, W. Franklin, Bethany, Jesse, Briggs, B. Franklin, Bogan, Isaac C., Bogan, P. P., Boram, W. H., Bobo, Jason, Canaday,

C., Canaday, David, Sr., Canaday, David, Jr., Clefton, Wesley, Dillard, Wm., Eubanks, Shelton, Eubanks, Charner, Foster, W. A., Foster, I. F., Gee, P. M., Gossett, T. G., Goodlin, W. P., Gossett, Henry, Gist, D. C., Grass, J. C., Hembree, Ervin, Hollingsworth, Benj., Huckabee, W. P., Huckabee, James M., Huckabee, Philip, Huff, John, Huff, W. M., Haselwood, A., Haselwood, Thomas, Huges, Thomas H., Huges, E., Holcomb, Wallace, Jennings, Elias, Kelly, I. H., Lamb, Marion, Lamb, Robert, Lamb, John, Lamb, David, Lamb, Elijah, Lancaster. F. M., Lancaster, J. B., Lawson, Lemuel, Lawson, Munro, Lawson, J. H., Lawson, Elijah, Lawson, Charles, Lawson, Franklin, Lawson, Levi, Myers, G. W., Powell, James W., Prickett, H. P., Pool. Wm. M., Prince, Spencer, Prince, Franklin, Ray, Robt. F., Ray, Jeremiah, Ray, B. C., Rains, Wm., Rook, James, Rook, Franklin, Robinson, G. M., Sparks, William, Starns, W. A., Stone, H. C., Smith, Nimrod, Smith, Wm., Sumner, I. M., Sumner, F. S., Sumner, John, Sumner, Mattison, Templeton, Jno. A., Waldrip, W. M., West, B. E., West, W. McD., West, Jno. P., West, Isaac T., West, C. P., West. E. I., West, W. C., Whitton, John, Willard, Benj., Willard, William, Wilbanks, F., Wilbanks, T., Whitmore, J. F., Whitmore, E. H., Whitmore, Thomas, Whitehead, James, Whitehead, Stephen, Yarborough, Hiram, Young, George, Young, Thomas, Young, Francis W.

COMPANY "C."

CAPTAINS: Lewie, F. S., Lewic, J. H., Griffith, D. J. LIEUTENANTS: Swygert, Y., Lewie, S. T., Fulmer. W. W., Spence, S., Jumper, J. B., Shealey, Lewis. SERGEANTS: Kyzer, S. W., Lewie, E. W., Derrick, H. F., Sanders, W. F., Lammack, J. S., Leaphart. F. E., Jumper, J. W., Butler, J. W., Derrick, D. S., Anderson, F. S., Hare, J. W., Heister, M. W. C., Price, H. L. CORPORALS: Sease, D. T., Earhart, C. B. W., Black, J. W., Oswalt, F. Wade, Huer, W. B.

PRIVATES: Adams, I. P., Alewine, Philip, Alewine, W. W., Alewine, W. H., Alewine, J. L., Addy, M. W., Addy, S. L., Addy, E. I., Addy, J. W., Amick, F. R., Amick, H., Anderson, E., Anderson, J., Black, S. L., Blum, John, Busby, Tillman, Caughman, D. S., Craps, J. W., Craps, H. H., Crout, John, Crout, Ephraim, Crim, R. F., Derrick, A. E., Derrick, W. T., Derrick, Oliver, Fridell, J. M., Griffith, Allen, Hyler, N. W., Hare, D. T., Hare, L. P., Hallman, E., Hallman, W. B., Hartly, J. L., Hendrix, J. P., Hendrix, G. W., Hite, D. W., Hite, Noah W., Holeman, D. P., Jumper, D. A., Jumper, W. T., Jumper, H. F., Kelly, G. J., Kelly, Jasper, King, Luke, Hyzer, Henry L., Hyzer, J. T., Hyzer, J. S., Laurinack, Samuel, Laurinack, J. J., Laurinack, Noah, Laurinack, Paul, Long, L. W., Laurinack, E., Long, W. A., Long, J. W., Long, W. W., Long, Jacob, Long, I. A. Mettze, J. E., Nichols, Levi. Nichols, L. E., Nichols, Wesley, Oswold, Wilson, Oswold, James, Oswold, L. B., Oxner, N., Price, R. E., Price, Danl., Price, Jacob, Price, G. W., Sr., Price, D. W., Price, R. I., Plymale, W. W., Rysinger, David, Rysinger, Noah, Rysinger, Geo. D., Rysinger, Wesley, Rawl, L., Rawl, Christian, Rawl, O. D., Rawl, Franklin, Sanford, Wade, Sanford, S., Salther, H., Snelgrove, M., Lybrand, Wm., Sease, M. T., Shull, John, Seay, Danl., Shirey, I. P., Snyder, John, Shealy, Albert, Shealy, E. H., Shealy, Littleton, Shealy, Wiley, Shealy, Henry, Shealy, A., Shealy, P. W., Smith, Henry A., Swygert, E., Taylor, Ruben, Taylor, I. L., Taylor, David, Vansant. Addison, Warren, T. I.

COMPANY "D."

CAPTAIN: Warren, Thomas J. LIEUTENANTS: Davis, James M., Lyles, James V., Schrock, I. A. SERGEANTS: Burns, O. B., Somers, Adolphus, Huckabee, J. J., Davis, J. J., Fisher, C. A. CORPORALS:

Springer, Rudolph, Stewman, P. A. H., Wolf, Eugene, Young, Jno. W., Crosby, Geo.

PRIVATES: Ammons, H., Brannon, John, Brannon, Wm., Sr., Brannon, Wm., Jr., Brannon, David, Bradley, John, Brown, Wm., Corbitt, J. C., Corbitt, H. F., Copell. W. H., Copell. J. B., Copell, S. B., Creighton, E. E., Creighton, H. L. Collier, F. J., Evins, John, Evain, Samuel, Fulghum, James, Falkuberry, John, Ford, E. J., Fletcher, David G., Gardner, Lewis, Gardner, James L., Graham, Wm., Griffin, Stephen, Gaymon. John B., Hays, Joseph, Hays, E., Hayes, James, Harrall, Jim, Harrall, John, Hornsby, Joseph, Hornsby, Samuel, Hornsby, S. W., Hough, Hollis, Hinson, John, Sr., Hinson, John, Jr., Hunter, A. A., Hall, Russell J., Johnson, Ben F., Johnson, W. B., Jackson, Douglas, Jordan, W. H., Jordan, D., Kirkley, D. C., Kemp. Tira. Kemp, Warren, Kelly, B. P., Kirby, A., Kirby, J. W., Munn, A. J., McInnis, N. M., Mattox, James, Mattox, Isaac S., Mattox. Sam., Mattox, Geo. W., McLeod, N. A., Moneyham, John, Marsh, Gates, Marsh, James, Marsh, John, McCullum. H. B., Minton, C., Minton, Jno. B., McGuire, Henry, Outlaw, Jno. E., Parker, Wm. E., Parker, Redding, Parker, R. B., Richburg, J. J., Ray, James, Scott, Hasting, Scott, Manning, Shedd, Jesse P., Smith, J. W., Spradley, W. J., Spradley, John, Shaylor, T. S., Shaylor, C. H., Shivey, Jos., Turner, Jno. F., Hassein, A. Von, Wilson, Joel, Wilson, Henry, Wilson, Paul H., Williams, A. W., Williams, B Frank, Watson, W. W., Warren, Wm., Watts, C., Watts, Jno., Workman, W. H. R., Waddell, N. T., Ward, John, Watts, Frank, Young, Jno. W., Yates, Saml., Yates, Willis.

COMPANY "E."

CAPTAINS: Davis, J. B., Dawkins, W. J., Kirkland, W. W. LIEUTENANTS: Smart, Thomas H., Martin, Joseph B., Pearson, J. W., Hoy, J. B., Blair, C. B. SERGEANTS: Pettigrew, J. H., Blair, W. McD., Robinson, K. Y. CORPORALS: Gladney, J. D., Bridges, W. A., Gladney, Samuel.

PRIVATES: Aiken, W., Aiken, D. M., Bagley, J. S., Bagley, Lee, Barker, W. J., Barker, S. C., Butner, J. J., Barrimeau, J. J., Bridges, F. C., Packer, James, Cloxton, Wm., Cotton, W. J., Cotton, Joe, Crossland, Wm., Crossland, A. T., Camack, Samuel, Camack, A. F., Coleman, Robt., Coleman, H. T., Crumpton, W. C., Crumpton, T. H., Crumpton, W. S., Clarke, J. S., Crawford, Rob., Carlisle, Jno., Dickerson, W. P., Davis, J. P., Davis, Ross, Evans, J. W., Fenley, W. P., Fenley, D. D., Gladney, Amos, Gladney, John, Gladney, J. F., Gladden, W. A., Gibson, T. D., Greer, C. D., Hamilton, D. G., Hodge, J. M., Hodge, R. B., Hodge, A. F., Hodge, J. C., Hutchinson, J. B., Hutchinson, J. P., Hunt, C. M., John, J. A., John, James, Kirkland, W. F., Kirkland, L. M., Lyles, L. R., Lyles, W. W., Lyles, A. C., Long, W. W., Long, J. J., Ligon, T. N., Morris, T. S., Martin, R. L., Murphy, W. E., Murphy, S. A., Murphy, E. E., Murphy, Jno. R., Moorehead, W. J., McCormack, Hugh, McConnell, W. H., McClure, John, McDowell, Alex., McCrorey, James, Neil, J. H., Pettigrew, W. T., Pettigrew, A. R., Pettigrew, D. H., Pettigrew, G. B., Poteet, Lafayette, Price, Fletcher, Price, J. W., Parrott, R. L., Pearson, G. P., Powell, R. M., Rabb, J. W., Richardson, J. D., Sprinkler, Hiram, Smith, D. A., Smith, J. W., Smith, W. E., Seymore, Jno., Tidewell, B. N., Veronee, C. B., Varnadoe, Henry, Wylie, J. T., Wylie, T. C., Wylie, Frank, Wylie, James, Walker, Danl., Walker, Alex., Williams, G. W., Yarborough, T. J., Yarborough, W. T., Yarborough, I. T.

COMPANY "F."

CAPTAINS: Boyd, C. W., Jefferies, Jno R. LIEUTENANTS: Norris, James, Walker, S. S., Steen, Geo., Jefferies, J. D., Hart, W. D., Wood, Moses. SERGEANTS: Rowland, Jas. A., Boyd, R. W., Kendricks, M. S., Lipscomb, Smith, Shippey, Dexter, Wilkins, W. D., Jones, B. F., McKown, G. W. CORPORALS: Spears, G. S., Morgan, George, Balue,

Thomas, Mays, Jno., Littlejohn, I. H., Reavs, Z., Vinson, Richard, Jones, N. C.

PRIVATES: Alston, M. K., Bailey, T. J., Berbage, D. B., Blanton, Ambrose, Blanton, D. D., Brown, Wm., Burgess, Thomas, Betenbough, Joseph, Betenbough, Jno., Blanton, N. A., Burgess, L. I., Cellars, Wm., Clary, Herod, Clary, G. B., Clary, Singleton, Clary, Wm., Carter, E. L., Dukes, I. C., Edge, Jno., Fowler, B. F., Fowler, Jno., Fowler, R. M., Fowler, Wm., Fowler, Richard, Fowler, W., Farr, F. M., Goudlock, T. D., Griffin, Thomas, Goforth, W. M., Hames, L. A., Horn, Asbury, Horn, Elias, Hughey, J. R., Horn, Wash., James, Wash., Jefferies, Hamlet, Jones, James, Jeter, S. A., Jones, S., Kirby, Wm. D., Knox, James, Kendrick, T. J., Knox, Morgan, Knox, Thomas, Lee, W. A., Leonard, Wm., Littlejohn, C. T., Littlejohn, Henry, Littlejohn, M. R., Lockhart, J. C., Lockhart, J. N., Lenoad, J. M., Lockhart, R. M., Maberry, Saml., McCafferty, G. A., Macornsor, D. R., Mayes, L. C., McKown, F. M., Millwood, J. C., Millwood, J. H., Millwood, Morgan, Moorhead, J. T., Moorhead, W. G., Mosely, D. P., Moseley, W. D., Murphy, M., Murphy, S. M., Peeler, J. R., Page, J. L., Page, R., Peeler, A. J., Peeler, D. M., Perkinson, S., Phillips, S. G., Puckett, I. H., Pearson, I. A., Phillips, G. M., Phillips, J. T., Phillips, T. J., Rodgers, W. N., Scott, H. W., Scott, T. E., Scates, L., Spencer, D. N., Sprouse, W., Stroup, T. H., Sartor, T., Shippey, M., Spencer, J., Sanders, A. J., Thompson, M. D., Wakefield, L., Ward, I. L., Ward, I. N., Wilkins, R. S., Wilkins, T. T., Ward, W.

COMPANY "G."

CAPTAINS: Chandler, J. B., McCutcheon, J. LIEUTENANTS: Haselden, W. M., Barron, B. P., Timmons, F. M., Cooper, F. E. SERGEANTS: Fulton, T. M., Wilson, W. J., Eaddy, T., McClary, J., Gamble, H. D., Cox, W. G., Lenerieux, F. M. CORPORALS: Brown, J. J., Johnson, M. M., Burrows, J. T., Nesmith, J.

PRIVATES: Autman, J. A., Altman, I. C., Abrams, I. B., Abrams, W., Ard, R., Ard, J., Ard, F., Avant, O. R., Barrimeau, B. T. L., Barrimeau, J. J., Baxley, O., Bratcher, A., Brown, J., Brown, A. W., Brown, D. L., Bowden, H., Buckles, H., Buckles, L., Buckles, J., Burns, J., Burrows, I. T., Burrow, W. S., Carter, E. W., Carter, A. W., Carter, A. B., Carter, J. D., Carter, T., Colver, J., Cox, L., Cox, F., Cox, W. I., Cox, J. R., Cox, J. T., Cox, I. G., Cockfield, J. C., Christman, G. W., Cribb, C., Cribb, D. W., Donahoe, A. W., Eaddy, I. F., Eaddy, W. S., Eaddy, G. J., Eaddy, D., Ferrel, F., Flagler, A. P., Gaskin, J. J., Gaskin, E. V., Gaskin, J. C., Gaskin, C. A., Gaskin, A. M., Gist, G. G., Gordon, H., Graham, J. McC., Graham, W. L., Gurganus, J. E., Hanna, G. W., Hanna, R., Hanna, J. F., Haselden, S. B., Haselden, A. J., Haselden, J., Haselden, J. R., Haselden, W. B., Haselden, J., Hudson, J., Hughes, ——, James, J. A., June, T. G., June, A., Johnson, E. H., Kinder, H. H., Lambert, B. F., McDonald, ——, McAlister, W., Marsh, J., Matthews, J. J., Matthews, W. W., Matthews, J., Maurice, R. F., McConnell, W. S., McDaniel, J., McLellan, A. K., Miller, J., Owens, J. A., Perkins, W. G., Paston, H. A., Ponney, J. A., Ponney, M., Scott, A. W., Scott, J. C., Scott, G. C., Spring, G. W., Spivey, H. E., Stone, P. T., Stone, T. B., Tanner, T. A., Tanner, J., Thompson, S. B., Thompson, J., Tomas, J., Tilton, H., Venters, L., Venters, J., Whitehead, N. M., Whitehead, J.

COMPANY "H."

CAPTAINS: Sims, W. H., Farr, W. P., Briggs, W. R., Farr, F. M. LIEUTENANTS: Barley, J. L., Porter, J., Parr, W., Howell, M. SERGEANTS: Savage, J., Greer, F., Barley, J., Smith, H. CORPORALSS Fair, G., Coleman, B. C., Morgan, D. V.

PRIVATES: Adams, A. R., Adams, B., Adis, J., Adis, Wm., Adis, R., Alverson, W. G., Bentley, John, Bentley, James, Burgess, F., Burgess, R., Bevell, W., Bevell, W. H. H., Bends, L., Barnes, M., Conner, W. E.,

Conner, W. E., Cadd, F. R., Cadd, W. F., Chapman, J., Davis, J., Davis, P. A., Dabbs, W., Dabbs, J., Edge, J., Farr, D., Farr, D. A. T., Farr, D., Farr, N., Fausett, K., Fowler, J. M., Fowler, T., Fowler, G., Fowler, M., Garner, G. W., Garner, W., Garner, C., Garner, L., Garner, J., Gault, H. C., Gregery, A., Gregery, F., Griffin, W., Griffin, D., Hawkins, W., Howell, W., Howell, S. J., Hames, E., Hames, J., Haney, J., Haney, F., Humphries, A., Inman, D., Ivey, Wm., Ivey, Wiley, Ivey, R., Milwood, Frank, Milwood, E. V., Milwood, James, Milwood, Wm., Mitchell, A., McKinney, G., Motte, Jno., Mott, Jeff., Nance, N., Palmer, J., Palmer, E., Parr, R. T., Parr, D., Parr, Richard, Savage, A., Sharp, C., Simpson, C., Smith, M., Smith, W., Smith, Jno., Stears, A. D., Stears, D., Sprouse, L., Sprouse, Jno., Sprouse, A., Tracy, J., Vaughn, K., Vaughn, A. L., Vinson, J. W., Vaudeford, H., Vaudeford, W. M., Vaudeford, J. W., Wishard, J., Wix, James, Wix, Joel, Worthy, C., Worthy, Richard, Leverett, J.

COMPANY "L."

CAPTAINS: Koon, J. H., Derrick, J. A. LIEUTENANTS: Frick, R. W., Derrick, F. W., Lake, J. T., Fulmer, H., Monts, F. W., Davis, R., Wessinger, H. J., Lybrand, J. N., Keisler, Wade, Shealy, W. C. SERGEANTS: Wiggers, H. J., Frick, A. J., Lindler, S. P., Eargle, J. A., Long, P. D., Derrick, J. F., Frick, S. J., Frick, L. A., Wessinger, W. F., Amick, H. L. CORPORALS: Fulmer, C. N. G., Wessinger, N. J., Ballentine, C., Bowers, A. J.

PRIVATES: Amick, J. Wesley, Amick, Joseph W., Amick, James J., Amick, S. D. W., Amick, E. L., Amick, V. E., Amick, G. H., Amick, D. I., Amick, L. J., Amick, J. I., Bickley, J. H., Bickley, D. W., Bickley, J. A., Bickley, J. I., Busby, W. T., Boland, S. B., Ballentine, W. P., Ballentine, J. W., Coogler, D., Crout, J., DeHart, D., DeHart, J., Derrick, D. I., Derrick, F., Derrick, J. A., Dreher, G. L., Epting, D. W., Eargle, G. E., Feagle, George, Fulmer, L. J., Fulmer, W. P., Fulmer, D. J., Frick, I. N., Griffith, A., Ham. D., Hodge, A., Holman, W. W., Jacobs, J. E., Keisler, J. J., Koon, G. F., Koon, J. B., Koon, H. M., Koon, S. D., Koon, S. W., Koon, W. F., Koon, J. F., Koon, John F., Koon, Walter W., Koon, Hamilton, Koon, J. D., Koon, J. F., Koon, H. W., Lindler, S. G., Lindler, Jacob, Lindler, John, Long, G. J., Long, J. J., Long, J. W., Long, Jno. W., Lybrand, J., Monts, G. M., Mayer, A. G., Metz, O. F., Perkins, W. S., Risk, W. I., Risk, J. A., Sutton, J., Shealy, N. F., Shealy, M., Shealy, G. M., Shealy, G. W., Shealy, S., Shealy, J., Shealy, W. W., Smith, G. W., Talbert, J. W., Turner, C. B., Wiley, E., Wheeler, J. W., Wheeler, L. G., Wessinger, H. J., Wessinger, J. A., Wyse, W. M., Wiggers, A., Wiggers, J. D.

COMPANY "K."

CAPTAIN: Bird, H. J. LIEUTENANTS: Rodgers, W. M., White, A., Taggert, W. H., Smith, W. A., McCaslan, W. M., Henderson, O. SERGEANTS: Dean, R. A., Smith, S. B., Jennings, J. C., Freeland, S. E., McBride, S. S., McBride, J. B., Calvin, A. P. CORPORALS: Deason, A., Ballard, F. S., McCaine, J. K., Hendrix, M. F., Berdeshaw, W. C., Dorn, J. J., Bird, M., Attaway, S.

PRIVATES: Adams, J. Q., Bearden, W., Bangham, W. W., Bell, E. B., Bouchillon, H. M., Bouchillon, J. S., Bull, W. W., Bussey, T. J., Bird, D., Bird, W., Brown, R., Brown, W. M., Brown, E., Brown, M., Brown, J., Bussey, D., Bodie, J. R., Carr, N., Caldwell, J. W., Corley, J. A., Corley, C., Collins, J. F., Crawford, J. R., Cothran, J. M., Crestian, J. T., Covin, O. W., Cook, S., Curry, W. L., Dean, F., Devore, S., Devore, J. S., Devore, J. W., Doollittle, J. E., Doollittle, S., Ennis, J. O., Ennis, G. W., Ennis, T. W., Elam, J., Evans, J., Freeland, J. P., Frith, T., Gardner, W. T., Gardner, A. H., Glansier, F., Griffin, E., Hamilton, W. M.,

Harrison, H. C., Harrison, J., Hasteing, J., Harris, A., Henderson, C.,
Henderson, J. E., Hendrix, H. H., Hughes, J. S., Hill, T., Horn, S.,
Hannon, W., Holsomback, H. H., Hill, J., Hemphill, ——, Hardy, J.,
Holloway, W. J., Ivy, T., Irvin, J., Johnson, E. C., Jeno, M., Jennings,
C., King, W. M., King, T., King, S., Lawton, F. E., Lawton, J. W.,
Lawton, A., Lawton, L., Ludwick, W. C., Lukewire, H., Mathis, T. E.,
Mayson, R. C., Mayson, P. A., Mayson, J., Mayson, J. C., Martin, H.
D., McCain, W. J., Miner, J., Miner, W., Merriweather, R., McKinney,
J., McKelvin, G. T., Martin, A. M., McCannon, W. R., Moore, J. D.,
Medlock, A., Newby, G. W., Purdy, J. H., Price, W. C.; Price, R.,
Price, H., Rich, J. S., Robertson, J. B., Robertson, H., Rearden, L.
D., Rodgers, P. A., Rodgers, P., Sperry, E. C., Shadrack, T. N., Shan-
non, W. N., Scott, W. D., Shover, W., Steadman, J., Sheppard, L.,
Towles, E., Tompkins. S., Tompkins. W., Timmerman, F., Taggart, P.,
Vaughn, J., Vaughn, D., Weeks, C., Whitton, C., Walker, B. C., Walker,
C., Whatley, E., Weeks, S., Weems, J. T., New, S., Smith, W. H., Rob-
ertson, J. S., Davis, W. M., Reynolds, J. M., Crawford, J. W., Vaughn,
W.

ROLL OF THIRD BATTALION (JAMES).

Field and Staff.

LIEUTENANT COLONEL: James, G. S.
MAJOR: Rice, W. G.
COMMISSARY: Senn, R. D.
ADJUTANT: Harris, W. C.
QUARTERMASTER: James, B. S.
SERGEANT MAJOR: Ligon, G. A.
QUARTERMASTER SERGEANT: Ligon, R. B.

COMPANY "A."

CAPTAINS: Rice, W. G., Townsend, J. M. LIEUTENANTS: Anderson,
J. W., Anderson, D. W., Anderson, Jno. W., Murchison, B. K., King, A.
A. SERGEANTS: Craig, J. D., Wilcutt, B. F., Moore, G. W., Anderson,
J. J., Calhoun, J. W., Hunter, W. S., Nickols, R. J., Anderson, J. S.
CORPORALS: Davenport, L. P., Elmore, L., Teague, L.
PRIVATES: Anderson, P. K., Anderson, A. W., Anderson, A. T., An--
derson, J. B., Burns, W., Busby. J. S., Calhoun. J., Calhoun. J. W.,
Chaney, T., Chaney, J. R., Craddock, J. R., Cannon, B., Clardy, B. S.,
Connor, L. D., Davis, J., Davis, W. D., Davis, A., Davis, T., Davis, B.
F., Dodson, W., Elmore, Massalome, Elmore, J., Elmore, Maston, El-
more, G., Fooshe. J. A., Fooshe. J. D., Foose. J. C., Finley, J. H., God-
dard, J. E., Goddard, W. E., Graves. W., Golding. J. J., Griffin, W. H.,
Griffin, E. W., Hines, G. W., Hill, M. S., Hill. B. T., Hill, N., Hodges,
M., Knight, J., King. R., King, J. J., Lomax, W., Lipford, A., McGee, L.
H., Martin, L., McPherson, J. M., Martin, L., Nelson. J. M., Nelson, E.,
Nelson, W. A., Norman, J., Nichols, J. H., Nichols, J., Owens, B. L.,
Owens, J. T., Owens. E. N., Pinson. E. M., Pinsom. C. F., Puckett, W.
H., Puckett, S. D., Puckett, K. C., Redden, Hazel, Rampv, J. M., Red-
den, Harry, Saxon, P. A., Shirly, D. A., Shirley, Tully, Sims. Thadeus,
Sims, S. C., Taylor, J., Taylor, Jno., Taylor, G., Watts, W. D.

COMPANY "B."

CAPTAINS: Williams, J. G., Ligon, R. B., Watson, O. A., Wells. W. A.,
Pitts, W. S. LIEUTENANTS: Roberts, J. C., Fuller, A. A., Ligon. J. W.,
Miller, C. M., Dunlap, R. S. SERGEANTS: Davis, J. W., Watson, J. E.,
Starnes, R. C., Waldrop. R. G., Nance, W. G., Bryson, H., Wright. W.
W., Dunlap, R. S., Griffin, R. S., Grant, G. W. CORPORALS: Milam, A.

R., Cox, M., Sims, L. S., Fuller, J. C., Walker, F. M., Jones, J. A.,
Nance, R. G., Fuller, W. B.
PRIVATES: Austin, I. G., Austin, I. S., Boazman, W. M., Boazman, B.
S., Brown, T. S., Bailey, J., Butler, R. P., Boozer, J. J., Butler, W. L.,
Brown, H. R., Benjamin, S. R., Bailey, M., Crawford, J. W., Coleman,
T. T., Coleman, O. A., Calhoun, T. H., Cook, W. I., Cole, W. M., Dan-
iel, T. D., Duncan, J. G., Dalrymple, J. H., Dendy, E. G., East, O. D.,
Fuller, A. S., Fuller, P. A., Fuller, E. P., Fuller, J., Fuller, E., Finley, S.
J., Goodman, B., Goodman, B. B., Griffin, E., Harvey, J. H., Hitt, H. L.,
Hitt, P., Hitt, Robt., Hazel, G., Hazel, J., Hollingsworth, R. S., Hollings-
worth, A., Hughes, J. H., Hand, W., Hacot, B. C., Irby, W. L., Kissick,
F., Ligon, J. S., Ligon, G., Ligon, J., Lindsey, D. W., Lowe, I. G., Lake,
R. S., Mates, W. M., Miller, W. P., Madden, W. C., Myres, Z. E.,
Milam, H. W., Milam, J. A., Milam, W., Nelson, M. L., Nelson, J. F.,
Nelson, A., Nelson, J. M., Nelson, W., Nance, F. W. N., O'Neal, J.,
Pitts, G. W., Pitts, F., Reed, J. Y., Reed, B., Roberts, J., Richardson,
W., Smith, M., Snow, A. J., Thompson, W., Williams, R. E., Winne-
brenner, G., Wells, W. J., Wheeler, M. A., Watts, E. C., Watts, J. G.,
Waldrop, W. E.

COMPANY "C."

CAPTAINS: Shumate, J. J., Hudgens, W. L., Irby, G. M. LIEUTEN-
ANTS: Woods, T. R. L., Henderson, M. W., Cooper, J. N., Fuller, H. Y.,
Wadkins, H. H., Baldwin, S. B., Fuller, A. C. SERGEANTS: Boyd, W.
L., Hudgens, A. W., Donney, J., Bolt, W., Cooper, T. P. CORPORALS:
Culbertson, Y. J., Anderson, D. S., Stone, W. W.
PRIVATES: Abercrombie, J. C., Andrews, W. W., Avery, S. K., Avery,
J., Adams, J. P., Boyd, J. Y., Burton, J. J., Bolt, S., Bolt, Saml., Bolt,
Jno., Bolt, James, Bolt, Franklin, Brown, G. M., Brooks, J. P., Brooks,
N. P., Baldwin, J. E., Baldwin, D. H., Baldwin, V., Burgess, E. R.,
Blackwell, J. H., Box, W. I., Cooper, H. H., Cooper, J. Y., Cooper, J.
A., Cooper, D. M., Culbertson, Y. S., Culbertson, J. B., Culbertson, M.
M., Culbertson, W. P., Culbertson, T. H., Culbertson, W. S., Culbert-
son, J. R., Culbertson, J. M., Culbertson, J. H., Cheshire, L. H., Che-
shire, C., Cannon, W. N., Cannon, R., Duvall, J. H., Dugnall, W.,
Elledge, J. P., Fuller, I. M., Godfrey, I., Hudgens, R., Hudgens, C.,
Hellams, C. C., Henderson, L., Hill, W. T., Johnson, M., Johnson, B.
F., Jenkins, J. A., Jenkins, R., Jones, B. F., Jones, J. B., Knight, W.
D., Lindley, H., Lindsey, T., Lindley, W., Mitchell, M., Murff, M.,
Micham, A., Moore, L., Moore, M., Moore, Jackson, Moore, Frank,
Moats, W. C., Morgan, W., Manley, B. T., Manley, P. J., Moats,
T. A., McClellan, J. A., Malvey, P. W., Medlock, A., Nash, W. M.,
Nelson, W. Y., Nelson, J. W., Nelson, F., Pitts, J. W., Pitts, J. S.,
Puckitt, G. W., Puckitt, W. A., Robertson, J., Robertson, H. D., Ryley,
J., Ross, A., Ross, T., Saxton, F., Shumate, R. Y., Shumate, L. J., Shu-
mate, H., Sullivan, H., Stevens, J. P., Terry, B. F., Taylor, H. P., Tay-
lor, B., Vaughn, B., Watkins, T. J., Watkins, L., Walker, J. A.

COMPANY "D."

CAPTAIN: Gunnels, G. M. LIEUTENANTS: James, B. S., Kirk, C. E.,
Allison, R. W. SERGEANTS: Harris, J., Potter, B. L., Dial, D. T., Arm-
strong, D. CORPORALS: Shell, J. H., Allison, J., Ramage, F., Simmons,
W.
PRIVATES: Adams, J., Adams, Robert, Armstrong, S., Atwood, M.,
Abrams, G. W., Babb, William, Babb, Doc, Babb, J., Belle, L. G., Bar-
ger, H. M., Boyd, E., Boyd, D. W., Bailey, A. P., Brownley, J. R., Bur-
dette, G. W., Bishop, W., Bishop, J. W., Bailey, M. S., Bishop, J. C.,
Blalock, R., Chappell, W., Chambers, J. B., Cunningham, M. C., Cun-
ningham, R. A., Curry, I., Cason, M. J., Crisp, A., Duncan, R., Epps,

W., Eutrican, W. M., Evans, W. R., Garlington, C., Gunnels, W., Graham, A., Hollingsworth, J. I., Hollingsworth, A. C., Hellams, W., Hellams, Y., Harmond, F. F., Harris, S., Hatton, T. J., Hollingsworth, W., Joyce, J. C., Jones E. P., Jones, H. C., Johnson, Dr. J. P., Kelly, F., Knight, D., Langston, Henry, Loyd, T., Madden, D. C., Martin, J., Mason, A., May, J. P., Metts, M. B., McCawley, Martin, McCawley, James, McKnight, W. D., Milam, W. S., Munroe, W., Neal, A. T., Owens, J. H., Owens, L., Parks, A. R., Peas, Jno., Potter, Moses, Price, James, Ray, J. J., Rook, S., Rowland, A., Richardson, Jno., Shell, E. C., Shockley, J., Shockley, R., Simmonds, J., Starks, D., Spears, R. S., Spears, G. T., Speake, J. T., Speake, J. L., Stoddard, W., Taylor, A. S., Thomas, J. H., Tribble, F. E., Wesson, Thomas, West, S., Whitton, D. M., Winn, C., Wolff, W. Y., Harris, W. C.

COMPANY "E."

CAPTAINS: Hunter, Melnott, Fowler, W. H., Ware, H., Burnside, Allen. LIEUTENANTS: Riddle, A. J., Cooper, E., Cox, M. C., Henry, B. L., Moore, P. SERGEANTS: Fowler, W. D., Farburn, N., Mills, J. A., Armstrong, D., Owens, M. CORPORALS: Riddle, M., Ball, S. P.

PRIVATES: Balle, L. G., Bramlett, C., Bramlett, H., Bramlett, J., Bramlett, R., Brown, J., Bryant, T. T., Bryant, W., Burdett, J., Burns, J., Burns, R., Cheek, J., Cook, W. C., Cox, S., Culbertson, B., Culbertson, M., Farrow, T., Fleming, P., Fowler, J. R., Frank, J., Fowler, W., Garner, J., Garrett, P., Garrett, W. A., Gillian, W., Gideons, J. L., Guinn, M., Gray, J., Grumble, W., Hand, W., Handback, M., Handback, W., Higgins, A. H., Holcomb, A., Holcomb, H., Holcomb, J., Holcomb, S., Holcomb, Wm., Hunt, ——, Hunt, ——, Kernell, Wm., Knight, J., Long, J., Long, T., Martin, J. R., McNeely, J., Miller, J. D., Moore, G., Newman, B., Newman, S., Osborn, W., Owens, A. Y., Owens, G., Owens, T., Owens, Y., Park, J. H., Park, T., Patton, W. P., Powers, B., Powers, P., Prior, L., Riddle, D., Riddle, F., Riddle, G., Riddle, L., Riddle, M., Riddle, N., Riddle, W., Robertson, J. R., Ropp, H., Spelts, R., Stuart, B., Stuart, J., Stuart, John, Stuart, Joseph, Stuart, Robt., Sumerel, M., Sumerel, T., Sumerel, W., Switzer, L. O., Thompson, W., Todd, R. J., Garrett, J., Morgan, S.

COMPANY "F."

CAPTAIN: Miller, D. B. LIEUTENANTS: Percival, E. S., Morrison, R. S., Freidburg, Joseph. SERGEANTS: Percival, F. H., Kirkland, R. S., Diseker, J. H., Keough, P. H., DeLoria, A. CORPORALS: Friday, S. D., Montgomery, G. B. W., Scott, F. J., Cathcart, W. J.

PRIVATES: Altee, J. W., Barefoot, Sion, Bates, O. B., Baugn, Wm., Boyer, Moses, Bull, Thomas, Burroughs, W. D., Bellinger, Wm., Cloffy, P., Campbell, James, Cooper, Jesse, Cooper, Thomas, Curlee, John, Dennis, H., Denkins, Saml., Flemming, A. H., Forbs, J. G., Friedman, B., Fulmer, W., Gardner, J. H., Glaze, Jno., Glaze, Allen, Gladden, L. T., Hickson, Sam, Howell, R. E., Jones, David, Legrand, W. W., Lever, Geo., Marsh, Edward, McCauley, J. B., Miles, E. H., Miot, C. H., Moye, J. E., Munson, W., Moore, Allen, Neely, Jno., Norman, Chas., North, S. R., Percival, G., Percival, N. N., Purse, T. P., Pollock, J. L., Reiley, James, Rembert, Jno., Reaves, Jno., Ross, Thos., Sill, T., Saunders, J. W., Senn, Dedrick, Schultz, W. C., Smith, T. N. C., Smith, Sol., Spriggs, H. V. L., Stokes, E. R., Jr., Turner, W. T., Taylor, Wm., Taylor, Jno., Thrift, Robt., Tradewell, F. A., White, E. C., White, G. A., Williamson, T., Williamson, D. W., Wardlaw, W. H., Aughtry, Jno., Davis, Andrew, Elkins, James, Elkins, Spence, Hammond, E., Lee, John, Sealy, Wm., Wooten, Danl.

COMPANY "G."

CAPTAINS: Irby, A. P., Whitner, B. M. LIEUTENANTS: Gladney, Wash, Robinson, J. S., Shedd, J. P., DesPortes, R. S., Jennings, R. H. SERGEANTS: Martin, D., Ashford, J. W., Gibson, H. T., Trapp, Laban, Watt, B. F., Trapp, L. H., Mason, W. N. CORPORALS: Beard, J. M., Robinson, Wm., Blair, A. F., Craig, T. N. A., Craig, Wm. PRIVATES: Aiken, Jim, Aiken, H. G., Aiken, H. N., Aiken, Robt., Brown, U., Brown, J. W., Brown, T. G., Brown, J. R., Blair, Thos., Blair, A. F., Boyd, John, Boney, Jesse, Bull, Thomas, Brown, Chas., Beard, James, Brown, Frank, Crawford, R. B., Crompton, Thomas, Carman, Sam., Carman, Jesse, Crossland, H. J., Chandler, W., Craig, Wm.. Crossland, Jasper, Carmack, Warren, Davis, T. C., DesPortes, J. A., Douglass, C. M., Douglass, W. T., Douglass, S. M., Flanigan, Z., Gladney. B., Gladney, W. R., Gradick, Jesse, Gibson, H. J., Gibson, Green, Hamilton, Wm., Hogan, Pink, Hawes, Tatum, Haigwood, Jeff., Haigwood, R. M., Hook, W. T., Hopkins, Wm., Irby, W. F., Irby, Wm., Johns, Wm., Jennings, Robt., Lyles, B. F., McConnel, Butler, McClure, Jno., Millings, Rus., Mann, Thos., Martin, Jno., Morgan, Wm., Mason, W. N., Millings, J. N., Moore, Nathan, McKintry, T. B., McConnell, A. C., McCreight, S., McCrady, M. H., Milling, Hugh, Martin, Newton, Martin, Wm., Nelson, J. T., Paul, J. T., Porter, C., Pouge, W. C., Robinson, James, Robinson, W. W., Robinson, I. Y., Robinson, S. N., Robinson, W. I., Ragsdale, E. R., Rabb, Calvin, Russel, Jno., Shedd, W. H., Scott. Jesse, Tinkler, George, Tinkler, Wm., Turkett, T. W., Trapp, U. C., Wilson, Dave, Withers, James, Weldon, Wm., Veronce, C. B.

ROLL OF TWENTIETH SOUTH CAROLINA VOLUNTEER REGIMENT.

Field and Staff.

COLONELS: Keitt, L. M., Boykin, S. M.
LIEUTENANT COLONELS: Dantzler, O. M., McMichael, P. A.
MAJORS: Mimms, A., Partlow, J. M., Leaphart, G.
ADJUTANTS: Chisolm, R., Hane, W. C., Wilson, Jno. A.
QUARTERMASTERS: Kinard, Jno. P., Woodward, T. W.
COMMISSARY: Heriot, Jno. O.
SURGEON: Salley, A. S.
ASSISTANT SURGEONS: Fripp, C. A., Barton, D. R.
CHAPLAINS: Meynardie, E. J., Duncan, Y. W.
SERGEANT MAJORS: Quattlebaum, T. A., Quattlebaum, E. R.
QUARTERMASTER SERGEANTS: Barton, T. F., Wannamaker, F. W.
COMMISSARY SERGEANT: Solomons, J. T.
ORDNANCE SERGEANT: Phillips, T. H.

COMPANY "A."

CAPTAINS: Partlow, Jno. M., Woodin, C. H. A., Lee, Jno. LIEUTENANTS: Talley, Dyer, Williams, D. O., Norton, E. R., Siddall, Jno., Barr, S. A. SERGEANTS: Lusk, Newt., Wilcox, F. H., Knee, Hermon, Wilson, Mack. CORPORALS: Ansel, Harmon, Smith, C. M., Norrell, John, Fisher, James.
PRIVATES: Anderson, John, Appleton, Wm., Atkinson, Thomas, Burrell, Miles, Beiman, Henry, Bracke, Henry, Bramlett, Wm., Ballinger, Wm., Babb, ——, Brace, ——, Bowlin, Thos., Brown, Lee, Butler, Levi, Craine, Wm., Craine, Isaac, Cannon, S. C., Carpenter, Wm., Crow, Isaac, Dawkins, ——, Darby, Thos., Ellenburg, Jno., Elrod, ——, Ellis, G., Fisher, Wm., Fisher, B. P., Heddin, J. P., Heddin, Isaac, Heddin, D. B., Holcomb, ——, Hembree, Wm., Handcock, Thos., Holly, James, Ivester, Anderson, Knight, Jno., Kelly, Wm., Kelly, W. N., Lusk, Jno.,

Lyda, Jno., Owens, Riley, Partlow, Pickens, Patterson, Wesley, Powell, Ashley, Randolph, S. H., Reid, Samuel, Reid, Massey, Reid, James M., Rochester, W. T., Richie, D. L., Sanders, Elijah, Smith, Ezekiel, Smith, D. W. S., Teague, Wm., Teague, Isaac, Turner, Pickens, Vinson, D., Vinson, Jno., Ward, Nathaniel, Woodsin, C. H. A., Wilson, Mack.

COMPANY "B."

CAPTAIN: McMichael, P. A. LIEUTENANTS: Barton, B. H., Whetstone, N. C., Cox, J. R. SERGEANTS: Inabinet, D. J., Way, A. H., Myers, D. D., McCorquodale, ——, Donald, J. A. CORPORALS: Shuler, J. W., Murphy, J. C., Grambling, A. M., Buyck, F. J.

PRIVATES: Arant, J. T., Bair, J. S., Bair, S. H., Barber, W. E., Bars, W., Baxter, D. F., Bolin, J. E. A., Bolin, J. S., Boltin, J. H., Boltin, E. A., Bonnet, J. D., Bonnet, W. R. E., Bozard, D. B., Bozard, J. D., Bozard, C. F., Brantley, E. W., Brodie, J. W., Brodie, John W., Brodie, Judson, Brodie, J. R., Buyck, J. W., Clayton, W., Collier, L. P., Cook, J. M., Cox, A. M., Crum, J. W., Crum, A. F., Culalasieur, N. W., Dantzler, G. M., DeWhit, M., Dixon, W., Dixon, Henry, Dukes, T. C., Elbrooks, H., Fair, G. S., Fair, J. W., Felkel, J. R., Felkel, J. A., Friday, P. D., Grambling, F. H., Grambling, J. H., Grey, A., Haigler, J. A., Heiner, H. W., Herron, R. R., Holman, A. C., Horger, J. F., Houck, J. J., Houser, J. D., Hutchins, J. C., Hutchins, J. A., Huff, G. W., Hunkerpicler, T. N., Hunkerpella, L., Jackson, J. F., Jackson, J. C., Joyner, D. F., Judy, H., Judy, H. L., Keiser, W. J., Keiser, F. D., Leaird, H. D., Lyles, T., Mack, J., Metts, D. G., Metts, G. W., Metts, W. J., Murphy, H. H., Murphy, L., Murphy, H. B., Murphy, P., Noble, S., Patrick, J., Patrick, D. W., Patrick, E., Patrick, S. P., Patrick, V. V., Pearson, J. H., Pooser, F. N., Pooser, E. H., Rast, J. A., Rast, J. C., Rast, J. L., Rast, T. F., Rast, J. S., Rast, G. D., McReady, E., Reay, M., Riley, H. W., Riley, O. B., Rutlin, W. W., Rutland, A. E., Rutland, H., Seagler, J. E., Sellars, G. D., Shuler, J. W., Smoak, R. F., Smoak, A. B., Smoak, M. T., Smoak, G. W., Stellinger, T. W., Stellinger, F., Till, H. F., Till, J. J., Walsh, J. J., Wannamaker, H. C., Wannamaker, F. M., Way, R. F., Way, J. D., Wolf, W. S., Zeigler, H. H., Zimmerman, D., Bonnett, J. D., McMichael, O., Smoak, G. W., Knights, J. D., Huff, D. W., Wethers, M. L., Kennerly, L. D. S.

COMPANY "C."

CAPTAINS: Leaphart, G., Haltiwanger, G. T. LIEUTENANTS: Huffman, J. E., Eleazer, W. S., Haltiwanger, H. M. SERGEANTS: Houseal, W. F., Metts, S. S., Eleazer, J. M., Haltiwanger, J. H., Burkett, T. CORPORALS: Hipps, I. A., Williamson, W., Addy, T. M. G., Ballentine, S., Haltiwanger, D. K., Smith, S. L.

PRIVATES: Arnick, T. W., Arnick, I. A., Arnick, W. R., Arnick, D. W., Addy, J. B., Addison, H. T., Archart, H. M., Baker, J., Black N. L., Black, W. E., Bookman, S. W., Bouknight, W. J., Bouknight, J. W., Busby, L., Busby, W., Buff, H. J., Buff, J., Bickley, H. W., Bouknight, J. M., Bundrick, J. M., Bundrick, J. A., Bristow, J. M., Cumelander, W. N., Cumelander, A. W., Sr., Cumelander, A. W., Jr., Cumerlander, J. S., Cumerlander, S. C., Counts, H. A., Caughman, J. C., Coogler, J. P., Coogler, R. E., Clocus, H., Counts, H. A., Daly, J. T., Daly, W. A., Dean, J. A., Derrick, J. H., Derrick, J. S., Derrick, W. C., Derrick, J., Derrick, H. D., Derrick, J. D., Derrick, G. J., Derrick, S. W., Dreher, O. A., Dreher, E. J., Eleazer, R. J., Eleazer, G. B., Epting, D. J., Epting, J. H., Eargle, J. J., Eargle, A. D., Eargle, J. D., Eargle, J. W., Eargle, A. D., Fulmer, W. F., Fulmer, J. F., Farr, G., Farr, B., Freshley, G. W., Frick, E. D., Geiger, J., Geiger, D. W., Geiger, F. S., Geiger, J., Geiger, M., Geiger, E. W., Geiger, G. M., Geiger, J. A., Geiger, L. S., Haltiwonger, G. C., Haltiwonger, J. S., Haltiwonger, G. J., Haltiwonger, D. J., Haltiwonger, J. E., Haltiwonger, J. J., Hiller, P. J.,

37

Hiller, S. B., Hiller, S., Hiller, J. A., Hyler, J. B., Hunt, N., Hameter, G., Jacobs, W. A., Jacobs, J., Kibler. A., Koon, W. W., Koon, J. F., Koon, J. L., Keitt, J. D., Lorick, J. D., Lowman, J. P., Lowman, S. G., Lowman, P. G., Lowman, J. S., Lowman, P. E., Lybrand, B. C., Long, D. E., Long, W. W., Mayer, G. W., Metts, G. S., Metts, G. S., Metts, J. F., Metts, M. S., Metts, E. C., Metts, J. C., Metts, R. A., Metts, J. T., Metts S. J., Metts, C., Metts, L., Metts. E. W., Mathias, L. S., Mathias, T. S. McCartha. R., McCartha, J., Monts, J., Nates, J. T., Nates. J. A., Nunnamaker, A. S., Nunnamaker, J. H., Nunnamaker, D., Nunnamaker, W. A., Revel. J. W., Shuler, P. I., Shuler, J. L., Shuler, J. R., Stack, W., Stack. H., Sheeley, J. D., Sheeley, P. P., Sheeley, D., Sheeley, J. J., Sheeley, J. M., Suber, W. F., Slice. J. J., Slice. J. W., Slice. J. D., Summer, J. W., Sr., Summer, J. W., Jr., Seigler. J., Seigler, W., Schmitz, J. D., Stone, H., Swygert. J. W., Taylor. C., Williams, W. H., Williamson, W., Whites. E. M., Whites, A. E., Whites, S. H., Wessinger, G. S., Wessinger. J., Wessinger. J. D., Weed. C. A., Weed, J. C., Youngenener, J., Leaphart. L.

COMPANY "D."

CAPTAIN: Donnelly, R. V. LIEUTENANTS: Livingston, B., Jeffcoat, N. P., Inabenat. T. SERGEANTS: Jeffcoat, H. W., Jeffcoat, J., Redmorn. I., Livingston, J. S.

PRIVATES: Axson. W. A., Axson. F. D., Bailey, G., Brown, W. F., Bonnett, P., Cartin, E., Casson. J., Carson, R. A., Carton. W., Carton, E., Carson. W. H., Cain, W. P., Carson, T. J., Carton, W., Cook, J. A., Cook. J. Q., Cook, S., Crider. T. J., Crider. A., Crider. A., Crun, V. V., Crun, H., Culler, J., Chavis. P., Chavis. J., Cubsted, J., Davis, J., Evans. A., Fogle, P. S., Fogle. P., Fogle, J. W., Furtick, G., Furtick, W., Furtick, I., Gantt. C., Hughes. M. I., Hughes, E., Hughes, J. W., Hughes, A., Hughes. W., Hutts. J., Hutts. Jacob, Hooker, J. W., Hooker L. S., Hooker. J. L. G., Hooker. J. O. A., Hooker. G., Harley, J. M., Harley, J. H., Harley, G. W., Harley, J., Harley, T. W., Hoover, J., Inabinett. G., Jeffcoat. C. A., Jeffcoat. J. J., Jeffcoat. E. D. A., Jeffcoat, J. W., Jernegan, L., Johnson, P. P., Johnson, J. W., Johnson, J., Jorner. J., Jorner. H. W., King, W., Kneese. J., Kneese. W., Livingston. G. H., Livingston. W. B., Livingston. R., Livingston. M., Livingston. J. H., Livingston. F. D., Mennicken, J. A., Mack, J. B., Mack, W. C., Mack. F. H., McMichael. R. V., McMichael. W., Mixon, L., Murph. T. W., North. J. F., Ott, J. T., Oliver. T. W., Pou, J. A. R., Pou, W. G., Pou, B. F., Pound. J., Price, P., Porter. D. A., Porter. E., Porter. J., Porter, J. A., Phillips. J. F., Phillips, J. T., Phillips, G., Peil. W., Reed. J., Reid. J., Reid. R., Reid, W. H., Rucker. R., Rucker, W., Redman. A., Redmond. F., Robinson, L., Robinson, J. T., Starns. J., Searight. J., Stabler, M., Stabler, H., Tyler. L., Wacor, W. L., Williamson. W., Williamson. E., Williamson. T., Williamson. D. R., Williamson. G., Williamson. W., West, W., Wise. D., Wise, J., Wise, J., Witt, W. P., Zeigler, A., Donnely, O.

COMPANY "E."

CAPTAIN: Cowan, N. A. LIEUTENANTS: Shirley, J. J., Pruitt, W. C., King. J. A., Mattison. J. F. SERGEANTS: Copeland, J. J., Clinkscales, F., Parker. J. P., Hall. A. M., Broom, W. J. CORPORALS: Kay, C. M., Hanks. Luke, Shirley, N. A., Acker, W. H., Parker, R. E.

PRIVATES: Armstrong. J. A., Ashley, J. T., Adams, A. B., Armstrong, A. S., Ashley. John, Ashley. J. R., Ashley, J. T., Ashley, E. W., Arnold, Joel. Anderson. T. W., Brock, R. B., Brock. J. L., Bannister. M., Brock, J. H., Brock. W. C., Bancum. A., Bannister, Thomas, Bannister, W. L., Bannister. J. H., Sr., Bannister. J. M., Bannister. J. H. Jr., Bannister, J. N., Broom, J. N., Broom, A., Bagwell. Baylis, Bigby. J. A., Coker. J. J., Cummings, C. C., Callahan, J. F., Cowan, W. M., Cummings, H. A.,

Callahan, J. R., Callahan, D. P., Coleman, Robert, Fox, F. J., Cobb, M.
A., Crasberry, A., Cox, Mac, Diver, B. F., Dunlap, W. F., Drennan, S.
A. Davis, A. M., Dalrymple, J., Drake, E. H., Elgin, H., Flower, J. Y.,
Fields, Stephen, Fields, T., Freeman, W. G., Gambrell, S. V., Gillespie,
A., Gilkerson, W. D., Gilkerson, J. A., Gantt, E. S., Grubb, C. C., Gam-
brell, P. M., Gambrell, E. H., Greer, J. W., Greer, George, Hawkins, R.
L., Hall, J. B., Haynie, S. P., Haynie, James, Haynie, J. C., Haynie,
Pink, Holliday, J., Harris, E., Hall, W. C., Hanks, J. M., Hanks, Tho-
mas, Harper, N., Johnson, W. G. W., King, D. P., Kay, W. R., Kay, M.
V. S., Keaton, J. J., Kay, J. L., King, J. D., King, J. D., Jr., Kay, M. H.,
Kay, J. B., Kay, W. S., Leopard, H. B., Lathan, J., Lusk, J. F., Mattison,
James, Mulligan, W. H., Mann, S. H., McDavid, J. Q., Martin, Samuel,
Mann, A. K., Martin, W. A., Morgan, David, Mattison, W. H., Massey,
J. C., Massey, S. B., McLane, John, Murdock, J. T., Murdock, Stephen,
McCoy, E. W., Morrison, G. D., Mitchell, John, Mitchell, E. M., Martin,
Welborn, Neighbor, J. T., Owens, A. W., Pruitt, J. B., Pruitt, Joshua,
Pruitt, E. O., Pruitt, E. D., Pruitt, T. C., Pruitt, J. P., Pearman, W. L.,
Pearman, W. C., Pearman, S. N., Pepper, E. K., Posey, R. L., Pack, J.
B., Pitts, J. G., Pruitt, B. F., Robinson, Isaac, Robinson, Jesse, Robin-
son, R. B., Robinson, J. A., Robinson, J. H., Robinson, G. B., Robinson,
J. M., Robinson, S. E., Robinson, R. B. A., Recketts, William, Ragsdale,
F. A., Saylors, J. N., Saylors, Isaac, Shirley, S., Smith, William, Shaw,
R. M., Shaw, C. M., Saylors, W. P., Saddler, Isaac, Saylor, J. W., Say-
lors, W. P., Saylors, W., Stone, A. H., Stone, J. B., Shaw, H. W., Shaw,
J. C., Shirley, F. F., Shirley, J. J., Shirley, J. M., Smith, J. N., Smith, C.,
Saddler, William, Southerland, W. F., Simpson, J. D., Seawright, John,
Seawright, J. S., Taylor, J. W., Tucker, L. P., Tucker, W. T., Tucker,
Wm. L., Todd, I. A., Tribble, L. W., Tribble, S. M., Thurkill, ——,
Vandiver, D. J., Williams, Ira, Woods, W. J., Wilson, J. J., Woods,
Robert, Wilson, R. C., Wilson, J. M., Wilson, W. R., Wilson, W. N.,
Wilson, J. R., Wright, C. J., Wright, J. W., Wright, T. T., Williamson,
M., Williamson, James, Walden, J., Willingham, A. P., Willingham, J.
N., Cowan, Andrew.

COMPANY "F."

CAPTAINS: Kinard, John M., Kinard, Wm. M. LIEUTENANTS: Sligh,
Hilary, Kingsmore, E. R., Cannon, W. S. SERGEANTS: Reid, S. W.,
Buzzard, B. M., Epting, J. N., Graham, F. D., Goree, W. O. COR-
PORALS: Richie, C. M., Dickert, Jesse C., Rikard, Frank D.

PRIVATES: Abrams, Z. P., Abrams, S. S., Abrams, Daniel, Baker, M.,
Barrett, B., Brooks, H. J., Boozer, Tim, Boozer, Henry, Brown, M. L.,
Beard, S. P., Buzzard, O. H., Buzzard, Jeff, Buzzard, W. F., Buzzard,
William, Bowles, W. H., Barre, S. C., Bedenbaugh, W. P., Cady, F. N.,
Calmes, C. Wash., Campell, Ed., Cannon, Geo. W., Chapman, D. N.,
Chapman, Henry, Counts, John C., Counts, Adam, Counts, A. B.,
Cromer, John R., Cromer, Jacob L., Cromer, Enoch, Cromer, R. Press,
Collins, A. B., Crooks, John, Denson, John F., Denson, George, Dickert,
Wm. T., Dickert, Marion, Dunwoody, S. H., Davis, John D., Dominick,
L. F., Ducket, John, Epps, Wm. T., Epps, Micajah, Eady, Wm. H.,
Folk, Ham H., Farrow, Wood H., Glenn, Wm. H., Glenn, John D.,
Glenn, William, Glenn, Daniel, Glymph, B. J., Greer, R. P., Gary, I. N.,
Gaunt, Jeff., Henson, H. O., Hough, Andrew J., Houseal, John I.,
Hentz, Julius D., Hawkins, George, Herbert, Sullivan, Jones, J. E.,
Jones, Lewis, Kibler, Adam, Kibler, D. W. T., Kissick, J. W., Koon, W.
F., Kinard, Miner, Kinard, N., Lane, J. C., Livingston, J. C., Livingston,
Robert J., Livingston, Ham, Lindsay, James, Martin, Cline, McGill,
Archie, McCullough, H. S., McCullough, W. P., Miller, J. F., Miller,
Joseph T., Miller, J. D., Montgomery, William, Moody, J. P., Nates,
Jacob, Norris, John E., Nichols, Andrew, Rikard, A., Rhodes, J. W.,
Rook, J. T., Rook, S. J., Rook, J. W., Ropp, A. J., Rumbly, A. J.,
Reeder, William, Sanders, J. M., Setzler, W. A., Sloan, John P., Stone,

J. William, Stone, Henry. Suber, D. F., Stewart, John C., Stewart, S. F., Singley, G. M., Singley, J. H., Bedenbaugh, Pink., Cook, C. J., Cowan, E., Sligh, Munroe, Spencer, M., Thomas, Ed., Thrift, John, Watts, W. Peck, Wedeman, J. D., Wedeman, Silas, Wheeler, J. F., Williams, Robert H., Wilcox, W. P., Wicker Lang., Wicker, D., Wicker, D. R., Wicker, T. V., Wicker, Pelt., Willingham, P. W., Wilson, J. S., Wilson, J. C., Wilson, H. C., Wilson, G., Wright, M. J., Wilcox, W. P.

COMPANY "G."

CAPTAINS: Boykin, S. M., Herriott, R. L., Mosely, A. LIEUTENANTS: White, L. A., Rhame, G. S., McCaskill, K., Belvin, W. T., Herriott, J. V. SERGEANTS: Lafan, M. L., McLeod, William, McCaskill, F. D., Boykin, J. J., Boykin, S. B., Hancock, W. J., Jones, G. W., Madison, K., Mathis, J. R., McEachern, J. R. CORPORALS: McEachern, W. D., Allen, J. C., Andrews, G. T., Farfield, R. E., Mathis, J. V., Eachern, W. C., Smith T. W. P.

PRIVATES: Atkinson, William, Atkinson, Wash., Andrews, E., Boykin, William, Boykin, Drewry, Boykin, S. L., Boykin, Elias, Boykin, M. H., Boykin, James, Boykin, C. M., Boykin, John, Brown, L. T., Brown, Joshua, Brown, C. S., Bradley, S. P., Bird, James, Baker, A., Brunson, J. L., Bradley, William, Croft, William, Croft, Wesly, Cannon, G., Corbitt, J. A., Collins, Alex., Caughman, Joe, Corbitt, J. N., Dorety, L. G., Dunlop, Dorety, William D., Manning, Dorety, Henry, Dorety, Dorety, Laton, Daniel, Dixon, Benj., Davis, G. P. W., Davis, J. D., Davis, Lucas, Davis, Offel, Davis, C. R., Dorman, George, Daniels, Wes., Daniels, Alf., Genobles, Rufus, Gaillard, Rufus, Gaillard, W. F., Hawkins, Wash., Harmon, James, Hatfield, Benj., Hatfield, William, Hatfield, Caleb, Hatfield, Charles, Hancock, Wesly, Hancock, E. J., Hancock, T. D., Hancock, G. W., Hancock, Lon, Hawkins, Will., Hutchens, ——, Hyott, James, Jeffers, Daniel, Jeffers, H. L., Jones R. L., Jones, C. L., Jones, Henry, Jones, W., Jones, Francis, Jeffers, John, Kirby ——, Lee, John, Lee, William, Lee, T., Lee, W., Mitchell, Robert, Mathis, William, Mathis, G. M., Mathis, G. D., Mathis, S., Mathis, Alex, Murph, Henry, Lee Will., Myers, George, Myers, T. S., Myers, P. A., McBride, McCutcheon, Robert, McCutcheon, John, Marsh, J., McCoy, Neighbors, H., Neighbors, David, Neighbors, Isaac, Neighbors, Thomas, Nichol, W., Oliver, Jesse, Partin, William, Partin, J. W., Rhame, Thomas, Rodgers, J. D., Rodgers, Latson, Rodgers, Manning, Smith, J. W., Scott, Tullis, Scott, Manning, Scott, Benjamin, Syfer, C. P., Shiver, T. J., Smith, Scott, J. L., Shiver, John, Sexton, Tidwell, Thomas, Tidwell, Adison, Tidwell, William, Watson, E. S., White, William, White, Henry, Watson, J. T., White, J. T., White, Thomas, White, Pake, Wacton, R. C., Watts, William, Boykin, M. S.

COMPANY "H."

CAPTAINS: Kinsler, Edward, Roof, S. M. LIEUTENANTS: Hook, E. E., Hook, R. T., Hook, J. S. SERGEANTS: Mills, Jack A., Sox Jeff., Senn, J. E., Senn, A. D., Roof, Henry J., Hook, J. D. CORPORALS: Roof, D. J., Dooley, James L., Sox, H. E., Griffith, D. T., Hutto, Britton E., Hutto, Paul D., Spahr, J. J.

PRIVATES: Bachman, C., Bachman, H. H., Bachman, R. H., Buff, M. W., Buff, T. J., Buff, M. R., Blackwell, C. E., Berry, Jacob, Berry, George, Berry, Treadway, Berry, John, Pell, John, Clark, P. P., Clark, J. D., Churchwell, Thomas, Cook, E. E., Cook, John C., Carter, Henry A., Clamp, J. T., Dooley, Jesse K., Dooley, Jacob E., Dooley, J. L., DeVore, Thomas, Fry, J. R., Fry, Tyler, Fry, Thomas A., Gable, Godfrey, Gable, E. E., Gregory, Franklin, Gregory, John G. A., Hook, M.

M., Hook, Jacob, Hook, J. V., Hooks, J. G., Herron, E., Hutto, Murphy, Hutto, F. M., Hollman, J. H., Howard, Alex., Huckabee, Oliver, Joyner, William, Kirkland, E., Leach, R. P., Leach, Iseman, Lybrand, D. W., Lybrand, M. H., Lybrand, J. H., Lever, Jacob, Lecones, G. D., Miller, S. S., Miller, Thomas, Mathias, L. M., Mathias, J. B., Mack, J. F., Mack, H. L., Monts, George, Parr, Starkey, Pool, Isaac, Pool, Hiram, Reeves, J. C., Roof, Jesse M., Roof, Benjamin J., Roof, T. J., Roof, J. L., Roof, J. W., Roof, T. E., Roof, Martin, Roof, Jesse, Ramick, John, Rich, Michael, Roland, John, Sharp. Uriah, Sharp, P. M., Sharp, Lewie, Sharp, Barney, Sharp, J. D., Sharp, Jacob, Sharp. Reuben, Sharp, Calvin, Sharp, R., Sharp, D. J., Sharp, Emanuel, Sharp, Felix, Senn, R. N., Senn, W. B., Senn, Jacob, Stuart, Robert, Shull, H. W., Shull, D. E., Shull, R. W., Shull, H. M., Shull, John W., Roof, L., Snull, John, Shull, D. P., Shull, M. A., Shull, J. E., Smith, T. C., Sox, E. G., Sox, C. S., Sox, J. E., Sox, D. M., Sox, Jesse, Sightler, William A., Spraler, W. A., Spraler, E. C., Spraler, F., Spires, J. H., Spires, D., Spires, Amos, Spires, J. H., Spires, I. J., Spires, Andrew, Spires. Henry, Spires, W. A., Spires, James, Stuckey, C. R., Stuckey, D. C., Stuckey, Wesley, Schumpert, D. P., Schumpert, N. P., Taylor, J. F., Taylor, J. G., Taylor, James G., Taylor, B. J., Taylor, Andrew, Wilson, George A., Wilson, Henry, Wilson. William, Wilson. David, Williams, Sampson, Williams, T. J., Williams, T. D., Williams, F. E., Wise, James F., Wingard, Thomas A., Younce, George, Zenkee, William, Zenkee, John C.

COMPANY "I."

CAPTAINS: Jones, J. M., Gunter, Elbert. LIEUTENANTS: Coleman, J. E., Gunter, M., Pitts, W. W., Gunter, Leroy, Gunter, D. B. SERGEANTS: Jones, N. F., Gunter, Zimri, Gunter, Emanuel, Jones. John, Gunter, Levi, Gunter, Elliott. Gunter, W. C., Wise, John W. CORPORALS: Gunter, Mitchell, Abels, Pierce. Garrin, Robert.

PRIVATES: Ables, Burk, Altman, James, Altman, Rufus, Altman, Ruben. Lennett. Tyler, Baggant, Freeman, Baggant, E. F., Brogdan, Jesse, Progdan, M., Progdan, William, Bryant, Mark, Burnett, Brazil, Burnett, D. P., Burnett, Willis, Burgess, Felix, Burgess. J. S., Braswell, George, Baltiziger, A., Blackwell, James, Burgess, N. J., Christmas. S. B., Creed, B. O., Cook, Chesley, Cook, Wyatt, Courtney, Young. Courtney, James, Fulmer, Adam, Fox, James H., Gunter, D.bal, Gunter, H. J., Gunter, Abel, Gunter, A. E., Gunter, Alfred, Gunter, Balaam, Gunter, Felix, Gunter, Joshua. Gunter, Lawson. Gunter, Macon, Gunter, Marshall, Gunter, M. B., Gunter, Stancil, Gunter, V. A., Gunter, W. H., Gunter, William, Gunter, W. X., Gunter, B. Ex M., Gunter, A. M., Gantt, M. A., Gantt, William, Gantt, A. B., Garvin, C., Garvin, E. J., Garvin, J. C., Garvin, Larkin, Garvin, Wesly, Garvin, W. R., Gunter, Riely, Garvin J. A., Gunter, Eldridge, Hall, Jeremiah, Hail, Wayne, Heartly, Willis, Heardy, M., Heron, Abner, Heron, David, Huckabee, J. F., Huckabee, John, Hydrick, Emanuel, Hydrick, John, Hutto, W. B., Hall, J. C., Hall, J. T., Jernigan, L. W., Jones, L. C., Jones, Gideon, Jones, J. B., Jones, John P., Jones, Stanmore, Jones, W. B., Jones, N. B., Jones, Watson, Jackson, J. M., Jackson, J. P., Jones, Ezekiel, Kennedy, William, Kennedy, Alex., Kirkling, E. S., Kirkling. G. W., Kirkling. Tillman, Kirkland. Hiram, Kneece, Jacob, Kennedy, Matthew, Kirkland, J. F., Mixon, D., Nobles, Ed., Pool, Elzy, Pool, J., Pool, Tillman, Pool, Elvin, Pool, John, Price, T., Rawls, Theodore, Rich, W. B., Richardson, Harrison, Richardson, W. B., Richardson, G. W., Rich, John. Sawyer, J. D., Sawyer, P. S., Sanders, John, Sanders, E., Starnes, Ezekiel, Starns, Wesly, Starns, Randy, Starns, John, Starns, Joshua, Storey, Wesly, Shelly, Melvin. Smith, I. B., Ward, A. G., Ward, John, Williams, G. W., Williams, Hiram, Williams, Rowland, Williams John, Williams, R. F., Williams, J. M., Wells, William, Wells, Thomas.

COMPANY "K."

CAPTAIN: Harman, W. D. M. LIEUTENANTS: Haltiwonger, S. A., Harmon, T. S., Harmon, M. H., Seay, H., Harmon, F. J., Leaphart, J. L., Harmon, M. D. SERGEANTS: Sease, J. R. W., Quattlebaum, T. A. CORPORALS: Hendrix, J. E., Brown, S., Wingard, H., Earhart, J. W., Taylor, M. L., Rawl, E. A., Keisler, L., Wingard, J., Shealy, L. F.

PRIVATES: Alewine, J., Amick, J., Berry, J., Black, J. R., Blackwell, B., Boles, S. F., Bonenberger, P., Brown, J., Busby, P., Caughman, J. T., Caughman, L. W., Caughman, N. S., Caughman, H. J. W., Crout, L., Crout, J. T., Crout, W., Crout, W., Corley, E. L., Corley, L. W., Corley, S. A., Corley, W., Corley, W. A., Calk, W., Cook, W. I., Cook, W., Crapps, S., DeHart, A. H., Eargle, A. L., Eargle, F. P., Eargle, G. W., Fikes, J. A., Frey, J. W., Gross, A. H., Gregory, J., Gable, J. D., Gable, D. T., Gable, M. M., Hipps, W. S., Hite, J., Hicks, D., Hicks, R. J. A., Harmon, P. B., Harmon, G. W., Harmon, M. B., Harmon, G. M., Harmon, J. W., Harmon, J. A., Hartwell, J. J., Heyman, O., Hallman, M. L., Hallman, S. T., Hallman, E. R., Hallman, A. J., Hallman, E., Holeman, D., Hays, J. W. P., Hays, A. W. N., Hays, A. D. J., Hendrix, G. S., Hendrix, H. J., Hendrix, J. E., Hendrix, J. S., Hendrix, S. N., Hendrix, T. A., Hunt, J., Jackson, N. L., Jumper, H., Kyser, D., Kyser, J. I. B., Keisler, H., Keisler, S., Keisler, C. S., Keisler, D. F., Kaminer, W. P., Kaminer, J. M., Kaminer, J. A. W., King, E., Kistler, A. T., Kleckley, H. W., Kleckley, D. D., Kleckley, J. T., Kleckley, S., Kleckley, J. W., Lominack, D., Long, J. C., Long, J. A., Long, A. M., Long, J. H., Livingston, S., Lybrand, I. W., Lucas, M. H., Lewis, T. J., Harmon, L., Lewis, G. W., Leaphart H. H., Miller, J., Mills, J. B., Meetze, G. A., Meetze, F. R., Mouts, S. P., Mouts, J. T., Mouts, J., Oswald, D., Price, W., Price, E. J., Price, I., Price, L., Quattlebaum, E. R., Rawl, B., Rawl, P. J., Rawl, J., Ranch, W. W., Ranch, C. S., Reeder, G. W., Reeder, J. W., Rich, ———, Roof, J. N., Roof, S. G., Roof, R., Satcher, S., Shealy, W. P., Shealy, U., Shealy, A., Shealy, J. J. B., Shealy, W. R., Shealy, N., Shealy, J. M., Shealy, P. W., Smith, J. W., Smith, A. J., See, J. B., See, D. E., Shirley, S. W., Snelgrove, C. P., Snelgrove, E. E., Steel, J., Steel, Z., Taylor, G. W., Taylor, J. W., Taylor, E., Taylor, W. C., Taylor, Z., Taylor, H., Taylor, H. W., Taylor, J. W., Taylor, J., Wingard, J. S., Wingard, T. J., Wingard, S., Wingard, G. W., Wingard, M., Wiggins, S. J.

COMPANY "L."

CAPTAINS: Sparks, A. D., Folton, C. P. LIEUTENANTS: Peterkin, J. A., Kinney, W. F., Moore, A. E. SERGEANTS: Hodges, G., Emanuel, E. M., Walsh, W. W., Covington, J. T. CORPORALS: Manning, J., Rowe, A. J., Montgomery, J., Allen, E.

PRIVATES: Allen, J., Bridges, J. W., Bristow, J. D., Bristow, J. M., Bristow, R. N., Anderson, T. F., Bethea, J. W., Buzhart, J. T., Buchanan, J. A., Calder, W., Carter, W., Berry, D. F., Carrigan, W. A., Clark, R., Cope, E., Cottingham, J., Cowan, W. T., Coxe, R. A., Croley, D., Croley, R., Culler, C. W., David, A. L., DeBarry, E., Bridges, J. H., Bridges, S., Dunford, A. J., English, C., English, J., Evans, T. A., Fowler, W. D., Frasier, C., Frasier, W., Goss, H. L., Grice, E., Grice, J., Grice, T. S., Graham, W., Graham, Windsor, Graham, W., Havse, D., Hearsey, G. R., Holeman, E., Henegan, A. B., Henegan, S. A., Hubbard, J. G., Hodges, T. C., Hodges, W. L., Graham, J. J., Ivy, L., Jackson, J., Jackson, A., Jackson, O., Kendall, R. A., Lemaster, B. B., Lipscomb, E., Lipscomb, W. R., Manning, E., Manning, I. R., Moody, G. W., McCaskill, K., McCall, D., McCormie, A., McCall, C. S., McCall, J. D., McCall, L. H., McCall, P. R., McKee, I. A., McGee A., McLeod, M., McAlister, J., McAlister, C., Mumford, W., Parham, I. H., Parham, H., Parham, H. A., Parham, W. H., Miles, G. W., Polson, C., Polson, J., Parish, J., Parish, H., Pearson, M., Pearson, P., Rascoe, W., McLane, G., McDaniel, J. R., McDaniel, W. W., Rodgers, H. J., Rowe, S. H., Cope, I. T., Byrd, J., Quick, A. W., Smith, H. B., Spears, H., Sports, G., Sports, J., Sturgis, J., Strickland, M., Stubbs, A. A., Stackhouse, W. R., Turner, I., Truwic, C. L., Ware, G., Wetherly, E., Wilkins, J., Willoughby, R., Willoughby, J. T., Woodle, J., Williams, S. V., Miller, P. A., Welch, H., Welch, T., Windham, R. E., Hinds, J., Hale, R. W., Wallace, G. T., Wallace, W., Webster, G. W., Webster, J., Wilson, M. R., Walsh, J. R., Wright, J. G., Watson, S., Watson, W., Wicker, J., Page, W. J., Lampley, J., Gay, J., Snead, L. P., Johns, P. M., Burlington, H., Stanton, J., Littlejohn, J., Murchison, R., Berry, F., Ivy, W. H., Hamer, J., Bethea, W. H., McLeod, B. F., McPearson, A., McPearson, M., Medling, J., Baggett, H., Conner, D., Conner, W., Covington, R., Covington, E., Covington, T., Proctor, C., Fletcher, J., Emanuel, J. M., Thomlinson, L., Thomlinson, J., Moore, B. F., Moore, T., Reese, J., Reese, John, Cottingham, A., Cottingham. J., Crabb, H. B., Leggett, A., Calhoun, J. C., Calhoun, H., Sparks, B. M.

INDEX.

Printed in the United States
117871LV00007B/38/A